OPERA BIOGRAPHY SERIES, No. 9

Series Editors
Andrew Farkas
William R. Moran

In the 1940s, officially retired, Ponselle assumed the comfortable role of Mistress of Villa Pace, entertaining visiting celebrities and holding soirees for Baltimore society. In her music room, she poses with her ornate, custom-made Knabe piano. PHOTOGRAPH BY THE HUGHES COMPANY, BALTIMORE. COURTESY OF LAWRENCE F. HOLDRIDGE.

Rosa Ponselle

A CENTENARY BIOGRAPHY

James A. Drake

James M. Alfonte, Photographic Editor

Chronology of Performances by Thomas G. Kaufman
Bibliography by Andrew Farkas
Discography by Bill Park

Amadeus Press
Reinhard G. Pauly, General Editor
Portland, Oregon

TO MAGALI
Estrella de mi corazón

ISBN 1-57467-019-0

Printed in Singapore

Amadeus Press
The Haseltine Building
133 S.W. Second Avenue, Suite 450
Portland, Oregon 97204, U.S.A.

Library of Congress Cataloging-in-Publication Data

Drake, James A.

Rosa Ponselle : a centenary biography / James A. Drake; chronology of performances by Thomas G. Kaufman; bibliography by Andrew Farkas ; discography by Bill Park; James M. Alfonte, photographic editor.
p. cm. — (Opera biography series; no. 9)
Includes bibliographic references (p.), discography (p.), and index.
ISBN 1-57467-019-0
1. Ponselle, Rosa, 1897–1981. 2. Sopranos (Singers)—United States—Biography.
I. Title. II. Series.
ML420.P825D783 1997
782.1′092—dc20
[B] 96-28709
CIP
MN

Contents

Preface

The twenty-second of January 1997 marks the centennial of Rosa Ponselle's birth. This book is her centenary biography.

Whatever other merits it may have, this work also has the nominal distinction of being the second book written about the same biographical subject, by the same author. In 1982 Doubleday and Company published the authorized biography of Rosa Ponselle under the title *Ponselle: A Singer's Life*. Rosa Ponselle and I were listed as its coauthors. Although Ponselle did not live to see the book in print, our collaboration produced a book that was well received by reviewers here and abroad. Though out of print, it has remained until now the only book-length work published on the life and career of the American-born soprano whose voice once invited the description, "a Caruso in petticoats."

This book is not intended as a replacement for *Ponselle: A Singer's Life*. There are substantial differences between the two, most obviously in their respective formats. Although *Ponselle: A Singer's Life* was published as a collaborative autobiography, it was written, submitted, and initially accepted by its publisher as a biography. The original manuscript, in keeping with the agreement that Rosa Ponselle and I cosigned on 14 March 1978, was submitted to the publisher as an authorized biography. On 1 March 1979, however, in response to concerns about marketing the eventual book, we revised our agreement (as the amended contract stated) to "enable the manuscript to be transformed into an 'as told to' book without significant further assistance from Mme Ponselle herself." As a result of this change, what came to be published and marketed as Rosa Ponselle's story "in her own words" was in reality a story that had been transformed from a third-person to a first-person narrative.

In contrast, the present volume includes not only an account of Rosa Ponselle's artistic achievements as one of the most acclaimed singers of this century but also the story of the peaks and valleys of her personal life. The 1982 autobiography told only as much of her personal life as her legal representatives would authorize for publication. Much, needless to say, was either withheld or sanitized. (Soon after the book's publication, Myron Ehrlich, a longtime friend and admirer of the singer, quipped that her personal life had been reshaped to "read like the average nun's.")

Because Rosa Ponselle's performing career as a professional musician spanned only twenty-seven of her eighty-four years (nineteen in opera, three in vaudeville, and five in concerts and other settings), this book focuses mainly on the years 1912–37. However, the highlights of the years preceding her first paid engagements in 1912—as well as the period separating her abrupt retirement in 1937, her occasional concertizing until 1939, and her brief reemergence in the mid-1950s, when RCA Victor induced her to make records again—are discussed in detail, both for reasons of continuity and cohesiveness and for the benefit of readers who may be unfamiliar with many details about Ponselle's life.

In this new book, through the use of a special format, I have preserved both Ponselle's own words and those of her friends and colleagues. The format gives the reader a glimpse of the challenges any biographer confronts—-the arduous and frequently sensitive tasks of extracting distant and sometimes painful memories, of interviewing other principals whose viewpoints and recollections may differ sharply, and then of ferreting out whatever evidence there may be for determining which viewpoints are factual and consistent. These are the routine but often grinding tasks that form the basis of biographical writing.

The format employed in these chapters follows the logic and sequence of the biographer's work. A section entitled "The Interview" allows Ponselle to speak for herself. Each "interview" is a composite of two or more interviews given by Ponselle, usually within the same time frame and in some cases with the same interviewer. The chapters preserve the question-and-answer format in which these interviews were originally conducted and recorded. Except for minor rearranging to keep similar topics together and in chronological order, Ponselle's words are quoted verbatim.

The next section of each chapter, entitled "Recollections," presents an interview with other principals who were directly involved with the events about which Ponselle speaks in her interview. These supplemental interviews involve Ponselle's colleagues, family members, and other close associates. Sometimes they corroborate Ponselle's recollections, and at other times they contradict them. These interviews are presented in the first-person narrative style favored by Studs Terkel and other oral historians. In all instances the words of the speakers are preserved in their original form, again with only minor rearranging of topics.

A final section in each chapter, entitled "The Written Record," surveys the written documentation pertaining to the events depicted in the chapter. Typically, this documentation takes the form of critics' reviews, contracts or other legal documents, newspaper and magazine articles, printed or recorded interviews, and surviving official personal correspondence between Ponselle and other principals in her story. With very few exceptions in these pages, I have resisted the impulse to interpret Ponselle's or other principals' actions, motives, and thoughts, preferring instead to let readers draw their own conclusions from the evidence.

Locating much of that evidence would have been daunting without the help of those contributions I have acknowledged in the research notes at the back of the book. Without the generosity of Myron Ehrlich, Hugh M. Johns, James M. Alfonte, and Anne J. O'Donnell, much important information that Ponselle shared with them over the years would be lost altogether; and without the help of Robert Tuggle, Director of the Metropolitan Opera Archives, a great deal else would have been difficult to locate and verify. I am also indebted to Walter E. Afield, M.D.; William Ashbrook; Arbe Bareis; Fred Calland; Mem Catania; Dr. H. Trevor Colbourn; Lanny Collins; Andrew Farkas; Bill Fletcher; Roland Forster; Warren F. Gardner; D. Lloyd Garrison; Eve Goodman; Lawrence F. Holdridge; Dr. Bob Jones, Jr.; Karen Kirtley; Charles Koelsch; Ilene Massey; Joseph Mitchell; Charles B. Mintzer; William R. Moran; David Norbeck; Edward Hagelin Pearson; John Pennino; J. R. Peters; the Rosa Ponselle Fund of Meriden and its Director, Valerie T. Bubon; Alphonse Ponzillo; Mrs. Stanley Rosoff; William Safka; Mrs. Daniel Sheen; and Mrs. Horace Valiante.

This book also contains supplements to assist future researchers, including a bibliography, a chronology of all Ponselle's known vaudeville, operatic, and concert performances, and a discography. In sum, this book is both a body of research, organized and presented to give as true and immediate picture of its subject as possible, and an invitation to readers to join in the engrossing search for the real Rosa Ponselle.

J. A. D.
Cocoa Beach, Florida

CHAPTER ONE

Wait Till You Hear Her!

In the annals of the Metropolitan Opera, the second week of November 1918 has more than a passing significance.

On Monday, a performance of *Samson et Dalila*, with Enrico Caruso and Louise Homer in the title roles, opened the Metropolitan's thirty-fifth season. The date of that performance (11 November 1918) also came to occupy, in the words of the late Irving Kolodin, "a place in history of other sorts than musical."[1] Earlier that day, news of the armistice ending World War I touched off patriotic celebrations on two continents. Even the stage of the Metropolitan Opera House was no exception to the celebrating: after the final curtain for *Samson et Dalila* had rung down, it was soon raised again—revealing Caruso, Homer, and the other cast members waving British, French, Italian, and American flags, and leading the cheering audience in an impromptu medley of patriotic songs.

Of the five operas scheduled during that opening week, four were familiar to most Metropolitan Opera audiences. The opening-night work, *Samson et Dalila*, had been revived for Caruso in the 1915–16 season; it was the thirty-first role the great tenor had assumed at the Metropolitan since his debut in 1903.[2] The second opera on the roster, *Madama Butterfly*, had been in the repertory since the winter of 1907, when Puccini himself had come to New York to attend the Metropolitan premiere. *Aida,* the third work scheduled, had been heard at the Metropolitan practically since its doors had opened in 1883. During the 1918–19 season-opening week, however, the significance of the *Aida* performance lay chiefly in the Metropolitan debut of Giulio Crimi, a Sicilian tenor whose "instrument [of] beauty, power and compass"[3] would soon be heard in the upcoming Metropolitan premieres of Puccini's *Il tabarro* and *Gianni Schicchi*.

Following the Wednesday evening *Aida*, a performance of *La fille du régiment*—a production that had been revived chiefly for soprano Frieda Hempel a year earlier—was to take place on Thursday. And for Friday evening, 15 November, the roster announced the Metropolitan Opera premiere of Verdi's *La forza del destino*—a work that had been in the repertoire of many European opera companies since its premiere in Russia in November of 1862, but which had not been heard by a New York City audience since an Academy of Music performance nearly forty years earlier.[4]

Coupled with the continuing celebration of the armistice, which went on throughout the week, the publicity surrounding a Verdi premiere at the Metropolitan made it unlikely that the debut of a young American-born soprano would attract unusual attention from the New York press. And, on balance, it didn't—notwithstanding the mostly favorable reviews the young Rosa Ponselle received from the critics, and the future promise they heard in her surprisingly mature voice. But in the ensuing nineteen seasons, as this youthful promise unfolded into a first-rank career, the date of 15 November 1918 came to be associated more with the debut of Rosa Ponselle than with the Metropolitan premiere of *La forza del destino*.

On the afternoon of 9 December 1971—more than a half-century after her Metropolitan Opera debut, and six weeks before she would celebrate her seventy-fifth birthday—Ponselle relaxed in the library of her expansive home in the rolling hills of the Green Spring Valley near Baltimore, Maryland. The design of the home, as Francis Robinson once wrote, "might have been lifted bodily out of Tuscany; and while the Maryland landscape bears no resemblance whatever to Fiesole, neither the white stucco mansion nor its Italian name—*Villa Pace*—is in the least out of place."[5]

From its name to its cross-shaped design, the home was an enduring testament to the significance of *La forza del destino* in Ponselle's personal life. The name came from the fourth-act aria "Pace, pace, mio Dio." On one of the two columns bordering the villa's main entrance, the first four notes of the aria were etched in the shape of roses. The floor plan of Villa Pace, a cruciform of four separate sections, each with an ambience and function all its own, had been inspired by the crimson cross that adorned her fourth-act costume in *Forza*.[6]

On this brisk December 1971 afternoon, Villa Pace was being readied for the Christmas season, in anticipation of a steady stream of visitors from one to nine o'clock in the evening during each of the twelve days of Christmas. In the library, on a loveseat bordering the fireplace, Ponselle sat in front of a microphone. Seated near her was Hugh Johns, a long-time admirer who lived in nearby Pikesville. Across the room stood William Seward, who donned headphones momentarily as he made a final check of the sound levels on a Tandberg recorder. A few minutes later, at the behest of the Columbia Records division of CBS, Seward would begin recording a special interview with Ponselle, intended for inclusion on a commemorative LP he was preparing for release on Columbia's Odyssey label.[7]

Seward, a New York-based record producer and writer, had first come to Ponselle's attention through Bidù Sayão, the celebrated Brazilian soprano with whom Seward enjoyed a close working relationship after reissuing some of her radio performances and recordings. As a courtesy, Bidù Sayão had sent Ponselle a copy of a *Traviata* broadcast Seward had issued as a limited-edition LP. In return, Ponselle had written a highly complimentary thank-you letter, expressing her delight not only with the performance but also with the sound quality of the recording itself. Soon this led to an exchange of letters with Seward, at his initiative as the album's producer.

In time, Seward became a consultant to Columbia Records, which retained him to produce five albums of historic recordings for a newly planned "Legendary Singers" series. One of the five albums was to be devoted to the earliest Verdi-repertoire recordings by Ponselle. When Seward sold Columbia's executives on the novel idea of recording the singer's personal recollections for inclusion on the new album, he approached her for permission to record an interview with her at Villa Pace. After she consented, Ponselle drew Hugh Johns into the discussions to help finalize the arrangements.

Like William Seward, Hugh Johns was not a professional musician but had acquired a formidable knowledge of opera and of opera singers through years of self-study. A public-school teacher, Johns was the son of prominent Baltimore-area physicians. He had become acquainted with Ponselle shortly after World War II, when he was a teenager. As with Seward, who was approximately his age, Johns had nurtured a boyhood admiration for the legendary singers of Caruso's era.

Because he lived in a community close to the Green Spring Valley, where Villa Pace was located, Johns' admiration for Ponselle was heightened by an occasional opportunity to glimpse her from a respectful distance. When he had discovered, at age fifteen, that her telephone number was listed in the Baltimore directory, he gathered the boyish courage to call her—and to his pleasant surprise, he found her approachable. Three years later, he was delighted to see that his idol had begun attending the same Catholic church to which his family belonged. After Mass one Sunday, he approached her gingerly and asked if he might escort her to her car; after a while he did this regularly, and on these brief occasions he would ask her questions about her career. Impressed by the scope of his knowledge, especially in light of his young age, Ponselle took an interest in him, and even arranged for him to study voice with Romano Romani, her mentor and coach. In time, Hugh

Johns became a "regular" at Villa Pace, and was usually asked to sit in on interview sessions when Ponselle granted them—including the interview that William Seward was now preparing to record.

Seward, who had just turned forty, had already witnessed the fanfare surrounding one of Ponselle's infrequent interviews. She did not grant interviews readily, and in no case would she agree to be interviewed anywhere but Villa Pace—a self-made rule she would not suspend even for *The New York Times*' Harold C. Schonberg when he came to interview her. On the relatively infrequent occasions when she would agree to any interviews at all, she would ask that they be scheduled no earlier than four o'clock in the afternoon, to accommodate her penchant for sleeping through the morning hours after watching television late into the night.

On such an afternoon, between four and five o'clock, the door of Ponselle's second-story bedroom would swing open, leading to the long staircase in the foyer of Villa Pace. In an instant, a bevy of perfumed and coiffed poodles would begin a raucous race from her bedroom to the bottom of the stairs; their shrill barking would startle the four or more Persian and Siamese cats, the singer's other favored pets, which silently roamed the villa's lower level. Soon Ponselle's very recognizable face and form would be seen on the balcony that bordered the foyer, and in a few moments she would reach the top of the steep staircase. Then, one by one, she would take the tiled steps in a calculatedly slow gait, her guests awaiting her below. If a guest happened to be someone she knew and valued, it would not be unusual for her to sing a few measures of "I Love You Truly," inserting the guest's name into the words of the ballad.

Her appearance, even late in life, tended to belie her age. Although her waistline had gradually thickened as her capacity for the vigorous exercise of her younger days had lessened over the years, her supple skin, dark hair, large brown eyes, and flawless, pearl-like teeth kept her reasonably young-looking. Her hair color, she would concede privately, had retained its coffee color "with the help of a little touching-up now and then," and her diminished eyesight caused her to rely on a pair of large, black-framed glasses for reading. On most days, however, she confined her daily reading to a cursory scan of two or three newspapers. At no point in her life was she an intensive reader. Usually, she preferred to have whatever she considered important read to her aloud.

Perhaps more than her appearance, Ponselle's energy, attentiveness, and animated ways made her age seem irrelevant. Even at seventy-nine her spiritedness made Luciano Pavarotti think of "a young spring chicken" when he first met her. "Friends told me that she was still a young person," the tenor said after spending an afternoon with her at Villa Pace in 1976. "But I tell you, I wasn't expecting this. She was a young person. She was my age—maybe even younger."[8]

In her relatively few formal interviews Ponselle tended to give measured answers to questions, but almost always in a lively tone of voice. Like her sense of usage and phrasing when she spoke, the sound of her speaking voice, which could range from a mezzo-soprano's to a baritone's depending on her spirits, gave little hint of her unique dramatic-soprano voice and her insightful musical phrasing. Her vocabulary was an amalgam of slang, especially the show-business jargon of Broadway and Tin Pan Alley, and a requisite amount of cultivated English. The style she favored could change abruptly in an interview. "Yeah" might be preferred to "yes," "no" might yield to "nah," the tempo of an art song might be described as "snappy," and a major operatic triumph might be labeled "a big hit."

Her speech patterns could also be unpredictable, depending on whether she was thinking in English or in Italian. When discussing a particular Italian opera or when listening to a Metropolitan Opera broadcast, she could summon her prodigious memory and recite in a pure Tuscan accent the text of most any section of a libretto, regardless of the character to whom the lines happened to belong. At other moments, when she was relaxed and engaged in fireside or poolside conversations with friends, she might anglicize her Italian pronunciation, making "Verdi" rhyme with "wordy."

Interviewers who came to Villa Pace expecting to find her music room and library overcrowded with recordings, scores, photographs, and other memorabilia were surprised to find no abundant evidence of her past surrounding the once-famous celebrity. Of the three largest oil paintings that adorned the first floor, two were of family members: her sister and her mother. The third, a full-length portrait of Ponselle in a concert gown—frequently mistaken for one of her *Traviata* portraits—did not entirely please her. "It's nice, but look at the first finger of my left hand," she would remark. "It's way too long."[9] Only a small number of signed photographs—of Caruso, Antonio Scotti, and two or three others—hung in her library, but they were mounted in a paneled alcove and could not be seen from other parts of the room.

The alcove also housed a sound system that friends and advisors had updated for her since the early 1950s. Beneath the turntable and amplifier were a small number of compartments for storing recordings. First-time visitors usually found it strange that the shelves contained very few of Ponselle's own recordings; she neither owned many of them, nor seemed to have much enthusiasm for listening to any recordings at all. "Don't ask me to listen to records," she would protest. "I have to work when I listen to them."[10]

On the infrequent occasions when she could be coaxed into a listening session, she would demonstrate what she meant by having to work. First, she would reach into the drawer of a nearby end table to retrieve an A′-440 tuning fork. Rapped sharply on the underside of the table, the fork would enable her to determine the key in which an aria or ensemble was being performed. Then she would listen to every note with a focus and precision not unlike a scientist viewing a specimen under a microscope.

Ponselle's memories of her career, like those of many other celebrities, tended to be purposely selective. Dates and sequences of events tended to elude her, as any interviewer soon learned when asking her such questions as whether *Il trovatore* entered her repertoire before or after *Andrea Chénier*, or how many times she sang with Titta Ruffo, Feodor Chaliapin, or some other illustrious colleague. Interviewers found it an advantage to bring original programs of her performances, photographs of her and her colleagues, or original pressings of her early recordings. Holding those artifacts in her hands, she seemed able to transport herself backward in time.

But as her interviewers also discovered, Ponselle's memories of the emotions she experienced during critical points in her life—especially her memories of painful events—could be so clear and intense that while recounting them she seemed to experience them all over again. Late in life, this eidetic recall of deep-seated emotions could reduce her to tears, abruptly ending an interview.

William Seward knew how to accommodate Ponselle's idiosyncrasies. In his interview for Columbia, he intended to use the same format that Hugh Johns had favored in a considerably longer session he had recorded with her in the summer of 1968. As Johns had done, Seward wanted merely to prompt her memory by asking a few brief questions that he hoped would invite lengthy and detailed answers on her part. His plan was to record a monologue, not a dialogue, which he and Columbia's recording engineers would edit to fit the opening band of the new LP of her earliest recordings.[11] At approximately four o'clock on an afternoon in October of 1971, Seward completed the last of his equipment checks. Moments later, the reels of the recorder began to turn, and the interview was underway.

The Interview

From interviews of Rosa Ponselle by William Seward (October 1971), by Hugh M. Johns (June–July 1968), and by Fred Calland (1977, precise date unknown), supplemented by the author's interviews (March 1973, June 1975), with minor editing.

Can you tell us a bit about your debut? How was—

Oh, I wouldn't know where to start! Just to think about it, I shiver all over. All I can say is that it was a miracle.

How was it that you were given a Verdi premiere as your debut role, when you had never even been on an opera stage before, let alone the stage of the Metropolitan?

This Theatre, when filled to its capacity, can be emptied in five minutes. Choose the nearest exit now and in case of need walk quietly (do not run) to that exit in order to avoid panic.

METROPOLITAN OPERA HOVSE

GRAND OPERA SEASON 1918-1919
GIULIO GATTI-CASAZZA, General Manager

SATURDAY AFTERNOON, DECEMBER 21ST, AT 2 O'CLOCK

LA FORZA DEL DESTINO

(THE FORCE OF DESTINY)
OPERA IN FOUR ACTS AND EIGHT TABLEUX
BOOK BY FRANCESCO MARIA PIAVE
(IN ITALIAN)

MUSIC BY GIUSEPPE VERDI

MARQUIS OF CALATRAVA	GIULIO ROSSI
DONNA LEONORA	ROSA PONSELLE
DON CARLOS OF VARGAS	GIUSEPPE DE LUCA
DON ALVARO	ENRICO CARUSO
PREZIOSILLA	SOPHIE BRASLAU
THE ABBOT	JOSE MARDONES
FATHER MELITONE	THOMAS CHALMERS
CURRA	MARIE MATTFELD
THE ALCADE	PAOLO ANANIAN
TRABUCO	GIORDANO PALTRINIERI
A SURGEON	VINCENZO RESCHIGLIAN

HOST AND HOSTESS OF THE INN, MULATTOES, SERVANTS, SPANISH AND ITALIAN SOLDIERS AND PEASANTS, ITALIAN RECRUITS, MONKS, BEGGARS, ETC.

CONDUCTOR . . . . . GENNARO PAPI

STAGE DIRECTOR	RICHARD ORDYNSKI
CHORUS MASTER	GIULIO SETTI
TECHNICAL DIRECTOR	EDWARD SIEDLE
STAGE MANAGER	ARMANDO AGNINI
PREMIERE DANSEUSE	ROSINA GALLI
PREMIER DANSEUR	GIUSEPPE BONFIGLIO

PROGRAMME CONTINUED ON NEXT PAGE

CORRECT LIBRETTOS FOR SALE IN THE LOBBY

HARDMAN PIANOS USED EXCLUSIVELY

Figure 1. On this autographed copy of the program from *La forza del destino*, Ponselle wrote: "This opera shall always be closest to my heart because it was not only my debut, but my Alvaro was none other than the greatest of *all* tenors. God bless his soul." COURTESY OF BILL PARK.

Well, I guess the title of the opera says it all: *La forza del destino*, the force of destiny. That was my destiny, apparently, to sing Verdi with Caruso at the Metropolitan. I don't know how to explain it any other way.

But wouldn't you agree that destiny seems to work through a willing subject, someone who not only accepts this destiny but also wants it and is prepared to do all the hard work to achieve it?

Yes, I would agree with that. Geraldine Farrar once paid me a very lovely compliment. When she was asked how a person could have a voice like

Rosa Ponselle, her answer was, "Only by a special arrangement with God." But in the very next breath she said, "And then you have to work very, very hard indeed." You get her point. Believe me, I worked hard, so hard that I never really had a life of my own in all the years I was singing. You also have to be somebody who is willing to suffer, to feel the pain that goes with all of it. Caruso used to say to all of us, "It's necessary to suffer in order to be great."

Was it Caruso who got you the opportunity to audition at the Metropolitan?

Yes. My sister Carmela and I were coaching with a very prominent teacher and manager, William Thorner, and he was friendly enough with Caruso that he was able to get him to come to the studio to hear us. We had been in vaudeville—in bigtime vaudeville, [on] the Keith Circuit. We were making big money, but we had decided to leave vaudeville and try to get into grand opera. You see, in vaudeville our act was really twenty minutes of big opera arias and duets.

Did you just coach with William Thorner, or did you actually study with him?

No. Thorner never taught me a single thing—I wouldn't let him touch my voice. I didn't coach with him either. I coached all my early roles with Romano Romani, who took Carmela and me under his wing when we were still in vaudeville. Thorner, you see, was really a manager and an agent. But he had very good connections with the Metropolitan, and he was friends with a lot of the singers. And to give the devil his due, he did persuade Caruso to come and hear us.

Obviously, Caruso liked what he heard. But did you know that at the time?

Oh, yes. After I finished singing, he walked over to me and said to me in a very matter-of-fact sort of way, "You'll sing with me." Well, you could've knocked me over with a feather. I said, "Sing with you? Where? When?" All he said was, "Maybe in a year or two, maybe later, but you'll sing with me at the Metropolitan." Then he sat down next to me—I was as nervous as a kitten—and he said, pointing to his throat, "You have it here," meaning that I had the voice it would take to sing with him at the Met. Then he pointed to his heart, and he said, "And you have it here," which was his way of saying that I had the quality of emotion, the depth of feeling, that it would take to be an artist. Then he raised his hand to his head, and tapped his temple with his finger. He said to me, "And whether you have it up here, only time will tell."

At that point, then, was it Caruso who spoke about you to Giulio Gatti-Casazza, the general manager of the Metropolitan Opera?

That's right. Caruso went back to Gatti-Casazza and told him about these two sisters from vaudeville, and that one of them (he probably said "the fat one," because I was as big as a telephone booth in those days) had just the right voice for Leonora in *La forza del destino*. You see, they had this big premiere coming up, and it was wartime so they didn't have any of the great European sopranos over here to sing Leonora.

How did Gatti-Casazza react?

Gatti said to him, "This young girl who has only heard two operas in her life and is out of vaudeville is going to come and do Leonora with you? You must have your head examined!" Caruso said, "Wait till you hear her, and you'll change your mind." And then Gatti said, "Well, I'll tell you this: if this American makes good, every door will be open to American potentials from that moment on. And if she doesn't make good, Signor Gatti takes the first ship back to Italy—the first ship back to Italy—and America will never see me again!" But Caruso said to him, "You wait. You won't have to take that ship back to Italy."

Did Gatti-Casazza engage you on Caruso's word, or did you have to audition?

Well, after we sang for Caruso, Carmela and I had two auditions at the Met. The first one was a formal thing—it was only a couple of days after Caruso heard us at Thorner's studio. A lot of the big stars at the Met came to that audition. Giovanni Martinelli was there, and Pasquale Amato, Adamo Didur, Frieda Hempel, Margarete Matzenauer, and Caruso came too. The second one, that was about two weeks later, [was] just for Gatti and some of the executives. That time, I didn't do so good.

Why not?

I fainted. Isn't that the limit! Here I am, a kid looking for the big break, and when it comes, what does Rosa do? Rosa passes out on the floor. What happened was, Gatti had asked me to prepare the "Casta diva" from Norma. I had never even heard of the opera (I didn't know Norma from Wagner in those days), but Nino Romani helped me prepare it. Gatti asked how long I would need to learn it, and Romani told him two weeks. So, at this final audition with Gatti I was asked to sing the "Casta diva," and I got through it fine, right up to the last few measures. Then, all of a sudden, I keeled over. The next thing I knew, Carmela was leaning over me with smelling salts. I don't know what caused it—nerves, maybe a touch of the flu, or maybe I just ran out of breath. But I was sure I had lost my chance. I mean, why would the Metropolitan take a chance on somebody like that? Yet the next thing I knew, Gatti took me into his office, opened the drawer of his desk, pulled out this piece of paper, and handed it to me. I said, "What's this?" He said, "It's a contract. You're going to sing here with Caruso." Well, I didn't know the first thing about a contract! I was just a kid, barely twenty-one, and this was all new to me. I signed the contract, and from then on, as I said before, it was the force of destiny.

How long did it take you to prepare Forza del destino, *and where did you prepare it?*

You see, I had several other roles that I was supposed to prepare for that coming season. We worked on *Forza* first, because that was going to be my debut role.

You worked with Romano Romani throughout the summer?

Yes. I rented a place at a beach not far from my hometown [in Connecticut], and Romani rented a cottage there too. Carmela and Edith [Prilik], who became my secretary, stayed with me in my place, and my mother also stayed with us for a time. But I had to keep away from the kitchen while she was there. You see, I made up my mind to lose a lot of the weight I was carrying around.

Did you follow a particular regimen?

A very good friend of ours from vaudeville—his name was Al Herman, a comedian—gave me a book called *Eat and Grow Thin.* When Carmela and I were starting out in vaudeville, Al Herman used to follow our act. We got to know him pretty well, and we knew each other's act from start to finish. One time, he thought he needed a new opener for his act, so he asked me if he could open with a joke or two about our act. He said he wouldn't even think about doing it if it would hurt my feelings, because the joke was going to be on me. He would come onstage and say, "You know those two sisters who were just out here singin' to you? Don't let'em fool you! They ain't sisters at all. The big one is the skinny one's mother! Why, that mamma is so big she can't even get into a telephone booth. And if you can't get into a phone booth, well there's no use talkin'!" You see, he felt so guilty about using that joke, even though it did get a lot of laughs, that he bought me a copy of *Eat and Grow Thin.* So I followed it, and I did a lot of exercising that summer—swimming, golf, tennis, and long, long walks—and sure enough, I was a lot lighter when I showed up for my debut.

The week of your debut was a history-making week. Were you at the Metropolitan on Armistice Day, when Caruso sang Samson?

No, but I heard about it, of course. People were celebrating everywhere! I had an apartment at that time (it was on Ninety-seventh Street near Riverside Drive), and there were parties going on day and night. But I was too busy rehearsing, too preoccupied with being ready for my debut, which was to be on that Friday.

You say that you were preoccupied. Would you say you were also worried?

Not at all. At the dress rehearsal, which was on Wednesday, I had no such thing as nerves. I was showing off, really.

How do you mean, "showing off"?

Well, I was a pretty good sight-reader, and in those days, if you sat me in front of a keyboard I'd give you a pretty good show. I was kind of brash, a brazen kid, kind of fresh and full of herself, so at some of the rehearsals I showed off a little to impress the conductor, Gennaro Papi. Oh, I would sight-play eight or ten pages of the orchestral score on the piano. And if I wanted to get Caruso going, all I had to do was run to the nearest piano and play my own arrangement of the Tomb Scene from *Aida*—in ragtime, like Scott Joplin would've written it. It used to drive Papi crazy, but it would always break up Caruso, who liked to have fun and who had an ear for popular music too.

Did you have another rehearsal on Thursday, or did you try to rest that day?

You know, that whole day is a blank for me. There was a luncheon for me after the dress rehearsal. That was on Wednesday. But on Thursday, the day before *Forza*, my world caved in on me. My mother was staying with me, and she made me a big breakfast that morning. My secretary, Edith (she lived with Carmela and me at that time) had bought some of the newspapers that morning because we wanted to see how the *Aida* had gone the night before. You see, a very famous tenor from Italy had made his debut at the Metropolitan that Wednesday night.

You're referring to Giulio Crimi?

Well, I wasn't going to say his name because the critics just tore him to pieces. Let's just say that he was a great artist, and I sang with him later, but they didn't like him and they gave him very bad reviews. Anyway, those newspapers were on my tray. If I hadn't read those reviews, I think I might have been just as bold at my debut. But after I put those newspapers down I thought to myself, what have I gotten into? If this is what the critics can do to an experienced artist—and here am I, with no operatic experience and fresh out of vaudeville? Why, they'll cut me to pieces! From that day on, I didn't know what peace was.

How were you faring on Friday, the day of your debut?

Well, I knew before I left the house that there was some voice there, but I said, "I'm going to die, so what difference does it make?" I was sure I was going to die on the stage. So, on the way down to the theater I saw my favorite color in all the windows and everything: any stray paper on the streets or sidewalks was purple, lavender, the color of orchids, which is my favorite color.

Probably from bunting and paper flags because of the armistice celebrations?

That's right. From the celebrations. I said, "Well if this is any omen, I'm going to live in spite of it all." By the time I got to the theater, I was motionless. I couldn't even raise my arms to put my makeup on—they had to put the makeup on me. My dressing room was all upholstered—it was thickly upholstered, with carpets and heavy draperies. No one warned me not to vocalize in your dressing room, but to go out in the corridor where it's all cement floors and nice high ceilings, and where you can get a real true assessment of what voice you're in. Well, I vocalized in my dressing room, and my whole voice was absorbed by all the draperies and upholstery. "Well," I said, "it's all over now—I've lost my voice!" I couldn't hear any of the overtones, but I didn't know at the time what caused it. I had no voice. I couldn't hear myself.

Once you were onstage, how did your voice feel?

I had a great deal of singing to do in the first act. I had a big aria, "Me pellegrina ed orfana," which is part of the dialogue between Leonora and her maid. And before that, I had the little duet with the father, the Marquis. Then Caruso, as Alvaro, made his entrance through the big casement window. He sees Leonora and sings to her, making love to her with his words. Then he sings, "Ciel! che t'agità?"—in English, "What are you so afraid of?" Well, in the midst of all this love-making—and these are very fast exchanges, back and forth—I said under my breath, "I'm dying! I'm dying"—"Sto morendo! Sto morendo!" And he would say in between these quick passages, "Coraggio! Coraggio! Io ti sostengo!" He was telling me that he would sustain me, that he would get me through this thing somehow. But he was dying in his own tracks, so it was the blind leading the blind.

Did you realize at that moment that Caruso was nervous too?

Well, I didn't know that Caruso also suffered to such an extent at every premiere, but I found out that night. I didn't even think of him that night because I thought I was going to die. And he was trying to give me help because I was his protégé, you know, so he felt a double responsibility. He didn't come to wish me well or anything, but I was too nervous to realize that he hadn't come near me before the performance. He was having his own traumas in his dressing room. The room, they said, was filled with smoke, because he smoked cigarettes incessantly (that's how the nerves reacted with him). But, luckily, that never showed in that God-given voice of his.

You survived the first act, and then you had the second act to challenge you.

The second act is a terrific fifty-five minutes of constant singing. After the Tavern Scene there is the big aria, "Madre, pietosa Vergine," then the whole scene in the monastery with Padre Guardiano, and then the Church

Scene where she sings "La Vergine degli angeli" with the Padre and the monks. Today, they do a lot of cutting in the second act (usually they cut the Tavern Scene,) but in those days, everything was left in, so it was fifty-five minutes of continual singing [with] a very taxing tessitura—it lies very high. There I was, a beginner, a baby. The tessitura is always on high B-naturals, so I had to run the gamut, never stopping. But the more I sang, the more my throat kept getting drier and drier. Every time I opened my mouth, my throat would stick together, and I thought for sure I was going to crack on every note. Some people oversalivate, but I couldn't salivate at all. Well, my mother, my sister, [and] my secretary were all in the wings, praying for me, with smelling salts all over the place. When I realized that I'd lived through that second act, I got on my knees, thanked God, and wept!

And when "Pace" came?

Oh, my! Then I could stand in the wings and listen to Caruso and enjoy him and the rest of the cast, because I was relaxed. My only concern was that I had an hour and one-half of rest, so much that the voice lowers and can get sluggish and cold. So I had to vocalize again, but the whole last act, including "Pace, pace, mio Dio," was just like eating peanuts. But do you know I was laid up for some days after, from the reaction? That's when I started to feel the weight of this mantle, this reputation. You see, there were standards, apparently, that I had set that night. From then on, I would have to live up to them.

Recollections

Edith Prilik

When Rosa Ponselle spoke of "my secretary, Edith" during her recorded interview, she was referring to Edith Prilik—one of very few women who, by Rosa's own reckoning, had known her the longest and had been a confidante during crucial periods in her life. Born in Odessa in tsarist Russia, Edith had just turned twenty and Rosa was still in her teens when Carmela had introduced them shortly after Rosa's arrival in New York for her vaudeville audition. Their relationship during Rosa's formative years as a performer was indisputably close, and this closeness made Edith an offstage witness to the sequence of events surrounding the fabled Ponselle debut—events which she recalled in a series of interviews recorded at her New York City residence in 1977 and 1978.[12]

There are two stories I could tell you about Rosa Ponselle's Metropolitan Opera debut. One of them is the real story, and the other is the one that she and

I sort of cooked up, mainly to help out her sister Carmela. That's the story you read about in a lot of opera books. It sounds like a fairy tale, you know: Cinderella goes to the Met, and such. Even Rosa likes to tell it that way; and, God knows, she's told it so many times that she probably believes it by now. But to know the real story you have to understand, first of all, that, between the two sisters, it was Rosa who ran the whole show. Now, to understand why, you have to know something about Carmela and how she got into the entertainment business, which happened around the time that I met her.

My family lived in a large brownstone on Madison Avenue at 128th Street. My father was a furrier who also owned part interest in several other businesses, so we lived pretty well. I had a cousin who was a piano accompanist on what they called the café circuit. In those days, and I'm talking about 1912–13, there were a number of very fashionable restaurants and cafés (Shanley's, Reisenweber's, Lorber's, Wallick's) that hired singers to entertain the patrons. They had what were called cabarets, almost like a small vaudeville bill, where up to a dozen musical acts might perform late in the evenings. On and off, my cousin accompanied singers at several of these popular places.

Even though I was under age at the time, I could afford to dress "older" and I would talk my cousin into taking me with her when she would play at these places. One night, she happened to be accompanying a soprano who was billed as "Miss Operetta" in the card they put on the menus. I was just mesmerized by this singer because I thought this was the most exquisite creature I had ever seen. And such a beautiful voice, on top of it all! One of the songs she sang that night was "Love Me, and the World Is Mine." I carried around a mental picture of her singing that song for weeks afterward, and I got so fascinated by this "Miss Operetta" that I told my parents I wanted to study to be a singer.

After a while, I began studying with a voice teacher named Signor Martino. He had a studio on Forty-fourth Street. He told me I had some promise as a very light lyric soprano, which, of course, made my head a little bit bigger for a while. But the weeks went by, and I wasn't making enough progress to suit him. Finally, he told me as nicely as he could to quit wasting my parents' money. I was only a teenager, but I got rather indignant with him and demanded to know why I wasn't good enough to continue studying with him. He said to me, "If you come back here at four o'clock this afternoon, I'll let you sit in on one of my lessons with a girl who is a professional singer, and then you can make up your own mind about what you want to do." I went back to the studio at four, and there stood "Miss Operetta," my idol. I found out that her name was Carmela Ponzillo. I sat through her lesson, but of course I wouldn't have had to sit there to know how great she was and how amateurish I sounded by comparison.

I think that Carmela knew she was being used by Martino to make me quit studying. She probably felt sorry for me, so she invited me to go with her to her next singing engagement. Well, I was walking on air, just being around her. In those days she seemed to have it all; she was ambitious, gifted, and unbelievably attractive. When she would walk down Broadway, men would crane their necks to look at her. She had the physique of a model, and she wore very modish clothes for that time; she favored tailored tweed suits that were cut like a man's but fitted to her figure, and she wore wide-brim hats made of a matching material. She had her hats made almost like a man's fedora, and she always wore them at a rakish angle. Her hair was so long it almost reached her thighs when she let it down. She used to wear it in swirled braids that were pinned up near her temples. I know for a fact that she used to be offered anywhere from twenty-five to as much as two hundred dollars by fashion photographers, just to be photographed in elaborate gowns and to pose with her hair down.

The better I got to know Carmela, the more I got the feeling that she was very lonely being in New York and away from her family. So, my family started inviting her to our house for Shabbos, if she didn't happen to be singing someplace on a Friday. We were Jewish, and though she was raised Catholic, she seemed very open-minded about our traditions, and she learned to love kosher food too. She used to talk about her family back in Meriden, Connecticut, so I knew that she had a brother a couple of years younger than she. I often heard her talk about her kid sister, Rose (not "Rosa," which came later), who was ten years younger and was the baby of the family. All in all, then, we got to be very close, even though Carmela was seven years older than I. To me, she was like a big sister I could look up to and admire.

When Carmela got into smalltime vaudeville, she introduced me to Gene Hughes and his family. He was her manager, and had gotten her into one of Proctor's theaters and several others that were a little more up-and-up than the ones she started in. She did a solo act that ran about fifteen minutes; she sang popular music, mainly ballads, and a few things from the operettas of that day. After a while her act sort of got stale, and Mr. Hughes told her she was going to have to change it. Carmela didn't seem to know what to do. Mr. Hughes told her to think about a "sister act," which he thought he could promote a little better. That's when she invited her little sister to come and audition for Mr. Hughes.

Carmela introduced me to Rosa one or two days after she had been in New York, and had already auditioned very successfully for Gene Hughes. I can't describe what my reaction was when I first saw this "little sister" I had been hearing about. I expected her to look like a smaller, younger version of Carmela, in other words, a raving beauty. But my very first impression, to be honest about it, was of a big, fat, greasy Sicilian peasant girl. You wouldn't have known she was any relation to Carmela at all. She dressed like she just got off the boat, and she ate like there was a food shortage coming any minute: no manners, no finesse at all. The only nice features she had were her teeth; they were as white and perfect as you'll ever see, just like Carmela's. It was a family trait. But if you had seen Rosa in those days, you would understand why Caruso's first nickname for her, when he met her at William Thorner's studio, was *scugnizza*. It means urchin—like those unwashed street kids in the slums of Naples. That's what she looked like in those days, nothing at all like the Rosa Ponselle that she became.

I was with Rosa and Carmela for at least part of every day. They ate dinner at our house. They took me to Meriden with them to meet their family. Sometimes I slept on the couch in their room at the boarding house where they were living, and on weekends they might sleep at our house. I was with them when Rosa was writing out the musical score for their vaudeville act. I was there when they picked out the material for the dresses they used in their act. I helped them when they were sewing the backdrop for the act. And though I didn't go on the road with them when they got on the bigtime circuit, I went to hear them as often as I could when they were doing their act in and around New York.

Even though Carmela was older than Rosa, it was obvious that Rosa had the drive and the brains; and Carmela, to her credit, was smart enough to do whatever Rosa said they should do. Now, Carmela would have been just as happy to sing in vaudeville. But Rosa wanted to go into opera, so she sold Carmela on the idea. Rosa went to hear all the big opera singers when they did concerts and recitals, and after one of these she and Carmela met Romano Romani. He had come over from Italy, and he was sort of a "boy wonder" as a composer. Many years later, in fact, Rosa got Covent Garden to premiere his opera *Fedra*. Now, the Cinderella version of this story says that William Thorner, who was supposed to be their teacher, got Caruso to come and hear them. That's not the way it was. The way they got to Thorner was really through Romano Romani; and, as I'll explain, it wasn't Thorner who was the first to tell Caruso about Rosa.

At the time I'm talking about, which was around 1916 or 1917, Romani was doing a lot of coaching and conducting, and he was also working for the Columbia record company. He conducted some of their recording sessions, and he consulted with them about new singers that Columbia wanted to record. Romani knew most of the opera crowd, and he also knew William Thorner because he brought singers to Thorner from time to time, and Thorner often used him as an accompanist during his lessons. Now, Thorner was part of the inner circle at the Metropolitan Opera. His studio was on Broadway, and he used to rent out space to a few other teachers and singers.[13] Victor Maurel, who had created Iago in *Otello*, was retired from singing in those days but had an art studio in Thorner's building. Adamo Didur, the Metropolitan basso, had a studio there too. All these men played cards at Thorner's, including Caruso.

Romani was the one who introduced Rosa and Carmela to Thorner. This was a big thing, because Thorner had the connections to get them an audition at the Metropolitan. But Thorner would hardly pay any attention to Rosa. He thought Carmela was the one who was heading for a big career, and he wouldn't give Rosa the time of day. But let's face it, Rosa looked like hell at that time and Carmela was a raving beauty. So, let's just say that Thorner had an interest in Carmela that didn't have a whole lot to do with her singing voice. Not that she was interested in him. She wasn't, except for what he could do for their careers. But he didn't care a thing about Rosa until he asked Victor Maurel to listen to them.

Maurel set him straight. He told Thorner that he was betting on the wrong sister. After that, Thorner started pushing Rosa's prospects at least as much as he did Carmela's. Then Didur heard them (his studio was on another floor, so it wasn't unusual for him to drop by Thorner's). Well, Didur was the one who really began to talk them up, especially Rosa. He's the one who told Caruso about Rosa, and then Caruso and Thorner got together and made the arrangements for Caruso to come hear Rosa at Thorner's place.

Now, the way we all told the story later on, it was as if Caruso was wanting to hear both Carmela and Rosa. But the truth is, the only people who were promoting Carmela were Thorner and Rosa and maybe Romani, even though he knew that Rosa was the one who had the real gift. Thorner, of course, had nothing to lose with the Metropolitan Opera people by talking up Carmela and Rosa both. It doesn't take a Philadelphia lawyer to figure out that if you can get two contracts instead of one, you also get two fees instead of one. And as far as I'm concerned, you can say the same about Nino Romani too. You could never convince me that Romani didn't stand to make some money on the side from Thorner, for bringing young singers like Rosa and Carmela for him to manage.

Rosa's interest in Carmela was sincere. The way she put it to Thorner was, "Where I go, she goes." And I think in her mind she really believed it could work out that way. She had Carmela prepare duets with her from operas like *Aida* and *La gioconda*, thinking that the Met would want the Ponzillo sisters just like Broadway had. But it didn't pan out at all. When they had their audition with Caruso at Thorner's place, he did listen to both of them, but because that's the way Thorner set it up. Caruso was polite to Carmela after their audition, but he singled out Rosa for all the attention. He even told Rosa she was going to sing with him someday. You can imagine how Carmela felt when she heard that.

Thorner did get Gatti-Casazza to audition both of them at the Metropolitan. Gatti didn't give Carmela much to sing on her own, although they did let her sing several duets with Rosa. But everyone was there to hear Rosa. Now, Rosa will tell you that Carmela was at the second audition that Gatti arranged for some of the well-known singers and the Metropolitan executives. The truth was, Carmela was dropped after the first audition at the Met. The second audition was for Rosa alone. But after Rosa got successful, to help Carmela save face we put out the story that both of them had gotten offers to be with the Met. The way we said it was that Carmela had decided not to take the offer, so that she could devote all her time to helping Rosa. There wasn't a grain of truth to it, but it made for a good story, and it seemed to explain why Rosa was getting all the glory while Carmela wasn't doing much singing anywhere.

Rosa had about three months to prepare for her debut, so she rented a summer house at a resort called Pine Orchard, in Connecticut. Rosa had several operas to learn for her first season. She was so thorough that she insisted on having the Met give her not only the piano-vocal scores but the orchestral scores too. She and Romani would work about eight or nine hours a day, not all at once, but maybe two or three hours at a time. They would take a break, and we'd all go for a swim, or maybe Rosa and Romani would play tennis.

I didn't have much of anything to do except read and paddle around in the water a little bit. I wasn't athletic like Rosa, so I didn't go in for tennis and golf and that sort of thing. Then Rosa dreamed up the idea that I should be her secretary, to help manage things for her. Except for the fact that I couldn't even type, it sounded good to me. They got me a typewriter, and while she was learning operas I was trying to learn how to type with more than two fingers. After her debut, of course, this became my full-time job. I would do all of her correspondence, and copy all the translations of songs and arias she did in her concerts. Before a performance, I would set up her dressing room and make sure everything was ready for her.

She also liked for me to read all her reviews to her, and to read every fan letter out loud. She wanted to hear every word of those letters, and some of them she would have me read to her two or three times. She wanted every letter answered too. But if you were a fan, don't expect her to sign her name on a picture, or sign anything else for you—that was a poor use of her time, and time was money as far as she was concerned. To save both of us time, she had a rubber stamp made of her signature; it said, "Sincerely, Rosa Ponselle." Every week I would make time for her correspondence, and I would type a pile of letters in her name. I would hand them to her, she'd read them over, and would hand them back to me. Then it was *whack-whack-whack* with that damned stamper, just like the Ford assembly line.

That summer at Pine Orchard, Rosa learned *Forza* in only two weeks; that's how fast she was. After that, she and Romani went over every bar of the whole score so many times that she knew everyone else's roles down to the last note. Later on, at the rehearsals for *Forza*, she was so well prepared that she wasn't even nervous. Part of that was because Caruso kept everything calm. He was always full of fun at rehearsals. He carried a pocketful of gold pieces, and he used to have fun with the girls in the chorus; he'd play up to them, give them a pinch on the fanny, and then wink at them and press a gold piece in their palms.

Caruso was absolutely crazy about Rosa. He could read her like a book. He knew what she was going through inside, and when things would get tense, he would call for a little break. Then he would take her to the piano and make her play for him. He'd make her play ragtime, or maybe he'd get her to play and sing a crazy little thing that he liked called "Under the Yum-Yum Tree." He'd sing along with her: "If I like-a you like-a you like-a me," those were the words; or he'd have her play "O terra, addio" in ragtime and sing it like a man, in her chest voice. After a few minutes of fun, they would go back to rehearsing again.

Now, it's true that after Rosa saw the reviews of Giulio Crimi's debut, she got into a panic. We had gotten to know Crimi, and Rosa had sent him a little note wishing him luck the day of his debut. That next morning, I gave her the newspapers, but I didn't even think about reading Crimi's reviews because they didn't really mean anything to me. To this day I don't know whether they were good, bad, or indifferent, but to her they were awful; and, of course, because she was a nobody at that time, she thought her reviews were going to be ten times worse. I went by her bedroom door around noontime, and she was just staring off into space. Her mother tried to calm her down, and we finally had to get a doctor to give her some sedatives so she could sleep. That next day, Friday, she still wasn't completely right, so she had me ask the Met's publicity people to put out the story that she was getting over a bad cold. That way, she hoped the critics would go easier on her if she messed things up.

Around four o'clock that day, Romani came to the apartment and had her do some vocalizing. Her voice was just fine, so Romani told her to rest awhile, drink some broth, then go on to the theater and not worry herself about it. I had gone over to the Met earlier in the afternoon, to get her dressing room all ready for her. By the time she got there, which was around six, she was really nervous, but thank God there wasn't enough time for her to dwell on her nerves. She was on stage before she knew it.

I took my seat in the audience, which was in one of the front rows not far from the pit. She asked me to sit in the center, near the stage, so I could report back to her about how she looked to the audience. I used to do the same thing when she was in vaudeville. But this time, when I took my seat, in the row behind me I heard these two society women talking about Rosa. They were saying that nobody had ever heard of her, that she couldn't be much good. Then one of them said to the other, "Well, you know, she's a drunk." I thought to myself, this is the famous Metropolitan Opera House? The place of

Mrs. Astor and high society? I turned around and glared at these two old dames and said, "How dare you! What the hell do *you* know about her?" That shut them up!

Rosa was very nervous in the first act, until Caruso came on stage. From then on, she got a lot more confident, and she was able to let out more and more of her voice. She really hit her stride in the second act. It was in the monastery scene, when she sang with the Padre and the monks. Now remember, this was the Metropolitan premiere of *Forza,* so the audience had never heard this music performed there. The Padre was José Mardones. At the beginning of the prayer with the Padre and the monks, when the harp is heard, there was hardly a sound in the theater. You could have heard a pin drop!

As she finished, Rosa had her hands folded. She was looking upward, in prayer. She held that pose while the orchestra played the final measures. Then the house absolutely went wild. The applause sounded like thunder rolling through the whole Metropolitan Opera House! To me, that was the moment when she stopped being Rose Ponzillo. From then on, she was Rosa Ponselle.

The Written Record

In January 1977, *Opera News* commissioned Thomas Pasatieri to interview Rosa Ponselle for a feature article commemorating her eightieth birthday. Pasatieri, a young American-born composer whose opera *Inès de Castro* had its premiere under Ponselle's guidance at the Baltimore Opera Company in the 1975–76 season, considered himself well acquainted with Rosa Ponselle. But until his interview with her, he had never had an opportunity to hear her tell the story of her Metropolitan Opera debut.[14] As with most interviewers who heard her relate the story of her debut, he was affected by Ponselle's dramatic, almost frenzied way of telling it. "Her own past triumphs and troubles [had] all quietly stirred again," he wrote at the close of his article, "and as I looked at her I saw the frightened little girl who became a legend."[15]

Few would take issue with Pasatieri's claim that Ponselle "became a legend" in opera performance, especially in her own country. But was the Rosa Ponselle of November 1918 the "frightened little girl" her interviewer was describing nearly sixty years later? And were the actual events of that now-famous evening the same ones that had mesmerized a host of interviewers over the years? Or, as Edith Prilik Sania suggested, had Ponselle told the Cinderella-like story of her debut so many times that she had come to believe it herself?

Over the years, four elements became integral to the story of Ponselle's legendary debut: that through the personal intervention by Caruso with Giulio

Gatti-Casazza, she had been given an audition and soon afterward a contract; that for her debut Gatti had assigned her a starring role with the great tenor in a Metropolitan premiere "without a single role to my credit and without any operatic experience anywhere," as she repeated in interviews; that the day before her debut she had been "paralyzed" by the critics' reviews of tenor Giulio Crimi's debut, and by the sudden realization that she might fail; and, lastly, that because of the success of her debut performance, the Metropolitan Opera became accessible to subsequent American-born singers with no prior experience outside their native country.

As in any other instance in which the sheer ability of a novice leads to an unprecedented triumph, the telling of the debut of Rosa Ponselle makes a gripping story, especially as she herself told it. But when the events leading to her debut are reconstructed from press reports, contracts, and contemporary accounts, it becomes evident that only one of the four elements of that story, namely, that her debut was an unqualified success from the critics' standpoint, is unarguably true. Most of the others have long since become a part of opera lore, and in most cases, as will be shown, are not supported by any known documentation.

The first of the scores of interviews Ponselle would give during her career appeared in the New York *Star* in January 1919, shortly after she had sung her seventh performance (an *Oberon*, on 17 January 1919) as a new member of the Metropolitan Opera:

> A friend who heard us sing took us to William Thorner. He is the well-known teacher who discovered Anna Fitziù when she was Anna Fitzhugh of musical comedy. They say he persuaded [Cleofonte] Campanini to give Galli-Curci her chance with the Chicago Opera Company. Mr. Thorner tried Carmela's voice and liked it. He didn't care much for mine. But we persuaded him to give me some lessons. He was surprised by my improvement and said: "Before six months have passed I can place you at the Metropolitan."
>
> I went every day to Mr. Thorner's studio for an hour's lesson. Then I went to Romano Romani's studio to be coached in the operatic rôles.
>
> One day a wonderful thing happened. I went to Mr. Thorner's and was presented to Caruso. I was mute, remembering how I had heard him sing; I could only bow and look and long to kiss his hand. He was affable to me, a poor unknown. He heard me sing. He said, "I will appeal to Gatti-Casazza about you."
>
> I was summoned to an audition. I sang three times. I was asked to come back in two weeks. The next time I sang four times. I was so nervous that as I finished the last aria I fainted. Carmela ran into the wings and caught me in her arms.[16]

Two months after her debut, Thorner's version of how he became her teacher was recounted in a *Musical America* feature story. Despite some understandable self-promotion on his part (and leaving aside any extramusical interest he may have had in Carmela), Thorner's recollections are consistent with Ponselle's. "Five months from the time that Miss Poncelle [*sic*] first came to Mr. Thorner's studio," according to the article, "she had her audition with Mr. Gatti-Casazza and was accepted on a generous contract by the Metropolitan."[17] In a companion interview, Thorner said of his star pupil and his approach to teaching her:

> Sometimes I am amused at the attitude of teachers who make a mystery of their art. For there is no mystery about teaching voice. It is very simple, as are all things that are worth while. Give me a student with talent, spontaneity and art, and I will produce a singer. Rosa Poncelle is such a one and she has the interesting art that will develop year by year, and [will] always hold new delights in store of her hearers. But she has talent, voice, and excellent memory and an inexhaustible love of study.[18]

Thorner made special mention of Ponselle's commitment to hard work. "Often we have begun our lessons at three o'clock in the afternoon and worked continuously until seven or eight o'clock at night," he said. "It is to such singers that rewards come."[19]

At the time, Thorner was among the most influential voice teachers in New York, and had testimonials from a number of leading singers of the day. Titta Ruffo referred to him as the "estimable teacher"; Andrès de Segurola spoke of "his great and constant success as a vocal teacher"; and Ernestine Schumann-Heink labeled him "the best vocal teacher I ever met." Even Edouard de Reszke, the basso half of the legendary de Reszke brothers with whom Thorner claimed to have studied, referred to him in a printed advertisement as "my good pupil."[20]

While Thorner billed himself prominently as "a teacher of singing" in music periodicals, some of his advertisements contained veiled references to his managerial role. ("Mr. Thorner," a November 1915 advertisement in *Musical America* stated, "secures positions for pupils in light or grand opera."[21]) His contracts reflected both of these roles. His written agreement with Ponselle, as with similar ones he had negotiated with other singers, required Rosa to state that Thorner was her teacher, not merely her manager, in any interviews or promotional events in which their relationship became the subject of discussion. It was only after protracted legal wranglings with Thorner, which began in 1924 and were not settled until 1928,[22] that she began to cite Romano Romani, not Thorner, as her first and only teacher.[23]

In 1949, nearly twenty years after her lawsuit with Thorner and some twelve years after she had left the Metropolitan, Ponselle gave an illuminating interview to record researcher John Secrist. The interview was conducted at Villa Pace and, fortunately, was preserved on an early-model wire recorder. At Secrist's prompting she reconstructed how and why Carmela and she had sought out Thorner. On this occasion her recollections were more sharply focused and less dramatically reshaped than they would be in later years, and they contain details and nuances that are missing from her subsequent interviews.

During the session, Ponselle reiterated to Secrist that she had studied voice with Thorner, but had coached her roles with Romani. But after she realized what she had said (and perhaps had remembered that the interview was being recorded and would be published in print), she began to hedge on how she wanted to characterize Thorner's role in her development. When Secrist asked her to clarify if she was saying that William Thorner had been her teacher, she replied haltingly, "I don't want to go into that because I . . . studied with him, but I didn't like his method, and the only reason I went to him is because he knew Caruso and Gatti-Casazza and all those people."[24]

She also made a statement to Secrist which suggested that she was the one who had asked Romani to give her voice lessons while he was coaching her. "As I coached with Romani," she said, "I realized that this man knows so much about voice, and I've worked with him ever since."[25] If so, she and Romani would have begun working together in a manner that clearly conflicted with the division of responsibilities that Thorner had devised for her: voice lessons with him and coaching sessions with Romani. Of necessity, she and Romani would have been forced to be secretive about these new arrangements until she could find a way out of her contract with Thorner.

Ponselle made no mention to Secrist of any interest in Carmela on the part of Caruso or Gatti-Casazza. But in at least two interviews she gave in the early 1970s, she maintained that she and Carmela had been given two auditions, and she herself had been given a third one before Gatti-Casazza had offered her a contract.[26] The first of these auditions, Rosa claimed, had been with Caruso at Thorner's studio, where the tenor had listened to both sisters sing. "[My] sister sang Laura's aria from *La gioconda*, and together we rendered the duets from Aida and La gioconda," she said.[27]

A second audition, as she remembered it, was scheduled a few days later with Gatti-Casazza at the Metropolitan Opera House. There, she claimed, she and Carmela were heard by a select audience of great singers including (and her list varied in different interviews) Rosa Raisa, Pasquale Amato, Titta Ruffo, Giovanni Martinelli, Frieda Hempel, Adamo Didur, Margarete Matzenauer, Giuseppe de Luca, and José Mardones. She felt sure that a third audition had taken place less than two weeks later, again at the Metropolitan. This audition, she said, proved to be the final one: "Gatti typed my voice right then and there, having heard the agility of the 'Di tale amor,' and courageously offered me a contract."[28]

A half-century after the fact, Ponselle was confident about these recollections, despite the inconsistencies some of them revealed. She was certain, for instance, that Titta Ruffo and Rosa Raisa had been in the small audience of artists whom Gatti-Casazza had assembled to hear her. Ruffo, however, had no affiliation with the Metropolitan Opera until the 1921–22 season and was not even in the United States in 1917 or 1918.[29] Also, it would have been most unusual for Rosa Raisa, the *prima diva* of the Chicago Opera Company, to have been invited to participate in an audition session at the Metropolitan.

Near the time of Ponselle's auditions in the spring of 1918, Raisa was concertizing at the Hippodrome in Manhattan; her baritone husband, Giacomo Rimini, was her assisting artist. As Raisa and Rimini were well acquainted with Romano Romani (whose one-act opera, *Fedra,* had premiered two seasons earlier in Rome, with Raisa in the title role[30]), it is feasible that Romani was the one who arranged for Raisa to hear Ponselle sing. With the exception of Titta Ruffo, then, it is entirely possible that not only Rosa Raisa but several other artists for whom Ponselle remembered singing actually heard her in an audition setting—at William Thorner's studio, however, not at the Metropolitan Opera House.

Although nothing was said about it in the critics' columns when she made her debut, many writers would eventually accord Rosa Ponselle the distinction of having been the first American-born, American-trained soprano, with no prior European experience and without ever having sung in opera anywhere, engaged by the Metropolitan Opera Company. Ponselle was usually more cautious in making this claim herself. In a 1960 radio interview for a Metropolitan Opera broadcast, for instance, Boris Goldovsky asked her if it was true that she had been "the first American artist in this country [who was] engaged to sing major roles at the Metropolitan without singing in Europe." "Well, I guess I was," she replied somewhat hesitantly. "I was given to believe I was, anyway."[31]

Well before Ponselle, however, Gatti had given a number of American-born singers an opportunity to join the Metropolitan's artistic ranks. "It is a pretty long list," judged *Musical America* in 1919, "and [it] includes among others Geraldine Farrar, Louise Homer, Florence Easton, Mabel Garrison, Rosa Ponselle, Thomas Chalmers, Clarence Whitehill, Paul Althouse, Sophie Braslau, Marguerite Romaine, and May Peterson—and in former seasons also included Riccardo Martin."[32]

Although the English-born Florence Easton did not rightly belong on the list, two more names should have been added to *Musical America*'s tally: Anna Fitziù and Vera Curtis, both of whose musical origins were in several ways akin to Ponselle's. The Virginia-born Fitziù also had begun her career on Broadway, and in a vaudeville "sister act." As Ponselle had told the New York *Star* in her first interview, Fitziù was studying with William Thorner at the time she was given a Metropolitan Opera audition.[33] But unlike Ponselle, Fitziù had made a successful debut in Italy before Gatti-Casazza awarded her a contract for the 1915–16 season. (This, too, may have been arranged by Thorner, who had a written agreement with the Chicago Opera's Cleofonte Campanini, by means of which the impresario promised to "take a personal interest in your pupils . . . and give them an opportunity to make a debut in my theatre at Parma, Italy."[34])

Fitziù was also given a starring role in a Metropolitan Opera premiere (as was Ponselle later): Enrique Granados' and Fernando Periquet's *Goyescas*, in which she created the role of Rosario in January of 1916. Regrettably, however, Fitziù's singing did not fare as well with many of the New York critics as did the "intensely Spanish . . . texture and feeling" of Granados' score.[35] "Her voice is not notable for warmth or expressiveness," said *The New York Times* critic, "but there were some passages that she sang with success."[36]

The Connecticut-born Vera Curtis, like Ponselle, had no previous operatic experience in her own country or abroad when Gatti-Casazza awarded her a Metropolitan contract in the spring of 1912.[37] As *The New York Times* reported in a five-column feature story a few weeks before her debut was to take place, the young American-trained soprano (she had studied with William L. Whitney in Boston and had spent a year at the Institute of Musical Art) was being given weighty responsibilities for a newcomer: "During the coming year in the Metropolitan company she will sing in German, English, French, and Italian. Her roles will include Aida, Mimi, Marguerite, Euridice, Nedda in *Pagliacci*, Santuzza in *Cavalleria*, Julietta in *Tales of Hoffmann*, Micaela in *Carmen*, Venus in *Tannhäuser*, six other German parts, and some less well-known roles in French and Italian opera, as well as works in English."[38]

When asked about her career ambitions, Curtis told the *Times*, "Oh, my ambitions are boundless. But it's too early to talk of those, isn't it?" Apparently, Gatti-Casazza shared her view that it was indeed "too early": after her debut (as the First Lady in *Die Zauberflöte* in November 1912), Curtis was given only minor roles during her first two seasons at the Metropolitan, and had to wait until the 1914–15 season before she was assigned a substantial role (Gertrune in *Götterdämmerung*, which she first sang in February 1915). But from then until the end of her Metropolitan career six seasons later, her singing was limited to secondary roles.

By spring 1918, as his newspaper interviews attest, Gatti-Casazza had long since concluded that debuts by American singers would be a necessity because of the war in Europe. "Before the war," he told *The New York Times* in April

1918, "all aspiring young artists and students went to Europe and in the opera houses there they learned all varieties of opera. That is finished now, for a long time; I doubt if such a state of things will ever return."[39]

Young American singers, he added, would be a feasible solution, but "when taught, [they] must have a place to appear; they need many theatres, and not only two isolated troupes in New York and in Chicago," because neither the Metropolitan nor the Chicago Grand Opera Company could "engage all the artists to whom Europe is closed." Whatever the war's eventual outcome, Gatti predicted, economic conditions will have changed and the great opera houses of Europe "will not be as brilliant after the war." "Mr. Gatti made it plain," said the *Times*, "that he had been thinking of the American side of the question—what to do with native artists asking [for a] public hearing."[40] The time was ripe, therefore, for a promising American singer to be awarded a contract by the Metropolitan Opera.

On 4 June 1918, after the third and final audition he accorded her, Gatti-Casazza offered just such a contract to the young Rose Ponzillo. Housed in the archives of the Metropolitan Opera, the eight-page contract lists all the roles and operatic works that Gatti gave her to prepare for her first season. Reproduced below as it appears in the contract, the list goes substantially beyond *La forza del destino*:

> The artist agrees to sing and perform as the Company or its representative may require, in the following roles or parts:
>
> *In Italian:*
>
> # AIDA .... Aida
> # Il Trovatore .... Leonora
> # Cavalleria .... Santuzza
> # Forza del Destino .... Eleonora [*sic*]
> La Gioconda .... Gioconda
> Tosca .... La Tosca
> Un Ballo in Maschera .... Amelia
> # Verdi's Requiem
>
> The roles marked by "#" are to be ready for production by the artist by November 11, 1918.

As Metropolitan archivist Robert Tuggle has pointed out, the terms Gatti-Casazza offered Ponselle were those of "a beginner's contract," and the salary he negotiated with her was among the lowest ($150 per week) that the Metropolitan was paying any of its sopranos or tenors at that time.[41] The contract obliged Ponselle "to sing and perform whenever required by the Company or its representative during the term of her engagement, i.e., three times per week and during two weeks, at the option of the Company, four times per week," although she would never be required to perform "more than twice in succession" and "never twice on the same day."

During the 1918–19 season, however, Ponselle would actually perform in only three of the works listed in her contract: *Forza*, *Cavalleria rusticana*, and the Verdi *Requiem*. But the contract also required her "to study and sing and perform in new and additional roles or parts," a provision that enabled Gatti-Casazza to assign to her two additional operas which premiered at the Metropolitan that season: Weber's *Oberon* and Breil's short-lived *The Legend*.

What is unclear in the contract is whether the role of Leonora in *La forza del destino* was the principal reason for Gatti's interest in Ponselle. In his autobiography, *Memories of the Opera*, ghost-written by critic Howard Taubman, Gatti did not say whether he had auditioned Ponselle for the part of Leonora, or whether he had merely given her a rather routine audition and had assigned the role to her sometime later. "I have been asked how I dared to give this inexperienced young artist so difficult a role to begin with," he wrote. "I will admit that it was a somewhat difficult problem, since the girl's only experience had been [in] vaudeville. But I took a chance. I decided to run the risk, although I felt a certain amount of assurance that the young singer was extremely musical and very sure of herself."[42]

Ponselle's own version, as she told it to William Seward and other interviewers, of why she was chosen for the *Forza* premiere was that because of the world war there were no European sopranos at the Metropolitan who could sing Leonora. Yet this does not explain why Leonora in Forza would not have been assigned to Claudia Muzio, who was on the roster in the 1918–19 season and was among the Metropolitan's highest-paid sopranos.[43]

As the Metropolitan *Annals* attest, Muzio had a starring role in another premiere that season. On 14 December 1918, less than a month after the *Forza* premiere with Caruso and Ponselle, Muzio created Giorgietta in *Il tabarro* at the world premiere of Puccini's *Trittico*. Ponselle's recollections of the events surrounding the Trittico, and in particular the casting of Giorgietta in *Il tabarro*, make clear that for this important premiere Gatti-Casazza approached Rosa to cover for the far more experienced Muzio:

> Right after Thanksgiving (it was the Monday after, in fact) Gatti called me at my apartment and asked me to come see him in his office right away. He must have called Romani too, because [Romani] was already there when I got to Gatti's office.
>
> Gatti said to me, "I have a personal favor to ask of you." I said, "Well, whatever it is, it's only for you to say and I'll do it." He said there

> was a problem, and he needed me to learn the role of Giorgietta for the premiere of *Il tabarro*. Of course, everybody at the Met knew that Muzio was going to sing it. But there was some problem that involved Muzio, according to what Gatti said to Romani and me. So I was [asked] to start preparing the role right away with Romani.
>
> We worked on it seven days straight—day and night, one long week. But then Gatti called me in again, and told me that things were back to where they were, meaning that Muzio was going to sing it after all, and so I wouldn't be doing it. His "consolation prize," you could call it, was to have me premiere [Joseph Breil's] *The Legend*. So, instead of Puccini, I got to create an opera that would smell up a cat's box.[44]

Apart from the disappointment of having lost an opportunity to create a key role in a Puccini world premiere, Ponselle felt no animosity toward Muzio; rather, they were mutual admirers and were quite friendly with one another.[45] But Gatti's dealings with the two over the Trittico give rise to intriguing questions about his intentions for *Forza*: was the role of Leonora actually intended for the experienced and popular Muzio, with Ponselle merely being a second choice?

The written record establishes that none of Muzio's contracts with the Metropolitan Opera, both prior to and including the 1918–19 season, makes any mention of *La forza del destino*.[46] She did not undertake *La forza del destino* until the summer of 1921, when she sang it at the Teatro Colón in Buenos Aires for what appears to have been her first time.[47] This does not preclude the possibility, of course, that Gatti might have considered assigning Leonora to Muzio. But there is no documentary evidence—contrary to what vocal historian Michael Scott and some other writers have conjectured—that the role was intended for anyone other than Ponselle.[48] "To maintain anything to the contrary when there is no evidence at all to support it," Metropolitan archivist Robert Tuggle has said, "takes away from one of the great artistic achievements in the history of the Metropolitan Opera."[49]

On Sunday, 3 November 1918, Gatti-Casazza announced two of the seven operas he had scheduled for the first week of the new season. The casts of both operas, *Samson et Dalila* and *La forza del destino*, would feature Caruso in the leading tenor roles. Speaking of *Forza* in an interview with *The New York Times*, Gatti expressed his delight "that the public shares my interest in the forthcoming presentation of a 'new' opera by Verdi."[50] Perhaps because of the disproportionate amount of advance publicity that had preceded Vera Curtis' uneventful debut, Gatti called no special attention to Ponselle when he announced the remainder of the season-opening roster.

On the opening day of the season, only a few hours before the news of the armistice would be flashed to the world press, *The New York Times* devoted a column to the "new artists [who] will appear nightly" during the first week's performances. On this occasion, minor attention was paid to Ponselle in the *Times*' coverage, but without any mention of her success on Broadway in big-time vaudeville. ("Rose [*sic*] Ponselle is an American girl, born in Meriden, Conn., of Italian parents, and is said to have a remarkable soprano voice."[51]) If Gatti-Casazza's plan was to let the critics "discover" Ponselle rather than to mount a promotional campaign before her debut, his plan succeeded when the New York press was invited to review the dress rehearsal of *Forza* on Wednesday, 13 November, and there discovered Ponselle.

The first article that any of the New York newspapers devoted to Ponselle appeared in the New York *American* the day before her debut, beneath a two-column photograph captioned "the new soprano . . . who created so favorable an impression among music lovers at the dress rehearsal yesterday":

> The story of Rosa Ponselle, who makes her debut at the Metropolitan tomorrow night, proves that romance still lives on the opera stage.
>
> Nine months ago Miss Ponselle was in vaudeville—"doing a singing turn." She has never seen an operatic score. She scarcely knew what grand opera was. Rosa Ponselle was born in Meriden, Connecticut, which is not exactly the home of grand opera, whatsoever its other attractions.
>
> The . . . quality of her voice was appreciated by a chance listener—William Thorner, coach and vocal teacher—the same man that discovered Anna Fitziù and persuaded Mr. Campanini to engage Mme Galli-Curci.
>
> Mr. Thorner saw at once the possibilities of Miss Ponselle's voice, and she was put into hard, persistent training five months ago.
>
> Now she is to appear as the leading soprano of the Metropolitan's first novelty—the revival of Verdi's *La forza del destino*, in which Caruso sings the principal tenor role. Her performance at the rehearsal yesterday delighted her hearers.
>
> The gods were very gracious to Miss Ponselle, of Meriden, for they not only bestowed on her a glorious voice, but they gave her the accoutrements of personal beauty and grace.[52]

This was the first publicity Ponselle had received since signing her contract with the Metropolitan. Wanting Rosa to see it for herself, Edith Prilik bought a copy of the *American* and gave it to her. In a column adjacent to the article and accompanying photograph there appeared a detailed review headlined, CRIMI SCORES INSTANTLY IN "AIDA." Ponselle's eye took in the headline, and soon she read the full text of critic Max Smith's review of the handsome Sicilian tenor's debut the previous night:

> The youthful Italian tenor caught the fancy of the crowd at the very outset though his singing of the trying "Celeste Aida" showed conspicuous evi-

> dence of nervous excitement. But much as Signor Crimi pleased his auditors, he did not monopolize all the honors of the evening.
>
> Not until he had reached the Nile Scene, at the close of which he had the satisfaction of facing a genuinely enthusiastic audience, did Giulio Crimi disclose his powers completely. Yet even then did one feel that he had not been able to attain his best. Frequently, he and the orchestra were distressingly at odds, and generally Signor Crimi lagged behind the beat of the conductor. No wonder!
>
> There was nothing in the least sensational about the new tenor's voice or his method of singing. But for that very reason, perhaps, did he win all the more favor from judicious listeners. To judge from last night's hearing, his voice is not of great power. But it is a voice of dramatic fibre, firm, masculine, clean-cut throughout its range without any vices, without any of those qualities that are less acceptable to American than Italian ears.[53]

With minor variations among them, the other major critics found the same assets and liabilities in Crimi's first Metropolitan performance. In *The New York Times,* James Huneker wrote that the tenor's "naturally resonant and agreeable organ was not heard at its best," owing to "choppy" phrasing and an "emission labored in spots."[54] In the *Herald,* Reginald De Koven found fault both with his singing and acting. "Mr. Crimi's stage presence is not impressive, he seemed almost furtive in this heroic role; his voice is typically Italian . . . and altogether did not impress me mightily. Though he sings with taste, his emission of tone is uncertain, and its quality therefore variable."

With the exception of the review of Crimi that was printed next to her photograph in the New York *American,* how many of these other reviews Ponselle actually saw or read at the time is open to question. In later years, she exhibited very little interest in other singers' performances and almost no interest in what critics said about them. But as she told William Seward and every subsequent interviewer, reading Crimi's reviews made her lose her confidence. "From that day on," she said to Seward, "I didn't know what peace was."

However much she may have fretted about the anticipated verdicts of the same critics who had found fault with Giulio Crimi, she need not have worried. Beginning Saturday and Sunday, 16–17 November 1918, all the major New York critics welcomed her with laurels. As Huneker wrote in *The New York Times*:

> The newcomer is an American born of Italian parentage. Her "home town" is Meriden, Conn. With her sister she sang in vaudeville, and last night marked her first appearance on the operatic stage. She is young, she is comely and she is tall and solidly built. A fine figure of a woman was the opinion of the experts; and in cavalier costume she was handsome and—embarrassed. Those long boots made her gait awkward; she was too con-

> scious of her legs, and her gestures and gait were angular. But what a promising debut! Added to her personal attractiveness, she possesses a voice of natural beauty that may prove a gold mine. It is vocal gold, anyhow, with its luscious lower and middle tones, dark, rich and ductile.[55]

Not that she was without vocal flaws, as Huneker made clear in the remainder of his review of her performance. He faulted her for "forcing the column of breath with the result that the tone becomes hard to the point of steeliness," and he also advised that the "note of monotony in the tone color that occasionally intruded must be avoided. Nuance, nuance, nuance. That must be mastered."

Her nervousness, Huneker said, was evident, "but after she sang 'Addio' in Act I she had her audience captured. Her scene and cavatina before the church was astonishingly mature for such a youthful debutante. And she sagged below pitch on her last note." Yet for all of that, Huneker judged the Ponselle instrument "a sweet, appealing, sympathetic voice, well placed, well trained, . . . a dramatic soprano of splendid potentialities." But, he concluded, "she has an arduous road to traverse before she can call herself a finished artist."[56]

The *Musical Courier* reported that she "upset all traditions by assuming a leading role at the Metropolitan, and without previous operatic experience, carrying it to triumphant success. It is no exaggeration to say that she made a sensational impression and was sensationally received."[57] The reviewer for *Musical America* fully concurred, labeling her "a young artist of incomparable charm, dramatic ability, the possessor of a voice of considerable power and fine musical quality." Neither her rather young age nor her lack of operatic experience were in evidence at her debut: "she has today all the resources of an experienced artist of the first rank, and with such a start she should go far."[58]

Even the most demanding of the longstanding New York critics, while underscoring the occasional technical faults that intruded into her debut performance, were univocal in their overall approval of her voice, technique, and stage deportment. At the New York *Sun*, W. J. Henderson, who had heard nearly every world-class singer from the 1880s onward, repeatedly underscored the promise he heard in the youthful Ponselle voice:

> If [she] never sang in opera before last night, she must have been born with a ready-made routine. However that may be, she is the possessor of one of the most voluptuous dramatic soprano voices that present-day operagoers have heard. Some day doubtless Miss Ponselle will learn how to sing, and then she will be an artist.
>
> At this moment she is almost naive in method. But she has the precious gift of voice and she has real temperament, not the kind that drives

> people into acrobatic excursions all over the stage and wild shrieks of vocal anguish, but the kind that makes itself felt in the eloquent quality of tones and the accentuation of melody.[59]

Henderson concluded his assessment with a comment that in retrospect seems prescient for her career and for the significance it has been accorded in Metropolitan Opera history. "Her début was very interesting," he wrote, "and we hope [it is] an incident of the evening having permanent importance."[60]

Henderson's review and the others that Rosa Ponselle received from her performance in *La forza del destino* attest to the stature she achieved, not only at her debut but throughout her first season with the Metropolitan Opera. Although she would have "an arduous road to traverse," as James Huneker had expressed it, the success of her debut, coupled with the ambitious list of works listed in her first contract—a total of eight of the most demanding roles in the *spinto* repertoire, most of which she had less than six months' time to prepare—only serve to underscore the confidence that Giulio Gatti-Casazza had invested in her. And as it would on many other occasions, history proved him right.

CHAPTER TWO

I Never Really Have Grown Up

In March 1933, a decade after she had become an international figure, Ponselle spoke nostalgically of her family and her childhood in Meriden, Connecticut. "Though I am in public life today . . . I never really have grown up from the child who used to be very sentimental about her home and her family," she said in *Good Housekeeping*.[1] The domestic scenes she reminisced about for the magazine probably took place in 1905 or 1906, a year or so before Carmela left the family home in Meriden to begin a career in New York.

In the article, Ponselle described her parents in vignettes drawn from their home life. Her mother, Maddalena Conti Ponzillo, had passed away in 1931, two years before the article was published. "Mother was a homebody," Rosa wrote of her, "and she took her responsibilities very seriously.

> You can understand how much work she had with six in the family to feed, including three healthy, outdoor children with such ravenous appetites that there was no limit to the quantity of bread and butter, potatoes and spaghetti they could consume. Grandmother helped at the cooking, but there were incidentals even in the kitchen and chores in general that only Mother could do. For instance, Carmela, Anthony, and I used to play tag and skate and roll our hoops and ride our bicycles—soiling our clothes so fast that they had to be changed at least twice a day—which gave Mother quite a heap of wash.[2]
>
> [After the supper table was cleared, Rosa continued,] it was Mother's idea of recreation to take out her sewing and entertain one neighbor or another who brought in her own towels or sheets or something or other to be hemmed by hand. [And while the neighbor and her mother went on with

their sewing, stopping only to] gesticulate over a bit of shocking local news, [her father, Benardino Ponzillo,[3] would be] sitting with his newspaper near the stove, or at the open door in the summer months. Carmela and I would be washing dishes and singing a duet. And sometimes we'd forget ourselves and let our voices rise to such a pitch that Father would stop his ears and threaten to go upstairs.[4]

[As she searched her memory for details of her home life, and as one incident prompted a recollection of yet another, Ponselle tried to capture these cascading images in picturesque phrases.] I remember the day Anthony gave a boy a sound beating for saying naughty things to me on my way home from school; the Christmas [when] my father bought me a second-hand bicycle because his heart had swelled when he saw his youngest well-poised on a borrowed one; and I shall never forget the first piano we bought from the bit of surplus money we had laid away in the bank. Up to then, I used to stand on a stool and play my fingers on the window sill.[5]

At the time these reminiscences were published, Ponselle was only in her thirties but was already far removed from the working-class life of her parents. In 1905, according to her brother's estimate, the Ponzillo family's gross annual income was approximately $1,500; and the family's assets, owing to their father's indebtedness, totaled no more than two or three hundred dollars.[6] By contrast, a mere twenty years later, Rosa Ponselle posted a gross annual income of $117,173, and her assets were assigned a certified value of $2,367,402.[7] Her continuously expanding wealth made possible a series of luxuries that neither she nor her parents could have imagined in 1905: luxuries such as a penthouse on Manhattan's fashionable Riverside Drive, a limousine-size Isotto Fraschini, an ever-growing collection of jewels, furs, antiques, *objets d'art*, and a personal staff encompassing a cook, a chauffeur, two housemaids, a wardrobe maid, her secretary Edith, and yet another secretary to assist Edith.[8]

By 1933, this privileged lifestyle apparently enabled Ponselle to look kindly upon her youth and adolescence and to recast them in pleasant and uncomplicated domestic scenes that would have been familiar to most of her readers. Most of these scenes, however, bore only a tangential relationship to the ones she described late in her life. These later descriptions are recounted in the coming pages—first by Ponselle, then by her brother. Their recollections of the same events differ, sometimes slightly and at other times more substantially. But taken together, they help clarify not only the circumstances but also the motives that led the Ponzillo sisters from their family home in Meriden to "the Mecca of vaudeville" in Manhattan, B. F. Keith's Palace Theater.[9]

The Interview

From the author's interviews of Rosa Ponselle (March 1973, June 1975, and December 1978). Transcribed with minor editing.

Would you agree that there were six people who helped you begin your career: your mother and father, your teacher Anna Ryan, your sister Carmela, James Ceriani in New Haven, Gene Hughes, who became your manager in vaudeville, and Romano Romani.

You forgot one. Mr. Halliwell—Richard Halliwell. He gave me my first paying job. And as for my father, well, I can't say that he did anything to help me. It was the other way around.

How would you describe your parents?

My mother was a living angel. I can't tell you how hard she worked, and what little she got in return for it. But one thing I'll be grateful for till my last day on this earth: that is, that because of her encouragement, my sister and I had the kind of life she used to dream about. And I'm thankful, too, that I made enough money to be able to give her a better life than my father could give her.

And your father?

Cold. Cold and hard, like a piece of stone. Some people are givers, and some people are takers. He was a taker. I never had anything in common with him.

What business was your father in?

He had several at different times. There was the fuel business; he had a wood business, and later on a coal business. He also had a couple of acres a few blocks from where we lived, and he grew vegetables and raised chickens there. And we had a grocery store and a bakery on the bottom floor of our house. My father, and later on my brother Tony, ran the fuel business and the bakery. Mother ran the grocery store. It was just a neighborhood grocery [with] canned goods, cheeses, cured meats, and bread from our bakery. I used to help her after school and in the summertime. But I was always taking samples—a little salami, a little cheese, a handful of black olives—and my mother used to kid me about my snacking. "Rose," she would tell me, "you eat up all the profits!"

Were there other relatives living with your family?

My father's brother, our Uncle Alfonso from Waterbury, lived with us for a while. He was a nice man; very kind, lots of fun, a hard worker, the salt of the earth. And when I was little, my grandmother on my mother's side lived with us.

Do you remember her well?

Oh, yes. She was a small woman, very quiet. You wouldn't even know she was there. She didn't speak [much] English (maybe a simple "yes" or "no," if that), but that was no problem because we all spoke the Neapolitan dialect at home. Her hair had gotten very thin and she was sensitive about it, so Mother bought her a dark red wig. She was the typical grandmother, always giving me sweets and other things I probably shouldn't have been eating. I remember one time, though, she got mad at me because I wouldn't eat baked beans. Being Catholic, you see, we couldn't eat meat on Fridays, so my grandmother used to make baked beans, which we would eat with whatever kind of fish we could get. Well, I got so sick of those damned beans that rather than eat them, one Friday I actually begged a dime from a stranger. I said I hadn't eaten for two days or something. I took the dime, went to a diner and bought myself a hamburger! Somehow, my grandmother found out about it, and she beat the hell out of me! Not once, but twice—first for begging money from strangers and then for eating meat on Friday!

Who were your best friends when you were growing up?

There was Lena Tamborini, who lived next door to us back in Meriden, and Juliet Dondero, who was the daughter of a very prominent Meriden family that helped our family a lot. I was a little closer to Lena. We used to pal around together when we were kids, and we stayed pretty close over the years. When she was little, she got the nickname "Red" because she had this mop of red hair. Lena's mother was another angel, and she was very, very good to us. She sewed a lot of my clothes, because Mama didn't have enough time, what with running the grocery all day. Lena's father ran a saloon. It was on the bottom floor of their house, like our little grocery was [for us]. Mrs. Tamborini had a little more free time than my mother did, so she did some of our sewing for us. Lena and I went to the public school together. She used to help me with my homework. To tell the truth, Lena did my homework for me. I wasn't the world's greatest student.

You and school just didn't get along?

That's putting it nicely. I didn't get as much schooling as some other kids because I went to work when I was around fourteen. I never got to finish high school. I'm not proud of that, mind you, but that's the way things went. For what little schooling I had, especially in the seventh and eighth grades, I only did well on the homework part [and that was] because Lena was doing it for me. We had a deal worked out. I would help her with music, which made no more sense to her than mathematics did to me, if she would do my homework. It worked fine until I had to take tests. The teachers used to say to me, "Rose, you do so well on your homework, but you do so badly on your tests!" But, you know, it was in school that I first learned about the voice and how it works. In one of our lessons, there was a drawing of the throat, and it showed the esophagus, the larynx, the supporting muscles, and such. Now, *that* fascinated me.

Did you sing in school?

Not if I could help it. The other kids made fun of the way I sounded. I never had what I'd call a little girl's voice, you know, that Shirley Temple kind of voice you expect little girls to have. As far back as I can remember, my voice always sounded like an adult's, and I'm talking about when I was, oh, maybe eleven or twelve years old. So, when I would sing in school with the other kids I sounded like some kind of freak, and they would make fun of me.

Did you take music lessons at school?

At the Columbia Street public school [in Meriden], we had a man who taught us music. He used to go from one school to the next, one each day of the week. Tuesday was our day with him. He would spend that whole day at our school, and he would spend about an hour with each grade. I used to live for Tuesday, because that was the only day I could enjoy. It was just drudgery for me to go to school. For one thing, it was hard for me to stay awake. I have always done better at night than in the morning, even when I was a little girl. But on Tuesdays I used to shine. The school had a portable pump organ for our music teacher to use. He would wheel it along, going from one room to the next. He would let me play for our class because I could sight-read almost as well as he could.

Was there a lot of music in your home?

No. Our family wasn't musical. Carmela and I used to sing with my mother during Sunday Mass at the Mount Carmel Church, our parish church. Mother had a nice natural voice, a very high, lyric-coloratura voice. I think if she could have studied, she might have sounded a little bit like Lily Pons. But in those days, women didn't have any chance; they got married young, had babies, and spent the rest of their lives doing chores. And when you were in business for yourself, like my mother was, you had even more to keep you busy. But my father, well, music meant nothing to him. We didn't have a phonograph, and we didn't have a piano till I was around eight or nine. Mother talked him into buying a used upright because my brother Tony and I were taking lessons from Miss [Anna] Ryan.

Did Anna Ryan actually teach you to sing?

No. She was a piano teacher, not a singing teacher. But when I think back, she must have known enough about singing to know how to let a natural voice develop pretty much on its own. That's what she did with Carmela. Miss Ryan had Carmela as a piano student, in fact, she ended up teaching all three of us.

Describe Miss Ryan for us.

Well, she was Irish, not that she was born there, but she came from an Irish family. She learned [to play the] piano and organ from a man who taught in Meriden (he was still teaching when I was a kid, in fact), and when she got to be in her twenties, she took up teaching as her profession. She wasn't what you would call pretty (she never married), but she was attractive in her own way. She played the organ in a parish that was full of Italians, but she got along with all of them, even though she was Irish to the last hair on her head. My mother always made lunch for her before she would give me my piano lesson every week. Miss Ryan loved the taste of spaghetti, but she never learned how to eat it right. Mother would have to cut up the spaghetti into little tiny pieces before serving it to her. We called that dish Miss Ryan's soup.

How did Carmela come to her attention?

Carmela used to sing in the choir at the Mount Carmel Church, and everybody told Carmela that she had a pretty voice. She liked music, so Mother got Miss Ryan to teach her. Carmela took piano, but Miss Ryan also taught her a few simple vocalises that she must have picked up somewhere. They were arpeggio vocalises. She would have Carmela sing them on different vowels, up and down the scale. I know because I used to hear Carmela practice them. Carmela didn't know it at the time, but I would practice those little vocalises on my own when I would be walking to school or outside running errands.

As you were learning those vocalises, did they seem easy or hard for you?

It didn't take anything to learn them. If you knew what a major chord was, you automatically knew the basic vocalise, and all you did was repeat it on different vowels. They didn't seem easy or hard. I just did them because I liked to do whatever Carmela did. I was at that stage where a little sister wants to do everything that her big sister does.

Were you able to do everything that Carmela was able to do vocally, despite the age difference between the two of you?

I must have been able to, because Miss Ryan mistook my voice for Carmela's. That's how I got "discovered." How it happened was that Miss Ryan stopped by our house to buy bread from our bakery. (She always bought from us because my mother gave her bread at half-price.) One day she came by the house, and she heard a voice coming from upstairs. It was spring or maybe summer, and all the windows were open. Miss Ryan thought it was Carmela singing, but it was really me—I was singing "'O sole mio," which Carmela had learned. At my next piano lesson, Miss Ryan told me to be sure to tell Carmela that she heard her singing "'O sole mio," and that she sounded even better than before. Well, I was just beaming; I was so proud. "Teacher, it was *me*," I told her. Well, you could've knocked her over with a feather. And from then on, she had me sing and play at all my lessons. Later on when Carmela went to New York City to start out on her own, I still kept working with Miss Ryan.

What took Carmela to New York at that particular time?

There wasn't much for her in Meriden, and she wanted a professional career. She did a little bit of modeling at a hat shop in Meriden, a place called Mrs. Hurley's, but she couldn't find much else to do in our home town. In New York her career developed pretty fast. She had only been there a couple of years when she got a part in a musical comedy. That was her first real break. When she would come back home to Meriden, I would be walking on a cloud because I wanted to be just like her.

Did Carmela help you get your first musical engagement?

Oh, yes. She started encouraging me to get work as a piano player. I had to earn my keep too, you know.

How old were you at the time?

Fourteen—I started to work when I was only fourteen. Still wet behind the ears, in other words, but I learned fast.

Did it take much persuading on Carmela's part to get you started in a singing career?

I didn't follow up on it at first. I wasn't outgoing like she was. So, finally she just took me by the hand and led me to the owner of one of the movie houses in town. That was Mr. Halliwell, the one who gave me my very first paying job, which was playing the piano for the movies. He owned a movie theater called the Star. In those days, remember, there was no such thing as sound pictures—the "talkies," as they used to be called, didn't come in until much later. They would use pianos in the smaller theaters to emphasize the action on the screen, and in the larger movie houses, they might even have a small orchestra.

Did you do any singing at the Star?

Not that I can remember. Mr. Halliwell owned three movie houses, and each one was bigger than the other. The one in Meriden, the Star, was the smallest. He had another one in Ansonia, which is southwest of Meriden. The Ansonia theater was a good deal larger than the Star, and it had a small stage so I did some singing there. The third one was in New Haven. The name of it was the San Carlino, and it was a full-sized theater. It had nearly a thousand seats, counting the balcony and the boxes. It had a pretty large stage, and there was also an orchestra pit. I did most of my singing at the San Carlino.

What would a typical performance at the San Carlino be like, compared to your performances at the Ansonia theater?

In those days, what they called song slides were very popular in movie theaters. They would make glass plates that had the lyrics of popular songs on them, and they would put these plates, these slides, in a projector so that the lyrics would appear on the screen. The piano-player would play the melody, and the audience would sing the lyrics from the slides. Now, at the movie house in Ansonia, they had two pianos: one below the little stage, which is the one I played while I was accompanying the movie, and then another one backstage, which they would wheel out in front of the screen between movies so I could also lead the audience in the singing. Now, at the San Carlino, which, as I said, was a good-sized theater, Mr. Halliwell always had a fifteen- or twenty-piece orchestra. It was an all-woman orchestra, by the way, which was unusual back then. Well, I would come on stage and sing between movies, at the intermission time. I would usually do four songs, and I was always trying to please two different audiences. One group were Italians, mainly immigrants who were about my parents' age, and then there would be a group of Yale students, because the campus was not too far away. I would sing two popular songs for the Yale boys, and then I would do two Italian songs, usually Neapolitan songs, for the Italians in the audience.

Was it through your San Carlino engagements that you met James Ceriani?

Indirectly, yes. I developed a sort of "Yale fan club" at the San Carlino, and many of these same young fellows used to go to the Café Mellone, which Mr. Ceriani owned. He started hearing about me through the Yale boys.

Please tell me what you can remember of the Café Mellone: what it looked like inside, and any other details about it that come to mind.

It was in a brick building that had three or maybe four floors. The café took up the whole first floor, and I think there were rented rooms on the upper floors. Inside, it was pretty big; there were enough tables to seat at least two hundred people, maybe even more. The stage was kind of like an elevated band box; it was above all the tables, and there was a railing all around it.

And Mr. Ceriani? How would you describe him?

He was probably about forty years old at that time. He was always well groomed, had a mustache, dark hair—a full head of hair, brown almost to the point of being black. He was about five feet ten, a little overweight, but muscular and very strong. He had a very expressive face, dark brown eyes, always very happy looking. Every once in a while [when] I would be studying Caruso's face (he had such a wonderfully expressive face), I would be reminded of how Jimmy Ceriani looked.

What led you to leave the San Carlino to begin singing at the Café Mellone?

Jimmy Ceriani came to hear me at the San Carlino, and afterward he invited me to have lunch with him at the Café. That very day, he offered me double the money I was getting from Mr. Halliwell. I went from forty dollars a week to eighty, which was a lot of money in those days. He was also very encouraging about what kind of career I could have. He was the first person who ever made me feel that I could really go someplace with my voice. He told me that he had heard Emmy Destinn many times at the Met and that my voice was in the same league as hers. I'll never forget that; I can't tell you how much his confidence meant to me.

When you accepted his offer to sing full-time at the Café Mellone, then, you had to leave home and move to New Haven?

Yes, I stayed with a cousin of my mother's for a little while, and then through Carmela I went to live with a young married couple, Margaret and Rocco Da Vino. He was an architect, very successful, and they were friends of ours. Of course, I had to get my father to agree to all this, since I was not of age yet, but Jimmy Ceriani came to our house and talked it over with my parents. He had a real selling job to do on my mother. He had to reassure her that she needn't be worried about her daughter's virginity. You know how mothers are. But she gave in and said I could live in New Haven, as long as I had someone watching me all the time. Mr. Ceriani convinced her that he would look after me, which he did.

And your father? How did he react to this?

He didn't really object too much because I would be sending most of my salary back home to Meriden every week. Between what I was making in New Haven and what Carmela was getting in New York, we started sending home a pretty good bankroll. Believe me, they needed it.

Although you were being "watched," as you put it, are we safe in assuming that you still managed to have an active social life?

I don't know what you want to call active, but I nearly married a Yale boy, if that's what you mean. His name was Frederick Stimson. He used to hear me sing at the Café, and I would notice that every time I came on he would put down his knife and fork, turn his chair around, look at me, and applaud me louder than just about anybody else. Apparently, he liked my looks, and he asked Mr. Ceriani if he would personally introduce us. He said he wanted to go out with me, and he gave his word that he would see me home safely. Mr. Ceriani knew him because he came to the Café Mellone so much, and he trusted him because he knew Fred to be a perfect gentleman. Fred used to meet me at a flower shop that my mother's cousin ran, and he would take me out to dinner on the nights I had off.

Did you become serious about him?

I'll say so! He even went to Meriden to get my father's permission so we could get married. He was from a very wealthy family (his father was a financier) and Fred wanted to marry me and take me to Italy, so I could pursue an opera career over there. It sounded real good to me, I'll tell you.

Would your parents have let you marry him at such a young age?

I think they would have. They liked him, that much I do know. Even my father liked him. Fred even drove to Meriden a few times to help out at the little sawmill my father had. Fred would talk to Daddy while he ran the saw for a while, and then they would change places. My Dad really liked him, but Fred's own father was the one who gave him problems.

In what way?

His father thought that no respectable woman should ever be in show business, so he did everything he could to break up the romance. He finally sent Fred to Europe for five or six months, just to get him away from me. But do you know how it all turned out? Several years later, his father and mother started going to the Met. They even became fans of mine, but they didn't realize that Rosa Ponselle used to be Rose Ponzillo once upon a time. One night they took Fred with them to the Met, and at intermission he said, "Remember the girl from Meriden you didn't want me to marry? Well, she's the one you're applauding!" That's a true story.

When you were still in New Haven, singing at the Café Mellone, was it Mr. Ceriani who first took you to the Metropolitan Opera House?

Yes, and that was probably the most important day of my life up to that time because that was the day I had my audition for vaudeville, the audition that Carmela had arranged for me with Gene Hughes, her manager. Jimmy Ceriani drove me to New York for the audition, and as an extra "treat," he took me to the Met.

Do you remember what the performance was, and who was in the cast?

Could I ever forget it? It was *Madama Butterfly*, with Caruso as Pinkerton and Geraldine Farrar as Cio-Cio-San. And you know, all during the performance Jimmy Ceriani kept whispering to me, "Now, take a good look at that stage, because one day soon you're going to be up there too." He wasn't just buttering me up; he really believed in me, and I wanted to believe it too.

I don't know quite how to ask you this, but I'm going to have to find a way that I hope won't offend you. It's about your personal life at that time.

My what? My "personal life"? I didn't have any. I had to work too hard. There was never time to have boyfriends and such like other young women had.

It's Mr. Ceriani that I need to ask you something personal about. There was some talk (I heard it from people who knew you in Meriden) that James Ceriani fell in love with you and that you had considered marrying him. I was even told that on one occasion, when he was leaving for a trip to Italy, you showed up with a wedding ring and passed yourself off as his wife.

Oh, that! It's true, but not the way you're making it sound. They wouldn't let you spend time with someone on board ship unless you were a relative. I had things to discuss with him, but they wouldn't let me board the ship with him unless I was a relative. At first, I said I was his daughter, but nobody would believe me because I looked a lot older than I was. So I went to a dime store and bought one of those "diamonds" that are made out of glass. That's how I got around the rules. But an affair? Not at all. Jimmy Ceriani was like a second father to me. Anyway, I never went in for that sort of thing. I was a good girl. I waited till I got married to be serious with somebody.

You're saying that you never had any kind of a romantic involvement with a man until you got married?

Well, that's not the same question. I'm telling you that I never had time to get serious with somebody. If I had had as many lovers as the gossip said I did, I wouldn't have had time to sing! It's nonsense because practically until I got married (and, remember, I was thirty-nine when I was married), I had my sister, my secretary, and even Miss Ryan, my old teacher, living with me. I never even had any privacy, you see. Now, what else do you want to know?

I guess I don't know how to ask it.

Oh, I know what you want to know. You want me to tell you who the first man was. That's what you want to know, isn't it!

I might have put it a little more gracefully, but yes.

Well, why don't you just come right out and ask me who the first man was?—and I'll tell you too.

All right. Who was the first man?

Adam.

And the first woman was—

Eve. That's one of the oldest jokes in show business. Remember, I used to be in vaudeville!

Recollections

Antonio P. Ponzillo

In the Boston Advertiser *of Sunday, 2 November 1919, there appeared a full-page feature illustrated with a photograph showing two men seated atop a horse-drawn coal wagon. The wagon bore the sign "A. P. Ponzillo Coal Company." The men in the photograph were Antonio Patrizio Ponzillo, then twenty-nine, and his father, Benardino Ponzillo. The focus of the feature story was the younger Ponzillo, described in the headline as "Simple-Minded Tony with a Million-Dollar-a-Year Voice, Brother of Rosa Ponselle, the Grand Opera Soprano." In the article, when asked why he preferred the coal business to a Metropolitan Opera contract, Tony Ponzillo replied, "When I want to sing, I sing. When I don't want to sing, I don't sing . . . I am a business man and my own boss." He remained his "own boss" for another decade, after which he sold the family's coal business and retired. He recalled his childhood and family life in two interviews recorded in 1977 and 1978.*[10]

If you ask me where the singing comes from in our family, I don't know how to answer you. They used to say there was a priest in the family, a monsignor way back there in the family history, who was supposed to have had a beautiful voice. Maybe so, maybe not; who knows? I could show you a room full of newspapers and magazines that would have you believe the Ponzillo family did two things all day long: that we worked, which is true, and that we sang all the rest of the time, which is baloney. If my old man heard you singing when you were supposed to be working and sweating, he'd crack you one! Music was a waste of time as far as he was concerned. If he ever went to hear Carmela or Rosa sing, I can't remember when, even after they got famous.

Benardino Ponzillo was my father's name (they called him Ben, for short), and my mother's maiden name was Maddalena Conti. The Contis and the Ponzillos were all from the Naples area, from a part of Caserta called Caiazzo. Mamma used to say she was just a little girl when she met Pop because she was still in her teens. Pop (in Italian we say "Papa," but in English we say "Pop") was twelve years older than Mother. Even though they had been neighbors in the old country, they couldn't get too friendly over there because the Italians had old-fashioned ideas about marriage. In the old country, if a boy and girl started getting friendly, the old people would arrange a marriage, and it didn't matter whether the boy or the girl wanted each other or not. So my father courted my mother over here, not in Italy. After they got married they lived in Schenectady for three or four years.

Carmela and I were born there. We were both June babies: Carmela was born in June of 1887, and I came along in June of 1890. I don't remember much about Schenectady because my parents didn't stay there very long. They left there about 1892, and they moved to New Haven, where my father got into the saloon business. He owned his own saloon there. They stayed in New Haven for a few years and eventually they moved to Meriden, where they ended up settling for good.

Meriden used to be known all over the country as Silver City because our factories put more plated silver in more homes, restaurants, and hotels than probably anywhere else in the country. There was a factory here called International Silver, which was the biggest in the world. It's all pretty much gone now, but around the turn of the century and up to the time of the Depression, there was a lot of work here in Meriden. The factories were going day and night, and everything was booming. That's what attracted my father. Where there were factories, there were immigrants working in those factories; and wherever there were factory workers, a saloon was a sure bet to make money.

The saloon business was a tough business, especially for Italians. The "blue-noses" in these towns hated saloons, you see, because they associated the saloons with the Irish and the Italians. The blue-noses thought all immigrants were nothing but trash. Now, if you were in the saloon business and you were Italian, you had it rougher because the Irish weren't going to like you too much. If you were an Italian "from the boot," a southern Italian like the Ponzillos, then the northern Italians weren't going to want you around, either. You had to have a pretty tough hide to be in the saloon business.

Pop stayed in the saloon business when he moved us to Meriden. The part of Meriden we settled in was called Dublin, because there used to be only Irish people living there. But by the time we moved in, it was anybody and everybody who had crossed the Atlantic. In those days, many of the Italian families would rent out parts of their houses to immigrants who were just starting out in the town. Pop couldn't afford to get us our own home until two or three years after we moved to Meriden, so we rented rooms till we got on our feet.

The first place we rented was the downstairs floor in a two-story house that was owned by a family named Suzio. They were one of two Italian families in Meriden who got to be very, very wealthy: the Suzios and the Donderos. The Suzios helped convince the Donderos to give my father a year's free lease on a building over on Pratt Street, where he opened up the first Italian-owned saloon in that part of town. The Donderos helped my father get the money to buy a small house with a deep lot at 159 Springdale Avenue. Rose wasn't born there. She came along before then.

Our house wasn't very big to start with, but Pop built on to it year by year. We had relatives living with us on and off, so we needed the extra rooms. For a little while, my Grandfather Conti, my mother's father, lived in our house. But he didn't stay in Meriden too long. He went back to Troy [New York], where he and my grandmother had been living, and he died there not too long afterward. My grandmother (her name was Fortunata Conti) lived with us until she died, many years later. On my father's side, his older brother, Alfonso, lived with us on and off.

Uncle Alfonso was a tough guy. I mean a *real* tough guy. I had to laugh when I heard that Rose said he was a wonderful man, gentle and kind, the salt of the earth. Maybe she's confusing him with Saint Francis of Assisi. My uncle was a dangerous man! In Southington [Connecticut], when he was working in a [steel] roller mill, he got into a fight with another worker, and he beat this poor guy nearly senseless! The sheriff ran my uncle out of town because of it. Then he moved to Waterbury, and got into the saloon business. But that's not the end of his story. He committed murder. That's the truth. He shot and killed his own son-in-law in cold blood.

Uncle Alfonso and his son Giuseppe (or Joe) were bootleggers. That's where the easy money was in those days, as long as you didn't get caught. Alfonso had a son-in-law, who was a Sicilian. This boy had married my cousin Luisa, who was Alfonso's daughter. Now, we used to say that there are two types of Sicilians: the nice type and the Mafia type. Well, this son-in-law was the Mafia type, but he was a handsome brute! One day, Uncle Alfonso and the son-in-law were sitting in the car out in front of Uncle's house, after one of their bootleg deliveries. It came time to divvy up the money, and the son-in-law said he wanted more than my uncle said he was entitled to. They got into a shouting match, and pretty soon, they're throwing punches. Now, the son-in-law always kept a revolver hidden under the car seat, and Uncle knew it was there too. Both of them went for the gun. Uncle grabbed it first, and he pulled the trigger and shot this boy dead! Murdered his son-in-law in cold blood!—and got away with it too. An Italian attorney who was famous around here, Eduardo Moscola, got him off. He told the judge it was self-defense. The judge said, "Case dismissed!"

My father got out of the saloon business about 1896 or 1897, and he started looking at some other ways to make money. Eventually, he ran two businesses right out of our house: a little grocery store, which was on the front half of the first floor, and a small bakery, which we built onto the back of the house. Mamma ran the store, and Carmela would help out when she wasn't in school. Pop ran the baking business, although he didn't do any baking himself. He hired another Italian immigrant to man the oven; his name was Francesco Cocchiao, but we always called him Cheech. Our little one-oven bakery was putting out one hundred and ten loaves of bread at a time. We sold them in our own store, and we also supplied a few other small stores in that part of town.

I went to work in the bakery when I was about thirteen. I learned the baking business "by request." One day when I came home from school, Pop said to me, "You tell the teach' you no come-a back there no more. Tomorrow you start-a with Cheech to bake-a the bread." That's how my father made "requests." Oh, boy, he was a pip! I worked for him for about eight years, but he paid me next to nothing. If I asked for more money, I'd get a beating on top of it. For the first few years, I didn't much care. I had already learned the trade; and besides, I was only a kid. But he refused me once too often, and I realized I wasn't getting anywhere. So I packed up my belongings and left. I just told him goodbye—no arrangements, nothing. I took the train to New York (this was in 1911), and I got a job selling gloves in Macy's.

Carmela had gone to New York three or four years before that, around 1907 or 1908. She was living at a very nice rooming house at 120 West Sixty-fifth Street. The woman who owned the place was a charming lady, and she took very good care of all of her boarders. She rented a room to me, so I could live in the same place with my sister. Later on, when Carmela and Rose were touring in vaudeville, they always rented rooms at that lady's boarding house. Every time they came back from the tour, she had their rooms waiting for them. As a matter of fact, Rose lived there until the time of her Metropolitan Opera debut, when she got her own apartment.

I don't remember Carmela ever doing much singing in Meriden. She really didn't have a singing career until she moved to New York. She got her start in cafés in Manhattan. These places hired amateur singers all the time, and they paid well too. She even made a record for Thomas Edison back then.[11] I don't know what became of it (I never heard it myself), but, you see, it showed that she was getting good notices. Carmela's first big success was at the Fox Theater, the old Academy of Music, on Fourteenth Street in New York. She was in a musical called *The Girl from Brighton*. I saw it several times, and what I remember most was that she had a solo number called "Goodbye, Rose."

Rose got her start in Meriden, at a little vaudeville theater that was down the street from us on Springdale Avenue. The name of the place was the Bright Theater, and it was built by a fellow named John Brown. It only lasted for a few weeks, maybe two months at the most, and then it closed up. But Rose played piano there. She didn't do any singing; she just played the piano. That was the first place where she ever played in public. You see, by the time Anna Ryan got finished with Rose, she was a very good pianist. She wasn't the best in Meriden (there were some excellent pianists and piano teachers in town then), but she was very, very good.

Rose was a natural musician. She could learn an instrument as fast as lightning. I used to play in a band with other Italian kids (just a street band, like a lot of Italian communities had), and the boys used to store some of their instruments at our house. I was always having to chase Rose away, because she would sneak into my room and try to learn how to play every band instrument. She was a whiz too. I used to play the clarinet, and one day I caught her up in my room playing with it. She couldn't have had that clarinet three hours, and she had already learned enough of the fingering to play a scale. Another time, the daughter of one of our neighbors was trying to learn the accordion. It used to set my nerves on edge to have to listen to that kid practice. Then one day I heard some pretty nice music coming from that accordion. That night, I found out that Rose was the one who had been playing it!

Carmela wasn't the musician that Rose was, but both of them had very, very beautiful voices. Now, there were a lot of differences between their voices, though. They will tell you that Carmela's voice was a dramatic soprano when she was young, but I never could agree with that. I knew both of my sisters' voices like the back of my hand. Rose was a true dramatic soprano, even when she was in her teens, but Carmela had a lyric mezzo-soprano voice; maybe you could say it was *lirico-spinto* because of its size when she was in top form.

Not that Carmela had such a big voice. Rosa was the one who had the really big voice. But Carmela's carried very well, which tells you that her method, her technique, was correct. A voice won't carry if it's forced. Carmela wasn't what I would call a typical mezzo-soprano, because she had a range that could go up into the soprano's register. But Carmela didn't really have what we call drive in the voice. Rose's voice had real dramatic drive. It's hard for me to explain about "drive." But if you ever heard Rose sing "Suicidio" from *La gioconda*, you wouldn't need me to tell you a thing.

As for me, well, I never wanted a singing career like my sisters did. I had a voice, and I was good enough to get an audition with Gatti-Casazza at the Metropolitan when I was only twenty-one. I didn't get a contract, because I had no repertoire. But my point is, I never had a singing lesson in my life, yet I was good enough to get a Metropolitan Opera audition, and this was long before Gatti-Casazza ever laid eyes on Rose and Carmela. But I saw that kind of a life for what it is. It makes a slave out of you, and it's full of phonies, full of people who are just out to use you. I didn't want any part of that. I went into the Army in the First World War (the 145th Squadron was my outfit), and I did a lot of singing for the boys at Kelly Field in San Antonio, where I was stationed. I did a turn in vaudeville, just like my sisters did, but I didn't do any serious singing after that. I got married in 1922, had a son, built a beautiful home here in Meriden, and made my career in the coal business.

I sold out in 1928, but I found out I didn't like being retired, so I decided to give voice lessons. I had a few students coming in from nearby towns, even as far as New Haven and Hartford. I didn't get any takers from here in Meriden, though. My prices probably scared them away. A few would call for information, but they wouldn't come for a voice trial. I figured I could do better in New York, because you're supposed to charge high prices there. In New York, if you don't soak people they think you're no good. I got together some money, and I rented a studio in Carnegie Hall, but the people there were just like the ones in Meriden: they called, but nobody ever came.

The Written Record

In November 1940, five years after her largely uneventful Metropolitan Opera career had ended, Carmela Ponselle made a brief attempt to write her memoirs. Six double-spaced pages into the manuscript, she abandoned the project and relegated it to a steamer trunk in the storage basement of her Manhattan apartment house. Neither the manuscript (fancifully titled *Romancing with the Gods, or How the Dreams of a Little Girl of Five Came True*) nor the few additional pages of handwritten notes she had appended to it contained even a hint of how she had gotten into vaudeville.

Prior to her association with vaudeville manager Gene Hughes, who was then handling a number of promising acts including a traveling group headed by his performer-wife,[12] Carmela seems to have appeared as a soloist in several of the then-fashionable restaurants and tea rooms in midtown Manhattan. Most of these establishments catered to Broadway theatergoers and regularly featured singers, dancers, and small orchestras. Although groups were often billed in the newspaper advertisements of several of these night spots (especially at Reisenweber's, where a group calling itself The Original Dixieland Jazz Band had become an overnight sensation in Manhattan), few others advertised individual performers by name. For this reason, apparently, there is no mention of Carmela in Manhattan restaurant or tea-room advertisements of the World War I era.

In later years, Carmela took pride in noting (as would her sister and brother when repeating it over the years) that she had gotten a leading part in a musical called *The Girl from Brighton.* More than fifty years later, Tony Ponzillo would vividly recall seeing the musical "several times," and remembered being especially touched by the song "Goodbye, Rose," which Carmela had sung as a solo. The first published notice of the opening of *The Girl from Brighton* contains no mention, however, of Carmela Ponzillo among the principals in the cast.[13]

The premiere of *The Girl from Brighton* coincided with the opening of the 1912–13 theatrical season. Throughout its opening week at the refurbished Academy of Music at Fourteenth Street and Irving Place, producer and Academy-owner William Fox promoted the new musical in the major New York dailies, highlighting the show's "great cast and chorus of 100."[14] By the end of its first week, the box-office receipts for the matinee and evening performances of *The Girl from Brighton* were impressive enough for *The New York Times* to feature a three-column photograph of cast members Kitty Flinn, Anna Orr, and Clay Smith in one of the show's production numbers.

Near the end of the second week, the *Times* made brief mention of "an especially effective number" in the show, in which one of the lead singers in the chorus sang "a ballad about broken promises of love" while casting the remnants of a bouquet of roses to her feet. Whether the ballad was titled "Goodbye, Rose" is not mentioned in the notice. But on the front page of its theater section, the Sunday edition of *The New York Times* featured a compelling photograph of the singer. The young woman with the cascading hair, gazing skyward with a forlorn look while clutching a handful of roses, was identified in the caption as "Carmela Ponzella, Academy Of Music."[15]

From 1919 through 1937, Rosa Ponselle's annual concert tours usually included performances in New Haven, Waterbury, Ansonia, and Meriden—the cities and towns where she had given some of her first performances, either in movie houses or in smalltime vaudeville. In Meriden, her concerts were usually accorded headline coverage by the local newspapers.[16] But in the few interviews she gave to Meriden reporters prior to 1922, she never spoke of her childhood. When she finally did so in the Meriden *Daily Journal*, she apparently saw no reason to hide the fact that the Ponzillo family's finances were what had necessitated her having to go to work:

> When I was sixteen, the course of my life was greatly influenced by the family mortgage. Oh yes, we had one. And the banker, true to form, was threatening to foreclose. So when a motion picture exhibitor offered me $12 to sing for his patrons I lost no time in accepting, though I did wonder if I could possibly be worth so much money. . . . Then came a proposition from a leading hotel [*sic*] in New Haven—$50 a week—think of it! That was too good to believe! We soon disposed of the mortgage.[17]

In April 1922, one month after the above interview with Rosa Ponselle appeared in the Meriden *Daily Journal*, the Boston *Sunday Post* published a detailed account of Ponselle's first professional engagements. The author of the account was Richard T. Halliwell, the theater owner who had employed her as a teenager:

> In an Italian neighborhood in New Haven I owned a movie house called the San Carlino, named after the opera house in Naples.
>
> I had two other picture places at the time, one in Meriden, called the Star, and another in Ansonia. One day, while I was at the Meriden house, my wife came into the theater and said: "I guess you'll have to get a singer of illustrated songs for this theater. This afternoon I dropped into the Crystal, and Rose Ponzillo is singing there. She has a wonderful voice, and it's bound to have an effect on your business."
>
> The Crystal was another Meriden picture theater, in fact my only competitor. I appreciated my wife's judgment and, while pondering over the matter that same afternoon, who should walk into the place but Rose.
>
> "Say, Mr. Halliwell," she began, "do you want to engage me to sing here?"
>
> "There's no need of rubbing it in, Rose," I answered. "Isn't it bad enough to be at that other theater taking my business with your voice without coming here to torment me with it?"
>
> "I mean it," she said. "I heard today they're going to fire me Saturday night and I thought I'd like to save them the trouble."
>
> And she did.
>
> I saved Rose the embarrassment of being discharged from her first position by engaging her on the spot. She was to sing Wednesdays and Thursdays in Ansonia, and the remaining days of the moving picture week in Meriden.
>
> But Rose never drew very well in Meriden. . . . Whether it was because of the class of people who patronize[d] pictures [and] did not appreciate good singing, or because of the fact that she was a girl whom they knew as a baker's daughter, I don't know; but she did not draw.[18]

At the theater Halliwell owned in Ansonia, however, the audiences were far more enthusiastic, so much so that the reception Rosa received in Ansonia led Halliwell to engage her for his New Haven theater as well:

> In New Haven, Rose made her debut [at the San Carlino] to a full house, the audience being divided between a few hundred Yale boys, and the rest, Italian-Americans. We had a ladies' orchestra. The theater had 1,000 seats, with a dressing room that any three-a-day performer would have scorned, because dressing rooms then, as now, were an unnecessary luxury in a moving picture theater.

> It was the custom then in small picture houses to have singers use songs illustrated with color slides, but I chose something a little beyond this for Rose.
>
> I asked her to sing "The Rosary."
>
> I think today it was one of the things that gave her, her big chance. Singers of illustrated songs rarely get far.
>
> I had only one slide for this song, one I had made for the occasion. It was fashioned in an oval shape, with a border of colored rosary beads. Rose stood in the center of the little stage, dressed in a simple white gown, and with this slide on the screen, the beads on the canvas encircling her, she sang "The Rosary."
>
> The effect was almost magical. As she came [down] from the stage the audience almost roared its applause and a few minutes later she came to me and said, "Oh, Mr. Halliwell, I think I have at last been successful!"[19]

"We used to make the trip from Meriden to Ansonia, a distance of thirty miles, in an open Ford auto," Halliwell wrote. "It was winter at the time, and I've wondered often recently whether or not [the] Rosa Ponselle [who] now rides to the theater in her limousine remembers when Rose Ponzillo used to suffer the intense cold of those return trips at night":

> Many times she was saved discomfort, if not actual suffering, because other occupants of the Ford shared wraps with her. But she bothered little about discomfort. She was singing, and that appeared to be all she lived for.
>
> Not long ago she came home on a short visit. The mayor and a delegation of citizens greeted her at the station. A public reception was tendered her in the city hall, and her admirers presented her with a beautiful chest of Meriden's own silver.
>
> Only a few years ago, when these people could have heard her for five cents, they didn't care to.[20]

It was in New Haven, Halliwell went on to say, that the owner of the Café Mellone, James G. Ceriani, tripled Rosa's salary in order to engage her to sing exclusively for his patrons. Ceriani confirmed the essentials of his salary negotiations with Rosa in a brief interview he gave to a Hartford newspaper in 1919. His account differed from Richard Halliwell's only to the extent that Ceriani remembered doubling, not tripling, her salary. Asked whether she was difficult to deal with in any respect, Ceriani told the reporter, "Oh, no. Rosa never did anything like that. She was an awfully nice girl."[21]

Meriden newspaper coverage of Rosa's engagements at the Café Mellone gave two different versions of her age at that time. In the Meriden *Daily Journal* of 31 May 1915, she was described as follows: "Miss Ponzillo has been employed as a cabaret singer at the Café Mellone for the past three years.

Before going to New Haven she sang illustrated songs at the Star Theatre in this city. She is twenty-two years old and attractive in appearance." Two days later the same newspaper interviewed Carmela, who had returned briefly to Meriden between engagements in New York City. "My sister . . . is working hard to get an education and has been working for over five years. She is not twenty-two either; she is only eighteen."[22]

Rosa Ponselle consistently claimed that she was born on 22 January 1897. But her birthdate remained a matter of some controversy throughout her life. The late Bruno Zirato, for example, remembered Ponselle's age as she told it to him when they met:

> I was organizing a benefit for Italian relief. It was to be held at the Riverside Theater. Everyone was to sing for nothing. Caruso agreed to come there to make drawings, sketches, which would be sold at auction to raise money. I met Rosa and her sister at the Riverside. They were in vaudeville. I asked them to come there to talk to me about appearing in the benefit. Rosa said yes, they would do it. This was in October of 1916. She was twenty-three years old. I know so because that is what she told me that day.[23]

Soprano Nina Morgana, whom Zirato married in 1921 and who would later sing with Ponselle, corroborated her husband's recollections. "It was common knowledge at the Metropolitan," Morgana maintained, "that Rosa was twenty-five, not twenty-one, when she made her debut."[24]

Although Ponselle's personal records at Villa Pace contained a typewritten copy of a birth certificate she had obtained in 1944, rumors persisted among some of her colleagues that the document had been "bought and paid for." Even her brother cast doubts upon her purported birthdate. "You don't want to pay any attention to that stuff about Carmela being ten years older than Rose," Tony Ponzillo maintained. "There was only about six years' difference between them. And I know what I'm talking about." [25] But as the Rosa Ponselle centennial approached, the Office of the City Clerk in Meriden made available to the author the handwritten original of her birth record. There in the precise script of Herman Hess, Meriden's Town Registrar in the 1890s, the birthdate for "infant Rosa Ponzillo" is listed for posterity as the twenty-second of January 1897.[26]

CHAPTER THREE

Kid, You Won Your Bet!

Rosa's audition with vaudeville manager Gene Hughes, which she claimed took place during the same period in which she first heard Caruso, can be dated with some measure of accuracy. The first published review the Ponzillo Sisters' act received, a notice appearing in *Variety* on 10 September 1915, suggests that the audition probably took place in the summer of that year, in time for the beginning of the 1915–16 theatrical season.

Hughes, the senior partner of Hughes & Smith (the management agency he had founded in 1909 with Jo Paige Smith), was a well-regarded talent scout who represented an assortment of vaudeville acts. During World War I, the Hughes & Smith roster included Poole's Basketball Girls ("A Sporting Novelty Act"), the Del Rey Sisters' dance team, Kenny & Hollis ("The Original College Boys"), the comedy team of Murphy, Van & Kenyon ("The 12 Cylinder Trio"), singing duo Fred & Lydia Weaver, and Nell O'Connell ("The Rosebud of Song").[1] For a brief time, Jo Paige Smith managed the budding adolescent dance team of Fred and Adele Astaire. But of all the acts she and Gene Hughes managed as partners, only the Ponzillo Sisters were to make a lasting mark in the history of vaudeville.

The Ponzillos and other Hughes-managed acts played what were known in show-business jargon as circuits, and otherwise known as vaudeville management-and-production conglomerates that owned their own theaters and retained a stable of acts under exclusive contract to perform in their theaters. Among the major national circuits of the 1910s—the Orpheum Circuit, the Poli Circuit, the Ackermann & Harris Circuit, Pantages' Circuit, Fox's, Proctor's, and Loew's—the largest and most prestigious was the Keith Circuit. The namesake of showman Benjamin Franklin Keith,[2] the Keith Circuit and its rival, the Orpheum, together defined what was known in the trade as the bigtime. The highest stratum in vaudeville's hierarchical structure, the bigtime was characterized (in the words of historian Charles W. Stein) by "a full week of the same show, usually two performances per day, one or more headliners or stars on every bill, eight or more acts on the program, higher salaries, higher administration fees and production costs."[3]

The Keith Circuit boasted not only the highest-paid stars in all vaudeville but also the best-respected booking manager in show business: Edward V. Darling, the *wunderkind* head of Keith's United Booking Offices, who personally chose which acts would play at the seven largest Keith-owned theaters in New York City and Boston. Darling also coordinated the bookings for all other Keith theaters from the East Coast through part of the Midwest.[4]

Darling was respected by his booking-office peers in the other circuits and was genuinely liked by most of the stars he booked—even those top-drawing acts who found him unyielding when they tried to pressure him for more money or for better billing. "A presentation to Eddie Darling is under way by about sixty vaudeville artists," *Variety* reported in June of 1917. "It is to be a testimonial of esteem . . . for the rather youthful Darling in his exceedingly difficult position of booking the large B. F. Keith theatres." Carmela and Rosa, whose "The Italian Girls" act was beginning to command more of Darling's attention, were among the sixty Keith Circuit performers who helped plan and contributed funds to the testimonial.[5]

The Ponzillo sisters' act seems to have changed relatively little between their debut at the Keith-owned Royal Theater in the Bronx in the autumn of 1915, and their later performances at the more prestigious Keith theaters on Broadway. Their twenty-minute act, or "turn," was crafted along the lines of other successful vaudeville routines. From the moment the curtain went up, revealing the act's simple but visually appealing setting (a grand piano situated in front of a royal-blue backdrop), the Ponzillos built the audience's interest and enthusiasm to what was called, in Broadway parlance, "the 'wow' finish"—a closing which, as once defined by vaudeville comedian Walter De Leon, was meant to "lift roaring waves of applause to sweep toward the stage; a finish that Philadelphia and Phoenix, Montreal and Macon, Boston and Baton Rouge will respond to as certainly as New York."[6]

During and after her operatic career, Rosa Ponselle rarely talked about her vaudeville appearances, except to say that the Keith Circuit (and in particular Keith's Riverside Theater, where William Thorner heard her and where she met her mentor Romano Romani) had been her pathway to the Metropolitan. Not that she avoided discussing her three years in vaudeville, nor that she downplayed them in any way. Quite the contrary, she was justifiably proud of having "played the Palace," a distinction that comparatively few

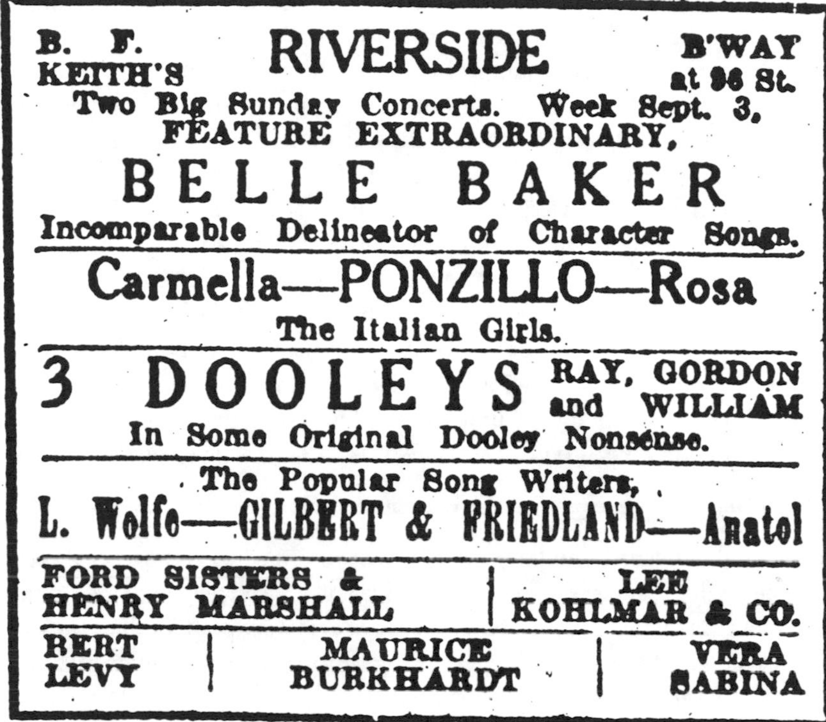
B. F. KEITH'S RIVERSIDE B'WAY at 96 St.
Two Big Sunday Concerts. Week Sept. 3.
FEATURE EXTRAORDINARY.
BELLE BAKER
Incomparable Delineator of Character Songs.
Carmella—PONZILLO—Rosa
The Italian Girls.
3 DOOLEYS RAY, GORDON and WILLIAM
In Some Original Dooley Nonsense.
The Popular Song Writers,
L. Wolfe—GILBERT & FRIEDLAND—Anatol
FORD SISTERS & HENRY MARSHALL
LEE KOHLMAR & CO.
BERT LEVY
MAURICE BURKHARDT
VERA SABINA

Figure 2. The Ponzillo Sisters' first bigtime vaudeville appearance, Keith's Riverside Theater on Broadway, 3 September 1917. FROM THE AUTHOR'S COLLECTION.

vaudevillians were able to claim. But most of her interviewers were interested only in her opera career, to which her years in vaudeville seemed only tangentially related at best. Yet it was on the Keith Circuit that she derived much of her self-confidence as a performer. And it was there that she learned the hard lessons of pacing and managing a burgeoning career.

The Interview

From interviews of Rosa Ponselle by the author (March 1973, June 1975, February 1977, and December 1978) and by John Secrist (1949, precise date unknown). Transcribed with minor editing.

What do you remember about your audition with Gene Hughes?

He had us come to his house. This was on a Sunday. He took one look at me and he pulled Carmela aside and said to her, "Who the hell are you kidding? She must weigh two hundred pounds! She's too fat for the vaudeville stage. This just won't work." I was waiting in the parlor, getting ready to sing, while this hush-hush conversation with Carmela was going on in the next room. Carmela kept telling him to wait till he heard me before he made up his mind. Of course, there I was in the next room, so he couldn't afford to be rude and just send me out the door—not with Carmela there, anyway. She got him calmed down, and he plopped himself into a chair and said, "Okay, show me what you've got." I sang "Kiss Me Again" from *Mademoiselle Modiste*, which I had sung many times at the San Carlino and at the Café Mellone. I accompanied myself on the upright in his parlor. Well, to make a long story short, as soon as I sang the last note he jumped out of his chair, grabbed Carmela and shouted, "I don't give a goddam *how* fat she is! When can she open with you?"

Had you and Carmela already conceived your basic act before you auditioned?

Not the specifics, but the general ideas, yes. She had come to hear me at the Café Mellone, and she talked over the idea of a "sister act" with me. Jimmy Ceriani was in on this conversation too. Sister acts were popular then, and Mr. Hughes felt sure he could get bigger billings for a sister act. He even told Carmela to hire somebody to pose as her sister, which is when she told him she had a real sister back home who could also sing. At first, we thought about just doing popular songs and some operetta in our act, but Jimmy Ceriani held out for opera arias. He reasoned that if we were doing opera while other acts were doing popular music, we would attract more attention. Gene Hughes ended up agreeing, so that's how we put it together.

Did it take you long to program your act?

The audition with Mr. Hughes was on a Sunday, and we had to be ready to go to the theater for a run-through the next Thursday. He didn't waste a minute. He got us a number two spot on a bill, so we had to be ready. On a nine-act bill, which was pretty standard in vaudeville, each of the acts had about fifteen minutes' stage time. We did six numbers. We started with the "Barcarolle" from *Les contes d'Hoffmann*, and then Carmela did "Musetta's Waltz" from *La bohème* as her solo. Next, we sang "Comin' Thro' the Rye" together. I made up a *fioritura* arrangement, full of runs and trills, most of it in [harmonic] thirds—you can hear it on the record we made for Columbia, which is exactly how we sang it in vaudeville, note for note. After "Comin' Thro' the Rye," I sang "Kiss Me Again," using the arrangement that Fritzi Scheff was famous for. That was my solo number. After that came the "'O sole mio," and for our finale we did the trio in the Prison Scene from *Faust*, but we sang it as a duet. I made up the arrangement—poor Gounod was probably turning over in his grave. It sounds corny, but it was a real grabber with the audience.

Did you play your own accompaniment throughout the act, or only part of the time?

Well, when we did our first turn on the Keith Circuit, we couldn't have an orchestra so I did all the accompaniment, which was easy because I could control the pacing all by myself. You see, timing was everything in vaudeville, and by "timing" I mean the buildup you took the audience through, leading up to your finale. We did our act with pit orchestras when we got into the bigtime, but there you had to depend on how much rehearsal time you could get and on how well the conductor could "read" how the act was moving. So it was easier for me to pace it right from the piano.

You said that Carmela sang "Musetta's Waltz" as her solo. Did you transpose it into a mezzo key, or did she do it in the original key?

She sang it just the way Puccini wrote it in the score. I'm glad you brought that up because Carmela, you have to understand, was not a mezzo-soprano until she got into opera. She was a soprano—and what a soprano! She had all the notes right up to and including the high C. She had a pocketful of high Cs. To be honest about it, she had a better top than I did in those days. We performed as sopranos, both of us, and we would exchange phrases in these duets. You could hardly tell our voices apart. That's what you hear on our very first records, too, although by the time we made them, Carmela was already preparing mezzo roles for opera and concerts. But she was *not* a mezzo to begin with, not until Thorner—the genius—changed her into a mezzo and ruined a good career.

How about the visual aspect of your act? Did you use a set? How were you costumed?

We designed our own costumes. We wore tailored skirts and blouses. The skirts were a royal blue, and the blouses were white. That was part of our billing. We billed ourselves as "Those Tailored Italian Girls." Our first costumes were made by a woman who had a shop way up in the Bronx. She was the only one we could find who could make them in less than four days. Now, we didn't need a set because we did our act "in one," so we weren't using very much of the stage.

What does doing an act "in one" mean?

The way that the bookers and managers figured your act was by how much of the stage you needed to use. The vaudeville theaters had at least two backdrops behind the curtain, and each one was several feet behind the other. If you did your act in front of the curtain, like we did, then you'd say that you did your act "in one," meaning that you were at the very front of the stage, with the curtain down, and you would be performing right in front of the curtain, or maybe with a backdrop or some piece of scenery that you would put between the curtain and the footlights. If you did your act "in two," it meant you needed for the curtain to be up, so that you could have some kind of scenery or props. If you billed yourself as doing an act "in three," it meant you were going to need practically the whole stage. Animal acts, especially ones with large animals, needed all the room they could get. Now, we did our act "in one," and we had our own backdrop—they called it a cyclorama in those days—and we designed and made the first one ourselves. We picked out the material. It was a royal blue, with gold trim. Carmela and I did almost all the sewing.

How many shows a day did you and Carmela do?

Two. The Keith Circuit had what they used to call the two-a-day. You did the matinee at two o'clock, and then you would do the second show at eight o'clock at night. There was also the three-a-day, and some places would have you playing four shows a day.

How long did your contract run?

Thirteen weeks. The big acts could negotiate a contract for double that [length], for a twenty-six-week run. But thirteen weeks was the rule, usually. If you were good, you'd get another thirteen weeks. If you weren't—if the audiences didn't like your material—you wouldn't get renewed. Sometimes they would even cancel an act in the middle of a run, if it wasn't going over the way it was supposed to. If they thought you had some promise, they would try to help you fix your act. But if not, you were out. Business was business. You see, if the management had a bad act in one spot on the bill, it would ruin the buildup and hurt all the acts that came after it.

Were you and Carmela in the smalltime circuit for a good while, or did you get a contract with the Keith Circuit early in your vaudeville career?

See, we weren't really in vaudeville more than two years, so it all came pretty fast. We were on what they called the "subway circuit" for a while. That was a group of theaters in the Bronx and in Brooklyn—there was the Shubert, the Montauk, and the Majestic in Brooklyn, and the old Opera House in the Bronx. Off Broadway there were several Proctor vaudeville houses; most of them were near subway stops. (The farthest one, I think, was way up at 125th Street.) Some of those Proctor [vaudeville] houses would have acts going all day long, from lunch time till maybe midnight. That's the way the smalltime ones operated. But we were with the Keith Circuit almost from the beginning.

How stressful did you find the traveling you had to do in vaudeville?

We stayed as close to New York as we could because that was the show business capital and that's where we thought our future was going to be. We played many of the bigger theaters in the East, and we went up into Canada several times—I remember playing in Montreal and also in Hamilton, Ontario. But we didn't play the West Coast, and we didn't go very far into the South. Chicago and maybe Milwaukee were about as far west as we went. If you played the West, you had a different booking office; that was the Orpheum Circuit, which handled the bigtime theaters from Chicago to California. But we had a good relationship with Keith's booking office in New York, so we stayed in the East. The traveling wasn't too bad, really. Now, sometimes they would book you so close together that you had to hope like hell that the train wasn't going to be late. But that didn't happen very often.

As best you can recall, how long did it take for you and Carmela to reach the Palace Theater?

We didn't play the Palace very often. We played the Riverside, at Broadway and Ninety-sixth Street. That was the next best thing to playing the Palace. When we played the Riverside our first time, it was quite an ordeal. We were so nervous! I was shaking, holding on to the curtain. Today it's hard to realize what it meant to play the bigtime vaudeville theaters in New York. Thousands of vaudevillians never got that chance. But there we were, playing the Riverside and the Palace, only two or three years after we started out in vaudeville.

I have been told that Carmela, although it's not well known, had gotten married while the two of you were in vaudeville. Was it while you were on Broadway, or was it before that time?

Before. It didn't last, you know.

Her husband, I understand, was a physician. Did you know him very well? And do you know how they met?

Sure. His name was Giamarino, Henry Giamarino, and he was a very good friend of Dr. [William F.] Verdi, who was my doctor. That's how Carmela met him. Dr. Giamarino was a surgeon—a very good one, very prominent—and he was practicing in New Haven at that time. But the marriage didn't "take," you could say, and they didn't stay together very long.

To the extent you might want to say, what came between them?

Vaudeville. He and Carmela had to get married in secret because his family didn't approve of "show people." They were narrow-minded Italians, the "old country" type. It turned out that he was just like his family. He didn't want Carmela to stay in show business. So they broke up, and she and I stayed on the Keith Circuit.

Do you remember some of the acts which were on the Riverside or the Palace bills when you and Carmela were appearing there?

You see, I was too nervous to think about any other acts. But I remember being on the same bill with the Dooleys—Ray Dooley, who was a comedienne and a friend of ours, and several of her brothers. The Dooleys were a big family, and they were all in vaudeville, even the parents. Ray was married to Eddie Dowling, who was on the Keith Circuit with us. He became a manager, and I think even a producer, but that was later on.

Did you stay with Gene Hughes' management throughout your vaudeville career?

I guess you could say that we kind of outgrew him. He couldn't get us the big bookings, mainly because he didn't handle the really big acts. And Mr. Hughes wasn't much on promoting you, either. If you wanted to advertise yourself, I mean, to have your picture in *Variety* with reprints of your reviews, like the bigtime acts always did, he wanted you to come up with the ideas, and he would also want you to pay for most of it. In other words, he had lots of good contacts and he got us started on the right track, but he couldn't get everything we wanted from the Keith management. But Mr. Hughes really believed in us, and we respected him.

Who actually did the booking for your act?

Eddie Darling, the manager [of the United Booking Office]. As our manager, Mr. Hughes dealt with him all the time, but he never seemed to be able to get us what we wanted from Eddie Darling. When Carmela and I were playing the Riverside and the other Keith theaters on Broadway, I got to know Eddie Darling well enough that I sort of became our manager—I used to deal with him personally, and we got along fine.

When you played the Palace, were you nervous?

Listen—if you were good enough to get the chance to walk on that stage at Forty-seventh and Broadway, what that meant was that you were one of the top acts in all vaudeville. Otherwise, you wouldn't be there. And the audiences—well, you were performing for probably the most demanding, most discriminating audiences that ever saw a vaudeville bill. You bet I was nervous!

It's sometimes said that the Ponzillo Sisters "headlined" at the Palace.

Not true. We couldn't get headline bookings at any of the Keith theaters on Broadway, even though we were getting more applause than some of the headline acts. It was easy to tell who the headliners were in vaudeville. They were usually the eighth act on a nine-act bill. Every other act was a buildup to the headline act, that's always how it worked. Now, the first and ninth spots on a bill were "no man's land" because the audience was either coming in or going out, and you had to contend with all the talking and moving around. But the fifth, sixth, and seventh spots were very good places on the bill, and, of course, the closer you got to the eighth spot, the bigger you were as an act. But the biggest billing we ever got at the Palace was sixth or seventh billing. We were never headliners there.

Who would have been some of the women who were "headliners" in vaudeville at the time you're speaking about?

Well, there were the old pros like Nora Bayes, Irene Franklin, Elsie Janis, Eva Tanguay, and Irene Bordoni; they were real celebrities. Then there was a younger bunch who were already pretty big by that time—Sophie Tucker, for instance, and Blossom Seeley and Belle Baker. They were at the Riverside with us. Carmela and I got acquainted with some of them, although we didn't socialize very much—most vaudevillians didn't. They were loners, most of them, because bigtime vaudeville was very, very competitive. Before you ever set foot on the stage you had to do whatever you could to make sure the producers, the managers, and the bookers were on your side, and then you had to worry about other performers stealing your audience from you. You didn't dare rest on your laurels. You had to work constantly to keep your material fresh, and you had to make sure your act was always in tip-top form.

Which of the women headliners stands out the most in your memory?

Oh, Nora Bayes! She would have even the toughest audience eating out of her hand! She had been around a long time. You could learn a lot by watching her.

The Ponzillo Sisters shared bills with a number of performers whose children became stars in the next generation. I'm thinking, for instance, of the Cansinos.

Oh, yes, they were tango dancers, the Cansinos. They had a daughter, Rita Cansino, who traveled with them on the Keith Circuit. When she went to Hollywood, she became Rita Hayworth. Another one was Jack Coogan, his act was called Mullen and Coogan. We played on several bills with Jack. His little boy, Jackie, was the one Charlie Chaplin picked to star in *The Kid.*

Of all the performers you saw in those days, the men and women alike, is there one that stands out the most in your memory?

Sure. Al Jolson. He was the biggest star in show business.

Did you ever perform on a bill with Jolson?

No. We were with Keith, but he was with the Shuberts, who owned the Winter Garden. That was Al Jolson's theater, you know. They even put up a runway that went from the footlights clear to the end of the orchestra seats, so that he could get right out there with the audience. Later on, when I was making records for Columbia, I was introduced to him. And a few years later, when I was singing on the radio a lot, I got to know him a little bit.

What made Jolson so memorable?

He had something that only the greats have. I don't know what you could call it, or even how to talk about it. When the curtain went up and Al Jolson would make his entrance from the wings, he'd be clapping his hands, the pit band would be playing all-out, and Jolson would come strutting down that runway. If you were there, it was just like electricity running through you! Even show [business] people reacted to him like that.

Did you run into any conflicts with other performers on the circuit?

Yes, with Eva Tanguay. It seemed that the better we got, the more Eva Tanguay complained about our act. She never said anything to our faces, but we kept getting the word that she didn't like all the applause we were getting. She would be the headliner, which meant that she had the eighth spot on the bill. But we would be on the seventh spot, and we would stop the show—we would steal all the applause. Ray Dooley and her brothers were always telling us that Eva Tanguay was bad news. See, if a top-draw star like Eva Tanguay would take a disliking to you, it could cause you a lot of trouble with the management. What kept us in good with Eddie Darling and the Keith people was that our act was literally stopping the show.

If you had to list two or three things from your vaudeville experience that helped shape you later on, things that stayed with you as a performer, what would those be?

Well, first of all, I learned to appreciate timing. Every great entertainer has great timing. One of the things I just love to do is to watch a comedian perform—especially Jack Benny, George Burns, or some of the others who came out of vaudeville like I did. You have to really understand timing to be able to appreciate what those men can do with a line. You want to know what the secret to comedy is? Making it seem like you're not doing anything at all. Take those wonderful long pauses that Jack Benny would do. It's a hell of a lot harder to keep an audience with you when you're not even saying anything than it is when you're dressed up in some funny costume, running around doing pratfalls. That's why Will Rogers was a great comedian. He kept everything natural. Like Jack Benny, he made you think he really wasn't doing anything special to make you laugh—that's the secret. Keep your act simple, natural, don't overdo it. I learned that in vaudeville.

In what other ways was it a learning experience for your operatic career?

Well, I learned to take care of myself in vaudeville, because nobody was going to do it for me. You had to be make sure that your backdrops, your costumes, your props, and all your baggage got to the right theater, and afterward you had to be sure they were packed up and shipped to the next stop on the tour. You had to learn to watch over all the details, to take care of your own business, and that was a very valuable lesson. I would say, too, that I learned how to play to an audience—how to pace things, how to build a performance to a climax. Where I put that to use was in my concerts. You see, a lot of opera singers don't particularly like to give concerts. But me, I loved doing concerts because each one was my own performance, nobody else's, and I could pace the program and work the audience any way I wanted to.

It's easy to tell from the way you talk about your vaudeville years that you thoroughly enjoyed them, and, obviously, you and Carmela did very well in vaudeville. What was it that made you leave vaudeville?

In one word, money. We were making seven hundred dollars a week when we were playing the Keith Circuit, and we were getting sixth or seventh billing most of the time. A headliner like Eva Tanguay or Nora Bayes could demand as much as two maybe even three thousand a week, and they would get it because they were filling the theater. But if you had an act that was stopping the show like ours was—not just once, and not in "tank towns" but on Broadway—then you should become a headline act. But that wasn't happening. Now, Eddie Darling, the booking manager, kept telling us to be patient and that in time he would give us top billing. Looking back, you could see his point; after all, we had made it to the Riverside and the Palace in only two years. But I was young and determined, and I wasn't willing to wait.

Were you getting some outside encouragement to leave vaudeville for opera?

Oh, sure. Nino Romani had been telling us that we should be in opera ever since he heard our act at the Riverside Theater. Another one who told us that was Mr. [Sylvester Z.] Poli, who owned one of the biggest theater chains at that time. He told us that we could have opera careers.[7] And then there was Bruno Zirato—he was Caruso's secretary—and he also told us that we belonged in opera. And, of course, Thorner was wanting us to get out of vaudeville completely. So, all these people were building up our confidence, and we were ready to take a gamble. So we decided to go on strike.

On strike? How do you mean?

We set a salary demand—$1,000 a week and not a penny less. We said if we didn't get a thousand dollars a week, we weren't going to perform on the Keith Circuit any longer. We knew, of course, that we stood to lose everything if they said no to us. I mean, you didn't go around threatening the Keith people, or any of the other circuits. That would be like some "B" movie star in Hollywood giving an ultimatum to [Sam] Goldwyn or [Louis B.] Mayer. If you did, you weren't going to be making movies anywhere else in Hollywood. And that's basically what the odds were for us with our "strike." If things didn't work out in our favor with the Keith people, it was almost a sure bet that we would be out of vaudeville altogether. But we took a gamble, and we delivered our thousand-a-week demand.

Did the management reject your offer out of hand?

No. They started dickering with us. They offered eight hundred, and we said no. They upped it to eight-fifty a week, and we still said no. The Dooleys and Eddie Dowling said that we were going to get blackballed if we didn't compromise with the Keith people. And the Keith booker, Eddie Darling, kept telling us we were crazy to hold out for that kind of money, and that nine hundred a week was going to be his best offer. Do you know what I said to him? I don't know what got into me, but I said, "You mark my words, Eddie, one day you're going to have to pay *ten dollars* a seat to hear me at the Metropolitan." He knew I had my heart set on opera. But he still thought we were crazy not to compromise.

And you didn't compromise?

No. Their last counteroffer was to pay us nine hundred dollars a week. We said no, which put us out of the Keith Circuit and out of vaudeville completely. We had a fair amount of money saved, so we knew we could get by for a year or more if we had to. But we were pretty sure that through Thorner's influence we could get contracts either at the Chicago Opera, through Maestro Campanini, or maybe even the Metropolitan if everything went right for us. As things turned out, that's pretty much the way it happened, so it was a gamble that paid off. Even Eddie Darling had to admit it, God bless him. Backstage after my debut in *Forza*, he was waiting in line in front of my dressing room. When he came in, it was like old home week for me. He didn't say a word at first, and then with a big smile on his face, he slapped a nice new ten-dollar bill on my dressing table. "Okay, kid," he said, "you won your bet!"

Recollections

Lena Tamborini

The only daughter of immigrants from Varese in northern Italy, Lena Tamborini (originally Elena, but anglicized to Helen) was Rosa Ponselle's closest friend during childhood. Until Lena married Henry Angle and left Meriden with her young husband in 1916, she lived next door to the Ponzillos in Meriden's predominantly ethnic west side. In two interviews recorded at her home in 1977 and 1978,[8] *she recalled the stressful circumstances that led Carmela and Rosa to pursue a career in vaudeville.*

Carmela and Rose didn't go into vaudeville just because they wanted to be in show business. It was either go to work or stand by and watch their family go broke. Rose's father got himself a bad reputation from the way he ran his businesses. He wasn't completely crooked, but he used only enough thievery so that he never got caught. Things got so bad that he stood to lose the house, which he had used for collateral when he bought land for their fuel business. That's when Carmela got Rose to go into vaudeville. They *had* to go to work. And with their talent, the theater was the place where they could make the most money. Eventually, of course, the money they made on the Keith Circuit not only saved their house and land, but made the Ponzillos rich compared to everybody else around here.

The families in our neighborhood lived pretty much day to day, but the parents were always hoping that their children would end up better off than they were. There were neighborhood schools for the kids (public schools in our case), because there were no Catholic schools around here then. But, like Rose, most of us had to go to work to help our families, so we didn't get to go to high school. Rose was street-smart all her life. In school she couldn't add two plus two, but when she was only in her teens, she was making deals with theater bookers that could make your head spin. If you got into a business deal with her, she would be eight miles ahead of you before you knew it. She had her father's sense of making money, but fortunately she had her mother's conscience too.

Rose was an attractive girl, but only the boys saw her that way. In school, in fact, some of the other girls were a little jealous of Rose because of the way the boys made over her. To the girls, she didn't look like much. She always looked kind of poor. She never had many clothes when she was a young girl, and what few things she had were awfully plain-looking. And we girls used to kid her because she was fat. But the boys in our neighborhood, and even some of the workmen, were naturally attracted to Rose.

There were some good-looking young men around here, mainly laborers, young fellows in their twenties, and Rose and I used to flirt with them all the time. We were only thirteen or fourteen, but we liked the men and they liked us. I got married young, but Rose stayed single, so she never had to stop liking men! Her brother Tony was a handsome guy, too, and he was real popular with the girls. But Carmela was the different one. She was one of the most beautiful women you could imagine. She had a real flair about her, too. But she wasn't attractive in the same way that Rose was. I don't know how to describe it exactly. I guess I would say that Carmela had the kind of beauty that you want to stand back and admire, but yet you can't get close to it. Rose, on the other hand, could attract men like a magnet, even though she was nothing but plain-looking compared to Carmela. Rose was sexy. Not that she tried to be, she just was.

Eight or nine years before she and Rose were in vaudeville together, Carmela was in a very bad auto accident. She was never the same afterward. She was visiting the Da Vino family in New Haven, and after a wedding she went joy-riding with Margaret Da Vino's brother, Frank, who had a touring car. They had been drinking at the wedding. Frank lost control of the car, and it turned over. Carmela was thrown from the car, but when it overturned, it landed in such a way that she was pinned under part of it. Frank somehow got the strength to lift the part of the car that was lying on top of her, but it had fractured her skull.

The hospital in New Haven telephoned the Meriden police, and they sent a policeman to tell Mrs. Ponzillo what had happened. She was taking care of me that afternoon, so she packed up Rose and me and took us on the train with her to New Haven. We got there about seven or eight o'clock that night, and we went straight to the Da Vinos' house, on Camp Street in New Haven. Carmela had to have an operation to relieve pressure on her brain, but she recovered after a while. Yet after that operation, something changed inside her—even Mrs. Ponzillo said so. I don't know how else to put it, except to say that Carmela had a kind of mental illness. It wasn't serious (she wasn't dangerous or anything), but she just wasn't completely normal.

That accident seemed to change her personality, too, and it affected her relationship with Rose. Carmela adored Rose, but another side of her resented all of Rose's success. She wanted to be as famous as Rose, as rich as Rose, equal to her in every way. But when things didn't work out that way after Rose got a Metropolitan contract, Carmela got mad because she thought Rose wasn't doing enough to get her into the Met. Out of spite, Carmela leaked a story to one of the New York newspapers about an incident that happened in New Haven, which was very sensitive as far as Rose was concerned. Rose's secretary, Edith Prilik, and Libbie Miller, who managed Rose's career, kept the story from going anyplace. But it caused Rose some embarrassment to have it dredged up again.

The incident had happened when Rose was singing at the Café Mellone. At that time, Rose was living with the Da Vinos, the same family that Carmela had been visiting when her accident happened. The Café Mellone stayed open very late on weekend nights, so Jim Ceriani used to drive Rose to the Da Vinos' after he closed up the place. One weekend, while he was inside cleaning up things, Rose was standing outside waiting for him. (It was about three o'clock in the morning.) Some drunk started to get fresh with her, and she told him to leave her alone. He kept it up, and finally he started tearing at her blouse, so she screamed for Ceriani. He came running, and when he saw what was happening, he slugged this drunk and knocked him flat. Apparently, when this guy went down, his head hit the curb. He never woke up. He died a day or two later.

Jim Ceriani was arrested for manslaughter, but he paid the bail and was released. They might have released him just on his own word, because he was in business and he was well liked. Later on, there was a trial and he was acquitted. But the incident made all the papers, including the ones here in Meriden.[9] It was treated like a scandal—you know, a teenage girl who sings at a café being pawed by some drunk at three in the morning, and the man who owns the place just happens to be there with her at that hour and ends up killing the drunk in a fistfight.

After the trial, there was some ugly small talk that got started about Ceriani and Rose having an affair. Personally, I never put any stock in it. Rose was only about seventeen or eighteen at that time, and Jim Ceriani was almost old enough to be her father. She wasn't experienced enough with men to know whether she was attracted to him or not. She probably had a crush on him. But, let me tell you, Jim Ceriani would have married her if she had been old enough. Anyway, the small-talk about them died out after a while. But it wasn't long after that, that Rose left the Café Mellone to go to New York and sing with Carmela in vaudeville.

I'm not saying that she was forced to leave New Haven by that incident. Carmela was encouraging her to do it anyway, and after what happened at the Café Mellone, it was the right time for her to make a move, so Rose decided to go to New York. I remember when Jim Ceriani came for her in his car—that was the day she left Meriden for New York to meet Carmela for an audition in vaudeville. Juliet Dondero, one of our other girlfriends, and I were waiting in front of the house with her. When Ceriani's car pulled up we gave her a big hug and wished her luck. Nobody in Meriden made much of it at the time, because she was taken for granted around here. But those of us who were close to her, believed in Rose, and it wasn't long until the Ponzillo sisters were playing the bigtime in vaudeville.

The Written Record

Once the most popular form of mass entertainment in America, vaudeville has since been reduced to images of cane-twirling tap dancers in striped coats and straw hats. As a result, the accomplishments of vaudevillians are neither understood nor appreciated for the most part. In the written accounts of many now-legendary performers who began in the two-a-day circuit, however, a sense of the talent, the drive, the determination, and the luck a performer needed to build a successful vaudeville career may still be glimpsed.

A number of these accounts underscore the sheer endurance required of vaudeville performers, especially of women who performed on the circuit:

> One special hardship . . . is the unbrokenness of the work, there being the same demand in summer that there is in winter, so that she may go on, if she needs the money, every week in the year, twice every day, even appearing in what are politely called sacred concerts on Sunday. One has to be pretty callous not to feel weary doing the same little act some six hundred times a year. Many a vaudeville actor, sick of this meaningless iteration, sighs for an opportunity in the "legitimate" [theater].[10]

Alfred Lunt was perhaps the most famous of the "legitimate" actors of Ponselle's generation whose early career was spent partly in two-a-day vaudeville. At twenty-one, Lunt had made his debut opposite Lillie Langtree in a twenty-six-week vaudeville tour. "Vaudeville," he would later write, "was a real show business. I have never seen any phase of the theatre in which everything counted so much. Vaudeville actors never let down for a minute. They fought to score each individual point, and if they failed to do it, they took the act apart to find out what was wrong and worked until it was right."[11]

Other contemporary accounts also suggest, as does Lunt's, that many who made the transition to other realms of show business never forgot their vaudeville experiences, especially the pain of failing during an audition or an engagement. The memory of a failed debut never left Fred Astaire, despite the phenomenal success of his six-decade career. Astaire began his career on the subway circuit in vaudeville with his sister, Adele, two years before Rosa and Carmela were to begin theirs. The Astaires moved into the bigtime in 1916, garnering laudatory reviews wherever they appeared. ("Their feet scarcely seem to touch the floor," said *Variety*, "and there is a snap, go, and personality in everything they do."[12])

In the 1917–18 season when the Ponzillo Sisters were appearing on Broadway, they and the Astaires often trailed one another in and around New York City. In late September 1917, three weeks after the Ponzillo Sisters had shared the bill with Blossom Seeley at the Riverside Theater, the Astaires appeared with Seeley at the Keith-owned Colonial Theater, which advertised "Palace stars at half the Palace prices."[13] In his autobiography, Fred Astaire recalled his and Adele's early years and spoke of their failure in their first significant engagement on Broadway, at Proctor's Fifth Avenue Theater:

> We rehearsed our music carefully, then waited until it was time to get dressed for the opening matinee. We were surprised and disappointed to find that our position on the bill was number one—opening the show.
>
> Our act was partly a sketch with all dialogue for the first five minutes. I knew the audience would be coming in on us and that the dialogue would suffer. We had the most dreaded spot on the bill. But Adele and I got together and decided to let nothing upset us. We hoped we'd be good enough at the matinee so that the manager would give us a later spot for the evening performance and the rest of the week.
>
> We were very nervous. Before we knew it we were on. The curtain went up and there was—to use the old vaudeville jargon—"nobody in the house." We were dismayed to see rows and rows of empty seats on the lower floor. Upstairs in the balcony and gallery the customers had arrived earlier, but they were paying little attention to us. Line after line of our comic dialogue went by without a snicker.
>
> As Adele and I went on with the act there was no enthusiasm whatsoever from the audience. They were now arriving in droves, with ushers slamming down seats. At the final exit of our closing dance number we received a sparse, sympathetic kind of hand, and returned to steal one bow. To make a horrible story more agonizing, what little applause there was stopped while we were out there, leaving us hanging. We had to get off in complete silence.[14]

When the next day's bill was posted, the Astaires could not find their name anywhere on the bill. "We went out and got the story from the manager," Fred Astaire recalled. "He said simply, 'I'm sorry, kids—your act wasn't strong enough. You've been cancelled.' That was it. There is no worse blow to a vaudevillian than that word, 'cancelled.'"[15]

Because vaudeville audiences encompassed the spectrum of American class structure at that time (factory workers, railroaders, recently assimilated immigrants, doctors, lawyers, bankers, and teachers), an established performer from the "legitimate" theater could find New York audiences difficult to impress. The first vaudeville appearance of the renowned Wagnerian soprano Johanna Gadski, whom the Keith management had lured with a $3,500 weekly salary,[16] attested to the challenges opera stars often encountered on the vaudeville stage:

> Madame Gadski . . . found the going rather tough, though doubtless the grand-opera star did not express it so, despite some children's songs she

> specially interpolated and announced. For her encore she sang the famous "Call of the Valkyrie" with which she is inseparably associated in the memories of countless grand-opera lovers. At the Metropolitan, and at Carnegie Hall, in almost any place except a vaudeville house, that electrifying bit of music would have brought a storm of applause crashing down upon the diva. But to the majority of Hippodrome habitués it was only an unfamiliar song. They applauded, and fairly generously, because it stirred them.
>
> Had Madame Gadski been more familiar with vaudeville, or better advised, she would have announced that number. She would have told that the song was "by that great old master, Wagner"; she would have explained briefly the situation of the play in which it was used and she would have identified herself with the excerpt. In short, she would have built up the number, interesting the audience in it before she sang it, preparing them in anticipation of a fuller appreciation.[17]

To a first-rank vaudeville star like Nora Bayes, the importance of "building up a number" with a vaudeville audience was self-evident. Rather than working to "hold" an audience, she maintained, "the situation is quite the reverse—they hold me":

> They represent the most comfortable and valuable relationship. They are my friends. It is therefore with intimate safety of friendship, that I go out upon the stage and shake hands with them. My performances are exactly like an intimate chat with one or two close friends, who sit around a table and enjoy themselves. I can think of no better symbol to express my own feelings toward the audience than that of a small party seated at a friendly table.[18]

However instinctive it may have been with Nora Bayes, this ability to hold, and to mold, an audience and to achieve a sense of intimacy with them in a two-thousand-seat theater came only after years of trial and error, and sheer hard work. As with most other headliners, the ego that fueled Nora Bayes' success left no room for any other performers when she felt her star stature threatened, especially by new acts that "stole" audiences with a show-stopping routine. Bayes even forced the resignation of a gifted young accompanist when he would not alter the melody of a song to suit her tastes. It mattered nothing to her that her accompanist—George Gershwin—had written the song she was insisting that he change.[19]

Nora Bayes displayed her ego in ways that often paled in comparison to Eva Tanguay, who routinely billed herself as "An Institution."[20] In Chicago during the 1916–17 season, when the Ponzillo Sisters appeared for the second time on a bill with Tanguay,[21] they experienced first-hand what the young Sophie Tucker had already learned a decade earlier in a confrontation with the temperamental and vindictive veteran. In 1909 Tanguay demanded (unsuccessfully) that the twenty-five-year-old Tucker be removed from the Ziegfeld *Follies*, on the grounds that she was stealing Tanguay's audiences.[22]

As Heywood Broun, then a drama critic for the New York *Tribune*, soon learned after printing an unfavorable review, Eva Tanguay did not exempt critics from her tirades. "Miss Tanguay is billed as a 'bombshell,'" Broun wrote after seeing her new wartime act. "Would to Heaven that she were, for a bomb is something which is carried to a great height and then dropped."[23] The following week, Tanguay took out a full-page advertisement in *Variety* and launched a broadside attack on the critic:

> And now that Mr. Broun has criticized me, why not I criticize him? First, I suggest an *Eat and Grow Thin* book for him—and, may I add, as a vaudeville critic he might have been a great war correspondent. Have you ever noticed when a woman succeeds how they attack her until her character bleeds? They snap at her heels like mongrels unfed, just because she has escaped being dropped into Failure's big web. They don't give her credit for talent. They don't discount a very hard start. They don't give her credit for heartaches and pains; how she grimly held tight to the reins when the road ahead was rocky and dreary—how smiling she met every discouraging sneer.[24]

Tanguay concluded what she termed her "rebuttal" with this assessment of Heywood Broun, printed in thirty-point type: "YOU are dirt 'neath my feet, for I have beaten YOUR game and it's a hard game to beat."[25]

Neither Rosa nor Carmela kept any memorabilia from their vaudeville years—no playbills, promotional photographs, correspondence, and not even reviews of their appearances. Nor do they seem to have advertised in the theatrical trade papers, as most other acts did from time to time. But their career on the Keith Circuit can be reconstructed from the pages of *Variety*, *Billboard*, *Clipper*, *The New York Times*, and other major New York newspapers of that day. What the record discloses, however, is a markedly different sequence of events than either of the Ponselles would recall in later years. For instance, there is scarcely any mention of their act in any of the vaudeville bills in and around Manhattan between 13 September 1915, when their act debuted at the Royal Theater,[26] and the 1917–18 season, when they began appearing with some regularity at the larger Keith theaters on Broadway.

As *Variety* and *Billboard* attest, the sisters spent the 1915–16 and 1916–17 theatrical seasons on tour, gradually refining their act until the Keith Circuit management was convinced they were ready for Broadway. Their touring appearances remained sporadic, however, especially when compared to the week-after-week performing records amassed by the Astaires, the Marx Brothers, the Cansinos, Sophie Tucker, and others who began their careers near the time the Ponzillo Sisters began theirs. Whether they were unable to get steady bookings because of Gene Hughes' conservative management style (as Ponselle suggested here) or because Rosa was unwilling to risk leaving her high-paying position at the Café Mellone is largely guesswork, unfortunately.

Songwriter Irving Caesar, lyricist for such popular songs as "Swanee," "I Want To Be Happy," and "Tea For Two," became acquainted with the Ponzillo Sisters after seeing them on Broadway in the 1917–18 season. His impressions of their act remained vivid nearly six decades later. "It was visually very effective, before they even made a move onstage," Caesar recalled. "Everything was a cool, limpid shade of blue—the backdrop was blue, I think even their blouses were a pale blue. It was really effective. Everything was kept visually simple." For Caesar, the highlight of the act was Rosa's singing of "Kiss Me Again":

> Rosa got up from the piano bench as the orchestra played the opening measures of the verse. Now, remember, this was a very big hit, and was always associated with Fritzi Scheff, whom no one would have thought capable of being equalled in the coloratura passages by any other vaudeville singer, especially some young Italian-American, piano-playing kid.
>
> You can imagine what went through audience members' minds between the time the orchestra started playing and [when] Rosa began to sing the first line of the verse. First, almost everybody knew that opening, and how hard it was—so they were probably thinking, "Well, this spunky girl has guts. Let's hope she can get through this without falling on her face. If only she were Fritzi Scheff, she might be able to do it well." That's probably what was going through a lot of minds.
>
> Then Rosa would sing the first few couplets, which aren't terribly demanding. There was the audience's first surprise, you see. This girl had the *higher* voice of the two. Up to that moment, the girls' voices sounded so much alike that those of us in the audience couldn't tell who had the higher and who had the lower voice. But in "Kiss Me Again," it was clear that Rosa was a real soprano, not a mezzo.
>
> Rosa would then launch into those sacred Fritzi Scheff coloratura runs, with the near-octave drops into the lower voice. That's when the hammer hit, right there. You would see people straighten up in their seats, and there would be looks of astonishment. The verdict was: this girl has an immense voice—bigger than anything you'll hear from a vaudevillian—yet she can sing as light as Tetrazzini when she wants to.[27]

"When Rosa would begin the refrain," Caesar remembered,

> she would invariably take the last note of the verse and diminish it, taking it down to a whisper. Then she would sing the line "Sweet summer breeze,

whispering trees," which drops way down into a contralto range—and it was as if someone had welded Schumann-Heink's lower voice to Tetrazzini's upper one. This was the most gorgeous, most ample sound you could possibly imagine. [The composer of *Mademoiselle Modiste*] Victor Herbert treated me like a son and frequently took me to the theater with him, [Caesar said.] I was with him when he heard Rosa sing "Kiss Me Again" at the Palace Theater. Afterward, he said that he had never heard it sung better.[28]

Although the young Ponselle bore no physical resemblance to the petite Fritzi Scheff and would have rekindled no memories of what critic Carl Van Vechten called Scheff's "saucy chic" on stage,[29] any favorable comparison to the original Fifi of *Mademoiselle Modiste* was a high compliment to a vaudeville newcomer. Scheff, for whom Herbert wrote the role of the milliner Fifi, had arrived at the Metropolitan Opera in 1901 after a successful career in Germany, where she had made her debut in Frankfurt four years earlier.[30] Her association with Herbert, who had already written leading roles for her in the two previous operettas, *Babette* and *The Two Roses,* reached full fruition when *Mademoiselle Modiste* opened at the Knickerbocker Theater in New York on Christmas Day 1905, eventually logging 252 performances during its first run.[31]

"Kiss Me Again," the most enduring melody in the score, had been modeled after Adele's narrative in Act Three of *Die Fledermaus*. Although Fritzi Scheff had initially objected to the song when the composer played it for her in manuscript form ("It is written too low at the beginning," she complained to Herbert), she sang it so definitively that, as Van Vechten wrote, she became "the toast and the tea, the hors d'oeuvres and the dessert; in other words a sensational success."[32]

Whether or not the young Rosa Ponzillo patterned her own performances of "Kiss Me Again" after Fritzi Scheff's, Herbert's popular *arietta* launched her career more than any other selection in the Ponzillo Sisters' act. Even after she made the transition from vaudeville to opera, both the popularity of "Kiss Me Again" and, apparently, Rosa's own association with the song in bigtime vaudeville led Columbia's management to ask her to record it. (Edith Prilik's diary entry for the recording session, which took place in New York City on Monday afternoon, 26 July 1920, reads, "This recording by Mme Ponselle is of the music she made famous on the Keith vaudeville circuit, at the Palace Theater."[33]) Although she did not perform it with any frequency, "Kiss Me Again" remained in her concert repertoire well into the 1930s. As late as 1937 she included it among the selections she sang on the *RCA Magic Key* program.

However well Herbert's lilting melody served Rosa as a solo on the Keith Circuit, neither "Kiss Me Again" nor the other selections the Ponzillo Sisters had incorporated into their "turn" were any guarantee that their twenty-minute act would be accepted by audiences accustomed to bigtime vaudeville entertainment. Considering the sheer number of new acts that were regularly given tryouts in and around Manhattan (Keith Circuit magnate Edward F. Albee once estimated that "of all our acts seventy percent [are] new ones"[34]) and considering the demands and expectations of New York–area vaudeville audiences, it is significant that the Ponzillos' debut was given a reasonably lengthy review in *Variety*, then the most widely read trade paper in show business.

Reviewing their debut performance at the Keith-owned Royal Theater in the Bronx, *Variety* commended their singing and musicianship, while expressing some concerns about the overall pacing of their act:

> This "sister act" with appearance and other qualifications, should rearrange its song repertoire before striking out for the bigtime houses, where it certainly belongs. . . . The act features ballads, and also the more familiar duets from the opera. The performers are the Ponzillo sisters, who are said actually to be sisters. Both possess rather pleasing voices, with a wide range that is well used, but owing to bad judgment in numbers the central part of the turn lags. The third number could be dropped at once, for the girls do not handle it as well as the others, and at the same time it would be just about enough to shorten the act to its proper length. The larger of the two continually plays a grand piano, joining her partner for a well-harmonized chorus, also handling a ballad splendidly for her only solo number.[35]

While generally commending their act, the reviewer made clear that the simplicity in costuming that Rosa and Carmela had tried to achieve with their tailored white blouses and royal-blue skirts was not as appealing as they might have thought: "The girls should have worn a more appropriate costume for the early season opening."[36]

As the pages of *Variety* attest, throughout 1916 and 1917 the Ponzillos performed in Keith theaters in the northeast and midwest. Their itinerary during the spring of 1917, which took them from Providence (Rhode Island) to Montreal and Hamilton (Quebec and Ontario), to Chicago, Milwaukee, Grand Rapids, Detroit, and Youngstown (Ohio) in an eight-week stretch, is typical of the route that the United Booking Offices under Eddie Darling assigned to acts like theirs. As did other vaudevillians hoping for Broadway and the bigtime, Rosa and Carmela could use these "hinterland" performances to refine their act. A detailed review followed their appearance on 25 January 1916 at the Keith-Orpheum Theater in Pittsburgh:

> Out of the assortment of offerings, four numbers stood clearly and distinctly as surpassingly good. Of these four, the Ponzillo sisters, billed as Italian girls, but possessing perfect English accents and mannerisms, received an

> ovation thoroughly deserved with a song repertoire combining operatic arias, ballads and even a syncopation or two of the better sort.
>
> These Ponzillo sisters are—or were—strangers to Pittsburgh. They possess voices of wonderful tone-sweetness, unusual range and flexibility, sufficient power for even a vaudeville stage, and the ability to handle them in a manner that left nothing to be desired. One of the voices would probably be classed as a pure contralto, although the owner [that is, Carmela] soars into the upper registers easily, gracefully, and musically. The other sister's voice is a dramatic soprano of almost identical tonal quality. When the two sisters sing in unison it is almost impossible to distinguish between their voices. Most of their repertoire was made up of operatic numbers, showing excellent taste in selection and unusual artistry in rendition.[37]

The sisters' selections, costumes, and color schemes on their Keith Circuit tours remained much as they were when the act first appeared at the Royal Theater. Yet on accasion a costume change would accommodate a new piece of music, as when they incorporated the "Flower Duet" from *Madama Butterfly* into their act in Grand Rapids. Rosa recalled the occasion in 1979 for the University of Michigan's Musical Society, then celebrating its centennial. "My first visit to Michigan . . . took place [in] 1917," she said in a dictated letter, "when Carmela and I played in vaudeville in Grand Rapids. We dressed ourselves in geisha costumes and sang, among other selections, the 'Duet of the Flowers' from Puccini's *Madama Butterfly*."[38] The local reviewer took note of their costuming:

> The matinee audience, ready for the right sort of entertainment, had its wishes fulfilled when "The Italian Girls" sang their medley of opera songs. The big surprise came as the two sisters, so identical in voice and mannerisms, slipped behind a large rice-paper screen placed opposite the piano onstage. While the orchestra played an Oriental strain, behind the screen the girls transformed themselves into lovely Mmes. Butterfly, with their kimonos and tiny slippers and hair held tight with long vertical combs. As they bowed to the audience in the familiar way of the Japanese, they sang the familiar duet from the Puccini opera. The costumes were mandarin, the voices golden.[39]

The Riverside Theater in Manhattan became the site of the Ponzillo Sisters' debut as a bigtime act on Broadway. Sharing top billing with Belle Baker (the headliner, billed as the "Incomparable Delineator of Character Songs") and the Three Dooleys ("Ray, Gordon and William, In Some Original Dooley Nonsense"), they opened at the Riverside on Monday, 3 September 1917.[40]

Although the sisters' first performance was a success with the Broadway audience ("The concluding turn of the first part was presented by the Ponzillo Sisters who were forced to deliver three encore selections," said *Variety*[41]), they were taken to task by *Variety*'s women's editor, Patsy Smith, for their unimaginative costuming. In her popular column "Among the Women," Smith chided the sisters for their "severe headdress," for "hair dressed most unbecomingly (like Indian maidens)," and, in Rosa's case, for having chosen "a black velvet draped affair [that] makes one of the sisters look twice the size she should."[42]

The audience's response notwithstanding, the Ponzillos were neither held over for a second week at the Riverside, nor did they receive any other booking on Broadway the following week. They were not given another booking at the Riverside during the third or fourth weeks of the new season; instead, the piano duo of Van and Schenck took their place on playbills featuring the Avon Comedy Four, Blossom Seeley, and the popular dance team of Adelaide and Hughes.[43] Nor were the Ponzillos appearing at any of the other Keith theaters in the area—the Colonial, the Alhambra, the Prospect, or the Orpheum and Bushwick theaters in Brooklyn. By the second week of October 1917, however, "The Italian Girls" were back at the Riverside. But their biggest triumph came at the end of the month: on Monday, 29 October, they appeared for the first time at the Palace Theater.

When *Variety* printed the Palace playbill the previous Friday (as was the custom in the theatrical trade papers), one spot was left for the United Booking Offices to fill by Monday afternoon. The rest of the bill had already been announced and featured the dance team of Maurice and Florence Walton as the headline act. Also on the bill were Blossom Seeley ("Jazz Melodical Delirium Tremens Running Wild"); Seeley's one-time partner, manager, paramour, and husband for a time Rube Marquard (formerly a star pitcher for the New York Giants[44]) and his newest vaudeville partner William Dooley of the Three Dooleys; the comedy team of Cressy and Dayne, and a new blackface team, Swor and Avey (or "burnt-cork act," as these were now being labeled in the marginally increased sensitivity of the times).

By Sunday morning, 28 October 1917, when *The New York Times* printed the now-finalized playbill, the Ponzillos were listed prominently as "Carmela & Rosa Ponzillo—Two Fascinating Italian Girls with Grand Opera Voices, in a New Programme of Superb Selections." Reviewing the Monday afternoon performance, the *Times* was not sufficiently impressed to mention the sisters at all, focusing instead on "the ever nasal Blossom Seeley" and Rube Marquard, "now teamed with William Dooley, an entertainer who sets a pace several miles beyond Mr. Marquard's wildest dreams."[45] *Variety*, on the other hand, gave the bill a detailed but hardly flattering review:

> Not a great show but it rounded out a pretty long evening . . . consuming more time than anything else. The show was strong in sections, with some

of the comedy insertions especially well received although the song deluge came close to swamping everything else.

After intermission Camel [*sic*] and Rosa Ponzillo sang entertainingly. Nobody seemed to fancy the gestures the girls are using and they might invest a nickel's worth more to make their present repertoire of hand poses a little more varied. The girls go in for distinctive dressing with the smaller of the girls [Carmela] wearing a clinging, shimmering black outfit that had some of the men forgetting she was there as a vocalist and not as a model of some sort. The girls did better with one section of their song routine than with others.[46]

The *Variety* reviewer's comments about Carmela's "shimmering black outfit" aside, women's columnist Patsy Smith once again found nothing to admire in the sisters' costuming. In her *Variety* column of 2 November 1917, she wrote, "Carmela Ponillo [*sic*] is still wearing the velvet gown with the shockingly bad lines for her figure—a full tunic chopped off just below the knees—and sister Rosa is wearing her dresses shorter." As it was, *Variety* never had another occasion to review the Ponzillo Sisters at the Palace. Contrary to their own recollections, as well as to those of other entertainment-industry figures who in later years would recall seeing their act at the Palace, the ten performances Rosa and Carmela gave during the week of 29 October–3 November 1917 marked their one and only appearance at Keith's celebrated Broadway theater.[47]

When she mentioned her vaudeville career in interviews, Rosa Ponselle invariably underscored the "gamble" that she and Carmela had taken when they delivered an ultimatum to Eddie Darling and the United Booking Offices. In her first tape-recorded interview (with John Secrist, in 1949) she told the very same version that she would later repeat to the *Times*' Harold C. Schonberg and to other interviewers. A verbatim transcript of her comments to Secrist captures the emphasis she accorded the risks she believed they were taking:

We were negotiating for a thousand dollars a week, because Eva Tanguay was getting three thousand a week, and we were getting the standard. It seemed that Eva Tanguay was on the bill with us wherever we went in the bigtime, in vaudeville. We stopped the show, literally, but she was getting the money. So we went on strike. We got the managers up to eight hundred, but we wanted a thousand. We literally stopped the show wherever we went. Eva Tanguay used to stand in the wings, you know, and she was getting in the papers, being reviewed the next day [with the reviewer] saying, "Eva Tanguay gets the money, and the Ponselle, or Ponzillo, girls stopped the show."[48]

Mat. Daily at 2
25, 50, 75c.

2,000 CHOICE
SEATS, 50c.
Except Sat. and Holidays.

B·F·KEITH'S
PALACE
BROADWAY AND 47TH STREET

EVERY NIGHT
25, 50, 75c, $1, $1.50

1,000 ORCHESTRA
SEATS, $1.00
EXCEPT SAT., SUN. AND HOLIDAYS.

TWO BIG CONCERTS SUNDAY, 2 & 8 P. M. Beginning Mon. Mat., Oct. 29.

Super-Splendid International Engagement of Stepping Stars, Back on a Short Furlough From the French Front, Where They Did Their Bit, Come

MAURICE and FLORENCE WALTON

with Dancing Reminiscences of the Battle and the Entertainments they gave the Wounded in the Red Cross Hospitals.
See their new War dances, "Waltz der Front" and "Chasseur's Fox Trot."
MAURICE, WHO IS IN THE FRENCH AMBULANCE CORPS, WILL DANCE IN UNIFORM BY GOVERNMENT PERMIT. MISS WALTON IS OFFICIALLY DECORATED WITH THE BERRY OF THE CHASSEURS. NEW PARIS GOWNS FROM PAQUIN AND CALLOT SOEURS. SPECIAL ORCHESTRA.
DANCERS AND DANCES WITH TRUE DISTINCTION.

XTRA FEATURE. Two Fascinating Italian Girls with Grand Opera Voices.

CARMELA & ROSA PONZILLO

IN A NEW PROGRAMME OF SUPERB SELECTIONS.

XTRA FEATURE—HAPPY TRIO OF HIGHLY GIFTED ENTERTAINERS.
Three Attractive Personalities Who Are Delighting Vaudeville Fans.

RUBE MARQUARD AND WM. DOOLEY

Assisted by HELEN CLEMENT in SONGS, DANCES AND COMEDY.
DONE WITH ORIGINALITY AND PUT OVER WITH AN EFFECTIVE PUNCH.

ADDED FEATURE. ADDED FEATURE.

WILL M. CRESSY AND BLANCHE DAYNE

In "A CITY CASE," by WILL M. CRESSY.

JOHN (Extra Feature) WEST
SWOR & AVEY
Impersonators of Southern Negroes.

ADDED ATTRACTION.
MILT COLLINS
As "The Patriot." By Aaron Hoffman.

PHINA & PICKS. MEEHAN'S DOGS.

EXTRAORDINARY FEATURE. Superb Syncopated Singers Entirely Surrounded by Jazz Melodical Delirium Tremens of Ragtime Running Wild.

BLOSSOM SEELEY

Assisted by JAZZ FIELDS, JAZZ SALISBURY, JAZZ DAVIS, JAZZ LOPEZ and JAZZ THORPE in "SEELEY'S SYNCOPATED STUDIO."
Wherein the Art of "Jazzing Things Up" Reaches Its Entertainment Limit.
Oh! Hearken to that Jazz Cornet.

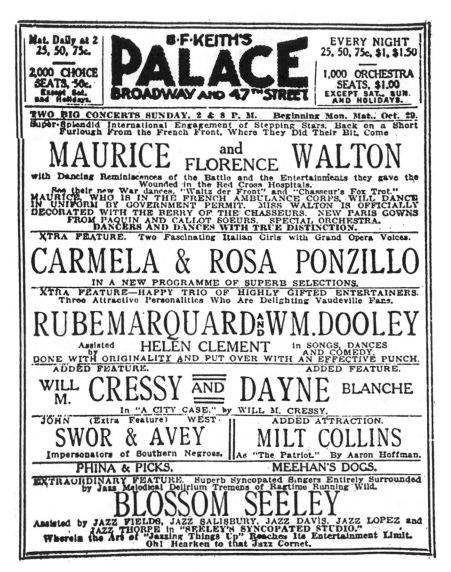

Figure 3. The Ponzillos arrived at "the Mecca of vaudeville," Keith's Palace Theater, on 29 October 1917. They were a last-minute substitute act, and at week's end were not reengaged. As the fine print of their billing indicates ("Two Fascinating Italian Girls with Grand Opera Voices,") they were already envisioning operatic careers. FROM THE AUTHOR'S COLLECTION.

Although no reviews yet discovered in newspaper archives attest to the Ponzillo Sisters' garnering more applause from an audience than Eva Tanguay, Rosa was unwavering in her belief that she and Carmela, by defying the Keith management, had taken the boldest step in their career. "When all of this happened," she told Secrist, "I said to the manager, 'One of these days you're going to have to pay plenty to hear me sing.' I had no idea what I was talking about. He said, 'More power to you.' That was Eddie Darling."[49]

In this and other interviews Ponselle always implied that this strike had not only ended the Ponzillo Sisters' lucrative vaudeville career, but had also forced them to live off their savings while studying with William Thorner, trying to learn everything they could about opera performing from Romano Romani and hoping that a break would somehow come their way before they depleted their savings. But as anyone who knew Rosa Ponselle would readily attest, she was rarely one to take risks where income was concerned, especially at that point in her emerging career when she and Carmela were supporting not only themselves but their parents as well.

Their need for a substantial and continuous income (and, of course, their having the means to earn it, with a bigtime act that paid them eight hundred dollars a week) makes it difficult to understand their unusually brief performance record on Broadway. Paradoxically, the more successful they became, the less they performed, particularly during their third and final season in vaudeville (1917–18) when their appearances at the Riverside and the Palace solidified their reputation as a bigtime act. As it was, out of an average of forty weeks available to them on the Keith Circuit, the Ponzillo Sisters performed for a mere six weeks in the 1917–18 season. Between November 1917 and March 1918, they were heard only twice on Broadway: at an all-star Sunday concert at the Century Theater on 26 November 1917 and at a war-relief concert in the Winter Garden on 6 January 1918, where they shared the bill with Ed Wynn, Fred and Adele Astaire, the Cansinos, and other bigtime acts.[50]

With the exception of these two performances (both booked separately from their regular schedules on the circuit and only one, the Century all-star concert, paying them any fees, the other being a benefit), the Ponzillos virtually disappeared from the Keith roster for nearly six months. Their whereabouts during these "missing months," though puzzling at first, can be traced through the court-case summaries of Ponselle's eventual separation from William Thorner's management. According to the briefs prepared by Nathan Burkan, who represented Rosa when the case was heard by the New York State Supreme Court in 1928,[51] she and Carmela were spending the bulk of their time studying with Romano Romani and sporadically with Thorner.

As Thorner would tell *Musical America* in a 1919 interview, Rosa first came to his studio in November 1917, the month during which, as her vaudeville performing record shows, she and Carmela gave their last regularly scheduled performances on the Keith Circuit for nearly six months. "Five months from [that] time," *Musical America* reported, "Miss Poncelle [*sic*] . . . had her audition with Mr. Gatti-Casazza and was accepted . . . by the Metropolitan."[52] In an interview she gave the Boston *Sunday Globe* not long afterward, Rosa confirmed not only that she had first come to Thorner in November 1917 but also that he assured her she would be "at the Met or the Chicago Opera in five or six months."[53] Apparently, then, she auditioned and was "accepted" by Gatti-Casazza in late March or early April 1918, even though she did not actually sign a contract until the first week of June, after Thorner and Gatti-Casazza had completed their negotiations for the roles Gatti wanted to assign her.

As the vaudeville bills in *Variety* attest, the Ponzillo Sisters made no appearances on the Keith Circuit in the 1917–18 season (with the sole exception of their January appearance in the all-star benefit) until mid-March 1918 when they returned to the site of their debut (the Royal Theater in the Bronx) for ten performances during the week of 18–23 March. Their next appearances, as announced by Eddie Darling from the United Booking Offices, were to take place at the Alhambra from 1 to 6 April and at the Colonial Theater the following week. But during the last week of March 1918, *Variety* reported that "the Ponzello [*sic*] Sisters cancelled the Alhambra . . . for this week because of illness."[54] The trade papers again reported on 7 April 1918 that the sisters had to be replaced at the Colonial Theater, owing to their continuing illness.[55]

They never appeared again on a vaudeville stage.

A telling entry among notes kept by Edith Prilik from that period suggests that illness was not the reason for the sisters' two-week indisposition. At three in the afternoon on Wednesday, 3 April 1918 (approximately five hours before Rosa and Carmela would have gone on stage at the Alhambra Theater had they not cancelled), Rosa went with Romano Romani to the Columbia Graphophone Company studios to make a test recording. The aria she agreed to record that afternoon, "Pace, pace mio Dio" from *Forza*, hinted that her "gamble" with the influential Thorner had now paid off and that Keith's youthful booking manager, Eddie Darling, was about to lose a ten-dollar bet.

CHAPTER FOUR

An Overnight Prima Donna

"Rosa Ponselle," critic Oscar Thompson wrote, "began a prima donna."[1] Written in 1937 near the end of her career, Thompson's comment reflected the future promise that the New York critics had detected in the Ponselle voice and technique at the time of her debut. Whether or not Thompson's statement accurately reflected the consensus among the major critics about Ponselle's artistic stature at the outset of her career (and in light of Henderson's and Huneker's reviews of her debut, it would be difficult to argue that it did), Ponselle herself dismissed any such "prima donna" stature out of hand. "A prima donna has a repertoire," she said when reminded in later years of Thompson's comment. "As for me, I didn't even know the stories of half the operas they gave me to prepare when I made my debut. How could I have been an overnight prima donna if I didn't have a repertoire?"[2]

Ponselle's initial Metropolitan Opera contract, it will be recalled, required her to learn seven operatic roles and one sacred work, namely, the title roles in *Aida*, *La gioconda*, and *Tosca*, the Leonoras of *Il trovatore* and *La forza del destino*, Santuzza in *Cavalleria rusticana*, Amelia in *Un ballo in maschera*, and, finally, the soprano part in the Verdi *Requiem*. She was to have prepared all but *Gioconda*, *Tosca*, and *Ballo* by the date of her debut and was to have mastered the latter-mentioned roles as soon as was feasible afterward. In addition to the Verdi *Requiem*, which she performed for the first time in April 1919, she was also given a second sacred work to prepare: Rossini's *Stabat Mater*, which she first sang in January 1919.[3] She was also given three additional operatic roles to prepare in her first season: Rezia in Weber's *Oberon*, Giorgetta in Puccini's *Il tabarro*, and Carmelita in Joseph Breil's *The Legend*.

In sum, then, she was required to prepare twelve works during her first Metropolitan season.

The toll that this continual preparation of new roles took on her energy and stamina would become evident in the terms she asked William Thorner to negotiate in her second-year contract. Her salary was necessarily a first consideration in her second-season negotiations. Her income was an immediate concern, not surprisingly, because after she left vaudeville for the opera stage, she had watched her income plummet to $150 per week from the $750 weekly fee that she and Carmela had commanded on the Keith Circuit. For her second season, therefore, she requested that Thorner negotiate a new salary that would be paid on a per-performance rather than weekly basis.

In view of the success of her debut season, the Metropolitan management granted Ponselle this concession. Consequently, instead of being required to sing as many as three times per week for a mere $50 per performance, such as during her first season, she would be paid $100 per performance fee for the 1919–20 season. But perhaps more tellingly, she asked for and received a contractual stipulation that she would never be required to sing two different roles in succession with less than fourteen days' rehearsal time being guaranteed her.[4] Her motives for negotiating this prolonged rehearsal time appear to have been twofold: on the one hand, she had no interest in reacquainting herself with the stress—physical, emotional, and vocal—to which she had been subjected during her first Metropolitan season;[5] and on the other, as will become clear in this chapter, she had also devised a plan to increase her income substantially by reducing the number of her Metropolitan appearances, thereby allowing more room in her annual schedule for lucrative concert appearances.

There were additional strains, too, that eventually she had to rectify. Chief among these was the management of her career, for which William Thorner had been contractually responsible since the date of her first Metropolitan Opera contract.[6] On the day she had accepted her contract, she took with her the following letter to General Manager Giulio Gatti-Casazza:

> With further reference to the contract entered upon between your company and myself this date (June 4, 1918) I herewith authorize you to retain from my salary during the season of 1919/1920 and eventual subsequent years of my engagement with the Metropolitan Opera Company, Ten (10%) Percent in favor and at the disposal of Mr. William Thorner, my authorized representative and teacher.[7]

Thorner had prepared the letter for her signature earlier that day. The contents of the letter, interestingly, make no mention of any payment of management fees for the 1918–19 Metropolitan season. The explanation for this lies in the management agreement Ponselle had signed with Thorner, which did not call for him to receive a percentage of her first-year earnings at the Metropolitan.[8] In lieu of a percentage, she had agreed to pay him a flat fee for his management services during her initial season at the Metropolitan.[9]

During her first three seasons, Ponselle grew increasingly dissatisfied with the manner in which Thorner represented her interests. She was especially critical of the contractual requirement that she must claim him as her teacher, a distinction she now chose to reserve solely for Romano Romani. She also resented Thorner's having persuaded her to sign a recording contract with the Columbia Graphophone Company rather than with the more prestigious Victor Talking Machine Company, for which the one artist whom she admired the most, Enrico Caruso, recorded exclusively.[10] She remained critical, too, of Thorner's inability to secure either a Metropolitan Opera or Chicago Opera contract for her sister Carmela.[11] These frustrations now led her to retain a young concert-management staff member, Libbie Miller, to book her annual concert tours. Eventually, she invited Libbie to replace Thorner entirely and to manage all aspects of her career.

If Ponselle's early years at the Metropolitan were marked by such passing stresses and frustrations, they were also years of steady growth and improvement for her as a singer and as an artist. Of her debut in *La forza del destino*, she spoke of "the weight of this mantle, this reputation" she had achieved on the evening of 15 November 1918.[12] In the ensuing four seasons, what now awaited her were the challenges of ten new roles. Her recollections of these early roles, recorded more than fifty years afterward, afford insights not only into her own performances but also into those of the first-rank singers of the years immediately following World War I, with whom she was frequently cast.

The Interview

From interviews of Rosa Ponselle by the author (March 1973, February 1977, and December 1978), by Hugh M. Johns (June–July 1968), by William Seward (December 1971), and by Fred Calland (1977, precise date unknown). Transcribed with minor editing.

You sang your first Santuzza in Cavalleria rusticana *about three weeks after your debut in* La Forza del destino. *What do you recall of your first Santuzza?*

That role was always one of my pets. To begin with, it's a good score; there's not a bad bar of music in it. It's also good theater. It's always done on a double bill, so it's often thought of as a short opera. But it's a compressed opera, not a short opera. It goes from one dramatic moment to the next—no breaks, no resting points, no musical "filler" in between.

What was especially attractive to you about Santuzza?

Well, it's a very earthy role. You can really get into the part and do something with it. Santuzza used to be a relief for me to sing, compared to some of those old-style roles I was given in my early years at the Met. It's a kind of primitive role, really, so when I was doing Santuzza I didn't have to be so concerned about being "grand" and queenly and that sort of thing.

Vocally, how difficult was Santuzza for you?

Other than Carmen, it was the easiest role I ever sang, which is one of the reasons why I did it so many times. The music lies very comfortably for my particular voice—right smack in the middle, which was always the easiest part of my range.

Very soon after your first Cavalleria, *you sang Rezia in the first Metropolitan production of Weber's* Oberon. *Was it especially challenging to learn and perform the role in English rather than in German?*

I would have preferred to sing it in German. It was originally written in English, you know, but it was done in German most of the time. Right after the world war there was still a lot of anti-German feeling, so Gatti decided to give it in English. But once I learned the part, it wasn't any more of a challenge to sing the role in English.

Is there any particular secret to singing in English?

Just that when you sing in English, you have to spit the words out. You want to do that in any language, really, because you need to make every word clear to the audience without allowing any of your tones to sound unmusical. In opera, it's always thought that the tone is the most important thing. But if you know what you're doing, you don't have to sacrifice diction for the beauty of the tone.

Was Oberon *given as a grand opera at the Metropolitan, or was there any of the spoken dialogue in the production?*

No, as a grand opera. I think [Artur] Bodanzky, the conductor, wrote the recitatives. They were very good, very much in character with the rest of the score.

It was in Oberon *that you and Giovanni Martinelli were first paired. Do you recall when you first met him, and what your first impressions were of him?*

I must have met him at one of the studios, maybe it was at Thorner's, but I can't be sure. What I remember most was his great warmth. He had a terrific personality—very magnetic, very charming. He had a great presence, on the stage and off. He wasn't really tall (most tenors aren't), but he had broad shoulders, a wonderful face, a big smile, and of course that mane of wavy hair. He was always full of laughter, full of fun, just like a big boy.

When you sang with Martinelli in Oberon, *would you have predicted that the two of you would become such a great box office draw together?*

In *Oberon*? Well, I realized that our voices and our styles blended nicely, of course. We had a sense of how each other did things. Voices don't always go together well, and sometimes styles aren't always compatible, either. But ours were. It was always a great pleasure to sing with Martinelli. Always.

There are two tenor parts in Oberon. *Martinelli sang Huon, and Paul Althouse sang the title role.*

Well, yes, but they're not comparable roles. Althouse didn't have to sing dramatically like Martinelli did.

Paul Althouse sang with you not only in Oberon, *but he was also your Turiddu in your very first* Cavalleria rusticana. *Were you impressed with Althouse as a singer?*

No, I can't say that I was. I mean, I could say that he sang well, that the quality of his voice was pleasing, that it was a nice healthy voice, and a very reliable voice. But was I impressed with him? No. You would have to know what I mean when I say I am "impressed."

Were there particular moments in Oberon *that you especially liked, and were there moments that gave you any difficulty?*

Everybody likes the overture, of course, and Huon's arias are very tuneful. I liked one of Oberon's arias, which is almost like a lullaby—and Althouse did that very nicely, by the way. I liked the Harem Scene, because of my costume. I wore dark pants that were made out of a gauze-like fabric, and I had a turban that was very attractive. In terms of the score, for me the most difficult moment was "Ocean, Thou Mighty Monster." It was staged from the top of a mountain cliff overlooking the ocean. As Rezia, I had to sing the big dramatic recitative from the cliff. And "Ocean, Thou Mighty Monster" has a high C in it, so I was always wondering whether that note was going to come out all right.

After Oberon *came Joseph Breil's* The Legend.

Ugh!

Do you remember anything about it?

No, thank God!

Did you like the score at all?

No. Did it have one?

What was the music like? Is there a particular word you would use to describe it?

Yes. Lousy.

What about the central character, Carmelita?

Lousier.

Was she a peasant girl or something?

Oh, sure. Not a princess or anything. In an opera like that, you don't get queens.

Do you remember how you were costumed as Carmelita?

I think I remember a feather sticking out of her somewhere.

Did you ever go back and look at the score in later years, just to see whether your opinion might have changed?

No. I couldn't.

Do you mean that you couldn't bring yourself to look at the score again?

No, I mean I burned the damned thing!

Am I right in assuming that the role of Carmelita in The Legend *was not a role you would have allowed in your contract, if you had had a choice about it?*

I never had to sign a contract for a certain opera.

How did you negotiate your roles, then?

That's not how it worked. You signed a contract for a certain number of weeks, at a certain salary per week or per performance. There would be several roles in your contract, but you could be given other ones to sing too. You didn't negotiate one role at a time, at least I didn't. Today, of course, a singer might do one opera at the Metropolitan one week, and then sing in Vienna the next week, and then have to be in Chicago or San Francisco for the next two weeks and so on. Because of the differences in travel time, singers today probably sign contracts for certain operas, but not in my day. If you were at the Metropolitan, you were there for the whole season, and you sang what the management gave you to sing.

Terrible —

This Theatre, when filled to its capacity, can be emptied in five minutes. Choose the nearest exit now and in case of need walk quietly (do not run) to that exit in order to avoid panic

GRAND OPERA SEASON 1918-1919
GIULIO GATTI-CASAZZA General Manager

FRIDAY EVENING, APRIL 4TH, AT 8 O'CLOCK
TRIPLE BILL

THE LEGEND

LYRIC TRAGEDY IN ONE ACT
(IN ENGLISH)

BOOK BY JACQUES BYRNE — MUSIC BY JOSEPH CHARLES BREIL

COUNT STACKEREFF . . . . LOUIS D'ANGELO
CARMELITE, HIS DAUGHTER . . . . ROSA PONSELLE
MARTA, A SERVANT . . . . KATHLEEN HOWARD
STEPHEN PAULOFF . . . . PAUL ALTHOUSE
SOLDIERS
CONDUCTOR . . . . . . ROBERTO MORANZONI

PLACE—A MYTHICAL BALKAN COUNTRY. (TIME—EARLY RUSSIA)
SCENE: HALL IN THE COUNT'S CASTLE

Scenery and Costumes Designed by Norman Bel-Geddes.
Scenery Painted by James Fox. Costumes by Louise Musaeus.
Properties by the Siedle Studio.

Rosa Ponselle

Figure 4. "As heavy as unleavened dough" was one New York critic's assessment of Joseph Breil's short-lived *The Legend,* which the Metropolitan management assigned Ponselle during her first season. Her own assessment, handwritten on the program, is more succinct: "Terrible." COURTESY OF BILL PARK.

But didn't you have any say about your roles at all?

Not at the beginning. Maybe some others did, but I didn't. Plus, I never asked for anything. I took whatever Gatti-Casazza gave me. To me, he knew what was right for me, and I trusted his judgment.

But would you have agreed to sing a role in the premiere of The Legend *if you had any choice in the matter?*

Oh! Never!

Why did you do it, then? Was it that you weren't in a position to tell the management that you didn't even care to see that opera, let alone to sing in its premiere?

I wasn't in that position, no. But I wouldn't have done that to the management anyway. It would have been un-American, in my way of thinking. Gatti-Casazza and the directors had their reasons for giving that so-called opera. The management had to cater to the American composer every now and then, rather than just doing Verdi and Puccini and such. So, if they had to produce it, it made sense that an American should sing it, and my being an American gave them a good excuse to have me sing it. My view was, just sing the damned thing and let the critics take care of things. I made sure the audience got every word of it, even if it killed me to put it over. Afterward, the critics put a stop to it pretty fast.

Was Carmelita in The Legend *the role you liked the very least of all the ones in your repertoire?*

There was a very close second—that [*La Notte di*] *Zoraima* thing by [Italo] Montemezzi. I never could believe that the composer of *L'amore dei tre re*, which I loved to sing, could have turned out something as bad as *Zoraima*. But Gatti asked me to create it, and Montemezzi wanted me to sing it, so I did it. Unfortunately.

Puccini's Trittico *premiered the same month you sang in* Oberon *for the first time. Let me ask you about each of the three operas. Do you remember Geraldine Farrar's performance in* Suor Angelica?

Could I ever forget it? Never! I can never hear that opera without seeing Farrar in my mind's eye. The other one who impressed me in *Suor Angelica* was Flora Perini; she sang the part of the aunt [La Principessa]. But Farrar's performance was the highlight [of the *Trittico*] for me.

Which were the most memorable performances in Il tabarro *and* Gianni Schicchi?

I remember Claudia Muzio in *Il tabarro*, and she was marvelous in it. I would like to have done it, and it would have been a great honor. But you couldn't take anything away from Muzio's Giorgetta. And in *Gianni Schicchi*, what I remember most was Giuseppe de Luca's performance. But, of course, anything de Luca did with a character was bound to be great.

What about Florence Easton's performance in Gianni Schicchi*? Would you rank her characterization with Farrar's and Muzio's in their performances that evening?*

Vocally, it was just fine; you couldn't fault it. But I thought she was too matronly for the part of a girl in her teens. Physically, she was too big to be able to do a sixteen-year-old girl and have you believe it.

As you have said in a number of interviews, you and Geraldine Farrar were a "mutual admiration society." In Suor Angelica, *was her voice still in its prime? And did her voice sound like it does on recordings?*

I don't know when her prime was supposed to be, so I don't know how to answer that question. It was never a big voice, you know. You can't go by those old-type [acoustical] recordings, because the men's voices registered a lot better than women's voices did. What I miss in Farrar's records is that lovely middle part of her range. The [acoustical recording] horn didn't register her middle. She had an excellent top (and it comes through on some of her records), but the middle of her voice was as beautiful as any you'll hear.

In your second season, was the role of Rachel in La Juive *your most important role?*

Yes, and it was Caruso's last big role. We also did several more performances of *Forza* together.

Did Rachel take any more time for you to prepare than Leonora in Forza*?*

No. By then I was quite familiar with the French language, and I coached part of the role with Wilfred Pelletier. I'm a pretty good parrot—I can imitate what I hear. I was singing in French by then too. I was doing some French songs in my concert programs. The language was no trouble, really.

It's been written that Caruso went to extraordinary lengths to be sure of his characterization, including consultations with a rabbi, to be sure of the Passover Scene and other religious-oriented parts of the score. Did you have to go to similar lengths to prepare your characterization of Rachel?

No, not at all. The two roles aren't alike in that way. Eléazar is extremely difficult—very, very dramatic. And the religious parts of the role have to be exact or the performance won't be believable. But Rachel is just a young Jewish girl, or at least she's been raised as a Jew, although of course she's really the daughter of the Cardinal. But she has no religious rituals that she has to direct, no big prayers that she has to chant.

But knowing your reputation for preparing roles, I can't help but think that you had to do some research for your own benefit, to be able to identify with the character of a fifteenth-century Jewish girl.

Rachel doesn't take that kind of preparation. Let's face it, it's a good role as far as it goes, but it's not Norma. For the Jewish aspects, I knew about Jewish religion and customs from Edith [Prilik], and also from my manager, Libbie Miller. Both of them were Jewish. And by the way, a lot of people at that time thought I was Jewish too. I mean, my secretary was Jewish, my manager was Jewish, and people used to say to them, "Come on, what is Ponselle trying to hide? She's Jewish, so why doesn't she admit it?" Maybe in *La Juive* that rumor helped me out.

Would you agree with most critics that in terms of the roles in which you saw Enrico Caruso, his Eléazar in La Juive *was the finest of all his characterizations?*

Not just his finest, it was the finest characterization that *anybody* could have done. I have never seen anything that surpassed it, not then, and not since.

Regrettably, we have only one recording by Caruso in La Juive, *his "Rachel, quand du Seigneur." Is the way he sings the aria on that recording the way he did it in his performances?*

No, not really. What I get from that record, mainly, is the baritone timbre of his voice. He could have passed for a baritone anytime, and nobody would have known the difference. But when Caruso would sing "Rachel, quand du Seigneur" in our performances, he would use far more dynamics than what you hear on that recording. He would vary the tempo much more than he could on a record. Everything went by the clock when we made records in those days, you see. We only had three or four minutes, and then the wax [that is, the blank recording disc] would run out. So when we made records, we had to take everything at a faster tempo. But onstage in *La Juive*, Caruso varied the tempo so that he could use more emotion. He let that God-given voice of his convey the emotion.

What made his Eléazar stand out so much, even when you compare it to many of his other great roles?

Well, he prepared all of his roles very, very thoroughly, I'm sure. If you ever saw his Canio, for instance, it would break your heart and scare you to death at the same time. I can still see him as he finished "Vesti la giubba"—that wild, terrified look in his eyes, the sobbing, and the rage boiling up inside him! But his Eléazar went even further, somehow. He *was* Eléazar when he was singing it. It was one of the very, very few characterizations that I would say might never be equalled, let alone surpassed. Not by anybody, anytime.

So that I can understand your frame of reference, would you give me some examples of characterizations that you've seen which you consider unsurpassable or unequalled?

Ones that I would rank with Caruso in *La Juive*? In my time? Oh, it won't be a very long list. There would be Feodor Chaliapin in *Mefistofele*—and also in *Boris*, of course. And Caruso's Canio in *Pagliacci*, as I've said. I would also say that Muzio's Aida, plus her Maddalena in *Andrea Chénier*, could not be surpassed, and the same for Rosa Raisa in *I gioielli della Madonna*. Mary Garden's Thaïs, her Louise, and also Geraldine Farrar's Cio-Cio-San; they belong up there with the others too. And I would put Lotte Lehmann's Marschallin in *Der Rosenkavalier* on the list. And Adamo Didur as Archibaldo in *L'amore dei tre re*, also. And in the opera you were asking me about, *La Juive*, I would also say that Léon Rothier's Cardinal Brogni was a characterization that has never been surpassed.

There are a few surprises on your list—and some that strike me as a surprise because they're not on your list at all. For instance, you didn't mention Giuseppe de Luca's Rigoletto, or Antonio Scotti's Scarpia. Did you see both of them in those roles?

Yes. But I'm thinking of the singers of my time who had truly great voices, and who also were great actors. I'm thinking about the ones who were more than great actors, really, the ones who *became* the characters they were portraying. That's the highest test of all. Now, Scotti, who was a great actor, didn't have the quality of voice that I'm thinking about. But, yes, his Scarpia was a really great characterization. And Giuseppe de Luca had one of the greatest lyric baritone voices—and, yes, his Rigoletto was one of the finest characterizations you could hope for. But, don't forget, when you're talking about Rigoletto, you have to think about Riccardo Stracciari as Rigoletto. And Titta Ruffo as Rigoletto. And as great as de Luca was as a baritone, his voice wasn't in their league, which makes it hard for me to say that his Rigoletto ranks up there with Stracciari's or Ruffo's.

What about Melchior and Flagstad as, say, Tristan and Isolde? Would you also include them on your list?

I don't know enough about their repertoire. The heavy Wagnerian operas, the ones from *The Ring*, require more voice than acting. I'm not sure whether you would call that type of acting a characterization, not in the sense that I'm talking about anyway. Of course, Kirsten Flagstad had one of the greatest voices ever. She could have sung anything and it would have been right up at the top. But, as I said, I don't know the [Wagnerian] repertoire very well. I get lost in those librettos. I have to read the stories ten times before I can figure out which of those characters in *The Ring* is the mother or father or sister or brother of which other one.

One of the surprises in your list, at least to me, is that you have spoken about two roles that were associated with your own career—Aida, and also Maddalena in Andrea Chénier*—and you said that Claudia Muzio did them unsurpassably. Were you including your own conceptions of Aida and Maddalena when you put Muzio on your list in those particular roles?*

Sure. Of course I was. But in those two roles I just don't think Muzio could be topped.

Are there any of your own characterizations that you feel should belong on your list?

Well, I would like to think that my Norma, and my Violetta, and also my Carmen would be considered as [being] in that league.

When I was asking you about Oberon, *you were telling me about the challenges of "Ocean, Thou Mighty Monster," and you spoke of your concern for the high C. You have said many times that your first performance of* Aida *was the source of your worries about high Cs. Your first* Aida *was at the Brooklyn Academy, during your second season at the Met. What actually happened to you in that performance?*

I was just getting out of a sickbed when I did *Aida* that first time. I was recuperating from the Spanish flu. I had been in bed all week, running a very high fever, but I made myself go to Brooklyn to sing *Aida* anyway. I was okay at first, and I took it easy as the opera progressed. But in the Nile Scene, I could feel my strength giving out. I could feel it in my diaphragm—I didn't have the [muscular] support, because of that flu. The high C in "O patria mia" is what we call an exposed high note. In other words, the approach to it is wide open, there's no room for error, and no way to cover yourself if something goes wrong. Now, I got on the tone all right—the pitch was right and everything felt normal for a second or two. But all of a sudden I could feel my [muscular] support going right out from under the tone. So I got off of the high C a lot sooner than I would have if all of my strength had been with me. I didn't crack the note or anything. I just didn't hold it as long, and that gave me a complex about the high C.

What I find interesting is that you sang it in Brooklyn in your second season, 1919–20, but you waited four years before singing it at the Metropolitan, and you only sang two performances at the Met, according to the Annals. *Yet you sang* Aida *twelve times on tour. What made it easier to sing on tour? Did you transpose the high C a half-tone down when you were on tour?*

Not at that time, no. You see, I didn't realize that other singers transposed. The way I found out was through [Tullio] Serafin. I was to sing *Aida* in Cleveland, and in the rehearsals Serafin could see that I wasn't comfortable with that C in "O patria mia." So he told me, "Why don't we take it down a half-tone for you?" I didn't know you could do that, but Serafin told me that Caruso, Ruffo, Martinelli, and lots of other singers took things down a half-tone, to fit their voices. I looked at him and said, "Now you tell me! You mean I could have been singing a B-natural in that aria all along? Well, this is a hell of a time to tell me!" But I was jumping up and down with joy after he told me. I was so happy that Edith [Prilik] and I went on a shopping spree in Cleveland. I treated myself to all sorts of costume jewelry; all with genuine stones, though. After I got back to New York, I said something to [Giuseppe] Danise about transposing. He said, "Of course! We all transpose when we want to." So from then on, I never even minded opening in *Aida* on tour. Later on, in fact, during our week in Cleveland I used to open with *Aida*, and close with *Norma*, or maybe the other way around, sometimes. I never worried about *Aida* again.

But that was on tour, not at the Metropolitan. Why didn't you just go ahead and sing a B-natural at the Met?

Because I was afraid the critics would find out.

I guess what I'm asking is, who cared? On tour, you transposed the aria, you've admitted that, so why not transpose it at the Met?

You see, I'm such a perfectionist and always so sensitive. If something goes wrong, it kind of stays with me. If I was going to do something at the

Metropolitan, whether it was *Aida* or anything else, I wanted to do it right. And if I transposed "O patria mia" in New York, I was sure the critics were going to find out about it. I didn't want that.

Would you agree that in Aida *there is a balance of difficult music—difficult arias and passages—where it's just as hard on the tenor as it is on the soprano?*

Most tenors are very nervous about the first act, because they have to sing "Celeste Aida" cold. Take Martinelli, God bless him, he hated to sing "Celeste Aida" because he wasn't warmed up yet. Now, I'm different when it comes to things like that. I would rather go right out on stage and sing the most difficult piece of music at the beginning. I'd rather get the hard one out of the way as soon as I could, and then be able to enjoy the rest of the performance.

Regrettably, we don't have a broadcast of your Aida, but we do have your studio recordings. There's a moment in the Tomb Scene I want to ask you about. In your electrical recording with Martinelli, your entering words— "Son io!" *—are sung with a sadness, a resignation in your voice. But some sopranos sing those words in* forte, *in an almost heroic, if not a defiant, way. What prompted you to sing it the way you did?*

[It's] very simple. First, look at how the first part of that scene is written in the score. From "La fatal pietra" almost to the beginning of Radamès' line, "Morir! si pura e bella!" it's all in a minor key—very sad, very heavy with gloom. Then look at the setting. The setting tells you everything about how to sing that line. Radamès knows that he's going to die. He can't possibly lift that stone that they've placed over the tomb. But before he was put in there and the tomb was closed, Aida somehow got in there. No one knows how she did it, but we know *why* she did it. She made a decision to die with him, because of their love. In that tomb they're slowly, slowly suffocating. With every breath they take, there is one less breath left to them. In those terrible circumstances, as Aida I would have no strength to sing "Son io!" in a big way. If I did, it would be all wrong.

Looking at the cast lists for your Aidas *on tour, your Amonasros included Pasquale Amato, Renato Zanelli, Giuseppe Danise, Michael Bohnen, Mario Basiola, and Giuseppe de Luca. You also sang a concertized performance of the Nile Scene with Riccardo Stracciari. Without asking you to compare them, would you give me your impressions of each one in the role?*

The best voice of all of them had to be Stracciari's. I didn't sing with him in the [opera] house, but I did concerts with him, and I made records with him. So I can't talk about his acting, but I can talk about his voice and his musicianship. His voice had a brilliance, a sparkle, that's hard to describe. It was like a shower of diamonds. Amato, of course, was one of the greatest baritones of that day, but he wasn't really in his prime when I did *Aida* with him. But you could tell what he must have been like, and, of course, his acting was excellent. I remember singing with Renato Zanelli, but not in *Aida,* so I don't remember anything about how he did Amonasro. Giuseppe Danise was an exceptional singer; he ranked up there with Giuseppe de Luca. In fact, it would be hard to choose between them for which one had the finer technique. They made as much out of Amonasro as could be done with that role. Mario Basiola and I were very good friends. I knew his family very well, and in fact I am the godmother of his son, who is also a baritone. I always enjoyed singing with Mario. He had a very warm voice [and an] excellent technique. He was a very good artist, and his Amonasro was all of those things.

And Michael Bohnen?

I was hoping you wouldn't ask. I never could stand Bohnen. Not as Amonasro, not as a singer, and not as an actor, either. I can't find a polite way to describe his technique (if you could call it that), but to me it sounded like he was vomiting his tones. His acting made no sense to me either. Some people actually compared Bohnen's acting to Chaliapin's. Not me. I thought he was as crazy as a loon.

Let me ask you, if I may, about some other singers, some American tenors in particular, who made debuts during your first seasons at the Metropolitan. I'm thinking, for instance, of Orville Harrold, who sang Léopold with you in La Juive. *What were your impressions of his voice, and of his singing overall at that time?*

His voice was a little hard to put a label on. It wasn't a pure lyric tenor voice. It was a little heavier than that—more of a *spinto* voice, really—but he could make it smaller, if he wanted to. He was a nice-looking man. A big man, not fat, but tall and handsome. He was in vaudeville, by the way, when Carmela and I were in vaudeville, but I didn't know him personally at that time.

Mario Chamlee made his Metropolitan debut in 1920. Were you favorably impressed by his singing?

Not much.

What was it that didn't seem to capture your interest? Was it Chamlee's singing, or perhaps his acting?

No, he was a good enough actor. He was sincere in what he was singing about, and his voice was altogether satisfying. But it was nothing very exciting, nothing to write home about.

Two other tenors who seem to have been well received at that time were Charles Hackett and Morgan Kingston. You sang with both of them. What were your assessments of their singing? Let's begin with Charles Hackett, if we may.

Now, *there* was an artist—a very, very good artist. [His] wasn't the most beautiful voice, particularly, but he had great technique, he was an excellent musician, and a true artist. I made records with him, and I knew his family too. He came from a very musical family—a very prominent musical family. I always thought highly of Charles Hackett in anything he did. And I liked singing with him.

And Morgan Kingston?

Why don't you ask me about someone else?

He wasn't one of your favorites, I gather?

Not in the least.

What was it? His voice? His interpretation? His acting?

Any of them, or all of them. Take your pick.

That's a wide field, for sure. But what didn't you like in particular?

The only thing I'll say about Kingston is that he was the Kurt Baum of his day. You know—strutting around the stage like a rooster, crowing out high Cs, things like that.

After your first Aida, *the next role you sang for the first was Elisabeth of Valois in Verdi's* Don Carlos. *Let me ask, first, what your impressions were of Elisabeth as a role. Did you like her? Was she a difficult character to create?*

It's [a] historical [opera], of course, and the characters are based on historical figures. There was nothing difficult about her as a character. There wasn't anything particularly difficult about her music, either. The only thing I didn't like was the end of her big aria. It ends very quietly—"Oh, cielo!"—and it ends low, very low.

Let me ask you about the cast, starting with Giovanni Martinelli as Don Carlos and Adamo Didur as Philip II.

They were both great. Didur's voice was no longer what it had been, but his acting, his characterization of King Philip, more than made up for it. Martinelli was a very fine actor, in anything he did, and he was in good vocal shape when we were doing *Don Carlos*. A little while later, though, (and I'm talking about the time when Gatti was getting ready to produce *Norma*) his technique wasn't always so secure.

That will come as a surprise to a lot of people. In what ways did you find his technique to be insecure?

Well, you wouldn't know this unless you sang with him a lot, but he wasn't too sure of the way he would place a tone in the upper part of his voice—from around F and G, where tenors get into the head register, on up to B-flat, B-natural, and high C. Once Martinelli got on the tone in that part of his voice, he was fine. But going from one tone to the next wasn't always easy for him when he was singing at a higher tessitura. Where it showed up the most was in very fast passages—like "Di quella pira" in *Trovatore*, where you have those sixteenth notes, and in the cadenza that Caruso made famous in "La donna é mobile." Martinelli couldn't sing those notes cleanly, like Caruso or let's say Gigli could. What Martinelli liked to sing were these very long phrases where he could tie one tone to the next very carefully, taking his time. He got a reputation for singing such long phrases, you know, but it wasn't always for the artistic reasons that some people thought.

A little later, you also sang Don Carlos *with Chaliapin as the King. How would you compare his Philip II in terms of Didur's characterization?*

Oh! Chaliapin was far more dominating on the stage than Didur was! Chaliapin's Philip was a marvelous characterization. And his [Chaliapin's] voice was much more distinctive than Didur's. But when Chaliapin was doing Philip II, the Metropolitan gave him more to sing than it did Didur. They restored the scene between the King and the Grand Inquisitor for Chaliapin. When we first did *Don Carlos*, you see, they cut that scene and they put in more of the ballet. But when Chaliapin came into the production, they cut the Fontainebleau Scene and they put back the part with the Inquisitor and the King. You should have heard Chaliapin in that scene, singing with [Léon] Rothier as the Grand Inquisitor. If you want to talk about great singing and great acting—that was unforgettable!

Descriptions of the Chaliapin voice seem to vary. There are a few who say that his voice was frayed by the early 1920s. And some have said that it was a powerful but rather hard or perhaps gruff-sounding voice.

No, no—*no*! Nothing could be further from the truth! It was mellow and warm, one of the warmest voices there ever was. To me, Chaliapin's voice was like honey: golden and sweet. The same with his pianissimos—and very few men singers could ever do a pianissimo like Chaliapin. His pianissimos were like honey when the last little bit clings to the spoon—a little thread that gets thinner and thinner until you almost can't see it, but it's still there and it still has that same golden color and sweetnes. Oh, Chaliapin's voice was one of the most beautiful voices ever!

Did you enjoy singing with Chaliapin?

I was a little scared of him, to tell the truth. There was something about him—he was a very powerful man—and I was kind of intimidated around him. When you were singing with him, you had to protect yourself because he would steal the scene. He was very subtle about it too. If you weren't watching, he'd take the whole stage away from you, and you wouldn't realize it until it was too late. When you sang with Chaliapin, you had to hold your own. But if you did, he respected you.

In your first Don Carlos, *Margarete Matzenauer sang the role of Princess Eboli. Your impressions of her?*

I was always impressed with her, and I saw her in all of her big parts, from Dalila to the German roles she sang. She was excellent in the German roles, and her Italian and French roles were always well-prepared, although I didn't think her voice fit Italian roles like it did the German ones. But whatever Matzenauer did was very good, and I couldn't have asked for more in a partner.

Let me ask you about some of the other mezzos you sang with during your first seasons at the Metropolitan. I'm thinking, for instance, of Jeanne Gordon.

Poor Jeanne Gordon! There was something wrong [mentally] with her. She lived her life in front of a mirror. She was always in the beauty parlor, always admiring herself. They say [she] was a mental case. I heard she ended up in an insane asylum. She didn't last long in opera. It was sad, too, because that was a great voice—a true mezzo, but with an exceptional high range.

You also sang frequently with Julia Claussen.

Whenever I think of the *Aida*s I sang, I always go back to Julia Claussen because she was the ideal Amneris. Like Matzenauer, she wasn't an Italian (Claussen was Swedish), but she sang Italian, French, and even big German roles. I think [Claussen] even sang Brunnhilde. In the Italian roles, which is where I sang with her the most, I thought that Claussen was more idiomatic than Matzenauer in her interpretations. Claussen had a huge voice, too, not a beautiful voice, but a huge voice and a very, very impressive voice. In the [opera] house, her tones were like big rays of light, going straight from the stage to the back of the theater. But, you know, it wasn't a natural voice at all.

In what way?

Well, [those] singer[s] who [are] just born with it, the ones who [have] the gift from the minute they [can] practically talk, it's always easy for them to sing—it's second nature to them. But it wasn't that way with Claussen at all. When we were on tour, she and I stayed at the same hotel a few times. I used to hear her warming up, and I couldn't believe my ears! She didn't sound anything like herself when she started to warm up. It took her a long time to get into the proper voice too. But when she got to the stage, you could hardly believe what you were hearing. Whenever I did a role with Julia Claussen, I was always very pleased.

What were your impressions of Karin Branzell and Sigrid Onegin?

Branzell's was a really beautiful voice. The timbre was beautiful. It was more of a contralto voice than the typical mezzo voice, at least as I remember her. But Branzell and I didn't sing together nearly as often as Claussen or Matzenauer and I did. Now, I can't really talk about Sigrid Onegin because I don't ever remember singing with her. I think she did more concerts than operas, at least in my time, and if I heard her it was probably in a concert. I can't really comment on her, but I know she was reputed to have a very beautiful voice.

And Gabriella Besanzoni?

I was very, very impressed by Besanzoni as a singer and as a personality too. She was one of those people who could walk into a room, and the whole room would light up. Vocally, she used to "Italianize" her singing a lot, which didn't always go over too well in New York. In Italy, you see, dramatic sopranos or mezzo-sopranos can deliberately create a break between their head tones and chest tones. It's done for a dramatic effect. The Italian audiences and critics accept it, even though it makes the vocal range seem unequalized. But over here, we want the voice to be equalized from top to bottom, with no audible break between the head and chest [tones]. So we consider it a fault if singers "Italianize" their technique by creating register breaks. Besanzoni did that at the Met, maybe a little too much for New York tastes. But I was certainly a fan of hers.

One of the first mezzos you sang with was Sophie Braslau. In your first Cavalleria, *she sang Lola and Mario Laurenti sang Alfio. What were your impressions of them?*

They were good singers and good voices, too, both of them. Mario Laurenti was nice-looking, and he made a good impression on stage. He had a lyric baritone voice, but you wouldn't put his voice next to [Giuseppe] de Luca's or [Giuseppe] Danise's, for instance. Sophie Braslau had an impressive sound, as I remember it, but to me she wasn't a "natural" in the Italian roles, and particularly not in a *verismo* opera. I liked her in concerts more than in opera. She had a good career, and, you know, she got a lot of help from Arthur Judson. They were "an item," as they say in the movie magazines, and Judson definitely helped push her career.

There is a soprano who made her Metropolitan debut about that time, whom I want to ask you about. I think you'll recognize her from my description. She was born in Czechoslovakia, she had blonde hair, she sang in Vienna a lot—

Did she sing *Tosca?*

As a matter of fact, she did.

Standing up, or lying down?

This wasn't much of a contest, was it! But seriously, Maria Jeritza and you were said to be rivals. What's your version of your relationship with Madame Jeritza?

Much of that stuff was made up by other people. Now, I'm not going to say that we got along like long-lost friends (not at that time, anyway) because we did have a run-in or two, but those things passed. And we weren't "rivals" anyhow, because we really didn't sing the same roles, maybe Santuzza and one or two others, that's all. But she did a lot of German roles, which fit her voice very well, and I did the Italian roles which fit mine. Later on, she and I became friends. We have a very close friend between us, Mrs. [Betja] Rosoff, who has known both of us for many years; in fact, Mrs. Rosoff knew Jeritza when they were both in Vienna. And Jeritza has been here [at Villa Pace] to visit, you know. We had a good time when she was here.

How would you appraise her voice, her singing?

It was a Slavic voice, so it had a completely different timbre than mine or other Italian voices. Her voice had a little bit of an edge to it too. To me, that made her a little less suited to the Italian roles. But in several of the German roles and especially in *Die tote Stadt*, which I think was written for her, you couldn't ask for better. In fact, I would say that her Marietta in *Die tote Stadt* is probably one of those characterizations that nobody else is going to do any better than Jeritza.

I'd like to turn, now, to Ernani, *which you sang for the first time in December of 1921. There is a rather widespread belief that* Ernani *was revived for you.*

Which isn't true at all. I don't really know if you could say it was revived for any one singer. If so, it was revived for Ruffo, or maybe for Martinelli. I think what happened was that Gatti felt that *Ernani* would be a good draw, good theater, and with Ruffo coming to the Met, he [Gatti-Casazza] probably felt he now had the right cast for it.

Let's talk about the cast for a moment, and then I want to ask you about the role of Elvira and how you prepared it. Although Titta Ruffo didn't do the first performance (he was ill, I believe) the cast included José Mardones as Dom Ruy Gomez de Silva, and Giovanni Martinelli in the title role. We've spoken about your partnership with Martinelli, and I'll want to ask you much more about his singing when we come to some of your other roles. But tell us about José Mardones, who had also been with you at your debut.

He had the greatest bass voice I ever heard. Nobody could even come close to that sound. It was like the lowest pedal on the pipe organ of a great cathedral—a real *basso profondo*. He had everything vocally: a huge voice, excellent technique, and a top that could go way up into the high baritone range. Now, he wasn't any kind of actor, but he was good for those "robe parts"—the toga roles, things like that.

Although Titta Ruffo didn't get to sing the first performance of the Ernani *revival, you rehearsed with him, and you sang with him many times.*

Many times? I don't think so.

Well, several times, anyhow. You did seven performances of Ernani *together. Was Titta Ruffo's voice in the same condition then as it was earlier in his career, as far as you were concerned?*

Well, I got a good idea of what that voice was like. I'd say it was close to what it probably was a little earlier. What was missing, though, was the ring in the tones. The *squillo* (that is, a ringing quality) was missing. At times his tones sounded kind of hollow. But the timbre, the color of his voice, apparently hadn't changed; he was a terrific musician. Overall, though, he was pretty shaky when he came to the Met. He was having an affair with this French girl, Yvonne d'Arle, which didn't help things. She was a pretty girl too. The poor thing died of cancer. He was a very sexy man, Titta Ruffo. He had girls galore.

Did you find him interesting in that regard?

What are you getting at?

Well, I've heard that he was interested in you and that maybe you were interested in him too.

Who told you that?

Your secretary, Edith—and she told me to tell you she had told me, just to see what you would say about it.

Well, tell her I don't know what she had in mind when she was telling you that.

Let me ask you something different, then. As a colleague, was Ruffo easy to get along with?

Oh, yes, as a person, he was rather serious. But when I was singing with him, I always thought of him as a great artist who was dealing with another artist who was pretty good (which was me) and I felt we had a good understanding. We were very compatible as singers.

If you were asked to assign a place to the role of Elvira in Ernani *among all of your roles, where would you place it? Would it be among your favorites, or among your least favorites, or maybe somewhere in the middle?*

Definitely *not* among my favorites. Anything that Verdi did deserves our admiration, but I would say the same about *Ernani* that I would about *Luisa Miller*. They're early Verdi, and the characters don't offer you much to work with. Dramatically, there's no real depth to them, just stock stuff, that's all.

Vocally, was Elvira a great challenge for you?

No, no, like falling off a log. And what's more, all the hard work comes in the first act. Once you've done the "Ernani, involami," it's like coasting from then on, except in some of the ensembles. But in those, at least, you're in good company.

In interviews you've given, you've been quoted as saying that for you, "Ernani, involami" was one of the easiest arias of all. Is that true?

Yeah, but that's not all I've said about it. See, there are other arias and passages that seem easy for other sopranos, but which aren't so easy for me. I've always said that. It all has to do with the way the music lies for your particular voice. And for mine, because I had the range for it, "Ernani, involami" was almost like a vocalise.

As I think you'll agree, your recording of that aria, especially your Victor electrical recording, is one of your best. Did you sing it that way in the opera house?

No, in the [opera] house I sang it at a much different tempo: I did it a lot slower on the stage. Take the trill on the middle F in the cabaletta to the "Involami" aria, for instance. On the record, it only lasts a few beats. But in the [opera] house, when it came time for me to do that trill, the musicians would put down their instruments, and [conductor Gennaro] Papi would just fold his arms to wait to see how long-winded I was going to be. I tried not to disappoint them, either. It's one of those moments where you can do that and still be in character. And the audiences loved hearing that trill, and seeing how long I could do it. So I would hold it and keep on holding it, and then on the upbeat, up would come Papi's baton. Some of the players used to kid me because they could tell what kind of voice I was in by how long I would hang onto that trill. If I held it a long time, which I usually did, they would say to each other, "Okay, now we can go home. She's in good form tonight."

After Elvira in Ernani, *you created the role of Margared in the Metropolitan premiere of Lalo's* Le Roi d'Ys. *Did you like doing Margared? Would you consider her one of your best roles?*

Not really. I didn't like her, and I didn't dislike her. There was nothing hard about the role: it doesn't lie very high, so even a mezzo can sing Margared. But she just wasn't one of my favorites, that's all.

What do you remember best about that premiere performance?

FIRE NOTICE.—LOOK AROUND NOW AND CHOOSE THE NEAREST EXIT TO YOUR SEAT. IN CASE OF FIRE, WALK (NOT RUN) TO THAT EXIT. DO NOT TRY TO BEAT YOUR NEIGHBOR TO THE STREET. *Thomas J. Drennan, Fire Commissioner*

Metropolitan Opera House

GRAND OPERA SEASON 1921-1922

Giulio Gatti-Casazza, *General Manager*

SATURDAY AFTERNOON, JANUARY 28TH, AT 2 O'CLOCK

ERNANI

OPERA IN FOUR ACTS AND FIVE SCENES

BOOK, FOUNDED ON VICTOR HUGO'S "HERNANI," BY F. M. PIAVE

(IN ITALIAN)

MUSIC BY GIUSEPPE VERDI

ERNANI	GIOVANNI MARTINELLI
DON CARLOS	TITTA RUFFO
DON RUY GOMEZ DE SILVA	JOSE MARDONES
ELVIRA	ROSA PONSELLE
GIOVANNA	MINNIE EGENER
DON RICCARDO	GIORDANO PALTRINIERI
JAGO	VINCENZO RESCHIGLIAN

Incidental Divertissement by
ROSINA GALLI, FLORENCE RUDOLPH, GIUSEPPE BONFIGLIO and CORPS DE BALLET

CONDUCTOR ... GENNARO PAPI

STAGE DIRECTOR	SAMUEL THEWMAN
CHORUS MASTER	GIULIO SETTI
TECHNICAL DIRECTOR	EDWARD SIEDLE
STAGE MANAGER	ARMANDO AGNINI

SCENIC PRODUCTION BY JOSEPH URBAN

PROGRAMME CONTINUED ON NEXT PAGE

CORRECT LIBRETTOS FOR SALE IN THE LOBBY

HARDMAN PIANO USED EXCLUSIVELY

Figure 5. Of Verdi's *Ernani,* which she first sang in December 1921, Ponselle wrote: "A great show piece, great music. Very demanding vocally—but found it easy for me." COURTESY OF BILL PARK.

Gigli singing "Vainement, ma bien aimée!" That was the best moment in the whole opera.

Do you remember the first time you had heard Gigli, and what your initial impressions were of him?

The first time I heard him was in *Andrea Chénier*. I don't think it was his debut (I don't remember that it was, anyway), but I was *so* impressed by the beauty of his tone. I had the same impression when I heard Galli-Curci the first time. With both of them, you could talk on and on about their techniques and their range, but what got to me about Gigli, just like it did with Galli-Curci, was how absolutely beautiful the color, the timbre, of his voice really was. And the way he sang "Vainement, ma bien aimée!" would make you think Lalo wrote it just for him.

Did you and Gigli get along well?

Oh, yes, right from the start. We were never close (not like I was with Martinelli), but we were good partners for one another. Gigli had an entourage with him all the time, you know. I didn't go in for entourages and that sort of thing myself, so it was kind of funny to see Gigli coming in to the Metropolitan with all of these people in tow. They were very loyal to him, and he took good care of them too. There was never any trouble between Gigli and me. He was the live-and-let-live type. If you stayed out of his way, he never got in yours. And, of course, that voice of his was just beautiful!

Frances Alda sang Rozenn in Le Roi d'Ys. *I've been told that there was some unpleasantness that occurred between you and Alda during* Le Roi d'Ys.

Not during the performance. Never. I never allowed myself to get pulled in to that stuff. But during the rehearsals, yes. We got off to a bad start, Alda and I, but it passed pretty quickly. What happened was, [Armando] Agnini, the stage director, was working with Albert Wolff, the conductor, about the staging. But Alda, who liked to fight, just took over the rehearsals. She didn't care what the conductor or the stage director said—she was going to do the staging her way. Of course, she was married to Gatti-Casazza, so everyone was afraid of what to say to her. She ordered me around in a couple of the rehearsals—"Stand over there, Ponselle! Watch what in the hell you're doing when you're moving, Ponselle!"—that kind of nonsense. Finally, I spoke up and said very calmly to the stage director, "May I ask who's in charge here—you or Madame Alda? I'd like to know because I can't follow two sets of directions. I can't be in two places onstage at the same time." After that, she left me alone.

As you think back to your first seasons at the Metropolitan, if you were asked to point to the one event that meant the most to you, what would it have been?

That's easy: singing with Caruso, that was the high point. Just being on that stage with him, standing right there next to him, watching every expression, taking in every gesture, feeling the emotion that he was creating, and hearing my own voice soaring with his!—nothing could ever take the place of that.

The date of his death was 2 August 1921. Do you remember where you were, and what you were doing when you heard the news of his death?

It makes me sad just to think about it. I was at a party in New Haven. Rocco Di Orio, a friend of ours, owned a big restaurant there, and he had this party for me. It was a wonderful evening, everything was gay and happy, and then somebody came in and said they just heard a newsboy outside saying that Caruso was dead. Everything got so quiet: nobody knew what to think or what to say. I was so upset that I had to go home to Meriden, to be with my mother. I wanted for my mother to take care of me, like I was a little girl again. That's how hard it hit me. It just seemed like the world had ended for me.

Did you feel that you knew him well as a person? Part of my reason for asking is that several of the Caruso biographies say that you were one of his close friends who, along with Scotti and some others, were brought to see him during his convalescence.

You won't find that story in the [Key and] Zirato book because it never happened. I don't know where that [story] got started. I think maybe it was in one of Mrs. Caruso's books. But whoever started it, [the story] wasn't true because I really didn't know him personally. I was too in awe of him to ever get friendly. Like everybody else, I always called him Commendatore when I spoke to him. We all treated him like you would treat a king. And as a singer, he was *the* king.

Did you see him socially very much—I mean, to talk with him about personal things rather than talking about music or roles?

The only time I ever had what you could call a personal conversation with him was on the train to Atlanta [in 1919], when we were on tour there. I saw him standing around outside my compartment (just by himself, kind of passing time) and he popped his head in after a while and asked if he could come in and talk. Well, I was so flattered that he even thought I was worth his time talking to, so I asked him to please come in. He got real melancholy during that conversation. And you know what he talked about the whole time? Ada Giachetti. The mother of his children. Now, he was already married to Dorothy [Park Benjamin Caruso] by then. But all that time in my compartment, the only thing he wanted to talk about was Ada Giachetti. I felt sorry for him, really. You could tell that some part of him was still in love with her.

Is there any way that those of us who never could have heard Caruso can ever fully understand what he meant to his art during his lifetime?

I wish you could, but I really don't think so. Caruso was the greatest tenor, the greatest singer, and the greatest artist I have ever heard. He was each of those things and all of those things. And now, all that we have left are his records. Some of them are better than others, as far as what you can hear of his voice—like the record [of the *Otello* duet] he made with Titta Ruffo, for instance. On that record, you get an idea of the size and the power of Caruso's voice. But still you can't rely on the old recordings. That's why I prefer to listen to his voice as I hear it in my memory. And I thank God for that memory.

Recollections

Libbie Miller

Born in Lithuania in 1895, Libbie Miller was five years old when her parents, who were orthodox Jews, emigrated to the United States. Her early academic achievements in the New York public schools qualified her for a scholarship to Hunter College, which became her alma mater. From 1918 to 1920 she worked as a booking agent for National Concerts, which she left when the Metropolitan Musical Bureau offered her the position of promotion director. When the newly formed Columbia Broadcasting System acquired the Metropolitan Musical Bureau, recasting it as a division of the Columbia Concerts Corporation, Libbie was named promotion director there.

In the 1920–21 season, Rosa Ponselle asked the Metropolitan Musical Bureau's chief executive, F. C. Coppicus, to assign Libbie to the management of all her concerts. By 1928, Libbie had formed her own management firm and was devoting most of her time and resources to Rosa, whose career she managed in all its aspects. Their association would end acrimoniously in 1938, when it became apparent that Rosa had no intention of resuming her Metropolitan Opera career. But as did Edith Prilik, Libbie enjoyed not only a professional relationship with Rosa Ponselle throughout her career but also a close personal one. In 1978 she discussed the plan that she and Rosa devised to increase Rosa's earning power exponentially in the mid-1920s.[13]

The concert business is what brought me into Rosa Ponselle's life. During her first two seasons, one of the concert booking agencies in New York at that time, National Concerts, was booking Rosa's concerts. William Thorner had arranged for one of National Concerts' executives, Arthur Ryan, to handle Rosa's first series of concerts. After her second season she signed with Columbia Concerts, where I was on the staff. At that time, which was in 1921, Thorner was still managing her opera appearances. At Columbia Concerts, we only managed her concert appearances.

Rosa wanted to do a lot of concerts. If you want to know why, you need to understand her background. She grew up in a family that lived decently sometimes, but lived quite poorly at others. I knew her family very well: I was at their house in Meriden many times, and often we had Rosa's mother with us on the train when Rosa was on tour. Between Rosa's father, who was a shyster, and her brother Tony, who had very little business sense, the Ponzillos never had any money they could depend on. Rosa and Carmela saved the family from financial ruin when they got to be successful in vaudeville. But when Carmela didn't get an opera contract, she didn't have a way of earning much money on her own. She wasn't marketable without Rosa, and Rosa ended up supporting her until Carmela could get a break of her own.

At the Metropolitan, Rosa had lots of expenses that she had never had to contend with before. She was paying Thorner, she was paying Romano Romani, she had coaches to pay, and after a while she insisted on [using] her own costumes because she didn't like the ones the Metropolitan would furnish. She and Carmela never had expenses of that kind in vaudeville. On top of that, she wasn't earning enough money to keep the Ponzillo family in the style they had gotten accustomed to, when the two girls were in bigtime vaudeville.

When Rosa first came to the Metropolitan, she wasn't making much money at all. All during the four years that Thorner managed her, in fact, Rosa never made what you would call big money from the Metropolitan. They started her at $150 a week, for twenty-three weeks. They gave her fifteen performances in the [opera] house, and five more on tour that year. If you allow for the fact that one of her performances in the [opera] house didn't bring her any money (it was a charity performance for the Metropolitan Relief Fund),[14] then during her first Metropolitan season she was earning about $240 for each performance. That may have been all right, at least on average. But what bothered her that first year was that she was having to spend too much time studying new roles and performing whenever they wanted her to, often with very little notice.

Rosa was always very astute when it came to money and business. It didn't take her any time at all to figure out what she needed to do in order to make a lot more money. It was actually rather simple. She wasn't making big money at the Metropolitan, so she would have to sing fewer performances there, but at the same time, she would have to parlay her Metropolitan Opera reputation into a concert reputation. If she succeeded in doing that and if she could be promoted well as a concert artist, which is where I came in to the picture, then she could do as many concerts as possible and make a lot of money on a "volume" basis, so to speak.

The first thing she had to do was to get the Metropolitan to agree to pay her by the performance and not by the week. Thorner got her that [provision] in her second contract. She started earning $100 per performance, instead of $150 for as many as three performances in one week. Next, she needed to get carte blanche from the Metropolitan to do as many concerts as she wanted to do before and after the regular season, and after the annual tour. This had to be negotiated, because the Metropolitan required most of the singers to submit all of their concert dates and bookings for [the Metropolitan's] review and approval. But she got the latitude from the Met that she wanted. That enabled her to start doing a lot of concerts. Now, when I say "a lot," I'm talking about one concert every two or three days for three months out of every year. That kind of a schedule would drive most opera singers to drink. But Rosa, remember, had been used to living out of a trunk on the Keith Circuit, so the traveling and the tight schedules didn't bother her in the least.

If you compare the number of concerts Rosa did during her first three seasons, you can see very quickly how well her personal business plan paid off. In her first season, her contract kept her from going on a concert tour until after the season was over, which meant the last week of April [1919]. So during that spring and early summer, she did only eight concerts—and at least three or four of those were joint concerts or part of a festival, which meant that she didn't get much of a fee. But during her second season at the Metropolitan, which was in 1919–20, she did five concerts in twelve days during the month of May. She did the same thing the following October, a month before the Metropolitan season opened.

In that second year, Rosa's concert fees went up from about $300 to $500 for each concert. But then in her third season, when she signed with us at Columbia Concerts, we negotiated higher concert fees for her. She began earning $750, and sometimes more, for each concert she gave. That season, too, she deliberately cut back the number of Metropolitan Opera performances she gave. That way, she could begin doing concerts as early as March instead of having to wait until May. In 1921 I booked eighteen concerts in a row for Rosa between the middle of March and the middle of May. Looking back through my records, I noticed that the only free time she wanted me to give her was the week of 25 April through 1 May, which was the week the Metropolitan performed in Atlanta. But right after that, on 3 May, she was back on the train, first to Houston for a concert, then on to Kansas and Denver, and finally back east for one last concert in Yonkers.

During that year, 1921, Rosa earned slightly more than $20,000 from her concerts. As I recall, she earned about half that amount from her Metropolitan Opera performances that season. But the very next year, 1921–22, we were able to negotiate her Metropolitan fees up to $1,000 per performance, and we not only booked more concerts for her, about twenty-five or thirty, but we also negotiated her concert fees upward to around $1,500 per appearance. So in that season, which was only Rosa's fourth one in opera, she earned about $50,000 from her concerts alone. Adding her Metropolitan fees and her royalties from her Columbia recordings, her income for 1922 went over $70,000.[15] That was almost twice as much as she and Carmela had ever earned on the Keith Circuit.

From that time on (and I'm proud to say this, because I was the one managing her career) Rosa's income went straight up. By the time she did *Norma* in 1927, she was earning $1,850 for each concert, and only two or three years later, I got her fees up to $2,500 per concert. It was nothing for her to earn $70,000 or $80,000 a year from concerts alone.[16] When radio got to be very big, which was in the late 1920s, it got even more lucrative for a singer of her stature to be on the air rather than on the concert stage. She was getting between $2,500 and $3,000 for a one-hour radio broadcast. Compared to giving a concert for that same fee—with the train travel, the expense of dresses, the fee for an accompanist, and the nervousness and all—doing a one-hour radio broadcast was a picnic. To Rosa, that was like having somebody bringing her wheelbarrows full of money for almost no work at all. But she didn't object to it in the least. Money was very important to her.

Yet Rosa and money were an odd couple. Money was important to her not just because she had her needs, but because she liked the challenge of making money. She also liked to spend it, but mainly on herself. That was a side of her that was always difficult for people who knew her to understand. She could be generous one minute, and the next minute she could be tight to the point of being cheap. Edith [Prilik] supervised most of Rosa's banking, and Rosa kept at her about the payment schedule for her bills. Every day you didn't pay, you accumulated one day's more interest on your money: that was Rosa's philosophy and that's how she wanted most things handled. She was terrible about tipping anybody; in fact, Edith used to follow Rosa around and leave extra tip money for waiters and servers, because what Rosa thought was a tip would have been insulting. When it came to her fees, she wanted to negotiate the most money she could possibly get. Yet she would also sing for nothing. She would agree to do a benefit at the drop of a hat, especially if it was for a charity that was raising money for children.

I traveled with Rosa on almost all of her concert trips and on the annual Metropolitan tours as well. Edith was always with her too, and Carmela went with us on several trips. Occasionally, she would even call up her school-girl chum, Lena Angle, and would have her travel with us, and, as I've said, Rosa's mother went with us too. Rosa always traveled in grand style. She was never one to deny herself any luxury, so we had the best of comforts all the time. On the trains, going from one concert stop to the next, she and Edith liked to do needlework. That's how they passed the time. Rosa wasn't much of a reader, although she did like to read the women's magazines that were popular at that time. She was especially fascinated by Hollywood and movie stars. She didn't just read movie magazines; you could say that she studied them.

I was the reader among us, so that's how I passed the hours. Rosa's mother, unfortunately, never learned how to read, and she was embarrassed about it. The poor dear would ask for a book, just to hold in her hands and look like she might be reading it. But if there weren't any pictures in it, and nothing but print on the cover, she might hold it upside down and not even know it. If Rosa saw it, she would go sit next to her mother and start talking to her about whatever came to her mind, and then very subtly, without taking her eyes off her mother, she would take the book, turn it right side up, and give it back to her mother to hold. Whenever I saw that happen, it touched me to see how sensitive Rosa was with her mother, and it brought into focus just how far life had taken Rosa by comparison.

Rosa got where she was almost entirely on her own. Her voice and her natural musicianship got her into the Metropolitan. But having a great voice is only the beginning. As Caruso told her, having the intelligence to know what roles are best for the voice and knowing how to build and manage a career are what count the most. Rosa didn't have much formal education (very little, actually) so she had to learn everything on her own. And when I say "everything" I mean the whole gamut from building a vocabulary to learning the social graces that a *diva* is expected to have. How she expanded her vocabulary was typical of the way she learned things. Whenever she encountered a word she had never heard, she would write it out phonetically, and then later, ask me what it meant. I would give her the basic meaning, and then she would ask me to make up at least two sentences using the new word. I would write them down, and then late at night, she would go over them until she had mastered them.

As much as I admired Rosa as an opera singer (no, not just admired her, I should say I revered her in opera) and as much as I would like to tell you that she was a great concert artist, the truth is she was not. I know it seems strange because, as I said, she loved to concertize. But what separated Rosa from the really great concert artists, singers like Lotte Lehmann, for example, was that Rosa hated to do what I would call a serious concert program. What she wanted to do in a concert was perform, not just sing. I think it was something she never got over from being in vaudeville. For instance, she wanted to be lighted in a rather dramatic way: she even carried her own custom-made stage lights. She tended to overdress, especially in her earlier years. She looked too gaudy for a serious concert singer: big hats, feathers, too many diamonds, too much *frou-frou*.

Her programs weren't like most other singers' programs. Someone like Frieda Hempel or Anna Case would do lighter songs at the beginning of their programs, to allow their voices to warm up. Rosa thought nothing of beginning a program with a very taxing aria, and *then* doing three or four songs. Her favorite first arias—imagine this—were "D'amor sull' ali rosee" from *Il trovatore*, "Un bel dì" from *Madama Butterfly*, "Pace, pace mio Dio" from *Forza*, and "Divinité du Styx" from *Alceste*. She'd pick one of those for her first piece [on the program]. And all that nonsense she's said in interviews about "O patria mia" in *Aida*—well, I could give you a stack of programs where Rosa opened with that aria.[17]

The arias she sang in concert, I should say, were never a problem as far as her acceptance was concerned. The problem was with the songs she chose. She would sing classical songs and lieder only because she had to, but what she really liked were songs like "Annie Laurie," "Beautiful Dreamer," and old-style popular songs that were not suitable for anything resembling a recital. She also favored Neapolitan songs, which were very popular and which she did very well—but, again, Paolo Tosti is not Schubert. Later on, she also tended to pick what I would call novelty pieces—songs like "The Night Wind" or "The Big Brown Bear," which are pure hokum. But in her mind, they were entertaining, and when she made up her mind about a song, you could forget about trying to get her to change it.

In the early years of her career especially, there was another fault in her concerts. It had to do with the structure of her programs. Rosa sang too little and gave too much of the program to her accompanist—to the point that it sometimes looked like she was making the concert into a joint recital with her accompanist. Now in those days, a famous singer would always give the accompanist a solo spot or two on the program, or, if not, they would have an assisting artist, who would often be someone just starting out in a career. Rosa didn't use assisting artists. She used accompanists, but she used to give them too much, in my opinion. She would sing an aria at the beginning of her program, and then she would sing three or four songs, but then she would turn the stage over to her accompanist, who would do three or four piano pieces. One or two would have been fine, but four of them was simply too much.

I'll tell you where that got started. In many of her earliest concerts, Rosa used Romano Romani as her accompanist. You can understand why: he was the one who really discovered her, so she thought of him as her mentor. They had this boyfriend-girlfriend sort of relationship (they weren't lovers or anything, just really fond of one another), and he was the one who had taught her most of the concert pieces she performed. So, when you add all that up, it was no surprise that Rosa wanted to feature him rather prominently in some of her concerts. But he didn't last as her accompanist. He was more of a prima donna than she was! Not that he was temperamental, just helpless, too used to having everybody wait on him and cater to him. He could hardly even dress himself! He thought that he should have a valet standing next to him all the time. Well, a half-hour before concert time Romani might need another tuxedo jacket because he forgot to pack one, or maybe he couldn't find his shirt, or his dress shoes, or whatever—and you would think it was a national emergency the way he would whine about it. The big problem was, he whined to Rosa—and I can tell you, she was in no mood to have to worry about his clothing a half-hour before going on stage. It wasn't long till she asked Romani to stay behind, and she hired another accompanist. But by then, you see, she had gotten accustomed to giving Romani so many solo opportunities during her concerts that she kept doing them that way.

After her accompanist had his first solo spot on the program, Rosa would come back on stage and do another big aria, but as soon as she finished it, she would leave the stage again and have her accompanist do another three or four piano pieces. Afterward, she would finish the program with four songs, and then she would do whatever encores she felt were appropriate to each particular audience. Her accompanists (after Romani, it was William Tyroler in the early days, and later on, Stuart Ross) were reputable accompanists, which is an art in itself, but they were hardly Rachmaninoffs as soloists. Now, later on she changed things, but in those early years, frankly, I had the feeling that most of her audiences tolerated her accompanist's solos only because they had no choice about it.

Idiosyncrasies of that kind made it a challenge to get good concert bookings for her in New York, but really, Rosa never cared about New York recitals. She liked getting on a train and going to other parts of the country to sing. I think she felt that the people who really appreciated her the most were the John Q. Publics from Vermont to Arkansas who were buying her records and, later on, were listening to her on the radio. Rosa was a real "democrat" in that way. And too, I think there was some part of her that actually missed the traveling, and the giving of one performance after the next, just as she and Carmela were used to doing in vaudeville. She was a great opera singer, yes, maybe the greatest of her voice type that we've ever heard. But never forget, Rosa was also an entertainer.

The Written Record

In November 1929, *The Etude* published a feature entitled "The American Girl's Chance in Opera." Written by Edward Ellsworth Hipsher, the feature was drawn from an interview Hipsher had conducted with Rosa Ponselle shortly after her return from London following her debut at Covent Garden. In the feature, Ponselle offered to beginning singers this counsel about the pacing of a career:

> One of the greatest obstacles in the way of success of our young singers in this day is the spirit of haste which urges them to want to get there too quickly. This cannot be too strongly or too often emphasized. Art is a slow growth, no matter what the medium of its expression; and the one who would achieve greatly must be patient and ready to devote years to the cultivation of this tender flower.
>
> The desire for fame, no matter at what cost, wrecks many a career. There must be no "burning of the candle at both ends." The singing and interpreting of a great operatic role makes demands upon the vitality of the

> artist, which can be scarcely comprehended by the uninitiated. To withstand this strain it is absolutely necessary that the singer preserve and develop mental, emotional and spiritual vigor. Otherwise, before the evening's performance is finished, there will be a diminution of powers. The audience will sense this.[18]

By the time these thoughts appeared in the pages of *The Etude*, Ponselle's career was in its eleventh year. She had been acclaimed on both sides of the Atlantic for her masterful portrayal of the title role in Bellini's *Norma*, the opera and role in which, in retrospect, the apogee of her career may have been reached. By the time she had sung *Norma*, therefore, she had experienced first-hand the "demands upon the vitality of the artist" that great singing makes. Through her early roles and the reactions they garnered from the critics—reactions that may be gleaned from their reviews, excerpts of which are reproduced below—she had seen demonstrated the maxim that "Art is a slow growth."

Ponselle's first appearance as Santuzza in *Cavalleria rusticana*, the role she would later describe as "the easiest . . . I ever sang," took place on Tuesday evening, 10 December 1918, during a touring performance in Philadelphia. A *Pagliacci* with Caruso as Canio, Florence Easton as Nedda, and Luigi Montesanto as Tonio completed the double bill. The Philadelphia-area critics were unreserved in their praise for her "splendid vocal endowment" and "purity of tones,"[19] and for the "intensity of feeling" and "careful attention to detail"[20] in her portrayal of Santuzza.

Judged from the perspective of *Musical America*, however, the overall performance was a failure for "Mr. Gatti's recruit from vaudeville," as critic H. T. Craven referred to the newcomer: "Of histrionic methods, she has yet much to learn, and this deficiency was especially striking last Tuesday, since she was absolutely new to the role of Santuzza. The part is capable of profoundly moving dramatic development, as artists like Emma Calvé and Florence Easton have eloquently proved. Golden opportunities were missed in the Ponselle interpretation, which was crude and unconvincing."[21]

Her dramatic shortcomings, Craven went on to say, removed all traces of "the smoldering southern passion" of this *verismo* masterpiece. Coupled with Paul Althouse's "manifestly un-Sicilian" Turiddu and an Alfio (Mario Laurenti) who "was not reassuring either vocally or dramatically," Ponselle's "dramatically discordant Santuzza" reduced Mascagni's score to "a string of familiar tunes."[22]

In *The New York Times* of 29 December 1918, the day after the Metropolitan Opera premiere of *Oberon*, critic James G. Huneker assessed the quality of singing he had heard. "Mr. Martinelli," he wrote, "sang the difficult measures, both martial and amorous, allotted him with energy and art. He was a gallant appearing knight. Mr. Althouse had an ungrateful role, and made the most of it. . . . The English diction of the foreign-born in the cast was understandable though unmistakably streaked with strange accents." Of Ponselle, "upon whose broad shoulders rested the hapless heroine Rezia," he wrote:

> To say that she has grown in artistic stature would only be the truth. Singing Verdi, especially with Italian blood in her veins, is not the same as delivering the majestic and tragic music of Weber. Miss Ponselle is too young, has had too little experience to sound the heights and depths of the mighty "Ocean" aria—itself at times too grandiloquent, not to say stilted; but with her dramatic temperament, musical intelligence, above all, with her beautiful, natural voice and its remarkable range, from a rich, velvety contralto to a vibrating, silvery soprano—well, for a newcomer on the operatic boards a few months ago, and with her artistic training and antecedents, we confess our hearty admiration for her brilliant future. Her scale is seamless, so equal are her tones from top to bottom. Her personality is pleasing, her acting immature.[23]

"Miss Ponselle," judged W. J. Henderson after hearing her Rezia, "ought to become one of the greatest singers of our time. She has the voice, the feeling, and the dramatic instinct." But his experienced ear detected a flaw in her vocal range, a flaw which, he ventured, would not be remedied by singing such dramatic operas as *Oberon*:

> Her vocal technique is by no means perfect, but it is far from being fatally defective. At this time her scale is well equalized because faulty methods have not yet accentuated the breaks between the registers. Her middle register is ravishingly beautiful in its full-blooded quality and its vibrant freedom. Her lower notes have the organ-like opulence of a contralto. Her upper register is her chief difficulty. Miss Ponselle does not approach . . . [upper tones] correctly, and apparently it is a matter of chance with her whether she gets a good tone or not above F. She ought to be singing pure lyric roles and exercising the flexibility of her marvellous voice in the use of elastic, florid music.[24]

The triple bill in which Ponselle's next opera, Joseph Breil's *The Legend*, was premiered at the Metropolitan Opera House in March of 1919 also included two other American operas: *The Temple Dancer*, by John Adam Hugo and librettist Jutta Bell-Ranske, which also premiered that evening, and Charles Cadman and librettist Nelle Richman Eberhart's *Shanewis*, an operetta that had been given a premiere the previous season at the Metropolitan.[25] James G. Huneker wrote at length about the two new works in the columns of the New York *World*:

> It would be idle to deny after a first hearing that "The Legend" was not legendary, but as heavy as unleavened dough. . . . Candor—which is the short, ugly word in criticism—compels us to state that [these] works would shine to advantage across the street from the Metropolitan Opera House; in a word, at the Casino, the home of light operatic entertainment.
>
> But the sanguinary element in these new librettos is arresting. Rose [*sic*] Ponselle stabs Paul Althouse in "The Legend," to save her stage father, Louis d'Angelo. He in turn is shot and Rose is bowled over by soldiers' bullets. Florence Easton poisens [*sic*] Morgan Kingston—possibly because of his chaotic phrasing in "The Temple Dancer," and is slain by the jealous god, Mahadeo, who looks like a glorified Vantine special sale in exotic brasses.
>
> The stories of these two novelties . . . are neither better nor worse than the average. Sung in English, they might as well have been sung in Choctaw. . . . By all means let us have opera in English, but let us have English that is singable.[26]

Huneker concluded his review by paying Ponselle a high compliment. "Miss Ponselle had to perform a lot of vocal stunts and only her extraordinary voice enabled her to compass most of the long-breathed phrases. She possesses a magnificent bellows. . . . This young woman is striding to her goal with seven-league boots. She is the only satisfactory 'find' of the present opera season."[27]

Although Huneker considered the role of Rachel in *La Juive* "wholly conventional, one of the 'O ciel!' kind," he concluded that Ponselle's "singing and acting are surer, better coordinated than even last season."[28] But the evening belonged rightly to Caruso as Eléazar, as W. J. Henderson's review amply attested:

> No one who is familiar with the achievement of the most popular tenor of this time would expect to be told that he met all the requirements of such a role as Eléazar. Nor would any one of the million devoted admirers of his voice care. Probably no one knows this better than Mr. Caruso himself. All he has to do to evoke thunderous applause is to linger on a high note and to emit a final phrase in the full power of his voice.
>
> Therefore, he commands the respect and admiration of all who regard operatic creations as of more import in art than their interpreters, for he has again and again shown himself a sincere seeker after genuine dramatic results.
>
> He had conceived the part in earnest study, and he sang and acted it with an art as far removed as possible from that of his more familiar Italian roles. There was dignity in his declamation and beauty in his cantilena. His chanting in the second act was a lyric utterance of exquisite character, while his delivery of the pealing air of the fourth act might have excited the envy of [the first Eléazar, tenor Adolphe] Nourrit himself.[29]

Concluding his assessment of the principals in the cast, Henderson dismissed Ponselle's Rachel in a mere two sentences. "Miss Ponselle did not fulfill the promise of last season. Her voice sounded much more constrained and less noble in tone, while her action was primitive indeed." Pitts Sanborn, writing in the New York *Evening Globe*, apparently concurred, but held hope for her improvement in subsequent performances of the role. "She will probably sing and act it with deeper significance as the season advances," he wrote. "Miss Ponselle may develop into a really great singer, but on Saturday she used only a modicum of the vocal resources Nature has so lavishly bestowed on her; nor did she sing with much color or expression, though she sang carefully and with some sense of the correct style."[30]

Only Huneker seemed to find merit in Ponselle's Rachel. In a none-too-subtle comparison of her voice with Caruso's, Huneker took another occasion to underscore his enthusiasm for her voice: "If the present recrudescence of the work proves successful it will be entirely due to the magnificent signing of Caruso, Rosa Ponselle, and the magnetic conducting of Artur Bodanzky. As a matter of fact, there are only two beautiful voices in the Metropolitan Company, and Rosa Ponselle's is the other one."[31]

"Rosa Ponselle, upon whose big shoulders rested ugly robes . . . sang with power, and a lovely, floating tone," wrote Huneker of her initial performance in *Don Carlos*. But on this occasion, an undertone of frustration with the slow pace of her artistic development was evident in his review. "Disappointing as she often is," he said, "you feel that the future is hers if she so wills it. She is in sad need of competent coaching. The native richness of her vocal and dramatic endowments—for there is plenty of temperament, latent as yet—ought to bear wonderful fruit sometime. A Caruso in petticoats? Who knows what she may achieve with her labor rightfully directed (we repeat, rightfully)."[32]

Henderson, as was often the case, expressed his discontent more bluntly: "For the present it can be noted that Miss Ponselle was neither queenly nor tear-compelling, neither most musical nor most melancholy; [and] that Mr. Martinelli probably sang more high notes than he ever sang before in a single role."[33] But Henry T. Finck, Henderson's counterpart at the New York *Post*, meted out high praises to Margarete Matzenauer and Ponselle alike: "Mme Matzenauer . . . sang with splendid dramatic fervor, and throughout the opera her rich voice was enjoyed, as was the opulent organ of Rosa Ponselle, to whom fell some of the most effective numbers in the score. If she sang everything as well as she does some of the numbers, she would be a second Nordica. Under proper guidance [she] might become one."[34]

The *Tribune*'s assessment was similarly positive: "Miss Ponselle's velvet voice was poured out with ceaseless tonal opulence in Elizabeth's music, but not until the last act did she succeed in lending a touch of regal dignity to her impersonation."[35] But two years later, on the three occasions when Chaliapin took Didur's place as Philip II (twice in New York and a final time in Atlanta), the attention of the critics was riveted on his brilliant characterization. Wrote Pitts Sanborn:

> It is easiest enough to say that Mr. Chaliapin looked like a great historical portrait, or a portrait come to life. But words of that sort convey scarcely so much as a faint notion of his achievement. His Philip was at once the proudest, the craftiest, and the gloomiest of monarchs, and likewise the most imposing to see. Gloves of as white as a kid as ever graced the hand of man or woman were positively sinister as he wore them. He lifted a single one of his ten digits and it was as [if] the royal sceptre [were] raised on high. The very curve and angle of his silken knees held the fate of peoples balancing. His face was [a] cloistered, tortured visage . . . and the whitening russet of his hair betrayed that Spanish House of Austria which sought peace through bloodshed, and burned all heretics, to the greater glory of an approving god.[36]

In his review Sanborn also praised Chaliapin's extraordinary vocalism, especially as it was displayed "in the king's 'Ella giammai m'amo!' The single line 'Dormiro sol nel manto mio regal,' no one who heard it is likely ever to forget. Other basses have sung this air, some of them extremely well; Chaliapin lived it."[37]

Prior to her first appearance as Aida at the Metropolitan in late December 1924, Ponselle sang the role on tour exclusively, but only in three performances: her first *Aida*, at the Brooklyn Academy of Music on Thursday, 6 March 1919; a second one on Friday, 29 April 1921, during the Metropolitan's week-long touring season in Atlanta; and a third performance on Monday, 28 April 1924, on tour with the Metropolitan in Cleveland.[38] Her first in-house performance gathered rather little attention from *The New York Times*:

> Rosa Ponselle sang Aïda for the first time in New York at the Metropolitan Opera House last night before a huge and enthusiastic audience. She looked the part and sang admirably in a role which was well suited to her; a fact which was quickly recognized by the public. Miss Ponselle is advancing as a dramatic singer and knows how to modulate her voice according to the sentiments required of her.
>
> The Amneris of Ina Bourskaya was another striking vocal characterization; the duel of jealousy between the two women was sharply intensified as the opera proceeded. Miguel Fleta as Radames filled all the lyrical demands of the hero.[39]

Despite the trauma of the high C in "O patria mia" that Ponselle recounted in her interviews, the review of her Brooklyn Academy performance (by Edward Cushing in the Brooklyn *Eagle*) suggests that the Nile Scene went altogether smoothly for her: "With the consummate singing of Mr. [Pasquale] Amato pleading, as Amonasro, for her to save her people, Miss Ponselle sang and acted her 'Nile River Scene' with a pathos and realism unapproachable in our judgment."[40]

Perhaps the greatest tribute Ponselle may have received as Aida was the one paid her by George Cehanovsky, who became the most celebrated *comprimario* baritone in the Metropolitan's history, and whose wife, soprano Elisabeth Rethberg, many critics and colleagues considered the greatest Aida of the mid-1920s and early 1930s. Speaking of Ponselle in an interview, Cehanovsky stated firmly that "Aida was *her* role. I tell you, she did [great] things [with her characterization] when she sang it."[41] He had first heard Ponselle in *Ernani* when Titta Ruffo joined the cast. A half century later, Cehanovsky recalled the performance to Hugh M. Johns:

> I went for one reason only—to hear Titta Ruffo. It would not have mattered to me what he was singing. As it was, the opera happened to be *Ernani*, and, of course, Rosa Ponselle was singing Elvira. But by the end of the first act, I was more intrigued with Ponselle than I was with Ruffo. Listening to her, I was convinced that I was hearing one of the greatest voices there ever was. It was such a dark sound—and such a *big* sound—and so flexible, so easy! And let me tell you, in the duets of Don Carlos and Elvira, when she and Ruffo were singing in their low ranges, I could hardly tell where Ruffo's voice left off and Ponselle's began.[42]

In an interview conducted by James M. Alfonte for *Opera News* in 1956, Ponselle reminisced about her performances of *Ernani*. "I suppose it may shock some listeners to learn that every role is not equally dear to a singer's heart," she told Alfonte. "But we do have favorites, and Elvira in *Ernani* was not one of mine! Rather . . . I had to make myself like [her]."[43] During the years when she was actively singing the role, however, her views of Elvira seem to have been more positive on the whole if only because, as she told Alfonte years later, she had forced herself to like the role.

In a *Musical America* interview in 1922, for example, she compared the merits of Elvira and Margared in *Le Roi d'Ys*, and in doing so she confessed to having liked Elvira "rather the better": "Why? It is hard to say, except that I feel that the heroine of *Ernani* is truer to the feminine heart. She is sometimes proud, sometimes happy, sometimes pursued by villains! The bad sister in *Le Roi d'Ys*—well, she must spend all her time plotting and act[ing] like a tigress. . . . The music of Verdi has more of what one calls a 'punch,' though the tenor's Aubade in the other opera is very pretty."[44]

Perhaps because she succeeded in convincing herself to like Elvira, contemporary reviews of her first *Ernani* give evidence of her customary attention to detail in her characterization. But her vocal performance drew decidedly mixed reviews. Richard Aldrich ventured this assessment in *The New York Times*:

> A serious disappointment confronted many of the patrons of the opera last evening, when they found announced in the lobby of the Metropolitan Opera House the fact that, owing to sudden indisposition, Mr. Titta Ruffo, newly acquired as a member of the company, would be unable to make his first appearance, as announced, in Verdi's "Ernani." His place was taken by the versatile Giuseppe Danise, who is said to have sixty-five operas more or less at his fingers' ends. A very large audience, expecting to hear Mr. Ruffo, remained to hear "Ernani."
>
> The performance last evening had an abundance of the sonorities for which the opera is calculated, but the musical style upon which Verdi counted was none too much in evidence. There were several transpositions of the music made by which the tonality was lowered, presumably for the benefit of Mr. Ruffo. As to the style, it was perhaps least in evidence in Mme Rosa Ponselle's singing as Elvira. She sang, of course, with great volume, but she sacrificed quality to power; and had little conception of the claims of legato, such as should be exemplified, for instance, in "Ernani, involami," whose phrases she dismembered in an apparent attempt at dramatic expression. Mr. Danise showed familiarity with the part of Don Carlos, which he took at more or less short notice; he gave a dignified and suitable impersonation and sang with finish. Mr. Martinelli's Ernani was vociferous in voice and sufficiently picturesque and romantic in action; but he, too, had not the clearest conception of the style of the work.[45]

The New York *Globe* dissented, urging that in Elvira's music "the voice of Miss Ponselle was nothing short of glorious. It is a voice that has both the low range and the high range for this exacting role, and she seems to have made distinct progress as a singer."[46] Deems Taylor, writing in the New York *World*, generally agreed. "Miss Ponselle did much with the part of Elvira, which is a trying one on account of its wide range. Her upper voice was lovely but showed the faintest hint of effort. Her lower tones were so extraordinarily broad and dark that they aroused a suspicion that her true voice might be a mezzo-contralto. However, that idea is neither new nor popular."[47]

If Ponselle considered Beniamino Gigli's singing of "Vainement, ma bien aimée" to have been the most memorable moment in *Le Roi d'Ys*, Richard Aldrich's review of the first performance suggests that he concurred—without praising much of Ponselle's singing, however:

> Mme Alda, as Rozenn, presented a figure not unsympathetic, though her's [*sic*] is not the character in the opera that will evoke the deepest interest in the audience, even though her[s are] wholly justified claims to sympathy.

> Perhaps if Mme Alda sang with more beauty of tone and mastery of style she would secure more sympathy for the gentle sisterliness of the heroine.
>
> Miss Ponselle presented the turbulent Margaret [*sic*] as a dominating personality, full of passion of the robustest [*sic*] sort, and singing with an equivalent turbulence and passion and with no little violence done to vocal beauty. There was great musical value in Mr. Gigli's singing; more restraint and less persistence in the use of the fullest voice than he has sometimes shown; and in certain passages, as in his aria at the opening of the third act, "Vocinement [*sic*] ma bien-aimée," with beautiful refinement of art. But . . . as [Gigli] presents him Mylio is a rather aloof personage.[48]

"There was savagery enough in Mr. Danise's picturesque and vigorous Karmac [*sic*], the music of which he sang very well," Aldrich said at the close of his review. "Mr. Rothier added one more to his gallery of kingly portraits with much intelligence and skill."[49]

Throughout the 1918–19 opera season, perhaps because of the pressure she was under to learn new roles with comparatively little notice, Ponselle appears to have confined her concert appearances largely to the popular Sunday Night Concerts held at the Metropolitan Opera House. After one of these concerts, in which she was paired with José Mardones, the New York *Evening World* reported that "Miss Ponselle's singing brought encore after encore, and Mr. Mardones shared in the general satisfaction."[50] Her first solo concert in New York, which took place at Lewisohn Stadium in June 1919, was reported to have attracted an audience of seven thousand, for whom she was reported as having sung as an encore the "Stridono lassù" from *Pagliacci*.[51]

Two of the most interesting of Ponselle's early concerts took place within a day of each other during the first week of May 1919. In Charlotte, North Carolina, on Saturday, 3 May 1919, she and Riccardo Stracciari shared the stage for the closing performance of the annual Charlotte Music Festival. There, she and Stracciari "created a veritable tempest of applause," according to the local newspapers: "The concert last night was a triumph. Miss Ponselle . . . was the undoubted star of the festival and will, in years to come, be known wherever music is known, as the great American soprano."[52]

The evening before their joint concert, in a performance in Norfolk, Virginia, Stracciari and Ponselle had sung a concertized version of *Aida*. Newspaper reviews imply that only the Nile Scene was performed, with Stracciari singing Amonasro and Ponselle singing Aida in modified costumes and with local singers performing the other roles. After the performance, according to newspaper accounts, the audience created a demonstration substantial enough to have the management push a piano through the curtain so that she could sing encores to her own accompaniment:

"A laughing Aida." That again was Rosa Ponselle. Imagine a rather big, very dark young woman, with eyes that seem abnormally large, with cheeks and lips of Oriental fullness, and hair so jet-black that the white gown is not needed to make it also abnormally black; imagine this black, luxuriant hair so rolled underneath and upward as to appear to be bobbed. You have the ideal Aida, it is true, but you also have Rosa Ponselle.

Imagine this Aida, also a good-humored girl who is glad to sing anything the audience would like to hear and who likes to join the loan-workers in the aisles and wheedle substantial citizens out of large subscriptions; imagine this Egyptian seated at a piano, and playing her own accompaniment to "Comin' Thro' the Rye" and "Mother Machree" and a half a dozen others.[53]

In this post-concert vignette of Ponselle playing her own accompaniment, still in make-up and singing ballads that she had done at the San Carlino in New Haven or on the Keith Circuit with Carmela, the reviewer unknowingly captured a one-time vaudevillian "working an audience" and delighting in every moment of it. It was just this tendency that Libbie Miller had deplored in Ponselle's early concerts, and it occasionally earned Ponselle some disappointing reviews.

In autumn 1920 a joint concert with tenor George Meader in Columbus, Ohio, prompted critic Daisy H. Krier to write: "Miss Ponselle is a good little sport (she is not so very little, either), but the Metropolitan Grand Opera Company has not purged her entirely of the vaudeville spirit, which adds verve to her numbers. She smiled in a most comradely way on her audience, fanned her accompanist [William Tyroler] with her brightly colored fan, and was generally acceptable."[54]

A return appearance to Columbus two years later, in connection with the annual Lacey Concert Series held at the city's only music auditorium, prompted the same critic to take Ponselle to task for "gesturing, distractingly, while singing opera arias on the concert platform."[55] Irritated by the criticism, Ponselle responded in the pages of the *Musical Leader*: "I do not believe any composer wants an artist merely to stand on a platform like a wooden image and emit a series of sounds, no matter how perfect the technique and tone, without an effort through gestures to convey the meaning of the aria and the feeling which he himself had endowed it. Nor do I believe that 99 percent of the audience wants it."[56]

On other occasions, she took similar opportunities to defend her preferences for drawing-room ballads as legitimate entries on a concert program. As *Musical America* reported in 1922:

The artist declares that . . . she also likes the simple song. "Of English ballads and, especially, American songs, I am very fond," she says. "Why

PROGRAMME

I. Aria: "D'amor sull' ali rosee" (From "Il Trovatore") . *Verdi*

MISS PONSELLE

II. Tre giorni son che Nina . . . . *Pergolesi*
Chi vuol la Zingarella . . . . *Paisiello*
Träume . . . . *Wagner*
Hymne au Soleil . . . . *Georges*

MISS PONSELLE

III. Piano Solos:
Theme and Variations . . . . *Corelli-Ross*
Berceuse, A flat . . . . *Tschaikowsky*
Liebesfreud . . . . *Kreisler*

MR. ROSS

IV. Aria: "Ernani involami" (From "Ernani") . . . . *Verdi*

MISS PONSELLE

V. Piano Solos:
Prelude, A minor . . . . *Debussy*
Intaglio, Waltzes in Miniature . . *John Tasker Howard*
Pell Street (From the Suite, "Chinatown") *Emerson Whithorne*
Country Gardens . . . . *Grainger*

MR. ROSS

VI. Wings of Night . . . . *Winter Watts*
Eros . . . . *Grieg*
Lullaby . . . . *Scott*
Piper of Love . . . . *Carew*

MISS PONSELLE

KNABE PIANO

Figure 6. The unconventional repertoire and format Ponselle chose for her early concerts, such as this one at Cornell University in 1926, led to constant disagreements with her manager—not only about the choice of a highly taxing aria as an opening selection but especially about the preponderance of solos Ponselle gave her accompanist. COURTESY OF THE CORNELL UNIVERSITY LIBRARY ARCHIVES.

> cannot the artist sing the simpler songs with artistry? You couldn't guess the number I have recently sung for the phonograph! No, it is nothing operatic, or even a Neapolitan song, but 'Little Alabama Coon,' a song of the South and an old favorite."[57]

Performances in that day by Ponselle and many other singers of "Little Alabama Coon" and other once-popular songs of its kind (although racist by any standards today) were "not a personal statement," as popular-music historian Laurence Bergreen has written, but rather were "a reflection of the prevailing vaudeville and minstrel show conventions" of the early years of this century.[58] Yet even in that context the issue of what was most appropriate for the recital programs of a newly established opera singer—the drawing-room ballads of an Albert Von Tilzer or Chauncey Olcott, or the lieder of Schubert or Brahms—was an issue about which Ponselle and Libbie Miller would continue to differ for the remainder of their relationship as artist and manager.

In her comments to James Alfonte in *Opera News* in 1956, Ponselle discussed two of her later roles (Violetta in *La traviata* and the title role in *Norma*) as well as Elvira in *Ernani*, one of her early roles. To Alfonte, as she did on other occasions to other interviewers, she dismissed Elvira as "an early Verdi stock type" of character and then devoted the bulk of her reminiscences to Violetta and Norma—both were substantially more meaningful to her than Elvira or, for that matter, any of her earlier roles except possibly Leonora in *La forza del destino*. Although Leonora, Santuzza, and Aida would remain in her repertoire, the other early roles would soon recede in the wake of her success as Maddalena in *Andrea Chénier*, as Leonora in *Il trovatore*, and as the heroine of Ponchielli's *La gioconda*—characters which, as she put it, "were more like flesh-and-blood women, which gave me the chance to really make something out of them."

CHAPTER FIVE

Flashes of the Grand Manner

"Some of the best years I spent with Rosa," Edith Prilik recalled late in her life, "were the seasons that led up to *Norma*, when she was singing operas like *Il trovatore* and *Andrea Chénier* and *La gioconda*. She was young (she hadn't turned thirty yet), and she was single. Her records were selling very well. She was a good draw on the concert tour, and she was getting rich by most anyone's standards. Because she was shrewd with her money, or tight with it (except for what she would spend on herself), she was able to enjoy her life. The pressure she was under wasn't as bad as it got to be later on."[1]

Ponselle's newfound ability to enjoy herself was reflected in newspaper accounts throughout the early 1920s. In summer 1922, her preference for life out-of-doors had led her to take up trout fishing. During an outing in the woods and streams of Maine that summer, she caught what local newspapers labeled a "record catch of trout," including a "square-tailed speckled trout weighing 9 pounds and 3 ounces."[2] Fishing became the latest addition to her list of sports. "She is seen on the tennis courts often and plays a fine game," the Hartford *Courant* reported. "She is also an ardent golfer [and] spends an hour swimming each day."[3]

Within her immediate family, there appeared to be a new and hopefully permanent stability. On 22 February 1922, Tony Ponzillo married Lydia Babuscio, the daughter of a Manhattan produce supplier. When they exchanged their vows in an elaborate but private ceremony at the Church of St. Thomas in New York, Rosa was the maid of honor; Carmela sang the Bach-Gounod "Ave Maria" during the nuptial Mass.[4] As a gesture of affection for her brother, Rosa had paid not only for the ceremony but also for the equally lavish reception, held at her new penthouse on Manhattan's Riverside Drive.

After the wedding, as a gift to the bride and groom, she purchased a residential lot Tony had selected on Meriden's Bradley Boulevard and offered to underwrite the construction costs for any home he wished to build there.[5] Although she would later regret making the offer, she gave little thought at the time to the $40,000 she spent on her brother's lavish tastes and ill-conceived business ventures.[6] As a gesture of his gratitude, Tony asked Rosa to be the godmother when Lydia gave birth to a son, Antonio Gerard, in 1923.

Immediately after his marriage, Tony's livelihood appeared to take a new turn when, as the New York *Daily News* reported in July 1922, he announced that he "was abandoning his coal-driver profession for the vaudeville stage." He was preparing his solo act, the article said, with both of his sisters, but he was improving his vocal technique under Rosa's tutelage. "There in [Carmela's] apartment at 250 Riverside Drive," said the *Daily News*, "the celebrated singer has been training her brother's voice for the past six weeks in preparation for his coming début." "Tony is a very good pupil," Rosa was quoted as saying. "He never studied with anybody else until he started working with me." As to his repertoire, she and Carmela planned to have Tony sing "one opera aria, perhaps, in vaudeville."[7]

His debut at the Keith-owned Riverside Theater in Manhattan, where the Ponzillo Sisters had triumphed only six years before took place on Saturday evening, 14 April 1923. On the bill he was identified, for obvious reasons, as Antonio Ponselle. The reviews, like his performance, were tentative at best: "Ponselle sings a combination of Italian classics and modern English numbers. He is accredited with making a somewhat trembling curtain speech in which he tells his audience [that] this is his first professional appearance."[8] By summer's end, he had been quietly dropped from the Keith Circuit and had returned to the family coal business in Meriden.[9]

More lasting was the reemergence of Carmela Ponselle. With the exception of her Columbia recordings and some charity concerts, her career had all but ceased after 1918 when William Thorner was unable to secure a Metropolitan Opera contract for her. Carmela's new manager Maurice Frank gave a creative explanation for her "lost years" of 1918–23, which the newspapers reiterated: "After devoting her life to her sister Rosa's ambitions, she seeks fame for herself."[10]

Carmela's first operatic performance was in a pioneering radio broadcast of *Aida* in New York City on Armistice Day 1922: "A complete opera was broadcast by radio for the first time in New York last night, when the Western Electric station WEAF reproduced Verdi's *Aida* as it was given in oratorio form in the Kingsbridge Armory in the Bronx. In the cast were Carmela Ponselle, Amneris; Anne Roselle, Aida; Dimitry Dobkin, Rhadames; and Léon Rothier, Amonasro, supported by the Metropolitan Opera Chorus and Orchestra under Giuseppe Bamboschek."[11]

The WEAF *Aida* broadcast was said to have attracted an estimated 600,000 listeners, owing in large part to the participation of basso Léon Rothier and conductor Giuseppe Bamboschek.[12] For Carmela as well as for Maurice Frank, the successful *Aida* broadcast proved to be an important advance in the pathway to her concert debut in New York, which took place at Town Hall on 18 March 1923. Although the concert attracted a limited audience, the reviews Carmela received were at least favorable, if not overly enthusiastic. "Her mezzo-soprano voice, though a lyric organ in the main," said Henry T. Finck in the New York *Globe*, "shares a basic similarity of timbre and hue to that of her dramatic soprano sibling, and is agreeable in quality and impressively extensive in its upper range."[13]

A few months after her Town Hall debut, Carmela would be engaged for another concertized *Aida*, given at the Polo Grounds in the summer of 1923.[14] But two more years were to pass before she would be extended a contract by the Metropolitan Opera Company. In the interim, her sister's star was clearly on the ascent.

The Interview

From interviews of Rosa Ponselle by William Seward (December 1971) and by the author (March 1973, October 1977).

After Ernani *you seem to have allowed yourself more time to live a fuller life than you had been leading during your first few seasons. I'm thinking about your first trip to Hollywood in the summer of 1923 and your first summer in Italy that next year, things you simply didn't do in your first two or three seasons.*

Yeah, but nothing had really changed, you see. I still didn't have a repertoire, so I was still spending all my time learning the new roles that they kept piling on me year after year. And I was always adding certain touches to the roles that were already in my repertoire. I had at least two new roles to learn every year, sometimes even three. I always had too much to learn, too much to memorize and study all the time. I didn't socialize, you know. I didn't have time to enjoy myself.

What about Hollywood? I wouldn't think that you went there just to study.

Well, no. That was a pleasure trip. Now, I did do some concerts out there, not just in Los Angeles but also in San Francisco, so I did work a little bit while I was out on the coast. But I really went there to enjoy myself and to meet some people I had been wanting to meet.

Who were some of them?

I met Mary Pickford and Douglas Fairbanks; they gave a very nice dinner party for me at Pickfair when I came to Hollywood. I remember spending time with Gloria Swanson while I was out there. I met Pola Negri, and I was introduced to Clara Bow, and I met Charlie Chaplin too. I had a lot of fun with Charlie Chaplin. He was at Pickfair for the dinner that Mary Pickford and Doug Fairbanks had for me. I saw him again at United Artists when they took me there to see [the studio].

At that time, of course, Pickfair was the Hollywood equivalent of Windsor Castle. Was that the first time you had met Douglas Fairbanks and Mary Pickford?

Mary Pickford, yes, and come to think of it, I guess I hadn't really met Doug Fairbanks before then, either. But it seemed like I knew him, because Carmela knew him. He used to be in vaudeville. In those days the bigger circuits used to put scenes from plays, or sometimes a whole act from a play, on a vaudeville bill. Doug Fairbanks did plays in vaudeville. He was friendly with Elsie Janis, and Carmela met him through her. In fact, that was the first thing he asked me when they had me at Pickfair that night. He wanted to know how Carmela was.

What were your impressions of Pickford and the other women stars you met?

Mary Pickford was very pretty, of course, but in a dainty kind of way. She was still wearing her hair long, with all those waves and curls. You wouldn't say she was talkative—kind of reserved, but not aloof, just very nice to be with, and an excellent society hostess—as you'd expect, naturally, because of how important she was. Now, Gloria Swanson and I had met in New York, so I already knew her pretty well by then. Pola Negri, I just couldn't warm up to at all. She was very aloof, nose up in the air—that kind of stuff. Clara Bow was just the opposite: no airs at all, very down to earth. One time she said to me, "You ain't leaving the Met to come woik *here*, are ya?" That's how she talked. [She was] Brooklyn down to her shoe tops.

What was your impression of Charles Chaplin?

At first I was a little nervous around him. You have to remember that it wasn't too many years before that when I was playing the piano in Ansonia or New Haven for Charlie Chaplin movies (the same with Mary Pickford too). Of course, in person [Chaplin] didn't look anything at all like [his] character in the movies. His hair was quite gray, but he wasn't very old. He was a very good looking man, really, and he seemed *so* intelligent—like his mind was going a mile a minute. He wasn't a bad musician, either: he played the violin; he was self-taught, I think. What was odd about it was that he played left-handed, so he had the violin strung the opposite way from what you would be used to seeing. When they asked me to sing at Pickfair, he accompanied me for one song: the Massenet "Élégie."

Lawrence Tibbett, who was just beginning his career, auditioned with you while you were staying in Los Angeles. Do you recall who arranged the audition and what your first impressions were of Tibbett?

Frank LaForge called and asked me to do it. I auditioned Tibbett, and I thought he was very talented. You couldn't help but be impressed by his voice; it had a color all its own, and he had fine technique. But Tibbett was at that stage where a young singer is either going to make it, or he isn't. Knowing the odds involved in making it in an operatic career, I wouldn't have been surprised at his success *or* at his failure. If he hadn't have been totally dedicated, if he hadn't really wanted to make it, I mean, and if he hadn't gotten the right breaks at the right time, we might never have heard of Lawrence Tibbett. But, lucky for us, he did.

When you speak of a "break" for Tibbett, do you mean the famous performance of Falstaff *when the audience demanded that Antonio Scotti give Tibbett a curtain call?*

No. I was thinking about the little things, the small favors that somebody does for you, that lead to bigger things [and] help your career along. To me, that *Falstaff* story shows that Scotti was his own worst enemy. If he had been a real professional, he would have brought Tibbett out with him [for a curtain call]. No one in the audience would have made much out of it, because their performances as Falstaff and Ford depended on one another. Bringing out Tibbett would have been the natural thing to do and the professional. So, Scotti made a very big mistake that night. But I think that *Falstaff* story does Tibbett a disservice.

In what way?

For one thing, it makes it sound like Tibbett never had to work hard. You'd think he got the role of Ford by just walking in off the street and having it handed to him: no work, no study, just dumb luck. The other thing that bothers me is, it makes it sound like Tibbett also didn't have to work very hard after *Falstaff*, either. You get the impression [from the *Falstaff* story] that the Metropolitan just handed him all these roles, one right after the other, and he sang them, and everybody lived happily ever after. But Tibbett worked very, very hard. I sang with him, so I know.

Don't you think it's possible, though, that Tibbett sometimes created that impression himself? He seemed so easygoing in his interviews—very relaxed, sort of an all-American nice guy. He tended to give that impression, don't you think?

Well, you don't know how much of that was [the work of] his managers and the publicity people. And later on, don't forget, he also had the Hollywood people doing his publicity. Managers and promoters were always trying to make us seem like down-to-earth people who just happened to be opera singers, particularly those of us who were American singers. Tibbett got his share of that kind of publicity, and I got a lot of it too. But you can't create characters and sing the way that Tibbett did without very, very hard work.

As you look back on your first visit to Hollywood, how did the film community seem to react to you?

We were treated like visiting royalty, from what I remember. I think that had to do with [Geraldine] Farrar, more than anything else. She was the first opera singer who got to be really big in the movies. At that time, you know, moving pictures were still silent. She made a movie of *Carmen*. People today, even people who know opera, don't have any idea that Geraldine Farrar was a movie star while she was at the Metropolitan. But when you remember that she made a movie of an opera, a *silent* movie of an opera—well, even without her voice, Farrar became a movie star. That tells you something. So, you see, we all got treated like royalty—I mean, fancy dinner parties, the whole works—because of the respect that they still had for Farrar in Hollywood.

One of those "fancy dinner parties" made headlines that summer. I am thinking of the house-moving party that Howard Verbeck, the artist, gave in your honor when you visited Hollywood. According to the press clippings, you sang that evening with Paul Whiteman's band. Do you remember that party?

Do I remember it—oh, yes! [The Verbecks] lived in a very fashionable part of Los Angeles, and they had decided to move someplace out in the countryside. Well, rather than build a new house, they just decided to move the one they were already living in. So they threw this big house-moving party, and, yes, Paul Whiteman had his band there, not the whole band—just eight, nine, [or] maybe ten of his men. And by the way, I sang that night, but not with the band. I played piano with them. Paul invited me to [play]. You see, Paul and I already knew each other pretty well by then. I had just signed up to make records for Victor around then, and Paul was a big star for Victor.

What actually brought you to the Victor Company? After all, you had been making very successful recordings for Columbia, and Romano Romani, your mentor, was affiliated with Columbia. Was there some particular incident or circumstance that caused you to leave Columbia?

See, Victor had wanted me all along—right from the start, when I made my debut with Caruso. But I didn't know that until much later when [Victor Company executive] Mr. [Calvin] Child told me about it. But almost all the big stars, starting with Caruso, were with Victor. So, naturally, I wanted to be there too, after a while. It was a business decision, nothing more.

How were you kept from knowing that Victor wanted you?

Thorner was the one who did it. He's the one who signed me up with Columbia. I didn't know it at the time (I was pretty green, being new to opera) but Thorner got into a fight with Mr. Child over Galli-Curci's contract with Victor. See, Thorner also managed Galli-Curci at that time. Later on she sued him, just like I had to sue him. The story I got from the Victor people was that Thorner was trying to push some kind of deal for Galli-Curci, but he was using me as a pawn because Mr. Child wanted me under contract too. But there was I, greener than green and not knowing enough not to trust my so-called manager, so I never knew what was going on.

It's been suggested that one reason you went with Columbia in the first place was because they were willing to offer recording contracts to you and Carmela both, whereas the Victor interests would only consider a Red Seal contract for you.

No. That's not so.

Did Carmela ever audition for the Victor Company, to the best of your knowledge?

No. She was happy at Columbia. We went with Columbia in the first place because they wanted us to record duets (especially some of our vaudeville numbers) as well as the solo records that she and I made.

According to the Columbia catalogs, you did make two duets with another artist, Barbara Maurel. Which leads me to ask you why you might have chosen Maurel rather than Carmela for those particular recordings.

I had nothing to do with that.

But you had to approve it, am I correct?

I wanted Carmela, but they had other ideas.

Who had other ideas?

The Columbia [management] people.

What was their reason? Were they more interested in promoting Barbara Maurel than Carmela at that particular time?

You could say that. Matter of fact, that's not a bad way to put it, or you could just say that somebody in the front office had an interest in Barbara Maurel that had nothing to do with her singing.

What was your opinion of her singing?

Nothing that I want to repeat here.

Were your negotiations with Victor easy or difficult, as you remember them?

I didn't get involved [in the negotiating], except to approve the arrangements once they were already made. Miss Miller, my manager, handled all of my negotiations.

Comparing the two companies, did you have more say over what you wanted to record at Victor than you had at Columbia?

Well, maybe a little more, yes. You have to remember that I went with Columbia around the time I made my debut. I was just a fresh kid, a beginner, so I wasn't in a position to ask for much in those days. But by the time I went with Victor, I was already pretty well established. I do want to say, though, that I liked all the people I worked with at Columbia. They treated me wonderfully.

At either Columbia or Victor, whose responsibility was it to suggest what you might want to record?

Well, at Victor I usually suggested the songs or arias for any records that I wanted to make. Now, they would bring ideas to me (it was always a two-way street), but if I didn't go along with their ideas, I could say no. That was in my [Victor] contract. I had that negotiated because over at Columbia, they were having me record things that were pretty far outside my repertoire. At that time, you see, I was singing *Oberon* and *La Juive* at the Metropolitan. But the people at Columbia had me recording arias from *Madame Butterfly*, *Tosca*, *Pagliacci* and *Bohème*—none of which, of course, I ever sang on the stage.

When you went with Victor, did their ideas and yours coincide most of the time?

As I remember it, yes. For instance, one of the things that Mr. Child wanted me to do was to record some of the old standards like "Carry Me Back To Old Virginny." That [song] had been a big record for Alma Gluck. So, they had me remake several of her records. Because I used to sing some of those songs in my concerts, I liked the idea of recording them for Victor.

One of the more enduring puzzles about your recording career is that, according to Columbia's files for early 1924, you actually had two more recording sessions at Columbia after you had already begun making records for Victor.

What? I missed that [question]. What files are you talking about that say that?

Columbia's files. The recording logs, or files, that Columbia maintained.

No. There's something wrong with their files. When I left [Columbia],

I left for good and went over to Victor. That was that. Unless, maybe, [Columbia] wanted me to come back to remake something I didn't like when I recorded it the first time. I wouldn't have [had] to—that would have been up to me. But I don't ever remember going back to Columbia.

During the years in which you were recording for Columbia, you sang your first performances of William Tell, Andrea Chénier *and* L'africana. *According to the Metropolitan* Annals, *in fact, you did them all within a ten-week period in the 1922–23 season. Let me ask you about each of them, beginning with* William Tell. *If I am correct, the opera was revived that season, and had not been performed at the Metropolitan for twenty-eight years.*

Yes, and they revived it for Giovanni Martinelli.

You sang the role of Matilda. Was it a role you especially liked?

Well, there isn't too much [to the role] to like or dislike. I didn't consider Mathilde one of my best roles—no. I don't think I sang it more than two seasons, anyway. When I think of *William Tell*, I always think of it as a man's opera. After all, most of the main characters (Gessler, Walter Fürst, Arnold, and William Tell himself) are men's roles. Even the part of the boy, Gemmy, which is sung by a lyric soprano, is a pants role. For a dramatic soprano, Mathilde isn't a very demanding role, really, because it's not that long or complicated. Her big aria is "Selva opaca." We did *Tell* in Italian rather than French, so "Selva opaca" is "Sombre fôret" in the French score. That's her only real showpiece, "Selva opaca."

Which you recorded on the Columbia label during the time you were singing William Tell *at the Metropolitan.*

Yes. I don't like most of the records I made for Columbia, you know, but I kind of make an exception for "Selva opaca," even though I could only record one verse, as I remember. But it's a good record. I was pleased with it.

To pursue that thought for a moment, is it that you don't like your Columbia recordings or that you really don't like any of the old-style acoustical recordings you made for Columbia or for Victor?

You mean when we had the [recording] horn? I guess some of them are okay; some people like them, because they tell me so. That *William Tell* record sounds better to me than a lot of the other ones do. But whenever somebody plays [one] of my early records for me, there are two things that I notice right away: one is the interpretation on the record (my interpretations were not mature at that time, not like they were later when I was more experienced), and the other thing is that I sound like I'm singing inside a box. I keep wanting somebody to lift the lid and let me out.

In terms of overall demands, how does "Selva opaca" as an aria compare with the rest of Matilda's music?

That aria can fool you. Most of the time you only hear it on records and in concerts or recitals. If you were to go by what you might hear in a concert, let's say, you might get the idea that Mathilde could be sung by a lyric soprano rather than a *spinto* or dramatic voice. True enough, as an aria it doesn't require a dramatic voice, but take it from somebody who did [Matilda] in the opera house, you wouldn't want to try singing the whole opera with anything less than a pretty good-sized, mature voice.

Was the Metropolitan's production of William Tell *shortened considerably?*

Oh, sure. I've never heard of a *William Tell* production without the cuts in it. An audience couldn't sit through it otherwise. Not unless you're going to serve them breakfast the next morning. I think the original score has five acts. But even when it's done in four acts, which is what our production was, every act seems about as long as *Cavalleria rusticana*. That's one of the reasons you rarely see it—the length, and [another is] finding a tenor to sing [the role of] Arnold: those are the big problems with *Tell.*

Of the cast of that William Tell *revival—Giovanni Martinelli as Arnold, Giuseppe Danise as Tell, José Mardones as Walter Fürst, Adamo Didur as Gessler—which ones stand out the most in your memory?*

Oh, Giovanni Martinelli, *much* more than anybody else, and I'm not taking anything away from the rest of them. For instance, in the ["Troncar suoi dì"] trio, you should have heard Martinelli, Danise, and Mardones. What an ensemble those three voices made! Now, in the performances he might have taken the "O muto asil" a half-tone down—I don't know for sure. Most tenors are going to want to transpose "O muto asil" because of the *tessitura* and the high notes. But those long phrases were just right for Martinelli. In my memory, *William Tell* belonged to him. You could really say it was his opera.

What were your assessments of the other women singers who sang with you in the revival? I'm thinking of Flora Perini, who sang Hedwig, and Marie Sundelius, who did the part of the boy, Gemmy.

Well, both were singers who kind of specialized in those smaller roles. Of the two of them, Flora Perini was the better artist. She always did those types of parts wonderfully. Marie Sundelius I remember because she was in several of the operas that I did. You could say that she was very capable, very reliable, very important to the company, and that they relied on her for many parts. Is that putting it nicely?

In other words, a second-rank singer?

No, no—I wouldn't put it like that. See, I don't like things that sound like I'm saying a singer is "second rate." Nobody who was at the Metropolitan in my time was second rate. Maybe they sang second parts, but they were never second-rate as singers.

Do you recall any details about your costuming as Matilda?

Yes—how bad it was! The costumes I wore in *Tell* were the Metropolitan's, not my own, which is one of the reasons why I started having my own [costumes] designed and made. The ones the Met had us wear, we didn't have to pay for. We only paid for any accessories that we wanted to use. But you know what they say about things that are free. You get what you pay for. That's why I started spending a lot of money having the big designers make my costumes for me.

Was there a particular look that you were seeking—a certain style that you had in mind when you were planning your costuming?

Yes. Clean, simple lines, and the simpler, the better. That was the problem with those Metropolitan costumes: instead of [having] simple lines, they were what I would call snakey—too many curves, too many changes of direction in the lines. The eye likes to follow a smooth, relatively straight line. Those Met costumes were hard for the eye to take in because the lines were always shifting, and most of them had way too much of the baubles, bangles and beads—too much junk on them. You see, the wrong costume will distract the audience from your singing. Those Metropolitan costumes, because of their bad lines and all that stuff on the front of them, took the audience's attention away from the voice. The other problem was that the Met costumes were usually designed and made before any of the singers in the production had been picked. So if you didn't happen to look like the mannequin that they used when they made up the costume—well, too bad for you.

Did you design your own makeup as well?

It was the same story with makeup. If you didn't know or didn't learn a lot from the pros, you could be in trouble if you left it up to the Met to do your makeup. You should have seen what they did to [Margarete] Matzenauer and me in *Don Carlos*. First of all, the costumes were awful, but the makeup was the icing on the cake. Matzenauer and I had big, dark eyes, that was our natural look—what we were born with. But the brilliant makeup people at the Met loaded us up with thick eye liner, dark eye shadow, and big false eyelashes. And glitter, too, they put glitter on the eyelashes and in the eye shadow. By the time they got done, Matzenauer and I looked like a couple of raccoons.

Did you do your own costuming and makeup for L'africana, *which you also sang for the first time during the 1922–23 season?*

I had three costumes, I think, in *Africana*. The main one, which was very simple, I put together from what I wore in *Aida*. In fact, the [Mishkin] studio pictures of me in *L'africana* are often mistaken for *Aida*. I wore an African-type wig with that costume, and I had a metal headband (a bronze headband, with two or three feathers on one side), and it matched the armband and wristband that I wore on each arm. Of course, in *L'africana* I wore very dark makeup again, [as in] *Aida*. In the Prison Scene I wore a leopard-skin costume. I liked that one. In the last act, where Selika is put on the throne, I had a very elaborate headpiece and a long, flowing dress. I changed some of the details, of course, as the years went by.

How did you feel toward Selika as a role?

I liked her—yes, I would have to say I did. But it wasn't my favorite role by a long shot. I had to make myself like her.

Was Selika's music difficult for you in any particular way?

No, but as a character, Selika doesn't have any of the depth that Aida has, for instance. So I had to work extra hard to make myself feel like the Indian queen that she was supposed to be. To keep my inspiration going, I had to pick through the text to find sections that were more true to life, and I had to work very carefully on the music [that Selika sings] trying to make it more interesting vocally. The whole opera, you know, is only sustained by three things: the big tenor aria, the ballet, and the shipwreck scene.

The sets of that L'africana *production were designed by Joseph Urban and were said to be very elaborate. Do you recall many details about the sets?*

Not many, no. But I could never forget how [Urban] staged the first scene of the fourth act. This was a very lavish set [in] that opening scene. Not that anything Joseph Urban ever did was less than lavish, you know. Anyway, as the queen I was supposed to be carried out [of the temple] on a golden chair. There were supposed to be eight or maybe ten men to march me around on this golden throne. It was a great big chair, which was supported by long, thick poles so the men could carry it on their shoulders. In those days I wasn't what you'd call petite—not thin and trim like I was when I went to Hollywood years later for my *Carmen* screen tests. So, as you can imagine, this throne thing made me nervous, which is putting it mildly. All I could foresee was me being eight feet off the ground, and having one of those men trip over the next one's feet. *Crash!* Into the orchestra pit I would go head-first! I could see it all in my mind.

Were you able to get the staging changed?

I had some funny discussions (well, funnier now than they were then) with Joseph Urban about that damned throne. I tried to get him to change the throne chair to a golden carriage. No, this isn't Cinderella, he said. So I told him, how about a chariot? We'll put in the program that Act Four is set in Rome instead of Madagascar. The libretto would stump a Philadelphia lawyer, so nobody would know the difference anyway. I was only half-kidding too. But the big throne chair stayed anyhow—and fortunately, we didn't even have a near disaster with it. But let me tell you, I checked it and double-checked it before every one of those *Africana* performances. If the thing so much as squeaked I had the carpenters there in a hurry, tightening up every screw.

Musically, were there special moments that you recall in your early performances of L'africana*?*

Yes, any of the scenes that I did with [Beniamino] Gigli. You know, *L'africana* was really his opera.

And yet I have heard you say that you were not always fond of his singing of "O paradiso!"

Well—yes, that's true. He would step out of his character, go to the footlights, sing the aria (and I mean he sang it beautifully, when it comes to [the use of the] voice), but then at the climax there at the end of the aria, in the line "*tu m'appartieni . . . a me, a me!*," he would hold on to those last three notes so long that it would ruin the effect. I thought it was very inartistic. He had nothing to prove by showing how long he could hold those notes. It wasn't like Gigli to do that in his other operas, not the ones I did with him anyway. Usually, he tried to be very artistic. And with that beautiful voice of his, you always wanted him to use it in the best artistic way.

Were you impressed with Gigli's acting?

Well, I always thought of him as a great singer first and not really as an actor. He kept his place, didn't move much, and some of the time he would sing directly to the audience like they used to [do] in the old days. But with that voice, who cared? One thing I remember about singing with Gigli in *L'africana* is that he would always try to get to the "hot spot" on the Met stage. At the Metropolitan there was a spot on the stage where the voice [felt and] sounded especially good. It was on one side, and we all knew where it was. When any of us had an aria, or maybe even just a special phrase we wanted to put over, we would head for that spot. In *Africana*, Gigli would inch his way over to that spot, even in some of the ensembles! Of course, some of the others in the ensembles didn't want to be outdone, so you'd see them work their way over to where Gigli was. Pretty soon, you had a small crowd all bunched up around that one spot on the stage!

The Metropolitan Annals *show that you sang* L'africana *with Giacomo Lauri-Volpi three times and that you also did one performance each with Giovanni Martinelli, Mario Chamlee, and a bit later on, there was a performance with Frederick Jagel.*

That's strange, because I don't ever remember singing it with anybody but Gigli.

I think that's understandable, because in the twenty-six performances of L'africana *that you sang at the Metropolitan, according to the* Annals, *twenty-one of those performances featured Gigli in the role of Vasco da Gama.*

And nobody could sing it better than Gigli. Not in my time, anyway.

Not even Martinelli or Lauri-Volpi?

Some voices just seem custom-made for certain roles—that's the way it was with Gigli in *L'africana*, as I heard it. But let's not forget, when you're talking about Gigli and Martinelli, you're talking about the two best tenors of my time—after Caruso, of course. Anything that they did was bound to be great.

You didn't mention Giacomo Lauri-Volpi, I noticed. I'm interested in your views about Lauri-Volpi because he sang with you reasonably often in a number of the operas you were singing during that period: L'africana, Il trovatore, Andrea Chénier, *and* La gioconda. *Yet in interviews, you have rarely said anything at all about his singing.*

Well, what do you want me to say?

Well, what about his singing? Did you like to sing with Giacomo Lauri-Volpi?

I didn't think about it one way or the other. See, I didn't make up the casts. Gatti-Casazza and the people who ran the Metropolitan made up the casts, not me. If Lauri-Volpi was in the same cast that I was in, okay, that was that.

In my interviews with your secretary Edith and with Libbie Miller, your former manager, I was given a blunter version of what you thought of Lauri-Volpi.

Oh? What did they tell you?

I believe the phrase that Edith and Libbie quoted from your description of Lauri-Volpi was something on the order of "that swell-headed s.o.b."

They told you I used cuss words like that? *Me?* [She laughs.] I certainly don't remember saying that. See, they were probably just telling you what *they* thought of Lauri-Volpi: they're both very intelligent women, you know, so I wouldn't want to disagree with them. Frankly, I could never stand Lauri-Volpi's singing.

Was it his technique? Did you fault his vocal production?

Oh, no. Give him his due: he had plenty of technique. The proof of it was that he could do a diminuendo even way up in the high range. You can't do that without excellent technique, and you have to be in tip-top shape too. But, really, all he had were high notes. I think of his voice [as being] kind of like a pyramid turned upside down. It wasn't an even voice from top to bottom. The quality just wasn't there in his low tones, and I didn't like the sound of the tones in the middle, either. But the higher up he went, the more focus he had in the voice. And *oh*, how he loved the sound of his voice! Romani used to call him Narciso. Do you know the story of Narciso?

Do you mean Narcissus, the mythological boy who fell in love with his reflection when he looked into a pond and saw his own face?

That's what Romani and I used to say about Lauri-Volpi and his love for his own voice. He thought he was God's gift among the tenors, just like Narciso staring into the pond.

What about his musicianship?

Lauri-Volpi wasn't any kind of a musician, as far as I could tell. He got by on instinct, I think. And he was very unpredictable. From one night to the next, he just sang an aria whatever way he felt like singing it, which would give you fits if you were in a duet or an ensemble with him because you had no idea what he might do.

Is that what happened between you in Il trovatore*? There was a well-publicized incident where the two of you supposedly had a falling out over how long he held the high note at the end of the trio that closes Act One.*

Not "supposedly." It really happened.

Give me your version of the incident, please.

Well, if that trio is done in key, then Manrico has to sing a D-flat at the very end, and so does Leonora. Count di Luna takes a harmonic note with those D-flats. Now, those notes aren't supposed to be sustained. Everybody is supposed to take their own high note, hold it for no more than maybe four beats so that everybody is together, and then you get off the note together. Leonora is supposed to faint then, and Manrico and di Luna draw their swords because they are going to duel. Then the curtain closes. Well, there we were, the three of us, and we all took our high notes, but di Luna and I (Giuseppe Danise was singing di Luna, I think) held the note like we were supposed to, and [then] we let go of it. But not Lauri-Volpi: he held it until the curtain had already closed, the conductor had put the baton on his stand, and the orchestra had started to put away their instruments.

We're exaggerating just a trifle?

Oh, no. I would only be exaggerating if I said that he held it until the audience was already home in bed and fast asleep.

In roles like Manrico, or perhaps Andrea Chénier, how was Lauri-Volpi's acting compared, say, to Gigli's?

Oh, Volpi tried to be full of fire and passion and such, but he overdid it. To me, his acting looked hammy. But you really wouldn't want to talk about either Lauri-Volpi or Gigli as actors. If you want to talk about tenors who were excellent actors, you want to talk about Martinelli, or [Aureliano] Pertile, or [Lucien] Muratore, but not Gigli or Lauri-Volpi. Gigli had the best voice of them all, but he wasn't an actor. Volpi wasn't much in either department. He did have a very good physique, though, very trim. Now, Gigli was just plain fat, but it was kind of becoming [on] him. He had a very sweet face, like a grownup choirboy. He was short, though, like Lauri-Volpi was. I think Volpi wore built-up shoes and boots, when we had to sing together, because I was taller.

Incidentally, did Caruso also wear built-up shoes when you sang with him?

Why, no. Caruso wasn't a short man. Did you think he was?

Yes, for some reason. I think that's the impression many people seem to have of him from photographs of him in various roles.

No, Caruso was around five feet nine. That was a little more than the average for men at that time, and it was on the tall side for a tenor. I remember that in *Forza*, when I was wearing high boots, I was almost at eye level with him.

It's been suggested that the Metropolitan premiere of Andrea Chénier *in March 1920, which went to Gigli to sing with Claudia Muzio because of Caruso's declining health, had really been intended by Gatti-Casazza for Caruso to premiere with you as his Maddalena.*

Caruso, yes. But me, no. Even Caruso couldn't have found fault with the cast of Gigli and Muzio. Gigli's voice was still on the *leggero* side at that time, so he didn't have all the passion, the drama in his Chénier, that he came to have later on. But Muzio had it all. To me, she was the greatest of all Maddalenas.

Were you somehow less pleased with your own Maddalena?

Less pleased? No, I was satisfied with it. In fact, I liked it a lot. It was a very popular opera, of course, and was still new at the Met in those days. Plus, Maddalena is a very believable character, which gave me an opportunity to really do something with her, compared to Elvira in *Ernani* or Selika or some of the other roles I was doing at that time. But I still go back to Muzio when I think of Maddalena. It just fit her like a glove—nobody could touch her Maddalena.

You sang Andrea Chénier *with Martinelli, Gigli, Lauri-Volpi, Giulio Crimi, and Miguel Fleta, although primarily with Gigli.*

I don't remember singing it with Fleta. I remember his voice—a very good *lirico-spinto* as I remember it—but I can't place him in *Andrea Chénier*. It must have been only once, maybe on tour or something, when he stepped in for Gigli. Now, Crimi I remember very well in that role. His voice was warm and rather mellow, an all-around good *spinto* tenor voice. Yet it wasn't what I would call a luscious sound, and it didn't ring—no *squillo* to it. But he was a good artist, and he was very satisfying as Chénier. Martinelli was an excellent Chénier—he was excellent in anything he did—and the blend of our voices was always just right. You need that especially in the very last scene, when they sing "Vicino a te": the voices of Maddalena and Chénier have to blend perfectly if that scene is to come off right. They have to be able to sing at the same volume (which is full out) and they have to be able to sustain those notes together, which means that their breath control has to be up to the requirements. That's the only place where Gigli and I weren't a perfect match in *Chénier*.

What was the basis of the problem? Was it that Gigli didn't have the breath control?

No. He had the breath control, for sure. But his voice was more lyrical, so I had to make myself hold back a little so that the blend of the sound would be right. In that moment especially, you don't want to be thinking about holding back. You see, whenever you have to be concerned about your partner instead of being able to let out what's inside you, you're going not only to be working harder than you should have to, but also to compromise yourself, and you'll lose some of the drama.

But with Giovanni Martinelli, perhaps even Giulio Crimi, the blend wasn't a problem?

No, never, and while I'm on that [subject], I just thought of something very good that I can say about Lauri-Volpi: he was good in that scene—his timbre wasn't broad, but his high notes carried very well. When I was singing "Vicino a te" with him, I didn't have to hold anything back at all. I didn't have to worry about how long he was going to hold any high notes, either. After all, if he wasn't going to cut off the high notes, the guillotine would cut off the source.

Your roster of the baritones who sang Gérard with you included Titta Ruffo, Giuseppe de Luca, Giuseppe Danise, Mario Basiola, and Armando Borgioli. I'd like to know your thoughts on their singing and characterizations.

I can give you a very short answer: Ruffo was the best of all of them. None of the others even came close. Danise would be my second favorite. He was very acceptable as Gérard, but he didn't have enough temperament in the role—in other words, he wasn't Titta Ruffo. You should have heard Ruffo in the Tribunal Scene, and right before it in "Nemico della patria." When he sang "Nemico della patria," it brought the audience right out of their seats! The performance came to a stop. They wouldn't stop applauding. As I'm talking to you, in my mind I'm seeing him in that scene just this minute. There aren't enough words—no words to describe it.

After Andrea Chénier, *but before* La gioconda, *you sang Leonora in* Il trovatore *for the first time. I can't help but imagine that Leonora was one of your favorite roles.*

Oh, I always liked *Trovatore*. Of course, it was a staple in the [Metropolitan] repertoire, and it was a favorite in the house and on tour. But I would have to say that Leonora is not one of the roles that I would single out as anything special. I liked the opera better than I liked the role. Muzio sang it as much or more than I did at that time. Frances Peralta did a number of them too, and when Elisabeth Rethberg came to the Met she did a lot of *Trovatore* performances. So, Leonora wasn't a role that was associated with me particularly, it's just that the public that followed my career expected me to do Leonora, and I delivered.

How would you describe the differences in Muzio's, Peralta's, and Rethberg's singing in Il trovatore*?*

Muzio had that throb in the voice—I don't know how else to describe it. Now, her production wasn't the most natural—she had a strange way of producing her tones. To get them "in the mask," as we singers like to say, Muzio would raise her cheeks and show her upper teeth, which made her look like she was smiling all the time. It was one of those things that you can't really criticize because it was her own way of doing things and it worked okay for her. I always thought her tone could've been even more beautiful if her production had been a little more natural. As a singer and an actress, though, there were many things that she did that were so great [that] you couldn't ask for better. Leonora in *Trovatore* was a very good part for Muzio—not her best part, but only because [Leonora] isn't like Aida or Maddalena or Tosca. Rethberg was one of my pets, of course. Her voice just shimmered: a beautiful, shimmering, silvery timbre. I didn't have many opportunities to hear her in *Trovatore*, so it's hard for me to say what was unique about her way of doing Leonora. Frances Peralta had a big voice—very good size to it. She didn't have the quality that Rethberg had, but it was a good voice, a satisfying voice.

Did you know Peralta well as a person?

Every time I think of Peralta, I think of her sickness and what a strong person she was. I didn't know her socially, but I liked her, and we used to keep up with one another through our dresser (the same woman used to dress both of us at the Metropolitan). One day the dresser told me confidentially that Frances Peralta had cancer. She said that the tumors were enlarging and that the costumes had to be altered to help cover them up. But do you know, Peralta never once complained, not once. You would never have known she was even sick. I'll never forget how courageous she was.

As you think back to your performances of Il trovatore, *were there any parts of Leonora's music that you found especially difficult?*

Not at that time, no. Later on, I wasn't too comfortable with "D'amor sull' ali rosee." That's because of the trouble I had with the high C in "O patria mia" during my first *Aida*. That spooked me until I found out it was all right to transpose. So after a while, I took "D'amor sull ali rosee" a half-tone down, and it felt just fine.

I can't help pointing out the irony in your being concerned about the high C in "D'amor sull'ali rosee" but not about the high D-flat in the trio at the end of Act One.

But they're very, very different. It's the approach that makes all the difference. Take "O patria mia," for instance: it's what you call an exposed high C. You attack it in the middle of a very long phrase that lies very high, and you're there all by yourself on stage—no trios, no chorus, very little orchestral accompaniment at all. That's completely different from the trio with Manrico and di Luna where you sing the D-flat. You're not the only one singing, and you don't stay on the note either—unless you're Lauri-Volpi.

What moments in Il trovatore *stand out the most as you reflect on the role of Leonora?*

I absolutely loved the last scene. I'm thinking of her music in the death scene, where the poison is slowly killing her. Those ascending passages she sings—up and up and up, *mezza voce*, slowly, very slowly, one long breath—I *loved* singing it. To tell you the truth, sometimes in that scene I would hardly be conscious that I was even singing. It felt like I was in some other world.

Another favorite moment of mine was the "Miserere," especially when Martinelli was singing Manrico with me. The audiences couldn't get enough of it. On tour, as long as Maestro Serafin wasn't conducting, we could get away with doing an encore of the "Miserere." The second time around, I would take the optional high C in the second part. Martinelli and I would go to town on that one! But in the opera house, Serafin wouldn't allow any encores, ever. He was right, of course, because they tire the singers and they stop the flow of the drama, but that doesn't mean they're not fun to sing.

Tullio Serafin first entered your professional life when you went to Italy for the first time, which was in the summer of 1924.

Yes. I went there to prepare *La gioconda* with him. He was coming to the Metropolitan that year, and he was going to be conducting me in *Gioconda* so I wanted to prepare it with him. He wasn't going to be in New York until around the time the [1924–25] season was ready to start, so I met him in Italy and worked with him over there.

When you say you "prepared" La gioconda *with Serafin, do you mean that you studied the role with him?*

No. I had already learned the score with [Romano] Romani, and I knew pretty well how I was going to do the role by the time I got to Italy. But I needed to prepare all of her music with Serafin because I had never sung with him before.

Did it take you very long to learn La gioconda?

No. But how long it takes to learn something from the score doesn't really have a lot to do with how you're going to sing it. Being a good sight-reader and [having] a good memory for music, I can learn a score pretty fast. But even when you're a fast learner, you just get the music up there in your head, that's all. It takes a good while for it to settle in, to go deeper and deeper inside of you. The music has to become so much a part of you that you can *live* it. At least that's how it was for me.

How long did that "settling in" process take with Gioconda?

Well, I can give you an answer, but it's going to sound like I'm bragging, so I'll have to explain what I mean. The truth is, it didn't take very long. That's because Gioconda, you see, is not a particularly demanding character. She's not like Violetta in *Traviata*, or Santuzza, or Carmen—not a real-life character with a lot of depth to her, in other words. It's her music that's so demanding. It's very, very heavy—almost like singing Wagner. It takes *so* much emotion out of you! If you don't watch yourself, if you really let yourself go, I mean, you won't have enough left for the last act. I used to fight with myself during *Gioconda*. I'd tell myself before each scene, "Now, hold yourself back a little here, Rosa—save it for the last act."

You sailed for Europe on the U.S.S. Leviathan, *which docked in Southampton, according to the newspaper accounts of your travels that summer. Did you go directly to Venice after you arrived in Southampton?*

No. I had never been to Europe, you see, so I wanted to take in as much as I could [and] we made several stops along the way. Of course, there were a lot of invitations that had to be considered. We, Edith [Prilik] and I, went to Paris for at least a week, maybe two weeks.

Do you recall any specifics about your stay in Paris?

Yes, how much money I spent! I did a lot of shopping there (I certainly remember that), but we saw some of our friends too. We were with Jeanne Gordon for a day or so. She had a beautiful apartment there. But the big time we had was with Chaliapin. We were his guests part of the time we were in Paris. He took us all around. Wherever he went he always had the best of everything—the best food, the best wines, the most elegant places, the most fascinating people. Believe me, when Chaliapin showed you Paris, you *really* saw Paris! We had a wonderful time.

And from Paris you went on to Italy?

Yes, to Livorno first. We met up with [Romano] Romani there. He had a villa in Livorno, a beautiful place overlooking the sea. We were there a few days, and then we all went to Rome. I was at the Vatican where I had an audience with the Pope (a private audience, which wasn't easy to get). After that we went to Naples so that I could visit some of my mother's family in Caserta.

How much did the Ponzillos in Caserta know about your Metropolitan Opera career and how successful you had become?

I couldn't really tell. See, my mother couldn't read or write much, and these poor people couldn't either. Mother sent along some clippings, but they were in English, of course, so they weren't worth anything except for the pictures of me. Plus, in the clippings I was Rosa Ponselle, not Rose Ponzillo. So, they probably didn't know anything. They were just dirt-poor farmers, but my old aunt seemed real glad to see me. I say "old" because she looked like she was about eighty, what with her skin all wrinkled from the sun. But, really, she couldn't have been much over fifty. It was the hard life they had to lead over there. It made them old before their time.

According to newspaper accounts of the trip, one of your purposes for going to Naples was to place a wreath on Caruso's tomb. Do you remember your visit to the Del Pianto cemetery where he is buried?

Oh! Good God! I didn't want to go anywhere near it! I mean, not that I didn't want to pay my respects. He was the king, and I will always be sad that he had to die when he did. I'm sad for him, sad for me, and sad for all the people who should have heard that voice the way I was able to hear it. But what those Neapolitans who ran that cemetery did to poor Caruso! They embalmed him and put his body on display under glass, like some mummy in a museum case! I was told that they had him laid out in full evening dress and that they changed his clothes every year. Can you believe that? What the hell did they think he was going to do? Sit up and sing? And do you know that it took Mrs. Caruso years to have his casket closed? She had to beg them to close it up and let him rest in peace, so that she didn't have to look at his dead face every time she went to say a prayer at his grave! I mean, remembering the dead is one thing, but what those people did to Caruso was just damned morbid.

From Caserta and Naples, if I'm correct, you and Edith joined Romano Romani and the three of you went to Venice to be with Maestro Serafin.

That's right. Maestro and his wife had already taken a place in Venice. His wife, you know, was Elena Rakowska, a very good soprano and a very beautiful woman too. She used to sing the *spinto* Wagner roles, and she did Italian roles too.

Do you remember your very first impressions of the Maestro?

Of course, vividly. He was an idol of mine. We all idolized him. He was still relatively young back then—he was in his mid-forties or thereabouts. His hair was already gray; I remember that, because it made him look very distinguished. He was a very good-looking man, very attractive. All of us singers were in awe of him. Yet he had so much warmth in him that he made you feel secure all the time. Everything he asked us to do was *con amore* [with love]. There were never any of these outbursts that you hear about with other conductors.

Perhaps you have Arturo Toscanini in mind?

Well, I think everybody knows what his reputation was with singers. [Bruno] Zirato told me that Toscanini ruined so many watches by stomping on them when he got mad in rehearsals, they finally had to buy him a whole box of cheap watches so he would stop ruining the expensive ones! I was scared to death of him! That's why I never would sing under him. [Toscanini] used to send Zirato and others to talk to me about things he would like to do with me in New York or over in Italy, but I would always say no—very politely, of course. You see, I couldn't possibly sing if I was upset. You never even had to give a thought to that kind of thing with Maestro Serafin. He understood everything about you. You'd swear that he could read your mind when you were on stage. He could anticipate exactly what you were going to do, and he made you feel like the whole orchestra was your accompanist. That's why we all adored him.

When you did Gioconda *that next season, were there moments in your performances that made you especially aware of Serafin's supportiveness?*

There was a special moment that he and I both just loved. It's in Act One, when Gioconda sings the phrase, "Madre! Enzo adorato! Ah, come t'amo!" On the word *amo*, which is a high B-flat in the score, it's to be sung pianissimo. It's very difficult to carry it off just right because Gioconda, Enzo, and La Cieca all have to make their exit together, but Gioconda is supposed to hold that high pianissimo while they're going offstage. Now, in the performances, Serafin would watch me real closely to see just how I got on the high B-flat. He could tell by how I got on it exactly what kind of shape my voice was in, and just about how long I would be able to hold that high pianissimo while walking across the stage. In the rehearsals, you see, he would practice with me. He would watch my breathing, listen to my attack, and then have me do it several times so that he would be able to keep right with me, no matter what kind of voice I was in. When I was in the best voice, I would hold that pianissimo until we were all practically in the wings, and he would have the orchestra right with me, down to the last fraction of a second when I would let go of the note. That's what I mean when I say that Serafin was truly a singer's conductor.

Do you recall what your work sessions in Venice were like?

He and I would work about two hours, maybe three, in the middle of the afternoon. We did our sightseeing late in the morning and into the early afternoon. If we weren't too tired after the one session, that night we would do some more. But if it was too hot during the day, we did all of our rehearsing at night. Nino Romani would be at the piano. Maestro Serafin would sit directly in front of me when I was rehearsing. These were all work sessions, nothing really memorable, just everybody working hard and then taking time out to enjoy the city. Venice was beautiful in those days—no motorboats, only the gondoliers, and no gaudy signs all over the place for the tourist traps, which I'm told is what Venice is like nowadays.

Do you remember some of the sites that would have been of interest to you—the Cathedral of San Marco, the Ca' d'Oro, and the Canale Grande?

We saw them all. I remember one time in particular. We were out in a gondola, just the five of us—Romani, Serafin, Rakowska, Edith and I. It was near dusk, and it was just chilly enough that I took along my ermine coat, which I was very proud of. It was all white, a beautiful thing. As much as it cost me, I should have been proud of it too. Anyway, there we were, drifting along the Canale Grande, and everything was so beautiful and peaceful that I decided to sing a little bit. So I sang Tosti's "Serenata" while we were going along. Well, the water and the buildings along each side of the canal gave the voice such a wonderful resonance! Of course, one song led to another and another and another, and after a while, Rakowska started singing, too. Before long, we had a pretty good-sized crowd following us along the sides of the canal. "Who are you?" they would yell. "Tell us who you are, and where you're from!" By the time we were ready to get out of the gondola, there was a *big* crowd where we wanted to dock. But we didn't want to have to do any more singing—there wasn't going to be any free, on-the-spot concert. So, of course, we had to stay out on the water till they gave up waiting for us. That ruined the mood, but it was still an unforgettable time.

Of all the places you visited during your first trip to Italy, I imagine that your trip to Viareggio, when Puccini invited you to his villa, was the most memorable.

Oh! No question about it! That was the privilege of a lifetime. And *so* sad, you know—he died only three months later.

Who arranged your introduction to Puccini?

Romani. He knew Puccini very well. Romani, you see, had written two operas, *Zulma* and *Fedra*, when he was young. Both were successes in Italy. Some years later, you know, they premiered *Fedra* in London at Covent Garden, and I sang it with Serafin conducting. You see, Puccini and Mascagni were very impressed with Romani's work. Puccini was the one who helped him make the right connections to get the first one, *Zulma*, produced in Rome.

Were you aware of how ill Puccini really was?

Not really. Romani told us that [Puccini] had been sick, but we didn't know whether he was just getting over something, recuperating, or just what the situation was. Of course, I had never known Puccini, so I had nothing to compare what he seemed like then with what he must have been like before he took ill. He was still working, which made me think that he couldn't be too sick.

He was working on the score of Turandot*?*

That's right. In fact, just before we left his villa that afternoon, he let me sight-sing some of Turandot's music from his manuscript. Just certain lines that he was working on, nothing very extensive. It made me very excited to have that privilege. Of course, Rosa Raisa was the one who got to create it, and Jeritza [sang it] when they brought *Turandot* to the Metropolitan.

Do you recall how Puccini reacted to your voice and your singing?

It haunts me to think about it. Not long after we had arrived, he went to the piano and asked me to sing for him and gave me a choice of anything from his operas that I might want to do. So I picked "Vissi d' arte" from *Tosca*, which was always a favorite of mine. I sang it for him twice, and each time I varied the ending of the aria. Afterward, I asked him which ending he preferred. He told me he liked [either] way I sang it, which was quite a compliment. What haunts me [most] is what he said when I finished "Vissi d' arte" the very first time I sang it for him. He just stared at the keys for a moment, and then he said, "Che peccato! Che peccato no ho sentito questa voce primo!" He had put his hand on the side of his face, and he was tapping his finger against his temple when he said that. He said it softly but just loud enough for Edith, Romani, and I to hear him. The way he said it, [it] was like he was thinking out loud: "What a pity that I never heard this voice before now!" You can only let yourself wonder what he was thinking of.

Perhaps he was thinking about how you would have sounded as Turandot?

No, I don't think it was that. Raisa had just the right voice for Turandot. I don't think he had anything specific in mind for me. I felt that he was thinking about what might have been if he had heard me earlier, or if maybe he hadn't been sick and could have lived longer. That's why it still haunts me.

Recollections

Edith Prilik

As Ponselle's secretary, Edith was responsible for making all of her travel arrangements, and with very few exceptions, traveled with her both in the U.S. and abroad throughout Rosa's career. In the summers of 1923 and 1924, consequently, she traveled with Ponselle to the West Coast, where she gave her first series of concerts in California, and also to France and Italy, which Rosa visited for the first time in 1924. Her recollections, drawn from the author's interviews of July 1977 and November 1978, begin with Ponselle's fascination with Hollywood and the motion picture industry.

Rosa was always interested in the movies. Claudia Muzio was the only singer I can think of who was more of a movie fan than Rosa. Muzio never missed a new movie when the Met was on tour. Rosa was a movie fan because, as she used to say, that was the way she got her start in show business, playing the accompaniment in movie houses. So, naturally, she wanted to see Hollywood and meet some of the stars while she was concertizing on the West Coast.

She arranged to stay there for about six weeks in May and early June [1923], and then came back to Los Angeles again later in the summer for another two weeks.

There wasn't much in Hollywood at that time, nothing like there was later on when Rosa lived there for a while in the late 1930s. There wasn't any culture to speak of out there except for what they were putting on at the Hollywood Bowl, which was almost brand new at that time (it didn't even have a bandshell over it yet). At first, it seemed like they booked just about anything to help make the investment pay off. Lawrence Tibbett, who was from California and who auditioned with Rosa that summer, got a booking at the Hollywood Bowl, but hardly anybody had ever heard of him.[15] There were other singers who appeared there, but Rosa was the first real opera star to give a concert at the Hollywood Bowl.[16]

By the time she went to Hollywood, Rosa was already friendly with some of the film stars, especially Gloria Swanson and Lillian Gish. She and Lillian Gish had met long before then, back when Rosa was under Thorner's management. Lillian used to model occasionally for Victor Maurel, whose art studio was in Thorner's building. Lillian often came to hear Rosa during her first couple of seasons at the Met. Gloria Swanson was a great admirer of Rosa because Gloria was interested in singing. She and Rosa became very good friends, especially later on when Rosa was living in Hollywood. Gloria and Pola Negri didn't get along, so Rosa didn't like Pola Negri. But she got a kick out of Clara Bow. I think she sympathized with her because [Clara Bow] also had a ne'er-do-well father to support. We met him—a little runt of a guy. He said he was a trained baritone.[17] Everybody thought he was a nut, but they put up with him because of who his daughter was.

Like the people she was friendly with in Hollywood, Rosa had a taste for the high life, and in New York she began to live like a star. Her pride and joy was her penthouse at 90 Riverside Drive, near Eightieth Street overlooking the Hudson River. She had always wanted a place that would be large enough to entertain in, but private enough that she could live her life without much interruption. She hated to feel enclosed in any way, and she had a mania about the temperature—no room was ever cold enough to suit her—so she wanted to be able to open all the windows and doors without worrying about intruders. She [also] wanted a place that was soundproof so that she could sing whenever she wanted and could rehearse with Nino Romani any time she felt like it, day or night.

She had been looking around for quite a while when she heard about the penthouse at 90 Riverside from a friend of hers, an Italian real-estate speculator named Paterno, who owned a lot of residential property in that part of Manhattan. As soon as she saw it, she fell in love with that penthouse. The yearly rent was about $2,000, which today [1978] would get you a janitor's closet in a dark corner of the basement. It seemed like a small fortune to me (it was more than my yearly salary as her secretary), but Rosa was making more than that for every one of her concerts.[18]

One of the things Rosa especially liked about the penthouse was that the roof-garden area was large enough that she could ride her English bicycle around it. She and that bicycle were inseparable—even in the wintertime when she would ride it on the rooftop. In the summer, even on a day when it would be hot enough to fry an egg, she would put on shorts and a sleeveless blouse, pull back her hair with a bandanna, and ride her bike way up to Grant's Tomb and back. Until some of her fans got wise to her route and started following her in their cars, nobody much bothered her.

One afternoon she even rode her bike into Gatti-Casazza's office at the Metropolitan Opera House. At first, he thought this was some publicity stunt that Libbie Miller had dreamed up for the newspaper cameras, but Rosa told him that she rode that bike all over Manhattan. Oh, did he hit the ceiling! "Don't ever do that again!" he scolded her. "You're too valuable to be killed in Seventh Avenue traffic!" She put it away for about a week, and then she was right back in traffic again.

Between golf, tennis, and bike-riding, Rosa was the picture of health in those days. She had the constitution of a horse (she could eat like one too), but she was absolutely petrified of any kind of sickness. She rarely got sick during the opera season, but sometimes things would hit her out of the blue. Then she would make herself even sicker by worrying about being sick in the first place. That's what happened to her a few weeks before she was to sail to Europe for her first trip overseas. She developed what the New York doctors diagnosed as acute appendicitis, which meant that she would have to be operated on and wouldn't be able to go to Italy. She sent to Connecticut for Dr. [William F.] Verdi, a well-known surgeon who practiced medicine in New Haven and who had treated some of the Ponzillos in Meriden.[19] He diagnosed something else entirely, and he got her well without much of a fuss. From then on, Dr. Verdi was her personal physician, and she kept him on a retainer so that he would be available to her any time she needed him.[20]

Before she took her first trip to Europe, Rosa began making records for the Victor Company. I went to all of her recording sessions, first at Columbia and then at Victor. She never particularly liked making records, so when she got to the studio it used to take her a while to get into the right frame of mind. She missed singing to an audience, for one thing. And there was the clock to worry about. Everything had to be sung or played in exactly so many minutes, or the record would be ruined. That clock would nearly drive her insane, because she had to sing everything too fast, and she wasn't able to use much shading in her singing. She had to sing into what looked like a big funnel, with the orchestra grouped around her. Everything had to be sung loud, or else it wouldn't register on the record. Rosa's voice, though, was naturally big, so she [was] recorded very well.

When she would arrive at the recording studio, Rosa would be all business and would usually be in a hurry to get it over with. But after she did one or two "takes," she would get into the right mood, and then she would give it everything she had. By the time the records actually went on the market, which could be several months later, she had usually forgotten about them.

The Victor people had been after Rosa to leave Columbia for quite some time before she actually made the switch. She now says it was just a business decision, which it was, but she also says that she had nothing to do with the negotiations, that she left them to Libbie [Miller] to handle. Like hell! Rosa did all the negotiating from behind the scenes, and Libbie was just her "front." Everything that Rosa tried to negotiate always started off the same way: she wanted far more money than the other party was about to pay her. This was her motto: start high, don't come down unless you have to in order not to lose the deal, and above all, get as much [money] in advance as you can, which is why she didn't accept an offer from Victor right away. She wanted them to pay her practically as much as they had been paying Caruso. But after a while they came to terms, and they agreed to pay her an annual retainer in advance plus royalties on each record of hers that Victor issued.

The only thing she wasn't able to get from Victor was a contract for Carmela to make records for the Red Seal. In those days, Victor had the Red Seal for the great classical artists, and then they had black-label records for everyday popular music. Carmela got more and more jealous of Rosa and started demanding everything that Rosa had—and she would get very pushy with Rosa so that she would do [Carmela's] bidding. But the Victor people wouldn't take Carmela without an audition. They didn't like what they heard, so they said she would have to make black-label records, which Carmela wouldn't do because she wouldn't be getting [paid] what Rosa was getting.

When Rosa went to Europe for the summer [of 1924], we were overseas for four months. We left at the end of May, and we came back to New York near the end of September, a few days before Rosa was due to sing a concert in Canada. Our first European stop was Paris, which was everything we expected it to be. Chaliapin had a dinner party for Rosa, and the next day he took us to several important places. All the time we were with him, we saw the dignified side of Chaliapin, which is not the way Rosa viewed him, at first, when they were singing together in *Don Carlos*.

I don't think Chaliapin ever found out about it, but Rosa actually went to Gatti-Casazza in private to ask him not to cast her with Chaliapin in any more of the *Don Carlos* performances. What she told Gatti was that Chaliapin was too temperamental and that he made her too upset to sing well. But the real story was that Chaliapin intimidated her and was always upstaging her. Yet the more she got to know him, the more Rosa was fascinated by Chaliapin. He had a notorious reputation as a womanizer, of course, and this fascinated Rosa. She knew he was friendly with [coach and conductor] Wilfred Pelletier, who was married to [soprano] Queena Mario at that time. So Rosa went to see Queena and asked her what she knew about Chaliapin's reputation as a lover. "When you're in Paris," Queena said, "just ask any woman on the street. Chances are, she'll know."

While we were in Paris, Jeanne Gordon invited us to stay at her apartment. To say her apartment was lavish would be an understatement. The furniture, the art work, the accoutrements—all looked like they had been bought at Tiffany's. Yet when Jeanne was showing us the apartment (and it was nearly as big as Rosa's penthouse) she seemed very matter-of-fact about all the expensive furnishings. Rosa's eyes were as big as saucers all the time we were there. She couldn't figure out for the life of her how this was possible, because Jeanne Gordon made far less money than she did. Rosa even began to wonder if there was something wrong with her own financial investments. Later on, she was relieved to no end when she found out who had really paid Jeanne Gordon's tab. It turned out that for a while Jeanne had become the mistress of [financier] Bernard Baruch!

Our trip to Naples to see Rosa's family in Caserta was a nightmare. To Rosa, this was going to be like a homecoming, so she made a big production out of it. She hired two huge touring cars (one for us, and one for our luggage) because she wanted to arrive at their house in grand style. Her aunt on her mother's side, the Conti side of the family, was living outside Caserta. She was the only one of the Contis or the Ponzillos we could find, but before we got anywhere near where she lived, the roads gave out and we had to ride on muddy cattle trails. When we finally got to the place, it was nothing but a nails-and-boards shack with a tin roof. It was built on top of a pigpen. Her aunt and a couple of her cousins raised pigs for a living.

It was pretty clear that none of these people had the foggiest idea who Rosa was. But it didn't take them long to figure out that she was a rich relative. You can be sure that nobody else had ever arrived there in two touring cars! I couldn't wait to get out of there, but I was feeling carsick because of the awful ride. I asked her aunt if I could lie down for a while inside their house. Well, the smell of the pigpen coming up through the floor boards didn't do much for me, and my head had barely touched the pillow when I saw bedbugs hopping all over me! I got out of there as fast as I could.

We ate a simple dinner with her aunt and cousins, who said very little the whole time. There wasn't much to talk about, after all. They kept eyeing all the luggage Rosa had brought in one of the cars. For all I know, they probably thought the trunks were filled with money and that she was going to give them some. Anyway, when it came time to give out the gifts she had bought, she handed her old aunt a beautifully wrapped box. Inside was a little bottle of expensive Parisian perfume. Imagine—French perfume for a pig farmer! The old lady opened the box, took one look at the bottle, and said, "What am I supposed to do with *this*?" Fortunately, Rosa had a good sense of humor and could laugh about it afterward.

If any one incident tested her sense of humor that summer, it was what happened to her in Venice one afternoon when we were getting ready to take our afternoon outing in the gondola. We were in Venice for about six weeks, and Rosa had hired two gondolas (one for the afternoons, and a different one for the evenings) so that they would be at our beck and call anytime she and Maestro Serafin wanted to take a break from rehearsing *La gioconda*. This particular afternoon, the two of them were having a disagreement over some point in the score (I don't remember what it was), and neither one of them was giving an inch to the other. They weren't arguing in the sense of fighting with one another. It was more like they were debating rather than arguing.

They were carrying on this debate while they were walking toward the place where the gondola was docked. They would walk about twenty or thirty feet, and then they would stop while one of them would make another point. The more they debated, the more intense Rosa got. The rest of us—Nino Romani, Elena Rakowska, and me—were walking along behind them, just keeping to ourselves and hoping that one or the other of them would change the subject, but they were oblivious to where they were and what was going on around them.

As we got to the gondola, Rosa was still carrying on and Serafin was saying, in his polite way, "No, Rosa, I think if you look at it *this* way," and so on. The rest of us went aboard the gondola and sat there waiting. Finally, they realized that everybody else was ready to go, so Serafin gestured to Rosa to go aboard, but just as she went to step into the gondola, Rosa missed her footing and fell right into the Grand Canal! Worse yet, she was wearing her new white ermine coat. When she bobbed up from the water, she looked like a wet polar bear. We were all aching to laugh, but we didn't dare—yet it was Rosa who ended up laughing the hardest![21]

Our trip to Viareggio, where Rosa met Puccini, was the high point of that first trip to Europe. Nino Romani, who was well acquainted with Puccini, set up the meeting earlier in the summer. Puccini wasn't receiving people at that time because he had been sick, but he made an exception for Romani out of friendship and also because he was interested [in] hear[ing] Rosa. He knew, of course, that Romani wouldn't be bringing newspaper reporters or anything like that—this was going to be a private visit, nothing more. We went there on a Friday, and we were with Puccini most of the afternoon. We met Signora Puccini, and also their son [Antonio], who was staying there at the time. Puccini was very gracious the whole time, but he certainly didn't look well. He was thin, [his] cheeks looked sunken, and he moved kind of slowly. His skin color was terrible—very gray, like ashes.

Except for the time when Puccini asked Rosa to sing for him, we spent most of the time sitting on the veranda talking. Just before we left, I asked him if he would let me take a picture of Rosa with him. (I had gotten interested in photography, and I had bought a Kodak folding camera before we went on the trip). I had promised Rosa I would take pictures of Puccini with her. He was very nice about it, and let me take as many as I wanted. As it turned out, those snapshots became the last photographs ever taken of Puccini. A month or so after he died, we got a very touching letter from Signora Puccini, who asked us to send her copies of the photographs to remember him by. Naturally, we sent prints of everything we had taken of him.[22]

In the middle of the afternoon, Puccini wanted to rest for a little while, so he had one of his hired hands take us around the grounds of the villa. While we were going along, this man happened to mention that the gardeners had found a fox cub that morning. The little thing was very thin, so the gardeners figured that its mother had been killed. This fellow said they would have to destroy it, because it couldn't live on its own. Well, you never talked about any such thing as destroying an animal in front of Rosa! I never knew anyone who was crazier about animals than she was. She could have been happy running a zoo, which is what her houses looked like with all the cats and dogs and birds and such.

When we got back to the veranda, Rosa told Puccini all about the cub, and asked him if she could take it back to Venice with her and try to raise it. He sort of grinned and told her that the fox cub wasn't his, it was God's. So, we took the cub with us, and in no time at all, Rosa was treating it to the life of Riley; after a while, the fox was eating better than we were! Of course, like all cute little animals, it started getting bigger and bigger. By the middle of September it was the size of a small dog, which is how Rosa sneaked it through customs. She had it on a leash but was carrying it on her shoulder. When one of the customs men asked her whether it was a fox, she said no. He looked at her, then he took another look at the fox. Finally, he asked her what it was and what she was going to declare on the customs forms. Rosa batted her eyelashes and said, "Why, it's an Italian police dog."

The Written Record

In an era in which newspapers were still the primary sources of national and international news, Ponselle's increasing celebrity in the mid-1920s all but assured that her travels would be chronicled in the daily press. Consequently, most of the details of her first trip to Europe found their way into newsprint. As the *U.S.S. Leviathan* prepared to leave port on 24 May 1924, the New York *Sun* accorded her name a prominent place among the five hundred first-class passengers who had booked passage on the liner—a list that included the Reginald Vanderbilts, impresario Sol Hurok, basso Adamo Didur, actress Jane Thomas, railroad magnate H. E. Farrell, and U.S. Consul General Roger C. Treadwell.[23]

In a *Musical America* interview a few days before her departure, Ponselle said she intended to occupy her time in Europe with three priorities—"clothes, study, and amusement"—while also visiting with her family near Naples and paying her respects at Caruso's tomb.[24] When she returned to Manhattan aboard the *S.S. Duilio* on September 19, her brother Tony, his wife Lydia, and their two-year-old son were there to greet her at the docks. Holding her curly-headed nephew in her arms, Ponselle told the reporters that she and Carmela were "already preparing him for a musical career" and that his tousled hair reminded her of Giovanni Martinelli's trademark mane.[25] Even the fox cub, now two months old and named "Gioconda," merited a brief mention in the press: the *Times* reporting that she encountered the cub "while walking with Giacomo Puccini, the composer, in the pine woods near his villa,"[26] and the *Morning Telegraph* stating simply that she had captured it "in the mountains of Italy."[27]

The previous summer, Ponselle's first trip to Hollywood was also given its share of press coverage. In particular, the so-called house-moving party that artist Howard Verbeck and his wife had given for Ponselle was carried in most newspapers around the country. Under the headline "JOY RIDING IN A THREE-STORY MANSION," the Buffalo *Times* printed this account:

> At midnight, along fashionable Wilshire Boulevard, past the sleeping homes of Los Angeles society, rolled a three-story mansion, mounted on rollers and hauled by heavy motor trucks to which huge cables were hitched. At the shouts of workmen and the sputter of engines, sleepers awoke and rushed to their windows. They stared, they marveled, they chuckled. But what amused them was not merely the spectacle of a house on wheels; it was what was going on inside the house while it slowly sailed past, like a big ship.[28]

Several weeks after returning from Hollywood, Ponselle granted an exclusive interview to the Atlanta *Journal*'s Jessie Fulsom Stockbridge, who printed Rosa's opinions of the motion-picture stars she had met. Charles Chaplin, she told Stockbridge, was "good-looking and brilliant, [and] an ardent wooer, too, if one doesn't take him too seriously." She spoke highly of Gloria Swanson ("an intimate friend, I admire her very much"), but dismissed

Pola Negri as "too temperamental to be a good friend."[29] The core of Stockbridge's interview, however, was devoted to Ponselle's private life on the West Coast:

> While on tour in California, Miss Ponselle visited a friend in Los Angeles who has a large studio building attached to the rear of her home. Everyone on meeting our songbird would say, "Oh, you *must* know Richard Wayne, my dear, he is just the type for you!"
>
> He came to a party, and they danced together in the large studio. The lights were low and the pianist played "My Hero" from *The Chocolate Soldier*. Miss Ponselle began singing it softly as around they waltzed. Then came the big moment. The music stopped. Dick still had her in his arms and he said, "Rosa, I love you, will you marry me?" Without waiting for her answer he kissed her.[30]

According to the article, Wayne, a real-estate speculator and land developer, drove Ponselle "to the top of a high hill and . . . pointed out a lot of several acres" and assured her, "It's yours now." As of December 1923, Stockbridge wrote, Ponselle was still receiving from Wayne "a fat letter each week and a night telegram at every stop she makes," but was waiting to see "if there's anything to the saying that 'absence makes the heart grow fonder.'"

Based on Ponselle's later recollections of Richard Wayne, however, a different proverb—"Out of sight, out of mind"—ultimately prevailed.[31] Her friend Mona Bonelli, wife of baritone Richard Bonelli, who was living in Hollywood when Rosa first concertized there, has left a more believable account of the fleeting relationship between Wayne and Ponselle. "Dick Wayne was a friend of my husband's and mine, and it was I who introduced him to Rosa," Mrs. Bonelli told discographer Bill Park. "Rosa always had men around her—*always*—but what the newspapers reported about Dick Wayne was nonsense. True, he was a handsome fellow and very successful in real estate, but there was no marriage proposal or any such thing. He and Rosa spent some time together while she was in Hollywood, and there was nothing more to it than that."[32]

Prior to her trip to the West Coast, Rosa had her first brush with scandal. In mid-April 1923, Washington-area newspapers ran a story alleging that she and Lucien Muratore, the respected French tenor, were having an affair that threatened to end Muratore's marriage to soprano Lina Cavalieri.[33] Although Muratore denounced the story as "shamefully ridiculous,"[34] the story lingered for a time, to the distress of the three principals. It was not until two decades later, however, that producer and promoter Merle Armitage openly acknowledged that the Ponselle-Muratore incident had been contrived for box-office purposes:

> Disguising my handwriting, I penned a letter to a Los Angeles newspaper critic . . . a newsy letter obviously written by a man on a New York vacation. Sandwiched innocently in with comments on the theatre, opera, and a Renoir exhibit, I mentioned a dinner party where I was placed next to an executive of the Metropolitan Opera. "Here's an advance tip for you," I wrote. "Lucian [*sic*] Muratore next week will divorce Lina Cavalieri and marry Rosa Ponselle." The letter then proceeded with other gossip of the metropolis, and closed with a "warm regards, Mac," knowing that my critic knew a dozen Hollywood friends named Mac. This letter was rushed to New York and [was] immediately posted.
>
> Just what happened can only be surmised by the results. Our critic, having received the letter, read the morsel about Ponselle and, knowing that Ponselle was scheduled for near future concerts, was certain she had a scoop. . . . She rushes to the City Editor, he reads [the letter] and agrees with her [and] immediately wires the New York office which, in turn, cables the Paris correspondent. The correspondent jumps into a taxi and, a few hours after my letter reaches Los Angeles, is interviewing Muratore in Fontainebleu!
>
> When Muratore chivalrously praised Ponselle as being the finest living dramatic soprano, but said his relations with her were platonic, that he was NOT divorcing his wife to marry her . . . *that* was news, *international* news![35]

According to Armitage's account, "Ponselle was a front page queen for five consecutive days, and . . . [her] concerts in California were sell-outs" as a result of this fabrication. As to whether the box-office ends justified the means, Armitage wrote:

> Character assassin? The answer is contained in a letter received following this tour from Ponselle's New York manager, which said in substance that although Ponselle was unquestionably the world's greatest dramatic soprano, it took an anonymous rumor to apprise most Americans of that fact. She had received more national publicity through that device than had been secured in her whole subsequent career. As for Muratore, he was offered another and more advantageous contract with the Chicago Opera![36]

Ponselle's manager, Libbie Miller, attested in later years to Armitage's role as the perpetrator of the Muratore-Ponselle story. Yet Libbie maintained that she did not condone the invention of the "romance," nor did she recall commending Armitage's ingenuity in a letter.[37] That aside, Armitage's account is marred by a number of factual errors. At the time her West Coast concerts were booked in the autumn of 1922, Ponselle, according to Armitage, was "at the apex of her career . . . singing opposite Caruso at the Metropolitan"—although Caruso had died in August of 1921,[38] and Lucien Muratore, to whom the Chicago Opera supposedly had offered "another and more advantageous contract" as a result of the publicity, had left the Chicago company in 1922.[39]

The 1922–23 Metropolitan Opera season ended on Saturday evening, 21 April 1923; on the next day, the New York *Telegram* summarized its assessment with the headline, "Best Opera Season Since World War."[40] The final day of the season had featured a matinee performance of *L'africana*, with Ponselle and Gigli as Selika and Vasco da Gama, followed by an evening performance of *Aida* with Morgan Kingston as Radames, Frances Peralta as Aida, and Jeanne Gordon as Amneris. Because the Metropolitan's annual tour was set to begin a few days later in Atlanta, most of the company's principal singers had to rush from their dressing rooms to be at the Pennsylvania Station in time to board the 5:15 New Orleans Limited, which would arrive in Atlanta near midnight.

Among those who had to take an early leave, as *The New York Times* reported, was the general manager: "Mr. Gatti . . . received his ovation midway in the fourth act of the matinee. Then, while Miss Ponselle was singing her final scene alone under the deadly mancinilla tree, her companion [Beniamino Gigli] in his costume and make-up as Vasco di Gama faced a battalion of photographers, had his hands wrung by thirty friends in the street, kissed his wife and little son goodbye at the curb, and bolted in his own automobile down Seventh Avenue to the Pennsylvania Station."[41] But as the *Telegram* also reported, Gatti departed for Atlanta feeling quite contented: "Something like two million dollars has been received in the Metropolitan coffers since last mid-November. The differences between that sum and expenses is approximately one hundred thousand dollars—on the profit side of the ledger."[42]

Both for Ponselle and for the Metropolitan Opera, the revival of Meyerbeer's *L'africana* had been a successful undertaking, at least from the box-office standpoint. Richard Aldrich, reviewing the first performance in *The New York Times*, commented on the "enormous audience" that had come to hear "some of the foremost singers of the company" in "a handsome, even a sumptuous, production." But the music of *L'africana* and its libretto, Aldrich thought, "reaches almost the limit of the preposterous in the absurdity of its plot and the stupidity of some of the characters":

> Even the admirers and defenders of Meyerbeer in the past have scant words of praise for *L'africaine*. According to Clément, the libretto is "pitiful" as we have it; "what must it have been before it was retouched and remade?" Others have found it "absurd," its incidents "preposterous," some of its characters "unattractive." The listener of today can certainly find no better words for it. It must be put among the operas that live in spite of their librettos.

> As for the music, it seems on the whole poor enough now, though it would not be difficult to give it a higher place than that of *Le prophète*, which was "revived" briefly at the Metropolitan a few years ago. It has still all the earmarks of Meyerbeer's "eclectic" style; a lack, that is to say, of any real style, a too frequent deficiency in warmth and emotional sincerity, a lapse more than occasional into triviality, bombast, and bad taste.[43]

Although Aldrich considered "the most beautiful thing in the opera . . . the air sung by Vasco da Gama in the fourth act, 'O paradiso,'" he did not consider the role an ideal fit for the voice of Beniamino Gigli: "It makes exacting demands upon his voice that had better not be made. He will do well not to be 'Caruso's successor,' but to keep his extremely beautiful voice and finished style for music that is best adapted to it."[44]

A week later, Aldrich offered his readers a more pointed assessment of Gigli's apparent ambition to become the "new" Caruso. Acknowledging that the young tenor had done "much beautiful singing" since his arrival at the Metropolitan, Aldrich took Gigli to task for his "corroding ambition lately to pour forth volume and sonority; to reach and hold high notes till the rafters ring. . . . Here [in *L'africana*] it is perfectly evident that [Gigli] considers it his opportunity to be the successor of Caruso, and he bawls it out in every aria he sings."[45]

Although Ponselle's performances as Selika netted few extensive reviews at the time, most of the notices she received were favorable. Aldrich described her Selika as "powerful and robust, physically and vocally," and judged that she had sung the role "in wholly competent style."[46] The reviewer for the *American*, while reserving most of his praise for Gigli's Vasco, also found much to favor with her Selika: "Miss Ponselle brought to the fore as much of the princess as fairly could have been expected [and] vocally her performance was of a very high order. In common with Mr. Gigli, her employment of tonal shading, especially as demonstrated by her ability to enlarge or diminish a tone at will, was not merely evidence of a sound singing technique, but also was inerrant from a dramatic point of view."[47]

After performing the role several more times, Ponselle earned more favorable reviews, some of which attested to her continuing maturation as an artist. Reviewing a January 1924 performance at the Metropolitan, *Musical America* labeled her an "artist who has developed apace," and ventured that she sang Selika "in her best style . . . despite the limited opportunities afforded by the librettist, Scribe."[48] Olin Downes, a respected critic for *The New York Times*, expressed a similar regard for her Selika: "Miss Ponselle . . . won applause, in the first place because of the superb quality of her voice; secondly, because, although her artistry does not match her natural vocal endowment, she has improved as a singer in later seasons and has, at moments, hints and flashes of the grand manner."[49]

Despite being "heard by a large audience,"[50] the revival of *William Tell* on 5 January 1923 merited rather little in the way of enthusiasm from the critics.[51]

Only nine performances of *Tell* were given in the Metropolitan Opera House during the 1922–23 and 1923–24 seasons.[52] Giovanni Martinelli's Arnold, more than Ponselle's Matilda, consistently garnered the most favorable reviews. "Arnold is the high part par excellence for heroic tenors," wrote Pitts Sanburn. "And . . . Giovanni Martinelli sings it with a minimum of forcing, really reaching in it the apex not only of his scale but of his New York career."[53]

As was the case with Martinelli in *Tell*, Beniamino Gigli remained the attraction in *Andrea Chénier* for the critics and public alike. "The revolutionary poet is one of Mr. Gigli's best parts," wrote W. J. Henderson. "He is not temperamentally revolutionary, but he can sing the music well."[54] As for Ponselle's performance, Henderson had little to say—and did so in a mere one sentence: "Miss Ponselle, as Maddalena, was praiseworthy last evening."[55]

The *Musical Courier*, reviewing "the season's first appearances of Rosa Ponselle and Titta Ruffo," lauded each of the principals in the *Andrea Chénier* cast:

> Miss Ponselle was in strikingly fine voice and her acting had great animation and dramatic effectiveness. She was earnestly applauded and brought repeatedly before the curtain. Mr. Ruffo, too, sang superbly, employing his rich and powerful voice with notable artistry and infusing his acting with abundant emotion. The role of the unfortunate poet was enacted with great distinction by Mr. Gigli, and the latter's singing was characterized by power and purity of tone together with admirable phrasing and control of nuance. Both he and Ruffo were hailed with delight by the huge audience.[56]

Echoing Ponselle's fond recollections, *Musical America* reported that Ruffo "was clapped and cheered after everything he sang, and [the applause for] 'Nemico della patria' interrupted the performance for several minutes."[57]

To those who may have preferred a tenor who was (to borrow Henderson's phrase) more "temperamentally revolutionary" than Beniamino Gigli, the newly arrived Giacomo Lauri-Volpi fit the bill. Acclaimed by Pitts Sanborn for his "all-around excellence" and "fine stage presence,"[58] and by Olin Downes for his "manly, ringing" tone and "triple fortissimo" upper range,[59] Lauri-Volpi's trumpet-like high notes earned him a vociferous following with Metropolitan Opera audiences.

In the season's second *Il trovatore* at the Met, Ponselle sang Leonora and "was applauded to the echo." "Her gorgeous voice was never more beautiful," said *Musical America*. "She is in such absolute command of all her powers as a singer and as an actress that she electrifies with her clarion high notes, and inspires with her incomparable mezzo."[60]

The performance in which Giacomo Lauri-Volpi incurred Ponselle's lasting disfavor took place during a matinee performance of *Il Trovatore* on Thursday, 6 December 1928.[61] The incident was reported in soap-opera terms by the Philadelphia *Inquirer* a few weeks later:

> In the first scene of the first act, everything rippled along melodiously. Then came the second scene, Lauri-Volpi as Manrico, playing heavy lover to Miss Ponselle. . . . His rival is Giuseppe Danise, a Count, and [is] not successful at the romance stuff. Danise is a baritone.
>
> They are in a garden. Leonora discovers by lifting a mask that the Troubadour is none other than Manrico. Thereupon the Count challenges him to a duel. The scene ends with the trio rising to the D-flat region. That is, Leonora and Manrico hit that note.
>
> It is usually held for two beats. Sometimes three. On this occasion Miss Ponselle and Mr. Lauri-Volpi held it five together, but Lauri-Volpi kept on going—continued for three more beats to establish a record. No other prima donna ever suffered this experience on the Metropolitan Opera House stage. She thought with lightning alacrity. To conceal her embarrassment, she plunged into the action of the opera, fainting to separate the two duelists.
>
> But Lauri-Volpi was oblivious to her ruse. It all happened so swiftly. The audience burst into applause—Miss Ponselle broke into tears. As the curtain dropped, Miss Ponselle fainted. That was in keeping with her part. To many it seemed a realistic bit of acting.
>
> "Why did you shame me out there?" she remonstrated [to Lauri-Volpi]. "I finished long, long before you. Why, why did you do it?"
>
> She continued to weep. Attendants tried to pacify her. She was on the verge of hysteria. Lauri-Volpi hastened to his dressing room.
>
> Three assistant directors of the Met went to his dressing room and pleaded with him to apologize to Miss Ponselle. But Lauri-Volpi, also emotionally distressed, could say nothing.[62]

According to Libbie Miller, Lauri-Volpi's temper flared at the very mention of an apology. He would not apologize, he insisted, for what was nothing more than an artistic liberty on his part.[63] But when the New York *Daily News* printed its version of the incident and proceeded to quote Lauri-Volpi's "secretary" as having said that the incident was caused by Ponselle's inability to sustain her breath, Lauri-Volpi and Metropolitan publicist William J. Guard codrafted a letter to the *Daily News*' editor:[64]

> Dear Sir:
>
> I am deeply pained by the publicity given by the press to a trifling incident during last Monday's performance of *Il trovatore*. The impression was given that I intentionally held onto a final high note in the Trio ending

> the second [*sic*] act, thus causing a painful annoyance to my dear fellow artist, Rosa Ponselle. There is no artist I know for whom I have a higher regard and of whose brilliant success, as an Italian, I am proud. The statement that we had unpleasant words because I held the note longer than she did, is absolutely untrue as is the statement that I held my note "because her breath gave out." This is nonsense. Miss Ponselle's voice never gives out. I was quite unconscious of what happened for I was not standing near enough to know that she had ended her note before me.
>
> I trust that you will publish this note and do justice to both Miss Ponselle and myself, especially since the story was given currency by an individual claiming to be my secretary whereas I have no secretary. It would be shocking to leave the public under the utterly erroneous impression that we are not the best of friends.
>
> Very truly yours,
> LAURI-VOLPI

Although a draft was shown to Ponselle before it was delivered to the newspaper, she remained unmoved by his explanation that he "was not standing near enough to know that she had ended her note before me." As Libbie Miller recalled, Ponselle had said, "With his education, he can surely count the number of beats in the score, can't he?"[65] Realizing that some form of an apology was all but inevitable, Lauri-Volpi then wrote Ponselle the following letter, in Italian, and had it hand-delivered to her penthouse address:[66]

> I am genuinely sorry to learn through my friend Mr. Cimarra that a New York newspaper has dared to arbitrarily stir up an unfortunate incident that was, as you know, definitely over and done with, by the letter written by both Mr. Guard and me, in your presence, signed and sent to the press. Evidently, this newspaper has the intention of creating scandals; at any rate, it tries to pit artists against one another.
>
> I understand your justified disdain and I beg you to rectify the truth so that you will be convinced that I (who do not read the newspapers and who does not aspire to ridiculous publicity) am totally estranged from the machinations of some people who seem to harbor bad intentions.
>
> Please preserve our friendship and believe that I am sincerely your cordial admirer.

Handwritten on the stationery of the Ansonia Hotel, where Lauri-Volpi kept an apartment during the Metropolitan Opera season, the letter did much to pacify Ponselle, according to Libbie Miller. As the tenor's tempestuous ways became increasingly evident both on stage and off, however, other colleagues were not always as forgiving.

Although Ponselle's attitude toward Lauri-Volpi hardened over the years, the tenor's recollections of his performances with her were more balanced, in the main. While he admitted a preference for Muzio in a number of the roles he also performed with Ponselle (in *Voci parallele* he described Muzio's as "a voice of tears, and sighs, and restrained interior fire"), Lauri-Volpi continued to speak well of Ponselle during her retirement.[67] In 1978, reflecting on his association with her at the Metropolitan and subsequently in Florence at the first Maggio Musicale Fiorentino (or May Festival), he wrote of Ponselle: "This great soprano sang *La Vestale* at the Maggio [Musicale] Fiorentino with great success. I sang with her in *La traviata*: it was Ponselle's first performance in this opera at the Metropolitan, where we sang together during several seasons [in] *Il trovatore*, *La gioconda*, *L'africana*, *Luisa Miller*, and *Andrea Chénier*."[68]

Although in his memoirs and letters he was silent about the so-called D-flat tragedy, Lauri-Volpi did not entirely ignore the subject of high notes in his assessment of Ponselle's successes. Of her Aida he wrote that "Ponselle was stupendous," but added, "thereafter [she] avoided [*Aida*], perhaps because of the high range of the famous *romanza* in the Nile [Scene]."[69]

On Monday, 8 December 1924, *The New York Times* reported that "one of the greatest crowds in the history of the Metropolitan . . . attempted to enter that theatre last evening for an extraordinary concert [which] . . . far surpassed any other such assembly in persistent and frantic efforts to get in." The concert, said the *Times*, had been "arranged as a tribute of international stars to the memory of Giacomo Puccini."[70] Although the no-encores rule was difficult to enforce with so many first-rank stars on the same program, the behavior of the audience, according to the *Times*, "was noticeably modified by the nature of a memorial occasion."[71]

Beneath the headline "Great Throng Surges to Puccini Concert," the *Times* sub-headline read, "Mme Jeritza and Gigli Among the Many Stars in Excerpts from Favorite Puccini Roles." As was often the case in the mid-1920s, Maria Jeritza commanded headline coverage that no other Metropolitan soprano, including Ponselle, was likely to match when the attractive and flamboyant Jeritza was within range of the cameras. Although in later years Ponselle would dismiss rumors of her rivalry with Jeritza by insisting that they were "made up by other people," the version told by her secretary attests that the rivalry was indeed real—certainly on Ponselle's part, and apparently on Jeritza's as well:

> When Rosa was doing *Norma*, she was always tense and she wanted everything just so. It was my job to see that everything was the way she wanted it. Before each performance, and even before the big rehearsals, I would go to the opera house early enough to get her dressing room in order. At the old Met, the women's dressing rooms were on one side of the house, and the

men's were on the opposite side. Of course, not every star had her own dressing room. Because every singer of any importance thinks he or she is a star, no opera house could ever be big enough to house that many dressing rooms! So, the singers have to share, and they alternate using the same dressing rooms.

One afternoon I came to the opera house early, to get the dressing room ready for Rosa. She was to sing *Norma* that night. Well, the dressing room was locked. Jeritza was using it, and she was up on the roof [part of which had been turned into a rehearsal area] and was getting herself ready for *Cavalleria rusticana* or some other opera that was hardly that important, compared to *Norma*. Jeritza's dressing-room maid was nowhere to be found, and nobody wanted to interrupt Jeritza just to find out where the key was. It was getting later and later, and finally I got tired of the run-around I was getting. So I got together some of the stagehands, and I had them take the hinges off the door.

Right about then, Rosa arrived—and, of course, the dressing room wasn't ready. Well, she had a fit! When I told her that Jeritza hadn't vacated the dressing room when she was supposed to, [Rosa] threw an even bigger fit. She grabbed everything of Jeritza's that wasn't nailed down, and she threw it in one big heap, right in the middle of the hallway![72]

An undated clipping in one of Ponselle's scrapbooks provides a glimpse of her feelings toward Jeritza early in the latter's Metropolitan Opera career. A review from the Cleveland (Ohio) *News* was pasted in her scrapbook for the 1922–23 season. Its headline read, "Jeritza Fails to Achieve Triumph." "Let's have the truth," the report declared. "Cleveland's multitude at Public Hall revealed a disappointment at least during Madame's early selections." At the bottom of the clipping, a one-word assessment—YES!—was written in bold pencil strokes. The handwriting was Ponselle's.

In April 1920 the cover-page headline of the Columbia Graphophone Company's monthly supplement to its dealers announced the "First Ponselle Sister Duet." Listed as record number 78846 and retailing for $1.50, Rosa's and Carmela's rendition of the "Barcarolle" from *Les contes d'Hoffmann* gave Columbia buyers "the first opportunity of hearing the Ponselle sisters together." The editorial content of the supplement would have required not only the sisters' prior approval but also William Thorner's:

> One of the fairy stories of American musical history is the tale of Rosa and Carmela Ponselle. Everyone knows the famous Rosa has a sister and many have heard her sing. But not everyone knows it was the beautifully rich mezzo-soprano voice of Carmela which first attracted the attention of the well-known maestro, William Thorner, in New York. It was Carmela's voice which "soared like a released bird" after a few lessons. It was Carmela

> who persuaded the maestro to also accept her sister as a pupil. And, to make the story short, it is the Columbia Company which has the pleasure of exclusive contracts not only with Rosa but her sister Carmela.[73]

"Where the voices sing in unison," the copywriter added, "the effect is as of one beautiful voice. Where they divide it is but a double beauty."[74]

By May 1922, in half-page advertisements in many metropolitan newspapers, the Columbia interests were busily promoting fourteen recordings by Rosa Ponselle: "Casta diva" from *Norma*, "Kiss Me Again" from *Mlle Modiste*, "Maria Marì," "Old Folks At Home," the "Siciliana" from *I vespri siciliani*, "Values," the "Suicidio" from *La gioconda*, "La Vergine degli angeli" from *Forza*, "Un bel dì" from *Madama Butterfly*, "O patria mia" from *Aida*, "Voi lo sapete" from *Cavalleria rusticana*, "D'amor sull' ali rosee" from *Il trovatore*, "Keep the Home Fires Burning," and Tosti's familiar "Goodbye."[75] Also advertised were two duets that Ponselle had recorded with Barbara Maurel ("Whispering Hope" and "Abide With Me"), and another duet with Carmela—"Comin' Thro' the Rye," which had been a staple in their vaudeville act.

In June 1922 *Musical America* sent an interviewer to the Columbia studios to observe Ponselle during a recording session:

> Twenty-three stories above the bustle of Columbus Circle, a dozen musicians were perched on elevated chairs in a close semicircle before a funnel-shaped contrivance. It was the critical moment in the phonograph recording room when a voice is to engrave itself indelibly upon a "master" record. The time was a recent rather warm afternoon, and the voice was the justly celebrated one of Rosa Ponselle, soprano of the Metropolitan.
>
> The opulent tones of the artist rose in the "Ave Maria" of Desdemona, and the players bent to their task under the potent bâton of Romano Romani, and presently the task was ended. Miss Ponselle emerged cheerfully from the singer's most critical ordeal—for not even the keenest ear among auditors is so ruthless as the recording machine. It was evident that the artist loved singing in any form.
>
> "I would rather sing a whole opera for you than give an interview!" she declared solemnly a moment later. "I do not like to talk about myself. I am an artist—not an orator!
>
> "Do I like to sing for the phonograph? Yes, indeed. It is rather like singing for the radio. One does not see one's audience, and that is a pity. I love to sing directly for my audience. I think that the artist ought to speak to the public, as they say, 'heart to heart' . . . [and] I am at home with the people who sit in front of me."[76]

At the close of the interview, when asked about her plans for the remainder of the summer (1922), she replied, "Now, as to my vacation, you ask whether I am going to Europe: not this year." Europe, she said, would be in her plans for the following summer. "You see, I want a *real* rest. There would be too short a time before I fulfill my early concert dates."

In spring 1923, as Columbia released several new Ponselle recordings, reviews of the new discs appeared in a number of syndicated newspaper columns. Of her "Rachem" release, which she recorded for Columbia on 8 January 1921, reviewer Lawton McCall wrote: "Though the work of a living composer, this work has an elemental intensity of a human cry from some remote Old Testament era. It fairly grips the listener. Ponselle sings it with dramatic power and rounded richness of tone. And what soprano can more wonderfully combine compassion with vocal poise, [and] emotional thrill with lyric limpidity? Truly, Ponselle's singing of the vivid heart-wail fills one with a feeling of awe."[77]

Of her Columbia disc of "Tacea la notte" from *Il Trovatore*, which she recorded on 16 November 1922 with Romano Romani conducting, the same reviewer commented: "This is light lyricism of the sort that one associates with Maria Barrientos [but] Miss Ponselle executes the trills and floridity with coloratura deftness. Always there is that warmth of tone that is peculiarly Ponselle's, and in the slower passages there is a deep feeling which gives to the smooth-flowing melody a human significance more potent, perhaps, than Verdi dreamed of when he composed it."[78]

"There are records newly released this month," Lawton McCall concluded, "which, if unearthed thirty centuries hence, would be remarkable discoveries indeed. Imagine the amazement of a human being in that far future era hearing a dusty disc give forth the glorious voice of Ponselle!" Ironically, only three years later, in 1926, one such "dusty disc" had a profound effect upon a precocious eight-year-old boy. Fifty years later, the boy who had been so affected by Ponselle's singing—Leonard Bernstein—described his youthful reactions in a personal letter to the singer: "Yours was the first operatic voice I ever heard, at age eight, on an old Columbia 78, singing 'Suicidio.' Even through all the scratchy surface noise, that voice rang through in such glory that it made me a music-lover forever. I thank you every day of my life."[79]

Ponselle herself, as was seen earlier in these pages, had a low opinion of her acoustical recordings generally, and of her Columbia recordings in particular. Her dissatisfaction with their compressed tonal quality (the aural sensation of "singing inside a box," as she put it) was a concern to her as early as 1919. Speaking to a Hartford newspaper reporter in a preconcert interview that year, she said of her recordings, "It's work, the hardest kind of work, and especially so when you have a big voice. But, you know, only one-third of the volume is reproduced on the record, in any case."[80]

According to Libbie Miller, Rosa's decision to leave Columbia Graphophone and to accept a contract from the Victor Talking Machine Company was a business decision based upon two considerations. One was the widening chasm in the financial health of the two companies. Victor's well-known reputation for quality, which was undergirded by its exclusive contracts with most of the musical celebrities of the day and was bolstered by an aggressive and sophisticated marketing effort, had enabled Victor to assume the dominant position in the recording industry.

Although Columbia maintained a distant second place, its ability to keep its niche in the marketplace was worsened by the national recession of 1921. As Roland Gelatt claimed in *The Fabulous Phonograph*: "Columbia's ledger looked grimmer than ever. Gross sales, which had been forty-seven million dollars in 1920, dwindled to nineteen million dollars in 1921, and the red ink showed a net loss of $4,370,611. Francis S. Whitten, Columbia's chairman of the board, pleaded with its bondholders to accept a voluntary adjustment in interest payments . . . [but] in October 1923 the company went into receivership."[81]

The precarious financial health of the Columbia company, according to Libbie Miller, made it increasingly difficult for her to negotiate a more favorable contract for Rosa, especially as regards the issue of advances against royalties. "To Rosa's way of thinking," said Libbie, "a cash advance was like a bird in the hand, which was always better than waiting for other birds to appear in the bushes."[82] From the outset of her Columbia contract, Ponselle was paid an advance, against royalties, of $900 for every disc she approved for commercial release. Her financial ledgers for 1923 show that she earned a total of $6,750 in royalties from the Columbia Graphophone Company; the previous year, 1922, Columbia had paid her $12,487.50. The Victor Talking Machine Company, by contrast, not only gave her more latitude in choosing what she wanted to record but also agreed to pay her an annual advance of $20,000 against royalties.[83]

During the negotiations with Victor, as her secretary recalled, Rosa wielded as much influence as she could in order to help Carmela obtain a similar contract. Apparently, the decision-makers at Victor stipulated that Carmela must first agree to an audition. The company's recording logs list two test sessions as having taken place in New York on 3 December 1923, during which Carmela sang "Kiss Me With Your Eyes" and an "Ave Maria," with pianist Herbert Spencer as her accompanist. Both tests proved unsatisfactory and were rejected.[84]

On 5 December 1923, two days after Carmela Ponselle's audition session at Victor, Rosa made her first Red Seal recording. Amid a variety of other new releases (including recordings by pianist Olga Samaroff, the Victor Symphony Orchestra, radio balladeer Frank Crumit, comedienne Marie Cahill, and a then-new dance orchestra called Waring's Pennsylvanians), the first Victor recordings by Ponselle were announced by the company in a March 1924 press release: "Sentimentally, it is fortunate to be able to claim for America such an artist as Rosa Ponselle . . . and her almost awesomely great gifts should be a source of pride to us all. Her first Victor records, issued this week, are two great arias of the slave-girl princess from *Aida*—'Ritorna vincitor' (Return victorious) and 'O patria mia' (My native land). They are happily chosen for this artist."[85]

The following year, in *Victor Records*, the company's annual catalog, the editors wrote, "She pours into every syllable of song the sense of an intensely vital, human, responsive personality vibrating with the joy and the beauty and the tragedy of life. If any singer has the 'thinking heart,' it is she, and her records will attest it."[86]

Rosa's new presence in the Victor catalog, her brother Tony remembered, had a deeply personal significance for Maddalena Ponzillo. Unable to read, she was forced to content herself with the photographs that appeared in the catalog's Red Seal pages, a special section printed on pink paper for the user's convenience. "If Mother needed a little cheering up," Tony recalled, "she would pick up the Victor catalog and thumb through those pink pages until she found Caruso's photograph. She would mark the place [and] then would keep turning the pages until she came to Rosa's picture. Mother couldn't read a word on the page, God bless her. But if you saw her face, you could read her thoughts: Enrico Caruso was in that book, and her Rose was there with him."[87]

CHAPTER SIX

A Perfect Voice

In 1954, seventeen years after Ponselle retired from the opera stage, she was persuaded by the Metropolitan management to be interviewed on radio. Tape-recorded in Baltimore, the interview was scheduled as an intermission feature during a Saturday matinee broadcast of *Norma.* To ensure proper timing, pace, and overall flow, the contents of the interview were scripted weeks in advance of the broadcast. During the two-day taping session at Villa Pace, Ponselle's pre-performance nerves resurfaced, causing the technicians to stop and start the recording equipment until she could read her lines properly; but with sufficient splicing and editing, the resulting broadcast was seamless enough to enable her to tell friends that she "didn't flub a word."[1] When her interviewer, Boris Goldovsky, asked her which of her roles had been the most challenging, she had no need for the typewritten script: "Norma and Gioconda," she answered unhesitatingly.[2]

In the judgment of most critics, Ponselle's ascent to *prima diva* status began with *Gioconda* and reached its apogee when Gatti-Casazza revived *Norma* for her. The demands of the two roles, she told Goldovsky, were severe though markedly different. "Gioconda is a savage part, full of violence, and Norma is classical," she said. "Norma feels emotion just as strongly as Gioconda, but [in *Norma*] you have to turn every phrase with elegance, no matter how dramatic. Then, too, the coloratura in *Norma* is formidable for any soprano with a big voice."[3]

Between *Gioconda* and *Norma*, Ponselle would add two new roles to her expanding repertoire: Giulia in Spontini's *La vestale* in 1925, and a year later, Fiora in Montemezzi's *L'amore dei tre re*, a role she shared with Lucrezia Bori.

She would also revisit two of her earlier roles: Rachel in *La Juive*, in which Martinelli succeeded Caruso as Eléazar, and Leonora in *Forza*, in which Martinelli was again her partner. In both operas she was well received by the critics, but in *La Juive* she was understandably overshadowed by Martinelli, who performed the role "amazingly well, singing . . . with great vigor and power."[4] Although Leonora in *Forza* stayed in her repertoire, Rachel held no lasting interest for her and the role was taken over by Florence Easton, who had sung it with Caruso during the tenor's final performance of *La Juive*. In the meantime, Ponselle laid claim to *La gioconda*.

Favoring an out-of-town trial performance, she sang her first *Gioconda* on tour in Philadelphia on Tuesday, 9 December 1924, and repeated it at the Metropolitan Opera House in a matinee the following Saturday. Scheduled as a Christmas season benefit for the New York Nursery and Child's Hospital, the afternoon performance "was welcomed in [a] holiday mood," according to *The New York Times*. As the title-heroine, with Gigli as her Enzo, Ponselle was acclaimed "a direct and vital singer," and was judged "fairly superb in [the] famous 'suicide air.'" As her admirers had expected, she "found the melodrama's title role suited to her rich voice and to a temperament that is this young American star's Italian heritage."[5] Ponselle was "greatly applauded," the *Times* noted, "bringing down the house when soprano and tenor before the curtain played a game of tag to see which should leave to the other the honor of taking a solo [curtain] call." Gigli insisted that she go first, "but she cleverly gave him the last call."[6]

The post-curtain scene was much the same the next autumn when Gatti-Casazza again paired Ponselle and Gigli in a season-opening *La gioconda*, "an inevitable sop to fashion," in the opinion of the *Times*,[7] although it enabled the Metropolitan to post record-breaking ticket sales for an opening night.[8] Heavily promoted in the newspapers as an "all-American opening" because of the number of American-born singers in the cast, the performance was to have featured Ponselle, Jeanne Gordon, and Merle Alcock. But within hours of the performance both Gordon and Alcock became indisposed and had to be replaced by Margarete Matzenauer and Marion Telva.[9] "No jinx curbed the attendance, however, for it was necessary to turn away two thousand hopefuls," Grace Robinson wrote in the New York *News*. "There was a jam of limousines, a majestic parade up the red velvet stairs, the opening strains of *La gioconda*—and lo, the New York social season of the winter was on!"[10]

From the standees, who crowded along the railings at the back of the opera house, to the diamond-adorned social register members seated comfortably in their boxes (the Clarence Mackays in box 15, the E. F. Huttons in box 22, the Harry F. Sinclairs in box 28, and the Vanderbilts, Goelets, and Whitneys in the low-numbered boxes known as "Vanderbilt Row" in the society columns),[11] the audience's applause for Ponselle "was deservedly unceasing," said Pitts Sanborn in the *Telegram*, and was "scarcely less so for Gigli."[12]

As would be the case every time the two were cast as Enzo and Gioconda, however, Ponselle dominated the stage, both vocally and histrionically. Despite the "sheer beauty of voice" in Gigli's Enzo—and despite the fact that Gigli himself maintained that *Gioconda* "belongs to the tenor"[13]—critic Max de Schauensee judged that "the fickle spotlight suddenly shifted from Mr. Gigli to Miss Ponselle, who has since been estimated as the greatest Gioconda in New York operatic history."[14] Only when Titta Ruffo entered the cast on 9 January 1925 was the spotlight deflected. On that occasion, de Schauensee recalled, "the beauty of 'Cielo e mar' and the tribulations of the heroine were momentarily dwarfed as the audience shouted welcome to the new and huge-voiced idol." But even then, the most vociferous applause occurred during the first act when Ponselle created "a truly memorable dramatic moment and an enviable vocal feat" by holding a pianissimo high B-flat while making her exit in a slow walk across much of the Metropolitan stage. "I would sing the line 'Enzo! madre mia!,' and take a few steps, walking very slowly," Ponselle remembered. "Then I'd take a good long breath, stop, and stand still for a second or two, and then I would start the line, 'Enzo, come t'amo!' On the word *amo* I would take the B-flat in pianissimo, and I would walk all the way from the footlights across the stage holding that note." Serafin, she said, "would breathe with me—that's how well he knew my singing. He would pace the orchestra according to how long he thought I would be able to sustain that note, and he stayed with me at every beat."[15]

Neither *La gioconda* nor the upcoming debuts of three of Gatti-Casazza's newest acquisitions (Lauritz Melchior, identified in the *Times* as "the Danish tenor who has been singing Wagnerian roles at Bayreuth," Marion Talley, "the young lady from Kansas City, a singer of coloratura persuasion,"[16] and Carmela Ponselle, "a mezzo-soprano with a voice said to be near in quality to that of her celebrated sister")[17] were as newsworthy in the 1925–26 season as the Metropolitan Opera premiere of *La vestale*. Initially, most critics assumed that this would be the first performance of Spontini's best-known work anywhere in the United States. Within a week, however, the assumption was shown to be erroneous: the *Times* reported that according to documents from New Orleans and Philadelphia, in the 1820s the opera had been heard in both cities.[18]

The historic significance of *La vestale* was undeniable. Olin Downes wrote of its place in opera's "chain of evolution"—a phrase that had gained national currency six months earlier when Clarence Darrow, squaring off against William Jennings Bryan, had defended a Tennessee biology teacher who was on trial for teaching evolution. Operatically, Downes ventured, the evolutionary "case" for *La vestale* was compelling:

> *La vestale* was—is—an outstanding grand opera of the pre-Weber period. It is one of the most conspicuous links in the chain of operatic evolution, from Gluck to Weber and the Wagnerian opera beyond. Thanks to this work, Spontini held for some years a dominating position among European opera composers of the beginning of the nineteen century. In that period—to be exact, until the performances of Weber's *Freischütz* in 1821—he was one of the most important personalities of the lyric theatre. He gauged well the public taste of his time, and for a time satisfied it. He also anticipated in a genuinely creative manner some of the very reforms and musico-dramatic practices which later caused his most significant work to recede in the public esteem.[19]

With Weber's *Der Freischütz*, however, came "the melody and romanticism of the German people," against which "Spontini and all the influences he could bring to bear [were] powerless." But, as Downes reminded his readers, historic significance does not necessarily translate into good box office—and how well this century-old, nearly forgotten work would appeal to a modern audience would remain to be decided "when the faithful, duly assembled, will sit in judgment" at the Metropolitan Opera House.[20]

With a cast pairing Ponselle and Edward Johnson as Giulia and Licinio, with Serafin conducting, and with de Luca, Matzenauer, and Mardones in the supporting roles, the premiere was a critical success. Downes, in the *Times*, judged the production "one of the best the Metropolitan has recently given,"[21] and W. J. Henderson ventured that the role of Giulia had "furnished Rosa Ponselle with . . . the loftiest flight of her young career."[22]

But Giulia in *La vestale* was merely a prelude to the role Ponselle next undertook. "One of our most interesting and important revivals," Giulio Gatti-Casazza wrote in his memoirs, ". . . was that of Bellini's *Norma*, an opera which I was very proud to be able to present with adequate interpreters to the Metropolitan public. In the noble masterpiece, so difficult for the singers that few opera houses present it today, Ponselle was magnificent." Both in New York and on tour, the critics and public echoed Gatti's assessment. "As it is now," W. J. Henderson wrote after *Norma*, "she is without doubt the foremost dramatic soprano of the Italian opera."[23]

The Interview

From interviews of Rosa Ponselle by the author (March 1973 and February 1978), by John Secrist (1949; precise date unknown), by Hugh M. Johns (June–July 1968), by William Seward (December 1971), by John and Susan Harvith (July 1976), and by Fred Calland (1977, precise date unknown). Transcribed with minor editing.

Most opera historians are of the opinion that Norma *was the high point of your career. Do you agree?*

It was a great challenge. I still get butterflies when I think of it. I had a lot of sleepless nights, worrying about how I was going to do in *Norma*.

Vocally, was it the most difficult of all the roles you sang?

It put the most pressure on me, so [in] that way it was the hardest role. Not that all of it was hard. Some parts [of the score] were easier than others.

For instance?

The "Casta diva" and also the duets with Adalgisa weren't so difficult. But I'm only talking about what came easier for me. It might be different for other singers. Anyway, no matter who you are, *Norma* is very demanding. It takes a dramatic coloratura [voice], and you have to have very good preparation to do it right.

And from an acting standpoint?

You mean the character? Well, Norma isn't what I would call a living character—not like Santuzza, or Violetta, or Carmen. It takes some work to make Norma a real character—which you do by [accenting] how torn she is and [by] bringing out all the despair she feels, such as with [the fate of] her children and [as in] the confession she makes to the Druids at the end [of the opera]. The way the opera ends, you see, she reveals herself as a woman, not as the Druids' great leader.

How long did you actually study Norma*?*

I took two years to prepare it.

Did you do your preparation in Italy with Serafin, as you had with La gioconda*?*

No. I spent two summers at Lake Placid working on *Norma*. I had a friend, Ghizene Stephens, who owned a resort on the lake, and I rented a place there for those two summers. It was just Romani and I [during] that first summer, although my secretary, Edith, was with us on and off, and my sister came to visit occasionally. But this was work, not a vacation. Serafin and I had worked on *Norma* in New York, and then Romani and I spent that first summer working on things that [Serafin] had gone over with us [in New York]. The next summer, we had Marion Telva with us at Lake Placid. She came for five weeks, and we spent most of the time going over the duets between Norma and Adalgisa. We got so we could do them in our sleep!

You have said in some interviews that, in Norma *as with other roles, you could actually "see" yourself on stage and that you would develop your characterization and even your costuming [based] on what your imagination would reveal to you. Would you elaborate on that, especially as it relates to* Norma*?*

I would lie in bed very late at night—maybe three or four in the morning—and I would sight-read the score. I would sing it to myself—sing it in my head, in other words. The more I would concentrate, I could begin to see myself on stage. It was like looking at myself from the other side of the footlights.

How did you derive this picture of yourself? Where did it come from?

From the score, from the music, and [from] the words the character is supposed to sing. The music and the words would give me a picture in my mind. Once I had that picture in my head, I had something to create, something to develop. It would give me ideas about how I wanted my costumes to look, what colors I wanted to use, all those things.

Rosa Raisa sang Norma *with the Chicago Opera Company before the Metropolitan Opera revived the opera for you. Did you see Raisa's* Norma*?*

Oh, she was a *great* Norma! When I heard Raisa in *Norma*, it scared the life out of me. That's how demanding I thought it was. I never heard so much coloratura for a dramatic soprano—and so many high Cs!

Would you describe the difference between your voice and hers, and how this affected your conceptions of the role of Norma?

Raisa had a marvelous voice—a big, bright sound, especially at the top. It was a real dramatic soprano, and her voice was right for *Norma*. And what a top! She could sing high Cs all day.

For some reason—maybe it's traceable to her recordings—Raisa's voice is not as well regarded today as it obviously was in her time. Some writers have said that it was more a thrilling than a beautiful voice and that it was not well equalized. As you remember it, was her tone consistent from the lowest part of her range to the highest?

I thought she carried her chest voice a little too high. The middle [of her range] was more lyrical, and she tried to make it bigger than it really was. To do that, she carried her chest tones higher than maybe she should have, to compensate for the size [of her middle range]. I don't know if you would call it a break in the voice, but there was a difference in [the quality of sound at] the top compared to her lower range. The higher she sang, her tones got brighter and brighter. It wasn't a wide sound or a broad sound at the top, but her high notes had lots and lots of resonance and a nice *squillo*.

Were you worried at all about being compared to Raisa in Norma*?*

No, because after I heard her I told Romani and everybody else around me that *Norma* was one opera I was never going to do.

What changed your mind?

I found out later that there was a conspiracy to get me to do *Norma*. Gatti, you see, had been thinking about [my doing *Norma*] ever since my audition, when he gave me the "Casta diva" to prepare. That's how far ahead he was thinking. Then when Serafin came [to the Metropolitan] and I did *Gioconda*, that was another step [toward *Norma*] because it was very dramatic, very demanding. Then came *Vestale*, which was just the right preparation for *Norma*. In *Vestale*, you have to be able to handle the long [vocal] lines that Spontini wrote. *Norma* is full of those too. Where they're different is in the coloratura [demands]; *Vestale* doesn't have the coloratura that *Norma* does.

When did Gatti-Casazza first broach the subject of Norma *with you?*

Around the time I did *Vestale*. That's when Gatti told me they were ready to have me do *Norma*. So it was a conspiracy, as I call it, that Gatti, Serafin, and Romani were planning for me. But I was completely in the dark about it until I did *Vestale*.

You sang La vestale *at its Metropolitan Opera premiere. How did you react when Gatti-Casazza first approached you about doing Giulia? Did you have any familiarity with the opera at the time he initially discussed it with you?*

No. Nobody had given [*La vestale*] in New York before the Met put it on.

Do you recall your reactions when Gatti first mentioned Vestale *to you ?*

I talked about it with Romani—I talked about every new role with him. Doing *Vestale* was going to be a great challenge. The music is difficult. It's not so much the tessitura—although that's no piece of cake, either—but the vocal line and the breathing that's required in those long phrases are what's hard about it. I liked doing *Vestale*, though, and, naturally, I was flattered that Gatti wanted to give it to me, [its] being a premiere. That was the first time I was in a premiere where I was going to be the "star," if you could say it like that.

Aren't you forgetting Breil's The Legend*?*

Around here, dinner is served at seven o'clock. Don't ruin it.

In La vestale, *your Licinio was Edward Johnson. Later on, of course, the two of you had a different relationship as diva and general manager. What was your relationship like in* Vestale*?*

Oh, we never had any problem between us, not in *Vestale*. We had some differences about my staying at the Met, but that was a lot later. Eddie Johnson was a love and a good tenor too.

Would you consider him the equal, say, of Martinelli as a vocalist or as an actor?

You can't really compare them. Eddie Johnson's voice was much more lyrical than Martinelli's. Johnson sang some *spinto* roles, but he didn't have the *spinto* voice, not anything like Martinelli had. I always think of Eddie Johnson with Bori in *Pelléas et Mélisande* and *L'amore dei tre re* and in *Peter Ibbetson* with Bori and Tibbett. Johnson and Bori were quite a pair on stage. To me, Eddie Johnson was the Bori of the tenors—he was a good actor and a good artist, like she was. Not the most beautiful voice you ever heard but a very good artist—and a nice-looking man too.

Margarete Matzenauer sang the role of the High Priestess in Vestale. *Do you recall any details of her performances?*

I always liked to sing with her. We weren't close friends or anything, but we sang together a lot, and we were very good together. The blend of [our] voices was very nice in *Vestale*, and we could "read" each other too. Matzenauer was an excellent musician, you know. She was a wonderful partner in *La vestale*.

Do you recall the costumes you wore in La vestale*?*

It was like what you would see on a Madonna [statue]. The material was very sheer, more of a cream color than pure white. I played Giulia with dark hair in the Metropolitan production, but in Florence I played her with long blond hair. Over there, that's the way they wanted her to look.

How did your Norma *costume differ from the one you wore in* La vestale*?*

My *Norma* costume was very delicate. The material was very thin—it was flimsy, really—and it had a long train with mother-of-pearl beads on it. The pearls were hand-sewn onto the train, and there were some on the front of the dress too. I wore a cincture around the waist, and where the two ends were tied there was a little medallion with a jewel in it. I wore a dark red wig—it was an auburn red, kind of wild and unkempt looking. Most other sopranos portrayed Norma as a blond, you know, but I deliberately chose dark red because I wanted to make her seem almost unearthly, especially in the first act. That's where her power is really felt. After that, it's her womanliness that comes through.

Ezio Pinza made his Metropolitan debut as Pontifex Maximus in Vestale, *and he was also cast with you as Oroveso in* Norma. *What was your impression of his voice and artistry at that time?*

I didn't think too much about him, really. In *Vestale* I preferred [José] Mardones, but he left the Met not too long after that. Of course, Pinza had a nice voice, but it was a little different than it was later on. When he was in *Vestale* and *Norma* it was higher, a little lighter, but still a bass sound—just not as much as it became when he got older. Anyway, he was new, and he wasn't Mardones, so I didn't give him much thought.

Was Pinza a good actor at that stage of his career?

There's not much acting for the bass to do, either in *Vestale* or in *Norma*. Oroveso and the High Priest are just toga roles, as we used to call them.

Because you were the center point of the Norma *revival, were you given any particular say about the casting of the principals?*

No. Well, except for [Marion] Telva. I wanted her for Adalgisa.

How did you arrive at Telva as your choice?

I heard her at the Met, of course, and she sang one or two performances of *La vestale* with me on [the Metropolitan's annual] tour. I liked her voice, and I had her sing through part of the "Mira, o Norma" with me—this was at Romani's studio—and I thought we sounded wonderful together. You see, the timbres of Norma and Adalgisa have to be just right. That was one thing that bothered me about the Chicago production with Raisa.

Do you remember who was Raisa's Adalgisa?

[Gabriella] Besanzoni, in the performance I heard. That was a great voice too. But I didn't think the timbres of their voices were the right match. Besanzoni's timbre had a metallic edge to it, and it was a contralto sound. She and Raisa sang the duets in a higher key than we did, which made them sound too bright.

Meaning by "bright" that the sound was penetrating rather than mellow?

Yes. And that's why for me, Telva was just right to sing Adalgisa. Her voice was a perfect match for mine. It was a very mellow voice, and it was just dark enough that it didn't sound higher than mine.

I'm curious about two other singers who sang Adalisa to your Norma: Gladys Swarthout and Elda Vettori. How would you characterize the blend of your voice with each of theirs?

Oh, Swarthout was a good Adalgisa—no question about that. The color [of her voice] was a little light, but she was a very good Adalgisa.

And Elda Vettori?

I don't ever remember singing *Norma* with her. I remember her from *Traviata*, which was later [January 1935], but I can't place her as Adalgisa. If

I did it with her at all, it must have been a benefit or something, or maybe it was on tour. I can't tell you a thing about her in *Norma*.

Would Ebe Stignani, who sang Vestale *with you in Florence several years later, also have been a good vocal match for you in* Norma*?*

No. We were just right for each other in *Vestale*—even better than Matzenauer and I were at the Met—but Stignani's voice had too much soprano in it to sing Adalgisa with me. You see, I had just the opposite problem. I could pass for a mezzo. Stignani might have sounded more like a soprano than I did. *Norma*, you know, was originally done with sopranos in both roles. We don't know how the original [singers] sounded, of course. But to my way of thinking, Stignani and I would not have been right together in *Norma*.

As I'm sure you know, the mezzo quality of your voice led some critics to conjecture that your "natural" voice may have been a mezzo-soprano's. At any point in your career, did you ever give serious thought to making the switch to mezzo-soprano roles?

Not seriously, no. But it didn't stop me from envying all those mezzos. I used to stand in the wings and listen to them, and it would make me think how much I would like to have sung Amneris, Laura, Dalila, and all those wonderful parts. My voice was dark enough in color, and it was low enough in range too. As a mezzo, I could have let myself go dramatically without worrying about the next high C coming up.

As you hardly need me to point out, the score of Norma *has a number of high Cs in it. I have yet to read a review of your Norma in which your high notes were faulted in any way. Did you sing them in key?*

In *Norma*, just like *Aida*, I would put them down a half-tone, depending on how I was feeling. Serafin made some cuts [in the score] too. I had a technique that always stood by me, thank God, but high Cs had become an obsession with me in places. Every time I studied a new score, I'd look through it first to see how many high Cs there were in it. I would have loved to be able to sing high Cs like Raisa could.

Did Raisa come to hear your Norma*?*

Oh, yes! She was one of my biggest supporters. We were good friends, you know. She even called me in London and sent me a lovely wire when I sang *Norma* at Covent Garden. Raisa and I were a "mutual admiration society," as they say.

As regards Adalgisa, wouldn't your sister have been a good partner in Norma*?*

Well, Carmela did study Adalgisa. She never did it at the Met, but I know she studied it. She asked Romani to work on it with her.

Was the possibility of casting Carmela as Adalgisa to your Norma ever discussed by the Metropolitan's management?

It wouldn't have been appropriate.

Do you mean the discussion wouldn't have been appropriate? Or do you mean it wasn't the appropriate role for her?

She was [at her] best in things like *Cavalleria*—she was a very good Santuzza—but the classical operas wouldn't have been a right for her. She liked to do things by instinct. You can do that in *Cavalleria*, but Bellini is a whole different thing entirely. Anyhow, I was nervous enough in *Norma*. If I was singing it with Carmela, I would have been pulling for her, worrying [whether] she was going to get this or that phrase right, and I had enough to worry about all by myself.

What do you recall of Carmela's debut performance?

It was in *Aida*. She was a very good Amneris too.

In what operas did the two of you sing together at the Met?

We did *Gioconda* several times, particularly on tour. I think that's all she and I did together.

Once Carmela was on the Metropolitan roster, the "gamble" the two of you had taken when you left vaudeville had essentially paid off. It must have been cause for celebration within the Ponzillo family.

Well, it took a little longer than we bargained for. There was some illness that slowed things down for her, but she came through it fine and she came to the Met. She stayed there for about ten years, I think. She was a good artist in what they gave her [to sing], but they could have given her more [roles] that would have shown what she could really do.

Which roles do you feel she excelled in?

She was at her best when she could be dramatic, especially in parts like Amneris and Santuzza. She would have been a very good Tosca too. She prepared it; she studied it—I know because I heard her sing through parts of it. But when you're stuck with that mezzo label, nobody ever thinks of you for *Tosca*. Romani used to tell her to go to Europe and make a career over there as a dramatic soprano. But she wanted to do everything her way, and she had a manager [Maurice Frank] who had his hooks into her too. We would tell her to go to Europe, to sing in Italy, and her manager would talk her into staying here as a mezzo. He didn't want to lose his 10 percent. It doesn't take a genius to figure that out.

Were the two of you still living together at the time of her debut?

Oh, yes. My place on Riverside Drive was pretty big. It was a penthouse, very spacious and well designed, so there was plenty of room.

Did you get to see your family in Meriden very often in those days?

Mother would come to New York and stay with me every once in a while. But she and Daddy were homebodies, and with my being so busy I didn't really get to see them too often. But if I had a concert in Hartford or Waterbury, I would stay an extra day or so to spend time with them.

Were those good years for your family, as you look back?

Things were pretty much the same. Mother and Daddy had closed the bakery, but Daddy and my brother still had the fuel business—coal and wood, but mainly coal—so there was money coming in. There was a grandchild to spoil—my nephew, Nino. I loved his mother, Lydia, the same as if she had been a sister to me. We were very, very close.

Returning to Norma, *there are two moments in the opera—one musical and the other a highly dramatic moment—that I would like to ask you about. The dramatic moment I have in mind occurs near the end of the opera when Norma sings the words* "Son io!" *thereby confessing her guilt to the Druids. I'm told that you sang those words in a prolonged, high* pianissimo. *Everyone I've spoken with who saw your Norma has never forgotten the emotion you conveyed in that moment. Was it an emotional moment for you as well?*

Oh, very emotional! I had to hold back [my emotions] all through *Norma*, but especially in that scene. I had to fight back tears! When you think about it, *Norma* has all the emotions a woman can have. There is religious devotion, passion, friendship, a mother's love, self-sacrifice—all those emotions in one role.

The scenes with the children must have been a challenge too.

Where she has decided to kill them, but she can't bring herself to do it. Oh, yes—very emotional. I always wanted children of my own, you know, but it just wasn't meant to be. I doted on children, and at the Met, the little ones who played the parts of the children were wonderful.

The other moment I want to ask you about has to do with the ending of the "Casta diva." Raisa, at least on one of her studio recordings, ended the aria with a trill. You didn't do that on your Victor recording, but did you do a trill at the end of the aria in the opera house?

A trill? Oh, no—that would be all wrong! It would stop the flow of the musical line. A trill is an ornament, really, and it only belongs in certain places, but not at the end of "Casta diva."

Do you like your Victor recording of "Casta diva"*?*

No. The way I sang it on that record isn't how I did it on the stage. I always sang the second verse twice as slow and half as loud as the first verse, but I couldn't record it that way. They told me you would hardly hear the tone, it would be too soft, and the tempo would be too slow for one side of the record. The clock was always the problem—that damned clock on the wall. Everything [recorded in the 78 r.p.m. format] had to be done in four minutes, which meant that I could only [record] the first verse. But without the second verse, you don't get [a sense of] the dramatic contrast I used in the [opera] house.

Fortunately for us, you made two recordings from Norma *for the Victor Company. In general, were you pleased with them?*

With the "Mira, o Norma" I made with Telva, yes. You have to be able to read each other's minds to get the pacing of those duets just perfect. I found a way to keep us together that was foolproof. We held each other's hand, and just ahead of the beat I would squeeze her hand, so that she would stay right with me. We were so used to doing them like that, we even held hands when we recorded those duets.

Your Victor Norma *recordings were made with the then-new electrical process. Do you have any specific recollections of making records for Victor when the new process was first introduced?*

The microphone, you mean? I remember that the Victor people told me all about how much better the sound would be with the microphone.

Did you like the sound of the new electrical recordings, compared to the ones you recorded by the old method?

They were a little easier to do. There wasn't that awful [recording] horn to contend with. But the clock was still up there on the wall, so you had to speed up everything. And in ensembles, the balance between voices wasn't always good.

Even in some of your own recordings?

Yes. Take the *Aida* records I made with Martinelli, for instance. Neither one of us was completely satisfied with them. We did the Tomb Scene twice. The first time [in an acoustical-recording session at Victor on 8 February 1924] they had Martinelli [positioned] too far forward and I was too far in the background, so the balance was all wrong. We did the Nile Scene, too, and neither it nor the Tomb Scene [was] good enough, so I wouldn't give permission to put them out. A little later, when they brought in the microphone [as electrical recording was being introduced at Victor early in 1925], they had us come back and record the Tomb Scene again [in an electrical recording session on 17 May 1926]. When they played the test [recordings] for me I still didn't like the balance, so I wouldn't approve them. Finally, they set up a three-way call with Martinelli, [studio conductor] Rosario Bourdon and me, and Martinelli talked me into approving them. He said, "Look, Rosa, it's great singing, and the musical public will accept the balance problem." So I gave in.

What is your opinion of your Victor "Red Seal" ensembles from Forza *with Pinza and Martinelli, and also the* "Vergine degli angeli" *that you recorded with Pinza?*

The trio is a pretty good recording, as I remember it, but I don't like the "Vergine degli angeli" [record] at all. Somebody in the studio turned up the volume on my microphone, which made me sound like I was singing *Gioconda,* which is hardly the way I would sing a prayer. In the [opera] house I sang it in mezza voce, which is how it's marked. That record is bad—my part of it, I mean, not Pinza's. He sounds just wonderful on that record.

Were you pleased with your two recordings from La vestale*?*

Very pleased. I haven't heard them in a long time, but they were pretty good records. Even [on] the best ones I made, though, I still don't hear the full sound of my voice. That's why I like to listen to the records they made from my radio broadcasts like *The Chesterfield Hour*, which I did with André Kostelanetz, and especially my *Traviata* and *Carmen* [Metropolitan Opera] broadcasts. When I listen to those, I can hear more of my voice than I can on my records. By the way, Eddie Johnson just loved those *Vestale* records. The manager of our Lyric Theater here in Baltimore was a very good friend of Eddie Johnson. Fred Huber was his name. He [had been] with the Lyric since World War I. Johnson used to tell young singers, "Every student of voice should listen to Rosa Ponselle's records from *La vestale* at least once a week, because they are examples of perfect singing." Fred Huber heard Johnson say that many, many times, and he quoted him verbatim.

In Norma, *your Pollione was Giacomo Lauri-Volpi. Would he have been your first choice if you had been able to put together your own "ideal cast"?*

I wanted Martinelli.

Did you and Lauri-Volpi have any difficulties during Norma*?*

No, not like [in] *Trovatore*. He had the high notes [for Pollione]. The high C in "Meco all'altar di Venere" was easy for him—but I would have loved singing it with Martinelli.

Do you have any idea why Lauri-Volpi was chosen instead?

Gatti knew I didn't like singing with Lauri-Volpi, but he [Gatti] tried to tell me that it would work because Volpi and I didn't get along too well. He thought it would help the tension that develops between Norma and Pollione in the story. When Norma confronts him about his affair with Adalgisa, she becomes a raging tigress, and I'll admit that some of those insults, which Norma hurls in her rage, came a little easier when I was looking at Lauri-Volpi! But, really, he was okay as Pollione. And anyway, Martinelli was having some problems at the time.

Do you mean vocal problems?

He wasn't singing too well, no, but that wasn't the problem I'm talking about. His life had gotten complicated around then. He was having this affair with Colette d'Arville. She had been a singer—she did light things, I think, at the Opéra Comique. I met her and got to know her a little, but I don't think she was singing much around that time. I don't know what she was doing, really. I guess the polite way to say it is that she was an "international consort." She was a pretty girl, and Martinelli was head over heels about her. Everybody knew [about] it, and some of us thought it was affecting his singing. I never thought he was quite the same [vocally] after that. His range was still okay, but there was a hardness in his tone from then on.

Between La vestale *and* Norma, *you were cast with Martinelli in two operas that you had sung with Caruso:* La forza del destino *and* La Juive. *How did Martinelli fare in those roles, given the standards Caruso had set?*

Well, you can't compare [their] voices. You really can't compare anybody with Caruso, vocally. I liked Martinelli's Eléazar, though. It wasn't Caruso's, but it was a pretty good likeness. I didn't do *Juive* with Martinelli that many times. I think [Florence] Easton did Rachel with him more than I did.

Were you impressed with Easton's Rachel?

I don't remember seeing her do it. You see, I never had time to go to other people's performances.

But you did hear Easton sing, so I am interested to know what you thought of her. Were you impressed with her singing overall?

So-so. She was very serviceable and sincere and that sort of thing. She could do more roles than almost anybody at the Met in my time, and she was a very fast learner. I don't think a singer can do that many roles in that many languages and styles without having them sound an awful lot alike, but in

Juive, I'm sure she was very serviceable. And Martinelli's Eléazar was very, very good.

In Forza, *which you sang with Martinelli at that time, Lawrence Tibbett is listed in one of the casts as Fra Melitone. Were you impressed with the rapid progress Tibbett had already made by then?*

Oh, sure, and like I told you before, nobody handed it to him on a silver platter. Tibbett was a hard worker. I can still see him with that funny false nose he wore as Melitone. You know, even then he was already beginning to create a real character, even in a small part like Melitone. He made as much out of that part as anybody could.

How about Martinelli in Forza*? How would you rate his Alvaro?*

Good, but not as good as his Eléazar. There isn't much to the character [of Alvaro] compared to what you can do with Eléazar. And Martinelli, God bless him, didn't have the kind of voice that Caruso had. He would tell you that himself. I read someplace what [Martinelli] told some fan of his who asked him about Caruso. This person said to him, "Don't you really think that you were as great as Caruso?" Martinelli said, "You can put Gigli and Lauri-Volpi and Pertile and Martinelli together in one singer, and that *one* tenor still wouldn't be fit to kiss the shoetops of Enrico Caruso!" I have heard him say things like that with my own ears. You see, that quote tells you everything about Caruso, and everything about Martinelli.

Do you agree with what he said?

Absolutely. If you're going to talk about tenors, you have to put them into two groups. In one, there is Caruso. All the others are in the second group. And that's not taking anything away from the rest [of the great tenors]. It's just that there was only one Enrico Caruso.

I can't help asking whether you realize that there are critics, historians, and singers who say that very same thing about Rosa Ponselle.

You mean when they said I was "Caruso in petticoats"? That was very nice.

I guess what I'm asking is whether you realize the extent of your own fame. From James Huneker and Tullio Serafin until this very day, there are those who say that the voice of Ponselle was the most beautiful of its kind in this century.

What? "In this century?" I'm not *that* old!

Putting aside all modesty, if you can, how do you think of yourself when you look back on your achievements as an artist?

That I was born with something that others didn't have—meaning my voice—and because of the voice I had, I could do things that some other [sopranos] couldn't.

What do you believe made your voice so distinctive?

I guess I would say the color, the timbre, and [the fact] that I had a pretty good range, and I could carry that dark sound clear up to the top and then way down low without any break in the voice. I never had to force [the voice]. I could just open my mouth, and it was there.

Your brother and sister have said that you had almost the same singing voice when you were very young.

Yes, and so did they. Carmela never needed any singing lessons. She'd have been better off if she'd never had any at all, because Thorner and his so-called lessons nearly ruined her. But you can hear what she sounded like from our [Columbia] records. You can hear the family resemblance [in our voices]. And my brother, to give him his due, never had a singing lesson in his life, and he had a nice *spinto* voice. So we were all born with it, you see.

But what about all the work you put into your roles?

I worked hard, that's true. But you have to remember that I loved what I was doing. I didn't always like the pressure of having to perform, but I always loved to sing.

How much maintenance did your voice require? For instance, did you do a lot of vocalizing each day?

No. I never vocalized more than ten minutes, and I never sang, not even vocalises, between my performances. I always walked to the theater, and when I got there, I vocalized [for] only about ten minutes before going on stage. My vocalises were my actual performances! But my voice always stayed right up there because I was always so busy.

What sort of vocalises did you use?

It depends, but most of the time I would sing phrases that had vowels in them that were good for the voice. When I warmed up, I would stay in the middle of the range until everything felt just right. I always concentrated on the vowels, especially the *oo* sound, which is the hardest for most of us, yet it's the foundation for all the other vowels. If you can sing a good *oo*, your placement is right, and if you're having a little trouble getting things right, the *oo* sound is the one to work on.

How do you keep the voice equalized from the low to the high range?

I have never had much of a problem with that, but I'm careful not to carry the chest voice up too high. When I do use the chest [voice], I always cover the tone. I call it putting a lid on it.

Do you believe there are separate registers for the chest and so-called head voices?

Well, they mix in the middle of the range. That's what you call the *voce misto*. I don't put much emphasis on registers, though, because you want to think of the voice as having the same sound from top to bottom. You want to think of it as one voice, not two. Plus, you can color the tone lots of different ways in each part of the voice.

Do you think of your voice as being a big voice, volume-wise?

A big voice? I don't think anybody ever had any trouble hearing me, if that's what you mean. I would call it a heavy voice more than a big voice, and I had to carry that heaviness all the way to the top. If I had thinned out the sound, I probably could have sung high notes easier than I did. But my voice was always heavy, which meant that I had to keep it heavy throughout the range for the big roles, and then I would have to make myself keep it light in the more lyrical parts. In *Traviata*, for instance, I always had to say to myself, "Light! Light! Keep the voice light, Rosa!"

They say that no singer can truly "hear" himself or herself. How can you tell whether your voice sounds the way it should?

By how it feels in the front of the face—that's what we call the mask—and especially how it feels in the cheekbones. Sometimes, I can also get an idea from the resonance I can hear coming back to my ears. But it's what you feel, not what you hear, that is what a singer has to go with. You have to memorize the sensations you have when your placement is just right, and you never want to change your placement to accommodate how you're feeling from one day to the next. You have to "home in" like radar on your [vocal] placement, no matter how you're feeling and no matter what your ears are telling you. If you start changing the way you produce your tones because your voice doesn't sound right to your own ears, you'll be fooled by it and soon find yourself in trouble. But if you stay "on the beam," as they say, it will see you through.

Is there any way you can describe to those of us who aren't singers how those sensations feel to you?

When everything is going right and you're in tip-top shape, it almost feels like the front of your face will come off when you're singing fortissimo. When you sing pianissimo, it's like pulling a thread through your nose. That's how I would put it. Of course, you're using your whole body, especially the diaphragm, and you feel those wonderful vibrations in the mask, and even on the top and the back of your head.

Do those sensations become even more intense when you're singing in an ensemble with other large, resonant voices?

It can, yes. It could almost make you dizzy, if you weren't lost in the music and the character.

Are there specific moments you can recall when the blend of your voices gave you that almost dizzying sensation with other singers?

Yeah. You should have heard Caruso, Mardones, and me in *Forza*. You really missed something!

When you were preparing a new role, did you have to do much vocalizing to get ready for your coaching sessions?

After I was up for a while, I would try out my voice in the shower. If it sounded okay and everything felt all right, I didn't do any more vocalizing until I was getting into my makeup and costume. You have to be very careful about where you vocalize. If there's too much fabric around—a lot of carpeting, upholstery, drapes, and such—you won't hear any resonance in the tone. As I told you, I found that out the hard way when I tried to sing in my dressing room before my debut. You see, the tone needs to have space around it, so you want to do your vocalizing where there are bare walls and good hard floors.

Between La vestale *and* Norma, *you added another new role to your repertoire when you sang Fiora in* L'amore dei tre re *for the first time. Did you like the role?*

Oh, yes! I loved the music, and I loved the text—and the music matched the text perfectly. The text is like poetry. One of my favorite parts of [the text] is when Archibaldo, the old king who is blind, gets angry with himself because he knows about the affair that's going on between Fiora and her lover. He sings, "If I must be blind, let me truly not see." I always loved that.

The role of Archibaldo, the king, became another early success for Pinza, as I recall.

Not when I was doing it. [Adamo] Didur did Archibaldo. He was just wonderful in that role.

Who was your Avito?

Gigli—who was wonderful, of course. And Giuseppe Danise [sang] Manfredo. I thought it was the best of all his roles.

What do you recall of your costuming?

I loved my first-act costume. I wore a white dress, very sheer, with pale blue flowers going up from the hem. The length had to be just right, because I wanted it to touch the floor [but] not be too long. The reason was that the flowers had stems, so it gave the effect of the flowers growing up from the ground—like I was standing in the center of a field of flowers. The blossoms were blue, and the center of each one—the part of the flower where the pollen is, in other words—were made out of little silver balls. I wore a long cape, or cloak, over the dress. [The cape] was vented on one side, and it had strips of ermine on the right side of it. I wore a crown with it, but not too big—just enough to frame my forehead, [but] not high enough to call too much attention to it. It was quite a nice effect, really.

There are photographs of you in L'amore dei tre re *in what appear to be four or five different costumes. Did you make changes within any of the acts?*

No. I had one costume for each act. In the second act, I wore a pink dress, very clinging, a princess line [style]. It had a long train, and there were jewels all around the back and sides—ruby stones, mainly—and they flared out onto the train of the dress. The cloak I wore with it was made out of silk velvet—a royal red silk velvet. Later on, I had new costumes made for the first and second acts when the Met was going to update the production. But nothing ever came of it, so I never used them.[24]

It is said that in the last act, where the murdered Fiora is laid out in the tomb, many other sopranos who sang the role would pick someone from the chorus to lie there in the tomb throughout the final act. But my understanding is that you opted to lie on the bier yourself. Is that true—and, if so, what was your reasoning?

Well, if I was going to do a role, I was going to do the whole role. I wouldn't have felt like I had done the performance if I hadn't done the tomb scene. Anyway, by the last act my work was all done, so the pressure was off me and all I had to do was lie there. Look at it this way: how often do you get to be at center stage for a whole act without even having to sing a note?

Recollections

Nina Morgana Zirato

Born of Sicilian parents who had emigrated to Buffalo, New York, a few years before her birth, Nina Morgana (1892–1984) first appeared in public under the billing "The Child Patti" at the Pan-American Exposition in 1901. A second-tier soprano at the Metropolitan Opera for fifteen seasons, Morgana made her debut in Rigoletto *in the 1920–21 season, which was Caruso's last. After she had studied with Teresa Arkel and had sung coloratura roles successfully in Alessandria and Milan, Morgana became Caruso's choice as one of his assisting artists in a highly publicized series of concerts in the United States. In June 1921, scarcely two months before Caruso's sudden death in Italy, Morgana married the tenor's secretary, Bruno Zirato, who in later years became the general manager of the New York Philharmonic and also served as Arturo Toscanini's representative in the United States.*

Essentially self-educated and invariably self-assured, Morgana was well acquainted not only with Ponselle but also with Claudia Muzio and Rosa Raisa, both on stage and off. She spoke candidly about all three legendary sopranos in this interview, portions of which were recorded shortly after she celebrated her ninetieth birthday.[25]

I have known Rosa Ponselle for more than sixty years. I knew her as a colleague at the Metropolitan, where she was a *prima diva* rivaled only by Maria Jeritza. I heard Rosa in most of the roles she sang, and as with Jeritza, with whom I sang Micaela in *Carmen* many times, I also sang with Rosa on several occasions. I was her Inez in a number of *L'africana* performances, with Gigli as Vasco da Gama and Rosa as Selika, and when another singer was indisposed, I also sang one performance of *La Juive* with Rosa on tour, when the opera was brought back into the repertoire for Martinelli. So I believe that I am in a position to speak knowledgeably about her career.

At the Chicago Opera, where I was engaged by Cleofonte Campanini the season before I joined the Metropolitan, I also heard and came to know Claudia Muzio and Rosa Raisa. Just as I regarded Rosa Ponselle as both a great artist and a personal friend, I felt the same toward Muzio and Raisa. While I admired all three of them, I like to think that I have no illusions about them as artists, and that I can talk about them in a fair and balanced way. I don't idolize singers just because they happened to sing in the same era in which I sang. To some people, the past always seems better than the present. I am not one of them. I don't believe in a so-called Golden Age.

And who am I? I sang at the Metropolitan for fifteen years, and I did both coloratura and lyric-soprano parts. I was not a star by any means—certainly not a Ponselle, a Muzio, or a Jeritza—but I did sing principal as well as secondary parts. I was a very quick study—sometimes I was often given a role to learn in less than two days because of casting changes. Since I could learn a role quickly, Gatti relied on me in the same way he relied on Queena Mario, who did most of the same lyric parts that I sang. She was a very good artist, too, although she was not Italian. Her birth name was Tillotson, not Mario, and she traded the lovely name Helen for the perfectly stupid name Queena, which she made up. (Once I made her mad by asking her, "If you have a brother, is his name Kinga?")

I have always tried to be forthright in my opinions about myself, and about any singers I have heard, even when my opinions displease others. Once

I offended Bruno, who was then my fiancé, over something I said to Caruso. I can assure you that no one respected Caruso any more than I. It was Caruso who had sent me to my teacher in Milan, Teresa Arkel, after I auditioned for him in Buffalo in 1908. Later, when I was engaged to Bruno, Caruso invited me to be his assisting artist for many of his U.S. concerts. When Bruno and I were married, Caruso served by proxy as our *compare d'anello*, or best man, as we say it in English.

Caruso's singing was so instinctive that I sometimes felt his instincts overruled his superb musicianship. At supper after a performance of *Elisir d' amore*, he said to me, "Tell me, *Mona*, was I good tonight?" (Caruso called me *mona*, which is Italian for "nun," because I was so prim and proper around him!) He had asked for my opinion, so I gave him a truthful but not especially flattering answer. "*Ma'st'o*," I said, using the Neapolitan for "Maestro," to show my respect for him, "why is it that you seem to prefer to sing three phrases in one breath, when it would be more musical to sing only one or two at most?" I was being honest, but I'm sure that Bruno wanted to reach across the table and choke me!

It was in connection with Caruso that I first heard about Rosa Ponselle. She and her sister, who were singing in vaudeville, had been invited to participate in a wartime fund-raising event to which Caruso also had been invited. I was one of several opera singers who were being asked to perform without a fee at the bazaar, and as most everyone else did, I did my part in raising money for war relief whenever I was given the opportunity.[26] A few months before this benefit performance had been scheduled I had returned from Italy, where I had made my La Scala debut as Amina in *La sonnambula* in the previous season [1915–16].

The benefit was to be held at one of the vaudeville theaters in Manhattan. To most opera singers, and certainly to me, vaudeville was what today we would call very lowbrow, the sort of entertainment intended for the *hoi polloi*. When Bruno told me where I would be singing, I made a rather curt remark about vaudeville theaters, because I was accustomed to singing only in opera houses and concert halls. To pacify me, Bruno said, "But the Ponzillo Sisters sing here."[27] He acted as if I should either be reassured or impressed, but I had never heard of the Ponzillo Sisters—and when he explained who they were, I had to hold my tongue at the thought of being compared to a pair of vaudevillians. For all I knew—or cared—they might have been fan dancers.

Two years later, Rosa made her debut in the Metropolitan premiere of *La forza del destino*. By a happy coincidence her debut occurred on my birthday, 15 November 1918. I had the privilege of hearing her from the Caruso box at the Metropolitan, where I was a guest of Dorothy Caruso. Like everyone else, I was absolutely thrilled by Rosa's performance! From the moment she finished her first aria, there was no question that [hers] was going to be a great career. During the next few years I came to know her quite well and, as I said earlier, I sang with her in two productions.

When I think of Rosa Ponselle, my memory presents me with two different women. There was one Rosa who could be very informal, very familiar, as a cousin or perhaps some other member of your own family might be. But there was also Rosa Ponselle the diva, who could be very self-absorbed, sometimes to the point of seeming rather pretentious. For instance, at our home in Chappaqua, Bruno and I once gave an intimate supper party for Pasquale Amato, to which we invited Rosa. While we were dining, Gatti-Casazza called Bruno on the telephone. Rather than having Bruno leave the dining room, our butler carried in the telephone and connected it to a special outlet, which we had installed near the dining table for situations of this sort. In those days, only the better restaurants had telephones that could be moved about, so it was unusual to see this in someone's home.

Rosa's reaction to this shows the two sides of her that I'm speaking about. When the butler carried in the telephone and began connecting the cord, Rosa sat straight up in her chair and immediately put down her fork, as if this were something extremely important that should be studied. Her eyes got wider and wider as she followed every movement the butler made until he handed Bruno the receiver. While Bruno was trying to converse with Gatti, Rosa said quite dramatically, "Why, I've never seen that before!" Then she began asking me all sorts of questions about this mysterious telephone of ours. "Where did you get that?" she demanded to know. She went on and on with her questions, as if Alexander Graham Bell had just invented the telephone before her very eyes. Although it would have been exceedingly impolite of me, I felt like chiding her for the way she was comporting herself. Finally, she announced to everyone, "Well, *I* have to have a telephone exactly like that."

I thought to myself, "And who do you think *you* are?" But then, I had to remind myself that she *was* Ponselle, and she had earned the right to make herself the center of attention when and if she cared to. Yet I can assure you that I chided her (but only to myself, not aloud) for carrying on in such poor taste at my table. To me it was very lower class, but Rosa could be that way, as anyone who knew her very well will tell you.

Carmela Ponselle, whom I knew even better than I knew Rosa, never had that pretentious side during the years when I knew her. Carmela and I got acquainted when both of us were studying with Dr. [P. Mario] Marafioti, who had been Caruso's throat specialist and who also taught voice to several of the singers at the Metropolitan. Carmela's weekly appointment was just ahead of mine. Sometimes we would wait for each other after our lessons so that we could compare notes and discuss our careers. I always enjoyed her company, sometimes even more than I enjoyed Rosa's when Rosa was being the diva.

But the diva, as I said, was only one side of Rosa's makeup. The other side of her could win over anyone with its friendliness and charm. Of the many examples I could cite, one very special memory comes to my mind. She was giving a concert in Detroit, and as it happened Bruno and I were in Detroit visiting my brother and his family.[28] When Rosa found out from Bruno that we would be in town, she sent us complimentary tickets to her concert. At the close of her program, as she often did, Rosa excused her accompanist and sat down at the piano to play her own accompaniment for her encores. She was a very good pianist, and she would invite the audience to suggest encores to her. That night, however, someone who was obviously not very knowledgeable asked her to sing "Caro nome." Instead of dismissing it, Rosa pointed toward the box where she knew Bruno and I were sitting. She told the audience, "I want you to know that Nina Morgana, one of our great coloratura sopranos, is in the theater tonight." Then she raised her arm and gestured in the direction of our box. "Now, there is the artist who can sing 'Caro nome' for you!" I was so taken aback I hardly knew what to say. Very few prima divas would do that for a colleague. But Rosa did—and I'll never forget her for it.

As a dramatic soprano, there is no question that Rosa was one of the greatest in our time. There are those, in fact, who say that she was a greater singer than either Raisa or Muzio. But the way I would choose to put it is that each of them had something the others did not have. Muzio, for example, had a different emotional impact on an audience than Rosa Ponselle had in the roles the two of them sang. On stage, especially in a role like Violetta in *Traviata*, Muzio always seemed more vulnerable than Rosa could. Rosa had a very forceful personality, a much stronger personality than Muzio's, and this affected how Rosa conceived and acted many of her roles. But Rosa was very much influenced by Claudia Muzio, and I think Rosa would admit it.

Muzio's voice did not have the extension in the lower range that Rosa Ponselle's had. Nor was Muzio's voice as large as Rosa's. But the size of a voice is important only so far as the demands of the score are concerned. In Muzio's case, her voice was well suited to the roles she sang, just as Rosa's was suited to most of the roles she chose. But where range was concerned, it was Rosa Raisa who had the high range of a true dramatic soprano, even more than Rosa Ponselle. I don't think that [Ponselle] would disagree with me, because Raisa's top was a wonder! There seemed no end to it, and the higher she sang the more powerful her voice seemed. Raisa's was such an exciting voice—not beautiful, not in the way Ponselle's was—but it was *very* exciting. It is true that there was a break that could be heard when she went from the middle of her range into her lower tones. But to those of us who learned to sing under Italian teachers, this was not something we considered a fault.

Madame Arkel, for instance, had no use for the so-called vocal registers. She considered them a fiction. When I was studying with her, she allowed me to attend a luncheon she gave for Frieda Hempel, who called on Madame Arkel for some advice. The subject of the vocal registers came up, and I heard Madame Arkel say to Hempel, "There are no registers unless we are prepared to agree that every tone is its own register." What she meant was that the vocal apparatus changes not merely in the middle of the range, but instead changes subtly with each tone a singer produces.

Teresa Arkel was not merely a great teacher but a *prima diva assoluta* in her time. She was accorded the same kind of respect as Lilli Lehmann. Even in retirement Madame Arkel's singing technique was so perfect that she could span a three-and-one-half octave range and could actually trill on *fa sopracuto* [F above high C]. I heard her do it no fewer than one hundred times! It is difficult to imagine how a soprano with that kind of range, and having mastered such a breadth of roles, could sing without having a slight break in what some singers today call the chest and head voices. But this was accepted in Italy, whereas American teachers and critics have always thought of it as a flaw in technique if there is any change of timbre or color anywhere in the voice. Some critics said this about Raisa's voice, just as they did about Callas later.

Rosa Ponselle had no break in any part of her range. In all my career, I never heard a more seamless and beautifully balanced dramatic soprano voice than hers. It was as smooth and even as Gigli's among the tenors, which is a great compliment as far as I am concerned. From Emmy Destinn to Maria Caniglia, no other dramatic soprano in my memory could maintain the evenness of tone quality from the highest to lowest tones, especially with so large a voice, as Rosa Ponselle could.

That is not to say that her voice was perfect in every way. Her top was not as secure as it ought to have been, although it was not always lacking in security. At the time of her debut, her top was very, very good. In *Forza*, *Africana*, or *Trovatore* her high notes came easily to her, and her voice was even larger than it was when she began singing *Norma*, or certainly *Traviata*. But later on, it would make Rosa very nervous if she had to sing above B-flat. I never felt that she lost any of her technique. It seemed as if she lost her confidence, not her technique, the more nervous she became. Even in *Norma*, she had two or maybe three scores prepared, each one in a different key, so that she could accommodate how her voice felt at each performance—or even from one act to the next, if she was more nervous than usual.

Any singer who is as nervous as Rosa was can be helped or hurt by a conductor—and I don't mean just in the orchestra pit. Singers who are temperamental and competitive, but not nervous about their abilities, are actually helped by demanding conductors who spare no one's feelings. Toscanini was that type of conductor. I remember vividly the first rehearsal for a performance of Beethoven's *Ninth Symphony* with Toscanini, in which I was to sing with Richard Crooks and Ezio Pinza. In the rehearsal, the baton did not last very long. Toscanini snapped it in two, and then threw his pocket watch on the floor and smashed it with his foot!

Toscanini pointed at poor Crooks and told him that he sang like a sick pig. Then he used a very crude Italian expression for Pinza. It would embarrass me to repeat it. He told Pinza that his singing had the same worth that the pig's food has after the pig has digested and eliminated it. And Toscanini did not spare me, either. He told me that Madame Arkel, whom Maestro had known very well in Italy, should have forbade me ever to mention her in public because my singing was a disgrace to her name! Then he told all of us to get out of his sight and not come back until we were prepared to give our very best. At the next rehearsal, I can assure you, Morgana, Crooks, and Pinza and everyone else associated with the performance sang better than we ever knew we could!

Tullio Serafin was just the opposite of Toscanini. Serafin had a wonderful touch with his artists. Everything he did was with encouragement, patience, and calm. I never knew him to raise his voice or to lose his temper with anyone. The only thing that displeased him was if someone was unprepared at a rehearsal. But even then, all it took was one disappointed look from that expressive face of his, and you could feel about one inch tall. Serafin was the ideal conductor for Ponselle because he knew how to deal with her nerves. Especially in *Norma*, where her nerves were put to a severe test, he had a great impact on Ponselle. Later on, of course, he did the same for Callas.

Serafin once said that there were three voices that he considered to be miracles: Caruso's, Ruffo's, and Rosa Ponselle's. Their voices could not have been taught by any teacher or coach. You're either born with that kind of voice, or you're not. Considering how very hard Rosa worked in all her roles, she certainly belongs along side Caruso and Ruffo. But we should keep in mind that although Ruffo and Caruso were unique, they too had their limitations. Ruffo, for instance, would sometimes "snarl" his low notes because they were not the best or the easiest part of his range. Caruso had his little devices—especially the way he would "scoop" into high notes by attacking them from below the tone before going to the center of the pitch. It was not correct, I suppose, to a voice teacher's ears. But it was as distinctive to Caruso as his handwriting was, and everyone applauded him for it.

There never has been a singer whose voice and technique were flawless, a singer who could do everything better than anyone else, past or present. But I am prepared to make two exceptions where Rosa is concerned: one is for her Norma, which in my mind remains unsurpassable, not just vocally but dramatically (and I say that after having heard Raisa's and in recent times Callas' and Sutherland's). The other exception I would make is for the unusual quality of her voice. I would express it this way: from the A-natural in her upper range to about an F an octave below it, the tones that Rosa Ponselle sang may have been the most beautiful that ever came from a woman's throat.

The Written Record

When the Victor Talking Machine Company hosted a surprise party for Ponselle in January of 1927, the lavish event was meant as a celebration of two milestones: her thirtieth birthday (on 22 January) and her assumption of the title role in *Norma*, which she was in the final stages of preparing under Serafin's direction. "The party took place at Liederkranz Hall, in a large rehearsal room," recalled Libbie Miller, who had arranged the event. "The Victor Company paid the tab. The party came off superbly. All the guests were in place and the candles on the cake were burning when we brought Rosa into the room."[29]

Impressive as it was, the Victor-sponsored party paled in opulence compared to the one given for Ponselle by Perle Mesta the following November, after the first performance of *Norma*. "I hurried to the Park Lane Hotel," Mesta later wrote, "where I had invited one hundred guests, including Lucrezia Bori, Lily Pons, Antonio Scotti, Beniamino Gigli, Ezio Pinza (who sang the role of Norma's father that night), and Edward Johnson. . . . The room was decorated entirely with orchids. I had sprays along the stairs, on the walls, and on the tables; there was an orchid corsage for each lady and when Rosa made her entrance in a beautiful white chiffon gown I draped a *lei* of white orchids around her neck."[30] By the time the $25,000 party broke up at six o'clock the next morning, Eddie Cantor and a number of vaudeville headliners from Rosa's Keith Circuit days had performed, and the popular Meyer Davis Orchestra had played through the night.[31]

A few months later, the I. Miller Company, a chic source of high-priced women's shoes with franchises across the United States, marked Ponselle's achievement by commissioning a statue of her Norma for the façade of the company's then-new headquarters at Seventh Avenue and Forty-sixth Street in Manhattan. Following a month-long newspaper poll in which readers were asked to name "the four greatest American women of the entertainment media," the honors went to Ethel Barrymore for drama, Marilyn Miller for the musical theater, Mary Pickford for film, and Rosa Ponselle for opera. To celebrate the occasion, the I. Miller executives obtained permission, from New York City's theatrically oriented mayor Jimmy Walker, to hold a block party between Seventh Avenue and Broadway, with the four stars as the company's guests of honor.[32]

By any reckoning, these were heady times for a singer whose career was only nine seasons in the making. Once a wide-eyed newcomer with few social graces, Ponselle was now courted frequently by the doyens of Manhattan society. Yet despite her celebrity status she resisted the temptation to believe her own publicity and remained, as her Metropolitan colleague Nanette Guilford put it, "friendly, open, generally relaxed and full of fun, and not at all haughty despite the fact that she was such a big star."[33] From her role in *La gioconda* through her phenomenal success in *La vestale*, these and other qualities of Ponselle's adventuresome personality regularly found their way into newsprint. But, as will be seen, the demands of *La vestale* and *Norma*, coupled with her unalterable perfectionism and fear of meeting her own self-imposed standards, frequently displaced her *joie de vivre* and began to erode her self-confidence.

Scarcely any evidence of this erosion, however, surfaced in the critics' columns. There, perhaps as never before, Ponselle was the regular recipient of highly favorable reviews. Assessing the Metropolitan premiere of *La vestale*, for example, Olin Downes attributed most of the success of the production's first performance to her singing. "She has never more completely justified her talents and her promotions," he judged. "The beauty, the range and opulence of the voice have been common knowledge, but Miss Ponselle has not invariably been finished and judicious in its employment. Last night her native temperament and intuition for vocal effect found full play in a highly expressive and artistic interpretation—one that was thoughtfully and finely proportioned, that took account of text as well as song, and histrionic representation. The applause of the audience was fully merited, and if Miss Ponselle had not finally come alone and repeatedly before the curtain there would probably have been a demonstration equal to the Tibbett affair of last season to force her to do so.[34]

In the *Tribune*, Lawrence Gilman echoed these comments. "Here was a singer," Gilman wrote, "who could sing Spontini's long, gravely sculptured melodies with the required sense of line and dignity of style, and with the formal and somewhat stilted pathos that is their quaint and special mark—as in her second-act aria, 'Tu che invoco con orrore'; for Miss Ponselle sang these passages of cantilena with admirable phrasing, with loveliness of tone, and severity of style, and she was no less admirable in those moments of true dramatic expression with which the score abounds."[35] Even W. J. Henderson, always more measured in his judgment-making than most of the other New York critics, maintained that *La vestale* had not only "introduced to the audience some music in the grand style of the historical French opera" but also had "furnished Rosa Ponselle with one of the best roles she has ever had. . . . It was her opera."[36]

Two seasons later, the acclaim Ponselle received in *Norma* made equally clear that this too was "her opera." In February of 1918, some ten months before her name would appear on a roster, critic James G. Huneker wrote a lengthy retrospective in *The New York Times* on the limited success of Bellini's operas at the Metropolitan Opera. By Huneker's reckoning, the generation of Metropolitan operagoers who had been accustomed to hearing Marcella Sembrich, Lilli Lehmann, and Italo Campanini had been treated to Bellini's best-known works—*I puritani*, *La sonnambula* and *Norma*—a mere twenty-four times in all.[37] Of these *Norma* had last been heard at the Met in 1890, with Lehmann in the title role. Her vocal performance at that late point in her career was not uniformly lauded. As Huneker wrote: "Frau Lehmann took many of the elaborate ornamental passages at a very moderate tempo and sang them with very evident labor, thus depriving them of much of the brilliancy which the smooth, mellow, pliable Italian voices impart to them."[38]

Nearly forty years later, the pre-performance publicity for the Metropolitan's revival of *Norma* began when the *Musical Leader* covered one of the dress rehearsals on Sunday afternoon, 13 November 1927. "From the moment Mr. Serafin's baton was raised, to the end of the opera about 3:40 p.m., a most enthusiastic crowd of music 'knowers' sat enthralled," the *Leader* said. "Particularly did Miss Ponselle outdo herself with the sort of singing that seems to come from instinct, because it was instinct with artistry of the untrammeled, smoothest, cream-voiced emotion with phrase after phrase getting its golden due." As Pollione Lauri-Volpi was "most excellent," the reviewer wrote, and Marion Telva "delivered her big part with sound beauty and beauty of sound for the most part." The *Leader* quoted Metropolitan basso Pavel Ludikar, who attended the rehearsal, as saying that he "never heard better singing than Miss Ponselle's that morning"—a judgment about which "everyone seemed to be in unison" at the conclusion of the rehearsal.[39]

The significance of *Norma* guaranteed that the first performance received full coverage by all the major newspapers. In the *Evening Post*, Charles Pike Sawyer wrote that Ponselle "never sang better in her life nor with better judgment. Her singing of 'Casta diva' was superb, the very acme of bel canto, and in her tragic moments or in agony the horror and distress was heartbreaking in voice and expression. It was a perfect voice perfectly displayed."[40] Edward Cushing labeled her "the greatest singer among the members of the Metropolitan Opera Company." "Listening to her," he said, "we do not regret that we were born too late to enjoy the Golden Age of musical performers in New York, for Miss Ponselle makes golden the age in which she lives."[41] In the *Evening World*, Richard Stokes wrote of the "lustre from the golden age of song" that Ponselle had brought back to the Metropolitan in this "most formidable role in Italian opera." As Norma, he wrote, Ponselle had "won the transcendent victory of her career."[42]

This tendency on the part of some critics "to stellify Miss Ponselle," as Oscar Thompson phrased it, led him to express reservations in *Musical America* about the rest of the cast. "It . . . would not have been true if certain other members of the present company had been selected for the other roles," Thompson believed. "Chaliapin, it will be recalled, sang Oroveso at one time. Whether he could be prevailed upon, today, to assume what he might now regard as a 'routine' Italian part, is another matter." These concerns aside, Thompson judged that "in several of the most important scenes, as the one given over to the honeyed duets of Norma and Adalgisa," both the production and the performance "possessed a satisfying measure of the rare quality."[43]

Olin Downes, praising the production as a whole in the *Times*, credited its success to Serafin and Ponselle—who, he wrote, "has probably the most beautiful voice of any soprano of her generation, and who has advanced remarkably as an artist. Her opening aria, 'Casta diva,' was one of the memorable moments of the evening, a moment of haunting beauty, an observance of style, and evocation of mood that recreated the exquisite old music [for] her hearers."[44] W. J. Henderson, never one to mete out unwarranted praise, said that Ponselle had "added to her repertoire an embodiment which will increase her fame. Her 'Casta diva' was a genuinely beautiful piece of singing. To be a great Norma is more difficult in these days of specialized singing than it was in the days of Pasta and Grisi."[45]

Leonard Liebling, writing in the *American*, ventured that Ponselle had "conquered her measures and listeners completely. In pomp of bearing and plasticity of gesture she was truly regal in the sense of Roman drama. Her singing calls for the highest praises. It was vocal art, intelligent, musical, appealing. She searched the heart and touched the imagination of the listener. Her tones were suave in quality and vibrant with feeling. She celebrated a true triumph after the monumental 'Casta diva' aria, and was recalled again and again after each act." In the *Herald Tribune*, Lawrence Gilman concurred:

> From the moment Miss Rosa Ponselle poured her lovely voice into the mold of "Casta diva," the prosperity of this revival was a foregone conclusion. Norma herself, despite the musical importance of certain of the duets, is very nearly the whole thing in Bellini's opera. And Rosa Ponselle by the fervor, the dignity and the tonal beauty of her embodiment—which in its finest moments had even a touch of that fabulous, transfiguring thing, the "grand style" of the immortals—enforced and made eloquent this predominance.
>
> How touching and simple she was in the scenes with her children; how movingly she sang the noble melody of "Teneri figli," one of the greatest airs in all of opera; and how she conquered by the restraint (which was there most admirably fitting) of her final scene of magnanimous self-sacrifice, when she tears the sacred wreath from her forehead and declares herself the guilty one.[46]

For Gilman, the most emotionally compelling moment in the opera was Ponselle's singing of the line "Son io!" at the climax of the drama. The line, "uttered in a pianissimo of extraordinary and subduing beauty, was unforgettable," Gilman wrote. Pitts Sanborn, writing in the *Telegram*, shared his sentiments. "It is doubtful whether she could ever surpass her magnificence of yesterday in the memorable closing scene."[47] Even among those who saw the scene repeatedly, the impression Ponselle left was indelible. "In the last act,"

Edith Prilik said, "when Rosa took off her crown of laurel and sang that line—'Son io!,' 'I am the culprit!'—I started to cry every time, even though I had heard it at every rehearsal and every performance."[48]

Conductor Wilfred Pelletier, whose admiration for Serafin led him to attend many of the rehearsals, had the same reaction. "What she did in that scene was more than singing. Even if she hadn't sung the line at all, and had just acted the words 'Son io!,' the impression would have been the same. She achieved in that moment what Caruso did in *Pagliacci*, Mary Garden in *Thais*, and Chaliapin in *Boris Godounov*. Ponselle *was* Norma."[49]

Oscar Thompson, writing about *Norma* in *Musical America*, maintained that it was "Miss Raisa's exploitation of the part in [her] Chicago performances" that had "caused rumors to be floated as far back as 1920 that Mr. Gatti was considering it . . . for Miss Ponselle."[50] In most interviews, Ponselle claimed to have seen Raisa's Norma in New York during the period to which Thompson was referring, and she had met her on that occasion through their mutual friend Romano Romani. At least two written accounts, however, suggest a later date and a different locale.

A contemporary news account appearing in the San Francisco *Examiner* placed the first meeting of the two singers in that city, in March of 1929. "With black eyes shining and with arms outstretched, Rosa Raisa and Rosa Ponselle, famous opera singers and warm friends, met yesterday afternoon in the lobby of the Hotel St. Francis," the news release read. "Raisa, with the Chicago Grand Opera Company, and Ponselle, with the Metropolitan Opera Company, both of Italian birth [*sic*], have had parallel careers in the hearts of America's musical people, where high places are held by both 'Rosas.'"[51]

According to Raisa researcher Charles B. Mintzer, however, the meeting occurred not in San Francisco but across the bay in Oakland, California, the last of seven touring stops for the Chicago production of *Norma* in the spring of the 1928–29 season. "Her close friend Rosa Ponselle recalled years later that during the first intermission she rushed into Raisa's dressing room asking 'how many more high Cs do you have?'" Mintzer wrote. "Raisa, nonplussed, answered, 'Oh, lots, and you can put in a D too if you wish!'"[52]

In every interview in which she mentioned Raisa (including those conducted by this writer), Ponselle maintained that she had first heard Raisa's Norma in New York in 1920, with Gabriella Besanzoni as her Adalgisa. Although Mintzer's and others' research indicates that Ponselle's memory, as was often the case, was imprecise (the Raisa-Besanzoni pairing occurred in a New York performance in January 1921, not 1920), the fact remained that Ponselle was in awe of Raisa's Norma both times she heard it. "Having sung it herself by the time she attended Raisa's California performance," James M. Alfonte has suggested, "Ponselle would have had a much deeper appreciation for the demands of the role."[53]

The success of Ponselle's own Norma, however gratifying, did nothing to relieve her mounting anxiety about the immensity of the role. "It was the old problem of having your prayers answered," recalled Libbie Miller, her manager. "Rosa wanted new roles with characters she could make something of dramatically, in operas that would get the critics' attention. She didn't mind living in the shadow of Galli-Curci because Galli-Curci was a coloratura and the two of them were never compared. But it grated on Rosa to have to contend with the popularity of Maria Jeritza, who made headlines every place she went. Rosa wanted her own headlines, and when Gatti-Casazza gave her *Norma,* she finally got them, but she paid the price with her nerves."[54]

This anxiety surfaced in an increasing petulance about the conditions under which she would perform. Helen Noble, in her autobiographical *Life with the Met*, recalled Ponselle's insistence that the Metropolitan's heating system was to be shut down on stage and backstage whenever she was scheduled to sing:

> Her dressing room had to be cold and the stage as well, or she said she could not and would not sing. Her secretary, faithful Edith Prilik, would call the opera house usually on the morning of a Ponselle performance to remind us to turn off the heat. We knew well it had to be done, and never forgot. The temperature of her dressing room was her own preference and no one minded the freezing atmosphere there, but that of the stage involved other singers: the chorus, the ballet—usually with but few clothes on—and all the backstage technicians and crew. But the prima donna's word is law at the Met and everyone else had to freeze and very often sneeze.[55]

Aimé Gerber, a Metropolitan administrator for four decades, also attested to Ponselle's "heat phobia" in his memoirs. "The temperature-testing of Rosa Ponselle's [dressing] room takes a form all its own," Gerber wrote, ". . . and all windows must be open and all heat turned off hours in advance of her coming."[56]

Another source of anxiety, as Helen Noble phrased it, was Ponselle's "terrible phobia about high notes. She was petrified with fear each time she stood in the wings waiting for her cue. She was so nervous she made all about her nervous. She was sure she would never make her high notes—yet they always came over without fail, pure and wonderful and magnificent."[57] *Norma* only deepened this anxiety, although Serafin's assent to lower-key transpositions and cuts in several parts of the score offered her a measure of mental relief. Most of these were notated in Marion Telva's copy of the score, to which Dallas critic John Ardoin was given access in 1976. Telva's handwritten notations verify what Ardoin labeled "Ponselle's well-known fixation and fear of high C":

> The first set of Cs comes in the cabaletta to "Casta diva" ("Ah! bello a me ritorna"). Following historic practice and Serafin's own particular tastes, the second verse of the cabaletta and its further Cs were cut. The first two Cs in the first verse of the cabaletta come during a long melisma on the word "cielo." The first needs only to be touched, but the second is sustained and crowns the phrase. The third C comes at the very end of the section; the note was not written by Bellini, but has become dictated by tradition. All three of these Cs can be heard on Ponselle's electrical Victor recording of the aria made in 1928.
>
> However, a question arises out of an early, acoustic recording of the aria made for the American Columbia some five years before her first *Norma* on stage. For the Columbia disc, the cabaletta is sung down a semitone, or in E major. . . . Thus, on the Columbia disc, the three Cs become three Bs. If, by chance, this transposition or another was later employed by Ponselle in live performances, then the first Cs she sang as Norma came in the second act duet "Ah! sì, fa core."
>
> The crucial top Cs in the second act (or scene two of Bellini's original Act 1) come in the polonaise "Oh! non tremare." A transposition for Ponselle begins over two pages earlier . . . thus the entire polonaise is dropped to B flat major.[58]

In the third act, as Ardoin demonstrated from Telva's score, Serafin had incorporated a transposition for the Norma-Adalgia duet "Deh! con te," and also had lowered the key of the "Mira, o Norma" duet—effectively "weeding out a further four high Cs for Ponselle." In all, Ardoin concluded, the artful use of such transpositions and cuts in the score made it possible for Ponselle to sing "fewer top Cs in *Norma* than are normally encountered."[59]

The Telva score aside, an earlier exchange of telegrams and letters between Gatti-Casazza and his assistant Edward Ziegler makes clear that Ponselle's high-note phobia definitely predated *Norma*. In June 1925, Gatti wired Ziegler from Italy that he had "persuaded Jeritza to sing *Jewels of the Madonna*," but believed that it would be "advisable to have Ponselle prepared also."[60] Ziegler was unsuccessful in persuading Rosa to take on the role—a rather predictable outcome, considering that she was essentially being asked to understudy her rival Jeritza. In a detailed letter to Gatti-Casazza, Ziegler gave this account of Ponselle's reaction to the assignment:

> You know what her mentality is, and her decision is made more firm by the fact that she is not allowed to use her voice for one full month. She says she can't possibly learn *Vestale* and the *Jewels* in the time available, as she begins her concerts [tour] in September. Having lost a number of concert dates by her sickness, she has got to fill these concerts now. Then she also talked about the difficulty of the role because of the many high notes, and finally she said that she had definitely asked you if she could sing this role and you

> had told her she was not to sing it, so that she could not possibly acquire the part now. I am very sorry of my failure in his matter, but . . . she has become even more obstinate in her decision.[61]

Gatti-Casazza seems to have both understood and tolerated Ponselle's anxieties, even as they worsened with *Norma*. Well-experienced in dealing with singers and their eccentric ways, he seems to have shared Olin Downes' view that (as Downes wrote shortly before the *Vestale* premiere) "nervousness is, indeed, almost an inseparable part of the artistic temperament, and it is extremely doubtful whether those who congratulate themselves on never suffering from it will ever transmit the thrill their art provides at quite its finest intensity."[62]

Downes, quoting from an article by Erik Brewerton in *The Musical Times*, went on to suggest that performers who seem to be without nerves, while less inspiring than their high-strung counterparts, "may, however, make better public performers in the long run, as they will have a solid power of endurance their nervous colleagues will lack."[63] Although neither Downes nor Brewerton made specific mention of Ponselle in their commentaries, the psychological profile Brewerton had outlined in his article fit her temperament exactly. But Gatti's chief assistants Edward Ziegler and Earle Lewis took a less clinical view of what they considered Ponselle's peculiarities. Ziegler, in particular, regarded her as both puzzling and frustrating to deal with, despite his enduring regard for her artistry. "Whatever is the matter with the woman," he told Helen Noble, "I will never know."[64]

Libbie Miller offered a more balanced assessment. "Rosa and Gatti found themselves in a precarious position with each other because of *Norma*. For about three seasons, both in New York and on tour, everybody wanted to see Rosa in *Norma*. That was fine in one sense because it meant that Rosa now had a singular importance to the Metropolitan's leadership. But in another sense it was sheer hell for her because Norma is not a role that any soprano in her right mind would look forward to performing time after time. Nevertheless, Rosa, and nobody else, was the 'star of the show'—which meant, of course, that Gatti had to rely on her more than ever. No one but Rosa was acceptable in the role, either in New York or on tour. So if she had to cancel a performance Gatti essentially had no alternative but to put on another opera with another cast at the very last minute."[65]

As Rosa continued to internalize the pressures she was feeling as a result of *Norma*, she began to experience occasional bouts of ill health—most of it psychosomatic in the opinion of those closest to her, though nonetheless quite real to Ponselle. "Especially after *Gioconda*, and definitely when she was doing *Norma*," Libbie Miller maintained, "Rosa had all the traits of a hypochondriac." Edith Prilik concurred, and related this incident from the 1924–25 season as an example of Ponselle's hypersensitivity about her health:

Rosa was supposed to open the Metropolitan tour in Atlanta in *Gioconda*. But before that, she was scheduled to sing a series of concerts in Oregon and Washington, and then in California. There was a smallpox outbreak in the Northwest, so her accompanist Stuart Ross and I got vaccinated. But at the time Rosa wouldn't have the inoculation. She never reacted well to any kind of vaccinations, so throughout the train trip she was agitated about whether to take the vaccine or not. Finally, she agreed to take the shot.

The inoculation was given in the leg at that time. Unfortunately, the spot on her leg where she took the injection got infected, but the doctors along the way said it was more of a reaction than an infection. They told her not to worry about it—which was like telling Niagara Falls to stop flowing. Every other minute, it seemed, she kept checking her leg.

There was no air conditioning on trains in those days, and since Rosa couldn't stand to be hot, she opened all the windows in her compartment and kept the door open during the heat of the afternoon. The train was somewhere between San Francisco and New Orleans when we saw a middle-aged woman in mourning clothes pacing up and down the hallway of the car. Out of sympathy, Rosa invited her to join us, and asked the woman if there was anything we could do for her.

"This is a very sad day, Madame Ponselle," the woman said. "I've lost my son to this epidemic." Rosa held her hand and tried to soothe her. "This smallpox is a terrible thing," Rosa said. Then the woman raised her head and sighed, "Oh, it wasn't the smallpox. The inoculation was what killed him!" From that moment on, Rosa was sure she was doomed! She insisted that the train let us off at the very next stop—she didn't care where—and when they let us off in some tank town she had me hire two ambulances, four nurses and two doctors to accompany her all the way to Atlanta. They were only too happy, of course, to be around a celebrity and get their pictures taken for the newspapers. The two doctors couldn't figure out what all the fuss was about—yet Rosa "died" all the way back to Atlanta. In fact, she had to cancel *Gioconda* and *Juive* in Atlanta because she insisted she was still sick. She wouldn't have sung at all in Atlanta that season if Colonel Warfield hadn't put up the money for a performance of *Cavalleria rusticana*, which was given as a double bill with *Tosca* on the last night of the Atlanta tour.[66]

Not surprisingly, this tendency toward hypochondria became more pronounced during *Norma*, and as her anxieties increased she hinted of having to cancel performances from time to time. Gatti seems to have viewed this more as a case of fear, a growing reluctance to perform for fear of failing to attain the high standards she had led critics and audiences to expect from her. He knew, however, that once Rosa was actually in the opera house her sense of artistic duty would impel her to perform and that as soon as she went on stage (as Helen Noble and others attested) all traces of fear swiftly disappeared. For that reason, Gatti often placed a telephone call backstage to be certain that his *diva* had arrived.[67] By Rosa's own admission she often circled the Metropolitan Opera House on foot as many as twenty times, with her car and driver in tow in case she needed to dodge autograph-seekers. It was her way, she said, of summoning the courage she needed to walk through the stage door.[68]

Family tensions added to Rosa's nervous condition when Carmela's long-anticipated Metropolitan Opera debut took place as Amneris in *Aida* in December 1925, with Martinelli as Radames and Elisabeth Rethberg in the title role. Eleven months earlier in January 1925, the Metropolitan stage became the site of the Ponselle sisters' first joint appearance since their vaudeville days. The occasion was one of the popular Sunday evening concerts at the Metropolitan. Fittingly, the first duet the sisters performed was from *La gioconda*. The United Press syndicate used this joint concert as an occasion to recycle some of the myths about the sisters' early lives in Meriden, transforming them into "daughters of a poor ice man"[69] and claiming that Carmela had gone into vaudeville "to pay for Rosa's education" in Meriden.

The real story, as those closest to the Ponselles recalled, could scarcely have been more different. "Carmela had gotten so that she couldn't stand Rosa being so successful, being in the limelight all the time," Edith remembered. "What was worse, Carmela wasn't making any money to speak of. She didn't get that many offers and engagements at that time, and she wouldn't listen to anyone about what to do with her career. Nino Romani urged her to sing in Europe to build up her reputation, and he had the connections to get her the right engagements over there. But no, she was bound and determined to do everything her own way. Yet all the while she was forced to live off Rosa."[70] According to Libbie Miller, "They were all living together in Rosa's penthouse on Riverside Drive—Rosa, Edith, and Carmela. It was a big place, but it wasn't big enough for two Ponselles."[71] Inevitably, the tension between the sisters began to affect their relationship. As Edith expressed it:

> Carmela kept after Rosa to get her a Metropolitan contract, but, as Rosa was always telling her, she [Rosa] didn't have that kind of pull. Yet Carmela wouldn't let up, and things finally came to a head at Christmas time in 1924. Nino Romani, Rosa, Carmela, and I were decorating the tree and preparing for Christmas Day when Carmela let out a shriek and ran toward the living room windows. She flung them open and screamed, "This is the end! If I don't sing at the Met, I refuse to go on living!" This was about the tenth time this scene had been played out, and Rosa was accustomed to it by now. "Go ahead and jump," she told her matter-of-factly. "Just don't bloody up the sidewalk—I can't stand messes!" Meantime, Romani and I finished decorating the tree."[72]

The reviews Carmela received at her debut could not have eased either sister's state of mind. "It would be manifestly unfair to pass final judgment upon the singing of Carmela Ponselle . . . for her nerves were unstrung and she did not do herself justice," said the *Evening Post*. "She was, however, most impressive in her opulent beauty and fitted well into the picture. It seemed at times as if she would have been more satisfactory had she not forced her tones, but that fault, which her sister had and is gradually eliminating, will probably be overcome."[73]

The *Tribune* considered it "a pity that she had to be pitted against that glorious-voiced singer, Elisabeth Rethberg," and also had to compete with Martinelli, "who was in fine voice and spirits."[74] Regrettably, neither singer gained a favorable impression of the elder Ponselle from that occasion. To their mutual friend Myron Ehrlich, Martinelli confessed that Carmela's tendency to be "the star, the conductor, and the stage director" had made him angry enough to "want to choke her" during the rehearsals.[75] The normally easygoing Rethberg voiced the same complaint to James Alfonte years afterward. Carmela, she said, had spent most of her time "giving me stage directions and ordering me around."[76]

Wilfred Pelletier was in the audience for Carmela's debut. He had also observed her during one of the *Aida* rehearsals. "It was out of regard for Rosa," he wrote in his memoirs, "that the [Metropolitan] administration chose to engage Carmela. Her voice had neither the *éclat* nor the quality of Rosa—no! A voice like [hers] comes alone once in a hundred years." Assessing Carmela's Amneris, he wrote, "Her interpretation was good—and nothing more." He concluded his assessment with a polite rhetorical question: "But isn't it already a lot, just to be the sister of a celebrity?"[77] In private, however, Pelletier was a good deal more candid. When asked how he would describe the qualitative difference in the sisters' artistry, he replied, "Well, do you know the difference between day and night?"[78]

If Carmela never garnered the artistic respect and public acclaim her younger sister enjoyed, she eventually found her niche at the Metropolitan and remained on the roster for a decade, achieving notable success in a limited repertoire. But by the time Gatti-Casazza eventually cast the sisters together in *La gioconda*, fulfilling at last the hopes they had nurtured in vaudeville, their relationship had already become distant and tense. After one of their joint appearances in this opera, W. J. Henderson paid them a professional compliment that also would have described their relationship offstage. "Together," Henderson wrote, "they made the fire fly."[79]

CHAPTER SEVEN

Sleepless Nights

Although Carmela ignored Romano Romani's advice that she should restart her career in Europe, Libbie Miller drew from his suggestion a related strategy for Rosa's career. In later years Libbie said:

> On this side of the Atlantic, there wasn't another soprano who could touch Rosa after she did *Norma*. Yet Raisa, Muzio, Jeritza, and the others had made their reputations not just over here but in Europe too. Rosa, of course, hadn't. Even before *Norma*, not only Romani but even Rosa Raisa and [her husband] Giacomo Rimini had tried to talk Rosa into singing abroad. But nothing ever came of it.[1] She didn't want to sing in Italy (she knew she would be a nervous wreck over there), but Covent Garden appealed to her. After *Norma*, knowing that she would need another "first" in her career, she began to think more seriously about London.[2]

While preparing *Norma* and weighing her options abroad, she added the role of Fiora in Montemezzi's "swiftly tragic yet deeply romantic" *L'amore dei tre re* to her repertoire.[3] When she sang the role for the first time on 29 December 1926, Gigli was her Avito in a cast that also featured (in the words of critic Olin Downes) "the powerful person of Adamo Didur . . . who had appeared in the opera's original [Metropolitan] production on 2 January 1914."[4] Amid the near-dozen curtain calls after the second act, Downes reported, Gigli and Didur "gallantly ran off some moments later to leave Miss Ponselle alone for her well-earned ovation."

In time, Lucrezia Bori would be given the majority of performances of *L'amore dei tre re*. Rosa, despite a memorable association with the role among fans, would only sing Fiora a mere four times with the Metropolitan. Yet for the 1928–29 season-opening performance (which coincided with the tenth anniversary of her debut), Gatti chose not Bori but Ponselle. He cast Martinelli as Avito and Pinza as Archibaldo, but neither artist, according to the *Musical Courier*, was able to match the vocal perfection and dramatic depth of her Fiora. "Her tones sounded as fresh and mellow as ever," said the *Courier*, and her "conception of the role . . . now makes it one of the most telling in her roster of singing impersonations."[5]

Until Gatti's cast lists made it apparent that Fiora would remain Bori's role, *L'amore dei tre re* offered Rosa the prospect of singing music considerably less demanding than *Norma*, yet it was in *Norma* that the public wanted to hear her. Gatti-Casazza complied by scheduling it in Brooklyn, Philadelphia, Washington, Atlanta, Cleveland, and Rochester during the 1927–28 Metropolitan tour. Wherever *Norma* was heard, the local critics, like their New York counterparts, had nothing but praise for Rosa's performance. Rochester critics judged it "the ultimate demonstration of classical vocalism,"[6] and in Cleveland the audience that overflowed the 9,000-seat Public Auditorium "shouted itself hoarse for an encore of the nobly sung 'Casta diva.'"[7]

Gatti kept *Norma* on the roster for the next season's tour, but only after Rosa was able to negotiate, through Libbie, an agreement giving her fewer *Norma*s to sing than during the previous tour. The new terms also provided for her to be cast on tour in operas that she found more congenial to her voice—notably *Cavalleria rusticana*, *Gioconda*, and *Aida*.[8] Her motives for wanting this sort of formal understanding with Gatti, Libbie believed, were traceable to the heavy demands of *Norma*, demands that had already begun to outweigh the feelings of accomplishment the opera initially had given her.

Moreover, as Libbie explained in a letter to the Metropolitan's Edward Ziegler, Rosa also needed time to learn two new roles: Donna Anna in *Don Giovanni*, which Gatti was planning to revive under Serafin's musical direction after an absence of twenty-one seasons, and the title role in Verdi's *Luisa Miller*, which would be heard for the first time at the Metropolitan on 21 December 1929. In *Don Giovanni*, Gatti would assemble one of the stellar casts of his long tenure, bringing together Ponselle (Donna Anna), Gigli (Don Ottavio), Rethberg (Donna Elvira), Editha Fleisher (Zerlina), and Pinza in the title role.[9] This and *Luisa Miller*, Libbie told Ziegler, weighed heavily on Rosa:

> We know you share our belief that Miss Ponselle has given her best to the annual Metropolitan tours. This has been especially true with Norma. The role needs no comment, as we all remember Mme Lehmann's remark that singing Norma is more difficult than singing all the Brünnhildes.
>
> Donna Anna soon will become her first Mozart role. I believe Mr. Romani has discussed with you his concern that the very demanding music

of "Luisa Miller" may present a great strain to her if it [Luisa] is added to Donna Anna and Norma in the same season and also put on the tour.[10]

Of the two new productions, *Don Giovanni* was given first, but without Ponselle's Donna Anna, owing to a respiratory illness and related vocal problems that had incapacitated her for nearly a month.[11] Gatti had delayed the first performance in the hope that she would improve, but was finally forced to go on without her. "Of Miss Leonora Corona, who substituted for the ailing Rosa Ponselle," wrote Lawrence Gilman, "it will perhaps be sufficient to say that she made Miss Ponselle's indisposition seem a costly thing indeed for the

METROPOLITAN OPERA HOUSE
GRAND OPERA SEASON 1929~1930
GIULIO GATTI-CASAZZA, GENERAL MANAGER

MONDAY EVENING, JANUARY 6, AT 8 O'CLOCK

DON GIOVANNI

OPERA IN TWO ACTS (TEN SCENES)
(IN ITALIAN)
BOOK BY LORENZO DA PONTE

MUSIC BY WOLFGANG AMADEUS MOZART

DON GIOVANNI .... EZIO PINZA
DONNA ANNA .... ROSA PONSELLE
IL COMMENDATORE .... LEON ROTHIER
DON OTTAVIO .... BENIAMINO GIGLI
DONNA ELVIRA .... ELISABETH RETHBERG
ZERLINA .... EDITHA FLEISCHER
LEPORELLO .... PAVEL LUDIKAR
MASETTO .... LOUIS D'ANGELO

Minuet by CORPS DE BALLET
Arranged by AUGUST BERGER

CONDUCTOR .... TULLIO SERAFIN

STAGE DIRECTOR .... WILHELM VON WYMETAL
CHORUS MASTER .... GIULIO SETTI
STAGE MANAGER .... ARMANDO AGNINI
NEW SCENIC PRODUCTION BY JOSEPH URBAN

Positively No Encores Allowed

Program Continued on Next Page
Correct Librettos For Sale in the Lobby
Knabe Piano Used Exclusively

My only Mozart role, a great opera

Rosa Ponselle

Figure 7. Program displaying the all-star cast the Metropolitan assembled for the 1929–30 revival of Mozart's *Don Giovanni*. "My only Mozart role, a great opera," reads Ponselle's handwritten comment. COURTESY OF BILL PARK.

Metropolitan."[12] (Even more costly would have been the damaging combination of Ponselle's and Elisabeth Rethberg's absences, which nearly had occurred as the result of a badly burned arm Rethberg was nursing. Rather than risk both stars' replacement by second-cast singers, Gatti called upon his persuasive abilities to convince Rethberg to sing the performance in spite of her arm being in a sling. But, wrote Lawrence Gilman, she "was not, unluckily, in her best form.")[13]

Ezio Pinza's Don Giovanni, a role in which he would later be heralded, was not well received in this production. The New York *World*'s Pitts Sanborn implored him to "cut out the hop-and-skip-and-jumping and compose himself more like a *grand seigneur*."[14] But when Ponselle joined the cast some four weeks later, her Donna Anna added a new dimension to the production. Said Olin Downes, "Such singing as she accomplished in a role far removed from the vocal and dramatic style to which she is accustomed was something of a revelation even to her most ardent admirers. . . . Last night she consecrated herself wholeheartedly to the essence of the Mozartean tradition, never projecting herself out of the picture, always maintaining an aristocratic elegance of line and aloof distinction and a careful coordination of vocal and dramatic elements with the performances of her associates."[15]

Luisa Miller premiered at the Metropolitan on 21 December 1929, a month after the first performance of the *Don Giovanni* revival. The critics, however, were as much interested in Ponselle's vocal state after her lingering respiratory illness as they were in Verdi's early-period work. Gilman thought the opera "far from foolproof" and ventured that its success with Metropolitan audiences would depend less upon the score than upon "a well sung performance."[16] With Giacomo Lauri-Volpi as Rodolfo, Giuseppe de Luca as Miller, Tancredi Pasero as the Count, and Ponselle as the heroine Luisa, the opera "received such a performance yesterday" in Gilman's words. In *The New York Times*, Downes wrote:

> The audience was agog to discover whether Miss Ponselle's voice, after her illness, was its old self; whether she would equal or surpass previous efforts. The voice was glorious to hear. The interval of absence made its exceptional texture and its superiority to other voices more apparent than ever. No doubt as a result of the throat trouble from which Miss Ponselle has been suffering there was the occasional suggestion of effort in her singing, the occasional spread of a tone when she coped with the fortissimos of Verdi's orchestra, and a little less "velvet" when she drove the upper register. These, and some slight inaccuracies of intonation in the early part of the performance, are certainly the relics of the immediate past. The incomparable voice has come back to the Metropolitan audience. The occasion of its return was an unusually trying role, one that demands range, volume, and highly dramatic expression throughout the opera.

> Meeting these demands, Miss Ponselle on a number of occasions did some of the best-considered singing that she has done on the Metropolitan stage. She sought dramatic meaning and not merely stage effect. When the occasion permitted, she produced beautiful piano and pianissimo effects. She achieved dramatic expression, sometimes by means of full-throated song, at other times by the emphasis of understatement when contrast, marked simplicity of address, and careful observance of nuance told the listener more than the ear-splitting fortissimo could.[17]

During the 1929–30 season, Ponselle would sing only one performance of *Luisa Miller* outside New York City—in Philadelphia, at the "other" Metropolitan Opera House. Even more so than for *Luisa Miller*, the large and expensive cast of *Don Giovanni* tended to anchor that production to New York City; in the following season only one performance would be given on tour (also in Philadelphia), but with Maria Müller replacing Elisabeth Rethberg as Donna Elvira.

Guilio Gatti-Casazza scheduled no performances of *Norma* on tour in the 1929–30 season. Whether this came as a result of Libbie Miller's letter to Edward Ziegler or was merely a concession on Gatti's part is not clear. The letter itself had been prompted by some unexpected news from London, conveyed to Ponselle through her friend Natalie Townsend. Two seasons earlier, Lieutenant-Colonel Eustace Blois had assumed the leadership of a new syndicate at Covent Garden.[18] He was now interested, Mrs. Townsend reported, in the prospect of bringing Ponselle to London in *Norma*.[19]

From that time on, not surprisingly, the thought of repeating this taxing opera before audiences in public halls in Cleveland or Rochester was no longer either attractive or lucrative as far as Ponselle was concerned. Instead, *Cavalleria rusticana*, *Aida* (with "O patria mia" comfortably sung a tone lower), and *Gioconda*—plus occasional performances of *Andrea Chénier*, *Trovatore*, *Forza del destino*, *Juive*, and *Ernani*, preferably with Martinelli, her favorite tenor partner at that time—would have to suffice for the tour.

Although there is no record of the exact date and circumstances of the first face-to-face meeting between Ponselle and Colonel Blois, their surviving letters—all of them handwritten and lengthy and chatty, now preserved in the Covent Garden archives—confirm not only the smoothness of their working relationship but also the attention and affection Rosa showered upon the silver-haired Blois. While genuine, this treatment was quite pragmatic in Libbie's estimation:

> Colonel Blois was an older man, tall and very distinguished looking, and as you would expect, he was rather formal. Rosa's familiarity and directness took him by surprise. One minute, she would treat him the way she treated Gatti-Casazza, very formal and deferential. The next minute she might treat

> him like a much older boyfriend. They developed such a relationship that for the roles she wanted to sing, she did all of the negotiating herself. She all but kept me out of it. By the time she was done, the Colonel had given her every opera she asked for.[20]

Libbie's contention is borne out by Ponselle's correspondence with Blois. She wanted (and got) six operas for her Covent Garden seasons. Four were already staples in her repertoire: *Norma*, *La gioconda*, *L'amore dei tre re*, and *La forza del destino*. Another, Romano Romani's one-act *Fedra*, had enjoyed nominal popularity in Italy following its 1915 premiere, with Raisa in the title role. With Serafin slated to conduct, Blois scheduled *Fedra*'s London premiere for 7 June 1931; two subsequent performances would also be given. Ponselle's letters suggest that *Fedra*, strangely, had been a relatively easy "sell"; yet *Forza* seems to have necessitated the full measure of her charms before Blois was willing to approve it. In mid-November 1929, while recuperating from a lingering respiratory ailment, she wrote to Blois from her Manhattan penthouse:

> Well, here I am in bed for a change getting over a cold which has hung on for exactly one month. Do you know that I haven't sung so far? Yes, my dear—I arrived in the good old USA and the very next day I was stricken with a very bad cold—and the doctor I had at that time said that it was merely a head cold, and that it was perfectly alright [*sic*] for me to sing, so I did. I sang two radio concerts and rehearsals at the Metropolitan Opera House for two weeks or more—until one fine day I couldn't talk. Imagine such a thing! He was doctoring my nose instead of my chest. *The brute!* You can just about imagine what discommotion [*sic*] I caused poor Gatti and Mr. Ziegler. Just one month and one week laid up—*that's all. Povera me*!
>
> However, the doctor assures me that in two or three days I can begin singing—I hope so—as it will give me only *one* week to rehearse and sing *Don Giovanni* on the 29th of November. It was to go on the 21st but Gatti was kind enough to postpone it in the hope that I will be well by that time. They are very eager for me to sing Donna Anna—so here's hoping that I can do it. Pray for me, will you? I know you will. You are always so kind and helpful in every way.[21]

She now made her pitch for *Forza* and capped it with a comment suggestive of a relationship that had already grown quite personal:

> So you are not so sure that you will give *La forza del destino*? Oh! I think that the English would like it very much. Why not try? It is very beautiful and quite new to London, which in itself would be a novelty.
>
> Now for a little attention to you. I can't tell you how much I appreciated your letter—in fact, the only fault is that you don't write often enough.

> Write larger next time and put the letter in a Thermos bottle so that the words will *not* cool off before they reach America.[22]

She continued her letter in the same affectionate vein, congratulating Blois on having been awarded the Order of the Commendatore by the government of Italy for his efforts in promoting Italian works at Covent Garden. "Now that you have been made Commendatore," she kidded him, "I do hope you won't high-hat me next year."

She closed the letter with a mention of the sixth role she had recently negotiated with him—a role which, despite her initial success with it, would eventually immerse her in the first major controversy of her career. "Will you promise to talk to me and be as nice as usual?" she asked Blois tongue in cheek. "God help you and *Traviata* if you are not!"

The Interview

From interviews of Rosa Ponselle by the author (June 1975, January 1977, and December 1978), by Hugh M. Johns (June–July 1968), and by Fred Calland (1977, precise date unknown). Excerpts from informal conversations at Villa Pace between Ponselle and James M. Alfonte (which were provided to the author by Col. Alfonte, along with his permission to quote from them) have been incorporated into the portions of the interview concerning the Don Giovanni *revival. Transcribed with minor editing.*

For the first decade of your career, you sang opera only in the United States. Surely you must have had offers from abroad. What led you to decline them?

There were plenty of offers. I had them from Paris, London, Buenos Aires, [and] even from La Scala. I did accept an offer to sing in Havana; I sang some concerts there, but not operas. At that time, I could have sung just about anywhere in Latin America or South America that I wanted. I had an offer [to sing] in Buenos Aires, as a matter of fact. This was before I signed with Covent Garden. [Claudia] Muzio asked me to sing in Buenos Aires.

Muzio asked you? Was she part of the management at the Teatro Colón?

She was trying to help out [impresario] Walter Mocchi. He had been doing "short seasons" in Buenos Aires; he would put on four or five productions in the spring and early summer at the Teatro Colón, and maybe one or two other [theaters]. He was having a tough time at the box office, so Muzio, who was very big in Buenos Aires, asked me to come there and help them out. She and I were friends, and I would have liked to do something for Walter

Mocchi if I could. I remember that he sent me a contract, but I had other obligations at the time so I couldn't accept his offer.[23] But there were always offers to think about from other places too.

Italy, being the "home country" of most of the operas for which you were known, would seem to have been a more logical choice for your first appearances abroad.

Oh, God! Singing in Italy scared me out of my wits. Just the thought of it! They [the Italians] might tear you apart, even if you were singing pretty well. It seemed like the more famous you were, the worse they might treat you.

Singing in Italy "scared" you. Why? Surely, you had no doubts about your ability.

No, it wasn't that. Once I got on the stage and the curtain was up, I stopped being myself and became the character. Once you're out there, you don't think about *you*. You don't think much, period. If you're in character, you're being the character. So, no, I wasn't worried once I got on stage. It was the suffering I had to go through to get there. And most of all I was worried about the audiences and how they would take to me. That made me suffer, worrying about that.

What was it about Covent Garden that finally made you relent?

I thought that the English [audiences] would accept me better than the Italians would. To me, the English people seemed more like an American audience. They might be restrained if they didn't think you were much, maybe they would applaud with two fingers [on] each hand instead of clapping with all ten, but they weren't going to humiliate you like the Italian audiences were known for—throwing things at you if you cracked a note, running you off the stage and maybe out of town.

Was there much negotiating you had to do with Covent Garden?

I left that to Miss [Libbie] Miller, my manager. I didn't get involved with the business end—I just went where they pointed me. I mean, I had a say about what I was going to sing; I was no beginner, after all.

Did you deal personally with Colonel Blois, the impresario at that time?

I had nothing but pleasant, social kinds of dealings with him. We got to be pretty good friends. I used to kid him a lot. You could have fun with him. His name was Eustace but I'd call him Useless, just kidding around. He wanted [me to sing] *Norma*, you see. He had [Tullio] Serafin help work on me to get *Norma* over there. That was fine with me, really, because that [role] was one of my pets. I was going to debut in *Norma*, and they gave me a choice of other roles that would fit their repertory and their needs. So for my first time at Covent Garden—I sang there three seasons in all—I picked *Norma* and *Gioconda*.

Did you become involved in any of the details of the productions?

I don't know what you mean.

The costuming, the design of the sets, details of that type.

I used my own costumes, either the ones I had made up for my performances at the Met, or ones that I had designed for my London performances. But other than that I never got involved with the other things you're talking about. Like I told you, I just went where they pointed me.

You were introduced to Melba just before your first Norma *at Covent Garden. If I'm correct, your full name is actually Rosa Melba Ponzillo, with Melba being your confirmation name. Did your introduction to Melba live up to your expectations of meeting such a legend?*

Oh, no! It was such a disappointment! And that story about my name being Rosa Melba is only half true, by the way. I did try to take Melba as my confirmation name but the priest there in Meriden—Father Ricci, who was our parish priest—let me have it over that Melba business. "There is no Saint Melba," he told me. [Do] you know how in the Catholic church the priest is supposed to tap you on the cheek to cast out the Devil when you're confirmed? Well, when it came time for the little tap, Rosa Melba had to became Rosa *Maria* right there on the spot, and instead of a tap, I got a good hard slap across the face. But to give that priest his due, he was right about one thing: there was no Saint Melba. I found that out when I met her.

Who arranged the meeting?

I asked Natalie Townsend to help arrange it with Melba's representatives. Natalie knew all the right people in London society. Her husband [Laurence Townsend] was the ambassador to Belgium and also to Austria around the turn of the century, which is how Natalie got many of her social connections. By the way, she was the one who introduced Perle Mesta into Washington society. That's how Perle got her start. Perle always thanked me for introducing her to Natalie.

Was your meeting with Melba planned mainly for publicity purposes?

No, no. I really wanted to be able to say I had met Melba because, no kidding, she was an idol. Miss [Anna] Ryan, my [piano] teacher, used to talk about Melba like she was from another world. I wanted to tell Melba what an inspiration she was to us when we were studying. So it was no publicity stunt just for the cameras. I was the one who thought it up. It was something I really and truly wanted to do.

Had you ever heard Melba in a "live" performance?

Just once. Carmela and I were still in vaudeville. Melba sang *Faust* in New York. Cleofonte Campanini, [impresario] of the Chicago Opera Company, brought her there.[24] That was the only time I heard her in person.

Were you impressed with her Marguerite?

No, but she was old then, and at that time, which was before my debut, I didn't know much about *Faust* or the French tradition.

What was your impression of her voice?

It wasn't a big voice, and it wasn't a small voice. It was beautiful, but it wasn't my kind of voice. There were too many still tones in it for my taste.

When you say "still tones," are you referring to a "white" voice?

To me, a white voice is very shrill, kind of like a train whistle. There's nothing musical about that kind of sound. What I'm talking about are tones that don't have much vibrato—they don't move, they don't vibrate; it's as if the tones stand still. That's what I call a still tone. It doesn't have much feeling in it. Melba's voice was like that, at least when I heard her.

When you were introduced to her, do you remember how you greeted Melba, and what she said to you in return?

When I came into the part of Claridge's where this private dining room was, I saw Natalie [Townsend] waiting for me outside the room. She nodded in order to let me know that Melba was already in there. Well, I went in—it was a pretty good-sized room, or it seemed like it at the time—and there was Melba standing over near one end of this large table, which was set with beautiful flowers. At first I thought she might walk over toward me and meet me halfway, but she didn't move a muscle. I remember thinking to myself, "Okay, she *is* Melba, so I guess that means I should be the one who goes to her, not the other way around." The closer I got, I felt she was kind of looking me over. She was stone-faced, and her expression didn't soften up when I finally got in front of her. I put out my hand, and kind of bowed a little bit—you know, she was *Dame* Melba, which to me was like being the Queen's first cousin or something. But before I could really say anything, she said to me very stiffly, "You must be the new singer from New York." The way she said it made it sound like she had never heard of me, let alone that we were going to be having a private dinner. Then she said something like, "What sort of voice are you supposed to have?" I could tell right then that she had no interest at all in talking to me, but I wasn't going to stand there and have her treat me like somebody who was bothering her for an autograph.

How did you respond?

At first I didn't know what I should say, but then I told her, "Well, Dame Melba,[25] they say my voice is a dramatic soprano." She said to me that she would be the judge of that! Then she wanted to know what roles I sang—as if she didn't already know from Colonel Blois and didn't read the newspapers. She didn't say much else, although she did tell me that I should never expect any applause at Covent Garden until the end of an act. "This isn't the Metropolitan," she said (you know, in case it hadn't occurred to me that I had already crossed the Atlantic). She went on to say that even she, the great Melba, never got applause after an aria. The rest of the night Melba spent most of her time talking to Natalie about Lord this, and Lady that, and Princess so-and-so, which was fine with me. You see, that priest in Meriden was right: there was no Saint Melba.

Do you know whether Melba attended any of your Covent Garden performances?

She was supposed to come to *Norma*, but she sent a letter saying that she couldn't be there because a friend of hers was dying. Some people told me afterward that Melba did show up incognito.[26] I hope she did, because it must have been a big surprise to her, the way the audience reacted. She had told me that the English never applauded anybody after an aria. Well, they gave me six minutes of applause after "Casta diva." Now, to somebody who's never been on a stage [before an audience], six minutes might not seem like a long time. But if you start counting it out loud—one second, two seconds, three seconds—then you'll know what six minutes means when you're standing there waiting to sing again. I know it was six minutes, by the way, because Edith [Prilik, her secretary] timed it with her watch.

Had anyone forewarned you about how to approach Melba?

Oh, yes, but I didn't pay enough attention to it at the time. John McCormack called me up at the hotel. (He and I were great friends; we played a lot of tennis together, and he was like a big brother to me.) Well, McCormack couldn't stand the sight of Melba. When he called me in London, the first words out of his mouth were, "Have you met that bitch yet?" I never once heard McCormack call her Melba. It was always "that bitch." I loved that!

Your former manager, Libbie Miller, told me that during your first season at Covent Garden, John McCormack repeatedly urged you to add Elisabeth in Tannhäuser *and Elsa in* Lohengrin. *Is that true?*

He thought those roles were just right for me, and, yes, he did talk to me about it several times. Another one [who felt the same way] was the [Gramophone Company's] recording man, Fred Gaisberg. He thought I should sing the lighter Wagner roles too. I had considered [doing those roles] a little before then, actually. I even thought about costumes for them, thinking that someday I would sing them. I did buy a costume from Salomea Krusceniski: it was for *Lohengrin*. I still have the cape for it; it's in storage downstairs with my costumes. I used to do "Dich teure halle" and Elsa's Dream in some of my early concerts. In fact, I recorded Elsa's Dream with Romani when I was still with Columbia, but I never got around to doing either *Lohengrin* or *Tannhäuser* on stage.

Going back to your first Covent Garden appearance, I would like to ask you about Norma. *When you have spoken about your New York performances, you have talked about the constant challenge of keeping your emotions in check during* Norma. *Was this easier or harder when you sang it in London?*

Well, it's hard anywhere. Even on [the Metropolitan] tour. London wasn't any different.

But were there any special challenges you faced at Covent Garden that you hadn't at the Metropolitan Opera?

Well, the casts weren't the same. I mean, the ones at Covent Garden were probably good singers, but not like [the singers at] the Met. But I don't want that to sound like I'm criticizing anybody. Oh yes, and there was a problem with the children. Did I ever tell you about the children they put with me in London?

No, I don't believe so.

Oh, that's a story! There was some rule at that time that they couldn't use children on the stage. I don't know whether it had something to do with child labor [laws] or what, but they used midgets to play the children in *Norma*. I didn't meet them until the rehearsals, you see, so I didn't know anything about this. Well, the little boy—or so I thought—was cuddly and cute, and in the rehearsals I would hold him close to me and caress him. I didn't know the difference, because if you put a wig and theater makeup on a child, you can't tell what's underneath it. Anyway, this "boy" would hug me *so* tight, like a child would cling to his mother. But he kept trying to kiss me! Then during one of the rehearsals he started playing with my breasts! Well, naive me, I said something after the rehearsal about how affectionate this little boy was, and everybody started laughing! That's when they finally told me that he wasn't a little boy at all!

I'd like to ask you about the singers who were cast with you.

I don't remember any casts. That was a long time ago.

Let me try some names, if I may. Irene Minghini-Cattaneo sang Adalgisa to your Norma. Do you recall anything about your performances with her?

She and I didn't get along. She caused a scene at the dress rehearsal for *Norma*. It got pretty ugly at the rehearsal and then afterward with some rumors that she started about me. But I don't want to go into that because I don't like to talk badly about anybody.

Perhaps we can talk about her voice and musicianship. Did Minghini-Cattaneo's voice make a lasting impression upon you?

You see, the trouble she caused at that rehearsal is the only thing I can remember about her. I don't like friction. It's very destructive. She made a scene because Colonel Blois and Vincenzo Bellezza, who was conducting *Norma*, said it was all right for me to be in the [dress] rehearsal without wearing my full costume, and Cattaneo couldn't stand that.

Was there some problem with your costume?

The [costume] I had in London was the same one that I had worn for my Metropolitan *Norma*s. Like I told you, it had tiny pearl beads sewn onto the train—hundreds of them, all hand-stitched. That made the costume very heavy, very bulky, and it was almost impossible to clean or repair it if something happened to it before the performance. That's why they wanted me do the dress rehearsal in street clothes.

What could possibly cause another singer to argue over something like that?

Well, you would have to ask her. I didn't know then, and I still don't know. She had a fit about it in front of the rest of the cast. I was speechless; I didn't have a clue that she knew or cared anything about what I was going to wear. But she got ugly about it, and she started this rumor that I was having an affair with Colonel Blois. She said it was the reason they made an exception for me at the dress rehearsal. Imagine a rumor like that! I was very hurt by what she said about me. I could never trust her after that.

You said you were hurt by what she said, which is certainly understandable, but the way you tell it now, it sounds as if you weren't really angry at her. Were you angry at the time?

Like I said, I don't like friction. If you get mad at somebody, it makes for more friction, and then it gets harder for everybody because they get drawn into it. I don't know what got into Cattaneo. She was a powerful woman, you know; she married the heir of a big music publishing house over there. She had a good voice too. I don't know what her problem was. The poor dear, maybe she just wasn't very sure of herself.

Minghini-Cattaneo was also cast with you in La gioconda. *Had things between you gotten better by the time you did* Gioconda*?*

How did you say that? "Between us"? She was the one who had the problem, not me. I never wanted any trouble with her or anybody else. As for *Gioconda*, I had so much to do, trying to keep my mind on my own performance, I didn't have time to think about her. As I remember it, though, the *Gioconda*s went all right. But let's just say I'd rather have been singing with my sister.

Because her voice would have been a better complement to yours?

No, not just that (but we sounded so much alike, Carmela and I, so of course our voices fit nicely together). What I mean is I could always rely on my sister, I could always trust her, which I couldn't [do] with Cattaneo.

Let me ask you about two tenors who were cast with you during your first Covent Garden season: Nicolo Fusati, your Pollione, and Francesco Merli, who sang Enzo in La Gioconda *with you.*

Who was that first one you mentioned? What was [his] name?

Nicolo Fusati. I believe he had been brought to Covent Garden for the Otello *that same season.*

You couldn't prove it by me. I wouldn't know him or his voice if he walked into this room right now.

What about some of the other principals in your first Covent Garden season. I'm thinking of the baritone Giovanni Inghilleri, who did Barnaba with you, and Fernando Autori, the basso who sang Alvise.

I don't remember a thing about them. I don't mean that they weren't good. In fact, I'm sure they were the best that Covent Garden could get at that time. The reason I don't remember them is because I only did two or maybe three performances with them, and afterward I never saw or heard of them again. It wasn't like the Metropolitan, where I was singing with many of the same artists year after year. At Covent Garden, I was nervous because of the pressure I was feeling to do well with the English audiences, and as I've said before, I didn't socialize like some other singers did. That's why I don't remember the ones you just mentioned. You know, I don't even remember Merli singing *Gioconda* at all. I can't even picture him as Enzo right now; it's a complete blank. All I remember singing with him was *L'amore dei tre re*: that was unforgettable, even the rehearsals.

How so?

I'll need the air conditioning turned up if you get me started on that. Whew! I forgot myself around him, even in the rehearsals. I was a bad girl: those love scenes were pretty close to the real thing. He wasn't behaving himself, either. We got to liking the rehearsals so much that we were forgetting who we were, or where we were. You know, it's funny how those things happen to you when you least expect them to happen. You're put in the same room, the same situation with someone, and all of a sudden you're attracted. You don't know why, and in a way you don't want to know. You know that expression "animal passion"? Francesco Merli and I were animal passion—on the stage, I mean.

And only on the stage?

[She sings] "Some enchanted evening, you may see a stranger . . ." No, only on the stage and in those rehearsals, every last one of them.

Ezio Pinza sang the role of Archibaldo in the London production of L' amore dei tre re. *His presence must have strengthened the cast.*

I wouldn't say that he was a great Archibaldo, but you couldn't fault him. When I think of Archibaldo, the first person who comes to my mind is [Adamo] Didur, who sang with me in some of my performances of *L' amore dei tre re*. To me, Didur could never be surpassed in that role.

The mention of Pinza evokes memories of Gatti's revival of Don Giovanni, *and the "dream cast" of Pinza as the Don, you as Donna Anna, Elisabeth Rethberg as Donna Elvira, Editha Fleischer as Zerlina, and Gigli as Don Ottavio. Do you recall how long it took you to prepare Donna Anna?*

Not very long. Not like *Norma*, if that's what you mean. I didn't find it a hard part, particularly.

You prepared it under Maestro Serafin?

Well, I prepared the score with Romani first, but I did some work with Serafin while I was in Europe, and then we worked on it in New York together.

What do you remember most vividly about that famous cast?

Singing with Rethberg—that was the best thing.

According to the Metropolitan Annals, *you were indisposed for the first performance but joined the cast about seven or eight weeks later.*

Indisposed? I'll say I was! I lost my voice for a whole month. I got what they thought was a bad cold in Europe, but the doctors over there got it all wrong. Finally, I called in Dr. Verdi, my personal doctor, and he got it straightened out. But I was in bed for a whole month.

Leonora Corona, who understudied you, sang Donna Anna that first night. Do you recall her working with you?

My understudy? I don't remember anything about an understudy. I didn't work with anybody but Serafin. How could I? I was sick as a dog.

I may have been wrong referring to her that way, but according to the Annals *Leonora Corona sang Donna Anna when you were indisposed, and Maria Müller sang Donna Elvira after Rethberg was unavailable for the role. You sang most of the performances with Müller, I believe.*

Who?

Maria Müller, the soprano.

Oh, the washerwoman.

The "washerwoman"?

She used to beat time like a woman scrubbing clothes on a washboard.

Do you remember her voice? Was it any kind of voice at all?

How did you say that? "Any kind of voice at all?" That pretty well describes it.

So you wouldn't exactly place her in Rethberg's league.

Oh, no—please!

Were you impressed by Gigli's Don Ottavio?

Yes, yes, very much so. How couldn't you be impressed? And Schipa, too, I also sang some performances with him.

There was a backstage aspect of the Don Giovanni *revival that I want to ask you about, but I'll try to ask it delicately. I'm told that it was common knowledge at the Met that Pinza, who was married, was having an affair with Elisabeth Rethberg during that time. You were friends with both of them. Did their relationship interfere with the production?*

I wasn't friends with Pinza. I didn't socialize at all. I never had time.

But you considered Elisabeth Rethberg a friend.

Yes, but we didn't socialize. We respected each other.

Pinza was a handsome man, debonair and very self-confident. If there is any truth to even a fraction of the stories about his conquests, most women seem to have found him quite irresistible.

You see, I didn't know the person that you're talking about. The Pinza I remember was the one who used to come and go at the Metropolitan with cotton stuffed in his ears, wearing a big muffler and a heavy coat even in mild weather. He was so afraid that he might get sick. And "debonair"?—he wasn't debonair. He dressed like a *cafone*. (We don't have a word like that in English—it's like "fool.") He didn't have any manners, no culture at all. I don't think he knew how to eat with a knife and fork in those days. Grace Moore practically had to teach him how to eat in polite society. They used to say that she finally got him out of one-piece underwear too. Grace was a smart girl, you know. She saw through him. He had no morals at all. Girls, girls, girls—any size, any shape, any age, any color, it didn't matter to him. And what he did to his wife! He used to keep her waiting during rehearsals while he would hide out with some chorus girl, or ballerina, or whoever he could get his hands on. He would drop off his wife at the Thirty-ninth Street side of the Met, tell her to wait for him, and then he'd sneak out through the Fortieth Street side to meet some girl or other. And to think that poor Elisabeth Rethberg believed that line of his!

Did you ever have a problem with Pinza yourself?

During *Don Giovanni*, I used to stand in the wings and listen to Rethberg sing "Mi tradi," which was my favorite aria in the whole opera. While I was standing there, I was so taken up with her singing that I didn't realize that Pinza had come up behind me. Soon I felt his hand around my waist, making its way up to my breasts. He started whispering in my ear how we would be so wonderful together—the same thing he told every woman he met on the street. I grabbed his arm and pushed him away. I had to clench my teeth so that my voice wouldn't carry. "*Porco!*" I said. On the stage he could look and act like a king, but offstage he was a pig.

Verdi's Luisa Miller *entered your repertoire during the same season that you first sang Donna Anna. Do you consider Luisa one of your best roles?*

No. You have to admire anything that Verdi wrote, but I don't think you could say that it was one of his best. I did it because Gatti asked me to.

During that same time period, one of the roles you created at the Metropolitan was Montemezzi's La notte di Zoraima. *When you were singing at Covent Garden, the London newspapers reported that Montemezzi was in the audience at your first performance of* L' amore dei tre re, *and that he was brought on stage for a prolonged ovation after one of the acts. Do you recall that?*

Oh, sure, he was at several of the rehearsals too, and Bellezza went over parts of the score with him.

Did you and Montemezzi become well acquainted?

Yes, especially at St. Moritz. He and his wife located a villa for me there, and I saw a good bit of the Montemezzis when I was in the mountains taking a vacation. I got interested in mountain-climbing while I was in St. Moritz, and I tried to get Montemezzi to go on a climb with us, but I couldn't talk him into it.

At that particular time, did he mention to you, or perhaps even approach you, about La notte di Zoraima*?*

If he did, I wish he hadn't. God, that *Zoraima* thing was awful, and the critics tore it to pieces.[27] When I think of Montemezzi, I try only to remember what a beautiful opera he gave us in *L'amore dei tre re.*

During your second Covent Garden season, you sang L' amore dei tre re *and you repeated* Norma *with essentially the same cast that you had at your London debut. But the highlight of the season as far as the critics were concerned (and I suspect, the highlight from your standpoint as well) was your first appearance as Violetta in* La traviata.

In the back of my mind, you see, I had been thinking about doing my first *Traviata* in London rather than at the Met.

That's intriguing. You had sung your first Norma at the Met, and then you took it to London, and now you were thinking about singing your first Violetta for Covent Garden and singing it at the Met later on?

I can't say it was that clear. I just wanted to do Violetta at Covent Garden and then bring it to New York. But I needed to see for myself how things went with the English [audiences] first. *Gioconda* went very, very well, and as for *Norma*, it was a *big* success. After that, I felt the time was right for me to sing *Traviata* over there.

What made you turn your attention to the role of Violetta, especially after your triumph in Norma*?*

I was attracted to *Traviata* because to me there was a lot of dramatic potential there. I didn't worry about the vocal score—especially not after *Norma*, which tests your coloratura singing to the highest. I knew I would *sound* different because the timbre of my voice was darker and heavier, yet I could do all the coloratura. So I felt I could really create a very distinctive Violetta, vocally and also dramatically. There was some concern that I was too large for the role. At five feet seven in my bare feet, I was too tall, they thought. But I controlled my weight pretty well then, and with the right costuming, I knew I could look the part all right.

You have acknowledged that there were those who were not in favor of your taking on the role of Violetta. How did you overcome their concerns?

Well, Gatti didn't want me to do it at first. He didn't think my voice was right for it. The Metropolitan [audience] was used to hearing it [sung] by Galli-

Curci or Bori: light voices, in other words. That's why Gatti didn't think the audiences and the critics would accept a dramatic soprano in *Traviata*. But I got a lot of encouragement from Serafin. I would have to say that he was the one who encouraged me the most about *Traviata*. He said I had the voice for it because I was a dramatic soprano with coloratura [technique]. Serafin used to tell me that, in the days when Verdi wrote *Traviata*, they didn't divide up the soprano voice into the coloraturas, the lyrics, the spintos, and such. If you had the right technique, you could sing them all. That's why sopranos like [Lillian] Nordica and Lilli Lehmann had over one hundred roles that they could sing.

Did you draw upon any other conceptions of Violetta—say, Bori's or Muzio's, for example—in your own portrayal of the role?

Not theirs, no. Bori's Violetta was her own, and it wasn't anything like mine. [Hers was] all very *leggero*, very light, because that was the kind of voice she had. She was a tiny person, too, so she made Violetta fit her voice, her size, and her personality. Bori was like a cameo. That's how I would describe her and also her Violetta.

And Muzio's conception of the role?

That's a different story. Muzio's Violetta was more like the role as I imagined it—and Muzio was a great Violetta, for sure. But mine was different from hers too. She played [Violetta] tragically all through the score. But I added hope to her: I wanted Violetta to live, not to die. When she finally dies, I wanted the audience to feel it.

Was that your own insight as to how the opera should end?

No. I got it from Gemma Bellincioni. She sang *Traviata* at La Scala years and years before I came along, and they say that she was Verdi's favorite Violetta. I worked with her when I was preparing the role.

What brought you to Bellincioni?

See, I always like to go with the best authorities when I'm preparing a new role. That's why I went to Albert Carré for *Carmen*. I talked over a couple of possibilities with [Tullio] Serafin and Nino Romani, and I decided I would go to Bellincioni or Rosina Storchio for help with *Traviata*.

What made you decide on Bellincioni?

It was just that my voice and the way I thought about Violetta was more like Bellincioni's than Storchio's. I heard some of Bellincioni's records, and even though they were the old [acoustic] type, you could hear what a wonderful *spinto* voice she had. Later on when I went to Naples to consult with her, she sang a little bit for me (she had to have been in her late sixties or maybe past seventy at that time), and I could get a pretty good idea of her voice. She reminded me a lot of Muzio, in fact, but she used her chest voice a lot, and in that way she reminded me of [Rosa] Raisa. Now, Storchio's voice was more of a lyric coloratura, from what I understand. But she was a great singer and a great Violetta, so I'm sure I would have learned a lot from her. I felt closer to Bellincioni, and I have to credit her with helping me create Violetta the way I wanted to portray her.

Where did your sessions with Bellincioni take place?

In Naples; I spent about two or three weeks with her. This was in the summer before I did [*Traviata*] at Covent Garden. She was so nice to work with: very kind, very supportive, and she never tried to force her thinking on me about anything. In fact, when I sang through part of the score for her, she applauded me so sincerely and said to me, "*Diva mia*, there is nothing that I can give you that you don't already have." Talk about feeling flattered! I said to her, "Madame Bellincioni, will you 'mark' the first and last act for me, and just let me watch how you move and how you phrase?" Bellincioni mouthed the words, and sang some parts of the score in chest voice for me. Then I asked her about the sets in the last act, and especially how she portrayed Violetta in the final moments of the opera. When she "marked" the last act for me, it was like seeing the opera for the first time. She was doing what I had been trying to work out in my own mind, but she was adding little touches that made it so moving! When she finished I said to her, "Do you mind if I do the last act your way?" She said she would be honored; so I did the last act just like I saw her do it, and to me it was exactly right.

Surely, you must have been pleased with London's reaction to your Traviata.

Oh, yes! I kept adding to it—a little bit here, an extra touch there—before I sang it at the Metropolitan. When I came back to Covent Garden for my third season, I did *Traviata* again, along with *Forza del destino* and also Romani's *Fedra*, which was its London premiere.

Your Alvaro in Forza *was Aureliano Pertile. How would you assess his performance in the role?*

Oh! One of the greatest! I would have to say that after Caruso, he was my favorite tenor to sing with. He didn't have the most beautiful voice, but it was what he did with it. Pertile was one of the best actors I can remember. He really became the character he was singing, and he was so careful, so supportive and cooperative with the other cast members—just like Caruso was.

Tancredi Pasero sang Padre Guardiano. Did you like his singing?

I always liked him. I sang with him at the Met, of course; he did some of the *Norma*s with me. It wasn't a *profondo* voice like Mardones' was, and it wasn't as beautiful a voice as Pinza's; [it was] a little lighter in color than Pinza's, but a very, very nice voice. His vibrato was a little too rapid, as I remember it, but it was an even and well-centered vibrato, so it was all right.

If I may return for moment to the subject of Fedra, *which was written by your teacher and mentor Romano Romani, let me ask you to clarify for us whether yours was the first performance of the opera in London, or whether it was the premiere of* Fedra.

Oh, no, I didn't create the part. Nino [Romani] wrote it years before I did it. He wrote it for [Rosa] Raisa. The premiere was in Italy, but I sang it the first time it was given in England. Nino wrote a special aria for me, "O divina Afrodite," for the Covent Garden premiere. He wrote it on the liner while he was crossing the ocean, and it was a nice piece of music too.

The cast of Fedra *included Antonio Cortis, Cesare Formichi, and Elvira Casazza. What do you remember about their performances?*

Who was the first one you mentioned?

The tenor Antonio Cortis.

I don't remember much about him, except that he was a tenor and that he gave a good performance. But it wasn't a distinctive voice, at least not as I remember it.

What about Cesare Formichi and Elvira Casazza? My understanding is that she was related to Gatti-Casazza. Did you know her well?

Not at all. I couldn't place her voice if I heard it. But Formichi was in the Italian premiere of *Fedra*. It was a light baritone; he was a good enough artist.

Because Fedra *is not a part of the [active] repertoire, the story line isn't known to most of us. What are the moments that meant the most to you in the story?*

Well, the curtain went up with me (I mean my character) reclining on a chaise and staring blankly at the audience while some business was going on behind me on stage. The high point of the libretto is the murder scene, where Fedra stabs her *sorella di latta* [milk sister] as we say in Italian. The *sorella di latta* is sung by a lyric soprano. I wore a bronze crown with blue sapphires on it, and I had my hair piled high on my head. I wore my hair red in *Fedra:* a red wig, not my own hair. In the back there was a long spike, I guess you could call it, that had a bronze top with sapphires on it. As Fedra, after my big aria ("O divina Afrodite"), I pulled out the long spike and allowed my hair to fall down to my shoulders. Then I took that long spike and stabbed my *sorella di latta* with it. I didn't show any emotion right after I stabbed her; no emotion was called for because Fedra was so cold-blooded. Instead, I calmly put my hair back up, and I put the spike back in my hair to hold it in place. Then comes a duet: the mother of the *sorella di latta*, who sees that Fedra is agitated about something but doesn't know that she has murdered her daughter, sings a duet [with Fedra] in which the mother tries to calm her.

For want of another way to put this question, was Fedra *negotiated as a favor to you and therefore to Romani, or was it something that Covent Garden really wanted?*

Look, if they hadn't wanted to give it at all, they wouldn't have given it. It's as simple as that. I didn't demand it. That was never my way of doing things. We only suggested it, and Colonel Blois said yes to it. The [London] critics thought it was great. They couldn't figure out why the Metropolitan hadn't given it. By the way, both Richard Strauss and Igor Stravinsky were in the audience at one of my *Fedra* performances. Strauss came backstage afterward, and I was told by friends that Stravinsky was also there.

After one of your Traviata *performances in London, you were introduced to another legend, Luisa Tetrazzini. Can we assume that this proved to be a much happier occasion for you than meeting Melba?*

Oh, yes! [Tetrazzini] was a "pet" of mine. I heard her when I was just a kid. Miss Ryan took me to hear her. At Covent Garden, I had my picture taken with her in my dressing room.[28] [The Spanish dancer] La Argentina[29] was [in the photograph] with us. I had an enlargement sent to Tetrazzini, and I got such a lovely note from her about it. But, you know, when I met her it was sad in a way, because she was—well, how can I say it?—she was down when I met her.

Do you mean "down on her luck"?

Luck didn't have anything to do with it, not unless you mean bad luck. Her trouble was men. She had one lover after the other, and from what I understood at the time, they lived off her. They took her money, and then they left her. She was too easy with men.

Did you have the impression that she was just getting by, money-wise?

To look at her, you wouldn't have thought so. She was dressed nicely. She was pretty big around the middle, but she dressed very tastefully. She had a lot of pride too. She wasn't singing opera any more, not that I heard about, anyhow. They told me her voice was pretty much gone by then. I think she was singing in what we would call vaudeville over here, but the English don't call it that. But do you know [that] she brought me a big spray of roses? That's the kind of person she was. She couldn't have been nicer to me. Violetta was one of her best roles, you know. When she told me wonderful things about my Violetta, I was really touched. She was nothing like Melba.

A Photographic Portfolio

Rosa Ponselle as Norma, 1927.
PHOTOGRAPH BY HERMAN MISHKIN.
SAFKA & BAREIS COLLECTION.

Plate 1. These two snapshots, taken in 1914 outside a relative's home in New Haven, are the only photographs known to exist from Ponselle's teenage years, when she was appearing at the popular Café Mellone. *Above:* Rosa (left) and Carmela with Horace Valiante, who was appearing in smalltime vaudeville at Coney Island. Valiante was studying with William Thorner and shared the sisters' operatic ambitions. PHOTOGRAPHER UNKNOWN. COURTESY OF VINCENZA VALIANTE AND LAWRENCE F. HOLDRIDGE. *Below:* Rosa, seventeen, with her mother in New Haven. Although mother and daughter would become decidedly more stylish as Rosa's income skyrocketed in the 1920s, this snapshot lends credence to vaudeville manager Gene Hughes' harsh comments about Rosa's appearance when she auditioned for him. PHOTOGRAPHER UNKNOWN. COURTESY OF VINCENZA VALIANTE AND LAWRENCE F. HOLDRIDGE.

Plate 2. One of the few authenticated vaudeville portraits of Rosa Ponselle, 1917. The Ponzillo Sisters' costumes varied more than their act, which remained basically the same during their three seasons on the Keith Circuit. PHOTOGRAPHER UNKNOWN. SAFKA & BAREIS COLLECTION.

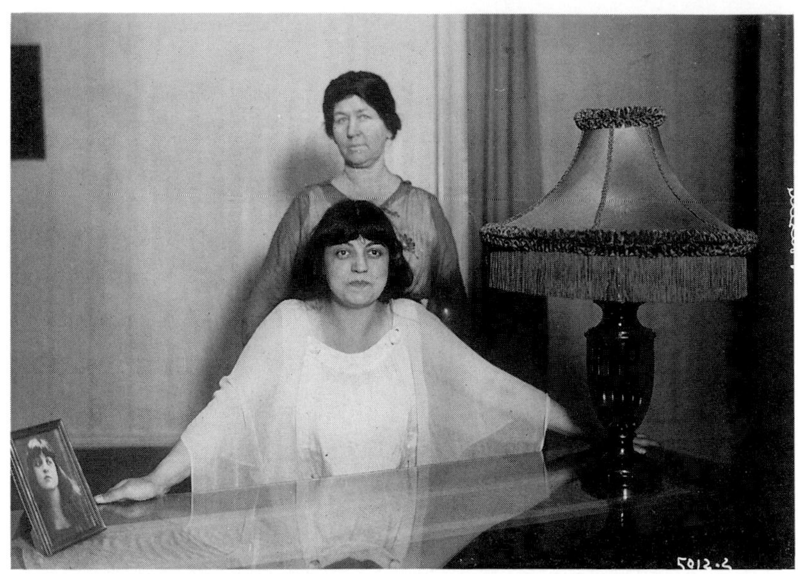

Plate 3. Ponselle with her hometown teacher Anna Ryan, who taught piano and rudimentary voice lessons to all three Ponzillo children. PHOTOGRAPH BY BAIN NEWS SERVICES. USED BY PERMISSION OF CULVER PICTURES, INC.

Plate 4. Voice teacher and manager William Thorner with the Ponzillo sisters, 1918. Rosa (right) would later claim, despite evidence to the contrary, that Thorner played no significant role in her vocal development. PHOTOGRAPHER UNKNOWN. COURTESY OF THE METROPOLITAN OPERA ARCHIVES.

Plate 5. Rosa Ponzillo, 1918. Her slimness suggests that this was taken shortly before her Metropolitan Opera debut. PHOTOGRAPH BY SAMUEL LUMIERE. USED BY PERMISSION OF CULVER PICTURES, INC.

Plate 6. Ponselle in profile, 1919–20. Her hairstyle, dubbed "the Ponselle Bob" by the press, became a near trademark in the early years of her career. PHOTOGRAPH BY SAMUEL LUMIERE. COURTESY OF LAWRENCE F. HOLDRIDGE.

Plate 7. As Rezia in *Oberon*, 1918–19. PHOTOGRAPH BY WHITE STUDIO. COURTESY OF OPERA NEWS.

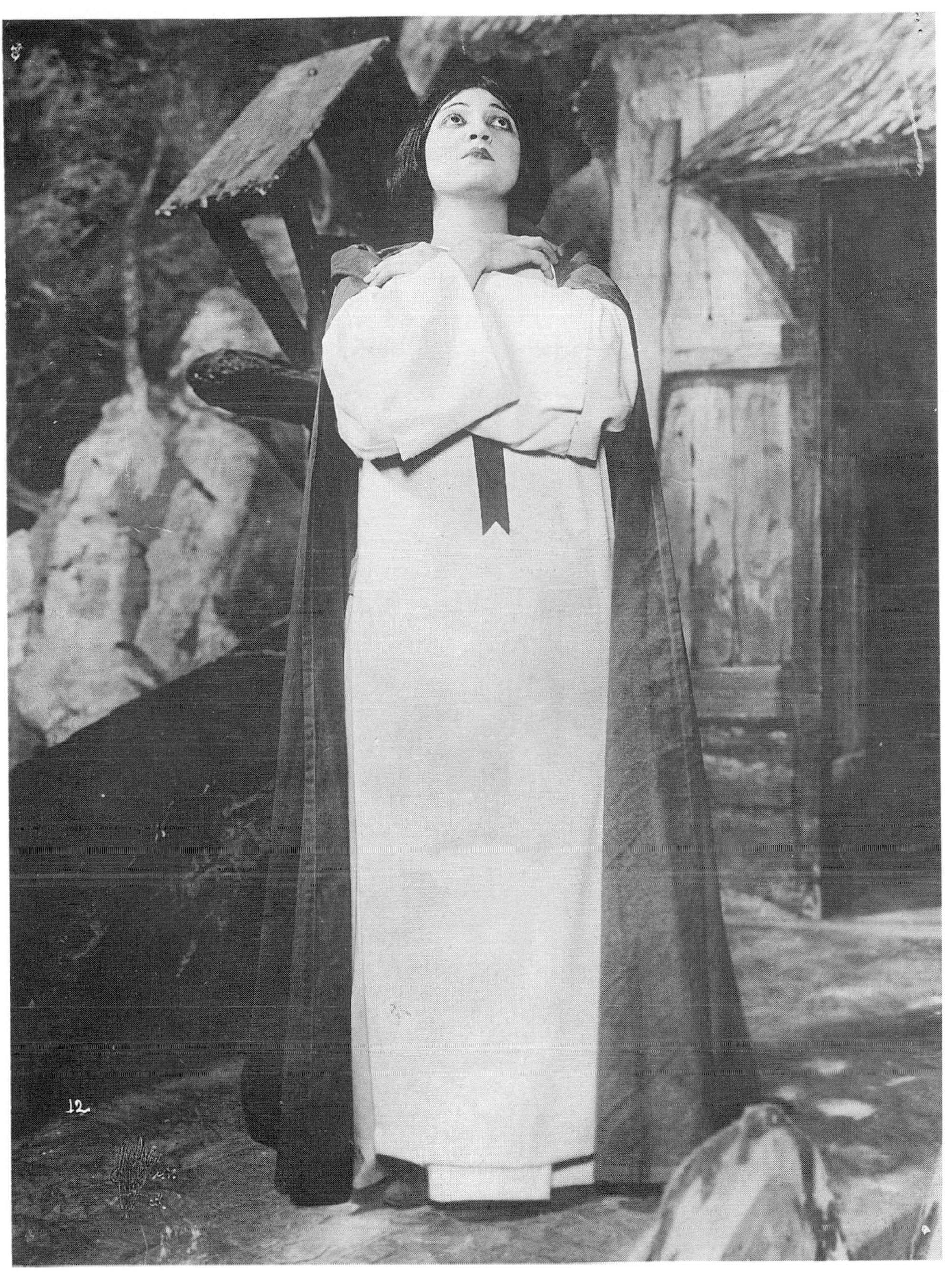

Plate 8. As Leonora in *La forza del destino,* November 1918. PHOTOGRAPH BY WHITE STUDIO. SAFKA & BAREIS COLLECTION.

Plate 9. As Rachel in *La Juive*, opposite Caruso as Eléazar, 1919–20. Although Ponselle's Rachel left the New York critics generally unimpressed, they lauded Caruso's moving portrayal of the embittered goldsmith. PHOTOGRAPH BY WHITE STUDIO. COURTESY OF JAMES M. ALFONTE.

Plate 10. As Maddelena in *Andrea Chénier,* Act One, 1921. Ponselle played Maddelena as a blond, but the wig she had commissioned was not yet ready when this publicity photograph was taken. PHOTOGRAPH BY HERMAN MISHKIN. SAFKA & BAREIS COLLECTION.

Plate 11. As Elvira in *Ernani*, which she first sang in the 1921–22 season. PHOTOGRAPH BY HERMAN MISHKIN. COURTESY OF JAMES M. ALFONTE.

Plate 12. As Margared in *Le Roi d'Ys* with Frances Alda as Rozenn, 1921–22.
PHOTOGRAPH BY WHITE STUDIO. COURTESY OF THE METROPOLITAN OPERA ARCHIVES.

Plate 13. As Matilda in *William Tell*, 1922–23. Ponselle's fluctuating weight, which peaked at nearly 200 pounds in 1922, was not helped by such stock Metropolitan Opera costumes as this one. In time, she would commission well-known fashion designers to custom-make her costumes. PHOTOGRAPH BY WHITE STUDIO. COURTESY OF HUGH M. JOHNS.

Plate 14. As Gioconda, Act Three, 1924–25. Ponselle purchased costumes for *La Gioconda* and also for *Lohengrin* from soprano Salomea Krusceniski. PHOTOGRAPH BY HERMAN MISHKIN. COURTESY OF THE METROPOLITAN OPERA ARCHIVES.

Plate 15. The only known photograph of Ponselle with Claudia Muzio, whose emotional characterizations influenced some of Ponselle's own. As with Rosa Raisa, Ponselle considered Muzio not a rival but a friend. PHOTOGRAPH BY MAY HIGGINS. COURTESY OF BILL PARK.

Plate 16. In Atlanta, on tour with the Metropolitan. Seated (left to right) are Ponselle, Frances Alda, and Kathleen Howard. At far left, standing, are baritone Giuseppe Danise and tenor Armand Tokatyan, who prepares to embrace Alda's hand. At center is conductor Wilfred Pelletier, and at far right, shipping magnate A. Davis Warfield. PHOTOGRAPHER UNKNOWN. SAFKA & BAREIS COLLECTION.

Plate 17. A high point of Ponselle's early career came in August 1924, when she and Romano Romani visited Giacomo Puccini (left) in Italy. Ponselle holds a fox cub she discovered while walking in the woods surrounding Puccini's estate. PHOTOGRAPH BY EDITH PRILIK. COURTESY OF THE METROPOLITAN OPERA ARCHIVES.

Plate 18. As Giulia in *La vestale*, Metropolitan Opera, 1925–26, with tenor (later general manager) Edward Johnson as Licinio. In *Vestale*, said one critic, Ponselle took "that big step forward" as a singer and and artist. The next step was *Norma*.
PHOTOGRAPH BY HERMAN MISHKIN. USED BY PERMISSION OF CULVER PICTURES, INC.

Plate 19. At Lake Placid, 1927, taking a break while preparing the *Norma* duets with her Adalgisa, mezzo Marion Telva. PHOTOGRAPH BY UNDERWOOD & UNDERWOOD STUDIOS. COURTESY OF ROBERT TUGGLE.

Plate 20. At the zenith of her career as the ill-fated Norma, with the child actors who portrayed the priestess' children in the Metropolitan revival of Bellini's demanding classic, 1927–28. PHOTOGRAPH BY HERMAN MISHKIN. COURTESY OF ROBERT TUGGLE.

Plate 21. Ponselle as Norma with Gladys Swarthout as Adalgisa in a Met dressing room on 19 March 1935, Ponselle's last public performance of *Norma* (Act Three). The occasion was the gala for Giulio Gatti-Casazza, the general manager who had presented Ponselle in her debut. PHOTOGRAPH BY WIDE WORLD PHOTOS. COURTESY OF ROBERT TUGGLE.

Plate 22. Joining Ponselle to celebrate her twenty-fifth birthday in January 1922 are (far left) Giuseppe de Luca, Yvonne D'Arle, Giovanni Martinelli. Clustered around Ponselle at center are Titta Ruffo (at her immediate right), Romano Romani, and conductor Giuseppe Moranzoni. At far right, standing above the group, is Carmela Ponselle. PHOTOGRAPHER UNKNOWN. COURTESY OF MYRON EHRLICH.

Plate 23. The Victor Company hosted this surprise party for Ponselle's thirtieth birthday in 1927. Eight-year-old Gloria Caruso cuts the cake with help from Nina Morgana. Grouped around the cake are (left to right) Romano Romani, Ponselle, Ezio Pinza, and Libbie Miller. At right are Giuseppe de Luca (holding bouquet), Giulio Setti (behind de Luca), Mario Basiola, and Mario Chamlee. At far left, Louise Homer smiles in the direction of the camera. PHOTOGRAPHER UNKNOWN. COURTESY OF JAMES M. ALFONTE.

Plate 24. As Fiora in *L'amore dei tre re*, from a studio photograph taken in her Manhattan penthouse. Although she sang Fiora infrequently, the role served her well at the Metropolitan and at Covent Garden. PHOTOGRAPH BY THE NEW YORK TIMES STUDIO. COURTESY OF JAMES M. ALFONTE.

Plate 25. Carmela Ponselle in London, c. 1928–30. "TOPICAL" PRESS AGENCY LTD. COURTESY ANDREW FARKAS.

Plate 26. Striking a demure pose in a concert gown, 1928. PHOTOGRAPH BY HERMAN MISHKIN. COURTESY OF JAMES M. ALFONTE.

Plate 27. As Violetta in *La traviata*, Act One, Covent Garden production, June 1930.
PHOTOGRAPHER UNKNOWN. COURTESY OF JAMES M. ALFONTE.

Plate 28. For the 1933–34 season, Ponselle commissioned New York couturière Valentina to design this first-act costume for *La traviata*. PHOTOGRAPHER UNKNOWN. COURTESY OF ROBERT TUGGLE.

Plate 29. Ponselle wore Valentina's first-act design for *Traviata*, complemented by a powdered wig and her *Ernani* tiara, to a Metropolitan fund-raising gala in the 1933–34 season. For this elaborate and successful fundraiser, the Metropolitan stage was transformed into a grand ballroom in a Louis XIV setting. PHOTOGRAPHER UNKNOWN. USED BY PERMISSION OF THE BETTMANN ARCHIVE.

Plate 30. Ponselle in her dressing room at the Met, receiving flowers with former diva Luisa Tetrazzini (seated) and Spanish dancer La Argentina. Ponselle met Tetrazzini in London and again in New York after Ponselle's *Traviata*. PHOTOGRAPHER UNKNOWN. COURTESY OF THE METROPOLITAN OPERA ARCHIVES.

Plate 31. Ponselle's London success was aided by the three men pictured with her in 1931. Left to right: Col. Eustace Blois, then head of Covent Garden's management; Romano Romani, whose Fedra she created at Covent Garden that season; and conductor Tullio Serafin, who had guided her artistic development from the mid-1920s onward. PHOTOGRAPHER UNKNOWN. COURTESY OF LAWRENCE F. HOLDRIDGE.

Plate 32. A rare photograph of Ponselle on stage with Romano Romani following the London premiere of his *Fedra*, 18 June 1931. The partly obscured banner in the background, which her fan club had sent to London, reads: "To Rosa, *Fedra*, and Romani from the Ponsellites in New York." PHOTOGRAPHER UNKNOWN. COURTESY OF LAWRENCE F. HOLDRIDGE.

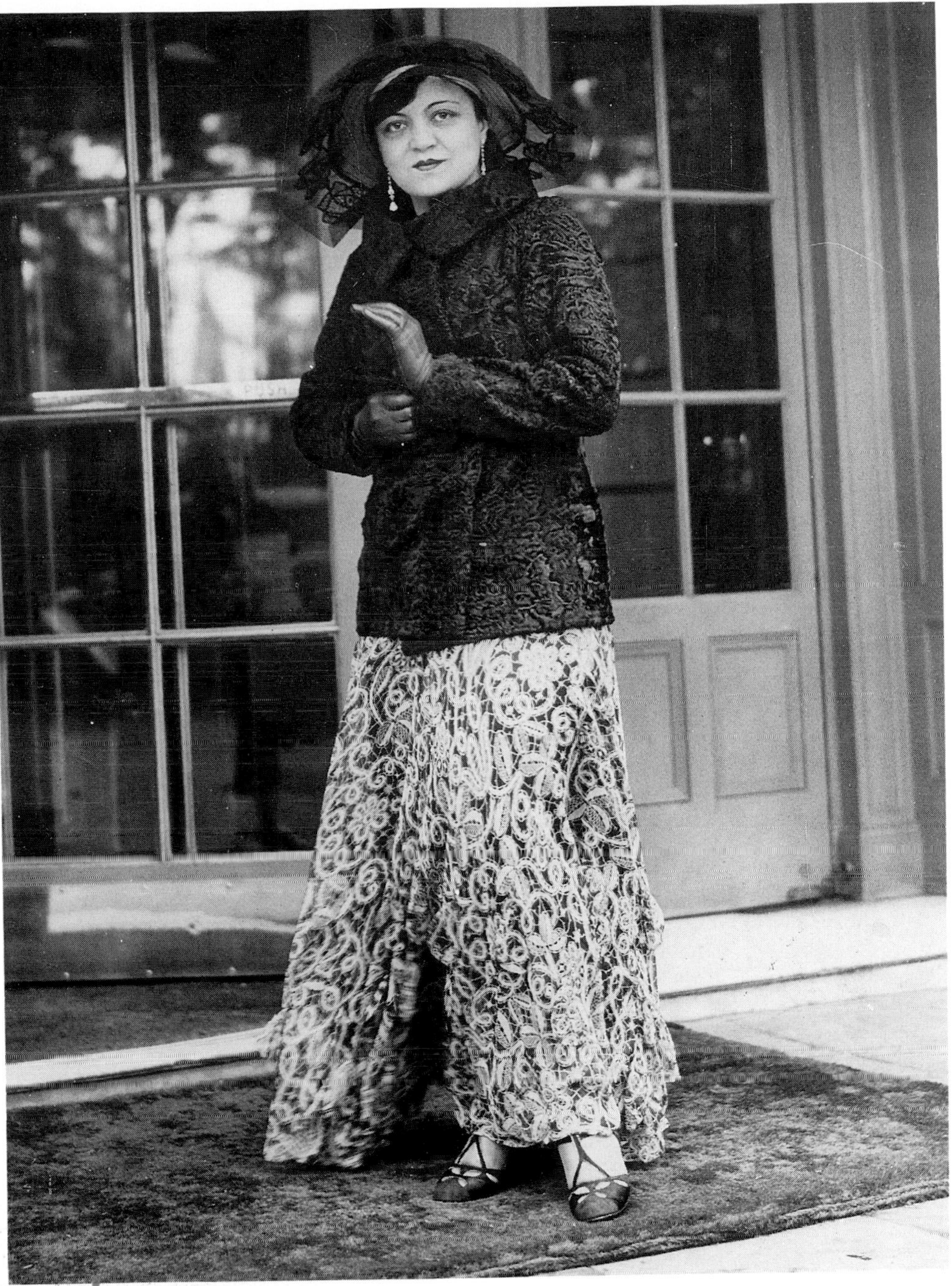

Plate 33. Ponselle leaving her hotel to join the king and queen in the royal paddock at Ascot on 19 June 1931, the day after the premiere of Romani's *Fedra*. PHOTOGRAPH BY PACIFIC & ATLANTIC PHOTOS LTD., LONDON. COURTESY OF LAWRENCE F. HOLDRIDGE.

Plate 34. As Luisa in the Metropolitan Opera premiere of Verdi's *Luisa Miller*, December 1929. PHOTOGRAPH BY CARLO EDWARDS. COURTESY OF ROBERT TUGGLE.

Plate 35. As Zoraima in the world premiere of Montemezzi's *La notte di Zoraima*, with Santa Biondo as Manuela, Metropolitan Opera, December 1932. Ponselle's high regard for the composer's plaintive *L'amore dei tre re* did not extend to *Zoraima*, which she labeled "horrible." PHOTOGRAPH BY CARLO EDWARDS. COURTESY OF THE METROPOLITAN OPERA ARCHIVES.

Plate 36. In May 1933 Ponselle accepted an invitation from the Italian government to reprise her much-acclaimed *La vestale* in the first May Festival in Florence. Between performances, the only ones she ever gave in her parents' homeland, she had a private audience with Mussolini. PHOTOGRAPH BY PETRELLI STUDIOS, FLORENCE. COURTESY OF LAWRENCE F. HOLDRIDGE.

Plate 37. Ponselle was thirty-five and single when she began a very public three-year affair with Giuseppe ("Pippo") Russo (far left), with whom she traveled openly while his wife and family remained in Italy. Here, Russo and Ponselle join tenors Giovanni Zenatello and Nino Martini (far right) at the premiere of the 1935 film *I Dream Too Much,* starring Lily Pons. PHOTOGRAPH BY WIDE WORLD PHOTOS. COURTESY OF LAWRENCE F. HOLDRIDGE.

Plate 38. Although both denied any romantic involvement between them, Romano Romani was a constant in Ponselle's life from her vaudeville years onward. They are shown in August 1938 at the M-G-M studios in Hollywood, where her influence helped secure a staff position for Romani as a vocal coach. PHOTOGRAPH BY WIDE WORLD PHOTOS. COURTESY OF LAWRENCE F. HOLDRIDGE.

Plate 39. Carle A. Jackson, son of Baltimore's mayor and ten years Ponselle's junior, promptly displaced memories of Giuseppe Russo when he was introduced to Rosa in April 1936. The couple was photographed at their engagement party, which Carmela (left) hosted in Baltimore in November 1936. PHOTOGRAPH BY THE BALTIMORE SUN. SAFKA & BAREIS COLLECTION.

Plate 40. "First impression," said *Time* Magazine of Ponselle in 1936, "was to wonder why anyone so flagrantly sexy as her Carmen should trouble to work for a living in a cigarette factory." PHOTOGRAPH BY THE NEW YORK TIMES STUDIO. COURTESY OF JAMES M. ALFONTE.

Plate 41. When preparing *Carmen,* Ponselle complemented the coaching and stage direction of Albert Carré with the choreographic expertise of George Balanchine, shown working with her in 1936. PHOTOGRAPH BY THE NEW YORK TIMES STUDIO. USED BY PERMISSION OF THE BETTMANN ARCHIVE.

Plate 42. For the last act of Ponselle's *Carmen,* Manhattan couturière Valentina designed a matador's costume, complete with tailored pants and an elongated version of the toreador's cap. Although the Metropolitan management demanded that the pants give way to a figure-hugging skirt, the costume remained controversial. PHOTOGRAPH BY THE NEW YORK TIMES STUDIO. COURTESY OF SAFKA & BAREIS COLLECTION.

Plate 43. Preparing for a CBS radio appearance on the *Ford Sunday Evening Hour*, Detroit, March 1935. PHOTOGRAPH BY BERT LAWSON. COURTESY OF LAWRENCE F. HOLDRIDGE.

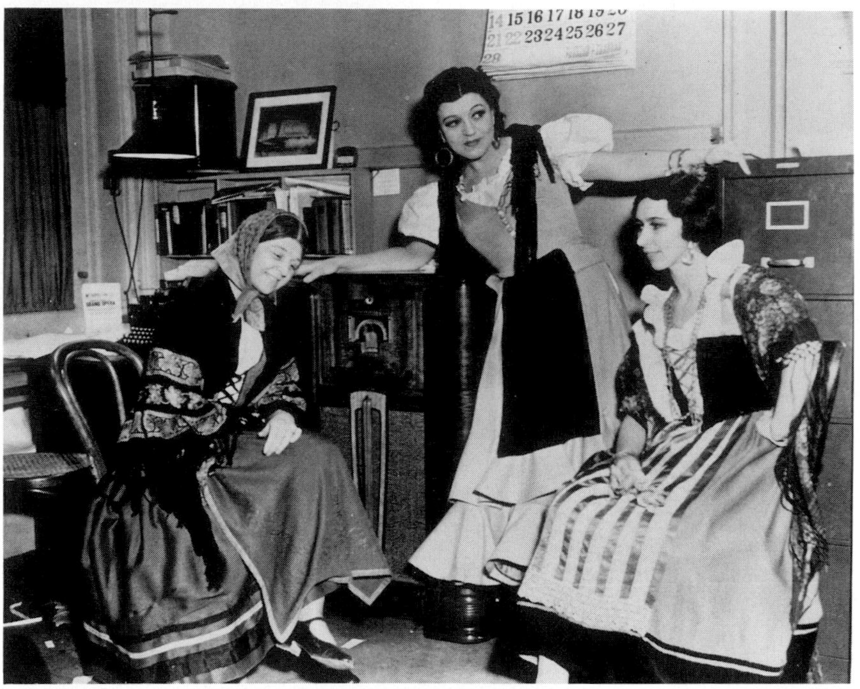

Plate 44. In costume as Santuzza, promoting the Metropolitan Opera's weekly radio broadcasts, with Irra Petina (right) and Anna Kaskas after a matinee performance of *Cavalleria rusticana* on 4 February 1937. This would prove to be one of Ponselle's final performances in the Metropolitan Opera House. Two months later, in *Carmen* on tour in Cleveland, she would sing the final operatic performance of her career. PHOTOGRAPHER UNKNOWN. COURTESY OF OPERA NEWS.

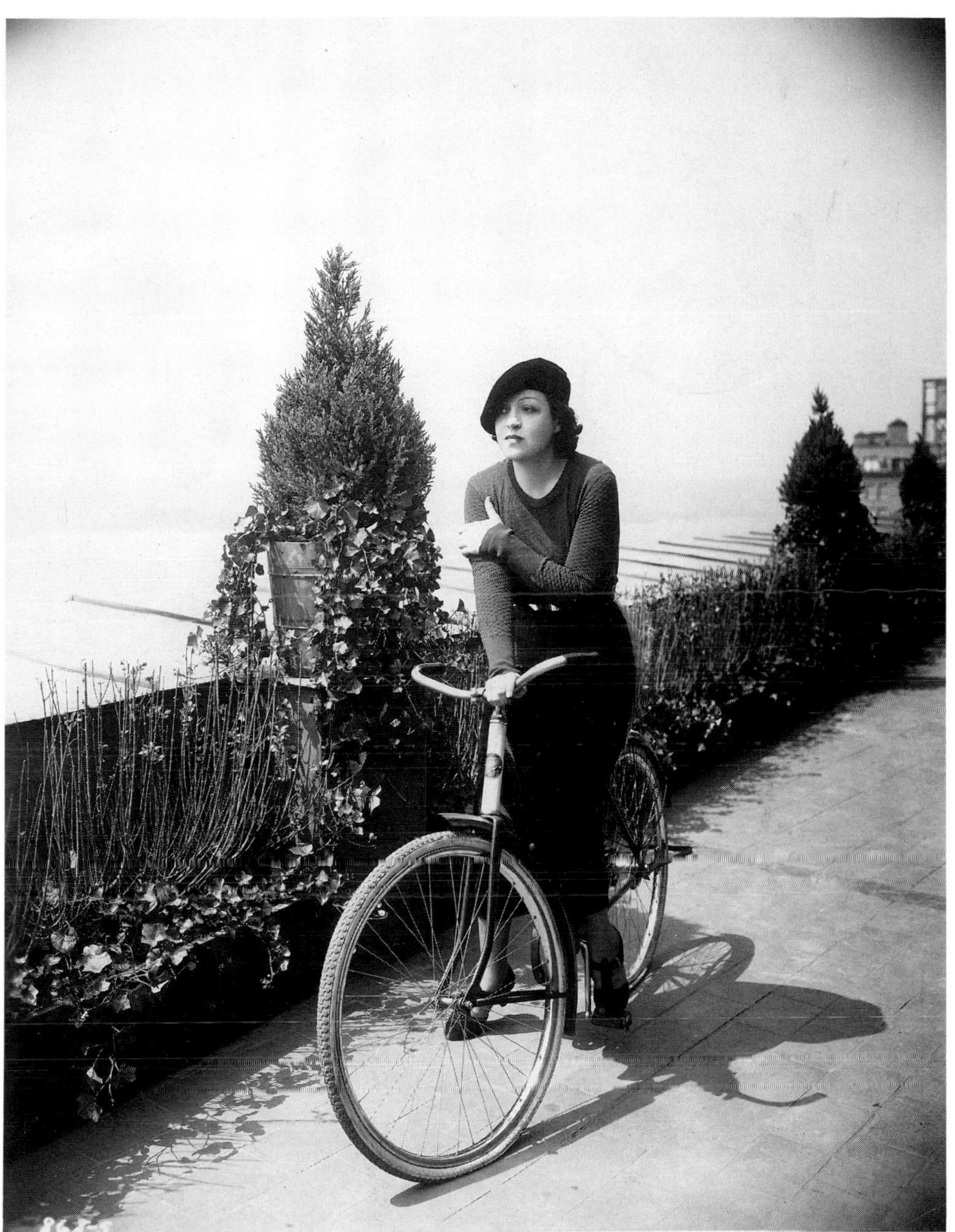

Plate 45. In New York and later in Holllywood, Ponselle bicycled several miles at a stretch whenever her schedule permitted. Partly to pacify Metropolitan manager Giulio Gatti-Casazza, who chided her for risking her life in Manhattan traffic, she rode her bicycle on the expansive rooftop terrace of her Manhattan penthouse, shown here. PHOTOGRAPHER UNKNOWN. COURTESY OF LAWRENCE F. HOLDRIDGE.

Plate 46. Visiting Joan Crawford, in costume for the M-G-M film *The Gorgeous Hussy*, 1936. PHOTOGRAPHER UNKNOWN. COURTESY OF ROBERT TUGGLE.

Plate 47. A frame from Ponselle's screen test for M-G-M, directed by George Cukor, December 1936. For this scene, Ponselle wore a shimmering gold costume Valentina had initially designed for the final act of *Carmen*. COURTESY OF OPERA NEWS.

Plate 48. A photo from Hollywood, 1936, inscribed to Rosa Raisa whom Ponselle regarded highly. The inscription, dated 1938, reads: "To the great artist and my dear friend Rosa—from the other Rosa who loves you dearly." PHOTOGRAPHER UNKNOWN. COURTESY OF CHARLES B. MINTZER.

Plate 49. Although undecided about continuing her career, Ponselle remained socially active in Washington through long-time friend Perle Mesta. In March 1940 Rosa joined Eleanor Roosevelt at the Women's National Press Club Dinner. Also pictured (left to right) are Press Club president Ruby Black and Bess Farley, wife of then-Postmaster James Farley. Ponselle's closeness to the Farleys led her to the Republican party when James Farley had a falling out with Franklin D. Roosevelt. PHOTOGRAPH BY WIDE WORLD PHOTOS. COURTESY OF LAWRENCE F. HOLDRIDGE.

Plate 50. At the annual Hunt Cup, a Maryland equestrian event in which Carle competed regularly after World War II. At left, watching the 1946 competition are Ruth (Mrs. Romano) Romani and Ponselle. At far right, seated next to Romani, is tennis pro Alice Marble, a frequent guest at Villa Pace in the 1940s. PHOTOGRAPH BY LLOYD GARRISON. COURTESY OF LAWRENCE F. HOLDRIDGE.

Plate 51. A decade after her retirement, Ponselle still attracted press attention wherever she went. She is shown here with Ohio senator Robert J. Barkley at a Washington event. PHOTOGRAPHER UNKNOWN. COURTESY OF LAWRENCE F. HOLDRIDGE.

Plate 52. Soon after her divorce from Carle Jackson, Ponselle became involved with Behrend Dryber (far right), whom she met in Washington diplomatic circles through Perle Mesta. With them (left to right) are Lloyd Garrison and Dr. and Mrs. Nicholas Ballich. A successful though controversial psychiatrist, Ballich began treating Ponselle for severe depression in the late 1940s. PHOTOGRAPH BY HUGH M. JOHNS. COURTESY OF JAMES M. ALFONTE.

Plate 53. By the mid-1950s, Ponselle was shaping the future of the Baltimore Civic Opera Company, where she became artistic director. Soprano Eileen Farrell visited Villa Pace when Ponselle was coaching a group of young singers for a local production. Left to right: Kira Baklanova, Joshua Hecht, Ponselle, Barbara Nuttall, Farrell, and accompanist-conductor Igor Chichagov. PHOTOGRAPH BY LLOYD GARRISON. COURTESY OF LAWRENCE F. HOLDRIDGE.

Plate 54. At Baltimore's Lyric Theater in 1955 with Baltimore socialite and best friend Sonia Parr; and Francis Robinson, assistant general manager of the Metropolitan Opera. PHOTOGRAPH BY LLOYD GARRISON. COURTESY OF JAMES M. ALFONTE.

Plate 55. In February 1962 Ponselle played host to "the other Rosa," legendary soprano Rosa Raisa (right). Hugh M. Johns joined the two for a brisk walk around the expansive grounds at Villa Pace. PHOTOGRAPHER UNKNOWN. COURTESY OF BILL PARK.

Plate 56. In 1957 Ponselle entertained soprano Elisabeth Schwarzkopf at Villa Pace following a concert she gave with the Baltimore Symphony. PHOTOGRAPH BY HUGH M. JOHNS. COURTESY OF JAMES M. ALFONTE.

Plate 57. Greeting soprano Zinka Milanov backstage at Baltimore's Lyric Theater, March 1953. At right is Anne J. O'Donnell, later of Columbia Artists Management. PHOTOGRAPH BY HUGH M. JOHNS. COURTESY OF JAMES M. ALFONTE.

Plate 58. Playing host to soprano Bidù Sayão (far left) and long-time secretary Edith Prilik Sania, April 1967. PHOTOGRAPH BY HUGH M. JOHNS. COURTESY OF JAMES M. ALFONTE.

Plate 59. Celebrating Christmas with Major (later Lt. Colonel) James M. Alfonte, December 1961. PHOTOGRAPH BY LLOYD GARRISON. COURTESY OF JAMES M. ALFONTE.

Plate 60. With Dr. Charles Kent, Peabody Conservatory, 1957. Of all the honors Ponselle received during her long retirement, she especially treasured her honorary doctor's degree from Peabody. PHOTOGRAPHER UNKNOWN. COURTESY OF OPERA NEWS.

You sang three consecutive seasons in London. After your third Covent Garden season, it must have been assumed that you were now willing to entertain other European offers. This leads me to ask whether you and La Scala considered each other.

Well, they made overtures (Miss Miller took care of those things), but I didn't want to go there because I still was afraid of the Italian audiences—and when I finally did sing in Italy, I saw how badly [the audiences] could behave.

You're referring to the first Maggio Musicale in Florence? Surely you didn't get any bad treatment from that audience, did you?

No, not me. Oh, that was a big success. That's when I did *Vestale*. No, I'd have to go pretty far to top that one! They were wonderful to me, but I saw them just tear apart—there are no other words for it—a very big star in that festival.

Who was it, if I may ask?

[Giacomo] Lauri-Volpi in *Puritani*, with Serafin [conducting]. I couldn't believe my own eyes and ears.

What exactly happened?

Well, first of all, Lauri-Volpi never liked to rehearse. On top of [that], he was like a rock—[he was] stubborn, wouldn't move an inch when he made up his mind about [something]. So he made up his mind that he wasn't going to rehearse with the rest of the cast for *Puritani*. I went to three or four of the rehearsals myself. It was an opera I didn't know too well, and I loved to watch Serafin at work anyway. [At] every one of the rehearsals I saw, Lauri-Volpi sat in the middle of that empty theater—he'd be sitting there with his wife, talking, doing as he pleased. Several times Serafin asked him if he would like to join the cast on stage. Volpi would just say, "No, Maestro, I know the role and I want to save my voice, so I'll just keep watching how it's being staged." Now, he was so damned stubborn about it that he wouldn't even go [on stage] and "mark" his big aria, "A te o cara." When we talk about "marking" (and singers have different ways of saying this) we mean going through the motions on stage but singing in half voice rather than singing in full voice. Lauri-Volpi wouldn't get out of his seat even to do that, not even for Serafin.

How did Serafin react? We can imagine Toscanini unleashing a hurricane if any tenor refused to rehearse.

But, you see, that was never Serafin's way. Everything he did was *con amore*. I was sitting close enough to the pit to hear Maestro say to the orchestra, "All right, it will be his neck if anything goes wrong, not mine." So the first performance came along, and everything was going along fine. Volpi seemed to be in good voice, and he remembered most of the stage directions. Then came the time for his big aria. Everybody in the theater, of course, was waiting for one note in that aria—it's a high D or maybe a D-flat, I don't recall which, but it's pretty damned high. It's in the second verse when the note comes—there's the tenor, the soprano, the full chorus, a beautiful moment—and when Volpi went for the note, his voice cracked. I tell you, that audience didn't wait one second—*not one second*—until they started hissing and booing him. He just stood at the front of the stage, defiant, and the longer he stood there, the worse [the audience] decided to get. Soon, they were tearing up programs and throwing them like confetti! They were yelling, hissing, booing, and before long they were throwing anything that wasn't bolted down.

How did Lauri-Volpi hold up under that kind of duress?

This was the worst demonstration of an audience humiliating a singer that I have ever seen. But, you know, Lauri-Volpi was no pushover. He stood there for a little while—I remember he folded his arms as if to say, "Okay, I'll just stand here and wait"—but when it got really bad, he just stomped off the stage. They said that between the stage and his dressing room, he broke everything that was in his path. The only thing I can say is, thank God I didn't witness that [incident] before my first *Vestale*. My God! I would have cancelled right then and there. With my nerves, it would have killed me!

But as it was, your Giulia was every bit as well-received in Florence as it was in New York.

Yeah, but that didn't take away the worries. I couldn't enjoy Florence like I would have wanted to, because I was worried—nervous—all the time.

Were you nervous when you were summoned to meet Mussolini?

Oh, yes! It started when I got the word that he wanted to see me. They told me he had heard my *Vestale* on the radio—it was broadcast in the big cities—and I guess, or was told, that at first he thought there was a political demonstration going on until he realized he was hearing the opera. I don't know whether he just happened to listen in right when there was big applause—like after "O nume tutelar," which [the audience] went crazy over. They told me [that] Mussolini thought there was some kind of rebellion going on till he realized what was happening. Anyway, that's what I was told by his [staff] people, [that] he thought there was some rebellion going on. Imagine that! Me, a rebel! The American Joan of Arc!

Do you recall what Mussolini said to you? Was it a long meeting?

I didn't think it was going to be long, but we ended up talking for quite a while. He had a car sent for me, and he said it was all right for me to bring someone with me, so I took Edith [Prilik], my secretary, with me. It was a pretty good distance by car from where we were in Florence to the palace where he had his headquarters, but I was nervous all the way. When we got to the palace, I think that his big office (or his study, I guess you could say) was on the second floor. Everything was very proper, very military, but what a beautiful palace! When I was ushered in to his study, he was sitting at this big desk way at the opposite end of this very long room. I don't remember a stick of furniture being in that room except his desk, which was very ornate and very large. There were a few chairs right near the front of it. This was a beautiful room—the walls, the ceiling, all very ornate—and it was so large [that] it took me a good while to get to his desk when he motioned for me to come closer to him. I must have looked nervous because as I started to walk toward him he said to me, in Italian, "Come ahead, come ahead! Don't be afraid of me." When I got to where he was (he had gotten up from his chair and had come around to greet me) I gave him my hand, and he said with a very nice smile, "You know, we think of you as a sister." He said that even though I was born in the States, he knew my parents were both Neapolitans; he even mentioned their full names, which floored me, and told me all about Caserta where they were from.

As you think back to that time, were you quite impressed by Mussolini?

You couldn't help but be impressed. Remember, this was long before Hitler got to him. I was convinced that Mussolini had Italy's interests at heart. These days, you know, you can't say anything good about Mussolini—not over here, and certainly not to the Italians, because of what he did with Hitler. I think he was tricked into it by Hitler. I still can't believe that he would throw in with a madman like that. And then when I saw those awful pictures in the magazines of how his own people killed Mussolini!—[they] butchered [him] like a piece of meat! I don't even want to think about it. I'll always have that [image] to haunt me.

I think you would agree that if there was an element of sadness to your performances of La vestale *in Italy, it was that your mother did not live to be there with you.*

That was the sorrow of my life. That's all she wanted, you know: to be in the audience when I sang in Italy, the country where she was born, but we lost her before I went over there.

Everyone I have talked to, even Carmela and your brother Tony, has spoken about the special bond between you and your mother.

She was too young to die: only sixty-two. Daddy lived to see the other side of ninety, yet Mamma had to die at sixty-two. But somehow she was with me in Italy—I'll always believe that. All during those big arias in *Vestale*, I would concentrate on the darkness near the back of the theater, above the audience. The harder I concentrated, [the more] I saw my mother's face. She was looking at me, smiling back at me from the darkness.

Recollections

Lena Tamborini

Back in 1929, if somebody called you long-distance it was like sending a telegram.[30] If you got one, you knew it must be bad news. You can imagine my surprise when our phone rang on a winter night in New Hampshire (that's where my husband, Henry, and I were then living) and the operator said it was long-distance from Meriden, Connecticut. I thought sure that something awful had happened to my mother, but when the operator connected the call, it was Rose on the line. She had stopped to see her parents in Meriden, and she was on her way back to New York. "Hey, Red!" she said. "How would you like to go to England with me next spring?"

I was so flattered that she wanted me to go with her that I hardly knew what to say. Henry wasn't any too thrilled about it, though, but I let Rosa take care of that. She called him every day for two weeks, she wrote him letters, she sent him gifts, whatever it took to get him to say yes to my going. She told him she would be paying for everything, so money wasn't going to be a problem. It wasn't long until he gave in!

I knew that Rose made a lot of money (after all, I read the newspapers), but to me she was still Rose Ponzillo from next door, so I didn't know what her life was really like until I went to Europe with her. My husband and I were just plain working people, so we didn't have any money to spare, not even for new clothes, which I knew I would need for such a special trip. But do you know that I never had to say a word about it? Rosa sent me to one of her dressmakers in New York and had a complete wardrobe made up for me. That's the kind of friend she was.

For the ocean-crossing, she booked first-class cabins for all of us—Edith, Libbie Miller, and me. In London we stayed at the Savoy. She included me in all the dinner parties, every place that it was appropriate to have me with her. She even had me with her in the receiving line when she was introduced to the King and Queen, after one of her *Traviata* performances.

For fun, when she wasn't rehearsing or being interviewed, the four of us girls would go see a movie. Edith or Libbie would arrange it ahead of time with the theater manager, who would arrange for us to have the balcony to ourselves. One afternoon we went to see a movie that we kept hearing about from some of the people Rose knew in London. It was called *The White Hell of Pitz Palü*, a German film about a love story set in the Alps.[31] We ended up seeing *Pitz Palü* two or three times. We couldn't get enough of it, and the men in it were just gorgeous! Finally Rosa said to us, "That's it! We're going to the Alps!" A day or so later, through some connections that Montemezzi, the composer, had in St. Moritz, she had gotten a chalet for us, almost exactly like the one in *Pitz Palü*.

To show you how far Rose would go when she wanted something, she had Edith track down the men who starred in the movie, and also the ones who filmed it, and she had two of them meet us in St. Moritz to teach us all about mountain climbing![32] That's how it was with Rosa—one day we're sitting in a theater watching a movie, and the next day she's getting us together with the stars we were seeing on the screen. It was like we were in *The White Hell of Pitz Palü* ourselves! We learned all about mountain-climbing, and we had some real parties up there in the mountains with those boys from the movie. We saw several other big stars in St. Moritz too. Grace Moore was there. She was a big fan of Rose's, and she stayed at our chalet for a day or two.

For all the fun we had in Europe (and we were there almost five months, from May through the end of September), Rose had a lot of pressure on her over there. Edith had always told me that Rose was nervous before she had to sing. If I hadn't seen it for myself, I wouldn't have believed it. But take it from me, it was the gospel truth. Libbie knew how to handle Rose. The rest of us just stayed in the background until after the curtain went down. Then she was the same old Rose, and she would start having fun again.

Libbie Miller was good for Rose. By that time, she was only managing a few singers because Rose was her biggest star. She also managed Grace Moore, but Grace used to complain to her that Rose got all the attention.[33] But Rose and Libbie weren't as close as Rose was to Edith Prilik. After that summer in Europe, though, I began to have my doubts about Edith. A couple months after we got back from England, Rose sang a few concerts before the Metropolitan Opera season started. Edith couldn't go with her for some reason, so Rose called me and asked me to travel with her as her secretary.

I knew enough about what Edith did after being in England with her, so I went along and did what I could to help Rose. But at nearly every place I went with Rose, the people I was dealing with—the local concert booker, the theater manager, the publicists—would pull me aside and say, "You're real nice to work with. You're not like that so-and-so Edith Prilik." Sometimes they would volunteer more about their experience with her. The gist of it was that Edith was very hard to get along with, and she kept people from Rose if she [Edith] took a dislike to them. From what I heard, the quickest way to get her to dislike you was if you didn't butter her up enough. The way it was put to me, Rose may have been the star of the show, but Edith wanted everybody to know that she was a big wheel too.

Rose's family was always putting pressure on her. Things in Meriden weren't too good, especially with Tony. There he was, Rosa Ponselle's brother, still living in Meriden while his baby sister was a rich opera star in New York. Tony had to be a big shot, so he started spending money to keep up with the Joneses. The trouble was, he didn't have any money of his own. He'd borrow on the coal business, and then he wouldn't be able to pay it back. Pretty soon the creditors would start dunning him, and then he'd have to go to Rosa for help.

I was at Rosa's penthouse several times when he went there to ask for money. He'd call me and ask me to go to New York and meet him there because he didn't want to have to ask her all by himself. It was kind of pathetic, really. He was a sweet guy, but he didn't know the first thing about money. He used to go around town telling everybody that he was a businessman, but the only kind of business he knew anything about was monkey business. He had too much pride to learn from anybody. Rose used to get furious with him, not to his face, but to Carmela and often to me.

Rose wanted to help Tony out, but she couldn't just hand money to him. She had to give him loans, even if she wasn't meaning to ever collect them. That way she could use them for tax purposes. But that meant there were papers that had to be signed, and she would have to get her lawyer involved. Tony always took it personally, as though she couldn't trust him, because she would make him go to her lawyer and sign papers. That hurt his pride. Rose could stand that, even if he sometimes drove her crazy with his bad investments and such. But there was something else that she couldn't stand at all: Tony would take things out on Lydia, his wife.

It got back to Rose that he would hit Lydia. Tony was hot-headed, and we all knew it. Sometimes things between him and Lydia got real bad. This was very hard on Rose's mother, who tried to be good to all three of her children. She considered Lydia one of her own, too, but Mrs. Ponzillo knew what was going on—yet Tony was so headstrong that nobody could do much about it. Carmela would never take a stand on anything in the family, so she just went on her way. Mr. Ponzillo was no help. Tony had taken over the coal business from him because the old man wouldn't let him run it the way *he* wanted. Sometimes they hardly spoke to each other. Tony couldn't make a go of the business, not without Rose loaning him more and more money. So, you see, everything was up to Rose. She adored Lydia like a sister, and when she heard how Tony was treating Lydia, Rose lost whatever respect she had for her brother.

As long as Rose kept the money coming and as long as her mother was able to keep everybody in the family on speaking terms, life went along all right for the Ponzillos. But just when everything seemed to be holding together, Mrs. Ponzillo took sick. It wasn't much at first, just a bad cold that didn't seem to want to go away. But then it got worse, and her doctor in Meriden put her to bed. Then she got to feeling better and was up and around working, but pretty soon she got sick again. This time, Tony and Carmela called Rose, who brought in Dr. Verdi from New Haven. He confirmed that Mrs. Ponzillo had a serious case of pneumonia and that the chances of her coming through were not very good. Rose had him hire round-the-clock nurses to help take care of her.

When I found out from my mother what was happening, I called Rose and then I came home to Meriden to help out. Rose was on a concert tour (this was in October [1932], not too long before the Metropolitan Opera season was to start), but Carmela was able to go to Meriden. Mrs. Ponzillo gradually got worse and worse, and finally, Dr. Verdi called Rose and told her that her mother was not expected to live. Rose was on her way to Hartford [Connecticut] to do a concert, and Edith was traveling with her. Rose got to Meriden in the early afternoon and went to her mother's bedside right away. Mrs. Ponzillo was already failing by then.

Tony, Lydia, Carmela, and I were in the room when Rose came in with Edith and Libbie. Rose tried hard to cheer up her mother. "I have to sing tonight, Mamma, but I'll be close by," she told her. "Don't worry, you're going to get well, and I'll be back to see you real soon." She was fighting back tears while she was holding her mother's hand. Then she bent down to kiss her. Mrs. Ponzillo said to her, "You may see me, Rosina, but I won't be able to see you."

Rose left the room, ran down the stairs, and went to my parents' house next door. I never saw a woman cry so hard in all my life! My mother held her tight, I held her, Lydia held her—she was like a baby in our arms. Edith, meantime, was on the phone to the theater because she didn't know whether Rose would have to cancel. Libbie and Edith talked her into doing the concert, to get her mind away from her mother's condition for a little bit. They felt that she could lose herself in the music, once she got on stage.

Everybody said that she gave a beautiful concert that night, one of the best she had ever sung. But when it came time for her last encore, she sat down at the piano like she always did and began to sing "Home, Sweet Home." In one of the verses there was a line about a mother's love for her child.[34] She had sung it dozens of times before, but this time the words meant something very personal. As soon as she began to sing that line, her voice broke and she started to cry. She couldn't stop and had to leave the stage.[35] That was on a Saturday night. One week later, at the Sacred Heart cemetery in Meriden, I was at Rose's side, crying with her and praying with her as they lowered her mother's casket into the grave.[36]

The Written Record

Long after the shock of it had passed, the death of Maddalena Ponzillo continued to affect the lives of her family. Her husband, whose flinty exterior had never betrayed any hint of emotion, seemed to take her passing the hardest. Whether his grief stemmed from a genuine devotion that he had never been able to express to his wife (as Tony believed), or whether it was from guilt for the indifference he had shown her throughout most of their marriage (as Rosa maintained), Ben Ponzillo was inconsolable. "For the first time in my life," Tony remembered, "I saw Pop break down and cry. For a long time after her funeral, he just went through the motions of living."[37] Eventually, his volatile older brother, Alfonso, also a widower by then, came to live with him in Meriden. A few months after moving in, Alfonso renewed his earlier reputation for violence by threatening to beat up a meddlesome neighbor.[38]

For Tony, the slow downward spiral caused by his over-spending and lack of business sense took its predictable course. As the Depression worsened in the early 1930s, he was forced to sell the family fuel business; Rosa paid off most of his remaining debts and forgave her prior loans to him. "I would hate to count up how much of her money he ate up," Edith Prilik said. "He was always coming up with some new scheme to make money. He was going to try this, then that, but all he did was throw away good money after bad—her good money, not his. We could count on a call from him about once a month. 'Edith,' he'd say, 'you gotta help me out with Rose.' He wanted me to soften her up. Whenever he showed up in New York, I knew I would be making a call to the Fifth Avenue Bank to have a check cut for him."[39]

Briefly, Tony toyed with returning to the stage, but his previous failure on the Keith Circuit was too recent a memory for potential backers. At home, he was an inattentive father (his son and namesake was now in elementary school), and he was still capable of being an abusive husband. As time went on, his flashing temper and domineering ways made the petite, pretty Lydia more and more introverted.

Carmela helped sustain Tony and Lydia financially as best she could, but on the condition that they must never tell Rosa. Carmela's own career was reasonably stable throughout the late 1920s and early 1930s. In New York City and on the Metropolitan Opera tour, she received commendable, sometimes quite laudatory reviews, especially as Santuzza and Amneris. In 1929 *Musical America* reported that she and Chaliapin were among the first-rank singers who had been engaged "for twelve appearances with the All-Star Opera Company at the Manhattan Opera House in the fall."[40] Carmela had made no recordings since Columbia had dropped her and Victor had declined to issue her a contract, but she gave concerts with some regularity.

For Rosa as well as for Carmela, the death of their mother seemed to release them from a self-imposed obligation to keep their personal lives out of public view. Not long after her mother died, Carmela was introduced by mutual friends to Francis X. Bushman, the one-time silent screen star whose fortunes had waned in the advent of the "talkies." Although Carmela claimed to the press that their meeting had been "a case of love at first sight,"[41] she knew from newspaper accounts that the thrice-married Bushman had placed an advertisement that read "Wife Wanted" in Boston-area newspapers during an appearance in that city. Seven thousand women had supposedly proposed to Bushman in answer to the ad, which prompted Carmela to ask the Boston *Globe*, when a reporter confronted her about it, "Well, how about the seven thousand wealthy men who have proposed to me?"[42]

Late in January 1934, both denied rumors of their impending marriage, but on February 8 in Chicago, newspapers reported that Bushman had obtained a marriage license. "Now a partner in a retail liquor firm," said the Chicago *Times*, "Bushman appeared at the marriage license bureau alone, gave his age as 47 and that of Miss Ponselle as 27."[43] Singing in Boston when the Associated Press distributed the Chicago news release, Carmela confirmed their engagement the next day. "He's marvelous; Bushy is the grandest person in the world," she said. Ten days later, however, "Bushy" changed his mind and decided to reconcile with his first wife, by whom he had fathered five children. "Carmela and I talked it over," Bushman told the Associated Press in Chicago. "She is big and fine, and she decided for the sake of the children we had better call it off."[44] "I always say," Carmela mused, "that love will find a way."[45]

About the same time Carmela began her involvement with Bushman, Rosa became immersed in a very public affair with Giuseppe "Pippo" Russo, the Italian-born chief executive of an imported-automobile franchise in New York City. Supposedly separated from his wife, who remained in Italy, Russo was married nonetheless. Although Rosa claimed that she had met him through business circles, those close to her said that the introduction had been arranged by Elena Rakowska, Tullio Serafin's singer-wife, who had suspected Rosa of having an affair with Serafin while the two were preparing roles in Europe.[46] The young, handsome Russo, Edith Prilik maintained, had been Rakowska's pawn in a game to distract Ponselle from the much older Serafin.[47]

Having fallen for Pippo Russo, Rosa threw herself into the affair with a passion and abandon that she had never shown in any of the flirtations she had had with men she had dated in the past. Russo's sudden presence in her daily life, however, soon created a rift within her staff. Edith took a dim view of his intentions: "Money, money, money—that's what he was after. He was just out for the buck. A gigolo, basically."[48] Libbie, on the other hand, liked him and approved of the relationship.

"I got to know Pippo very well," she recalled years later. "He had looks, and he had a lot of charm. He was married, yes, but he hadn't lived with his wife for years. Being an Italian and a Catholic, he couldn't get a divorce. I think Rosa would have married him otherwise. They spent as much time together as they could. He was with her practically every day when she was in New York. Because of his business, he traveled back and forth to Italy a lot, which made it convenient for him to happen to be in the same cities and the same hotels when Rosa was singing abroad."[49]

A newcomer to Ponselle's circle in the early 1930s—Myron Ehrlich, who had first met Rosa in 1919 as an eleven-year-old fan in his native Atlanta—recalled the more humorous aspects of her relationship with Pippo:

> His franchise, Italian Motors Limited, sold Italian luxury cars. He talked her into ordering this custom-built Isotto Fraschini. It was red, silver, and chrome, a mammoth thing. Of course, she couldn't drive it because the controls were too complicated. Not only couldn't she drive the car, Rosa couldn't even ride in it for more than a mile. She would get car-sick unless she was riding in the open air.
>
> Rosa liked to be spontaneous, so she'd decide on the spur of the moment that she wanted to go "motoring" with Pippo. Because she was fronting the money, he'd be at her penthouse in a minute. Here would come this behemoth of a red car; it looked like a fire engine careening down Riverside Drive. Rosa would get in, and off they would go. About a mile down the Drive, the car would come to a screeching halt. Rosa would be getting carsick. So she would get out and walk. The car would be rolling along beside her with him at the wheel. Then she'd get back in for a few blocks. Pretty soon she'd have to get out again and walk. In and out, in and out—six blocks in the car, and six blocks of fresh air to let her stomach settle down.
>
> Imagine paying that much money for a fancy custom car and then walking along next to it while your boyfriend drives the car that he sold you! The whole thing was a circus to watch. The two of them should have charged admission. Had Pippo Russo thought of it, he would have.[50]

Early in 1936 their affair ended after Russo began spending more time in Italy than Rosa would tolerate. Her reactions to their breakup were as impassioned as the rest of her involvement had been: she tore up every portrait he had given her, and in any group photographs in which he appeared she used scissors to cut out his likeness. She destroyed all their correspondence, and except among her closest friends she refused even to mention his name.

Libbie Miller, however, preserved a letter that Rosa had written to her from Florence at the height of her affair with Pippo. Rosa had hastily written the letter from her villa after her final appearance in *La vestale* at the Maggio Musicale. (Libbie, who also managed Rosa's friend La Argentina, was unable to travel to Florence because she had to manage the popular Spanish dancer's North American tour.[51]) The letter Libbie received from Rosa not only attests to her feelings for Pippo Russo but also captures her wide-eyed reactions to what proved to be her first and last performances in her parents' homeland:

> *Villa Cristina, to Miss Libbie Miller (Personal), 4 May 1933:*
>
> Darling Libbie,
>
> At last I am able to breathe, with these two performances out of my system.
>
> You can just imagine the sleepless nights I have put in—the suffering—all for what? Just foolish, that's all. These damn nerves get the best of me all the time—even after all these years. But thanks to God (as there most surely is one) when I got out on the stage, a certain feeling of calm came over me just as it did at my London debut three years ago. It would be needless to try to explain my triumph. It was simply outstanding. I was as you know a bit afraid of *Vestale* inasmuch as it is a great classic piece—nevertheless it is also true, that it could be a flat tire. It is not an exciting popular type of music—therefore it was for me a double achievement to have triumphed irrespective of this handicap. Not only did I triumph—but also the opera itself. Both performances were broadcasted [*sic*] all over Europe. What a pity America didn't pick it up.
>
> They tried (the public) to make me repeat the prayer in the second act—but since encores in grand opera are forbidden here in Florence, the public after an ovation and cheers lasting all of four minutes finally had to give up in despair. But at the second performance they were (God bless them) simply determined to break the tradition and clamoured until an encore was conceded. This was something I shall never forget. They all got up and screamed to the maestro who was directing and whom they adore—"Please, oh please, Maestro, let us hear her as much as we can—we beg you on our knees to permit her to sing the encore—the Lord knows when we shall have this angel from heaven again."
>
> They all screamed and implored him—he tried to be severe and not break the rule—and at the same time [he was] overjoyed at my success. [Then] the public became rebellious and simply wouldn't permit the opera to proceed. I can't tell you how exciting it was. The maestro then got furious at the public because they were blaming him so finally he turned around and yelled to them to shut up, then they would be given their encore. It took even a long time before they could be silenced for fear their wish should not be granted. Then at the end of the act, the ovation was simply overwhelming.
>
> All Florence is in an uproar. Good Lord—you would think [I] was some other hero such as Lindbergh, such is the adulation I am receiving. Now the trouble starts—all Italy [is] sending representatives from all over to offer me all sorts of inducements to sing in their cities.
>
> You can well imagine Rosa accepting—can't you? They even will accept concerts—anything as long as I sing. All Italy is clamouring for me. A great tribute indeed. I give all sorts of excuses, trying to ward them off

somehow or another. It was well worth my efforts I must confess, as such a satisfaction as I had here has never before been quite as gratifying as this.

Enough of me now—with all this I am still a coward. Pippo simply lost his heart to you. I know and appreciate the comfort you are bestowing upon him. He never fails to speak volumes regarding this, each time he writes.

We will remain here until the end of the month. [Carlo] Delacroix [the director of the Maggio Musicale] and the elite of all Florence are entertaining me royally and showing us around. Princess Strozzi is going to give a big reception in my honor at the famous Palace Strozzi. Here is where one finds the real nobility—with real ranks—natural and humble. They have made a goddess of me—such is their appreciation for fine singing and fine art. As for Florence—it is simply too beautiful and poetic to put in mere words.

Flowers keep pouring in every day from people I don't even know. Women and men alike call at the hotel to kiss my hand and leave flowers. I manage to be out all day so as not to have to tolerate [it]—this [is a] sacrifice too.

Oh, if you knew how thrilled I was at your telegram—the "gang" that congregated at Pippo's to hear the results of my debut—also that one sent the day of Pippo's birthday. How do all you guys get together? I'm sure it is your doing as usual, knowing it will make both Pippo and me happy. It was sweet—and I cried with joy. I will close now, as we are going out to see some churches. Give my love to the Cottillos, Billy, and the entire "gang." As for Pippo I will permit you to deliver direct kisses to him—and [I] promise not to be jealous. For you, all my love and appreciation, as ever, from your Prima Donna.[52]

As effusive as Ponselle found the Florence audiences, their British counterparts had made her the toast of London when she made her debut at Covent Garden in *Norma*. She had arrived in London during the week of 13 May 1929 and had made her first visit to historic Covent Garden on Sunday, 19 May. *The New York Times*' Charles Selden went with her and relayed his report to New York City by wireless that evening:

Miss Ponselle, accompanied by Miss Libbie Miller, walked to the opera house and strolled for a half hour back and forth through the funny aisles of the fruit and flower market near by while waiting for the appointed opening of the stage door.

"I never ride in a motor [car] when I can walk," she explained, "and it is silly to stay indoors in England when the sun does consent to shine. I have done just two things since I arrived—taken long walks out of doors in clear weather, and I have walked just as far in the art galleries when it rained."

One other thing that Miss Ponselle has done was to have tea yesterday with Dame Melba, who is going to attend the performance of *Norma*. The two women, both great singers, had never met before.

The two singers sent a wreath today for the funeral of Lilli Lehmann in Berlin. It was Mme Lehmann, by the way, who sang *Norma* in Covent Garden the last time that London heard that opera thirty years ago.[53]

Selden then became an audience of one as Ponselle had a stagehand push a small upright piano from the wings to the center of the stage. When Selden asked her to sing something he would be "sure to recognize without the aid of a program," she accommodated him with an impromptu performance of "Annie Laurie." "That is the best song to warm up a voice that was ever written," she said.[54] After singing snatches of arias from *Norma* to hear how her voice sounded at different dynamic levels, she displayed to Selden her sense of detail about matters of staging. "Before leaving," he wrote, "she borrowed a two-foot rule from a stagehand who had appeared, did some measuring for herself from the footlights, and explained exactly where she wanted the altar used in the first act of *Norma*."[55]

Nine days later on Tuesday, 28 May, Londoners heard her for the first time. Waiting in line and hoping for a ticket that afternoon was Ida Cook, then a stenographer at the Law Court; a budding short-story writer, she would soon embark on a career as a romance novelist, under the penname Mary Burchell. "We were in a fever pitch of excitement," she wrote years later, "when, just before the queue moved in, a tall, striking—indeed, almost melodramatic looking—figure sauntered up Floral Street and stood for a few moments at the corner. The whisper went round that *this* was Ponselle, though we found it hard to believe that the star of the evening would just stroll up like any of us. I was commissioned to walk past and take a good (though surreptitious) look at her and see if I could identify her as the *Forza* Leonora we had last seen on the stage of the Metropolitan. This I did. But, we were still in some doubt until she walked along the street and in the stage door. That settled all disputes."[56]

While Ponselle's reputation in the United States, especially in *Norma*, had all but ensured sellout performances in London, neither her Italian roots nor her American reputation had guaranteed her a favorable reception with the critics. The most experienced of them, Herman Klein, expressed his reserve in the columns of *The Gramophone*:

> Interest in Bellini's once-popular *Norma* has been re-aroused by the fact that it is shortly to be revived at Covent Garden for the Italian-American prima donna, Rosa Ponselle, whom we have not yet heard here except through a few records made presumably by the Victor Company in New York. These have certainly won admiration, though I cannot recollect finding in them all the phenomenal qualities attributed to the singer herself by certain New York critics. It may be, of course, that she is a "real wonder," the "queen of the Metropolitan sopranos," an artist who "makes Golden

the Age in which she lives," and so forth. But on the whole it will be safer not to judge her by her gramophonic efforts, brilliant though they may be, and wait until we have heard and seen the lady herself.[57]

Klein, born in 1856, had studied voice with the legendary Manuel Garcia and had heard the *Norma*s of Theresa Tietjens and Lilli Lehmann. When he heard Ponselle's, it was not until her second performance, and she was not in her best voice. Still, he found her musical interpretation quite unlike any other *Norma* he had heard:

> Speaking for myself, I may say that my ability to form a calm, dispassionate judgment concerning the new American soprano was materially aided by the absence of first-night excitement. In other words, I did not hear her until her second appearance [but] . . . she happened to be suffering from a slight cold, contracted, so I was told, midway between the two performances.
>
> The trouble was plainly perceptible in the medium register. It was also responsible, I fancied, for the extraordinary extent to which Mme Ponselle relied upon her *mezza voce*. Very rarely indeed did she allow herself the indulgence of declaiming a passage with the full voice demanded by the nature of the utterance and the music. During the greater part of the opera, in fact, she was singing everything in this subdued, quiet manner, so utterly unlike the one depicted by Pasta or Grisi. There were moments when it sounded not only beautiful (it was always that) but particularly appropriate. Such, for instance, was the long-drawn phrasing of the wonderful opening to *Casta diva*; no singing could possibly have been lovelier under any conditions. Again, the famous duet for the two women, *Mira, o Norma*, where Adalgisa stands pleading for the lives of the two children, holding each one by the hand, whilst Norma reclines on a couch with her head buried in the pillows, the living embodiment of grief and remorse.
>
> You might wonder whether she has even heard the appeal addressed to her in the so-familiar melody; and then, without a movement or gesture to indicate its source, you suddenly hear the distant echo of an exquisite tone answering in softest *pianissimo* with the same notes sung to the words, "Ah, perchè, perchè la mia costanza vuoi scemar con molli affetti?" (Why seek to bend my resolution with gentle words?) The effect of that soft entry was intensely pathetic, indescribably beautiful, and I could not remember to have heard it done exactly in that way before.[58]

Reviewing her debut performance in the London *Times*, Ernest Newman, the well-known and influential critic, wrote:

> Here is that rarity of the operatic stage, an artist who can not only sing but create a character. After Miss Ponselle's performance one understands better than before the attraction that this part has always had for sopranos of intelligence.

Not only is her voice one of great beauty but she also has the art of making it convey every nuance of the mind without its ever for a moment losing its pure singing quality. The range of psychological inflection in it seems unlimited. It is a curious voice in some ways, with a contralto timbre in its lower register, with a real high soprano up above. She is not only a mistress of coloratura technique in the abstract, but has the rare gift of being able to make coloratura dramatic and psychological. Sung as she sings it, we begin to have an inkling of what it was in the old coloratura that made it for our ancestors not a mere vocal display but the carrier . . . of dramatic meaning.[59]

Charles Selden, for *The New York Times*, wrote of the "unusual demonstration" that had taken place in the staid theater after Ponselle finished the "Casta diva":

Just how much of a triumph it was is best indicated by telling the prediction of Nellie Melba, which did not come true. Mme Melba was with Miss Ponselle shortly before the performance, cheering her up [!] and warning her of the ways of London opera audiences.

"It will not be like the Metropolitan in New York," said Mme Melba, who had many triumphs of her own at Covent Garden, "and above all, don't expect any applause for your great aria 'Casta Diva.' For never in the history of opera has a London audience interrupted the performance in the middle of an act by any demonstration whatever. They wouldn't clap the Angel Gabriel until the curtain was down and the proper time for applause had arrived."

That was the prediction that didn't come true. Within two hours after it was made, Miss Ponselle sang her "Casta Diva" and in response to the loveliness of that voice a London audience forgot a tradition of this ancient theater and applauded. It was not only from the upper altitudes of the galleries that this amazing demonstration came, but from boxes, orchestra, and circle stalls.[60]

Selden placed this second meeting between Melba and Ponselle as having occurred immediately before Rosa went onstage to sing *Norma*. No newspaper accounts in London, however, made any mention of Melba's having attended Ponselle's debut or any of her other performances. On the contrary, a handwritten note which Melba hastily jotted to Natalie Townsend (and which Mrs. Townsend in turn forwarded to Rosa) indicated that Melba could not attend the opening-night *Norma* but was hoping to hear a portion of the final rehearsal:

Claridge's, London, 26 May 1929

If I can come Thursday evening, may I come in during [the] dress [rehearsal]? I am frightfully sad, for one of my dearest friends is dying, and

> I am with her a great deal. This evening there is a consultation and I must be there. Their [*sic*] *very* poor and I am calling in a big man; but I am afraid there is no hope—will you tell P[onselle] how sorry I am but I hope to go to her next performance. I have sent flowers—tell her I *know* she will have a *big* success because she is a very great artist—I am sorry but I know you will understand and miss me.[61]

About the same time Melba's letter was being delivered to Ponselle at the Savoy, a much appreciated message arrived by telegram from another legendary singer. "In passing on my way to Berlin," wrote Geraldine Farrar, "I want to add my affection to the wishes of those of your new admirers over the seas; may the English laurel crowns you plant for us grow as fully as do those of your own land—and may happiness attend their gardening."[62]

The evening after her first *Norma*, Ponselle was given a supper party at Claridge's by her Washington friend Natalie Townsend. "I am very happy," she told the awaiting press at the Claridge. "I have sung in old Covent Garden and an English audience has been very kind to me. That's one of the experiences that I've wanted all my life."[63] Inside the private dining room, she was greeted by the twenty-five guests Mrs. Townsend had invited on this special occasion. Only two among them were singers: Elisabeth Schumann, who was then appearing in *Don Giovanni* and *Der Rosenkavalier* at Covent Garden, and Melba, who had given her farewell performance there three years before.[64] The remainder of the guest list, according to the *Musical Courier*, encompassed visiting European royalty and London nobility, including the Italian Ambassador, the American Charge d'Affaires, Lords Leesdale, Colebrook, and Mounteagle, Lady Cunard, and Prince and Princess Bismarck.[65]

The public interest stimulated by Ponselle and *Norma* led Colonel Blois to arrange with the BBC to broadcast one of the performances. Although much of Europe was able to tune in, the broadcast signal was not relayed across the Atlantic. But two seasons later, by transatlantic arrangements between the BBC and the Columbia Broadcasting System in New York City, American listeners were able to hear Ponselle's Covent Garden performance of *La forza del destino* on Monday, 1 June 1931, and also her *Traviata*, which aired nine days later.[66]

The King and Queen heard her in both operas that same season. In a cable from London, the *Musical Courier* described her Leonora in *Forza* as "sheer perfection from every point of view," and noted that "King George, Queen Mary, King Alfonso and the Duke and Duchess of York, along with many other notables, joined the capacity audience in tendering an ovation to this great American artist."[67] Two weeks later, according to the *Courier*, the King and Queen heard *Traviata*, "it being the second time Their Majesties had heard the great American singer."[68] "The King showed enthusiastic appreciation of Mme Ponselle's magnificent singing," the *Daily Telegraph* reported, "and when the final curtain had fallen she curtseyed before the royal box in acknowledgement of the applause."[69] After the *Traviata* performance, King George and Queen Mary received her and subsequently invited her to join them in the royal box for the races at Ascot.[70]

While she was in the midst of her final rehearsals for *Norma*, Ponselle made a new friend of the Wagnerian soprano Frida Leider, who was singing Wagnerian roles at Covent Garden that season. Leider found herself taken as much by Ponselle's personal charm as by the dramatic power of her *Norma*. "We had arranged to have lunch at the Savoy, and the previous evening she had come to hear my Isolde," Leider wrote in her memoirs. "Rosa was not only an interesting artist, but an engaging personality. Warm-hearted and overflowing with life, she captivated me from the beginning. When I walked into the Savoy, she rushed to me spontaneously and cried, 'You belong to us.' Her Norma, which I then heard in London, was the last word in perfect technique and beauty of voice."[71]

The next season (1931), Leider heard Ponselle again, this time in *Forza* and also in Romano Romani's *Fedra*. "Shall I congratulate you first, or Maestro Romani first, on your splendid collaboration," Leider wrote after the *Fedra* premiere on 18 June 1931. "This is a wonderful new work, especially for a great actress such as yourself, and the score is the work of a truly fine musical mind."[72] While the London critics were not quite so effusive about *Fedra*, their reviews momentarily bolstered Romani's confidence, especially the prospect of recouping some of the money he had lost during the stock-market crash two years earlier.[73] Herman Klein, in the columns of *The Gramophone*, said of the premiere:

> Covent Garden owed this novelty to the kindly offices of Rosa Ponselle, who justly perceived in the title role a magnificent opportunity for the display of histrionic powers beyond any that we had suspected. True, her Norma and Gioconda had in a measure prepared the way; but not until now had there been legitimate ground for acclaiming her as a great tragic actress. I take for granted that everybody has a notion of the purport of that dreadful Greek story which forms the subject of Racine's immortal tragedy. Not since Sarah Bernhardt enacted the unhappy Athenian queen who fell in love with her stepson have I seen anyone, actress or singer or both, save Rosa Ponselle, possessing the requisite dramatic genius for the portrayal of this character."[74]

If Ponselle's *Fedra* and *Norma* indelibly impressed Frida Leider, *Traviata* did the same for two other singers who rapidly became Ponselle admirers: Alexander Kipnis, the acclaimed Russian basso who was then singing in the same repertoire as Leider at Covent Garden, and a young Zinka Milanov, who had made her debut in 1927 in her native Yugoslavia. Nearly fifty years after hearing Rosa's Violetta, Milanov said "Ponselle was magnificent . . . in *Traviata* because the voice was light but not white! The voice has to have a dramatic but not a loud sound, and this comes in the *color* of [her] sound."[75]

Kipnis, who attended the dress rehearsal preceding Rosa's first *Traviata* at Covent Garden, said years later, "Rosa Ponselle had the greatest dramatic soprano voice I ever heard. She had everything—a very warm, very beautiful quality, and a lovely pianissimo even in the highest tones. In addition to the warmth and beautiful color of her voice, all of her tones had such evenness—the high tones as well as the middle and the lowest tones were of the same fullness, the same color, the same roundness. Ponselle was also one of the greatest soprano actresses there ever was."[76]

While Herman Klein and the other London critics were counted (as Geraldine Farrar had put it) among Ponselle's "new admirers over the seas" after her triumph in *Norma*, these same critics were even more effusive in the reception they accorded her Violetta. "We were told that Rosa Ponselle was singing Violetta for the first time on any stage," Ernest Newman said in the London *Times*,

> but one found it difficult to believe it. Nothing finer has been seen or heard at Covent Garden this season. Violetta suits her in every way. The notoriously poor constitution of the suffering lady gives Mme Ponselle the best of dramatic pretexts for turning on her softest tones and showing us what she can do in the way of modeling a mere quarter-inch canvas. Mme Ponselle proves to us once more that the finest singing—given a good voice to begin with—comes from the constant play of a fine mind upon the inner meaning of the music: her Violetta is so exquisitely sung because it is so subtly imagined. Even coloratura, as she sings it, ceases to suggest the aviary and becomes the revelation of a human character.[77]

The *Daily News & Chronicle* reported that after "Ah! fors è lui" the audience gave her "an ovation lasting nearly ten minutes."[78] The *Observer* found her "at her absolute best" and judged that "Violetta gives her a fitting opportunity not only for coloratura singing, but for graceful, vivacious movement."[79] In the music columns of the *Daily Mail*, Richard Capell offered this assessment:

> The part makes a combination of demands that makes the most of her attributes. For the actress it is a psychological problem on which she brings an acute intelligence to bear. For the singer, its emotional stresses offer scope for the suppressed passion she expresses in a pianissimo. And above all that, she is of the very few who can perform the almost impossible feat of making

coloratura singing seem a natural, or at least plausible, mode of expression, instead of the feat of virtuosity it usually is. The Lady of the Camellias turns out to be Mme Ponselle's great part.[80]

The *Daily Express* summarized what most of the other London newspapers had printed about this latest success of "one of the greatest singers, present or past." "*La traviata* was a failure when it was produced in 1853. It was a success last night at Covent Garden, when Rosa Ponselle proved herself an actress as well as a glorious singer."[81]

This extraordinary reception from the critics, as Ponselle's correspondence with Eustace Blois makes clear, was the result of intense preparation on her part—not merely of the role, musically as well as dramatically, but of every detail of the production. Amid the demands of her Metropolitan contract, the Met's spring tour, and her usually taxing concert schedule, none of it had come easily. "I wanted so much to work on *Traviata* this winter," she wrote to Blois in February of 1930, "but it couldn't be done—just couldn't. I tried so hard to be excused from the Met tour, but they simply *will not* hear of it."[82] She went on to describe her schedule and the pressure she was feeling—all the while conveying to Blois specifics of the set designs, color schemes, and even the orchestral instrumentation:

> I can't sail before May 9th it seems, as much as I tried. [I will be] arriving London about the 16th. I hope you will give us plenty of stage rehearsals for *Traviata* as I won't have a chance to prepare it here. *You will, won't you?* I do *want to do it well* you know. They [the Metropolitan] wanted me to do it on tour here but as I have promised, I wouldn't do it elsewhere before London, and furthermore I'm not ready with it histrionically: I do want to put it over big—don't we? *You!*
>
> I saw [Covent Garden stage manager Charles] Moor last week in Boston and gave him an idea of what I would like the scenery to be like—or rather the way Bellincioni had it. It is very interesting in detail—all very significant. I forgot to mention to him the color of the *walls* in the bedroom scene, last act—if possible, please have them a real mysterious lavender, more on the orchid shade. This color with my costuming of white is very impressive. And then the lighting of cold blue lamps and the reflection from the fireplace help to make Violetta a more pathetic figure.
>
> Another great favor I ask of you is to get after the *orchestra pitch*. Have your German director keep pulling it down until you get it to A'-435 and *keep* them down. Get them to *adjust their instruments* before beginning your season—of course using the A'-435 new clarinets.[83]

The morning after her first *Traviata*, Francis Toye, the esteemed Verdi specialist, summed up the results of such detailed preparation. "The London public," he wrote, would have never discovered the beauties of *La traviata* but for Ponselle. To hear her sing the coloratura, acting every note of it, is in itself a lesson that every singer should take at any cost. All through the part she brings her great intelligence to bear on the vocal line wherein lies the major part of the expression, so that Verdi's sense of poetry and psychological insight are as clear as crystal. Her acting, too, is superb; she looks as lovely as a picture by an old master; altogether her performance is perhaps the most remarkable of operatic interpretation in the world today.[84]

CHAPTER EIGHT

A No-Come-Back Girl

Buoyed by her London reviews and revitalized by the Alpine scenery at St. Moritz, Ponselle felt thoroughly confident during her return voyage to the States that she had nothing to fear from the Manhattan critics when she brought her *Traviata* to the Metropolitan Opera. But when she ventured the role for the first time (at a matinee benefit on 16 January 1931, with Lauri-Volpi as Alfredo and de Luca as the elder Germont), neither she nor anyone who had read the transatlantic news stories of her triumph in London could fathom the reviews she received in New York.

Olin Downes mirrored most of the critics' sentiments. An unwavering Ponselle admirer in prior roles, Downes expressed reservations about her choice of Violetta as a new role, while granting that it "may well lend itself to different interpretations":

> Miss Ponselle's conception of it had many elements of interest, and, logically for such a singer and such a voice, it departed widely from the more recent interpretations witnessed in this city.
>
> The splendor of the voice itself would accomplish much for the role, and there is nothing in the music that need be beyond the technical capacities of this rarely gifted singer. With Miss Ponselle the interpretation of Violetta is not a question of vocal technical capacity, but rather one of taste and style. This commentary can take no account of Miss Ponselle's delivery of the early scenes and the more brilliant passages of the score. In emotional moments she was often eloquent. In later scenes, specifically those of the third and fourth acts, her treatment of the music inclined to exaggeration and to the spasmodic delivery of phrases. There was apparently the inten-

> tion, in certain passages, to lighten the tone arbitrarily and, with sudden intentions of delicacy, to make it unnecessarily frail. In its sudden and sometimes gusty alternations this singing suggested a manner more appropriate to *Trovatore* than to *Traviata*, and certainly not a métier which found Miss Ponselle at her best or at her ease in the delivery of dramatic but also polished music.
>
> Had she taken the whole opera on a very realistic and passionate plane the logic and unity of her conception might well have had a convincing if unusual effect. As it was, the treatment of the music wavered between two styles, the refined style being rather unconvincing, while a tendency to sensationalism preponderated. This was not justice to Verdi's music, nor was the death of Violetta the extremely touching passage that it can be.[1]

"Either Miss Ponselle has not yet made this part fully hers," Downes speculated, "or it is one for which she is not specially gifted." He came to his own tentative conclusion: "The latter assumption is probably the correct one."[2]

Downes' senior counterpart at the New York *Sun*, W. J. Henderson, offered an assessment that seemed a point-by-point rebuttal to everything the British critics had praised in Ponselle's Violetta:

> Miss Ponselle's voice is quite well enough suited to the music. It is not a heroic organ, but rather a lyric one with dramatic power and color. One can hardly fancy it in Isolde or Brünnhilde, but singers who have successfully sung those roles have also been admirable as Violetta. Miss Ponselle's version of the part was one which in the hands of a woman of genius might have been triumphant. There are well-established traditions of *La traviata* and a genius might throw them overboard with impunity. But the risk is not to be taken lightly.
>
> Miss Ponselle elected to disregard the fact that Verdi's music in this opera is essentially lyric. It was conceived on the lines of sustained cantabile with smoothly flowing phrases and nicely balanced rhythm. The eminent soprano endeavored to make every number passionately emotional by introducing methods verging closely upon the declamatory. She modified the melodic flow of "Ah! fors' è lui" by spasmodic utterances. She took the "Sempre libera" at an exceedingly swift pace. She dragged out the opening measures of "Dite all giovine" till they were cold and heavy. She sobbed and struggled and panted and even talked in some of the subsequent scenes. She indulged in violent contrasts between piano and forte, making explosive transitions from one to the other.
>
> Her first act was her best. Her last was her weakest. Her attempt at transforming Verdi's plaintively pathetic conception into hard-breathing tragedy was most unfortunate. But throughout the opera she made it clear that she was sincere in her conviction that a compelling interpretation of Verdi was to be accomplished by the means she had chosen. There was

> never any evidence of empty search after superficial effect. Her mistake was to attempt to escape the well defined limitations of the style.[3]

"Verdi's music," Henderson ventured, "lays bare the soul of his Violetta; it has to be sung as he wrote it." Some two weeks after his initial review, he devoted an essay review to his analysis of the faults of Rosa's conception of the role:

> Miss Ponselle has a highly individual method and one which exercises a potent spell in the theater. But such a sharply defined personal [method] is not unlikely to erect obstacles in the path of a singer striving to enrich her repertory. Miss Ponselle manifestly aimed at a reconstruction of the obvious style of Verdi's music in *La traviata*. Instead of adapting her own style to the music, she sought to adapt the music to her way. She made a gallant effort to do something that could not be done without destroying the musical nature of the work.[4]

"The public has been officially informed that Miss Ponselle had an 'ovation,' the likes of which has not been known since the now fabulous day of Caruso," Henderson said in conclusion. "Miss Ponselle was indisputably a sensation at her first appearance as Violetta. But it is the conviction of this music lover that . . . [she] has made a mistake about the possibilities of Verdi's Violetta."[5]

Henderson's colleague at the *World-Telegram*, Pitts Sanborn, took Ponselle to task for "violent onslaughts on Verdi's melodic line," although he conceded that she had "accomplished some beautiful singing" in the process.[6] Only Lawrence Gilman, among the major critics, had more positive than negative comments about her *Traviata*. "Verdi's ideal Violetta, it appears, was Patti's," he wrote. "But, if Verdi had heard this young impassioned Violetta? Hers is an eloquent and moving performance."[7]

Giacomo Lauri-Volpi and Giuseppe de Luca sang, respectively, Alfredo and Germont *père* to Ponselle's Violetta in her first Metropolitan *Traviata*. Neither garnered much praise from the major critics, but the keenly observant tenor, his own shortcomings as Alfredo aside, soon concluded that Violetta disclosed Ponselle's weaknesses, both vocal and mental. Describing her voice as "a human violoncello" with a range "as solid as a shaft of granite," Lauri-Volpi used her Giulia in *La vestale* as a benchmark in his analysis of her limitations in *Traviata*:

> There were two notes which were not secure; two simple notes at the upper end of the scale, otherwise so compact and solid; the B and C natural were not immediately available at all times, nor was she always able to sustain them. . . . The struggles of this stupendous voice in the first act of *Traviata*,

> and in the "Amami, Alfredo" in the second act caused the downfall of her will. Thus the Metropolitan, and the entire operatic world, lost the most distinguished Giulia, the most exquisite *Vestale*, that the history of opera has ever recorded. Her mad assumption of the role of Violetta in effect strangled the mythical Giulia.[8]

Citing her "restless temperament, the limits of her voice, [and] the specific density of her sound" as evidence, Lauri-Volpi judged that "none of her qualities was in the least suited to an approximation of the fragile, tender, timorous Parisienne."[9]

In time, with the exception of W. J. Henderson, most of the major critics found more to commend in Ponselle's Violetta as she continued to refine the part. But Philadelphia critic and commentator Max de Schauensee, who had heard her in every new role since Leonora in *Forza*, detected something ominous in the vocal style with which she approached Violetta:

> When Rosa prepared *Norma*, she lightened her voice compared to what it had been in *Forza* and her other early roles. She also used the *mezza voce* more than she did in any of her earlier roles—but that was appropriate in *Norma* because of the way she approached the character and the music.
>
> When she sang Donna Anna, on the other hand, I felt that we got to hear more of her "old" voice than we did in *Norma*. She achieved a finer balance between the size of her voice and the style which Mozart requires. Her Donna Anna was unforgettable. I have always thought that in *Don Giovanni*, more than in *Norma* or any other role, Rosa did the finest singing of her career. But when she prepared *Traviata*, she lightened her voice even more so than she had for *Norma*. After she did Violetta, to me her voice was never the same.
>
> Rosa always complained about high notes—yet they were a wonder to behold in the days when she was singing with Caruso. But after *Traviata* I don't think she felt secure above a high A, or maybe on a good night a B-flat. Whether it was a loss of nerve, or perhaps a loss of [tonal] support, is still a matter of debate. But her uncertainty about her high notes, plus her interest in doing more of what she used to call real flesh-and-blood women rather than the old static roles, made her very choosy about what roles she would sing.[10]

In 1931 Rosa returned briefly to the best-known of her "old static roles" when the Metropolitan celebrated the centennial of *Norma*. The performance, a matinee, was given on Saturday, 26 December 1931, one hundred years to the day after Bellini's masterpiece had premiered in Milan. The premiere itself, as Olin Downes recounted in a detailed piece in *The New York Times*, had been a fiasco; the original-cast principals (Giuditta Pasta as Norma, Giulia Grisi as Adalgisa, and Domenico Donzelli as Pollione) were in poor vocal condition as

METROPOLITAN OPERA HOUSE
GRAND OPERA SEASON 1930-1931
GIULIO GATTI-CASAZZA, GENERAL MANAGER

MONDAY EVENING, JANUARY 26, 1931, AT 8.30 O'CLOCK

LA TRAVIATA
OPERA IN FOUR ACTS
(IN ITALIAN)
BOOK BY F. M. PIAVE

MUSIC BY GIUSEPPE VERDI

VIOLETTA	ROSA PONSELLE
FLORA BERVOISE	MINNIE EGENER
ANNINA	PHILINE FALCO
ALFREDO	GIACOMO LAURI-VOLPI
GIORGIO GERMONT	LAWRENCE TIBBETT
GASTONE	ANGELO BADA
BARON DOUPHOL	ALFREDO GANDOLFI
MARQUIS D'OBIGNY	MILLO PICCO
DOCTOR GRENVIL	PAOLO ANANIAN

Act III, Ballet Divertissement by
RITA DE LEPORTE, GIUSEPPE BONFIGLIO, MILDRED SCHNEIDER
and CORPS DE BALLET
Arranged by ROSINA GALLI

CONDUCTOR	TULLIO SERAFIN
CHORUS MASTER	GIULIO SETTI
STAGE MANAGER	ARMANDO AGNINI

Positively No Encores Allowed

Program Continued on Next Page
Correct Librettos For Sale in the Lobby
Knabe Piano Used Exclusively

Figure 8. "Next to 'Norma'—my 'pet,'" Ponselle wrote of *La traviata*. But documentary evidence indicates that by 1931 she was eager to remove the vocally taxing *Norma* from her repertoire. COURTESY OF BILL PARK.

a result of too many rehearsals.[11] But the centennial performance, Downes wrote, was an unequivocal success—especially for Ponselle:

> In the best of all possible worlds, in which everything was for the best, we would have only such performances as the Metropolitan Opera Company gave yesterday afternoon of *Norma*.
>
> Miss Ponselle was her old self and more. . . . We never heard the music of *Norma* so completely in her voice as yesterday, or the voice itself so opulent and brilliant in this difficult music. She also gave the acme of dramatic significance and grand style to the recitatives. Her singing grew in

> authority, confidence and effect as the voice warmed, and the occasional slur or sideways attack of a high note disappeared. The quality of this rare voice in itself was a delight; some of the technical deeds of derring-do were thrilling from the standpoint of sheer execution, but it is only just to say that at no time was technical dexterity sought as an end in itself; always the resources of the voice and technique were at the service of dramatic expression. Furthermore, in deportment and in acting Miss Ponselle carried out the implication of her song. Her bearing and gestures were noble.[12]

This day-after-Christmas matinee, like the one the Metropolitan gave of Humperdinck's *Hansel and Gretel* on Christmas afternoon, entered the history books for yet another reason. A front-page story in *The New York Times* reported that on Christmas Day, "the melodious strains of Humperdinck's opera . . . were carried without distortion to millions of radio listeners in the United States and abroad."[13] So successful was this experiment, said the *Times*, that "the last two acts of Bellini's *Norma*, with Rosa Ponselle in the title role, will be carried over the National Broadcasting Company this afternoon at 3:45 o'clock."[14] Because Christmas Day 1931 fell on a Friday, the next-day *Norma* performance was aired on Saturday afternoon—and with it began a tradition that for six decades has brought the Metropolitan Opera into listeners' homes throughout the United States and Canada.

Although the technology of commercial broadcasting was entirely new to the Metropolitan in 1931,[15] Ponselle was already a reasonably experienced radio performer by the time *Norma* was heard over the airwaves. Four years earlier, on New Year's Day in 1927, the Victor Company had announced her radio debut on *The Victor Talking Machine Hour*. Originating from the Broadway studios of station WEAF, the broadcast also featured her friend John McCormack, as well as pianist Alfred Cortot and violinist Mischa Elman.[16] For singing a mere five selections (one aria, "Pace, pace mio Dio," plus two sacred songs and two ballads), she was paid $2,500—more than she made for singing an entire opera at the Metropolitan.[17]

A year later, on New Year's Day 1928, she made another appearance on the Victor program, this time with Martinelli and Pinza. In the "Miserere" from *Trovatore* her partner was Martinelli. Ezio Pinza joined them for the final trio from *Forza del destino*. (Three weeks later at the Victor laboratories, they would record the trio for the company's Red Seal label.) During *The Victor Hour* broadcast, radio columnist Carl Dreher sat in the control room and wrote his impressions of Ponselle's performance:

> She does not appear at all nervous as she faces the microphone, although there is some tension in her attitude—mainly energy and determination. She stands about three feet from the microphone and not much farther from the conductor, who is one of the regular maestri from the Metropolitan. The

orchestra of about thirty-five is behind her, and a mixed chorus of about the same number in back and to one side, fully thirty feet from the transmitters; but they come through very well.

Miss Ponselle weaves back and forth as she sings, varying her distance from the microphone according to the loudness of the passages. During piano portions she advances to a point where her mouth is about eighteen inches from the transmitters, while when she wants to hit a note hard she may get as far away as four feet. . . . Her assistant supplies the loudspeaker ear for her. When he considers that she is getting too close he moves his hands apart with the familiar "So big!" gesture of the fisherman; when she is too far from the pick-up he advances the parallel palms of his hands to within a few inches of each other, and when she is hitting it right the coach signals with a short vertical gesture, palms down, quite like an umpire saying "Safe!" to a runner who has just slid into a base.[18]

Rosa found the new medium ideally suited to her, Edith Prilik recalled. "Singing a couple of arias—in any key that she felt like—and doing two or three ballads on top of that, didn't even seem like work to her."[19] Never one to ignore a potential source of income, Rosa told Libbie Miller to seek out more radio opportunities. New offers came regularly, so much so according to Libbie that by the end of the 1932–33 season three-fourths of Rosa's income stemmed from radio programs and concert appearances.[20]

By February 1934, she had appeared on *The Atwanter Kent Radio Hour*, *The Cadillac Hour*, *Heinz Hall of Fame*, and General Electric's *Twilight Hour* and *Sunday Circle* programs. That month, she received a lucrative offer that would enable her to concentrate on one series of programs, rather than making occasional appearances on a variety of radio shows. The new offer was for a thirteen-week series to be sponsored by Chesterfield, a then-popular cigarette brand. If the series proved successful, the sponsor was willing to commit to a longer contract. When *The Chesterfield Hour* went on the air in April 1934, *Musical America* reviewed the first three weekly broadcasts:

Miss Ponselle sang with her accustomed brilliance an aria from *Fedra* by Romano Romani, the "Swiss Echo Song" and "A Perfect Day." On her second program were "Comin' Through the Rye," "Home, Sweet Home" and "Addio del passato" from *La traviata*. For the third event, she sang Dvorak's "Songs My Mother Taught Me," "The Nightingale and the Rose" by Rimsky-Korsakoff and an aria from *Sicilian Vespers*. This is Miss Ponselle's first long commercial broadcast and is evidently popular.[21]

"Not the least interesting part of the programs," *Musical America* said, "is the evident care with which André Kostelanetz, conductor of the orchestra and chorus, has prepared each list, so that they are expertly given and run off as smoothly as silk." Nearly fifty years later, Kostelanetz wrote in his memoirs about the challenges of broadcasting a voice as large as Ponselle's:

> Her voice was extremely powerful, like Birgit Nilsson's, and very expressive, a perfect combination for the opera stage. When she sang at rehearsal in the Hudson Theater on Forty-fourth Street, our broadcasting studio until the end of the Chesterfield series in 1938, it was glorious to hear. Acoustically, the Hudson was exquisite—no matter what we played, it sounded good—and, of course, Rosa sounded fantastic anyway. The only problem was that she was so loud I couldn't hear the orchestra. I gave the baton to Alex Cores, my assistant, and went into the control room. Her voice was coming through so strong on the high notes that the needle, which should register ideally in the center of the meter, was all the way to the right.
>
> Well, when I told our engineer how powerfully Rosa was heard in the hall, he suggested that she sing more softly. But I just couldn't imagine her voice, which was something close to a primitive force, having to be restrained. And I also did not feel justified in asking her to, in effect, reinterpret the whole piece just for the microphone. I decided it was the moment for an experiment: why not move the mike away from her and from the stage altogether, [and] hang it out over the sixth or seventh row? An hour or so later we were set up. Alex took the baton, and I posted myself in the control room once more.
>
> The effect was unbelievably beautiful. Rosa's voice was in all its glory, the orchestra was heard. And something else happened: the quality of the sound was immensely improved, the overtones were beautiful. We were all in a state of happy bewilderment that so simple a change, and one prompted by nothing more than a whim, could make such a significant difference.[22]

Ponselle's popularity with listeners enabled Kostelanetz to parlay *The Chesterfield Hour* from a thirteen-week series into a four-year run with consistently high ratings.[23] On Wednesday evening, 1 April 1936, Rosa sang her thirty-third broadcast with Kostelanetz, and was planning to do more. At eleven o'clock the next morning, she boarded a train to Baltimore, where the Metropolitan had scheduled three consecutive nights of opera that week: *Bohème* on Thursday, *Tristan* on Friday, and *Carmen* on Saturday. She had been singing *Carmen* for three months already—or, as she might have agreed, her *Carmen* had been the subject of three months' controversy—and hence she needed no special rehearsals for this Baltimore *Carmen*, except for a walk-through of the staging at the Lyric Theater. She had ample time, then, to relax and enjoy herself before her Saturday night performance.

On Thursday, the day she arrived in Baltimore, preparations were in place at the Lyric for a post-performance celebration honoring Lucrezia Bori, whose long and distinguished career with the Metropolitan was to come to an end that evening. Earlier in the opera season Bori had made what Irving

Kolodin would later term a "wise choice between a long career and an over-long career."[24] She had sung her final performance on the Metropolitan Opera House stage during a matinee broadcast of Puccini's *La rondine* on 21 March, two weeks prior to the touring performance of *La bohème* in Baltimore. Immediately after the final curtain, Baltimore's popular mayor, Howard W. Jackson, was scheduled to present Bori a silver jewel case as a token of the city's longstanding appreciation.

Before going to the Lyric that evening, the mayor had telephoned his twenty-nine-year-old son and told him rather forcefully, "If I have to go, then you're going too." Under protest, the young man reached into his closet for his tuxedo, but vowed to be "having a drink at the bar as soon as I could duck out of the box without making a spectacle of myself."[25] At six feet three, with a muscular 210-pound frame many of his friends likened to Gary Cooper's, Carle Jackson found it hard *not* to make a spectacle of himself. Recently divorced, he was never short of female companionship, but on this particular evening he decided to endure the opera alone.

Later that evening, he watched from his father's box as the mayor made his presentation to the diminutive Bori and in the process mispronounced her name three different ways.[26] Afterward, he herded his son backstage to greet the rest of the cast. While the Mayor pumped hands and chatted with Lawrence Tibbett, the Marcello of the performance, Carle Jackson stood and talked with the Lyric's long-time manager Fred Huber. Out of the corner of his eye, Jackson suddenly noticed an attractive woman walking toward an exit door not far from where he was standing.

"Who's the number in the gray dress?" he asked.

"Why, that's the great Ponselle," Huber told him.

"Who?" Jackson said quizzically. "I've never heard of her."

Huber laughed, explaining that she was one of the most famous singers in all of opera. Then he motioned to Rosa, who by then was almost out the door. "I need some fresh air," she said as Huber hastily introduced her to Jackson.

"Why don't you let this young man join you, Rosa?" Huber said. "Carle is an outdoor type like you are, and I'm sure he'd like some fresh air too."[27]

So began an intense mutual attraction that would permanently alter the course of Rosa Ponselle's life and career. In short order, Carle Jackson would not only displace permanently any lingering memories of Pippo Russo but also fill a void in Ponselle's life that neither fame nor money had been able to eradicate. The previous summer, on vacation in the Alps, she had described this void to Grace Moore. "When we last talked, in a little restaurant high above St. Moritz," Miss Moore later wrote, "she tried to explain it to me: 'I am thirty-nine years old,' she said, 'and have never had any fun. I worked and sacrificed all my life for this career, so I think I had better start now before it is too late.'"[28]

The fun began on Friday, the day after Fred Huber introduced Carle to her. He called on her at her hotel, and after a long lunch the two went for a vigorous walk in downtown Baltimore. The following evening, he sat in the mayor's box and watched her transform herself into the sultry, tempestuous Carmen—and afterward, Fred Huber remembered, Rosa made certain that her young suitor was near her while she received visitors and signed autographs backstage.[29]

For the next six months she tried to maintain a discreet relationship with Carle, but the two soon grew tired of dodging reporters' questions about their eventual plans.[30] By mid-November 1936, she was sufficiently serious about Carle to want to spend the rest of the month with him in Baltimore. To avoid inquisitive reporters, she asked Carle to take a short-term lease in his name, rather than hers, for a well-known estate in the Green Spring Valley area outside Baltimore. She passed the Thanksgiving weekend with the Jackson family, and afterward she telephoned Libbie Miller and gave her permission to release news of her engagement to Carle.[31]

Two weeks after Thanksgiving, in a private ceremony in her penthouse on 13 December 1936, Rosa officially became Mrs. Carle Andrew Jackson.[32] In a rare display of fatherly interest, Ben Ponzillo stirred from Meriden long enough to give his daughter's hand in marriage. Afterward, at a reception Libbie hosted at the Waldorf-Astoria, three hundred guests drank champagne-toasts to the bride and groom.[33] For a time, the newlyweds lived in Rosa's penthouse, with Carle commuting to Baltimore twice a week by train in order to attend to his father's insurance business. But a few months later, he and Rosa would leave New York for Hollywood, in search of a new direction for her career.

The Interview

From interviews of Rosa Ponselle by the author (March 1973, June 1975, March 1978, and December 1978), by Hugh M. Johns (June–July 1968), by William Seward (December 1971), and by Fred Calland (1977, precise date unknown). Transcribed with minor editing.

What attracted you to Carle Jackson?

Well, he was quite tall, very good looking, an all-American type—and very charming too. I guess he had everything that I was looking for at that time.

Did you know you were right for each other immediately?

It wasn't love at first sight; we took our time, but we knew there was a real attraction between us. Everybody knew it too. We didn't hide it too well, I guess.

At first glance, the two of you wouldn't seem to have had a lot in common. He wasn't a musician and had no involvement in the arts at all, but yet you seemed to have a lot of other qualities in common.

He was an outdoor type, just like I was. Give me fresh air and nice scenery and plenty of exercise, and I'm a happy girl. He was a sportsman: he was quite a horseman, he foxhunted, and he was a hell of a polo player. When we lived in Hollywood, he played polo with some of the best players out there, and they all admired him. The studios wanted him for the movies, you know.

How did that come about?

All they had to do was look at him! He could ride a horse like the wind, and he had the looks and the physique for the movies. In fact, [the studios] wanted to make him into another Gary Cooper, but things changed and that didn't happen.

After the two of you began to be seen together in New York and Baltimore, there was a lot of speculation in the newspapers and the trade papers about whether you and he were planning to marry. Although Carle had lived in public life, what with his father being a politician, your life was that of a celebrity. How did he cope with that?

After a while he couldn't stand it. I was more used to it, of course, but I didn't like discussing my private life with a newspaper reporter. We wanted to spend as much of our time as we could together, but that wasn't always possible. So one thing led to another, and we decided to get married.

I have heard several versions of how he proposed to you. Would you clarify the record by telling it as you remember it?

Through Carle, I rented a home here [in the Green Spring Valley] from a very wealthy man, Charles Morton Stewart, a friend of Carle and his family.[34] I wanted to be able to spend more time here, you see. Anyway, one day I was getting my hair done at a little salon; I was under the dryer when the hairdresser handed me a note. It was from Carle and it said, "I'm outside in the car. Come out and talk to me." I got in the car, and that's when he asked me to marry him.[35]

You were married in December of 1936.

December the thirteenth.

It was a private wedding?

Just my father, my sister—my immediate family, in other words. Of course, his family was there too—his father and mother and his brother, Riall, who was a little younger than Carle. Riall was his best man. Carmela, of course, was my maid of honor. Richard Crooks was there too. He sang at our wedding. He and Carle had become good friends. But, yes, it was a private wedding. We weren't trying to sell any tickets.

Where did you go for your honeymoon?

Canada. Just the east coast of Canada, mainly. We were gone for a week and it snowed every day, so we had to stay inside our hotel room all the time—ha, ha! We rented toboggans, went skating, and had a good time.

Where did you both decide to live after the wedding?

At my place on Riverside Drive. He was in a family business—the insurance business, which his father had started—so he could be in New York part of the time and then in Baltimore the rest of the time. Later, of course, we moved here to Baltimore and built Villa Pace, but that was after we lived in Hollywood for a little while.

A great deal had transpired in your career by the time you met your future husband. You had come back from London after your triumph in La traviata, *and after performing it at the Metropolitan, you decided to undertake Carmen as your next role. But let me ask you about* Traviata *first. Were you pleased with how your Metropolitan performances of* Traviata *went?*

They sold a lot of tickets, I can tell you that much.

I think it's only fair to say that the New York critics weren't as enthusiastic about your Violetta as the London critics had been. Would you agree about that?

I didn't pay any attention to any critics. They didn't like Bellincioni's *Traviata* either. She told me all about it. What matters is the audience, not the critics, and the audiences couldn't get enough of my *Traviata*.

You sang Violetta on one of the Metropolitan Opera broadcasts. Lawrence Tibbett sang the elder Germont, and Frederick Jagel sang Alfredo on that occasion. Do you remember that performance?

Yes. I have the records that Larry Tibbett had [made] of it. He found them in one of his trunks. He gave them to [specialty-recording producer] Eddie Smith, who called me right away to tell me. I was so excited that I couldn't wait till he finished putting them on the new [long-playing] records.[36] So I made him play them for me over the telephone. That was quite a [phone] bill too!

This many years later, what do you think of your performance?

I think most of it is pretty good, but I was just getting over an attack of pharyngitis when Gatti and Ziegler had me scheduled for that performance. I was all set to cancel because of the pharyngitis, but Gatti called me at my penthouse and begged me not to. He had [Frederick] Jagel for Alfredo, and Tibbett for the father, and with my being in the performance, it was going to be an all-American cast. So he begged me not to cancel, and, of course, I could never say no to Gatti. But when I listen to that performance there are things I don't really like, compared to how I did things in my other *Traviata*s.

For example?

In the Letter Scene, when I heard it again I said to myself, "Come on, Rosa, you could do better than that!" I just didn't put enough of myself into it that day. The "Libiamo" wasn't one of my best. I don't like the "Amami, Alfredo" either—it's not dramatic enough, not at all like I usually did it. But I liked the way the rest of the first act came out, especially "Ah! fors è lui" and "Sempre libera," and of course the scenes with Tibbett as the father. The death scene, too, I was pleased with that.

I need to ask you something about the "Sempre libera" as it is heard in the recording of the broadcast that Eddie Smith issued. I have been told that you asked him to rerecord the "Sempre libera" a tone higher than you were actually singing it. Is that true?

Really? Who said that?

Eddie Smith told me.

Oh, well, so much for little secrets. Yeah, it's a tone higher. I usually sang it a half-tone up, but I was getting over pharyngitis at the time so I transposed it down. But on the record it's a full tone higher. Because of that pharyngitis attack, I asked Gatti to make one concession if I would not cancel. I wanted the "Ah, fors' è lui" taken down a half-tone, and I wanted to do "Sempre libera" down a whole tone because I wasn't feeling up to par. But I forgot all about that, and when Eddie Smith played the "Sempre libera" for me it sounded too low. That's what made me want him to take it up a tone. You know, when [Renata] Tebaldi did *Traviata* here [in Baltimore], she also took "Sempre libera" down a tone because she wasn't at her best that night.

What was your opinion of Frederick Jagel's Alfredo?

It was all right, but he didn't have the lyric voice or the style for it. He was reliable and a good colleague. He did so many roles, you know, practically everything from Bellini to Wagner. When you do as many [roles] as he did, you can't expect them all to be good.

You were doing a lot of radio work by the mid-1930s. Some singers complained that it was not fulfilling because there was either no audience, or usually a small one. Yet you seemed to have enjoyed singing on the radio.

But most of the time, you see, I had a big audience. When I was doing *The Chesterfield Hour*, we were broadcasting in a regular theater, so there was always a good-sized audience.

You had a long association with André Kostelanetz during The Chesterfield Hour *series. In later years, he became more associated with lighter music, at least on recordings. How would you rate him as a conductor, based on your work with him in the 1930s?*

Oh, one of the best! He was a singer's conductor; he was always right there with you, breathing with you, always getting the orchestra to do just what you wanted. He was like Serafin in that way. I *loved* his orchestral arrangements. I liked everything I did with him.

Did your radio shows generally require a lot of rehearsals?

No. Most of what I did on radio were things I already had done, so I didn't really have to prepare too much. But some of those pieces I was practically singing right from the page. I didn't have a lot of time to spend in rehearsals.

In general, do you prefer your radio performances to your commercial recordings?

Oh, much more. As I told you before, I'm not that fond of many of my recordings. The tempos were either too fast or too slow because of that damned clock on the wall. But on radio, I sang most everything just like I sang it at the Metropolitan or like I would sing it in one of my concerts.

According to the Metropolitan Annals, *in addition to* Traviata, *you did broadcasts of* Norma, Trovatore, Don Giovanni, Africana, *and* Carmen. *Except for your* Carmen *broadcasts, of which there are four, only* Traviata *and fragments of your* Don Giovanni *broadcasts are known to have survived. Do you like the* Don Giovanni *excerpts?*

My "Non mi dir" isn't on it. That was the best moment for me.

As far as what can be heard of your performance as Donna Anna, do you like it?

I don't remember it that well because I kept waiting to hear "Non mi dir" again and it wasn't there. I was so disappointed about that.

Schipa sang Ottavio in that performance (this was after Gigli left the Metropolitan), and Müller did Donna Elvira rather than Rethberg. This many years later, how did their performances sound to you when you heard them again?

Schipa had the voice and the style for that role. It was a beautiful voice—a short voice, not a big top to it or anything, but a lovely timbre. His legato [singing] and his attention to words was superb, and I always admired the details, all the little touches that he put into his characters. Who was the other one you asked about?

Maria Müller's performance as Donna Elvira.

She sounds better than I remembered, especially in the recitatives, which she handled better in Italian than I would have thought. Her voice sounds very forward, too, but that might be the microphone or something. In my case, I sound like I'm practically in the wings in most of the ensembles.

You were outspoken in your criticism of Gigli when he left the Metropolitan rather than take a 10 percent salary cut that the rest of you agreed to in order to help keep the Opera Company solvent during the Depression. Did you try to talk to him about it at the time, or perhaps try to persuade him to take the cut?

You see, I didn't get involved in anybody else's business, but I thought it was a terrible decision that he made. He had bad advice. They said that [Fiorello] La Guardia influenced him.[37] When I was asked what I thought about it, I said it was the wrong thing for Gigli to do and it would hurt the Metropolitan.

How did you personally feel about the salary cut?

What was there to feel? Gatti asked all of us to take a cut to help out the Met, so I did. What I was getting [paid] was already a lot lower than what I was making before the Depression.[38]

In some of your earliest radio broadcasts you were already singing arias from Carmen. *What took you from the frail and delicate role of Violetta to Carmen, which is one of the most earthy roles in all opera?*

She was a real woman—full of fire, a woman of hot-blooded passion—not anything like those queens and princesses they used to give me to sing. I loved Carmen as a character, and the music fit my voice like a glove. That was the only one of my roles that never made me lose a wink of sleep—no worries at all—as easy as pie.

During the time you were preparing Carmen, Giulio Gatti-Casazza retired from the Metropolitan as General Manager. How did you feel when you first heard about it?

He told me about it himself. We had a wonderful relationship, like father and daughter. He took me to his office one day and told me that he was going to retire and that Mr. Witherspoon was going to be the new manager.

You already knew Herbert Witherspoon?

Oh, yes, and I was looking forward to working with him too. He had a nice way about him. I felt like I could trust him, and I thought he was really going to build my career. He was his own man, I'm sure, but in some ways he reminded me of Gatti. He [Witherspoon] understood artists because he was an artist himself. But it wasn't meant to be—he died suddenly, and then Eddie Johnson became the general manager.

Did you feel the same way toward Johnson that you did toward Witherspoon?

I guess you could say it took us a while. Of course, I had sung with him in *Vestale*, so I knew him as a colleague. He could be a love—very warm, very friendly—but there was another side of him that was arrogant, very impressed with himself. I didn't much like that side of him. We got along fine most of the time, but I knew it was never going to be like what I had with Gatti.

Was Johnson favorable to your doing Carmen?

Oh, yes, it was good box office.

Did you ever discuss doing Carmen with Gatti-Casazza?

He wasn't too keen about it, but he didn't say no to it.

I have been told that your mentor Romano Romani was not at all in favor of your doing Carmen. Is that true?

We had a little spat over that. Romani didn't think it was right for my voice. At the time, I didn't like it because I was looking to him for support. We didn't see each other, or even talk to one another, for several months after that. It wasn't until my wedding day, in fact, that we got back together again. I made up my mind that I wasn't going to get married without Nino being there, so I had several friends go find him in an Italian restaurant in Manhattan that I knew he liked. Sure enough, he was there, and we patched things up. But I prepared *Carmen* with Albert Carré, who had worked with Bizet at the Opéra Comique when they first did *Carmen*, so I knew I would get everything just right.

It's been said that you also prepared your conception of Carmen with Maria Gay. Did you base a lot of your Carmen on her conception of the role?

Not at all. She came to some of the rehearsals, and she was very supportive of the way I wanted to do *Carmen*. I asked her how she did certain things when she was doing *Carmen*, but that was all. She gave me some bracelets which she had worn [as Carmen], and I did use those because I liked them. I knew her very well, of course, and [her husband Giovanni] Zenatello too. From time to time they would bring new singers that they were working with, so that I could hear them and give an opinion about them. But I didn't prepare any of *Carmen* with her because I did all my work with Carré. I had a contract with him.

Do you have any idea where the notion came from that you had worked with her, or that she had somehow influenced your Carmen?

Not the slightest. You see, that was never my way of doing things. When I prepared Norma, I did *my* Norma, not somebody else's. Why would I work as hard as I did? You don't have to work hard if you're going to imitate or copy how somebody else does something.[39] I didn't copy her Carmen. That would have been the farthest thing from my mind!

What about other Carmens before you? How would you compare their approaches to the role? I'm thinking, for instance, of Geraldine Farrar, or Mary Garden, or perhaps Maria Jeritza's Carmen.

I saw Farrar's Carmen, and it was wonderful. What an actress! Now, she didn't have the best voice for it (she did Carmen as a soprano, of course), but she colored her voice to fit the music, and she managed to carry it off. She was one of the best Carmens.

And Mary Garden? Did you see her in the role?

She was good, but I couldn't get past her looks. She always looked the parts she played, even her facial features seemed different in each of the parts that I saw her do. But for some reason she couldn't get the look for Carmen. There wasn't enough gypsy in her Carmen.

And Jeritza's?

I didn't see her in *Carmen*, but that was the same production that I used: the same scenery with the changes that I wanted, and of course, my own costumes. I think they were still using that production at the Met after I was gone. Somebody told me it's the same one that [Risë] Stevens was using until [Rudolf] Bing came in.[40]

Returning to Albert Carré and your preparing Carmen, *where did you actually do most of your work with Carré?*

At St. Moritz. I took a suite at the Palace Hotel, which was my favorite place. This was in the summertime. I also had a suite at the hotel for Carré and his wife[41] so it would be easy for us to work.

Can you describe for us a typical work day with him?

I would get up around ten and have something to eat, something light because I was slimming down for the role. After that I would get some exercise, usually some walking or hiking. Then we would start working about noon, and we would keep going until six or seven at night. Then we would have supper, and maybe work some more if I wasn't too tired, but I wasn't just working with Carré that whole time. I went through the score and worked on the staging with him, of course, but I also had a French coach for my diction, and I worked with La Argentina, mainly, and some Flamenco dancers she knew for the dance scenes in the second act. Sometimes I worked two and three hours on the dances. I had a lot to learn—not just the dances but the castanets—and I wanted everything authentic. Lucky for me, I was a pretty good study.

Did you also work with George Balanchine on the dance sequences?

Yes, but that was in New York. He did the ballet [choreography], but he gave me some good ideas for the second-act dancing. I was never a dancer until *Carmen,* and I was going on forty years old, but with La Argentina for a teacher I did pretty well in those dance sequences, if I do say so myself.

There is some debate over which version of Carmen *you actually did—the dialogue version, such as the Opéra Comique productions, or the all-music version we usually hear. Which one did you actually do?*

Neither one, exactly. I would have preferred the dialogue version, but the Met didn't want it so I couldn't do it. But I put some dialogue in my Carmen. In fact, Carré encouraged me to improvise the dialogue. If you listen to my [Metropolitan] broadcasts of *Carmen*, you'll hear differences in each one of them.

Do you remember your first-night Carmen*? How did you feel about your performance?*

Oh, it went very well—a sellout—but unfortunately I wasn't in my best voice. I had the flu the week before. In fact, I was so sick that I had to cancel the dress rehearsal, but I was happy with the way everything went, even if I wasn't in tip-top shape myself.

Martinelli sang Don José to your Carmen that evening. How would you characterize his Don José at that point in his long career?

Martinelli had sung it with Farrar, you know. His voice wasn't as fresh as it was [when he sang it with her], but it fit the role very well, and we were always a good team.

René Maison was a frequent partner as Don José. How would you rate him in the role compared to others you sang with in that role?

He was my favorite Don José. He was at the Paris Opera before he came to the Met, so he really knew the style of Bizet. He had worked with Carré, you know. Our interpretations fit together hand in glove. He was a very, very good actor. He was a big man, very tall, one of the tallest tenors I can remember singing with. And strong! Do you know that one time he threw me around so hard that he almost broke my arm? It happened right here [in Baltimore]. In fact, it was the same night that I met my husband, right after *Carmen.* Late that night I had trouble sleeping because my arm kept hurting me. It was swollen, so they thought I might have broken it. They took me to Johns Hopkins the next morning, but it wasn't broken, just a hairline fracture.[42] Poor René Maison, he was *so* upset about it! "Don't worry about it," I told him. "I loved it because it was great theater." But I'm glad he didn't do it to me the next time!

How would you compare his José to those of Charles Kullman and Sydney Rayner?

I didn't think too much of Kullman in that role—not enough passion in his singing. But I thought Sydney Rayner was all right, not like Maison, but good enough.

Pinza was the Toreador to your Carmen during your first performance. What do you recall of their singing that night?

Oh, Pinza was great! He was the best of all the Escamillos I sang with. It's unusual to hear a bass doing that role, but he had the range for it. His acting, the way he looked and moved—and he certainly looked the part—everything about it was all very, very good.

Your first Micaela was Hilda Burke, who was making her Metropolitan debut that evening. What do you recall of her performance?

I don't remember anything at all. I mean, I know who she is (she was married to [stage director] Désiré Defrère), but I couldn't tell you a thing about her in *Carmen.* There was another Micaela I did it with, [Natalie] Bodanya, who reminded me a little of Bori. She is on one of the [recordings of the *Carmen*] broadcasts I did [and] she was pretty good.

You mentioned your Metropolitan Opera broadcasts of Carmen. *The first of the four broadcasts occurred soon after your first performance in the role. What is your opinion of that performance overall?*

Oh, I was in terrible shape! I was still sick, very sick that day, but I went on with the performance anyhow. You can hear it in my voice—it's unsteady, and sometimes I'm not singing in tune. I'm flat several times, and you know I never sang flat. If anything, I used to sing just a little bit sharp every once in a while, but *never* below the pitch. Yet in that performance, I didn't have the strength, the support, like I usually had.

You have often spoken of favorite moments you had in various roles. Did you have one in Carmen?

Oh, yes. I always liked the Card Scene, which Carré told me to take at a slower tempo. He told me, "That's the only place in the score, Rosa, where the quality of your voice can be heard." My single favorite moment in *Carmen* is in that same act—Act Three—which is set in the mountains. The gypsies light a campfire and Mercedes and Frasquita come and sit down in front of it, but José is sitting away from them, all by himself, just staring into space. My first solo line in that act comes then: "Que regardes-tu donc?" I'm saying to him, "What are you staring at?" I *loved* that line, and I waited for it in every performance.

The way you speak about Carmen suggests that of all the roles you did, it was your favorite in every way.

Well, you have to put Violetta up there, too, but I loved doing Carmen.

Which leads me to ask you how you reacted when you saw how the critics responded to your conception of Carmen?

You mean Olin Downes? He gave me a bad review. But most of the others liked my Carmen. Olin Downes had it in for me because of my manager.

You're saying, then, that Olin Downes' review was based on a personal problem with Libbie Miller? What was the problem between them?

I don't want to get into that now, but he wanted me to sing some sort of lecture series that he was putting on, and he wanted me to sing for a very low fee. I couldn't do that, you see, because if I did that for his benefit then I would have to do it for everybody else's, and that wasn't the way I liked to operate. So Miss Miller told him that I couldn't sing for that fee, and he got mad at her. He took it out on me in *Carmen*.

And you feel that his review, which has been quoted in various books over the years, was basically the only negative review you received in Carmen*?*

I didn't read reviews. Edith or Miss Miller would tell me about them—but I know that Downes *hated* my Carmen. Yet he has to get some of the credit for the money that it made for the Metropolitan. You see, he got the public curious about it because of that bad review. "If Ponselle is so bad," they said, "then we have to go and see this *Carmen* for ourselves." He created a demand, you see, and my *Carmen*s were always sold out. The audiences could never get enough of it.

Hollywood seemed to think so too. Were you quite interested in the prospect of filming your Carmen?

Very much so.

What made you decide to pursue a movie career?

I didn't. They came after me.

They? Do you mean the studios, or specific producers?

Mr. [Louis B.] Mayer and the people at M-G-M. They wanted to do a film of my *Carmen*. They were making movies with Jeanette MacDonald and Nelson Eddy at that time. Those were very popular with the public.

Did you know Jeanette MacDonald?

Oh, sure. We were friends. She was such a love!

What was your opinion of her voice?

You know, I didn't think about her as a singer. She had a nice enough voice, but I always thought of her as an actress, an entertainer, more than a singer. The same with Nelson Eddy. To me he was a movie star first, and a singer second. He and I got to know each other, but not like I knew Jeanette. He invited me to some of his parties at his house in Hollywood. I used to see Larry Tibbett there. Nelson Eddy had recording machines all over his house, and he would make private records of all of us singing together.

Did you move to Hollywood when you began discussions with M-G-M?

No, I was still living in New York on Riverside Drive. I took a bungalow at the Beverly Hills Hotel while I was talking with the studios. I spent most of the summer in Hollywood. Later on, after I got married, my husband and I lived there for a couple of months. But I never moved out there—not permanently, I mean.

During your stay in Hollywood, I've read that you became a sort of mentor to several well-known movie actresses who either had been singers or else wanted to be. I'm thinking of Irene Dunne, Joan Crawford, and Gloria Swanson. You knew them well?

Oh, they were friends; I saw Joan practically every day, and I saw a lot of Gloria too. I didn't socialize as much with Irene Dunne, but we spent time together at parties and other events. There were others, too, especially Janet Gaynor, Irene Rich, and Constance Collier. I knew Constance from New York, but I used to see a lot of her in Hollywood. My husband and I were friends with Lionel Atwill and his wife, Eva.[43] We knew them from here [in Baltimore]. Her family had built a home here years before then, and she and Lionel Atwill lived in it when they were here in the East. We were friends with Edward G. Robinson too. He was quite a fan of mine, and he was very much a man of the arts, nothing like [the characters] he played in his movies.

You had met Gloria Swanson during your first Hollywood stay in 1924.

No, before that. We knew each other in New York. She used to come to the Met to hear me too. This was even before she went out to Hollywood. She was still making movies in New York and New Jersey in those days. So we were old friends by the time you're asking me about. When I was in Hollywood, she used to come to my bungalow and listen to me go through my paces. She had done some singing, and it was a nice little voice, but she was an actress not a singer—a very smart woman, you know, a very good businesswoman and *very* witty.

And Joan Crawford?

We've been close friends all these years. She is a great lady and a great friend in my book. You know, someday they will talk about all the charity work Joan Crawford has done. She'll never talk about it; she's a very private person in that way. Of all the people I knew in Hollywood, I was closest to her. When I would be practicing, Joan would come over to my house, and I would have her sing a few pieces with me. I rented Barbara Stanwyck and Frank Fay's home; it was on Angelo Drive, and Joan lived across the street. This was after I got married, and my husband and I were living out there for a while.

Around the time of your wedding, according to documents I've seen, you made two screen tests: one for Metro-Goldwyn-Mayer, which we have seen, but also one for Paramount Pictures. Do you remember that Paramount test?

What? For Paramount? I don't remember that. Are you sure about it?

Libbie Miller gave me copies of letters from Boris Morros, Paramount's musical director, and in one of them Morros mentions your screen test.

I remember Boris Morros, of course, but I don't remember doing a test for him. All I know about is the one I did with George Cukor, but that was for M-G-M.

Do you recall details about that M-G-M test?

Yes. I did the "Habanera" and the "Chanson bohème" for the cameras. There were two parts to the screen test. They had me model different gowns and improvise some dialogue. George Cukor was directing me, talking to me out of the range of the camera. Then they had me do the arias in costume. They had a set built for me. I used my own costumes.

Were you pleased with the test?

Oh, yes. George Cukor liked it, and so did Mr. Mayer. But I couldn't sign [a contract] at that time because I had to go back to New York. I had to sing my performances at the Met, then I had the tour to do and radio and concerts on top of that. So I couldn't make any commitments because of the Metropolitan. That's what held me back.

Looking back, do you regret that now?

I was married by then, which changed things. Like a good wife is supposed to, I wanted to be with my husband. And not too long after that, I left the Metropolitan. That was one of the reasons why I left, you know: I was married, and I wanted to spend more time with my husband.

There are so many things I want to ask you about your retirement, I hardly know where to begin. One of the more prevalent views is that you were very hurt by the reviews of Carmen, *so much so that it made you not want to continue singing.*

Oh, it hurt!—of course it did, but that wasn't why I left. I was already planning to do *Adriana Lecouvreur*, but then Eddie Johnson and I couldn't agree about it. So, you see, I was already looking down the road. And like I said, *Carmen* was a big hit with the public—that's what really counted, not what critics said about it. The one who hated it, Olin Downes, had his own motives, but they had nothing to do with *Carmen.*

What actually happened between you and Johnson over Adriana Lecouvreur*?*

It wasn't really Eddie Johnson, it was Mr. Ziegler who didn't want *Adriana* at the Met. I think if Eddie had had his way, he would have backed it. But Ziegler had more say about it, and he opposed it because he said it hadn't made any money back when Caruso and Lina Cavalieri did it. But times had changed, and I felt that the public would really go for *Adriana.*

What attracted you to the role?

Oh, it's a wonderful score—like Puccini in a lot of ways. Adriana is a famous actress (she was a real person, a historic character), so there are great dramatic possibilities there. It's such a great story—totally different from *Carmen*, of course. There's so much that can be done with that role. I really, really wanted to do it, but Ziegler said no, and Johnson wasn't strong enough to go against him with the [Metropolitan] board. He and Ziegler wanted me to sing *Norma* again, and I didn't want to do that anymore.

Yet your Norma was one of the triumphs of your career, and you wouldn't have had to prepare a new role like Adriana.

But I didn't want to do that; I wanted to go forward, not backward. After *Traviata* and *Carmen*, I wanted another meaty acting role—and, of course, I wanted one that fit my voice to a tee, which is another reason I wanted to do *Adriana Lecouvreur*. *Norma* is a great opera, a masterpiece, but there is no way that you can compare Norma as a character with Adriana. Norma is very stylized acting. She doesn't have real blood in her veins like Adriana does.

It's often rumored that Johnson wanted you to sing Desdemona to Martinelli's Otello in the revival the Met was then planning. Is that true?

There was some talk about it (not with me, but with Miss Miller), but nothing came of it. I would have done it. I used to sing her prayer and the "Willow Song" in my concerts and in some of my radio broadcasts. It's a good role, and I would have liked doing it with Martinelli, but I wanted to do Adriana much, much more.

Do you remember which roles you and Edward Johnson discussed along with Adriana?

I said I would do *Gioconda, Ernani, Don Giovanni, Africana, Cavalleria, Carmen,* and *Adriana Lecouvreur*. But he wouldn't go along with *Adriana*, and after that I decided it was my time to leave. I had a life to live; I wasn't getting any younger.

In her memoirs, Grace Moore wrote that you told her in St. Moritz that you had worked so hard throughout your career that you had never had time for fun. Do you recall telling her that?

I don't remember that specific conversation, but that was exactly how I felt.

Reconstructing things from that period, you and Carle went to Hollywood during the time you were negotiating with the Metropolitan. Were you still considering doing the film of Carmen *for M-G-M?*

I was still thinking about it, and like I told you, the studios also had an interest in Carle at that time.

When you finally made your decision to leave the Metropolitan (and according to my research, you were still in Hollywood when you informed Johnson of your decision), were you actually intending to retire, or were you just planning to take a break?

I wasn't thinking of retiring at all. I had Hollywood on my mind at that time, plus, I was getting ready to do a lot more concerts. I had been working with Artur Bodanzky, studying lieder, because I wanted to do different types of concerts than I had been doing.[44] Things weren't going anywhere between Eddie Johnson and me, so I was prepared to wait—I was willing to stay out for a season if I had to. I thought they would eventually come around and let me do *Adriana Lecouvreur*. But it wasn't meant to be, I guess.

I have been told that Johnson met with you privately, actually took you for a long walk in Manhattan, and tried his best to persuade you to come back that next season. Is that true?

That's right. Eddie Johnson and Ned Ziegler came to see me at my penthouse. We talked for quite a while, and then I suggested that we get some fresh air, so the three of us took a long walk. We walked for a long time that night. I remember it very well.

And you and Johnson just couldn't come to terms?

I said, "Eddie, I'm a no-come-back girl." And I never went back.

Recollections

Libbie Miller

Everything started to change when Rosa met Carle Jackson. I didn't personally have anything against him (we got along fine at first), but they were totally mismatched. He was so much younger than she was. He had no connection with the music world; in fact, he didn't even like music. He had been married and divorced already, and he had a son to raise. He had married his first wife when he was practically out of high school, but they filed for divorce after only a few months. The story I heard was that she was pregnant when they got divorced, but they didn't know it. So they got back to together, remarried, and tried to make it work, but they couldn't make a go of it. They had a son.

[When Rosa and Carle married,] the boy was about eight or nine years old and was living with his mother. Naturally, Carle still needed to be a father to him. Rosa, of course, had never even been married, let alone had any responsibility for children, so all this was going to be completely new to her. I couldn't fathom how she was going to make all these adjustments with the kind of demands that her career put on her.

What made Rosa want to marry Carle was that he was very good-looking, a man's man, and the kind of challenge that Rosa liked. She couldn't push him around. She always had men in her life, but they would come and go. Usually she got tired of them, or else they got tired of following her all over the countryside because of all the attention she demanded. That's why she and Pippo broke up; he could never do enough to please her. The first time she tried that stuff with Carle (this was right after they met), he set her straight in a hurry. She told him, "Of course, I'll see you at all the stops along the Metropolitan tour." He looked at her and laughed! He said to her, "If you want to get ahold of me, you have my address and telephone number, so you can either call or write. Take your pick." Well, she wasn't used to that from a man, and it made her all the more attracted to him: he became a challenge.

Once they got married, Carle took over her life—and she let him, starting with where they were going to live. She was paying about $1,500 in rent for her penthouse at 90 Riverside Drive when she and Carle decided to get married. Yet she wasn't there half of the time, but was supporting two other people who were living with her. Carmela was still there, and Edith Prilik lived with Rosa too. Well, Carle wasn't going to have any of that. If they were going to live there as husband and wife, then Carmela and Edith would have to move out. So Rosa rented a place up the Drive for Carmela,[45] and Edith moved out not too long afterward.

Edith hated Carle for that, and believe me, Edith was a bad enemy to have. I used to call her the machinator. She knew how to manipulate Rosa, and she would play people against one another to get her way. But Carle saw through her, and he made Rosa tell her that she was going to have to move out. Once she was out of their house, he started working on Rosa to get rid of her entirely. The first thing he did was convince Rosa that Edith's secretary ought to be let go. It wasn't personal, it was just that it made no sense to him. If Edith was supposed to be Rosa's secretary (and that was her title all those years), he couldn't understand why the secretary needed a secretary.

Then he started telling Rosa that she shouldn't be paying for a secretary at all. That's where he and I had our first run-in. He told Rosa that if I was her manager, I should be handling all her affairs, including answering her fan mail, doing all of her correspondence, and taking care of all the other details that Edith had always handled. Well, that wasn't part of my working agreement with Rosa, and I wouldn't go along with it. I had moved from National Concerts, of which I was the manager, to the Metropolitan Musical Bureau, which used to handle the concert bookings for the Met singers. But because of Rosa, I started my own bureau, and gradually I let all my other artists go to other agencies because managing Rosa's career was a full-time job for me. So, being on my own, I didn't have a big staff (just a secretary and a receptionist) and I was in no position to take on all Rosa's appointments and fan mail, which was a very big job. I told Rosa that, and Carle let go of it for a while.

But he was still looking for a way to get rid of Edith, and of course she knew it. The way Edith would get back at him was by playing on Rosa's jealousy. If Carle was out of Rosa's sight and was seen with another woman (anybody at all) Edith would immediately tell Rosa about it and try to convince her that he was having an affair. Carle had a reputation for being a playboy in Baltimore, which Rosa knew, and that made it easier for Edith to work on her in order to get back at Carle. Edith would always pick a time when Rosa was the most prone to getting upset, usually the day of a performance. Rosa would be beside herself with jealousy over the thought of Carle being with another woman, and she would go off the deep end. She might even cancel a performance over it. The whole thing got to be a soap opera!

Some of Rosa's friends blamed Carle for her leaving the Metropolitan, but that wasn't so. Rosa ruined her career herself, and I had to stand by and watch her do it. Looking back, I don't think she wanted to sing at all anymore. She used to say that she loved to sing, but she hated to perform. She got so that she didn't like having her life planned for a year or so in advance. But she was at the peak of her career. Hollywood was interested in her, she was still one of the biggest draws at the Metropolitan, she was very popular on radio, and she was planning to expand her concert schedule, which was very lucrative.

If she had listened to me and to others who were trying to convince her to compromise with Edward Johnson, she could have had a top-notch career for at least another ten years. But she got it in her head that she didn't need the Metropolitan Opera anymore. Her reasoning was that she was already a big star, a big name, and therefore she could plan her own career without having to deal with anyone who wanted her to do things that she didn't want to do. And if that meant Johnson, Ziegler, and the whole Metropolitan Opera Company, well, so be it. That was the frame of mind she was in, and trying to get her out of it was like talking to the trees.

Hollywood dropped her because she was totally unreasonable about the money she wanted for doing a film of *Carmen*. I had deals going at Paramount with Adolf Zukor, through Boris Morros, and at M-G-M through Irving Thalberg. Thalberg and Morros both attended a concert Rosa gave at the Hollywood Bowl, and they went crazy over her. That was the time when they were making big-budget movie musicals, and when they saw her, they began thinking about a movie for her. After that concert, Boris Morros sought me out and made a point of talking to me about his interest in Rosa. The next day, he had a letter delivered to me at the Beverly Hills Hotel, where Rosa and I were staying, and in it he made clear that he wanted to talk business.

When I showed Rosa the letter she was interested, but she wasn't really that enthusiastic about it. It wasn't anything she had against Paramount (it was a major studio, so that impressed her), but it was because she knew Thalberg was also interested in her for M-G-M. One thing that you never wanted to do with Rosa, and I learned this the hard way, was to have two offers for her to deal with at the same time. She never wanted to make a decision, and she would do anything to avoid it. If we had two deals going, she would go back and forth between them and try to play them against each other, anything she could do to delay having to arrive at a decision. After a while, of course, they would just go away.

That's what she did with Paramount and M-G-M. Boris Morros arranged a screen test at Paramount, and I was told that everybody in New

York liked it. But Rosa already thought she could pick between Paramount and M-G-M, depending on who would give her the most money, so she wouldn't let me talk to Morros until I got a feel for what Mr. Mayer might offer her at M-G-M. But I couldn't get it through her head that these people were master dealers and that we were playing by their rules. Also, I had been told something privately that I wasn't about to tell her, because it would have set her off: one day [as] I was talking casually with Boris Morros, we drifted into the subject of what kind of money she might want. He was quiet for a moment, and then he said to me, "But, Libbie, what am I going to do about that face?"

Her features created problems with her screen tests. First of all, she had a very wide face, and she was all eyes and teeth and hair. She was thinner than she had ever been (she weighed 139 when she tested for M-G-M and Paramount), but on film she photographed heavier, like everyone does. Her profile looked terrible on film. She was always sensitive about her nose—she didn't like it because it didn't have much of a bridge.[46] In *Norma*, to make her profile look more sharply defined, she wore a nose-bridge made out of mortician's wax. She used to use that in some of her studio photographs too, because she liked the way it made her look. But this was Hollywood, not the Metropolitan, and in Hollywood faces and shapes counted for just about everything. So, when Boris Morros made that comment about her face, I knew that if Paramount wanted her, she wasn't going to be able to name her price—which is just what she tried to with Louis B. Mayer.

I had been talking with Irving Thalberg all along, and he had arranged her screen test. But he died suddenly before it was made—her test was scheduled for October [1936], and he died in September.[47] After they shot her screen test, Mr. Mayer personally took up the discussions with me. That's when Rosa stepped in, against my advice. She insisted that she was going to close the deal herself. Mr. Mayer arranged a meeting with us in his office, and it started off very nicely. During the small talk, he brought the conversation around to M-G-M's interest in her. He said, "You know, Rosa, we're not used to dealing with a real opera star like you. We're used to talking contracts with these movie singers and their agents, so we don't really know where to start when we talk with you about money." Of course, that was a clever strategy on his part to get us to make the first move.

I was getting ready to say something to turn it around again, to have him name a starting figure. That's just common sense when you're in a deal. He wasn't born yesterday, so I'm sure that he knew I was going to try to get him to commit to something first. But before I could open my mouth, Rosa said to him very matter-of-factly, "I want a quarter of a million dollars: I'll want half of it in advance, and the other half, if the picture is good, you can pay me in semiannual sums. Libbie can work out the details with you." And with that, she smiled and got up and left!

Needless to say, there was dead silence after she left the room. My God, they weren't paying Clark Gable that much money! I was sitting there like a bump on a log, so I started making small talk until I could get myself together. Mr. Mayer looked at me and said, "You know, Libbie, I admire your client." I said, "Well, she's a great admirer of yours, Mr. Mayer"—I couldn't think of anything else to say. Then I told him that I would talk to her and try to get her to come up with something more reasonable. Finally, Mr. Mayer said to me, "Well, I'm glad you see it that way. The only way your client could have come up with that figure is by adding up all the numbers in the Los Angeles telephone book!"

When I told Rosa what he had said, she just brushed it off and told me to go back to Paramount and see what they would give her. What she couldn't, or wouldn't, understand is that those studio heads and producers were a close-knit group. On the outside, of course, they made it look like they were all-out competitors. But most of them had known each other since they were in the garment district in Manhattan, just off the boat, and they shared information with each other. But try to get that across to Rosa! I was sure that what she pulled with Louis B. Mayer was going to get back to Paramount and that it would kill any chances we had there.

In the end, that's what happened. She wouldn't budge on her salary demands with M-G-M, which made it impossible for me to nail down anything with Louis B. Mayer; plus, she started touting Carle for a movie career. First of all, that did nothing but draw attention away from the deal I was trying to get for her. It was like changing the subject in the middle of a conversation. But also, it wasn't even realistic. In Hollywood, good-looking men who wanted to get into films were a dime a dozen. Carle had the kind of looks that are appealing in person but that don't photograph as well. On top of that, he had a bad speaking voice—a kind of high-pitched voice with a little gravel in it. In the silent-movie days, he might have had a small chance, but not in 1936.

At M-G-M, then, nothing was going anywhere. Rosa wouldn't budge, and Mr. Mayer was sure that she had taken leave of her senses. Meanwhile, at Paramount, Boris Morros kept delaying things. He came up with every excuse I had ever heard: Mr. Zukor was overseas; Mr. Zukor was back now, but some vice president that had to be in on the decision was overseas; the home office in New York couldn't agree on a role for her; they couldn't agree on which script they should think about; money was suddenly tight: every excuse in the book—I heard them all. Finally, and just as I predicted, M-G-M and Paramount lost all interest in her.

Meanwhile, we had the Metropolitan Opera to deal with. *Carmen* had put her through hell, and she wanted to put it behind her. Whether she will admit it or not, the reviews [the critics] gave her *Carmen* nearly threw her into a depression. It wasn't just Olin Downes' review; it was all of them. Now, it is true that Downes and I had had some differences over the fees he asked Rosa to accept for an engagement he wanted her for, but Rosa caused the problem herself.

Olin Downes had a concert series under his own name in Brooklyn at that time, and he was also one of the directors of the Endowment Series at Town Hall. He invited her to do a concert for the Endowment Series, and he told me he was also interested in her for his Brooklyn series. He said that the Endowment Series' funds were somewhat tight, but they could pay her $2,000. I gave him a tentative yes. When I told Rosa, she had a fit. She told me flatly that she wouldn't accept a penny less than $2,250, but she made me tell Downes that her fee would be $2,500, or else she wouldn't sing.[48] Not only did that make me look very bad, but it was also a dumb thing for her to do. Olin Downes had always been one of her best supporters, and God knows, she didn't need the money. But if Downes had agreed to $2,500, she would have turned around and made me ask for $3,000 just to see if he would do it. That was Rosa's style. She was always so tight with a dollar that she could never see the bigger picture.

It wasn't just Olin Downes' review that devastated her—it was almost all of them. We used to read all of her reviews to her of every new role she sang. There would always be a big party after the first performance, and the next day Edith and I would collect all the newspapers, cut out the reviews, and read them to her over a glass of red wine. That was our little ritual, and we did it for *Carmen* just like we did with every other role. But those reviews were terrible. I can't remember any of the really important critics saying much of anything good about her first few performances. Believe me, that was devastating to her.

By the time Rosa sang what turned out be her last *Carmen* [on tour in Cleveland on 17 April 1937], she was already eager to move on to something new, something that would make the critics write about the "old" Ponselle. That's where *Adriana Lecouvreur* came in: it fit her voice; it was an acting part; and as with *Traviata* and *Carmen*, she would be the star of the show. That was the main reason why she didn't want to consider doing Desdemona. The opera is called *Otello*, not *Desdemona*, and it was going to be Martinelli's show, not hers.

What tells you a lot about her eventual feelings toward *Carmen* is that she only sang about half as many Carmens as she did Normas.[49] Yet *Carmen*, as she always said, was like a vocalise for her, whereas *Norma* was so much work, so exacting vocally, that she wanted to drop it from her contract. Carmen was easy for her, yes, but that was the only role she had ever done that caused rumors to get started about her voice. The rumor was that she had lost her top completely and was doing Carmen because it was a mezzo role. Like rumors tend to be, that one wasn't true. Yes, she had lost a little bit at the top, but her voice was basically intact. Some people just couldn't accept [hearing] it in *Carmen*.

With all these troubles over *Carmen*, all that Rosa wanted to do was to make a movie of it in Hollywood, to make a lot of money from it, and to never sing *Carmen* again. She didn't even want me to mention it in her contract negotiations for the 1937–38 season. She kept delaying those negotiations because she kept thinking that M-G-M would eventually see the light and give her the terms she wanted. When she was dealing with Edward Johnson, then, she needed something to buy time, so she used *Adriana Lecouvreur* as a lever.

She knew from Ned Ziegler's reaction that there was almost no chance the Met was going to underwrite a revival of that opera. Johnson had the *Otello* revival coming up, and he was spending money in the Wagnerian repertoire to take full advantage of Flagstad's popularity. But as long as Rosa could keep negotiations going and avoid having to make a decision, she could keep all her options open. The way she did that was to keep changing the list of roles she would agree to sing. In one round of discussions with Johnson, she would offer to sing *Gioconda*, *Africana*, and *Cavalleria rusticana*, plus *Adriana Lecouvreur*. He would come back with *Norma*, which was always big box-office when she was doing it.[50] But she didn't want to even think about the pressures of singing *Norma*, so she would change her mind and offer to add *Ernani* or *Don Giovanni* to the list—provided, of course, that Johnson would agree to revive *Adriana* for her. It went round and round.

She couldn't come to agreement on much of anything with Johnson for the 1937–38 season, but I did get her to agree to allow him to keep her name on the Metropolitan roster. I was still hopeful that we could get past *Adriana Lecouvreur* and compromise about the roles she would sing. But during the spring and summer of 1938, Rosa and Carle kept flitting back and forth to Hollywood, and we made no headway in our negotiations for the 1938–39 season. She got to the point that she wouldn't even make a decision about allowing her name to stay on the roster. By that time, I was practically tearing my hair out because I was losing money faster than I could count it. She was my only artist, and I was dependent on my percentage of her fees for my income. But she wasn't doing much of anything except cavorting in Hollywood with Carle. My livelihood didn't mean anything to her, of course, because she had more than three million dollars in assets and didn't have to work at all.[51]

Early in October 1938, Edward Johnson wired her in Hollywood and said he had to have a final decision about keeping her name on the roster. They had held up the presses just for her, and the time had come for a yes or no. Johnson had Earle Lewis telephone her and try to talk her into leaving her name on the roster, and, obviously, I was doing everything I could to talk her into it too. She liked Earle Lewis, but she told him she didn't want to be a part of the Metropolitan anymore. So, the day after she got Johnson's wire, she sent him a telegram saying that because they couldn't agree on anything, she saw no reason to keep any ties to the Metropolitan Opera.

That telegram was her letter of resignation. In her mind, of course, she was now free to do all the concerts and radio shows she wanted. As far as she was concerned, she was now beginning a new phase of her career, and it was going to be a very productive time in her life because she could run things her own way and never have to deal with the Metropolitan again. But she was deluding herself. She didn't want to work anymore—she had Carle, and she wanted to play. She wouldn't accept what I had been telling her all along: that without the label "Metropolitan Opera Company" attached to her name, she could never command the bookings or the fees of the past. So, it wasn't a new beginning at all. It was the beginning of the end.

The Written Record

The downward spiral that marked the end of Ponselle's operatic career was amply documented in newspapers and music periodicals, in correspondence to and about her, and in the memories of those closest to her. Most of the principals in her professional and personal lives in the late-1930s (Libbie Miller, Edith Prilik, Lena Tamborini, her sister Carmela, her brother Tony, her husband Carle Jackson, film director George Cukor, and a number of her Metropolitan Opera colleagues) were still living and in good health, for the most part, when she celebrated her eightieth birthday in 1977. Their recollections of the final years of her career, from the controversy over her Carmen to her dealings with Hollywood and the Metropolitan, help to augment the documentary record of the events that brought to a double-bar ending a two-decade reign as one of the most acclaimed singers in the history of the Metropolitan Opera.

Her Carmen, the final and most controversial role of her career, is thoroughly documented from its conception to its (and, one is tempted to add, her) execution. The record shows that the most intensive period of her preparation commenced in late-June 1935 when she and Albert Carré began their summer-long work sessions at the Palace Hotel. The hotel's chief executive, Hans Badrutt, welcomed them with a private luncheon in their honor on Saturday, June 22; Pippo Russo, who had arrived the day before, and Grace Moore, also staying at the Palace, were among the select invitees.[52]

Shortly afterward, Carré entered into a leather-bound copybook the first of what would prove to be more than three hundred pages of notes, drawings, and stage directions for Ponselle's Carmen. Her own notes, written on hotel stationery and penned in a barely legible scrawl as compared to the delicate hand of Albert Carré, began the next evening after their initial session had ended. Carré made his final entry on Saturday, August 17, 1935.[53] At eight o'clock that evening, Ponselle capped her summer's work (and, according to

Libbie Miller, paid for most of her stay at St. Moritz) by singing a well-attended concert at the Palace Hotel.[54]

In May, a few weeks before she left for Europe, Rosa had several preliminary sessions with the only designer she would have even considered for *Carmen*: Valentina, the eccentric Russian-born former actress who in one decade had risen from posing as a store-window mannequin to a premiere position in the New York fashion world. By 1935, Valentina and her husband, producer and entrepreneur Georges Schlee, were sought-after guests in a widening social circle of theatrical and film personalities. One of Garbo's biographers, Hugo Vickers, depicts Valentina's impact on high fashion near the time she and Ponselle began working together:

> Irene Selznick said there was nothing grander than a simple Valentina dress. . . . Valentina made only to order, though she did create an annual collection for I. Magnin for a while and launched a perfume called My Own. She went on to dress Katherine Hepburn, Mary Martin, and Gloria Swanson. Clients included Paulette Goddard, Rosalind Russell, and Norma Shearer. She was her own best publicist, wearing clothes so that others wanted to wear them. She designed costumes for Judith Anderson in *Coming of Age* in 1934. These were better received than the play. She also undertook *Idiot's Delight* with Lynn Fontanne, who copied her mannerisms and speech, and the stage version of *The Philadelphia Story*, which was so stylishly popular that she was inundated with orders for clothes like those worn by Hepburn for five years after.[55]

The designs that Valentina showed Ponselle for the first three acts of *Carmen* were distinctive but not far removed from the tradition of other Carmens: an ankle-length skirt with a green print, to be worn with a black sash and white blouse in Act One; a sultry-looking Flamenco dress of bold red, accentuated by vertical pleats, for Act Two; and a tailored maroon skirt to be worn with a matching jacket trimmed with black appliqué for the third act.[56] But Valentina's fourth-act design, a near replication of the Toreador's costume, led to an immediate controversy between Valentina and the Metropolitan management when she presented her rendering of the costume. As Ponselle explained years later:

> For the last act, I was expecting to see a hoop skirt like other Carmens had worn. That's what she gave me; it was gold lace, ankle-length, very nice, but when I told her I liked it, she said it was boring. Then she had a model come in wearing a costume that would make your eyes pop out. It was a matador's costume, like the Toreador is supposed to wear. It was all black, [made out of] black velvet with gold embroidery on the jacket. The pants were real pants, as tight as a matador's, and [the costume also had] a long stole with a blood-red lining. The stole went clear to the floor—no, even

> longer than that, so that it would flow behind me when I moved with it. And Valentina also designed a sort of exaggerated version of a matador's cap for me.
>
> The idea she had was for me to wear a red carnation set against all that black velvet, to heighten the effect. She said to me, "They'll see that one little red carnation all the way to Verona!" I couldn't wait to wear that costume. But the people around Eddie Johnson at the Met told him if Carmen wore pants it would break tradition too much, so he said no to it.[57]

Seeking a compromise, Valentina soon designed a black velvet, tight-fitting skirt which, from the audience, looked like a matador's pants. In an interview six years later in 1941, Valentina explained her rationale for the design:

> I made a decisive departure from the established convention, and . . . in the heated controversy that followed, I was accused of having attempted a stunt. This was not the case: the idea came to me as a logical development of certain considerations. While in Spain, I learned that very often girls used to attend bullfights in their riding habits. The gypsy Carmen would not be averse to flaunting her conquest of the most admired man of the hour. And Manet's woman toreador may have lurked in the back of my mind.[58]

"The appearance of Rosa Ponselle in that costume was met first by a gasp from the audience," Valentina wrote, "and then by enthusiastic applause which showed immediate appreciation, although criticism followed from the more conservative operagoers." The stark yet sleek costume attracted considerable press attention, and, as Valentina recalled proudly, "the bolero became the fashion of the day."[59]

Reviewing the first performance of this newest *Carmen*, Pitts Sanborn took note of the "startling costumes"—including Valentina's controversial costume for Act Four, which Ponselle wore somewhat hesitantly—and predicted that they were "bound to be talked about" in fashion circles.[60] Of the evening's *Carmen*, however, Sanborn found nothing complimentary to write:

> Miss Ponselle in her first public essay depicted the gypsy baggage in terms of a Tough Girl of old-fashioned vaudeville. The brazen air, the killing glances, the arms akimbo, the noisy bravado were all there. And if the dancing seemed only mildly funny, her acrobatics and pugilistics were almost worthy of an eminent predecessor [Maria Jeritza]. If you can lie down on your tummy to sing a prayer, what's to prevent your doing so to read a fortune?
>
> It is altogether likely that the music of *Carmen* lies badly for Miss Ponselle's voice. In any event, her tones last evening were too often thin and brassy. Nor did she seem altogether aware of the vocal requirements and possibilities of the part. Otherwise a singer of her attainments hardly would have made such sad work of the "Seguidilla."[61]

Martinelli's Don José, which Sanborn had heard when the tenor sang *Carmen* with Farrar, "was as the shadow of a great rock in a weary land, thanks to the tenor's seriousness of purpose and artistic integrity." Pinza, Sanborn judged, "sang in better vocal condition" than in other recent performances, despite being "not an ideal Escamillo." And Hilda Burke, making her debut that evening, "offered a coquettish and flirtatious Micaela" with "a voice of sufficient volume and agreeable quality" and French diction "distinctly above the general level" at the Metropolitan.[62]

In the *Evening Post*, Samuel Chotzinoff took note of the public interest in the new *Carmen*, a level of interest "attested by a house jammed to the doors." Tickets, he reported, were nonexistent even among the usual retinue of scalpers outside the Met. Inside the opera house, Chotzinoff found much more to commend than had Sanborn:

> Miss Ponselle, looking picturesque and slim, did all the things one expects Carmen to do and did them with communicative zest. She ogled the soldiers, stuck her elbows in their stomachs, negotiated shimmies, threw missiles, spat out orange peel, fell into tantrums, yawned, giggled derisively, grew seductive and blanched at the thought of approaching death. Yet her actions appeared to be spontaneous rather than studied, and the audience responded to her waywardness as it comprehended the mainsprings of that fascinating character. I found no time to stay and witness the manner of her departure from her turbulent world, but I have no doubt that her death was as sensational as her life.
>
> Vocally, there was much to admire in her vibrant and plenteous lower tones, but I could not help noticing a slow tremolo in her upper register, in forte, especially. . . . I can safely recommend it to opera lovers as well as students of feminine psychology.[63]

In the Brooklyn *Eagle*, B. H. Haggin, like Pitts Sanborn, found her vocal performance up to her usual standards, but found considerable fault with her characterization:

> It is my impression that Miss Ponselle achieves her characterizations not through dramatic instinct but through study, and that a good deal of study has gone into her Carmen. The method has produced some good results in some instances; in this one, however, it has produced an impersonation of an impersonation—the external characteristics and mannerisms of the conventional operatic Carmen—the head-tossing and shoulder-shrugging and hip-twisting, all not proceeding from any inner reality, and all therefore without external coherence and credibility. The fault with the Card Scene, then, was not its conception—for Carmen is a hussy, not a philosopher, even here—but in its exaggeration of the conception. The best was the fierce intensity of the last scene with José. And there were some good

> points: the excellent dancing, the costumes (except, possibly, that of the last act, which one might expect to be less severe and more gaudy), and of course the sumptuous voice.[64]

No admirer of Martinelli at that period in the tenor's long career, Haggin labeled his Don José "portly, iron-gray haired and in other ways unconvincing, except in the despair of the last scene, and constricted as usual in voice," in contrast to Pinza's "exuberant and rich-voiced" singing as Escamillo.[65] But it was not Haggin or the Brooklyn *Eagle* that mattered the most to Ponselle—it was *The New York Times* verdict, which Olin Downes expressed at length the following morning:

> We have never heard Miss Ponselle sing so badly, and we have seldom seen the part enacted in such an artificial and generally unconvincing manner. Her first act was more carefully composed than what followed. It had less exaggeration, fewer mannerisms, some interesting detail, and clean diction. She used a little of the spoken dialogue of the original version of the opera with good effect but already showed a cheerful disregard of laws of good singing, for which she has won richly deserved eminence. She also played fast and loose with time and with rhythm, and this to an extent unnecessary for any genuinely expressive purpose. It appeared that Miss Ponselle had determined at any cost to quality of tone, to pitch, to vocal style, to be "dramatic." This unfortunate intention only served, of course, to defeat the very ends it was designed to promote. Especially from such a voice and such an artist are these methods unnecessary and inadvisable, for Miss Ponselle is primarily a singer and secondarily an actress, and not all her efforts put her in the dramatic frame.
>
> Her dancing need not be dwelt upon, although in the Inn Scene it raised the question of whether Spanish gypsies preferred the Charleston or the Black Bottom as models for their evolutions. The sum of her acting was affected, overdrawn, often inept. There was bad vocal style, carelessness of execution, inaccurate intonation. The principal virtue of this figure was its slimness, for Miss Ponselle has heroically reduced, and is now a tall and personable gypsy. That is her Carmen's principal distinction.[66]

In the *Daily News*, Danton Walker, a consistent and unabashed Ponselle admirer, seemed to sense what Downes and most of the other Manhattan critics were about to put into print:

> The more pedantic among the critical fraternity may, and probably will, tell you this morning that Rosa's characterization was a bit vulgar. But so what? If Carmen wasn't vulgar, what was she? A factory girl who discovered that sex was her trump card and who played it—to her own destruction—would not be, in the words of Bert Lahr's song, "definitely too, too

refayned, but definitely." She was a roughneck first to last, with a bawdy wit and a native gaiety which most of the Carmens missed, but which our Rosa suggested superbly.[67]

In the Hartford *Courant*, Pierre Key accepted her characterization for what it was, but argued that the distinctiveness of the role made it difficult to compare Ponselle's with other Carmens:

> Miss Ponselle's estimate of Carmen quite clearly viewed that character as a cigarette girl of the roughest of the rough-and-ready sort. Impudent, contemptuously swaggering, and coarse—above all else. Selfish and self-centered, too; and as thoughtless over breaking a masculine heart as though it were only so much china. . . . It differed in virtually every respect from the Carmens of Emma Calvé, and Mme Bressler-Gianoli; from the Carmen Geraldine Farrar gave us, and that of Mary Garden as well. Being so markedly different . . . no comparison with any other interpreter of the part would seem to be in order.[68]

After reading most of the reviews the next morning and afternoon, Geraldine Farrar felt compelled to write to Ponselle. Probably referring to Downes' review in particular, she wrote encouragingly:

> Do not let your spirits be dampened by any press comments. I found the *base* of your Carmen well-grounded, full-blooded—and knowing something of nerves you did it *so* well; time will make all smooth and you will have a *definite* success; I liked all the dresses save the *last act*—which is not as flattering to you as it should be. And one counsel as a true admirer of your glorious voice—*do* keep up your vocal routine in Donna Anna and Norma: Carmen is a *vocally lazy* role and needs the expansion of a larger octave to counteract it. Be happy in the result of your study and ambitions.[69]

At the second performance of *Carmen* on 5 January, Pitts Sanborn found hardly more to commend than in her first outing a week earlier. "Miss Ponselle's singing—leaving aside the exaggerated antics she so freely dispenses as acting—lacked color, variety, and style. Her voice had little of its once lovely quality. In only a few instances, such as [at] the first phrases of 'La-bàs, la-bàs dans la montagne,' [in] part of the Card Scene and one or two sequences near the end, did the luscious roundness emerge."[70]

Time Magazine, which accorded the Metropolitan Opera regular coverage in its pages at that time, weighed in with a summary based on the major critics' assessments:

> First impression was to wonder why anyone so flagrantly sexy as her Carmen should trouble to work for a living in a cigarette factory. She sang the

> "Habanera" belligerently, as if defying the world. She turned on bewildered Don José like a tigress, sidled up to the captain of the guards like an old-time cinema vamp. The stage scarcely seemed to hold her. Ponselle's voice is naturally sumptuous, but she was too busy ranting to do justice to Bizet's music.
>
> In fairness to Miss Ponselle, disgruntled critics would have done well to point to the fact that there have been few successful Carmens. The redoubtable Lilli Lehmann sang the role like a Brünnhilde. Adelina Patti was completely unsuited to it. The most effective impersonation was by fiery Emma Calvé, though purists fussed at her because she took liberties with the music. Farrar's popular Carmen lacked the finesse of many of her other roles. Mary Garden was not at her best in the part. Maria Jeritza failed to stand the test.[71]

"Those who disliked Ponselle's performance last week," *Time*'s music editor concluded, "did not damn her as a singing artist but rather as a dramatic actress."[72] Nonetheless, as *Time* noted, the controversy caused by this newest production of *Carmen* still made for good box-office. As the Metropolitan ledgers attest, Ponselle's *Carmen* generated average ticket sales of $10,580 per performance, against the season's per-performance average of $8,155. The following season (1936–37), her *Carmen* continued to draw $10,028 per performance against the season average of $9,568. *Carmen* even managed to rival the per-performance intake ($10,940) that the lustrous presence of Kirsten Flagstad, then in her second season, was attracting in the Wagnerian repertoire.[73]

Ponselle's brief and unsuccessful foray into film-making, which was stimulated by Hollywood's interest in her *Carmen*, began not in the autumn of 1936, when both Paramount and Metro-Goldwyn-Mayer arranged screen tests of her in the role, but rather in 1930, when a telegram arrived from Lawrence Tibbett's management, the Evans & Salter agency, which was then finalizing a promotional campaign for his new film, *The Rogue Song*. Seeking reactions from other Metropolitan stars (a number of whom were invited to a private screening in New York), the agency asked Rosa for a written endorsement for use in newspaper releases. Too busy to attend the screening, she sent Libbie and asked her to compose something to suit the agency's purposes.

The resulting telegram, addressed to Tibbett in care of Evans & Salter, went through at least two drafts before Rosa and Libbie could agree on what should be said. "Bravo! Bravissimo! Your performance in *The Rogue Song* is most excellent," Rosa (or rather Libbie) wrote. "I was happily surprised at the progress made in talking pictures, especially in the progress of recording the singing voice. My very best wishes for your continued success."[74]

From the exchange of notes between Libbie and Rosa about the wording, it is apparent that Rosa wanted to be more effusive in her endorsement than

Libbie felt the film deserved. "If you want you can say 'Your performance in *The Rogue Song* was wonderful,' instead of 'most excellent,'" Libbie advised. "Personally, I wouldn't because I really don't think so. I think it was very good, but no more."[75] As usual, Rosa's word choices prevailed, but she readily agreed to Libbie's insert about the evident progress of recording technology in the still-infant sound films of the time. "I brought in the part about the progress made in the talkies," Libbie explained, "because I thought that would be a good hint to all the companies that you might be induced to make one."[76]

The telegram had scarcely been signed and sent when Rosa received an unexpected wire from an old acquaintance from Carmela's and her vaudeville days. The message was from Eddie Darling, the former booking manager for the Keith Circuit, now a producer and agency head in Hollywood. Because of his close working relationship with Evans & Salter and other New York agencies, Darling had an involvement in the *Rogue Song* campaign.[77] Seeing Rosa's telegram and sensing exactly what Libbie's inserted sentence meant, he promptly wired Rosa from Hollywood. "If you will make a test for the talkies either in New York or Hollywood," he wrote, "I feel almost certain a terrific contract will materialize from same."[78] He asked her to wire him immediately at the Beverly Hills Hotel where he was then living.

That same day, Libbie sent a brief, noncommittal response in Rosa's name. ("Thanks for the telegram. Someday I may consider making talking pictures. Regards, Rosa."[79]) But however noncommittal she was to Darling, from then on Rosa took every opportunity to underscore her interest in Hollywood and movies in general. An interview she gave to a New Orleans newspaper prior to a concert appearance there in 1934 was typical of her enthusiastic, lofty pronouncements about Hollywood. "To consider movies merely an entertainment is a great mistake," she opined. "They are instruments of education, sugar-coated education, but tremendous educators nevertheless. The movies are inescapable influences. The kind of influence depends just as much upon those who control the child as those who control the industry."[80]

Whether or not Hollywood took any notice of her public statements, Rosa received no expressions of interest (except, of course, Darling's) until her *Carmen* transported her from the critics' columns to the fashion pages.[81] Then came her Hollywood Bowl concert on 2 June 1936, after which events at Paramount and M-G-M began to unfold. The next day (as Libbie Miller had accurately recalled), Paramount's Boris Morros had this letter hand-delivered to the Beverly Hills Hotel:

> Dear Libbie,
>
> I am sure you will excuse me for addressing you this way, as I felt from the very first moment I met you that I am your "Landsman," and that goes a long way with me, particularly after meeting so many "prima donna

> secretaries," "prima donna managers," and "prima donna otherwise" in my long life. I think you are exceptionally charming and a good business manager. I am sure you have contributed to Miss Ponselle's success last night, and I graciously bow to you.[82]

M-G-M's charming and personable vice president Irving Thalberg also came courting after the Hollywood Bowl concert and kept in touch with Rosa periodically throughout the summer. The most influential figure in M-G-M's executive ranks at that time, Thalberg and his wife—film star Norma Shearer, for whom he had just produced *Romeo and Juliet*—held a dinner party in Ponselle's honor at their home. The black-tie event took place on Wednesday, 2 September 1936. The next morning, Thalberg had this handwritten letter, accompanied by a large bouquet of flowers, delivered to Rosa at the Beverly Hills Hotel: "It is impossible to tell you how much you contributed to last night's affair—you were warmth, beauty, talent, and generosity. You changed a formal affair into an intimate house party and a magnificent concert at one time."[83]

The morning after he wrote to Ponselle, Thalberg and his wife left Hollywood for what was to be a brief getaway up the California coast. As film historian Thomas Schatz has written, Thalberg was depressed about the poor box-office returns for his wife's latest film, which had been released a month earlier:

> To subdue his disappointment over *Romeo and Juliet*, he . . . decided to get away for a few days. Over the Labor Day weekend, he and Norma and several other couples and industry friends holed up at the Del Monte Club on the Monterey Peninsula. Most of the time was spent playing bridge, Thalberg's abiding passion outside the movie business. They played into the wee hours throughout their stay, and the long evenings in the cool California air left Thalberg with a head cold, which grew worse when he returned to Los Angeles. By the following weekend he was bedridden, and within another few days he had contracted pneumonia. For almost anyone else this would have been a difficult illness, but for a thirty-seven-year-old filmmaker with a bad heart and chronically weak constitution, it proved fatal. Early Monday morning, 14 September 1936, Irving Thalberg died at home in his sleep.[84]

Ponselle was on her way back to New York, preparing for a concert and an upcoming appearance on *The General Motors Hour* later in the month, when news of Thalberg's death reached her on the train. Libbie, who was traveling with her, immediately wired Rosa's condolences to Norma Shearer.[85]

Meantime, Libbie began to be concerned about the fate of the dealings she had had with Thalberg over the prospect of filming Rosa in *Carmen*. He had assured her that a script had already been commissioned and had promised

Libbie that a screen test would be arranged soon—a promise that he had reiterated at his dinner party for Rosa, only twelve days before his death.[86] Rosa worried, too, until she received a package from George Cukor, whom Thalberg had assigned to supervise the test. "Here is *Carmen*, newly translated," Cukor said in a handwritten note appended to the tentative script. "It would be thrilling to see you do it on the screen, and my great hope would be to have something to do with the picture."[87]

A week later, Cukor confirmed that the arrangements for the screen test were now complete; it would be filmed in mid-October.[88] The actual shooting took place on Tuesday, 13 October 1936.[89] Four decades later, George Cukor recalled working with Ponselle and remembered the reactions her screen test generated within the executive ranks at M-G-M:

> When she arrived in Hollywood that summer, which is when I was introduced to her, she was the one dinner guest everybody who was anybody wanted to have. She was the real thing, a genuine opera star. Tibbett had been a success in movies, of course—but Rosa Ponselle was in a different stratum, you might say. She was talked about in almost the same breath as Caruso had been. And what a presence, what a style she had! Very few people, men or women, could walk into a room and instantly command the center of attention like she could. And it came to her naturally. She didn't do anything to cause it. You just gravitated to her.
>
> Irving Thalberg was very interested in filming *Carmen* with her. We were doing very well with musicals at M-G-M at that time. Two that were released that same year [1936]—*Rose Marie* with Jeanette MacDonald and Nelson Eddy, and *San Francisco* with Jeanette and Clark Gable—made big money for M-G-M. I think *San Francisco*, which of course was a great story, made about five million dollars, which was more than twice what a successful film was expected to make in those days. Thalberg's interest in Ponselle and *Carmen* stemmed from the earning power that those two films, especially *San Francisco*, had proved.
>
> Her test went very well. As a screen test it wasn't anything unusual, not really different from what we generally did—some interior shots with her in different gowns and hair [styles] and makeup, some long shots and some close-ups to see how she could be made to look. And then we shot some scenes of her in costume for *Carmen*. Thalberg, of course, never lived to see the test. But Louis B. Mayer, who took over everything after Irving died, liked the test enough to want to do the film.[90]

Cukor said that he had never learned why the *Carmen* project had never materialized. "But from what I saw and heard while I was working with Rosa," he added, "I can tell you that she would have done it very, very well. She made a real impression on Hollywood. When some of us who were around in those days get together to reminisce every now and then, we still talk about her."[91]

Whether Paramount Pictures was as serious as M-G-M is far less clear from the written record. Correspondence between Boris Morros and Libbie Miller confirms that a screen test was made of Rosa at Paramount, probably in November 1936 a few weeks after the M-G-M test.[92] Morros made reference to the test in a letter written a few days before New Year's, in which he summarized for Libbie the studio's position on a contract for Ponselle:

> It isn't off and it isn't on—with the only explanation that the Home Office was not favorable to the price at all, in spite of the fact that Mr. Zukor and I liked the test. Mr. [Leopold] Stokowski also saw it and liked it.
>
> I hope that Rosa's marriage will not be a handicap in her career, and sincerely wish her all the luck in the world, always.
>
> We expect all the executives to be here on January 7th, during the Paramount Jubilee celebration, and will discuss the above matter again in the presence of everyone, and will write you again as soon as I have the opportunity.[93]

Morros' subsequent letters, according to Libbie, became less frequent and more vague, ultimately amounting to what she called "the Hollywood brushoff."[94] As with Louis B. Mayer and M-G-M, Ponselle's uncompromising insistence upon negotiating unrealistic terms also put off Adolf Zukor and Paramount, minimizing her chances for a film career.[95]

Returning to New York blissfully preoccupied with Carle Jackson's attentions, Rosa put her hopes of a Hollywood career on hold as she and Libbie prepared for her contract negotiations with Edward Johnson. Although she continued to enjoy superficially cordial relations with the new general manager, she confided to Libbie and Edith that Johnson's comparative inexperience as an administrator, his less than sterling artistry (by her standards) as a performer himself, and his boy-next-door familiarity in contrast to Gatti-Casazza's *grand seigneur* bearing, made her wish all the more that Herbert Witherspoon had gone on living.[96] But she had no way of knowing how perilously close Witherspoon had come to dropping her altogether from the Metropolitan roster. Yet Johnson, who was then serving as one of Witherspoon's assistant general managers, had been privy to those discussions and knew how close indeed his predecessor had come to not renewing Rosa's contract.

Witherspoon's worksheets—four in all, typewritten and undated, most of them bearing the title "Artists to let go"—are now housed in the Metropolitan Opera Archives. On what appears to be the first of these worksheets, he listed both Ponselles among the female singers he was considering dropping; although most of the rest were secondary artists (the names included Philine Falco, Dorothea Flexer, Elda Vettori, and Nina Morgana, among others), the popular and much-acclaimed Lily Pons also made the list.

In the context of the Metropolitan's history during the 1934–35 season, the decisions Herbert Witherspoon faced—which artists he should renew, and which he should let go—were not of his own making. By 1934, the Metropolitan had posted losses in excess of one million dollars, and during the 1934–35 season—Giulio Gatti-Casazza's last as general manager—the company lost more than a quarter-million dollars.[97] The chief cause of these staggering losses was the depressed economy that followed the Wall Street crash of 1929. But the sizeable fees still being paid to leading singers and conductors in the depths of the Depression were worsening the Metropolitan's financial duress.

In March 1935, the month during which Gatti-Casazza's long reign would draw to a close, the Julliard Foundation (a philanthropic outgrowth of the fortune accumulated by textile magnate A. D. Julliard, a large portion of whose assets funded the performing-arts school bearing his name) came to the Metropolitan's aid, eventually underwriting a quarter of a million dollars in financial relief.[98] Ultimately, the Julliard interests succeeded in having Witherspoon, a former conservatory head and a recent member of the Julliard School faculty, appointed as Gatti's successor as the Metropolitan's chief executive officer.

In the negotiations between the Foundation and the Opera, the Julliard directors imposed a number of conditions upon the Metropolitan. One required an annual operating budget with "every promise of operating without a deficit."[99] Another called for increased opportunities for promising young American singers at the nation's premiere opera house. As the new general manager (and, at that, a man who owed his selection for that prestigious post to the very same organization that had imposed these conditions), Witherspoon had no choice but to enforce them.

His reasons for including Rosa among the leading singers he was considering for nonrenewal were principally her high fees and her limited, self-selected repertoire. "Unless [she] sings Carmen," he remarked to his associates at the time, "she is practically useless for the repertoire under consideration."[100] But on what appears to be his next worksheet, in which he noted which artists he had met with and had agreed to retain, Witherspoon put a question mark after Rosa's name. And on what seems to have been his final worksheet (indicating which singers definitely would be let go), the only Ponselle named on the list was Carmela. Her contract was allowed to lapse.[101]

Following Herbert Witherspoon's sudden death from a heart attack on 10 May 1935, it had fallen to Johnson to finalize not only Rosa's but most other artists' contracts for the upcoming 1935–36 season. As of Wednesday, 15 May 1935, the day after Witherspoon's funeral and Johnson's first day as his successor, those the United Press labeled "the big three"—Pons, Ponselle, and

Tibbett—had not been reengaged.[102] But by Saturday, 17 May, the news services were reporting that Ponselle had been the first of the three to be reengaged and that Johnson had personally confirmed that Tibbett and Pons would also be returning.[103]

During this first phase of their new relationship as general manager and *prima diva*, Johnson and Ponselle occasionally dealt with one another face to face rather than using Libbie Miller as an intermediary—a strategy Libbie encouraged, feeling that it would eventually give Rosa an edge in contract negotiations. The first official communication Johnson sent Rosa, a telegram that followed a ten-day negotiating session in May 1935, suggests that the strategy worked initially:

> DEAR ROSA: I TRIED TO GET YOU ON THE PHONE BUT TWO IMPORTANT MEETINGS, PRESS AND [THE METROPOLITAN OPERA] BOARD, WITH A NUMBER OF APPOINTMENTS UNFINISHED, KEPT ME FROM SAYING GOODBYE. LET ME EXPRESS MY THANKS AND APPRECIATION FOR YOUR COOPERATION AND LOYALTY. AFFECTIONATELY, EDWARD JOHNSON.

Throughout the following season (1935–36), relations between the two remained cordial and uneventful. But subsequent letters and telegrams between them betray Johnson's growing impatience with Rosa the longer she and Carle stayed in Hollywood. "Rosa had no interest at all in doing anything," Edith Prilik recalled, "except going to parties, playing tennis and golf, watching Carle play polo, and lolling around the swimming pool at the house they were renting."[104]

Edith, contemptuous of what she considered Rosa's slothfulness—and still seething at Carle for his overt attempts to limit her role in Rosa's life—brought matters to a boiling point when she telephoned Rosa from New York and told her exactly what she thought of her Hollywood lifestyle.[105] Even more imprudently, she laid the blame for Rosa's indolence squarely upon Carle—who, when he heard what Edith had said, told Rosa to fire her immediately.

"Rosa, of course, wouldn't do it herself," Carle remembered. "She said she couldn't bring herself to do it, but I can assure you that I didn't mind doing it at all. I had already put enough pressure on her to move out of Rosa's penthouse, which she did. As far as I was concerned, firing her was long overdue."[106] Carle discussed the mechanics of dismissing her with his attorney, who recommended a generous severance payment and, in return, a written commitment from Edith that she would neither disclose the amount publicly or make any public statements about her twenty-three-year association with Rosa. The amount of the severance offer was ultimately left to Rosa, who signed a personal check from the Fifth Avenue Bank on 24 September 1937 and included with it a brief, handwritten note offering the check "as a token of my appreciation for your years of service."[107] The check was for three thousand dollars.

Several days after Edith received it, she went to her typewriter and aired her feelings in a long letter to Rosa:

> Many thanks for your check which arrived a few days ago. This token—as you call it—was a bit staggering, so much so that I could not answer you immediately. I really had anticipated you in a more generous mood when one considers all the facts and circumstances. I must clear myself first and for all time, but before I do, I want you to feel as I do, without rancor. And if the truth hurts remember it's the truth.
>
> I'm going to start about nineteen years ago with the real Rosa. The one I would have given my life for, if necessary. At 307 West Ninety-seventh Street, when you made your debut. Think hard and you will recall the promises you made to me. For one entire year you did not pay me a salary because you earned such a nominal sum, and I was satisfied. Your future was most promising. You were to rise to great heights, and I was to be with you and share in all your joys and sorrows. You as the Prima Donna and I as the friend-companion-secretary-Mother-sister-nurse-maid-and-chief-cook-and-bottle-washer. Knowing that you would become the greatest living woman singer of the century (and my judgment was justified) I put all my eggs in one basket, as it were. I gave you everything that it was humanly possible to give, loyalty, devotion, friendship, consideration and sisterly love. I was at your beck and call—day and night—everything and everyone was pushed aside. You and your career were of the greatest importance. Nothing else mattered.
>
> For eighteen years I clipped coupons and looked after your bonds. You know that banks charge for clipping coupons. This alone should have brought me an [extra] income of $200 per year for eighteen years.
>
> I watched your pennies and dollars just like a falcon watches his prey.
>
> Four years ago another person [Giuseppe Russo] walked into your life and became your financial advisor. Until then, you had accumulated a very large fortune, instead of showing losses as everyone else did. And perhaps you can recall how bad I felt when you told me that you didn't need [Fifth Avenue Bank president] Mr. Hetzler's advice or mine any longer.
>
> All of this does not come under the heading of the duties of a secretary but under the heading of finance-plus. However, I had always hoped that someday your magnanimous nature would assert itself and you would prove to me that you really appreciated my interest.
>
> What about the income tax? The interest on your bonds from 1920 to 1932, which was not reported on your income tax returns? That alone enabled you to accumulate an additional fortune. This of course does not include a number of other items which we omitted and which saved you a considerable amount of money. Didn't that prove my loyalty conclusively to you?

> And further:
>
> That after nineteen years of unswerving loyalty and honesty—honesty when I know other people without the love and interest I had in you, might have been dishonest—I find myself practically destitute.
>
> That for fifteen years I never deviated from the one cardinal feeling I had, that someday you would make an arrangement whereby my future would be made comfortable. This hope was almost a religion with me, and the thought that you would not fulfill this hope never occurred to me. That was the degree of faith I had in you.
>
> Rosa, in considering the above, do you honestly feel in your heart that you could on the Day of Judgment say that you had kept faith with me? Could you then too say honestly, that you love me as much as you claimed when you spoke to Albert, Mina Horne, Lydia and a few others?
>
> Think over carefully all that I have written and you will agree with me. I'm sorry that circumstances beyond my control have made this letter necessary.[108]

In the event her appeal to Rosa's emotions might not be successful, Edith added these lines in closing: "By the way, it is strange how quickly news travels. I am sure you will be interested to know that a newspaper syndicate has heard that we have severed our connections and has made me a very flattering offer for a series on 'My Life with a Prima Donna.'"[109] Moreover, to bolster her claims of inequity, she included three of Rosa's checks to underscore the point. The first was a photostat of Rosa's severance check for $3,000; the second, a $5,000 check Rosa had written to Rosa Raisa's husband, Giacomo Rimini, apparently as a personal loan to Rimini and Raisa, in July 1935; and the third, which Edith surely intended as a get-even measure against Carle, was an $8,000 personal check Rosa had written in April 1935 to Giuseppe Russo, ostensibly as a business investment.[110]

Rosa's reactions to the letter and enclosures, according to Libbie, were entirely hostile. "Edith showed her true colors for once," Libbie said. "That was the hand of 'the machinator'—preying on Rosa's fears, trying to make her feel guilty, and threatening her on top of it! And that reference to Rosa's 'magnanimous nature' is laughable, considering how selfish Rosa was with money. She was tighter than old man Rockefeller, and Edith knew that better than anybody. She was the one who used to traipse after Rosa in restaurants, doubling and tripling the measly tips that Rosa always left."[111]

Rereading a copy of the letter forty-one years later, Carle recalled his reactions at the time Rosa received it:

> I didn't give a damn what she wrote, or what the hell she thought. I had her figured out from the start. She had the easiest job in history, the way I looked at it. Rosa was paying her about $7,000 a year in salary. I was mak-

ing $11,000 back then, which put me way up the scale in the mid-thirties. But here was this woman making $7,000 a year, living rent-free in a huge penthouse, having all of her meals made by a live-in cook any time she wanted anything, and all of her clothes and her travel expenses were being paid by Rosa. That was a real gravy train, having a so-called job like that.

Prilik was a nasty little bitch. I got to the point that I wouldn't have wasted the saliva to spit on her, but she never could do anything wrong in Rosa's eyes. Every time I would catch [Edith] pulling something, if I said anything bad about her, Rosa would go off like a cannon. It wasn't until later, when it came time to get rid of her and Prilik sent that letter, that Rosa finally wised up and saw what a little shrew she could be.[112]

Rosa's equally hostile reaction to the letter (not only to the disclosure of her "loan" to Pippo Russo, but especially to the thinly veiled threats of exposing what amounted to income-tax evasion on her part) led her to meet Edith's plea with stony silence. She refused to answer the letter, much less to increase the severance offer. Edith eventually cashed the $3,000 check, but refused to sign any agreement swearing her to silence.

Initially, Rosa's anger caused her to retaliate by refusing to speak to Edith again, but before long, she found herself missing her longtime confidant.[113] A few months later, when Edith announced her engagement to Albert Sania, an insurance executive and entrepreneur whom she had met in Hollywood, Rosa had softened to the point that she wanted to share in Edith's newfound happiness. During the 1937 holiday season, the two were reunited in California through the intercession of Mina Horne, a mutual friend; and on 19 May 1938, when Edith married Albert in Hollywood, Rosa stood at her side as Matron of Honor. But as their friend Mina had cautioned Edith before her reunion with Rosa, the closeness she and Rosa had once enjoyed could never be rekindled. "Rosa sure misses you, honey," Mina said, "but as long as Carle will be around, he will be the boss, and no one will be too near her."[114]

In mid-October 1937, soon after Rosa and Edith had reconciled, Edward Johnson was on the telephone repeatedly with Libbie Miller, urging her to relay word to Rosa in California that the Metropolitan must have a decision about leaving her name on the roster. Libbie did so, placing a call to Rosa but talking instead to Carle, who happened to answer the telephone. After he and Libbie discussed Johnson's urgent request, Carle telephoned William Matheus Sullivan, the Manhattan attorney who had helped bring the Julliard Foundation money to the Metropolitan during the financially troubled last year of Gatti-Casazza's tenure[115] and who was also handling Rosa's legal affairs at the time.

Sullivan, after speaking long-distance with Carle, sent a letter to Edward

Johnson on 14 October 1937, summarizing Carle's and his conversation. The letter hints that Carle, either at Rosa's urging or at his own initiative, was now serving as an intermediary in negotiations between Rosa and the Metropolitan. "Libbie Miller tells me that she has told you what has transpired to date with Rosa," Sullivan told Johnson. "Carle assured us the other night that he thought he could even promise us a performance of *Norma*. We told him that we did not expect miracles but simply definite action on her part for next season."[116] When five days passed with no word from Rosa in California, Libbie sent Carle a telegram on 19 October:

> CARLE: SULLIVAN AND I HOPED TO HAVE ROSA'S METROPOLITAN DECISION BY NOW. THEIR PROSPECTUS MUST GO TO PRESS 3 O CLOCK THIS AFTERNOON. THEY CANNOT POSSIBLY HOLD IT UP ANY LONGER. SULLIVAN AND I STRONGLY ADVISE LEAVING ROSA'S NAME IN. PLEASE ADVISE IMMEDIATELY. LIBBIE

By return wire, Rosa finally gave the necessary permission for the Metropolitan to retain her name. But her chronic indecisiveness was now spilling over to her concert dates, some of which she was hinting that she might cancel. This prompted Libbie to plead with Carle, in a letter dated 27 October, to "talk sense to Rosa and make her understand what she is doing to a career for which not only she, but all of us, have reputations to uphold."[117] If Libbie was anticipating either help or sympathy from Carle, he disabused her of any such notions in his curt response:

> I received your letter, this morning, enclosing clippings from various newspapers. I must say this upsets me the first thing in the morning when I have many things on my mind besides Rosa's career.
>
> I am not very thin-skinned and can take the best or worst but I am certainly getting bored and upset with receiving nothing but adverse criticism from you. I am not telling you how to run Rosa's career but I believe it has gotten to a point that if you would spend more time to build her up than that which you spend sending me letters and clippings from different cities, you would all make far more money if that is what you are interested in.
>
> I am reluctant in writing this letter but I have tried to tell you in a very nice way that I think your criticism is uncharitable, if not unjust. I personally am not interested in whether you ever book Rosa for another concert or an opera. As far as I am concerned, as long as you are her manager just tell me the results of what you have done and not what you had to overcome to do it. I have many problems in my business but I don't air them to the world.[118]

From then on, Libbie and Carle's relationship, both on paper and, less frequently, when they dealt face-to-face, rapidly degenerated into profitless wrangling. Throughout the spring of 1938, most of which Rosa and Carle spent living in Beverly Hills, Libbie prodded her to renew discussions with Johnson. Rosa said no and that she preferred to wait until September or October when the Met's prospectus would be prepared for publication and all negotiations would have to be concluded. She also instructed Libbie not to commit her to anything, but said she would be willing to consider a few concert dates. In mid-April, Libbie sent her this telegram:

> ROSA: SHALL MAKE NO FURTHER COMMITMENTS TILL YOU ADVISE TO CONTRARY ALTHOUGH MEANTIME LOSING SOME GOOD POSSIBILITIES BECAUSE OF PROCRASTINATION. SINCE YOU WILL DO SOME CONCERTS HOW ABOUT A BALTIMORE-WASHINGTON? PRESSING ANSWER. LIBBIE

She agreed tentatively to sing four concerts: two in New York City, one in Baltimore, and another in Washington, both of the latter with the National Symphony Orchestra.[119] (One of the two New York City concerts, ironically, was the Town Hall Endowment Series for which Olin Downes had solicited her four years earlier.[120]) But in September of 1938 when the time came for the Metropolitan to send its prospectus to the printer with all the artists' names who would be singing in the 1938–39 season, Rosa again delayed making her decision.

By Monday, 3 October, Edward Johnson had to have an answer from her. He had already heard from box-office manager Earle Lewis, who had phoned Rosa at Johnson's urging. She had told Lewis that she had no interest in continuing her career. Still hoping for a different outcome for her and for the Metropolitan, Johnson telephoned Libbie and asked her to call Rosa and persuade her to leave her name on the roster. Libbie had placed the call as promised, but Carle had answered the phone. He told her that Rosa had arrived at a decision, and he repeated it to Libbie. When she dutifully relayed it to Johnson, he wired Rosa in Beverly Hills at three o'clock in the afternoon that same day:

> GREETINGS. LIBBIE TELLS ME THAT CARLE TOLD HER DEFINITELY THAT YOU HAD NO INTEREST IN SINGING AT THE METROPOLITAN DURING THE COMING SEASON. EARLE [LEWIS] REPORTS THAT HE SPOKE TO YOU AND THAT YOU DEFINITELY DECLARED THAT YOU ARE NOT GOING TO SING AT THE METROPOLITAN. IN VIEW OF THIS DO YOU WISH YOUR NAME RETAINED IN OUR PROSPECTUS? PLEASE TELEGRAM AT ONCE YOUR DECISION AS WE ARE ABOUT TO GO TO PRESS WITH THE PROSPECTUS. REGARDS. EDWARD JOHNSON

The next evening, 4 October 1938, Libbie received a copy of the telegram Johnson had gotten a few hours earlier in his office at the Metropolitan:

> DEAR EDDIE: I DEEPLY REGRET THAT IN VIEW OF THE FACT THAT WE COULD NOT GET TOGETHER ON A REPERTOIRE LAST SEASON AND INASMUCH AS THE SITUATION REMAINS THE SAME I THINK IT BEST THAT YOU ELIMINATE MY NAME FROM YOUR ARTISTS LIST THIS YEAR. AFFECTIONATE GREETINGS TO MR. ZIEGLER, EARLE AND YOU. WITH BEST WISHES FOR A MOST SUCCESSFUL SEASON. ROSA

In Beverly Hills late that morning, on the patio of their rented home on Angelo Drive, Rosa had asked Carle to word the telegram for her.[121] After it was sent, they went their separate ways for the remainder of the afternoon: he to the polo field, and she to the golf course.

CHAPTER NINE

Some Enchanted Evening

After reading Rosa's final telegram to Edward Johnson, Libbie Miller had but one question to ask her: what did she intend to do with her career, or rather, what was left of it? Initially, she told Libbie that she wanted to concentrate on concerts and radio work, preferably on the West Coast. At Libbie's urging, however, she agreed to do a coast-to-coast concert tour. "But Rosa wasn't giving up on Hollywood by any means," Libbie remembered. "She insisted M-G-M might come through any day."[1]

Ponselle's autumn concerts in the 1937–38 season, the first she had sung after leaving the Metropolitan, were well attended and well received by local critics. In Worcester, Massachusetts, where she began the tour, reviewer Earle Johnson commended the "familiar rich hue, the warm vibrancy, and [the] rounded tone" of her voice,[2] and in Atlanta, Moselle Horton Young proclaimed that Rosa had "recaptured the city which in the days of the Metropolitan's annual season here worshipped at her feet."[3]

In Columbus, Ohio, *Dispatch* critic Samuel T. Wilson found her "in fine voice and buoyant spirits" when she appeared there on 12 November.[4] Wilson's counterpart at the rival *Citizen*, R. L. McCombs, praised her "meticulous care. . . . Every song, every phrase is studied for its great yield of emotional value."[5] And in Charleston, West Virginia, she was heralded for "a richness of tone that so many sopranos cannot achieve. Add her personal attractiveness and her flair for drama and you can appreciate why six encores were demanded of her—and there would have been more had she been willing."[6]

In retrospect, the Charleston critic's last line—"there would have been more had she been willing"—was an apt description both of her disposition and the state of her career by the 1938–39 season. Nothing associated with music (except a *Carmen* film, if it were to materialize) seemed to hold any appeal for her. In summer 1937, after giving a tentative yes to an offer from Covent Garden to sing "a minimum of six performances . . . [of] operas to be mutually agreed upon"[7] (according to correspondence with Sir Thomas Beecham), Rosa suddenly opted to discontinue the negotiations. Despite Libbie's mounting frustration at Rosa's lack of interest, she barely stirred herself to respond when the Chicago Opera made overtures for a lucrative, long-term contract. Rather, she sent a telegram to Libbie directing her to turn down the offer in such a way that the Chicago management would realize she was not at all interested, rather than thinking she wanted more money from them.[8]

After a year of watching her own income plummet because of Rosa's inactivity, Libbie decided to give her an ultimatum. "I wrote her a letter and told her that she could either resume her career and let me run it (not Carle) like I always had, or else I would be forced to drop her as my one and only client and start over with other artists."[9] Knowing the risks of giving Rosa any ultimatum (especially now with Carle increasingly in control of her life), Libbie expected the same hostile reaction that Edith Prilik had gotten. Rosa did not disappoint her. But this time, she went a step further: she refused to respond to Libbie at all, even to the point of not acknowledging her letter.

Incensed at this indifference and fearing that Rosa would eventually restart her career but with Carle as manager, Libbie retained an attorney and threatened to sue Rosa for breach of contract if she were to sing under anyone else's management.[10] As she anticipated, the threat brought a prompt and hostile response from Rosa's attorney; from then on, Libbie became the ultimate *persona non grata* in Rosa's life. In formal interviews, she would refer to Libbie only as "Miss Miller" and generally would change the subject as soon as she could. In private, depending on Rosa's mood, the mere mention of Libbie's name might trigger the angry retort, "Thank you for ruining my day!"[11]

For her part, Libbie eventually rebuilt her clientele and, in her words, "moved on with my life."[12] Although she had no interest in resuming her once-close relationship with Rosa, nevertheless she retained a residual softness toward her. But over time, Libbie would reach the conclusion that she had inadvertently given Rosa an ironclad excuse never to sing in public again by having threatened to take legal action.

Quite apart from the Chicago Opera and with or without Libbie to do her bidding, Rosa was hardly lacking for offers. Early on, the Peabody Conservatory invited her to become a member of the voice faculty. Far shrewder than the Conservatory's administration initially realized, Rosa knew very well that her presence in Baltimore would be a threat to the Peabody's voice teachers if she were to decide to take pupils on her own. She had no intentions of doing so ("I wish I had the patience to teach," she said, "but I'm afraid my confounded nerves won't permit such an undertaking."[13]) yet she did not hesitate to use any leverage she could command while negotiating with the Conservatory. The Peabody administrators compounded their problems by telling her that essentially she could name her own terms to join the faculty. Typically, she set her price unrealistically high, and she also imposed another condition on accepting a faculty appointment: "If they want me, they will have to take Romani, too," Rosa wrote at the time. "They certainly need someone like him here."[14] The Conservatory did not share her opinion, however, and negotiations were soon abandoned.

In the 1939–40 season, RCA Victor, for whom she had last recorded a decade earlier, offered her a new contract. Almost simultaneously, the National Broadcasting Company approached her about a series of radio programs similar to those she had done with André Kostelanetz. To avoid having to accept either offer, however, she pitted one against the other and also used Libbie's threat of a lawsuit when it served her purposes. First, she told NBC that she could not appear on radio until she completed her obligations to RCA, and then when she turned her attention to RCA, she set specific conditions for the recordings she would agree to make. "I have signed with RCA Victor," she wrote to Edith in November 1939. "They want me to make an album of three lieder, three French, three Italian, and three English songs. *Carmen* they definitely want to record sometime this fall, either in Washington or in New York."[15] By then, she had made a few recordings at RCA's west coast facilities on the M-G-M lot; all were with piano accompaniment only, with Romano Romani (then on the M-G-M staff as a vocal coach) serving as her accompanist. But when it came time to record the album RCA had specified, Rosa balked at the location of the sessions. "They want me in New York," she told Edith, "but on account of Libbie I can't go—for, as I told them, I couldn't sing while I am worrying about her lawsuit."[16]

When RCA countered with Washington, D.C., or Philadelphia as possible venues, she cited royalties as a problem. "If I go to Philadelphia and record with their symphony, then I must share my royalties with the orchestra. Otherwise, I can only record with piano there, which I'm not willing to do."[17] And when RCA's executives suggested the National Symphony in Washington, Rosa retorted that she would not "make records with just *any* orchestra."[18]

By the autumn of 1938, when Libbie had delivered her ultimatum to Rosa, the lengthening silence on the part of Louis B. Mayer made it increasingly apparent that a *Carmen* film would not be in the offing. Yet this did not deter Rosa from wanting to continue the rounds of Hollywood parties, polo games, and tennis matches to which she and Carle had easily grown accustomed. Late in October 1938, however, events in Baltimore conspired to end their six-month idyll in California. Fred Huber, the Baltimore theater director who had introduced Rosa and Carle, relayed the events in a letter to the Metropolitan's Edward Ziegler:

> Mayor Jackson was humiliatingly defeated. The defeat carried with it so much more of a sting because he lost the city by a 12,000 majority. His opponent Mr. O'Connor carried every legislative district in the city and twenty-three out of the twenty-eight wards. Now Rosa has no hope within the next four years of being the wife of the Governor's son. Whether he will survive enough to be again the candidate for Mayor remains to be seen, because "a night is a year in politics." He will no doubt make a deal of some kind whereby he will remain a factor in local if not state politics.[19]

Whatever eventual political role his cronies might carve for him, Howard Jackson suddenly found himself out of office, and in a sense, out of work for the first time since 1922, when he had been swept into office at the age of forty-five.[20] Now sixty-three, he knew that his prospects for a political future were inherently limited, so he decided to return full-time to the insurance business he had long ago turned over to his two sons to manage.[21]

With one son on an extended leave with his celebrity wife in California, the senior Jackson needed more help than his second son, Riall (whom he had named after Harry Riall, his founding partner in the business), could realistically provide. Briefly, "the mayor" (as he was still popularly called) considered hiring an experienced agent from another firm. But then he turned his attention to Carle and gave him a choice to make: "If you want to stay out there [in Hollywood] and play polo and tennis and get a nice suntan," the mayor lectured his eldest son, "then you can turn over your share in the company to your brother and me so I can get somebody else to replace you. But if you want to earn a decent living like other people have to, then make up your mind that you're going to have to come back here and earn your keep."[22]

Always the obedient son, Carle informed Rosa that they would have to return to Baltimore. She agreed—reluctantly—but still clung to the hope that in time Metro-Goldwyn-Mayer would offer her a contract. Needing a place to live in Baltimore, they began house-hunting soon after their return. During the work-week, Carle would stay at his parents' home and spend his off-hours scouting various properties. Later in the week, Rosa would have her chauffeur drive her from New York to Baltimore, and each Friday she and Carle would look at the houses he had selected. When none pleased her, they finally decided to build. Through James Piper, Jr., a local realtor and friend of Carle, they joined with another couple and bid on a large tract of land in the Green Spring Valley, a picturesque area of rolling hills and sparsely populated farm land dotted by historic homes and wealthy estates. Carle had the deed to the acreage recorded on Rosa's birthday, 22 January 1940.[23]

Although construction began almost immediately, the expansive estate Rosa had envisioned, which originally included not only a seventeen-room house but also a swimming pool, three garages, a barn, a chicken house, a meat-dressing building, a dairy house, and a climate-controlled underground-storage area for her costumes and memorabilia,[24] had to be scaled back and redesigned several times. As a result, the estate (which Rosa had already named "Villa Pace," from the *Forza del destino* aria) took more than a year to build. Meantime, she and Carle lived on the property in an old clapboard house, which they had nominally modernized with the thought of renting it to a tenant farmer when their new home was completed.[25]

With no singing engagements in the offing to worry over, Rosa immersed herself in the pleasant task of furnishing Villa Pace. She retained the H. Chambers Company, a local firm, to design the interiors. Within a few weeks, the decorators submitted four floor plans for each of the home's living areas. With the designs now in hand, Rosa contacted her young friend Myron Ehrlich, who had since relocated from Atlanta to New York City, and asked him to accompany her on a buying trip in and around Manhattan. Ehrlich recalled her often idiosyncratic purchases:

> One of the first places we stopped was a Steuben glass retailer. Rosa wanted twelve fingerbowls for her dining-room service. The salesman told her they would cost ninety dollars. She turned to me and whispered, "Ninety dollars! My God, I can't spend that kind of money now that I'm not singing!" Then she proceeded to look around the place a little while. She saw a blown-glass bowl she liked, then some glass candlesticks, and a half-dozen or so decorative glass pieces. She wrote the man a check for over $1,000 and smiled all the way out the door.

By far the most entertaining experience Ehrlich had with Ponselle came, he recalled, at the Anderson Gallery, where an auction for priceless antiques and art work was scheduled to take place:

> As soon as we walked in, we saw Giovanni Martinelli and his girlfriend, Colette d'Arville. They were so happy to see Rosa again—and because I had known Martinelli for some time, we all stood there and talked for five or ten minutes. Martinelli kept looking over his shoulder, and finally said to Rosa, "[Frances] Alda is here. If you don't want to talk to her, you had better not let her see you."
>
> Rosa said, "I don't even want to look at that old bitch after the terrible things she said about my Carmen in her book!"[26] But she had no more than finished saying that when I saw Alda waving and coming right toward us. Of course, as soon as Rosa saw there was no escaping her, it became "Alda dearest" and "divine Rosa" while they made over each other. But instead of wanting to talk, Alda told us that we just *had* to go with her—and she meant right then—to see her new house, which was at Madison Avenue and Sixty-third Street.
>
> Alda had her chauffeur waiting outside, so she herded us into this

> enormous car. Out of deference I sat in one of the jump seats, facing the two of them. Alda went on and on about her house—and when she stopped to take a breath I said to her, "You know, Madame Alda, when you and Caruso and Chaliapin were singing at the Metropolitan, it was truly a golden age. But now it seems as if we're living in the tin age."
>
> Well, that was all the prompting she needed. "This is a perceptive young man, Rosa," Alda said. "God save us all from so-called singers like Grace Moore—that *goat*! And don't get me started on that godawful Tibbett, either! I saw him awhile ago in *Tosca*. If that son of a bitch had barked one more note as Scarpia, I'd have left the theater even sooner than I did!"
>
> When we finally got to Madison and Sixty-third, Alda took us into the foyer of her house and rang for all of her servants. They came scurrying from everywhere, it seemed, and she made them stand in line next to one another. "This is Rosa Ponselle, and she has the most beautiful voice in the world!" she shouted at them. "Now, all of you take a look at her and then get the hell back to work!"[27]

Villa Pace was no sooner completed than the attack on Pearl Harbor took the nation into World War II and Carle into the U.S. Navy for what would become a four-year tour of duty. For most of 1942, however, he was stationed in Baltimore and was allowed to live at Villa Pace until receiving his orders to go to sea. Meanwhile, Rosa began to involve herself in "Valley society," as the wealthy set from the Green Spring Valley was often termed in the press.

At first, the well-publicized construction of Villa Pace, which looked quite out of place amid the antebellum estates for which the Valley was known, gave rise to derogatory comments in society circles about Rosa's "Italianate taste."[28] Added to the fact that the United States was at war with Italy, the garish-looking (to some) Mediterranean villa, coupled with the amount of press attention it and its diva owner were receiving, did not sit well within conservative, privacy-conscious Valley society.

In time, Sonia Parr helped Rosa change those initial impressions. The wife of industrialist Ral Parr (for decades a wealthy and prominent Baltimorean and owner of a massive Valley estate called Laural), Sonia Parr had been introduced to Rosa at a party in Hollywood in 1937. Forty years later, she remembered her sudden awkwardness when they were introduced: "I had been accustomed to being around movie stars and artists generally," she said, "but to me Rosa Ponselle was a larger-than-life figure, and I had always wanted to meet her. But when I was just about to be introduced to her, I found myself getting very nervous. I remember that I was standing next to a grand piano when she said hello to me, and in my nervousness, I knocked over a cocktail into that piano."[29]

From the 1940s onward, Sonia Parr and a select group of other prominent women formed the hub of Rosa's social circle. Her intimates in those years included Betja Rosoff, a Russian-born singer and pianist who had spent most of her career in Vienna and numbered Maria Jeritza and Leo Slezak among her friends; Burtie Hoffman, whose husband Hugo was one of Baltimore's wealthiest men and whose estate called Gramercy adjoined Rosa's acreage; Nancy Symington Perrin of the old-line, politically prominent Symington family; Katherine Latimer Stewart, whose estate, Cliffholme, was on a ridge adjacent to Villa Pace; Grace Campbell, whose husband H. Guy Campbell owned several stone quarries and other businesses; Ruth Rosenberg, sister of Amoco Petroleum founder Jacob Blaustein and wife of Henry Rosenberg, who founded Crown Central Petroleum and was a major donor to Goucher College, the Baltimore Symphony, and other local causes; and Clarisa Mechanic, sister of the popular radio bandleader Blue Barron and wife of Morris Mechanic, who owned Ford's Theater, the Baltimore version of the historic theater in Washington, D.C.

With these and other friends including (from the 1950s onward) donors, executives, and performers from the Baltimore Opera Company, with which her name would be associated for the remainder of her life, Rosa Ponselle passed her retirement years amid the stately but comfortable surroundings of Villa Pace. It was there that during the war years she would offer her services to various wartime causes, there that her marriage to Carle would come to an end in 1951 after several separations in the late 1940s, there that she would receive and entertain numerous guests, including singers and instrumentalists, stage and screen personalities, regional and national political figures, and even a few well-known athletes, and there that the Baltimore Civic Opera (as it was then known) would become her creative outlet after her divorce, with its young, mostly local singers becoming an extended family to her.

It was at Villa Pace on 22 January 1977 that a houseful of distinguished guests gathered for a three-day weekend to celebrate her eightieth birthday. Her seventieth and seventy-fifth birthdays had been marked by similar celebrations, and they too made the news wires because of her enduring reputation and fame. But her eightieth birthday became the last occasion when her health, though already declining by then, would enable her to entertain so many of her friends and former colleagues on such a grand scale.

Midway through the evening, she was interviewed for CBS television by Merle Comer, a Baltimore news anchor at that time. (Another newswoman at a competing station in Baltimore, a very young Oprah Winfrey, had been given a different assignment that weekend.) Later that night while seated in front of the fireplace in her walnut-paneled library, Rosa spoke of her career, her later recordings, and the new directions her life had taken after her departure from the Metropolitan Opera.

The Interview

From interviews of Rosa Ponselle by the author (January 1977, December 1978), by Ruby Mercer (1955, precise date unknown), by Hugh M. Johns (January 1977), and by William Seward (December 1971, January 1977).

How does it feel to have such an important birthday as this one?

Well, I never used to mind birthdays that had zeros on the end, but I don't know what to think about one that has an eight in front of it.

Do you feel eighty?

Not when I'm sitting down, no. But when I have to stand up I know I'm not a kid anymore. There's something wrong with my ankles and feet, but [the doctors] don't have it figured out yet. So I'm not as steady as I used to be, and I don't walk so well. But that doesn't bother me too much right now because I don't mind being inside by these nice, big fireplaces in this winter weather. I'm a homebody, you see.

Considering what a beautiful estate you have here at Villa Pace, we can sympathize with your being a homebody. Is the estate much like it was when you built it, or have you made changes over the years?

I used to have more land than I do now, not that what I have isn't enough, but some time ago I sold several acres. Years ago, Villa Pace used to be like a farm. We had dairy cattle, sheep, lots of animals. We bred dogs—dalmatians at first, then poodles later on. For a time we were even going to raise our own beef, but I got so attached to the cattle that I wouldn't allow them to send them to market! And our dairy cattle—oh, that's another story. I would walk down by the fields every day. While I was walking I would sing to the cows, and they would come to the fence to greet me!

Your swimming pool and also the tennis court adjacent to it have been sources of exercise and relaxation. Did you add those when you built Villa Pace?

I put them in not very long after the main house was finished. My pool is spring fed, which I wanted because I like to swim in very cold water. The water temperature in that pool sometimes goes down into the sixties. I use it until practically Thanksgiving Day. As long as it isn't snowing, I want to be in the pool. The tennis court I don't use anymore, but I used to play all the time. In fact, one of my very dear friends at that time was Alice Marble, the tennis pro. The first weekend that I opened the tennis court, Alice came here to play. I had quite a workout that weekend!

Should we ask who won?

I had no intention of playing against her. But after we finished eating lunch, she said in front of the other guests, "It's time for you and me to try out the new court, Rosa." I said, "What? Me play against you? Why, you'll beat the hell out me!" So she said, "Well, I'm not playing at all unless you play against me." As you can imagine, I couldn't score a point against her! But I got even with her that night, after went back to the house. At that time, you see, Alice had gotten the bug about singing, and she was trying to make a second career out of it. She had this little tiny voice, and she learned to play the guitar well enough to accompany herself in some Spanish songs. She had gotten an engagement at the Rainbow Room in New York around that time. After dinner the conversation turned to music, and Myron [Ehrlich], who had come down from New York that weekend, asked her how her act was going at the Rainbow Room. A little later, everybody asked me to go to the piano and sing. But I said, "Oh, no—I won't sing unless Alice sings first." The poor dear! She was as nervous as a kitten, having to sing in front of me!

Everything about Villa Pace seems to reflect a different facet of your personality. The downstairs area is very Mediterranean, as one would expect in an Italian villa. But your bedroom, bathroom, and dressing room are Art Deco.

Oh, yes, I loved that look. I had a bedroom somewhat like it in my penthouse in New York, and I wanted it here, too. And I wanted a fireplace in the bedroom, which I think is just wonderful. My dressing room and bathroom are on the large side, but I like lots of space. I had everything made just the way I wanted it, even the shower. You won't see another shower like mine very often. And do you know who gave me the idea for it?

The architect? Or maybe your contractor?

Nope. Al Capone.

As in Al Capone, the Chicago mobster? Where in the world did you get to know Al Capone—or shouldn't I ask?

I met him at a charity event for children. This was in Chicago. I was doing a concert near there, and I was invited to come and help raise money at this event. Capone was an opera fan—he gave a lot of money to opera, but probably under the table. Most of the singers in Chicago knew him. Raisa and [her husband, baritone Giacomo] Rimini knew Capone. I met him and he was very nice, very polite, not tough-talking or anything like that. He asked me how I liked to relax. I told him that if I get near water, I'm a very happy girl. That's when he told me about this shower that he had in his home. Instead of just one nozzle, he had a shower with a nine or ten nozzles in it. That way, you feel the spray from head to toe. I had one like his put in the master bedroom of my penthouse in New York, and when we built Villa Pace, I had them make a similar one for my bedroom.

Do you ever get tempted to take a trip to New York City, just to see Riverside Drive and go by the building where your penthouse was located, or maybe visit old friends there, or perhaps tour the new Metropolitan Opera House at Lincoln Center?

No, I have everything I could want or need right here, so why would I want to go anywhere? Nothing would be the same there [in New York] anyway. I'm sure the new Met is very nice, but it wouldn't mean much to me. I never sang there—never had anything to do with it at all.

How about Meriden? Do you ever think about Meriden and wonder what it's like today?

I'm still in touch with my girlhood friends there. Lena called me yesterday, and I heard from Juliet [Dondero] too. I keep track of things through them. But I would never want to go back there and see that cemetery with my mother's grave and terrible things like that—too many memories!

Your sister Carmela couldn't come for your birthday celebration, but you talked to her on the telephone. How is she?

She's quite hard of hearing, so it's not easy to talk to her. I didn't realize it until I thought about it, but she's going to be ninety—ninety years old this June. That doesn't even seem possible to me. She takes after my daddy's side of the family: most of the Ponzillos live to be quite old. Carmela says she doesn't get around too well, so she has somebody who looks in on her and takes care of her meals. But she tells me she can't sing at all anymore. I don't understand that. I don't know why she can't.

Your own voice certainly seems intact. How does it sound to you?

When I'm in tip-top shape, everything feels right and it still sounds pretty good. You won't hear any break from head to chest, and the *mezza voce* will be right there. But if I'm not in good voice, I can't sing a *pianissimo* and there will be a little break between the head and chest [voices]. Of course, I don't have a top like I used to, but I can go as low as a bass in the chest [voice]. When I used to do all those high notes like I had to in *Norma*, I used to cross my fingers that they would come out! But, really, my voice has stayed pretty much the same. The big difference is that when I was singing at the Met and doing concerts and radio programs, I was in good voice every day. But now there aren't so many days in a row when I'm in good voice.

The last time you sang before a large audience, I believe, was at a rally here in Baltimore for Dwight D. Eisenhower, when he was running for the presidency for the first time. Do you remember that event?

Oh, yes! It was here at the [Fifth Regiment] Armory. John Charles Thomas and I were campaigning for Ike. They had our voices piped to the crowd outside through loudspeakers. I know it because he and I were singing Stephen Foster's "Old Folks At Home" when the motorcade brought Ike and Mamie to the Armory. Mamie told me that as soon as they got near the Armory, they could hear us because of those loudspeakers. And Mamie said to Ike, "I know that John Charles Thomas is supposed to be here, but that can only be Rosa Ponselle singing with him! I'd know her voice anywhere!" When they got inside the Armory, Ike sent for me and asked me to sing Schubert's "Ave Maria" for him. Well, you could have heard a pin drop while I was singing it, and Ike sat there with tears in his eyes the whole time. I know because I was singing it to him, looking right at him. And do you know what else I sang for him? "Some Enchanted Evening," which Pinza had sung in *South Pacific* on Broadway. That song was a big hit for him, and I used to love singing it too. But when I did it for Ike, I changed the last line to make it about him. The line in the sheet music is, "When you have found him/Never let him go." But I changed it to, "Now that *we've* found *him*/Never let him go!" Oh, how Ike loved that!

You have known and sung for an impressive list of U.S. presidents. The first you met, if my information is right, was Warren G. Harding. Do you remember the occasion?

How could I forget it? That was [in 1919] when they dedicated the tomb of the Unknown Soldier. I met President Harding just before the ceremony started. General Pershing was there too. Oh, what a sad, sad day! I can still see those men in their uniforms, carrying that wooden casket! And those mothers crying and wailing when that casket passed by! And to think that I had to sing after hearing those mothers crying like that! To this day I don't know how I got through it.[30]

You seem to have had a rather close relationship with Franklin D. Roosevelt, especially during his first and second terms.

I knew him before he got elected. You see, I was good friends with Jim and Bess Farley. In fact after I left the Met, the few times that I would go back to New York to visit, I would stay at the Waldorf with the Farleys. Jim Farley was running that first campaign for FDR [in 1931–32], which is how I met him. Gigli and I sang for FDR on board ship when I was going to Europe to sing at Covent Garden. Gigli and I took the same ship and FDR made the crossing with us.[31] I remember that he invited me to sing at a celebration they gave for him during his first term.[32] And later on, Larry Tibbett and I sang at his inauguration concert when he got elected. We sang part of the "Nile Scene" from *Aida*.

You knew President Truman?

Oh, yes! I met him through Perle Mesta. In fact, she got him to perform with me at one of her parties. I sang, and Harry Truman was my "accompanist."

As you know, some of your singer friends who are Democrats kid you about being a rock-ribbed Republican. But in the days when you were supporting FDR, obviously you weren't a Republican. What prompted the change?

Do you remember President Eisenhower's campaign saying, "I Like Ike"? Well, I liked Ike. I couldn't warm to [Adlai] Stevenson, but they say he was a brilliant man. To me, Ike was the greatest.[33] With the Russians and Communism to watch out for, I thought Ike was the one to do it. He and Mamie and I became friends, and I gave him all the support I could both of the times that he ran.

The 1952 rally at which you and John Charles Thomas sang was tape-recorded by one of your admirers and was made into a long-playing recording.

Yes, Lloyd Garrison made that recording. But Lloyd was here regularly [at Villa Pace], and he always had his recording machine going. He made a recording of the rally for Ike, and I sent copies of it as a Christmas present to my friends in Washington, New York, and here in Baltimore. He also made [a recording] of my open house during the twelve days of Christmas (that was the next year, I think). I had my singers from the Baltimore [Civic] Opera here. I had an electric organ brought in, and in the foyer, we sang a lot of carols and also some timely pieces like "Panis Angelicus" and other things. Carmela was here too. In fact, she and I sang "Silent Night" together. And that, you see, made for another nice album that we put out to help make some money for the Baltimore Opera.

Your privately published recordings, if my information is correct, eventually led to the now famous long-playing albums that RCA Victor induced you to record in 1954.

Yes. They wanted me to come to New York to make those records, but I didn't want to do that so they came here instead. Those albums were made here in the foyer, like my Christmas record was. I had the rug taken up so that we'd get a nice bright sound, and [the RCA Victor engineers] turned my dining room into a recording studio. Oh, there were wires all over the place around here! And do you know that the man they sent down here to oversee things was one of the same men who recorded me during my career? Mr. Lynch was his name. That was such a pleasant surprise to see him again after all those years.

Before you made your RCA Victor LPs, the last time you had been in a recording studio was in Hollywood in 1939. Do you remember your Hollywood recordings?

I made those with Romani at M-G-M, where the Victor people had a recording place. He was teaching out in Hollywood at that time. I had introduced him to the M-G-M people, and they had hired him to teach some of the stars how to sing. He taught a good many of them: Ann Sothern, Ilona Massey, Eleanor Powell, Deanna Durbin, Douglas MacPhail, Joan [Crawford]. While I was out there [in Hollywood], I arranged with the Victor people for me to make some records.

Were you pleased with them?

I didn't think too much about them at the time. The night before Romani and I made them, Jeritza gave a big party for me in Beverly Hills, so I didn't get very much sleep. I got up quite late, and my voice was still low, low, low. But some of those records are pretty damned good. I like "The Nightingale and the Rose." I remember that one in particular. But I didn't like the Schubert "Ave Maria" record. I should have done one or two more [takes]. I sound like I'm just sight-singing it, and it's way too loud. I'm supposed to be praying, after all.

Those, of course, were 78 r.p.m. recordings, which limited you to about four minutes' singing. How did you like making long-playing recordings?

I must admit it was a nice experience, really. I just wish we had had those when I was still singing at the Met.

Your accompanist on almost all the selections you recorded, excepting the ones on which you accompanied yourself at the piano, was Igor Chichagov, who is also here tonight. Did you and he have a regular schedule for completing those sessions?

No, I never sang unless I was in the mood. But when Igor and I got started we kept right on going, usually. [*He replies yes.*]

Let me ask you about some of the selections you included on the first of your two LPs, Rosa Ponselle Sings Today. *One song you chose was "Rosemonde" by Mario Persico. How did you come to include that among your choices?*

Bidù Sayão was visiting with me here. This was during one of her concert tours. She said, "Rosa I have something for you, and you *must* sing it for me." She gave me the manuscript for "Rosemonde." It was written for her. I fell in love with it immediately. I promised her that if one day I did record [it,] I would sing it to her. So in my mind while I was making that record, I was singing it to Bidù Sayão.

You also chose Saint-Saëns' "Guitares et mandolines" for that first LP. Had you sung that before?

Oh, that's one of my favorites! I used it as an encore in my concerts. Looking through my music to see what number we could find to follow the "Rosamonde," I wanted something that would be contrasting in color.[34] So we ran across "Guitares et mandolines" and I said to Igor, "Oh, here's a little encore that I'm very partial to. Let's try it!" But he said, "Rosa, unless you let me practice it, my fingers will never get around this accompaniment!" I told him, "Let's try it anyway." So we had two or three readings of it, and Mr. Lynch was recording it. Afterward he said, "Here it is, Miss Ponselle," and it was accepted. It's quite lovely, really.

You never seem to have done much lieder, yet you chose Brahms' "Von ewiger Liebe" for that first album. What made you decide to include it?

That was one I had never done. In fact, I did very little German lieder in my entire life. But I have always loved and admired "Von ewiger Liebe." About a year or so before I made that record, Jimmie Alfonte (he was Captain Alfonte at that time, but he's now a Colonel), who is a dear friend and also a record collector, said to me, "Rosa, you *must* sing this 'Von ewiger Liebe.'" I said that I could never hope to compete with those great [lieder] singers I've heard in my time, but Jimmie insisted.[35] Then Robert Lawrence came down a few weeks later, and I told him what Jimmie had said, and he agreed with him. So that's how I came to do it on the album.

In that same vein, what significance did "Mir träumte von einem Königskind" have to you?

That was brought to my attention by another friend of mine, Kurt Schiffler, who was then in Washington and was quite an exponent of German lieder himself. He had a lovely, lyric-baritone voice and just lived for music. He brought that music to me.

Your performance of Schubert's "Erlkönig" earned you high praises when that first LP was released. Had it been in your concert repertoire?

That really brings back memories! Many years ago in Switzerland, when I used to spend most of my summers at St. Moritz, I had a Belgian maid who spoke German fluently, and also French, Italian, and English. When I would be mountain climbing, I would try to memorize the "Erlkönig" because I wanted to start doing it in concerts. She would be right along side of me to correct my pronunciation and to give me the exact meaning of each and every word. But singing "Erlkönig" was comparable to singing *Norma* for a concert number in my estimation! Half the pleasure, though, was trying to get the three distinct voices for each of the characters in the song. I did "Erlkönig" for many years in my concerts.[36]

How did you create the necessary somberness of tone when you recorded Beethoven's "In questa tomba oscura"?

I just made myself think of a black tombstone, and of the poor victim who lies underneath that stone. She was jilted by her lover, and he has come there to repent and weep over her tomb. But the voice of her soul says, "You cry in vain! You should have thought of me when I was alive, and your tears are futile and do nothing but wet my poor, cold ashes! Go—go—and let me rest in peace," she sighs. When I was singing it, I just let myself feel that I am wallowing in self-pity, but that I am content to lie there in peace.

You also chose to record Wolf-Ferrari's "Rispetto" on that occasion.

He composed *Jewels of the Madonna*, you know, and so many lovely songs too. But I never sang anything of his other than this little encore number, which I used to include in my concerts. It's a very flirtatious number, very short and snappy.

Was Donaudy's "O del mio amato ben" an almost automatic choice?

Strange to say, that was one of the first songs I grew to love at first sight, at first hearing. I heard Giuseppe Danise sing it in, I think, a Sunday evening concert at the Metropolitan. I started to include it in some of my own concerts because I loved it so much.

Several of your song selections on both of your RCA albums were more associated with tenors. I'm thinking, for instance, of Tosti's "Aprile."

I had never sung that before. That one was Jimmie Alfonte's discovery. He brought a recording of Gigli singing "Aprile," and I liked it so much that I wanted to try it myself. There might be one other female voice [on a recording] of "Aprile"—by Tetrazzini, I think, but I'm not quite sure. Other than that, they're all done by male singers.

On your second album, Rosa Ponselle in Song, *you recorded several Tosti songs, including the lovely "Ideale." As you know, most tenors sing the last two notes in "Ideale" an octave higher than they're written in the score. You chose the ending Tosti wrote. Did you try it both ways?*

No, no. I mean, I could have done it that way, but why? It ruins the whole mood of the song when you end it an octave higher. It's a very, very sad song; you want to hang your head when you finish it. Tosti knew what he wanted, and that's why he wrote that low ending for it.

You also included Tosti's "'A vucchella" on your second album. Was that an encore in some of your concerts?

Oh, I've been singing "'A vucchella" practically since day one. I used to do it at the Café Mellone back in my New Haven days. It's almost like a vocalise to me.

Many reviewers found it interesting that in your first RCA album you chose to include "Bois épais," from Lully's Amadis. *Had you listened to Caruso's recording of the aria?*

Oh, yes. I was looking to do something quite different, and I liked the music so I recorded it.[37]

There are two songs by Geni Sadero on your first album. The first is "Amuri, amuri." Your interpretation is so very emotional that I can't help asking how you managed to record "Amuri, amuri."

Well, the song is about a peasant woman who's been jilted by her lover, and she's delivering her products to the market in a cart pulled by a mule. The little mule's name is Nicuzzu. On the way home she has time to think about herself, and she goes on lamenting, "Oh, love! Oh, love! What have you done to me?" Then she pulls in her emotions and says to herself, "Come on, let's stop this nonsense." But then she breaks down again. And all the while she keeps saying to her mule, "Let's get along, Nicuzzu! Let's get home!" I'll tell you how I recorded that. I did my own accompaniment on that one. I sat down at the keyboard, got myself into the right mood for that piece, and then I recorded it. I was spent afterward! I may have done it a second time (I don't remember because we were recording night and day it seemed), but if I did, I would have waited a day or so before trying it. It was hard to keep my emotions under control when I was singing it.

The other Sadero song you recorded on that first album was "I battitori di grano." How would you describe the text and mood of that piece?

In English it's the "grain-threshers," if there is such a word. It's another little peasant song, about a young lady who's going to the village well to fetch water. And one of the grain threshers says to her, "Where are you going, pretty maiden?" She answers very innocently, "Oh, I'm going to fetch water to drink and to cook with." It's a short little number, but very nice. You know, I coached that song, and also "Amuri, amuri," with Sadero herself, so I knew just what she wanted.

You often sang Roland Farley's "The Night Wind" in your concerts. But you did it a bit differently on your RCA album.

Making the record of that song was one of the most amusing things I've ever done. That [song] was so closely associated with me that I could never leave the concert platform without having sung "The Night Wind." But on that RCA recording I finished it quite differently. The climax of the song is almost at the very end, and it goes up to a high A. Then you do a *glissando* downward, like the wind quickly dying down. Well, this time I kept on going lower and lower and lower, until I finally had to stop. I think I went clear down to a low D in the bass-baritone range. I found it quite amusing, so we left it that way [on the recording].[38]

You sang Teresa del Riego's "Homing" in some of your radio broadcasts, and you also included it in your first RCA album.

Another one of my pupils at that time, one of my "chicks," was Barbara Nuttall, who had a very beautiful mezzo-soprano voice. She said to me, "Miss Ponselle, what would be more fitting than for you to sing 'Homing' on this new LP of yours! After all, you *are* coming home to us by way of this record." I thought that was quite appropriate, so I decided to put it on the album.

I suspect that "Drink To Me Only With Thine Eyes" was in your repertoire for many years by the time you sang it on your first LP.

That brings back such memories! When I was a young girl in New Haven, singing at Jimmy Ceriani's café, I attended a John McCormack concert. That was the first time I ever heard him. I remember that I had to stand—there was standing room only, not that I could afford much else. One of the songs that made the deepest impression on me that night was when he sang "Drink To Me Only With Thine Eyes." And all my life, whenever I've heard it, I think back to that little girl from yesterday who I once was.

Recollections

Carle A. Jackson

On Wednesday, 1 March 1978, the towering figure of seventy-one-year-old Carle Jackson swept into the main dining room of the Green Spring Inn, a private country club to which he had belonged for nearly forty years. Silver-haired, six feet three, and still lean and tapered ("I weigh 212 pounds stripped, which is exactly what I weighed when Rosa and I got married"), he shook hands with any number of long-time friends as he made his way through the noon-hour maze of tables to a more private corner of the room. With no more preface than a firm handshake and a clear indication of his willingness to talk on the record ("Hell, my life is an open book anyway," he said, "so I'll tell you whatever I can remember"), he spent the next two hours candidly discussing his life with Rosa Ponselle.

Though happily married for seventeen years at that time ("My present wife and I were married in December of 1960," he said wryly, "and they tell me the fifth time is a charm"), he had to interrupt the interview several times when women of various ages stopped by his table to greet him or, in two cases, to introduce themselves to him. After the fourth such interruption he felt it necessary to say, "Look, I don't want you to think that I had this planned. You might be thinking that somebody staged this." Suitably reassured, he resumed his narrative about his fourteen-year marriage to a woman he described alternately as "alluring," "bright," "shrewd," and "sometimes just impossible."

When I was in my early twenties, if anybody had told me that I would have ended up marrying an opera singer, I would have laughed out loud! So would anybody who knew me back then. Nobody in my family was opera-minded, then or even now. But when Rosa and I met, there was such an instantaneous attraction between us that I really didn't care what she did for a living.

I kind of think she liked that in a way. She knew I wasn't some star-struck guy who was dying to meet her. Hell, I didn't even know who she was when I was introduced to her. But I was very attracted to her—the way she looked, the way she moved, everything about her. Yet that was nothing compared to what I felt when I saw her *Carmen* a couple of nights after we met. This was the sexiest woman I thought I had ever seen! I decided then and there that I was going to have her, and she made it very clear that she wanted me just as much.

I have always been a sports type. I still ride horses nearly every day, and I play a pretty good game of polo for my age. I like adventure, like to test myself, to "rough it," as Teddy Roosevelt used to say. I get that from my mother. But I never got to spend time with my father like other boys did. Because he was mayor, his professional life was one long series of luncheons, dinners, and other public events. I hardly ever saw him without a dinner jacket: he had three of them, one hanging in his office, one at home, and a third one at the cleaners. That restricted his time with the family, but he tried to make it up to my brother and me by giving us things and condoning just about everything we did. If I wanted a horse, he'd buy it. If I wanted a car, I'd charge it to him. The same with my brother, who got interested in flying when he was just a teenager. Dad bought him a plane and even rented hangar space for him at the old Curtiss-Wright Airport here in Baltimore. Whether my father was right in giving us so much, I can't say, but he was a disciplinarian too. If you did something wrong in his eyes, he'd straighten you out right then, but he wouldn't make another reference to it as long as you lived. I respected him, and I said "Yes, sir" to him till the day he died.

Because of my father's schedule, it was my mother who was my real companion. She took me to ball games, she taught me how to shoot (she had been raised around guns and was a very good shot herself), and best of all, she got me fascinated with horses. She loved horses, and she was a born competitor. She had a huge black mare that could step a mile in two minutes and ten seconds, pulling an iron-treaded buggy with her and me in it. There is a park that surrounds a lake in Baltimore, and she used to take me or my brother down there in that buggy when we were just kids.

She'd take on all comers with that mare. "Nice rig you've got there," she'd say to somebody we pulled up next to. "But I'll bet your rig won't outrun this one, and I'll put my money on it too." About once a month my father would get a call from the Police Department, telling him, "Mayor, if you don't put a stop to Mrs. Jackson racing around that lake, we're going to have to bar her from the park." He'd get on her about it, and she'd promise not to race anymore, but a week later she'd be back there taking bets.

We had four other driving horses when I was a kid. At least two of them were always loose somewhere in Baltimore. My father would just hop out of his carriage and leave them, not bothering to tie them up or anything. He'd come out of some meeting or other, and his rig would be long gone. He'd call up Mother, and often she'd pull me out of school (she'd make up some excuse or other, which was fine with me) and together we'd go find Dad's rig and bring it back to his office.

Mother never could see me being married to Rosa. It was nothing personal against Rosa. Mother just thought she was all wrong for me because I was a sportsman and Rosa really didn't do anything like that. My father liked her well enough, but Rosa and my mother were so different that they could never see eye to eye about anything. What my mother thought was very important to me. I had very strong family ties—always—and my parents, especially my mother, were a priority with me. I went to see Mother every day, from about five until seven in the evening. If I was out of town, I called her long-distance. With my father being away so much at night, I didn't want her to be lonely, and above all, I never wanted her to need anything.

It became apparent to me that Rosa and I had entirely different views about family. For instance, when I met her father, I thought he was a fascinating old fellow, and the same with her brother Tony. I thought he had a lot of charm—a nice guy, the kind I might have liked to go to a bar and have a drink with. The way I met them was that I went to Meriden on the train. I went early in the morning, but while I was on the train I somehow spilled a bowl of soup down the front of my suit. I didn't have a change of clothes, so I showed up in Meriden looking like hell. But Rosa's father and brother made me feel right at home. I spent the day with them and came back to Baltimore on the night train.

Rosa's father spoke broken English, but we were able to communicate man to man, and I got to like him. After we got married, I used to beg Rosa to bring him to New York, but she never wanted him around. One time I remember that he, or maybe somebody he asked to do it for him, wrote her a letter asking for some money so that he could buy a new overcoat. He explained that he needed the coat to go to the utility company to pay his monthly bill. When Rosa looked at the letter, she told her secretary, "Don't send him any money. Tell him to mail his payments so he won't have to go out of the house."

Rosa and I got along okay at first. The attraction between us was so strong that it took awhile for us to cool down, if you get what I mean. But it wasn't long after we got married that we started having problems. The biggest of all our problems was her idea of a schedule. I had to be in my father's insurance-company office by eight o'clock in the morning. That was his rule, and he didn't mean 8:01, either. But she would sleep all day long. She would get out of bed around two or three in the afternoon, and then she'd be up most of the night. Her life was all upside down. By about midnight I would be half-crocked, and I would drink myself to sleep.

The opera crowd was all right, but basically they just weren't my kind of people. Lucrezia Bori was very nice—a great lady—and Mary Garden, whom we used to see in Hollywood, was always a treat to be around. So was Lily Pons. Lily was a good friend of Rosa's, and when she and André Kostelanetz were together, Rosa and I would go out with them. But the rest of the opera women were just not my type. Half of them didn't seem to know a word of English, and of course I couldn't understand any Italian, German, or French. And about the time you got so you recognized them at social gatherings, you'd go backstage and there was one of them wearing a pound of rouge, a phony-looking wig, and some costume that looked like the fairy godmother. I wouldn't recognize them, and then they'd complain to Rosa that I had ignored them.

The men were all right, too, but they weren't my type either. One of the nicest guys I got to know was Nino Romani, who had been with Rosa since her first day at the Metropolitan. Some people told me that they had been involved romantically at one time, but I never bought any of that. She told me there was never anything between them—I didn't ask her, which is the way things should be with your partner's past, but she told me without my even having to ask. About 1939, Nino married his wife Ruth, who was a very attractive girl (she was much younger than Romani), and they became very good friends to Rosa and me.

Giovanni Martinelli was a nice guy, but he was another one Rosa got annoyed at me about because I didn't recognize him one time. Rosa had introduced me to him after a performance, and he was wearing a brown wig and some strange costume when I met him. The next time we ran into him, we were at a restaurant in Manhattan. Martinelli was in a suit and his hair was snow white. When he said hello to me, I guess I looked at him like I didn't know him from Adam, so she got mad at me about it. Another fellow I really liked was [Richard] Crooks. He was an outdoorsman, and he and I used to go shooting together.

For a time after we got married, Rosa and I lived in her penthouse on Riverside Drive. I even moved a couple of my horses to Manhattan—I boarded them at the Central Park stables so I could ride on weekends and keep myself in shape. Rosa had a beautiful place, but it was like living in a hen house. Carmela lived there, and so did Edith Prilik. And every day, Libbie Miller, Rosa's manager, came there, sometimes for half the day, it seemed to me.

The first one who moved out was Carmela—that was my decision. She was flighty, an odd type. One time I was in the shower when all of a sudden, I saw a woman milling around in the bathroom. Thinking it was Rosa, I opened the door, and there was Carmela. I said, "Get the hell out of here! Can't you see I'm taking a shower?" She just waved her hand and said, "We're all God's children, dear, so there's nothing to be ashamed of." Well, I told Rosa that Carmela had better be living somewhere else by the next Friday, or else I wouldn't be coming back. Rosa found her a place up the Drive, so she was out of our hair, except when she needed more money. Then she would call Rosa and say, "Send me some flowers, dear."—that was her code for Rosa to send her more money.

Carmela was always talking about her career and spent a lot of time trying to come up with ways to catch up with Rosa. A lot of her schemes for promoting herself were far-fetched, and she never had enough money to make a go of them. One time she came to me for a loan for some type of special recording, maybe a film or something, that could be used on television. This must have been around 1940. Well, I didn't think television had any future at all, so I considered it another flighty idea on her part, and I said no to her. Basically, Carmela wasn't right mentally. I tried to get her some professional help, but it didn't seem to do much good.

Libbie Miller was the only one who didn't live in Rosa's "boarding house," as I used to call that place. She had an apartment at the Franconia Hotel, an office on West Fifty-seventh, and she earned her keep on a commission basis. But her ideas and my ideas about business were about as far apart as you could get. To me, she was a nag and a whiner. All she could talk about was how tough show business was—and on and on and on. Being on commission, her motive was to book Rosa everywhere and anywhere she could get her in, and for the highest fee, naturally. But she couldn't get it through her head that Rosa needed some rest and relaxation, especially after she got married. We were trying to build a new life together, particularly when we were out in Hollywood. But Miller would never accept that. She wanted Rosa working day and night, but Rosa was tired of the grind.

Miller and Prilik hated each other. They had been with Rosa a long time, and they had a lot in common—they were both Jewish, single, and had careers—but even that didn't seem to enable them to get along. They both knew that I was nobody to trifle with when I came into the picture. Later, they blamed me for stopping Rosa's career. Well, only Rosa—and nobody else—put a stop to her career. She wanted to make movies, do some concerts, make records, and do a lot of radio shows, but she didn't want to stay at the Metropolitan. In those days, she could get $1,000 for fifteen minutes' radio work. What was the point of staying at the Metropolitan Opera when she could get all the work she wanted without it?

We were very content being in Hollywood, and we would have stayed there if things had materialized for Rosa with the *Carmen* movie at M-G-M. But that didn't happen, and my father was on my back about being away from the firm for too long. When I didn't come back to Baltimore when he thought I should, he wrote me a very blunt letter telling me to come back home, to face up to my responsibilities, and to earn a decent living. As always, I said "Yes, sir," and Rosa and I headed back east.

We couldn't live in New York City because of my need to be in Baltimore with the insurance firm. Since Rosa wasn't singing at the Metropolitan any more, she didn't have to live in New York either, so she didn't renew the lease on her penthouse and we started looking for a house in Baltimore. I wanted to buy one that was already built, and I found a big house in the Green Spring Valley that would have been perfect for us. The asking price was about $55,000, but today [1978] you couldn't touch it for less than $600,000. She wouldn't have it. Too small, she said. I found a larger house, but she didn't want it either; she said it didn't fit her character. My idea of a house was a big, rambling Tudor house, or maybe a Georgian colonial, like many of the estates in the Valley. But what she wanted was something that looked like those villas she stayed in when she went to Italy. We had to do something fairly soon, so we agreed to build here in the Valley. With another couple, Rosa and I bought a one-hundred-and-fifty-acre parcel that had been carved out of a very large estate here in the Valley. In those days, and I'm talking about the Civil War period, the place used to be owned by a general named Felix Agnus. He called it Nacirema, which is nothing but "American" spelled backwards. There were about two hundred acres in the Agnus estate.[39]

A fellow named [James W.] Carter had bought it a few years before we bid on our tract. Carter tried to subdivide it and had attempted to sell off the lots by pitching a tent and gathering bids. About half of the people in the Green Spring Valley got mixed up with bids that turned out to be phoney or in conflict with other bids, and Carter's plans totally fell apart. That's when we bought the 150 acres. Rosa and I took the front fifty, and I sold back the other hundred to the other couple.[40] Later on, Rosa and I sold a few acres to Nicky

Ballich, a psychiatrist friend of ours who lived up the way, so that we could straighten out the property line.

Designing the house she wanted was a real nightmare. By the time she got finished telling the architects what she wanted, it was going to cost well over $400,000. The house she had in mind was about double the size of what is now Villa Pace. She wanted a marble terrace running the full length of the house, and she wanted balustrades, fountains, potted plants, and things of that sort all over the place. I nearly got sued because of her extravagance. I found out that she would call the architect, who was a friend of mine, and tell him whatever she wanted that day, and his staff would just add it to the bill. I didn't know anything about it until it came to start construction—and, of course, that kind of money was just out of the question. So we junked that idea, paid off the architect, and started over again with a fellow named Chester Snyder, who designed much of what is now Villa Pace.

I have seen and heard more nonsense written about how much that house cost, and I want to set the record straight. Someplace I read that it cost a half-million, and somewhere else it said that it took a million dollars to build it.[41] That's bloody nonsense! In the late 1930s you could have bought half of the Valley for a million dollars! The actual cost of building Villa Pace was about $86,000 for the main house and the outbuildings and maybe another $10,000 for the pool and tennis court. We had paid $20,000 for the land, so the whole place cost about $116,000 to build.

You have to understand that by Green Spring Valley standards, Villa Pace isn't all that big, and certainly not a mansion. It's like Pickfair, the estate of Mary Pickford and Douglas Fairbanks in Hollywood. Before I went there, I imagined Pickfair to be some sort of palace. But it was nothing more than a rather roomy hunting lodge with all sorts of amenities. The same is basically true of Villa Pace.

While the new place was being built, Rosa and I lived in what had been the guest house back in the days of Nacirema. But it seemed like it took forty years to complete Villa Pace. Rosa kept changing her mind about little details in the plans. One day she had to have this kind of cabinets in the kitchen; the next day those wouldn't do, and she had to have some other kind. Then it was the windows—either there weren't enough of them, or else none of them were big enough to suit her. It was that way from start to finish.

Furnishing the place was another ordeal. She bought several pieces from the William Randolph Hearst collection, which was being sold through Saks Fifth Avenue at that time. Rosa got the Hearst catalog, and the first thing she picked out was an ornate pair of candelabra that she wanted to put in front of the two-story windows in the living room. She gave me the number of the candelabra from the catalog so that I could go to New York and bid on them. She told me to pay whatever I had to, that money was no object because she had to have them. Well, I stayed at the "21" a little too long: I had too much to drink, and then went to Saks and bid a hell of a lot more money than what I thought two candelabra ought to have sold for.

"Oh, good!" she told me when I got back to Villa Pace. "When are they going to deliver them?" I told her I didn't have the faintest idea. Two weeks passed, then three and four, and still no candelabra. Then one morning this van pulled up in the circle outside Villa Pace, and the driver and two other guys unloaded a crate about the size of a piano. Our stableman, whose name was Jim, signed for the crate and pried the top open with a hammer. I had just gotten out of the shower, and I was looking out of the second-floor balcony watching all this.

When Jim caught sight of me, he motioned for me to come outside and have a look at it. Instead of the candelabra, I had mistakenly bought a huge wax horse with an Indian riding on it and a jaguar running along side ready to lunge at the horse. Believe me, *that* made for a happy weekend when Rosa saw it! Lucky for me, though, the horse had developed a crack along the neckline during shipping, so I was able to get the shipper to refund our money. I had wanted to hire a band, have a big cocktail party, and then build a bonfire to melt down the damned thing, but Rosa failed to see the humor in it.

I could never quite figure out what Rosa really felt about anything. She used to yell and scream and go into hysterics, often over nothing and at unpredictable times. After a while, I stopped paying attention to whatever she hollered about because I never thought she had deep feelings about much of anything. For instance, I bought a flock of sheep for us. Somehow, a goat got mixed up in the flock, and the dealer pushed it aside. "Doesn't the goat come with the deal?" I asked. When the man told me no, I said, "How much do you want for it?" He wanted ten dollars, and I offered him six. I brought the goat home, and Rosa thought it was the cutest thing that ever boarded the Ark. For a month or so, she would put a leash on the goat and walk it like a dog. We used to have dalmatians back then (around fifteen of them), and the goat used to go around butting them, cutting them up with his horns. I even tried sticking rubber crutch tips on the horns, but it didn't help. By then, Rosa had long since stopped paying any attention to the goat. The novelty of walking it had worn off, and she would just turn it loose in the fields. I would end up chasing it twenty miles on horseback trying to get it back. Finally, I got tired of chasing after that goat, so I gave it away.

That was in October. Eight months later, in June, we opened our swimming pool for the summer. She had some people over and she wanted to impress them, so she picked up the poolside telephone and called Jim down at the barn. "Bring up my pet goat for the guests to see," she told him. "What goat?" he wanted to know. "You know, my little goat, the one I take for a walk every day." He said, "Why, Mr. Jackson gave it away a long time ago."

As you can probably guess, all hell broke loose after that—another happy weekend at Villa Pace!

We hadn't been in the house more than a year or so when Pearl Harbor happened. I heard it on the radio with Rosa that Sunday afternoon, the seventh of December. I enlisted the very next day; my brother and I enlisted together. He saw a lot of action: he became a fighter pilot and flew more than one hundred missions. But I didn't get into the thick of it like he did, just a few skirmishes, nothing important.

When I enlisted I wanted to go into the Army, but I chose the Navy instead—yet I wound up in the Coast Guard when it was all said and done. I was going to be in the troop-movement end of the Navy, but I was asked by some Navy brass to get involved in the horseback beach patrols they were putting together. I never saw a horse, though, and wound up at sea. I was stationed in Baltimore for a while, but being the mayor's son I couldn't stay there because people would say that he was pulling strings for me. So I put out to sea from St. Augustine, Florida, and I was in the European theater for most of the war. I got out of the service on my birthday, 22 December 1945. My rank was Lieutenant Commander by that time.

Rosa took my enlistment badly. She didn't think it was necessary for me to join up. While I was at sea, she never once wrote to me, not a single letter or card for nearly four years. We weren't in touch at all; I just called her up when I got home to Baltimore. To be honest about it, I never wanted to go home. I was one of the very few guys who went to war and hoped he wouldn't come back alive—that's how bad I felt about our marriage and where it was headed, and not too long after that, it finally came apart.

I haven't seen Rosa in twenty years—not even from a distance. I hear about her from other people here in the Valley, but I wouldn't want to see her again. I would rather have her remember me like I used to be—I don't want her to see an old man now.

The Written Record

With Carle at sea during the war, Rosa began to socialize in Valley circles, following the lead of her friend Sonia Parr. Although her celebrity status made her a sought-after addition to most invitation lists, Rosa's "show-business hours"—her penchant for staying up most of the night and for sleeping until midday—made it difficult for her to adapt to Valley society's preferences for luncheons and afternoon card parties. When she began hosting her own soirées, however, she found that she was able both to utilize Villa Pace for the purposes she and Carle had envisioned and to control her social calendar.

Even when she entertained at home during the war years, she seldom sang, and almost never when someone asked.[42] If someone persisted, she would respond that now that she was retired she would sing only when the mood struck her. In her living room (or, as she preferred to call it, her music room), the walnut-finished grand piano that the Knabe company had specially made for her was tuned and serviced regularly. But it was not often that she raised the fallboard and sat down to play. On the infrequent occasions when she chose to, she confined whatever singing she did mainly to Neapolitan songs that appealed to her.

One of the few public occasions for which she agreed to perform was the opening of the USO in Baltimore at the beginning of the war. For the next three years, Rosa remained involved with the USO and seemed pleased with the continuing contact it enabled her to have with young men and women from the various military-service branches. Each Saturday night for the duration of the war, she would invite groups of them to Villa Pace, and in the summers, she would host pool parties for them.

Through the USO she also renewed acquaintances with other celebrities she had known earlier in their careers. Some were ex-vaudevillians who had prospered in radio or films after the demise of the two-a-day. Among those who came to Baltimore and Washington to entertain for the USO were Al Jolson, whom Rosa had idolized during his heyday at the Shuberts' Winter Garden; Sophie Tucker, who like Rosa and Carmela had felt the wrath of Eva Tanguay; Jack Pearl, the prevaricating Baron von Munchausen of radio fame and who had heard Rosa on the Keith Circuit; Jack Benny and his close friend, George Burns, whom Rosa and Carmela had known as Nat Burns when he played the Loew's and Keith's several years before he met and married Gracie Allen; and William Frawley, from the Keith act of Frawley & Moylan, who was now playing Joe Palooka's manager-friend "Knobby" Walsh in B-grade films, but would later earn his place in television history as Fred Mertz in the *I Love Lucy* series.[43]

Because Baltimore was a ship-building hub during the war, Rosa also did her part when new warships were launched. On one occasion she was escorted by aviation magnate Glenn L. Martin and joined a dais that included Orson Welles and Paulette Goddard, whom she knew through the designer Valentina.[44] Although Rosa had been asked in advance whether she would like to sing, she had chosen not to, preferring simply to lend her name and presence to the occasion. In her place, a local soprano who had made a wartime career of performing the national anthem at official ceremonies was asked to lead the crowd in singing. When Rosa impulsively joined in, unfortunately, the local singer was scarcely able to be heard.[45]

Libbie's threat of a lawsuit, which Rosa had now magnified into something akin to a no-trespass order barring her from Manhattan, gave her a ready-made excuse for staying away from New York City for most of 1939–40. In spring 1940, she made an exception, however, when Giuseppe de Luca invited her to attend a special performance of *Il barbiere di Siviglia* he was singing at the Metropolitan. Because Carle had no interest in going, she asked Edith Prilik (now Edith Sania) and Myron Ehrlich to join her in the box she was offered for the performance. Years later, Edith recalled Rosa's state of mind when she returned to the Metropolitan as a member of the audience:

> She was very nervous about going, but felt she owed it to de Luca to be there. She seemed surprised that when she entered her box, many people in the audience started to applaud just at the sight of her. That made her feel good, and she continued to do all right until she caught sight of Edward Johnson during one of the intermissions.
>
> By that time, Rosa had come to blame Johnson for most of her troubles at the Met. She heard that he had told a newspaper reporter that he liked working with Florence Easton better than with Rosa, because Easton had never caused him the trouble that Rosa had. Seeing Johnson brought that comment back to her, so she sat there fuming about him for the rest of the performance. She got herself so upset that she didn't even want to go backstage. Myron and I had to talk her into it.
>
> When we went backstage, everybody was glad to see her and made a fuss over her. But while we were waiting to see de Luca, we ran into Eddie Johnson. Somebody had told him that Rosa was there, so he went out of his way to greet her. But the moment he spoke to her, Rosa blew up at him. She started in on him about Easton, and what he had supposedly said to the reporter. Johnson was so taken aback he didn't know what to say. When she kept it up he said to her, "Rosa, I'm afraid I don't know what you're talking about." But that only made her madder.
>
> Then her temper got the best of her. She got so mad that she started hitting him, pounding on his chest! This was going on in front of the chorus, the ballet dancers, and the crew! Johnson backed away from her and went to his office. By then, Rosa was in tears because she knew very well what she had done and how it had made her look.
>
> After a while, she mustered the courage to go find Johnson and apologize to him. He took her into his office, and they stayed there for maybe half an hour trying to straighten things out between them. After that, I never heard her say a bad word about Eddie Johnson. But because of that incident, Rosa said she never wanted to see the Metropolitan Opera House again.[46]

True to her word, she stayed away from the Met and even from New York City, except for occasional buying trips for Villa Pace, for a Broadway play or two, and for a small number of parties to which she accepted invitations.[47] Her stays with the Farleys at their Waldorf suite became less frequent, and after Carle went to sea she especially missed their company—a situation that she remedied by offering Bess Farley one of the guest rooms at Villa Pace for several weeks at a time, as a respite from wartime Washington.[48] Rosa herself liked Washington, however, especially now that her friend Perle Mesta had become as much a celebrity as had the diplomats and other political figures for whom she hosted her much-publicized parties.

Early in the war, Rosa began to be concerned about Romano Romani, whom she corresponded with and occasionally telephoned in Hollywood. Before the war, his coaching and teaching had enabled him to prosper at M-G-M. By mid-1941, however, wartime sentiments had relegated musicals to the bottom of the production lists at most of the major studios.[49] But Romani had more to contend with than M-G-M's wartime production priorities: Louis B. Mayer had become increasingly suspicious of native-born Italians after Mussolini joined forces with Hitler and the Japanese, and rumor had it that Mayer wanted Romani, among others, off the M-G-M payroll.[50]

Rather than fire him outright, Mayer temporarily offered him studio space on a rent-free basis so that he could take on private pupils, including any M-G-M stars who might want to continue studying with him on a paying basis. But as Romani would remark later, as an Italian he was so offended by Mayer's offer that he chose to leave Hollywood entirely.[51] With his young wife Ruth, he accepted an invitation that Rosa had arranged from Hugo Hoffman, who gave the Romanis use of their guest house at Gramercy, his Valley estate. Soon afterward, they moved into the guest house Carle and Rosa had renovated at Villa Pace; he and Ruth stayed there for a few months, after which Romani began staying in New York City during the week, giving lessons in a small apartment he rented.

Although Romani did not know it when he began teaching in Manhattan, Ruth had become pregnant; the following March she gave birth to a son, who was named for his father. Rosa, sharing the Romanis' elation, became the infant's godmother when he was baptized. For the young mother, living at Villa Pace was most opportune. "Because of the rationing that went on during the war," Ruth recalled later, "we were concerned that the baby might not have enough fresh milk. But at Villa Pace, Rosa and Carle had their own dairy cattle, even a steady supply of goat's milk, so it was a great relief to us to be able to live there."[52]

Even after Carle returned from the war, Romani kept his apartment in Manhattan. During the week he gave voice lessons and held coaching sessions there, and on weekends commuted to Baltimore to be with Ruth and the baby. He continued to do so until 1951, spending a portion of the year abroad at Livorno (his family home in Italy) and then returning to Baltimore and New York for the remainder of the year. But for a while after Carle returned from the Coast Guard, the Romanis spent more time together in Manhattan, mainly to give Rosa and Carle sufficient privacy to renew their relationship.

The renewal went very poorly, almost from the start. For several months, Carle found himself missing the heightened sense of adventure and the structured life of the military in wartime. Moreover, he knew that he would be returning home to an unhappy marriage, and once he got there, he spent much of his time trying to avoid dealing with Rosa's emotional upheavals.[53] Although the two of them resumed their prewar entertaining, Villa Pace soon became a house divided. "If Rosa felt like singing, as she sometimes did, her friends would gather in the music room to hear her," recalled her friend Sonia Parr. "But as soon as she started, Carle and his friends would go into the library, pull the doors shut so that they wouldn't have to hear her, and spend the rest of the night drinking and playing cards."[54]

As the 1946 holiday season approached, Rosa seemed in a constant state of anxiety. Carle found it hard to give her complaints much credibility, however. "She was always complaining that she couldn't sleep," he said later. "She'd tell me that she had only gotten two hours, or maybe forty-five minutes' sleep. But she would rock the rafters with her snoring for eleven or twelve hours straight. The same thing with her appetite. She would carry on about how she was so nervous and upset that she couldn't eat whatever she had told the cook to make for dinner, but then she would eat a whole pie for dessert."[55]

Throughout November 1946, Rosa alternated between anxiety and depression. On the day after Thanksgiving, she did something that stunned Carle into the realization that her emotional condition needed to be taken seriously:

> On Saturdays, Rosa and I would eat our dinner in the master bedroom in front of the fireplace. I used to go on a foxhunt in the morning, and I would get home about four or four-thirty. Rosa would sleep late, and during the opera season, she would listen to the Metropolitan broadcasts while she was lying in bed. She would still have her nightgown on when the cook would bring the food up to our bedroom.
>
> Because the day after Thanksgiving was a holiday, I went foxhunting in the morning, came back around dark, and went upstairs to change and have dinner with Rosa. When I came into the room, though, she was still asleep, and her face had an unnatural expression on it. I tried to wake her up, but I couldn't—and it scared me. I called Dr. Nicky Ballich, a psychiatrist who lived just up the road from us, and he came right away. He took a look at her and said he thought she'd taken an overdose of some kind of pills. He gave her a shot, sent for an ambulance, and had her taken to the hospital.
>
> Word got out later that Rosa had tried to commit suicide, but I could never buy that. She had been taking sleeping pills ever since we lived in

> Hollywood. Out there, everybody was taking something or other; it was a pill peddler's paradise. I think she simply forgot that she had taken a big dose late that night, still couldn't get to sleep, and then took several more sleeping pills without counting them. But whatever it was, those pills did something to her. She ended up having to get shock treatments (Nicky Ballich talked her into them), and she was under guarded care for several months.[56]

This "guarded care," as Carle euphemistically put it, took place at the Seton Institute, a Catholic psychiatric hospital. No one other than Carle was allowed to visit Rosa during December and early January, owing to the electro-convulsive therapy sessions that she underwent every day for the first month of her confinement. The treatments, although effective in alleviating various forms of depression, were crudely administered, judged by later standards. A patient was strapped to a table and given a dose of curare as a relaxant. Then a rubber plate was inserted between the upper and lower teeth to prevent biting the tongue when the burst of electricity contorted the body into violent spasms, causing the patient to lose consciousness.[57]

Sonia Parr and Edith Sania were the first visitors allowed to see Rosa. "She looked like an old woman lying in that bed," Edith remembered. "There were big, dark circles under her eyes, her skin was sallow looking, and her hair was unkempt."[58] Sonia thought the scene pitiful, but Edith used the occasion to lecture Rosa about the cause of her problems. "I said, 'Look at you! So this is what has become of the world's greatest soprano! And do you know what put you here? In one word, *men*. You have always picked the worst men you can find, and then you let them take you for everything. This time you even married one of them!'"[59]

No matter how many times Sonia tried to restrain her, Edith kept up her litany until Rosa began crying and screaming. A nurse soon intervened and asked Edith to leave the premises.[60] Although Rosa retained few memories of her confinement at Seton, she would neither forget nor forgive Edith's thoughtless outburst. From then on, she would not permit Edith to stay overnight at Villa Pace. (At Sonia Parr's invitation, Edith would stay at Laural, the Parr estate.) And on the relatively few occasions when Edith and her husband would come to visit, Rosa spent as little time as possible alone with Edith.[61] If the Sanias came during the summer months, Rosa would subject them to long stretches at the pool, which Albert seemed to like, but Edith, who had never learned to swim, did not. On other occasions, Rosa would use various friends to help her avoid having much interaction with Edith.

"One afternoon when the Sanias came to Villa Pace," Hugh Johns recalled, "Rosa called me up and insisted that I had to come over right away.

I was waiting with Rosa in front of Villa Pace when Mrs. Parr's chauffeur brought them to the house. Because Edith went by her married name, I didn't recognize who she was, but I was flattered to be included. Practically as soon as I got there, Rosa said that we all should go for a walk up to the fields that adjoined her estate. She always walked very fast, very vigorously, but I was young and was used to walking with her. Yet Edith and Albert couldn't keep up with her at all. They were lagging way behind us, but Rosa kept right on talking to me and made no effort to let them catch up. From then on I noticed that, whenever Edith was around, Rosa was always nice to her, but it was as if she wanted to keep her at arm's length.[62]

A few months after Rosa was released from the Seton Institute, she received a setback during her recovery when news came from Meriden that Lydia, Tony's wife, had also suffered a debilitating nervous breakdown. Lena Angle, who had moved back to Meriden before the war, called Rosa with the sad news. "Late one night," Lena recalled, "the police found Lydia wandering the streets in a nightgown. She was incoherent, and had to be institutionalized."[63] Regrettably, Lydia never recovered her sanity or her health; she died a year later in 1948 and was buried in the Ponzillo family plot in Meriden's Sacred Heart Cemetery.

Rosa, still emotionally frail and unable to deal with so personal a loss, blamed Tony for having ruined Lydia's life.[64] From then on she began to distance herself from her brother. Several years later, when Tony remarried, she accepted his marriage as a fact but refused to see him when he showed up unexpectedly at Villa Pace with his new wife. When Tony eventually became estranged from Nino, his son, Rosa sided firmly with Nino; she remained close to him for the rest of her life. But as time passed, she grew more hostile toward his father. Eventually, she would neither accept nor return Tony's telephone calls.[65]

A year after her breakdown and confinement, Rosa had recovered remarkably well, although the psychiatric care she was receiving under Dr. Ballich became controversial in local medical circles. According to Walter E. Afield, M.D., a young Harvard-trained psychiatrist and frequent visitor to Villa Pace at the time, Ballich refused to disclose the identities of the drugs he was dispensing to Ponselle.[66]

Although she remained under Dr. Ballich's care throughout the late 1940s, Rosa still complained about her "confounded nerves," as she referred to them. Despite the gradual improvement in her mental health, however, the most important part of her life—her marriage to Carle—still remained troubled and showed little promise of improving.

As her friend Sonia Parr later assessed it, "All that Rosa and Carle had in common was a love of life, which each of them expressed quite differently, and a love of the home they had built together. Carle appreciated beauty and refinement in his possessions and was especially fond of the furnishings that Rosa and he had purchased or had had custom-made for Villa Pace. But he had no reason to marry a woman like her, nor had she any reason to marry him—or, if I may say so, to marry anyone at all. For as much as I love Rosa, and I do, I believe that God himself couldn't live with her."[67]

The marriage finally came apart shortly after New Year's in 1949. Sometime earlier, she had confronted Carle about two cancelled railway tickets she had found when she had sent one of his suits to be dry cleaned.[68] She was convinced that he was having an affair, and according to Sonia Parr, there were grounds for her suspicion:

> Another woman who was a friend of Rosa's came frequently to Villa Pace where she developed what I shall call a drinking relationship with Carle. After a time, it became clear to all of us that although she said she was Rosa's friend, the woman was after Carle.
>
> I don't think he was unfaithful to Rosa at that time. But I do know that for Rosa, infidelity had no place in her makeup. The last thing anyone would say of Rosa was that she was unfaithful, whether to her friends or especially to those she loved. But by nature, she was also a very jealous person. If another woman walked across the floor and Carle had an eye out for her, Rosa would become instantly jealous.
>
> I believe Carle knew that this other woman was pursuing him—he eventually married and divorced her—but he did not understand what effect it was having upon Rosa. In time, her suspicions grew, and after she confronted him, he left her.[69]

Years later, Carle confirmed that his departure was indeed abrupt. "I don't remember that we had any public scenes. We did our fighting in private. But one day I said that I was leaving, and that I wasn't coming back. Rosa said to me angrily, 'Let me help you pack!' But I told her I had already packed my bags. I walked out the door, and sometime later we were divorced. That was that."[70]

The crisis occurred during an evening when Rosa had invited the Romanis to dine at Villa Pace. As Carle made his way down the long driveway in his car, Rosa became hysterical. The Romanis summoned Sonia Parr, who in turn called Dr. Ballich at his home. Ballich arrived soon afterward and gave Rosa an injection of a strong sedative. Amid all this confusion, as Sonia Parr would recall, Romano Romani, who had witnessed other similar scenes, turned to her and said in his fractious English, "Meez Parr, why did Carle leave before dinner is served? Now his guests go hungry!"[71]

After Carle's departure in mid-January 1949 and amid legal wrangling that followed the separation, Rosa began to seek solace in the Catholic faith she had been raised in, but which she had largely abandoned during adulthood. Her confinement at the Seton Institute led to her return to Catholicism; the Sisters of Charity, who operated the facility, ministered to her daily during her two-month stay. Soon after her release in February 1947, she began to attend Sunday Mass regularly at the St. Charles Borromeo parish church in nearby Pikesville. To the delight of other parishioners, she lent her voice to the "Tantum Ergo," "Holy God We Praise Thy Name," and other sacred songs of the Catholic liturgy at that time.

In the early 1950s, Canadian-born Anne O'Donnell, who would eventually become an executive at Columbia Artists Management, came to Baltimore to audition for Ponselle. Although the audition was not as successful as the young woman had hoped, Rosa invited her to stay at Villa Pace while she was looking to make a career for herself in the United States. Miss O'Donnell often accompanied Rosa to Mass at St. Charles Borromeo:

> One Sunday morning we arrived after Mass had already started, and to my chagrin Rosa decided to sit in the front of the church, which meant that we had to walk clear to the front and make a spectacle of the fact that we were late. As it happened, the pew she chose was adjacent to the side altar devoted to the Blessed Virgin Mary. During the Mass, out of the corner of my eye, I happened to notice Rosa gazing very pensively—prayerfully, I thought—at the statue of the Blessed Virgin.
>
> She fixed her eyes on it so long that I couldn't help watching her. As I did, I wondered to myself what thoughts she was having, what prayers she was saying, as she looked so longingly at the image of the Virgin. Then she suddenly turned and whispered something in my ear. "Do you see that?" she said in a low voice, pointing to the statue. "She's wearing my *Vestale* costume."[72]

Whatever the depth of her renewed commitment to the tenets of her childhood faith, Rosa did not choose to deprive herself sensually when a new suitor, Behrend Dryber, began to offer her his attentions in 1949. She was sixty-two years old. The two had met through Perle Mesta, who had known the erudite, Holland-born Dryber in Washington diplomatic circles. At the time he was introduced to her, Dryber's U.S. citizenship status was in jeopardy, and he was lacking a place to live. Before long, he was spending most nights at Villa Pace. Although Ponselle's friends believed that she "was mad about him" at first, she eventually ceased returning Dryber's attentions but maintained a platonic concern for him.[73] After the passion of their early relationship had cooled, Dryber settled into the uncertain status of a professional guest at Villa Pace, where Ponselle allowed him to live on and off for the next two decades.

More enduringly, Rosa made a renascent return to music after Carle and she were separated. Prior to Carle's leaving and even before her hospitalization at Seton, she had done very little singing. One of the few such occasions occurred at a party given for them in 1946 by Gideon Stieff, a prominent Baltimore businessman, when she was reunited with Marion Telva, her Adalgisa in the *Norma* revival of 1927. With the encouragement of the pianist Alec Templeton, who offered to accompany them, she and Telva reprised the "Mira, o Norma" duet. Afterward, Templeton induced Rosa to sing the "Addio del passato" from *Traviata*.[74]

In March 1947, approximately six weeks after her release from Seton, she reluctantly accepted an invitation to a dinner party Fannie Hurst was giving at her expansive apartment in the Hotel des Artistes in New York, honoring Giuseppe de Luca as the fiftieth anniversary of his operatic debut approached. At the party, Rosa was reunited not only with de Luca, who was then appearing in a well-publicized series of recitals, but also with Giovanni Martinelli, who had retired from the Met the previous season. Edith and Albert Sania, Myron Ehrlich, and artist Luigi Luccioni were included among the invitees. During the evening, Martinelli and de Luca persuaded Rosa to sing through the final portion of the Nile Scene from *Aida* with them. Afterward, she told the Sanias and Ehrlich that she felt "ecstatic" about singing again.[75]

News of this impromptu *Aida* spread rapidly in Manhattan music circles. Several weeks later, Constance Hope gave a party for her and invited Robert Merrill, Blanche Thebom, and Leonard Bernstein to perform for her. "Blanche and I had just sung a duet, with Lenny accompanying us," Merrill recalled. "We were still standing in the bend of the piano when Lenny started playing 'Ritorna vincitor.' Rosa was sitting in a chair off to the side, and all of a sudden, she started to sing. My God! I had never heard a soprano voice like that!"[76]

"After 'Ritorna vincitor,'" Bernstein added,

> I got her to sing part of the "Suicidio" from *Gioconda*. The old Columbia recording she made of that aria was the first opera record I had ever heard, and I always regretted that I had come along far too late to hear her in *Gioconda*. But when she sang that opening phrase in full voice— *"Suicidio!"*— it nearly lifted me off the bench! Who can describe that sound in words? Powerful? Yes, but creamy and subtle and a hundred other things. Communicative? Yes, straight into the soul. But what does that mean to somebody who never heard her? When we start talking about art on that level— singing, painting, prose, poetry, art in any form—we're not talking physics, friends. Language doesn't capture voices and souls. There were others before Ponselle and others after her. I heard Cigna, Milanov, Callas, Farrell, and the others—I knew them, I conducted most of them, and they all had their form of greatness. But after I heard Ponselle, if you wanted to talk to

me about dramatic sopranos, don't talk to me about anybody else. Talk to me about her.[77]

During spring 1949, John Secrist was preparing to compile what was to become the first published discography of Ponselle's commercial and radio recordings.[78] Secrist was invited to travel to Villa Pace with a group of British visitors including Ida and Louise Cook, who had heard Rosa at Covent Garden and in Florence and had visited her in Baltimore two years before, and Dr. Dick Alexander, a London physician who offered to record Secrist's interview with Ponselle on a portable wire recorder.[79]

While at Villa Pace, the Cook sisters persuaded Rosa to allow Alexander to record her singing a few songs and arias. She found the quality of the wire recording and the state of her voice equally disappointing. "Do I really sound that bad?" she exclaimed to the Cook sisters. "You mean I'm that rusty and my *pianissimi* aren't what they should be?"[80] "There's nothing that a few weeks of practice wouldn't put aright," Louise Cook said, hoping to bolster Rosa's confidence. A few weeks later, she began working again with Romano Romani, and by autumn 1949, she felt confident enough to make a small number of private recordings with him as her accompanist.[81]

Several months later in March 1950, Lloyd Garrison visited her and demonstrated his new Webcor tape recording equipment and studio-type Shure microphones. Impressed by the quality of the reproduction, Rosa now took a more favorable view of allowing her singing to be recorded. Soon afterward, Garrison recorded her singing two arias: "Divinités du Styx" from *Alceste* and "O divina Afrodite" from *Fedra*, both with Romani as her accompanist, and nine songs ranging from such personal favorites as "'A vucchella" and "Dicitencello vuje" to "Bali Ha'i" and "Some Enchanted Evening" from *South Pacific* and "So in Love" from *Kiss Me, Kate*. The next year, she retained Garrison's services to produce a 78 r.p.m. disc for her, utilizing his tape recordings of her singing Bizet's "Agnus Dei" and Luzzi's "Ave Maria." She intended to send the disc as a Christmas present to friends in Baltimore, Washington, and New York.

Garrison and his equipment were also on hand in September 1952 when Rosa and John Charles Thomas serenaded General and Mrs. Eisenhower in Baltimore. This too she authorized Garrison to publish in disc form, but in the increasingly popular LP format. Again she sent the records to her friends at Christmas time. These and a privately issued LP of carols and sacred songs, which she recorded with several singers from the Baltimore Civic Opera the next holiday season (1953), were widely circulated among fans and collectors and eventually prompted both Capitol and RCA Victor to offer her recording contracts.[82]

Chiefly out of loyalty, she chose RCA, which accommodated her reluctance to travel by setting up a temporary studio at Villa Pace. There between 17 and 21 October 1954, with Igor Chichagov accompanying most of the selections, she recorded more than enough material for two LPs.[83] As Chichagov later acknowledged, the sessions took place with minimal rehearsing on Ponselle's part: "she would go through her old repertory and say, 'Yes, let's record this song.' So that [was] put in front of me, and we sang it through once and then we recorded it. And now when I hear some of these things [played] back, I think, 'My goodness, how terrible I played that thing,' because I'm not with her, and some places she has surprised me because she never sang the same way twice."[84]

When her first album, *Rosa Ponselle Sings Today*, was released in spring 1955, the reviews she received were uniformly commendable. "That Ponselle should have agreed to emerge from her self-imposed retirement and to record again for RCA Victor is a surprise and a very heartwarming one," reviewer Aida Favia-Artsay wrote in June 1955. "But that she should make her comeback with the freshness of voice she had at the zenith of her career—that is staggering!"[85] In *The Saturday Review*, Irving Kolodin heaped praises upon "the Ponselle of today":

> Any public career that ends, as Rosa Ponselle's did, when the singer is barely forty, has to be considered an unfinished story. What is wonderful to note, in this evidence of her art nearly twenty years later, is that the long *fermata* has left her well short of the double bar, marking a wise end to endeavor. Not only in the richness of the sound and the trueness of the emotion, but in the admirable discipline of what she has undertaken, the best in these performances of October 1954 mark the Ponselle of today as an artist to be reckoned with when the fine singers of '55 are totaled up.
>
> Needless to say, in a sequence of sixteen songs extending in time from Lully's "Bois épais" to Roland Farley's "The Night Wind," and in style from "Drink To Me Only with Thine Eyes" to Del Riego's "Homing," not everything is of equal quality or equal suitability to her still remarkable voice. I could well spare, for example, her efforts with Brahms' "Von ewiger Liebe" and Schubert's "Erlkönig"—both a little too melting and curvaceous for the kind of line involved. However, it is doubtful if any singer now well-known could surpass her versions of Donaudy's "O del mio amato ben," or Del Riego's "Homing" or Sadero's "Amuri, amuri," each a little masterpiece of tonal portraiture.[86]

Two years later when RCA released the second LP, *Rosa Ponselle in Song*, Kolodin was no less enthusiastic:

> [I]t is singing of ravishing sweetness and sonorous appeal, with that direct appeal to the listener which marks the elite among vocal interpreters of

> whatever type. It strikes me as freer, less tentative, more assured than the collection of 1954 issued as *Rosa Ponselle Sings Today*. Many singers in their prime would now envy her mordent in "Plaisir d'amour," not to mention the life and vitality she imparts to the Granados and Alvarez material. I doubt that she could have sung the Debussy and Delibes songs as sensitively twenty years ago. They show a concentration of expression rarely possessed by one with her sweep in *Aida* or *Forza*.[87]

Although most of Ponselle's contemporaries expressed similar enthusiasm for the two albums, a former colleague, the irreverent Nina Morgana Zirato, did not entirely share it. "Bruno and I have listened to Rosa's newest album, which he finds wonderful and I do not especially like," Morgana wrote to Bidù Sayão in 1957. "About the only selections that remind me of the Ponselle of old are 'Plaisir d'amour,' 'Nel cor più non mi sento,' and 'Ideale,' which I find better interpreted than any tenor's recording, including Caruso's. (Bruno disagrees but he is always loyal to his old boss.) Too many of her songs are taken in keys that at her age are too high for the natural placement of her voice. If Rosa makes a comeback, she shall have to content herself with being a mezzo."[88]

Rose Bampton, on the other hand, had only praise for both RCA albums. "I thought then, and I still do, that Rosa's interpretations of many of the songs were among the best I had ever heard," said Bampton, who had made her Metropolitan debut as Laura with Ponselle in *La gioconda*.

> Even though Rosa didn't sing any of her great arias on those records, the albums still give people who never heard Rosa in the opera house a better idea of the size of her upper voice than her old records could capture. When I have referred many of my [voice] students to Rosa's recordings from the 1920s, they have often said to me, "Her tone is beautiful but her voice doesn't sound very big, and her top sounds kind of thin." I wish the recording people could do something about those old records because they couldn't capture Rosa's high notes, which were just huge. But on those RCA albums, when she sings in her upper range at full volume it sounds much more like what I remember when I was on stage singing with her.[89]

Overall, Ponselle's two LPs posted respectable sales, although the second album did not generate sufficient revenues, apparently, to warrant the publication of a third.[90] Though a comeback was indeed rumored, Ponselle had no intentions of disrupting her comfortable, self-controlled lifestyle. When her longtime friend Frederick C. Schang, then president of Columbia Artists Management, approached her in 1955 with an offer to sing a series of concerts, she tactfully declined. When he persisted, she artfully refocused his interest and persuaded him to create the Rosa Ponselle Opera Quartet, featuring Baltimore-area singers who were studying with her. It was modeled after the successful Bel Canto Trio that had launched the careers of Mario Lanza, George London, and Frances Yeend. But when the quartet did not sufficiently impress the Columbia directors, she abandoned the idea.[91]

By that time, Ponselle had become identified in musical circles with the Baltimore Civic Opera, which she had joined formally as director of auditions in autumn 1951. As the small company began to grow, her title was changed, first to artistic advisor and subsequently to artistic director.[92] Dr. Leigh Martinet, son of Eugene Martinet, a former singer who had founded the Civic Opera in the 1930s, conducted almost all the company's productions from 1949 until 1961. With industrialist and arts-supporter Hugo Hoffman, whose estate was near Rosa's in the Green Spring Valley, Martinet and Elmer Bernhardt (then city comptroller in Baltimore) visited Ponselle in the hope of interesting her in the struggling company's future. In a 1978 interview, Martinet spoke of her initial involvement with the Civic Opera:

> We had next to no money to work with, but we didn't let being poor bother us. In 1950 we did an *Aida*, if you can imagine this, with an organ, a ten-piece "orchestra," and a stage that had a maximum depth of fifteen feet! With that kind of a history, of course, we didn't think we had a chance at getting the great Rosa Ponselle to even talk to us. But to our surprise, she accepted our invitation to attend the dress rehearsal for the *Traviata* we were giving that next season [1950–51].
>
> We were very nervous about having her. We were such amateurs that we thought she might laugh at us and turn on her heels and leave. Well, she not only stayed but she actually sang parts of the score to show the cast how to sing this or that phrase. She even gave them some impromptu coaching about how to make their movements look more natural on the stage—a few tips that were second nature to an artist of her caliber, but which she didn't seem to mind sharing.
>
> In the early 1950s the Civic Opera moved from an auditorium to the Lyric Theater in downtown Baltimore, where the Metropolitan Opera used to perform when it toured here. The move made it possible for us to transform ourselves from an amateur to a semi-professional opera company over time. But we needed vastly more money when we went into the Lyric. That's where Rosa came through for us. She opened Villa Pace to the public and used the admission charge to help not only the Opera but also the Baltimore Symphony. Just her presence generated substantial donations and also helped us build our subscription list. We never asked her to solicit money directly. But she was always willing to make the key telephone call, or bring some donor out to Villa Pace for dinner—whatever it took to help us get the money we needed.

> She involved herself completely in every detail of the musical preparation of our productions. Rosa was truthful with singers who auditioned. "It's not for you," she would say, but she was also very considerate of their feelings. For instance, she never allowed fewer than three singers to try out for a part. If there were only two, it meant that one had to walk away the loser. But she didn't like how that made the other singer feel, so to make sure that no one person would have to feel like a failure, there always had to be three singers trying for the same part. But before very long, because of Rosa's name and presence, we were never short of aspiring singers who wanted to come and audition.
>
> She was a stickler about tempo, interpretation, drama, and especially diction and pronunciation. Her dictum was, "Get lost in the text"—which meant that the singers' techniques had to be secure and polished to the point that they could concentrate on the meaning of the text. Their diction had to be correct so that the words would come out just right. But Rosa knew how to impart those details to young singers who were just starting out. Thankfully for us, she seemed to genuinely like doing it.[93]

Of the numerous singers Ponselle worked with during her long tenure as artistic director, several of them—including James Morris, Richard Cassilly, Lili Chookasian, and Spiro Malas—went on to achieve international prominence. Others among her brood of "chicks," as she called them—especially Gabriella Ruggiero, John Aler, and Richard Cross—attained an enduring prominence through recordings. Several already well-established singers also came to Villa Pace to seek Ponselle's guidance. Among them were the sopranos Raina Kabaivanska, Gilda Cruz-Romo, and Adriana Maliponte, who credited to Ponselle various refinements in their singing.[94]

Throughout the 1950s and late 1960s, Ponselle maintained her day-to-day involvement with the Baltimore Opera Company.[95] During the mid-1960s, however, she gradually withdrew as the company opted to hire experienced artists. By the late 1970s, the decline in her overall health precluded her continuing as artistic director.[96] But by then she had already passed into operatic legend. As Bruce Burroughs insightfully described her place in operatic history:

> The preservation on discs of [her] characteristic sound . . . has created not only a personal monument but a touchstone for the measurement of sheer beauty of voice. Commentary by those professional listeners who were of long experience when Ponselle was a beginner and who found her wanting, vocally and musically, must be taken somewhat on faith. If anyone before her possessed anything close to a timbre of such nurturing immediacy, the extant recording equipment was too primitive to do it justice, though one *can* discern more rarified stylistic accomplishment, purer vowels, and more

> highly placed, radiant tone quality in certain older sopranos. No matter. Ponselle, just by having the voice she had and using it as eloquently as she did, superseded all previous models and became herself the one that female singers, from coloraturas to contraltos, want to sound like. Ponselle is the archetypal "modern" soprano, whose sound is a universal ideal, whose style and manner are broad and general enough (but not in any sense careless or unconscientious) not to reflect in some limiting or archaic way the era in which she herself performed. She is uniquely the Soprano for all Seasons.[97]

Her own assessment was perhaps no less insightful. In the summer of 1978, when an interviewer asked her to comment on her 1926 recording of the "Ritorna vincitor" from *Aida*, she listened intently as her youthful voice brought to life Verdi's prismatic measures. Afterward, she leaned back in her chair and said detachedly, "I was a freak—a freak of nature."[98] She was then eighty-one years old. Three years later, having lived an expansive life and having given the most she was able to give to her art, she was laid to rest amid the hills and woods of the Green Spring Valley she loved.

Postscript

CARMELA PONSELLE died in a New York City hospital on 13 June 1977, a week after her ninetieth birthday. Until a broken hip debilitated her in 1976, she had remained in excellent health, which she attributed to her religious faith—a nondenominational blend, according to those who knew her well, of biblical Christian principles and the positive-thinking philosophy of Dr. Norman Vincent Peale. Her last significant performances were on radio between 1937 and 1940, on the CBS *Broadway Variety Hour* series. She is buried next to her sister, in a crypt in the Green Spring Valley. She had no children.

ANTONIO P. (TONY) PONZILLO died on 12 December 1978, at the age of eighty-eight. He was buried near the grave of his first wife, Lydia, in the Ponzillo family plot in the Sacred Heart Cemetery in Meriden. He spent his last years with his second wife, upon whose income and care he depended, living in a trailer park near Wallingford, Connecticut. At the time of his death, he had had no interaction with Rosa for approximately twenty years. Tony's son, Anthony Gerard Ponzillo, from whom he was also estranged, had a successful career with the Black and Decker Tool Company.

BENARDINO PONZILLO, the father of Rosa, Carmela, and Tony, died in Meriden on 26 April 1952 at the age of ninety-four. Until his ninety-second year, when he moved into a facility for the elderly, he lived at 159 Springdale Avenue, the home in which his children had grown up and the only residence he had ever owned. After the death of his wife, Maddalena, in 1932, he never remarried. Carmela and Tony accompanied his casket to the Sacred Heart Cemetery where he was buried next to Maddalena. Rosa did not attend his funeral.

ALFONSO PONZILLO, the volatile older brother of Benardino and the uncle of Carmela, Tony, and Rosa, died at the age of ninety-one in 1949. At the time of his death he was living with Benardino at the Ponzillo family home in Meriden, where the two brothers made their own wine, played cards with friends, and cultivated a backyard vegetable garden. Alfonso occasionally spent part of each month at the home of one of his five children in nearby Waterbury. Rather than ride in a car, the fiercely independent Alfonso often insisted on walking the eight-mile distance from Meriden to Waterbury.

EDITH PRILIK SANIA died in 1983 at age eighty-six in St. Petersburg, Florida, where she had relocated in 1980 after her health had begun to decline. She survived her husband, Albert Sania, by two decades; he died in 1962. They had no children.

LIBBIE MILLER died at the age of eighty-five in 1978—ironically, on 15 November, the sixtieth anniversary of Rosa's Metropolitan Opera debut. At the time of her death, she was still living at the Franconia Hotel in Manhattan, from which she managed her own concert bureau after she and Rosa severed their relationship. Libbie wrote (but did not publish) her memoirs, but made no mention in the manuscript of her years as Rosa's manager. She never married.

LENA TAMBORINI ANGLE died in Meriden in 1983, at the age of eighty-seven. She survived her husband, Henry, by three decades. She remained active in civic organizations in Meriden throughout her life.

ROMANO ROMANI died in 1958, at the age of seventy-four. By a twist of fate, he died at Villa Pace, where he and his son paid a brief visit to Rosa before a trip they planned to take to Italy. During his week-long stay at Villa Pace, Rosa had arranged for him to give voice lessons and to hold coaching sessions with several young singers from the Baltimore Opera. He was accompanying Celina Sanchez, a young soprano then studying with Rosa, when his head suddenly slumped and his hands dropped from the keyboard. He was buried three days later in a cemetery in the Green Spring Valley. His wife, Ruth, survived him by nearly forty years. His son and namesake, Dr. Romano Romani, Jr., is a founding partner in a large and successful political consulting firm in Washington, D. C. He has served in senior-level positions on the staffs of a number of U.S. Congress members over the years.

CARLE A. JACKSON died in Baltimore in 1995 at the age of eighty-eight. Until the last year of his life, when his health declined in the aftermath of an operation, he continued to ride horses and to participate (though less vigorously as he aged) in the outdoor life to which he was accustomed. Three months before his death, Carle and his fifth wife, the former Margaret Jefferson Crothers, celebrated their thirty-fourth wedding anniversary. Carle survived his only child, Edward ("Bimmie") Jackson, by thirteen years.

MAYOR HOWARD W. JACKSON never ran for political office after his defeat in 1938; he died in 1960 at the age of eighty-three. His wife, the former Ella Mae Galloway, Carle's mother, died at the age of eighty-seven in 1965.

ROSA PONSELLE died at Villa Pace on 25 May 1981, five months after her eighty-fourth birthday. During her long retirement, nearly every honor a performing artist could receive had been bestowed on her, including the coveted Order of the Commendatore from the government of Italy (1969), election to the U.S. Hall of Fame Society (1968), a Lifetime Achievement in the Arts award (1975), and honorary degrees from Peabody University, the College of Our Lady of Notre Dame, and the University of Maryland.

Until July 1979, when she suffered a debilitating stroke, she had remained in generally good physical health, although she continued to suffer from recurring mental depression. After the stroke, her speech was permanently impaired and she eventually became bedfast. Fortunately, her financial assets, which were valued at $2.5 million at the time of her death, enabled her to have long-term medical care in the privacy of Villa Pace.

It was at Villa Pace that her singing voice was last recorded (a few measures of the Tomb Scene from *Aida* in an impromptu duet with musicologist Edward E. Swenson), and it was also there that her last documented interview took place. On that occasion her interviewer was American bass Jerome Hines, who was then writing a book about singers. Although he had hoped to have Ponselle analyze her technique during the interview, Hines quickly realized that her impaired speech would make that impossible. Instead, he conducted the interview with Igor Chichagov, Hugh Johns, and soprano Kira Baklanova (a Ponselle student in the mid-1950s), who formed "a carefully selected team to aid and abet the interview."[99] While they answered Hines' questions, the frail diva, now mute and confined to a wheelchair, registered her agreement with an occasional gesture.[100]

In 1982, less than a year after her death, a foundation was capitalized in her name, and that September, Villa Pace was opened to the public as a museum. In 1984 the Rosa Ponselle Foundation began sponsoring international vocal competitions. Three years later, the Foundation was no longer able to sustain its operating expenses and was forced to authorize the sale of Villa Pace, which had undergone extensive renovation after a 1979 fire had ravaged portions of the interior. The sale of the estate in August 1987 signaled a symbolic close to the life's work of one of the twentieth century's greatest singers and most colorful personalities.

Notes

CHAPTER ONE: Wait Till You Hear Her!

1. Irving Kolodin, *The Story of the Metropolitan Opera* (New York: Alfred A. Knopf, 1953), p. 332.

2. Thomas G. Kaufman, "Enrico Caruso's Operatic Repertoire," in Enrico Caruso, Jr., and Andrew Farkas, *Enrico Caruso: My Father and My Family* (Portland, Oregon: Amadeus Press, 1990), pp. 709–10.

3. New York *World*, 14 November 1918.

4. Prior to November 1918, *Forza* apparently was not heard in New York City after 1881, nor anywhere else in the United States after an 1897 San Francisco touring-company performance. See Thomas G. Kaufman, *Verdi and His Major Contemporaries* (New York: Garland Publishing, Inc., 1990), pp. 482–96.

5. Francis Robinson, liner notes for *Rosa Ponselle Sings Today* (RCA Victor LM-1889).

6. Letter of Carle A. Jackson to Palmer and Lamden, Architects, 20 March 1940.

7. The commemorative LP, *Rosa Ponselle Sings Verdi* (Columbia Odyssey Y 31150), subtitled "A Tribute on Her 75th birthday with a Spoken Recollection of Her First Recordings," was released in 1972.

8. Author's interview with Luciano Pavarotti, December 1978. Pavarotti first visited Ponselle at Villa Pace on 4 April 1976.

9. The oil portrait is now housed at the Metropolitan Opera House in New York.

10. Author's interview of Rosa Ponselle, June 1975.

11. Columbia's audio engineers edited Seward's master tape without his involvement. Hence, the opening band of the LP inadvertently included six of Seward's own "offstage" questions and comments, plus several phrases that Ponselle demonstrated in her chest voice. Seward had assumed that these would be deleted.

12. From the author's interviews of Edith Prilik Sania (July 1977, August 1977, and November 1978). Transcribed with minor editing.

13. A half-page advertisement Thorner took out in *Musical America* (20 November 1915) lists his studio address as 2128 Broadway.

14. Author's interview of Thomas Pasatieri, 23 January 1977.

15. Thomas Pasatieri, "From the Villa Pace," *Opera News* (12 March 1977), pp. 17–18.

16. New York *Star*, undated clipping from the Metropolitan Opera press book, 1918–19 season. Ponselle said in the interview that she had just completed her seventh performance, which took place on 17 January 1919, in *Oberon*. Because her eighth performance (another *Forza*) took place on 27 Jan. 1919, it can be assumed that she gave the *Star* interview during that ten-day interval. (The author is grateful to Robert Tuggle, Director of the Metropolitan Opera Archives, for providing a copy of this interview.)

17. *Musical America*, 18 January 1919.

18. Ibid.

19. Ibid.

20. *Musical America*, 20 November 1915. Similar testimonials appeared in notices Thorner placed in numerous other issues of *Musical America*, *Musical Courier*, *The Etude*, and other professional music periodicals of the World War I period.

21. Ibid. See also the 28 December 1918 issue, which Thorner devoted chiefly to Ponselle.

22. Ponselle's contract with William Thorner extended from 30 September 1918 through 30 September 1922. On 1 December 1922, Ponselle signed a comprehensive managerial agreement with Libbie Miller, who left her employment at National Concerts, Inc., to become Ponselle's concert manager. Eventually, Libbie Miller would manage all aspects of Ponselle's career. Ponselle filed suit against Thorner in New York City in 1924. The suit was eventually decided in her favor, following the brief argued before the Appellate Division of the New York State Supreme Court by her attorney, Nathan Burkan, on 1 February 1928.

23. For example, see Ponselle, "The Power of Destiny," *Mentor* (February 1930), p. 70.

24. Interview of Rosa Ponselle by John B. Secrist (1949; precise date unknown).

25. Ibid.

26. Interviews of Rosa Ponselle by William Seward (December 1971), by Tom Villella (undated, probably 1972), and by the author (March 1973).

27. Tom Villella, "An Interview with Rosa Ponselle," in *Le Grand Baton: Journal of the Sir Thomas Beecham Society* (June 1975), pp. 25–26.

28. Ibid., p. 26.

29. Titta Ruffo, Jr., and Marinelli Roscioni, "Chronology of Titta Ruffo's Public Performances," in Andrew Farkas, ed., *Titta Ruffo: An Anthology* (Westport, Connecticut: Greenwood Press, 1984), pp. 222–23, 227.

30. Harold Rosenthal and John Warrack, eds., *The Concise Oxford Dictionary of Opera* (London: Oxford University Press, 1978), p. 130.

31. Interview of Rosa Ponselle by Boris Goldovsky, Metropolitan Opera broadcast (intermission feature), 11 March 1960.

32. *Musical America*, "Mephisto's Musings," 25 January 1919.

33. In an advertisement in the *Musical Courier* (12 April 1923), Thorner listed Fitziù, Ponselle, Galli-Curci, Anne Roselle, Yvonne D'Arle, and Marguerite Namara among his prominent pupils.

34. *Musical America*, 20 November 1915.

35. *The New York Times*, 29 January 1916.

36. Ibid.

37. A similar claim was made for Eleanora de Cisneros (*née* Eleanor Broadfoot) in her obituary. (*The New York Times*, 4 February 1934.)

38. *The New York Times*, 22 September 1922.

39. *The New York Times*, 21 April 1918.

40. Ibid.

41. Contractual figures cited by Robert Tuggle in *The Golden Age of Opera* (New York: Holt, Rinehart and Winston, 1983), suggest that the salaries for sopranos and tenors who had little or no experience in major opera houses ranged from $50 to $200 per week (pp. 137, 158, 179).

42. Giulio Gatti-Casazza, *Memories of the Opera* (New York: Charles Scribner's Sons, 1941), p. 202.

43. Tuggle, *The Golden Age of Opera*, p. 179.

44. Author's interview of Rosa Ponselle, March 1973.

45. This was attested by Edith Prilik Sania, in the author's interview of July 1977, and by Claudia Muzio's secretary, the late May Higgins, in a series of informal interviews that discographer Bill Park conducted with her in the 1970s.

46. Claudia Muzio's contract for 1918–19, in the Metropolitan Opera Archives, lists the following roles: Aida, Nedda in *Pagliacci*, Bertha in *Le prophète*, Tosca, Leonora in *Il trovatore*, Fiora in *L'amore dei tre re*, Santuzza, and Mimi in *La bohème*. Giorgetta in *Il tabarro* was apparently added to her repertoire after she accepted her 1918–19 contract. (The author is grateful to Robert

Tuggle, Director of the Metropolitan Opera Archives, for this and all other information concerning Muzio's contracts and roles cited in this chapter.)

47. Eduardo Arnosi, *La Unica* (Buenos Aires: Ars Lirica, 1986), p. 65. The date of Muzio's first *Forza* was 16 July 1921, according to the annals of the Teatro Colón. See Roberto Caamaño, *Historia del Teatro Colón, 1908–1968* (Buenos Aires: Editoriál Cinetea, 1970), p. 88.
48. Michael Scott, in his *The Great Caruso* (New York: Alfred A. Knopf, 1988), writes (p. 166), "The role of Leonora [was] originally to have been sung by Muzio." But Scott neither cites nor alludes to any documentary evidence for this claim.
49. Robert Tuggle to the author, 17 April 1995.
50. *The New York Times*, 3 November 1918.
51. *The New York Times*, 11 November 1918.
52. New York *American*, 14 November 1918.
53. Ibid.
54. *The New York Times*, 14 November 1918.
55. *The New York Times*, 16 November 1918.
56. Ibid.
57. *Musical Courier*, 21 November 1918.
58. *Musical America*, 30 November 1918.
59. New York *Sun*, 16 November 1918.
60. Ibid.

CHAPTER TWO: I Really Never Have Grown Up

1. Rosa Ponselle, "Home, Sweet Home Is What You Make It," *Good Housekeeping* (March 1933), pp. 45, 156.
2. Ibid., p. 45.
3. Printed references to the father of the Ponselles often misidentify him as "Beniamino" Ponzillo. The few surviving documents which were signed in his hand identify him only as "B. Ponzillo" or "Ben Ponzillo"—short for "Benardino," a corruption of "Bernardino," the Italian diminutive for "Bernardo."
4. Ponselle, "Home, Sweet Home," p. 156.

5. Ibid.

6. Author's interview of Antonio P. Ponzillo, July 1977.

7. "Financial Statement of Rosa M. Ponselle, Tax Year 1925," prepared and certified by the Fifth Avenue Bank of New York, February 1926. (Courtesy of the late Libbie Miller.)

8. Author's interview of Edith Prilik Sania, November 1978.

9. Author's interview of Irving Caesar, June 1977 (Edward S. Clute, cointerviewer). According to Caesar, the phrase "the Mecca of vaudeville" was used as a reference to the Palace Theater among vaudeville booking agents and managers, and occasionally by some of the performers.

10. Author's interviews of Antonio P. Ponzillo (July 1977 and November 1978).

11. According to the recording-laboratory logs maintained by the Edison Company for its then-new "Diamond Disc" series, a singer listed as "Carmela A. Ponzillo" was given a recording audition at the company's New York City laboratory on 7 December 1914. The logs indicate that three trial "takes" were recorded of Carmela performing a song entitled "In the Heart of a Rose." According to the Edison ledgers, all three "takes" of the song were rejected, and no copies are known to have survived. (The author is grateful to William R. Moran, founder and honorary curator of the Stanford Archive of Recorded Sound, for providing this information.)

12. *The New York Times*, 21 January 1917.

13. "The principal members of the company," said the *Times*, "are Raymond and Caverly, Harry First, Robert Dailey, Maude Rockwell, Sophie Petrayer, Kitty Flinn, and Anna Orr." (*The New York Times*, 8 September 1912.)

14. *The New York Times*, 1 September 1912.

15. *The New York Times*, 15 September 1912.

16. Ponselle's first concert in Meriden—actually a joint concert with Carmela—took place on Wednesday, 21 May 1919, at the Poli Theater. The concert was reviewed at length in the Meriden *Daily Journal*, 22 May 1919.

17. Meriden *Daily Journal*, 9 May 1922.

18. Boston *Sunday Post*, 9 April 1922.

19. Ibid.

20. Ibid.

21. Hartford *Daily Courant*, 28 December 1919.

22. Meriden *Daily Journal*, 2 June 1915.

23. Author's interview of Bruno Zirato, August 1972.

24. Author's interview of Nina Morgana, August 1972.

25. In October 1982, the author reviewed the parish baptismal ledgers at the Our Lady of Mount Carmel rectory. On that occasion the pastor confirmed that the names and dates appearing in the ledgers were copied from earlier records. The local diocese also confirmed that in many Italian-American communities at the turn of the century, parents were permitted to give their children's birthdates orally to a parish priest, without having to document them. In 1934 the original Mount Carmel church was leveled by a fire that also destroyed many original baptismal ledgers. Ponselle was a major donor when the church was rebuilt in 1934–35, which led to some speculation among her friends that an altered baptismal record was an implied "return favor" for her substantial donation.

26. The 1978 search was initiated at the author's request. A subsequent search (1991) was initiated and overseen at the author's request by Warren F. Gardner, retired editor of the Meriden *Record*. The unofficial birth-certificate copy in Ponselle's personal papers was obtained by her in 1941 and contains several errors regarding her parents.

27. Author's interview of Antonio P. Ponzillo, November 1978.

CHAPTER THREE: Kid, You Won Your Bet!

1. *Variety*, 30 December 1917.

2. B. F. Keith, "The Vogue of the Vaudeville," *National Magazine* (November 1898), p. 152.

3. Charles W. Stein, *American Vaudeville As Seen By Its Contemporaries* (New York: Alfred A. Knopf, 1984), p. 109.

4. The similarity in name between Eddie Darling (the Keith Circuit booking manager) and Eddie Dowling (husband of comedienne Ray Dooley and himself a Keith Circuit performer), both of whom Ponselle had a habit of referring to as "Eddie" without specifying which one she was speaking about, frequently led interviewers to confuse the two (including this author, in *Ponselle: A Singer's Life*). Dowling (born Joseph Nelson Goucher, 1894–1976), had a long and distinguished career as an actor, manager, director, playwright and film writer. For further information see *Who Was Who in the Theatre, 1912–1976* (Detroit: Gale Research Corporation, 1978), Volume II, pp. 695–96. The "other Eddie," the United Booking Offices' Edward V. Darling, briefly reentered Ponselle's career in the early 1930s (as will be seen later), by which time he had entered the motion-picture industry.

5. *Variety*, 15 June 1917.

6. Walter De Leon, "The Wow Finish," *The Saturday Evening Post* (14 February 1925).

7. At least three newspaper accounts published between 1925 and 1959, as well as the private papers of S. Z. Poli, suggest that he played a key role in Ponselle's early career. See *Everybody's Magazine* (November 1925), the Hartford *Courant* (23 October 1937), and the New Haven *Register* (5 April 1959). (The author is grateful to Donald C. King of the Theatre Historical Society for providing details in 1979 from segments of Poli's private papers.)

8. Author's interviews of Lena Tamborini Angle (July 1977, November 1978).

9. The incident occurred during the early morning hours of Monday, 31 May 1915. The trial was covered amply in the New Haven *Register* and Meriden *Daily Journal* during the week of 31 May–7 June 1915.

10. Norman Haygood, "The Life of a Vaudeville Artiste," *Cosmopolitan Magazine* (February 1901), p. 393.

11. Alfred Lunt, "Twenty-Six Weeks in Vaudeville," *Billboard* (26 December 1936), p. 20.

12. *Variety*, 29 June 1917.

13. *The New York Times*, 30 September 1917.

14. Fred Astaire, *Steps in Time* (New York: Harper & Brothers, 1959), pp. 36–37.

15. Ibid., p. 37.

16. *The New York Times*, 28 October 1924. The *Times* subsequently reported (16 November 1924) on Gadski's appearances at Keith's Boston theater, but the next month carried a story (8 December 1924) indicating that she was "compelled to cancel the remainder of her profitable season" on the Keith Circuit because she had been "suffering for a month past from ear trouble."

17. De Leon, "The Wow Finish," pp. 16–17.

18. Nora Bayes, "Holding My Audience," *Theatre Magazine* (September 1917), p. 128.

19. Edward Jablonski, *Gershwin: A Biography* (New York: Doubleday & Company, 1987), pp. 31–32.

20. *Variety*, 11 May 1917.

21. *Variety*, 13 April 1917. The sister's performances with Tanguay took place twice daily during the week of 16–20 April 1917 at the Majestic Theater in Chicago. They had first performed with the temperamental star at the Colonial Theater in Manhattan during the week of 8–12 May 1916.

22. Marjorie Farnsworth, *The Ziegfield Follies* (New York: Bonanza Books, 1956), p. 56.

23. New York *Tribune*, reprinted in *Variety*, 15 March 1918.

24. *Variety*, 15 March 1918.

25. Ibid. In some parts of Tanguay's diatribe, Broun's name is spelled "Broon." Whether this was a typesetting error (as was often the case in *Variety* at the time), or a bit of perverse lampooning on the star's part, can only be guessed.

26. Ponselle repeatedly said in interviews that Carmela's and her vaudeville debut had taken place "at the Star Theater in the Bronx," which she characterized as "a fleabag of a place." But no mention of such a theater is found in the theatrical listings of *Variety* and *Billboard*. Perhaps she was confusing this nonexistent Star "in the Bronx" with the motion-picture house of the same name in Meriden owned by Richard Halliwell, her first mentor.

27. Author's interview of Irving Caesar, July 1977 (Edward S. Clute, cointerviewer).

28. Ibid. Given the fact that the Ponzillo Sisters played the Palace for only one week (29 October–3 November 1917), composer Victor Herbert must have heard them during that brief time span—unless Caesar's recollections were in error and the incident had occurred at one of the other Keith theaters on Broadway.

29. Carl Van Vechten, "A Good Little Devil," in *Stereo Review* (May 1954), p. 35.

30. Harold Rosenthal and John Warrack, *The Concise Oxford Dictionary of Opera* (London: Oxford University Press, 1978), p. 358.

31. J. Walker McSpadden, *Operas and Musical Comedies* (New York: Thomas Y. Crowell Company, 1935), p. 540. However, Bloom, in *American Song*, lists the number of Broadway performances as 202 rather than 252.

32. Van Vechten, "A Good Little Devil," p. 35. In interviews over the years, Ponselle repeatedly said that in vaudeville she had always sung "Kiss Me Again" using "the arrangement Fritzi Scheff was famous for." Patterned after Adele's narrative in the third act of *Die Fledermaus*, "Kiss Me Again" (in the words of Joseph Kaye, Herbert's biographer) "is officially known as, 'If I Were on the Stage,' and . . . [it] really consists of a prologue and three acts," including a two-verse introduction, a gavotte, a polonaise, and a waltz. (See Joseph Kaye, *Victor Herbert* [New York: G. Howard Watt, 1931], pp. 152–153.) Ponselle's recorded version of the song contains the introduction, but omits the gavotte and polonaise in favor of the waltz (which begins with the lines, "Sweet summer breeze, whispering trees"). Regrettably, Fritzi Scheff, the original Fifi, did not make commercial recordings, although she continued to perform "Kiss Me Again" in regional theaters, supper clubs, and on radio long after the bloom of her voice was gone. She was last scheduled to sing it on Ed Sullivan's popular television show, *The Toast of the Town*, on Sunday, 18 April 1954. Ten days before the telecast, she died in New York at the age of seventy-five.

33. From a typewritten summary of Ponselle's Columbia Graphophone Com-

pany recordings, compiled by Edith Prilik from her diary entries, dated 4 December 1925. (Courtesy of the late Edith Prilik Sania.)

34. Hugh Leamy, "An Interview with Edward F. Albee," *Collier's Weekly* (1 May 1926), p. 11.

35. *Variety*, 10 September 1915.

36. Ibid.

37. Pittsburgh *Leader*, 26 January 1916.

38. Barbara Ferguson, ed., *100 Years of Great Performances at the University of Michigan* (Ann Arbor: University of Michigan Press, 1980), p. 82. Playbills listed in the *Variety* edition of 11 May 1917 show that the performance Ponselle speaks of took place at the Empress Theater during the week of 14 May 1917.

39. From an unidentified clipping in the scrapbooks of Rosa Ponselle, compiled by Edith Prilik.

40. *The New York Times*, 2 September 1917.

41. *Variety*, 7 September 1917.

42. Ibid. (Patsy Smith column)

43. *The New York Times*, 30 September 1917.

44. "Rube Marquard in Court," *The New York Times*, 22 September 1912.

45. *The New York Times*, 30 October 1917.

46. *Variety*, 2 November 1917.

47. Irving Caesar, Jack Benny, and George Burns, in their correspondence with Ponselle over the years, alluded to the sisters' appearances at the Palace. Caesar, especially, felt certain that he had seen the Ponzillos' act "several times" at the Palace. (Author's interview of Irving Caesar, June 1977.) But this was not the case.

48. Interview of Rosa Ponselle by John Secrist, 1949.

49. Ibid.

50. *Variety*, 6 January 1918.

51. See chap. one, n. 23.

52. *Musical America*, 18 January 1919. Based on an interview with William Thorner by May Stanley.

53. Boston *Sunday Globe*, 9 April 1922.

54. *Variety*, 29 March 1918.

55. *Variety*, 5 April and 12 April 1918.

CHAPTER FOUR: An Overnight Prima Donna

1. Oscar Thompson, *The American Singer*, p. 335.

2. Author's interview of Rosa Ponselle, February 1978.

3. *The New York Times* briefly reviewed the *Requiem* on 7 April 1919, praising the "quartet of voices of the best in Mr. Gatti's roster" including Ponselle, Margarete Matzenauer, Charles Hackett, and José Mardones. The *Stabat Mater* performance, which took place on 20 January 1919 at the Metropolitan, was announced in the press but was not reviewed by any of the major Manhattan newspapers.

4. Author's interview of Ponselle, March 1978. This stipulation appears in her Metropolitan Opera contract for 1919–20 (pp. 2–3, Section XIV), in the Metropolitan Opera Archives. See also Rupert Christiansen, *Prima Donna: A History* (New York: Viking Press, 1987), p. 208.

5. Author's interviews of Rosa Ponselle (March 1978, December 1978).

6. Letter of Giulio Gatti-Casazza to William Thorner, 11 June 1918. (The author is grateful to Robert Tuggle, Director of the Metropolitan Opera Archives, for providing a copy of this letter.)

7. Letter of Rosa Ponselle to Giulio Gatti-Casazza, 4 June 1918. (Courtesy of the late Edith Prilik Sania.)

8. Strangely, Thorner waited until 30 September 1918 to ratify a contractual agreement with Ponselle about the management of her career. No copies of this written agreement are known to survive, although most of its contents were reprinted in the court records of the Appellate Division, First Department, Supreme Court of the State of New York, pursuant to the case of *Ponselle v. Thorner*, which was argued before the court on 1 February 1928. (See chap. one, n. 22.)

9. Author's interviews of Rosa Ponselle (June 1975) and Libbie Miller (November 1978). Neither in Nathan Burkan's brief of 1 February 1928, nor in the abstract and summary of the case appearing in the *Law Journal* of 2 February 1928, is any mention made of the amount of the fee that Ponselle paid Thorner for his services during the 1918–19 season.

10. Caruso's exclusive contract with the Victor Talking Machine Company is referred to in varying detail in most of the commercial Caruso biographies. See, for example, Howard Greenfeld, *Caruso* (New York: G. P. Putnam's Sons, 1983), p. 155. For a detailed account of the tenor's association with Victor based upon intra-company documentation and other original sources, see William R. Moran, "Discography of Original Recordings," in Caruso, Jr. and Farkas, *Enrico Caruso*, pp. 603–5.

11. Author's interviews of Rosa Ponselle (March 1973 and June 1975).

12. See chap. one, p. 000.

13. From the author's interviews of Libbie Miller (August 1978, September 1978, and November 1978).

14. A reference, apparently, to the Metropolitan Opera Relief Fund concert of 3 April 1919, in which the second act of *La forza del destino* was performed. See *Annals of the Metropolitan Opera*, Vol. I, p. 285.

15. Tax records compiled by the Fifth Avenue Bank of New York for Rosa Ponselle for the year 1922 reported her gross income as being $69,463.17, of which a total of $10,633.95 was derived from her Metropolitan Opera performances, and $44,866.72 from her concerts. Ponselle paid $617 in federal income tax in 1922.

16. Tax records compiled by the Fifth Avenue Bank for Rosa Ponselle for the year 1927 reported a gross income for Ponselle in the amount of $141,404, of which a total of $37,444 was derived from her Metropolitan Opera performances, and $85,100 from her concerts and radio appearances. Federal income tax paid by Ponselle for the year 1927 totaled $356.07.

17. In a May Festival Concert at the University of Michigan in Ann Arbor on 14 May 1919, Ponselle appeared as soloist with the Chicago Symphony Orchestra under the baton of Frederick Stock. She sang three arias, in this order: "O patria mia" from *Aida*, "Un bel dì vedremo" from *Madama Butterfly*, and "D'amor sull' ali rosee" from *Il trovatore*.

18. Edward H. Hipsher, "The American Girl's Chance in Opera," in *The Etude* (November 1929), p. 802.

19. Philadelphia *Record*, 11 December 1918.

20. Ibid.

21. *Musical America*, 21 December 1918.

22. Ibid.

23. *The New York Times*, 29 December 1918.

24. New York *Sun*, 29 December 1918.

25. *The New York Times*, 13 March 1919.

26. New York *World*, 13 March 1919.

27. Ibid.

28. New York *World*, 23 November 1919.

29. New York *Sun*, 23 November 1919.

30. New York *Evening Globe*, 24 November 1919.

31. New York *World*, 23 November 1919.

32. New York *World*, 24 December 1920.

33. New York *Herald*, 24 December 1920.

34. New York *Post*, 24 December 1920.

35. New York *Tribune*, 23 December 1920.

36. New York *Globe*, 4 December 1922.

37. The high acclaim that Chaliapin's portrayal of Philip II received from the critics supposedly led to an angry confrontation, according to an apocryphal story widely circulated (and widely believed) among Ponselle's devotees, between Chaliapin and Ponselle during one of the *Don Carlos* dress rehearsals. According to most versions of this story, Ponselle became so angered at Chaliapin's purported scene-stealing that she became enraged and broke a chair over his head. Apart from the fact that Ponselle repeatedly denied to this writer and others that any such incident ever occurred, the prowess required of her to have lifted one of the set's medieval-style chairs—and especially to have "broken it over the head" of a man who was a half-foot taller than she—would have been extraordinary indeed.

38. Quaintance Eaton, *Opera Caravan* (New York: Farrar, Straus and Cudahy, 1957), pp. 283–93.

39. *The New York Times*, 26 December 1924.

40. Brooklyn *Eagle*, 7 March 1920.

41. Interview of George Cehanovsky by Hugh M. Johns (1979; precise date unknown).

42. Ibid.

43. James M. Alfonte, "Three Heroines for Ponselle," *Opera News* (24 December 1956), p. 27.

44. R. M. Knerr, "Rosa Ponselle Makes a Record—and a Few Remarks," in *Musical America* (15 July 1922), p. 5.

45. *The New York Times*, 9 December 1921.

46. New York *Globe*, 9 December 1921.

47. New York *World*, 9 December 1921.

48. Cited in Ruffo, Jr., and Roscioni, "Chronology of Titta Ruffo's Public Appearances," in Farkas, ed., *Titta Ruffo*, p. 188.

49. *Musical America*, 4 February 1922. Thompson's reference to Ruffo's having performed Iago "a year ago" refers to Ruffo's performance in a touring production of *Otello* given in New York by the Chicago Opera Company at the Manhattan Opera House in February 1921. For additional information, see Farkas, *Titta Ruffo*, p. 226.

50. *Musical America*, 4 February 1922.
51. *The New York Times*, 6 January 1922.
52. Ibid.
53. New York *Evening World*, 14 February 1919.
54. New York *Globe*, 30 June 1919.
55. Charlotte *Observer*, 4 May 1919.
56. Norfolk *Ledger-Dispatch*, 3 May 1919.
57. Ohio *State Journal*, 12 October 1920.
58. Ohio *State Journal*, 17 October 1922.
59. *Musical Leader*, 21 December 1922.
60. *Musical America*, 15 July 1922, p. 5.
61. Laurence Bergreen, *As Thousands Cheer: The Life of Irving Berlin* (New York: Viking Press, 1990), p. 54.

CHAPTER FIVE: Flashes of the Grand Manner

1. Author's interview of Edith Prilik Sania, August 1977.
2. Portland *Express-Advertiser*, 21 April 1923. An earlier account appeared in *The New York Times* upon her return to Manhattan during the last week of September 1922.
3. Hartford *Courant* (undated clipping, probably late August or early September 1923).
4. *The New York Times*, and also the New York *Herald Journal*, 23 February 1922.
5. Author's interviews of Antonio P. Ponzillo (July 1977) and Edith Prilik Sania (August 1977).
6. Author's interview of Edith Prilik Sania, August 1977. Although her financial records for 1923 to 1925 do not always identify Tony Ponzillo as the recipient of gifts or loans, Ponselle confirmed the $40,000 amount to Myron Ehrlich, James M. Alfonte, and the author on separate occasions.
7. New York *Daily News*, 31 July 1922.
8. Bronx *Home News*, 22 April 1923.
9. Meriden *Journal*, 25 April 1924.
10. New Haven *Evening Register*, 12 March 1923. See also *The New York Times*, 18 March 1923.

11. New York *Tribune*, 12 November 1922. In view of the fact that Rothier was a bass rather than a baritone, he probably sang Ramfis rather than Amonasro.

12. New York *Herald*, 12 November 1922.

13. New York *Globe*, 20 March 1923.

14. According to an undated clipping in a scrapbook belonging to Carmela Ponselle, this second concertized *Aida* took place on Wednesday, 20 June 1923.

15. In an essay published in Andrew Farkas, ed., *Lawrence Tibbett*, Thomas R. Bullard states (p. 20) that Tibbett was the featured soloist at two concerts given at the Hollywood Bowl in August 1923. "While in Los Angeles," Bullard writes, "he also arranged a private audition before Rosa Ponselle, then on a concert tour."

16. Merle Armitage, in *Accent on America* (New York: E. Weyhe, 1944), p. 90, states that Ponselle "was the first great artist to sing a concert in the Hollywood Bowl, using a stage improvised à la Sid Graumann."

17. David Stenn, in *Clara Bow: Runnin' Wild* (New York: Penguin Books, 1988), states (p. 5) that Robert (father of Clara) Bow, who "some were convinced was mentally retarded," had "a rich baritone singing voice [that he] used to entertain fellow wastrels. . . ." But the recollections of Rosa and Edith concerning Clara Bow probably stem from return trips to the West Coast in 1924 and 1925, since Robert Bow did not come to live with his daughter in Hollywood until the summer of 1924. Furthermore, according to Stenn, Clara Bow's stardom was not established until *The Plastic Age* was released late in 1925.

18. Financial ledgers kept by Edith Prilik Sania for fiscal years 1921 to 1924 show her annual salary as $1,800, an increase of $500 from her salary for 1923, and a $1,000 increase from the salary she earned in 1921. The rental amount for fiscal year 1924 for Ponselle's Riverside Drive residence totaled $2,100, compared to an annual rent of $1,780 when she began leasing the penthouse late in 1921.

19. During his student days at Yale in the mid-1920s, entertainer Rudy Vallée became a *pro bono* surgery patient of Dr. Verdi. In his second autobiography Vallée described how Verdi had "risen from a bootblack and newsboy and worked his way through Yale University to become a highly esteemed surgeon." (See Vallée and McKean, *My Time Is Your Time*, pp. 38, 51.) Once successful, Vallée, like Ponselle, referred numerous celebrity friends to Verdi's New Haven medical clinic.

20. Financial ledgers maintained by Edith Prilik Sania indicate that as early as 1921 Ponselle had begun paying retainers averaging $750 annually to Dr. Verdi for his exclusive services as a consulting physician.

21. Ponselle often told the story of her unplanned "swim" in Venice's Grand Canal, but persistently linked the incident to her impromptu singing in the

gondola with Tullio Serafin and Elena Rakowska. But Edith Prilik Sania, who was an eyewitness, insisted that the incidents were separate; additionally, Ruth Romani, widow of Romano Romani, confirmed to Hugh M. Johns in 1992 that her husband, who was also present on that occasion, told the same version of the incident that Edith had given. Hence, it is Mrs. Sania's version that is relayed here.

22. According to the Hartford *Courant*, 13 January 1925, the Eastman Kodak Company made custom enlargements of Edith's snapshots for the Puccini family. Intriguingly, the *Courant* also reported that Signora Puccini had sent Rosa a photocopy of an unfinished song that Puccini had written for her. Neither Edith nor Rosa ever recalled being told of this purportedly "unfinished song"—and neither the manuscript photocopy nor any document referring to it was ever located among Ponselle's personal papers at Villa Pace.

23. New York *Sun*, 24 May 1924.

24. *Musical America*, June 1924.

25. New York *Morning Telegraph*, 20 September 1924.

26. *The New York Times*, 20 September 1924.

27. New York *Morning Telegraph*, 20 September 1924.

28. Buffalo *Times*, 5 August 1923.

29. Atlanta *Journal*, 9 December 1923.

30. Ibid.

31. Author's interview of Rosa Ponselle, December 1978.

32. Telephone interview of Mona (Mrs. Richard) Bonelli by Bill Park, October 1992.

33. Washington *Herald*, and also Washington *Post*, 14 April 1923.

34. Washington *Herald*, 14 April 1923.

35. Armitage, *Accent on America*, p. 90.

36. Ibid., p. 91.

37. Author's interview of Libbie Miller, September 1978.

38. Armitage, *Accent on America*, p. 89.

39. Rosenthal and Warrack, *The Concise Oxford Dictionary of Opera*, p. 275.

40. New York *Telegram*, 22 April 1923.

41. *The New York Times*, 22 April 1923.

42. New York *Telegram*, 22 April 1923.

43. *The New York Times*, 22 March 1923.

44. Ibid.
45. *The New York Times*, 1 April 1923.
46. *The New York Times*, 22 March 1923.
47. New York *American*, 23 March 1923.
48. *Musical America*, 9 February 1924.
49. *The New York Times*, 28 December 1924.
50. New York *Herald Tribune*, 5 January 1923.
51. *The New York Times*, 5 January 1923. Reviewed by Richard Aldrich.
52. Kolodin, *The Story of the Metropolitan Opera*, p. 601.
53. New York *Telegram*, 13 November 1923.
54. New York *Sun*, 17 December 1923.
55. Ibid.
56. *Musical Courier*, 29 December 1923.
57. New York *Sun*, 17 December 1923.
58. *Musical America*, 26 December 1923.
59. New York *Telegram*, 22 April 1922.
60. The New York Times, 1 March 1924.
61. *Musical America*, 12 December 1927. (The performance was dated 7 December 1927.)
62. Ibid.
63. In the Philadelphia *Inquirer* and a number of the New York–area newspapers that printed stories about the *Il trovatore* incident, the date of the performance was given as Monday, 3 December 1928. But according to the Metropolitan *Annals*, a performance of *La bohème* rather than *Il trovatore* was heard on 3 December, and the 6 December matinee was the only performance of *Il trovatore* given at the Metropolitan Opera House during December 1928.
64. Philadelphia *Inquirer*, 20 January 1929.
65. Author's interview of Libbie Miller, October 1978.
66. Letter of Giacomo Lauri-Volpi to the editor of the New York *Daily News*, 8 December 1928. (Original letter courtesy of the late Libbie Miller.)
67. Author's interview of Libbie Miller, October 1978.
68. Letter of Giacomo Lauri-Volpi to Rosa Ponselle, 13 January 1929. Translation courtesy of Dr. Sabatino Maglione. (Typewritten transcription of the letter courtesy of the late Libbie Miller.)

69. Author's interviews of Nina Morgana Zirato (August 1972 and March 1978). In a letter to the author dated 1 December 1978, Lauri-Volpi wrote, "I remember Nina Morgana as the sweetest voice in the lyric-coloratura repertoire." (Translation courtesy of Andrew Farkas.)

70. George Jellinek, "Giacomo Lauri-Volpi," *Opera News* (July 1979), p. 23.

71. This was the firm impression given the author in interviews with Libbie Miller (1978), Nina Morgana Zirato (1973), and Edward J. Smith (1978). Smith was well acquainted with Lauri-Volpi from the 1950s onward and interviewed him on a number of occasions at the tenor's villa in Spain.

72. Letter of Giacomo Lauri-Volpi to the author, 1 December 1978. (Translation courtesy of Andrew Farkas.)

73. Ibid.

74. *The New York Times*, 8 December 1924.

75. Ibid.

76. Author's interview with Edith Prilik Sania, August 1977.

77. *Columbia Records, April 1920*, p. 1.

78. Ibid.

79. Dallas *Times-Herald*, 12 May 1922.

80. R. M. Knerr, "Rosa Ponselle Makes a Record—and a Few Remarks," *Musical America*, (15 July 1922), p. 5. The writer's reference to the studio orchestra being comprised of "a dozen musicians" was occasioned by the particular aria being recorded—namely, Desdemona's prayer, which is scored for an ensemble of strings. Most operatic recording sessions of the early 1920s utilized a larger number of instruments in the recording-laboratory orchestras.

81. Albany *Times-Union*, 24 February 1923. Manna (or sometimes Mana) Zucca had been introduced to Ponselle by Edith Prilik. In September 1912, when Carmela was appearing in *The Girl from Brighton* at the Academy of Music, *The New York Times* reported that Manna Zucca had been engaged for a forthcoming production of *The Rose Maid* on Broadway. The *Times* also reported that she had toured in the U. S. as a pianist at the age of 7.

82. Tampa *Tribune*, 29 March 1923.

83. Letter of Leonard Bernstein to Rosa Ponselle, 24 September 1976. The original was sent to Ponselle by Bernstein in care of Tom Villella, as part of a tribute to Ponselle on the occasion of her seventy-fifth birthday.

84. Hartford *Times*, 20 May 1919.

85. Roland Gelatt, *The Fabulous Phonograph: From Tin Foil to High Fidelity* (New York: J. B. Lippincott Company, 1955), pp. 210–11. Gelatt's book was writ-

ten for a general audience and contains no source-by-source documentation for the financial data cited here.

86. Author's interview of Libbie Miller, September 1978.

87. Financial Statements of Rosa M. Ponselle, Tax Years 1922, 1923, 1924, and 1925, prepared and ceritfied by the Fifth Avenue Bank of New York. (Courtesy of the late Edith Prilik Sania.)

88. No matrix numbers for these tests appear in the Victor recording logs. (The author is grateful to William R. Moran, founder and Honorary Curator of the Stanford Archive of Recorded Sound, for providing this information.)

89. Victor Talking Machine Company, 1 March 1924. (Copy courtesy of the late Libbie Miller.)

90. "Rosa Ponselle," in *Victor Records* (Camden, New Jersey: Victor Talking Machine Company, 1925), (nonpaginated).

91. Author's interview of Antonio P. Ponzillo, July 1977.

CHAPTER SIX: A Perfect Voice

1. Author's interview of Myron Ehrlich, March 1978.

2. Interview of Rosa Ponselle by Boris Goldovsky, Metropolitan Opera radio broadcast, 27 March 1954. In the radio performance of *Norma,* Zinka Milanov sang the title role.

3. Interview of Rosa Ponselle by Boris Goldovsky, Metropolitan Opera radio broadcast, 11 March 1960.

4. New York World, 19 December 1925.

5. *The New York Times*, 14 December 1924.

6. Ibid.

7. *The New York Times*, 1 November 1925.

8. New York *News*, 3 November 1925.

9. This last-minute change in casting nearly cost Leonard Liebling his credibility as music critic for the New York *American*. In a review published the day after the season-opening Gioconda, Liebling wrote, "Jeanne Gordon's rich contralto contributions [and] Merle Alcock's fervent utterances as La Cieca . . . helped materially to stimulate the appreciative spirit of the occasion." Neither Gordon nor Alcock, of course, had sung in the performance. Liebling partially salvaged his credibility by admitting in the review that he had left the opera house well before the end of the performance. "I looked for a spot where there was no singing," he claimed, "and wrote this report."

10. New York *News*, 3 November 1925.

11. Ibid.

12. New York *Telegram*, 3 November 1925.

13. Beniamino Gigli, *The Gigli Memoirs*, trans. Darina Silone (London: Cassell & Company, Ltd., 1957), p. 153.

14. Max de Schauensee, "Whose Opera is Gioconda?" in *Opera News* (26 February 1945), p. 30.

15. Author's interview of Rosa Ponselle, December 1978. The full effect of this prolonged pianissimo was usually lost on the audience. "Nobody got to hear the end of that long phrase but me," Ponselle remembered. "They would start applauding before I ever got to the curtain."

16. *The New York Times*, 1 November 1925.

17. New York *Evening Post*, 1 November 1925.

18. *The New York Times*, 13 November 1925.

19. *The New York Times*, 8 November 1925.

20. Ibid.

21. *The New York Times*, 13 November 1925.

22. New York *Sun*, 13 November 1925.

23. Henderson, *The Art of Singing*, p. 389.

24. A wine-colored velvet dress purportedly intended for Ponselle in *L'amore dei tre re* was included in a Metropolitan traveling display of costumes exhibited in various locales in the United States in the early 1980s. The dress, which may have been a Metropolitan Opera costume rather than her own, did not resemble any of the ones that were expressly designed for her.

25. Author's interviews of Nina Morgana Zirato (August 1972, November 1975, and November 1982).

26. Among several benefits in which Morgana participated was the United Catholic Works Charity Benefit of Sunday, 20 January 1918, with George M. Cohan, Eleanora de Cisneros, and Ethel Barrymore. Former president William Howard Taft was the guest of honor. (*The New York Times*, 19 January 1918.)

27. Although no date or program for this benefit has been located so far, Morgana's recollections were generally quite accurate and, in this case, they raise the intriguing question whether Caruso heard the Ponzillo Sisters at this benefit.

28. Charles Morgana, then a vice president of the Ford Motor Company and a long-time associate of Henry Ford, was one of the more influential automo-

tive-industry executives of his time. According to Carol Gilderman in *Henry Ford: The Wayward Capitalist* (New York: St. Martin's Press, 1981), Morgana was the company's "machine-tool expert who had roved the industry as Ford's chief technological scout" (p. 201).

29. Author's interview of Libbie Miller, August 1978. Both Miss Miller and Edith Prilik spoke of this surprise party as having taken place after a recording session. But Ponselle's only sessions at Victor that year were on 2 June, 13 June, 16 June, and 8 December 1927.

30. Perle Mesta, *Perle: My Story* (New York, New York: McGraw-Hill, 1960), p. 50. The famed hostess' memory apparently failed her as regards the presence of Lily Pons at the party: Pons did not come to the United States until the season of her Metropolitan Opera debut, which took place in January 1930.

31. Ibid., p. 50.

32. New York *Evening Post* (undated clipping). As recently as the spring of 1994, the building and its four statues—Barrymore's Ophelia, Miller's Sunny, Pickford's Little Lord Fauntleroy, and Ponselle's Norma—were suggested by Joseph L. Hopkins in *The New York Times* as prime candidates for the reclamation of Times Square. Hopkins characterized it as a "monument . . . to women who brought joy . . . to the entire country . . . [and who] over the passing decades have become part of our heritage." (*Times,* 1 April 1994.)

33. Author's interview of Nanette Guilford, January 1977.

34. *The New York Times,* 13 November 1925. The mention of "the Tibbett affair of last season" refers to the performance of Verdi's *Falstaff* during which the audience demanded that Lawrence Tibbett, singing the secondary role of Ford, be given a solo curtain call rather than to share curtain calls with the veteran baritone Antonio Scotti, who was singing the title role.

35. New York *Tribune,* 13 November 1925.

36. New York *Sun,* 13 November 1925.

37. *The New York Times,* 24 February 1918.

38. Ibid.

39. *Musical Leader,* 13 November 1927.

40. New York *Evening Post,* 17 November 1927.

41. Brooklyn *Eagle,* 17 November 1927.

42. New York *Evening World,* 17 November 1927.

43. *Musical America,* 19 November 1927.

44. *The New York Times,* 17 November 1927.

45. New York *Sun,* 17 November 1927.

46. New York *Herald Tribune,* 17 November 1927.
47. New York *Telegram,* 17 November 1927.
48. Author's interview of Edith Prilik Sania, October 1978.
49. Author's interview of Wilfred Pelletier, November 1974.
50. *Musical America,* 19 November 1927.
51. San Francisco *Examiner,* 18 March 1929.
52. Charles B. Mintzer, liner-note insert for the LP *Rosa Raisa,* produced by Rubini Records (1984).
53. Letter of James M. Alfonte to the author, 19 October 1993.
54. Author's interview of Libbie Miller, August 1978.
55. Helen Noble, *Life with the Met* (New York: G. B. Putnam's Sons, 1954), pp. 119–20.
56. Rose Heylbut and Aimé Gerber, *Backstage at the Metropolitan Opera* (New York: Thomas Y. Crowell Company, 1937), p. 263.
57. Noble, *Life with the Met,* p. 120.
58. John Ardoin, "A Footnote to Ponselle's Norma," Opera (March 1976), pp. 225–26.
59. Ibid., p. 226.
60. Telegram of Giulio Gatti-Casazza to Edward Ziegler, 25 June 1925. (The author is grateful to Robert Tuggle, Director of the Metropolitan Opera Archives, for providing a copy of the telegram.)
61. Letter of Edward Ziegler to Giulio Gatti-Casazza, 26 June 1925. (The author is grateful to Robert Tuggle, Director of the Metropolitan Opera Archives, for providing a copy of this letter.)
62. *The New York Times,* 1 November 1925.
63. Ibid.
64. Noble, *Life with the Met,* p. 120.
65. Author's interview of Libbie Miller, August 1978.
66. Author's interview of Edith Prilik Sania, July 1977.
67. Although Gatti was silent about these backstage phone calls in his memoirs, almost everyone who was associated with Ponselle at the time was aware of them. Among those who confirmed this to the author were Edith Prilik Sania, Libbie Miller, and Myron Ehrlich. Independently, James M. Alfonte heard the same version in informal conversations with a number of Ponselle's contemporaries in the 1940s and 1950s.

68. Author's interview of Rosa Ponselle, June 1975.

69. Washington, D.C., *News,* 8 January 1925.

70. Author's interview of Edith Prilik Sania, November 1978.

71. Author's interview of Libbie Miller, August 1978.

72. Author's interview of Edith Prilik Sania, August 1977.

73. New York *Evening Post,* 7 December 1925.

74. New York *Tribune,* 7 December 1925.

75. Author's interview of Myron Ehrlich, July 1977.

76. James M. Alfonte to the author, 19 October 1993.

77. Wilfrid Pelletier, *Une symphonie inachevée* (Ottowa: LEMAC, 1972), p. 104. (Translation courtesy of Andrew Farkas.)

78. Author's interview of Wilfred Pelletier, November 1974.

79. New York *Sun,* 22 December 1932.

CHAPTER SEVEN: Sleepless Nights

1. Based upon documentation quoted in Robert Tuggle's authoritative *The Golden Age of Opera*, p. 179, as early as 1919 the management of Covent Garden had expressed an interest in Ponselle, perhaps through William Thorner. When financier Otto Kahn relayed this interest to Gatti-Casazza, the General Manager replied that "it would neither be in the interest of this artist nor in the interests of Mr. Higgins to arrange her appearance in London this year."

2. Author's interview of Libbie Miller, September 1978.

3. *The New York Times*, 30 December 1926.

4. Ibid.

5. *Musical Courier*, 4 November 1928. The date of the performance was 29 October 1928.

6. Rochester *Times-Union*, 9 May 1928.

7. Cleveland *Plain Dealer*, 3 May 1928.

8. Author's interview of Libbie Miller, August 1978.

9. The casting for *Don Giovanni* was apparently not without its complications. Robert Tuggle, in *The Golden Age of Opera*, records (p. 216) that in June 1929 Gatti-Casazza was "informed by his assistant Edward Ziegler that Rethberg

didn't want to sing Donna Elvira because of Ponselle's presence in the cast as Donna Anna." But whether Rethberg's reluctance stemmed from her own interest in the role of Donna Anna (which she eventually not only sang at the Metropolitan but also performed at Covent Garden and Salzburg under Bruno Walter) or whether she feared being outshone by Ponselle is not clear. The late Ida Cook, who knew both women well, maintained that at no point was there any rivalry between them. To the contrary, Rethberg once reprimanded one of her guests for criticizing Ponselle's casual dress while bicycling through the countryside at Lago di Como. When the guest exclaimed that Ponselle "looked like a gypsy," Rethberg sternly said, "Stop! Stop! All I know is she is a wonderful colleague, and there aren't that many, and I won't have her criticized in my home!" (Interview of Ida Cook by Hugh M. Johns, 1967; precise date unknown.)

10. Letter of Libbie Miller to Edward Ziegler, 8 May 1928. (Date and summary of the letter courtesy of the late Libbie Miller.)
11. In June 1975 Ponselle told the author that a node was removed from one of her vocal cords while she was being treated for the respiratory illness.
12. New York *Herald Tribune*, 29 November 1929.
13. Ibid. Rethberg was forced to keep her arm in a sling during the first few performances of *Don Giovanni*.
14. New York *World*, 30 November 1929.
15. *The New York Times*, 3 January 1930.
16. New York *Herald Tribune*, 22 December 1929.
17. *The New York Times*, 22 December 1929.
18. The formation of the syndicate Blois managed, known initially as the Covent Garden Syndicate Limited, is given a detailed treatment in Harold Rosenthal, *Two Centuries of Opera at Covent Garden* (London: Putnam & Company, 1958), pp. 432–33, 453, and 458–63.
19. Author's interview of Libbie Miller, August 1978. Miss Miller maintained that it was Natalie Townsend who, at Rosa's prompting, had made Blois aware of her interest in singing at Covent Garden.
20. Author's interview of Libbie Miller, September 1978.
21. Letter of Rosa Ponselle to Eustace Blois, 16 November 1929. Used with permission of the Royal Opera House Archives, Covent Garden. (The author is grateful to William Ashbrook, editor of *The Opera Quarterly*, for obtaining copies of the Ponselle-Blois correspondence from the Royal Opera House Archives.)
22. Ibid.

23. The contract Mocchi had offered Ponselle was among her personal papers at Villa Pace. But among those who were close to Ponselle in later life, James M. Alfonte tended to the viewpoint that it was Muzio's enormous popularity in Buenos Aires—much more so than any "other obligations" to which Ponselle alludes—that kept her from accepting Mocchi's contract.

24. The performance, which took place at the Lexington Theater on Monday, 4 February 1918, marked the silver anniversary of Melba's Metropolitan Opera debut, according to *The New York Times* (5 February 1918).

25. Ponselle referred to Melba as "Dame Melba" rather than as "Dame Nellie," the correct form of address, whenever she retold this story. Whether she had long since forgotten which one was correct—or whether she remembered but used "Dame Melba" as a self-styled way of expressing her contempt—was never clear to this writer.

26. Ponselle's version of this story differed as she grew older. In 1955 she told James M. Alfonte that Melba had been spotted among the standees, poorly disguised, during one of Ponselle's *Traviata* performances. Ponselle told Alfonte that John McCormack had passed this on to her. (James M. Alfonte to the author, July 1995.)

27. Here Ponselle's memory has failed her. In August 1931 she and Montemezzi were photographed at the Palace Hotel in St. Moritz, reviewing the score of *La notte di Zoraima*. When the opera premiered at the Metropolitan on 2 December 1931, the major critics damned its "flat libretto," "hackneyed plot," and "unoriginal music." In one of its harshest reviews of a premiere, *Musical Courier* described the characters of *Zoraima* as "nothing more than typically sawdust puppets of the most ancient operatic manner," and its score as a series of "sentimental themes [which] often come close to lyricized drooling." (*Musical Courier*, 12 December 1931)

28. According to Myron Ehrlich, Ponselle's recollection of where she met Tetrazzini is inaccurate. The two met, he maintains, at a private party at the Ansonia Hotel in New York, on New Year's Eve 1931. (Myron Ehrlich to the author, August 1995.) Ehrlich's version is borne out by a story appearing in the New York *American*, in which reporter Grena Bennett wrote that Serafin, Martinelli, and Mario Basiola were among the other Metropolitan Opera singers who attended the party, along with Tetrazzini and Ponselle. (New York *American*, 10 January 1932.)

29. Billed as "The Foremost of the Spanish Dancers," La Argentina, as her name indicated, was Argentinian-born (Buenos Aires). Although she and Rosa shared Libbie Miller as their manager in the late 1920s, the two had known each other since their Keith Circuit days. La Argentina made her vaudeville debut at the Palace Theater on 20 May 1916. (*The New York Times*, 19 May 1916.)

30. From the author's interview of Lena Tamborini Angle, July 1977.

31. Originally titled *Die weisse Hölle von Piz Palü*, the film was codirected by Ernest Pabst and physical culturist Dr. Arnold Franck and starred Gustav Diessl and Leni Riefenstahl (who would subsequently earn a reputation as the most important of the Nazi film propagandists). In the words of biographer and film historian Barry Paris, *Pitz Palü* was "built around sentimental rescue plots . . . redeemed by the breathtaking beauty of glaciers and picturesque mountain chalets." See Barry Paris, *Louise Brooks* (New York: Anchor Books, Doubleday, 1989), pp. 321–22. For additional information about *Die weisse Hölle von Piz Palü*, see Siegfried Kracauer, *From Caligari to Hitler: A Psychological History of the German Film* (Princeton, New Jersey: Princeton University Press, 1947), p. 179.

32. In his biography of film legend Louise Brooks, Barry Paris cites contemporary accounts, including Brooks' own, that Sepp Allgeier, the film's principal photographer, was in the midst of affairs with Brooks and Riefenstahl during the production. Ponselle had invited Allgeier and one of the supporting cast members (not Gustav Diessl, the star of the film) to join Lena and the others in St. Moritz. See Paris, *Brooks*, p. 323.

33. In a letter dated 4 October 1978, Libbie Miller verified to the author that Grace Moore frequently chided her about the amount of attention she was devoting to Ponselle's management. Eventually, Miss Miller said, she discontinued managing Grace Moore and all other clients in order to devote full-time attention to Ponselle's career.

34. The couplet that caused Ponselle to lose her composure reads, "I gaze on the moon as I tread the drear wild / And feel that my mother now thinks of her child." In her Victor recording of "Home, Sweet Home" (made on 3 June 1925, but released only in the United Kingdom rather than in the U.S. in 78 r.p.m. form), Ponselle did not include the verse in which this couplet is sung. The only recorded version in which she included it was made privately at Villa Pace in January 1952, with Romano Romani at the piano. The recording has since been released in compact-disc form (Cantabile BIM-701), although the liner notes erroneously cite Ponselle, rather than Romani, as the accompanist.

35. The Meriden *Record* reported the incident on 17 October 1932: "Reports from Hartford said Miss Ponselle ceased singing and walked backstage and threw herself into a chair, crying 'I can't finish it.'"

36. In *Tristanissimo: A Biography of Lauritz Melchior* (New York: Schirmer Books, 1990), Shirlee Emmons cites (p. 296) a March 1963 letter which Ponselle wrote to Melchior upon the death of his wife, Kleinchen. In it Ponselle spoke of her mother's death: "I will never forget the night after my mother died I went into the living room to turn off the lights. There was adorable Kleinchen with a bottle of wine. She told us that she wanted to drink with us to the New Year because that was what Mother would have wanted us to do." Ponselle's memory must have failed her considerably, however, because her

mother had been dead more than two months by New Year's Eve. Moreover, she was in Meriden, rather than her Manhattan penthouse, for several days after her mother's funeral.

37. Author's interview of Antonio Ponzillo, July 1977.

38. Ibid.

39. Author's interview of Edith Prilik Sania, July 1977.

40. *Musical America*, 5 May 1929.

41. Boston *Globe*, 8 February 1934.

42. Ibid.

43. Chicago *Times*, 8 February 1934. Bushman conveniently subtracted twenty years from Carmela's age.

44. Meriden *Record*, 17 February 1934.

45. Ibid.

46. Author's interviews of Edith Prilik Sania (July 1977), Myron Ehrlich (July 1977), and Libbie Miller (September 1978).

47. Author's interview of Edith Prilik Sania, July 1977. Mrs. Sania claimed that Rakowska had arranged Ponselle's and Russo's first meeting over dinner in Bosca Chiesa Nova, in northern Italy, where the Serafins and Ponselle had adjoining suites in the same villa.

48. Author's interview of Edith Prilik Sania, July 1977.

49. Author's interview of Libbie Miller, August 1978.

50. Author's interview of Myron Ehrlich, July 1977.

51. Author's interview of Libbie Miller, September 1978.

52. Typewritten transcription of the letter courtesy of the late Libbie Miller, who retained the handwritten original in her personal papers.

53. *The New York Times*, 20 May 1929. Lehmann died in Berlin on 17 May 1929.

54. Ibid.

55. Ibid. See also *Musical Courier*, 25 May 1929.

56. Ida Cook, *We Followed Our Stars* (Ontario: Mills & Boon Limited, 1976), pp. 46–47.

57. Herman Klein, "A 'Norma' Revival," *The Gramophone* (May 1929). Reprinted in William R. Moran, ed., *Herman Klein and the Gramophone* (Portland, Oregon: Amadeus Press, 1989), p. 260.

58. Klein, "The Art of Rosa Ponselle," *The Gramophone* (July 1929). Reprinted in Moran, *Klein*, p. 268.

59. London *Sunday Times*, 2 June 1929.

60. *The New York Times*, 2 June 1929. Similar accounts appeared in *Musical Courier* (8 June 1929) and *Musical America* (July 1929).

61. Letter of Dame Nellie Melba to Mrs. Lawrence Townsend, 26 May 1929. (From the scrapbooks of Rosa Ponselle.)

62. Telegram from Geraldine Farrar to Rosa Ponselle, 30 May 1929.

63. *Musical Courier*, 6 June 1929.

64. Rosenthal, *Two Centuries of Opera at Covent Garden*, pp. 443–45, 778.

65. Ibid., 443—45.

66. *Musical Courier*, 30 May 1931.

67. *Musical Courier*, 13 June 1931.

68. *Musical Courier*, 4 July 1931.

69. London *Daily Telegraph*, 27 June 1931.

70. Author's interview of Rosa Ponselle, June 1975.

71. Frida Leider, *Playing My Part*, trans. Charles Osborne (London: Calder & Bypars, 1966), pp. 117–18.

72. Note from Frida Leider to Rosa Ponselle, 19 June 1931. (Typewritten transcription of the handwritten original courtesy of the late Libbie Miller.)

73. Ponselle confirmed Romani's financial straights in her letter to Eustace Blois of 19 February 1930: "I don't think Romani can come over this year as he lost very heavily in the stock market, although he hopes to save his pennies by then." (Used by permission of the Royal Opera House Archive, Covent Garden.)

74. Klein, "The Italian Season: *La forza del destino* and Other Operas," in *The Gramophone* (July 1929). Reprinted in Moran, *Klein*, p. 326.

75. *Opera News* (April 1977).

76. James A. Drake, "Kipnis Speaks: An Interview with Alexander Kipnis," *The Opera Quarterly* (Summer 1991), p. 90.

77. London *Times*, 14 June 1930.

78. London *Daily News & Chronicle*, 14 June 1930.

79. London *Observer*, 15 June 1930.

80. London *Daily Mail*, 14 June 1930.

81. London *Daily Express*, 14 June 1930.

82. Letter of Rosa Ponselle to Eustace Blois, 19 February 1930. (Used with the permission of the Royal Opera House Archive, Covent Garden.)

83. Ibid.

84. London *Morning Post*, 14 June 1930. Toye also contributed a review of Ponselle's first *Traviata* to the *London Listener's Music* on 15 June. "Indeed as an alliance between first class singing and first class intelligence," he wrote, "I do not think I have ever heard anything to surpass or even equal it."

CHAPTER EIGHT: A No-Come-Back Girl

1. *The New York Times*, 17 January 1931.
2. Ibid.
3. New York *Sun*, 17 January 1931.
4. Ibid.
5. Ibid.
6. New York *World-Telegram*, 17 January 1931.
7. New York *Herald Tribune*, 17 January 1931.
8. *The New York Times*, 17 January 1931.
9. Giacomo Lauri-Volpi, *Voci parallele* (Milano: Aldo Garzanti, 1955), p. 141. (Translation by George Nyklicek.)
10. Ibid., pp. 141–42.
11. Author's interview of Max de Schauensee, 23 January 1977. In a subsequent interview with Hugh M. Johns, de Schauensee reiterated his belief that Ponselle's best singing had been heard in *Don Giovanni*.
12. *The New York Times*, 27 December 1931.
13. Ibid.
14. *The New York Times*, 26 December 1931.
15. Ibid.
16. Though for experimental rather than commercial purposes, a prior attempt to broadcast from the Metropolitan stage had been made in 1910. On 9 January 1910, *The New York Times* reported that a performance "is to be heard by wireless telephony, if the present plans of Lee de Forest and the Metropolitan Opera Company are carried out." The performance, which took place on 13 January, was of *I pagliacci*, with Caruso as Canio. Although the range of transmission was limited to fifty miles, the *Times* reported on 14 January that "the steamship Avon and amateur experimenters at Bridgeport, Connecticut, reported they had picked up the broadcast."

17. *The New York Times*, 1 January 1927.

18. "Financial Statement of Rosa M. Ponselle, Tax Year 1927," prepared and certified by the Fifth Avenue Bank of New York, February 1928. (Courtesy of the late Libbie Miller.) Ponselle's Metropolitan Opera contracts, copies of which are housed in the Metropolitan Opera Archives, were issued (and therefore negotiated) annually from the 1918–19 through the 1923–24 seasons. From 1924 to 1930 she received three-year contracts; from 1927 to 1930 the Metropolitan paid her, on the average, $1,750 per performance. In 1930 she negotiated a four-year agreement specifying a $2,000 per-performance fee, but this agreement was amended in 1932 as a result of a voluntary salary reduction that the Metropolitan sought from its singers. From 1934 to 1937, her contracts were again negotiated annually, and she was paid $1,000 per performance. (The author is grateful to Robert Tuggle, Director of the Metropolitan Opera Archives, for providing this contractual information to James M. Alfonte and to the author.)

19. Carl Dreher, "Rosa Ponselle Before the Microphone," *Radio Broadcast* (April 1928), p. 429.

20. Author's interview of Edith Prilik Sania, July 1977.

21. Author's interview of Libbie Miller, November 1978. Based upon financial records to which the author was given access by Libbie Miller and also by Edith Prilik Sania, this substantial shift in sources of income was evident in Ponselle's tax records from 1927 onward. That year she reported a gross income of $141,404, of which radio and concerts accounted for $85,100. By 1928, she was receiving $3,000 for each radio appearance, and throughout the early 1930s, she continued to average $2,000 per radio program, despite the worsening Depression.

22. *Musical America*, 25 April 1934.

23. André Kostelanetz, *Echoes: Memoirs of André Kostelanetz* (New York: Harcourt Brace Jovanovich, 1980), pp. 72–73.

24. Ibid., p. 77.

25. Kolodin, *The Story of the Metropolitan*, pp. 462–63.

26. Author's interview of Carle A. Jackson, March 1978.

27. Quaintance Eaton, *Opera Caravan* (New York: Farrar, Straus, and Cudahy, 1957), p. 163.

28. The dialogue is reconstructed from news stories in the Baltimore *Sun* and Meriden *Record* of 30 November 1936, and from the author's interview of Carle A. Jackson, March 1978. Jackson's account differed only in one small detail: he recalled his exchange with Huber as having occurred during an intermission, rather than after the performance.

29. Grace Moore, *You're Only Human Once* (New York: Doubleday, Doran & Company, 1944), p. 138.

30. Meriden *Record*, 30 November 1936.

31. On 25 November 1936, *Variety* reported that "Rosa Ponselle, in Baltimore, is peeved over stories she is going to marry Carle A. Jackson, son of the mayor. Good friends of long standing, she explained, but no matrimonial plans."

32. Baltimore *Sun*, 30 November 1936. The version appearing in the Meriden *Record* of the same date indicates that "Miss Ponselle's sister, Carmela . . . broke the news at 'Finlagen,' the Green Spring Valley mansion where the bride-to-be has been staying."

33. Baltimore *Sun*, 14 December 1936.

34. Meriden *Record*, 14 December 1936.

35. A wealthy descendant of an old-line Maryland family, Charles Morton Stewart was one of Baltimore's most influential citizens at that time. His estate, Finlagen, was actually rented in Carle Jackson's name, to avoid questions from the press if Ponselle's name were to appear on the lease. (From the author's interview of Carle A. Jackson, March 1978.)

36. Carle Jackson remembered the event somewhat differently: "Rosa was supposed to go to Hollywood for three or four weeks, and we had already decided to put off talking about marriage until after she got back. When I pulled up in front of the hair salon, she was just going in or maybe coming out. She got in the car and I said, 'Look, we ought to do something one way or the other.' That night, we were supposed to go to a dinner party at the Supper Club in Baltimore. She told somebody at the party that I had just proposed to her. Word spread, and pretty soon somebody stood up to make a toast, and the band started playing the Wedding March. After that night, the news was off the vine." (Author's interview of Carle A. Jackson, March 1978.)

37. Ponselle's *Traviata* was first released in LP form by Smith in his privately sold *Golden Age of Opera* series of opera broadcasts and has been released on CD (Pearl Gemm CD9317, *Rosa Ponselle in* La traviata, and FT1513–14 *The Forties—Opera from America*). The performance has gained something of a cult following over the years. When the Metropolitan Opera released portions of her second-act scene with Tibbett in LP form, critic Will Crutchfield wrote, "Let me put it in this unpoetic way: If all the recordings of this scene were ranked from one to ten, with this one as ten, the very best of the others would be clustered somewhere between four and seven." (*The New York Times*, 13 October 1985.)

38. Ponselle is referring here to Fiorello La Guardia not in his later mayorial capacity, but rather as Gigli's personal attorney.

39. For information about Ponselle's contracts and per-performance fees, see

chap. four, nn. 15 and 16. The Metropolitan management's call for a voluntary salary reduction in 1932, especially the dealings among Gigli, Gatti-Casazza, and the Metropolitan's governing board, is a complex subject that exceeds the scope of this chapter, but is useful to an understanding of the period. For a summary of these dealings, see Kolodin, *The Story of the Metropolitan*, pp. 25–29. Kolodin's treatment of Gigli's refusal to accept the salary cut is drawn chiefly from contemporary newspaper accounts, however. For more authoritative information about Gigli's attempted compromises with the Met soon after he made his decision to leave, see Tuggle, *The Golden Age of Opera*, p. 175.

40. Ponselle seems to have forgotten, at least momentarily, that she had essentially copied her conception of the death scene in *Traviata* from Gemma Bellincioni.

41. Ponselle is referring to the 1951–52 Metropolitan Opera production, directed by Tyrone Guthrie.

42. Carré was married to the lyric soprano Marguerite Giraud, whom he had married, divorced, and remarried during a relationship that had begun nearly three decades earlier at the Opéra Comique.

43. On 6 April 1936 a story about the incident appeared in the Baltimore *Sun*, under the title "Ponselle Has Bone To Pick With Tenor."

44. Originally from Philadelphia, and the daughter of a partner of J. P. Morgan, Eva Roberts Stotesbury had been married to General Douglas MacArthur before she married Lionel Atwill. After their marriage, she and Atwill lived in the Green Spring Valley estate her father had built, called Rainbow Hill, not far from what would eventually become the site of Ponselle's home.

45. Ponselle and Bodanzky continued to work together sporadically until his death on 23 November 1939.

46. Carmela moved to 230 Riverside Drive where she would live for the next four decades.

47. During adolescence Ponselle's nose was accidentally broken by her brother, Tony. Years later she was told by her physician Dr. Verdi that she had a deviated septum, probably owing to the broken nose. Afraid that repairing the septum would somehow alter the timbre of her voice, she refused to have the condition corrected.

48. Among Ponselle's personal papers at Villa Pace was a letter, written by Libbie Miller to the M-G-M New York offices, in which she refers to one, possibly two earlier tests, apparently done in New York City in January or February 1935. From Miss Miller's letter it is clear that Ponselle sang "Carry Me Back To Old Virginny" and "I Carry You in My Pocket" in one test, and Massenet's "Élégie" in the second. Whether these were sound tests or actual screen tests is not discernable from the correspondence. Miss Miller had no

recollection of these tests when a copy of the letter was shared with her in November 1978.

49. A letter from Libbie to Rosa, dated 10 January 1934, suggests that Rosa gave her slightly more latitude at the time than Libbie would remember later. "While you say I should have discussed this with you," Libbie wrote, "I did not do so because the matter came up when you were so upset with Carmela's illness and several other things. I assure you that I shall not accept less than $2,500 unless I feel the engagement is very worthwhile—or else very necessary to break a big jump and of course shall agree to the $2,000 or $2,250 only if I am convinced that they cannot possibly pay the $2,500." To the best of Libbie's recollections, Rosa never performed in either the Endowment Series or the Olin Downes Series because she would not lower her fees. (Copy of the letter courtesy of the late Libbie Miller.)

50. According to the Metropolitan *Annals*, Ponselle sang twenty-nine performances of *Norma*, and fifteen performances of *Carmen*. She sang her last *Norma* on 25 January 1932, one month after the centenary performance at the Metropolitan. (See *Annals*, Tables, p. 178.)

51. The Metropolitan's box-office records bear out the popularity of the *Norma* revival. In the 1927–28 season, box-office revenues from *Norma* averaged $15,650 per performance, whereas the average per-performance gross was $12,809 that season. In 1928–29 *Norma* yielded an average of $14,712 per performance, compared to the season average of $13,812. (The author is grateful to Robert Tuggle, Director of the Metropolitan Opera Archives, for providing access to the original ledgers for the seasons discussed above.)

52. Estimates the author was given of Ponselle's cumulative wealth in the depths of the Depression by Libbie Miller and Edith Prilik Sania varied somewhat, although both agreed that by any measure Ponselle was wealthy. Both women also agreed that she had ridden out the stock-market crash without losing any of her assets, owing to the fact that William Hetzler, president of the Fifth Avenue Bank, who managed her stocks, had urged her to convert her holdings to bonds late in 1928. Edith Prilik Sania estimated Ponselle's worth at four million dollars in 1928–29, and she and Miss Miller independently concurred that Rosa's assets would not have decreased below three million dollars by the mid- to late-1930s. (Author's interviews of Edith Prilik Sania, July 1977, and Libbie Miller, November 1978.)

53. The date of the event, as well as a list of the invitees, was provided to the author by the late Libbie Miller.

54. The notebook Carré compiled, as well as several pages of Ponselle's handwritten synopsis of the libretto, were among her personal papers at Villa Pace when the author examined and copied them in March 1978.

55. Author's interview of Libbie Miller, November 1978.

56. Hugo Vickers, *Loving Garbo* (New York: Random House, 1994), p. 83.

57. Author's interview of Rosa Ponselle, November 1978. Ponselle clarified that she substituted her Santuzza costume for her Act One costume in *Carmen*. In Act Two, she occasionally wore a large Spanish-style shawl as an accent piece with the pleated Flamenco-style dress. The shawl was one of four that soprano Elena Rakowska, Serafin's wife, brought to Ponselle from South America. (Information courtesy of Hugh M. Johns, James M. Alfonte, and Myron Ehrlich.)

58. Author's interview of Rosa Ponselle, October 1977. Many years later, the stole Valentina had designed for the costume was loaned by Ponselle to the Baltimore Opera Company for a *Carmen* production she was coaching. The stole disappeared afterward.

59. Valentina, "Designing for Opera," *Opera News* (10 March 1941), pp. 22–23.

60. Ibid., p. 23.

61. New York *World Telegram*, 28 December 1935.

62. Ibid.

63. Ibid.

64. New York *Evening Post*, 28 December 1935.

65. Brooklyn *Eagle*, 28 December 1935.

66. Ibid.

67. *The New York Times*, 28 December 1935.

68. New York *Daily News*, 28 December 1936. Elsewhere in his review, Walker remarked that in the last act Ponselle "effected a blond wig." But in the act she had donned a gold-colored *recedilla*, or snood, which from the perspective of someone in the audience may have looked like a blond wig. A common accessory among Spanish women, the net-like *recedilla* was an authentic touch Valentina had added to the costume.

69. Hartford *Courant*, 5 January 1936.

70. Note of Geraldine Farrar to Rosa Ponselle, 28 December 1935.

71. New York *World Telegram*, 7 January 1936.

72. *Time* Magazine, 6 January 1936.

73. Ibid.

74. From the Metropolitan Opera box-office ledgers for the 1935–36 and 1936–37 seasons, excluding benefits and Sunday concerts. (The author is grateful to Robert Tuggle for providing access to the original ledgers for the seasons discussed above.)

75. The same content was sent in two telegrams, one to Hollywood in Tibbett's care, dated 30 January 1930, and the other to Evans & Salter in New York, which was dated 1 February 1930.

76. Memorandum from Libbie Miller to Rosa Ponselle, 30 January 1930.

77. Ibid.

78. Author's interview of Libbie Miller, November 1978.

79. Telegram from E. V. Darling to Rosa Ponselle, 31 January 1930.

80. Telegram from Rosa Ponselle to E. V. Darling, 31 January 1930.

81. New Orleans *States*, 25 February 1934.

82. During the controversy over her *Carmen*, the popular women's magazine *Vanity Fair* commissioned Edward Steichen to photograph Ponselle in her fourth-act costume. Steichen's color photograph appeared in a full-page spread in the February 1936 edition of *Vanity Fair*. A full-page black and white photograph of Ponselle in the same costume also appeared in *Vogue*.

83. Letter of Boris Morros to Libbie Miller, 3 June 1936. Reproduced with minor editing for punctuation. (Copy of the letter courtesy of the late Libbie Miller.)

84. Letter of Irving Thalberg to Rosa Ponselle, 3 September 1936.

85. Thomas Schatz, *The Genius of the System* (New York: Pantheon Books, 1988), p. 173.

86. Author's interview of Libbie Miller, November 1978.

87. Ibid.

88. Note from George Cukor to Rosa Ponselle, 25 September 1936. As Ponselle explained in reply on 28 September, however, M-G-M's condensed English version of the Meilhac-Halévy libretto, on which the tentative script was based, omitted the character of Don José!

89. Letter of George Cukor to Rosa Ponselle, 30 September 1936. (Date and summary of the letter courtesy of the late Libbie Miller.)

90. The title card for the test reads: "Screen Test #705. Rosa Ponselle. *Height*: 5' 7". *Weight*: 134. *Eyes*: Light Brown. *Hair*: Black. 13 October 1936."

91. Author's interview of George Cukor, February 1979.

92. Ibid.

93. The November 1936 probable date for the Paramount screen test was inferred by Libbie Miller from her correspondence with Morros.

94. Letter of Boris Morros to Libbie Miller, 29 December 1936. (Copy of the letter courtesy of the late Libbie Miller.)

95. Author's interview of Libbie Miller, November 1978.

96. Author's interviews of Libbie Miller (August 1978, November 1978). In later years, Ponselle said that Paramount still had an interest in her *Carmen* at the time she left the Metropolitan, but there is no known documentation or corroboration from Libbie Miller or others to support her recollection. In some interviews and in informal conversations with various friends, Ponselle also spoke of working with producer Walter Wanger at M-G-M. But Wanger left M-G-M in spring 1934, two years before Ponselle's own association with the studio began. She may have dealt with Wanger, however, as the chief executive of his own independent production company, which he formed (ultimately unsuccessfully) after leaving Metro-Goldwyn-Mayer. There is no known documentation, however, of any dealings between Wanger and her. (See Schatz, *The Genius of the System*, pp. 163–66, for an account of the circumstances of Wanger's departure from M-G-M.)

97. Author's interviews of Edith Prilik Sania (July 1977) and Libbie Miller (August 1978).

98. Kolodin, *The Story of the Metropolitan*, p. 34.

99. Ibid., p. 34.

100. Ibid., p. 37.

101. Quoted in Robert Tuggle, "Clouds of War," *Opera News* (July 1995), p. 14.

102. The author is grateful to Robert Tuggle, Director of the Metropolitan Opera Archives, for providing access to these worksheets.

103. The New York *Evening Post* reported that Ponselle had returned from the funeral only to find that her valuable Persian cat, named Tee-Tee, had leapt to its death from the roof of her penthouse after being chased by two of her dogs. "I am too much upset over the death of Herbert Witherspoon, General Manager of the Metropolitan," Ponselle told the reporter, "to talk about the death of a cat, even if I did love her." (New York *Evening Post*, 14 May 1935.)

104. United Press Syndicate release, 18 May 1935.

105. The contract, now housed in the Metropolitan Opera Archives, specifies the following roles that she agreed to perform: Selika, Fiora, Santuzza, Donna Anna, Gioconda, Violetta, and Carmen. But the terms of the contract clarify that she had only agreed to sing seven performances during this abbreviated season: two of *Cavalleria rusticana* and five drawn from the roles mentioned above. In a subsequent letter, however, the management and she came to an agreement that of the remaining five performances, "there shall be a minimum of two performances of *Carmen*." (Letter from Edward Ziegler to Rosa Ponselle, 4 November 1936.) (The author is grateful to Robert Tuggle, Director of the Metropolitan Opera Archives, for furnish-

ing to James M. Alfonte and to the author copies of the contract and letter of amendment.)

106. Author's interview of Edith Prilik Sania, July 1977.

107. Ibid.

108. Author's interview of Carle A. Jackson, March 1978.

109. Author's interview of Edith Prilik Sania, March 1978. (Mrs. Sania had retained a photocopy of the check as well as Ponselle's note and showed them to the author.)

110. Letter of Edith Prilik to Rosa Ponselle, 3 October 1937. (Access to a copy of the letter courtesy of the late Edith Prilik Sania.)

111. Ibid.

112. Ibid. Interestingly, the check to Rimini (Fifth Avenue Bank, check #A-511, 9 July 1935) was signed "Rosa Ponzillo." But the check to Russo (check #527-A, 30 April 1935) was signed "Rosa Ponselle." (Access to copies of the checks courtesy of the late Edith Prilik Sania.)

113. Author's interview of Libbie Miller, August 1978.

114. Author's interview of Carle A. Jackson, March 1978.

115. Author's interview of Edith Prilik Sania, July 1977.

116. Letter of Mina Horne to Edith Prilik, 23 September 1937. (Copy of the letter courtesy of the late Edith Prilik Sania.)

117. For an account of other dealings between William M. Sullivan and the Metropolitan during Edward Johnson's first years as general manager, see Kolodin, *The Story of the Metropolitan*, p. 33.

118. Letter of William M. Sullivan to Edward Johnson, 14 October 1937. Sullivan's reference to anticipating "word from Baltimore" is puzzling, since Carle was in Hollywood, not Baltimore, during that period. (The author is grateful to Robert Tuggle, Director of the Metropolitan Opera Archives, for providing a copy of this letter.)

119. Letter of Libbie Miller to Carle A. Jackson, 27 October 1937. (Copy of the letter courtesy of the late Libbie Miller.)

120. Letter of Carle A. Jackson to Libbie Miller, 4 November 1937. (Copy of the letter courtesy of the late Libbie Miller.)

121. Ibid.

122. Ponselle cancelled the Endowment Series concert two weeks before the scheduled November 30 date. Rose Bampton agreed to take her place. The announcement of the cancellation and Bampton's substitution appeared in

The New York Times on 15 November 1938, twenty years to the day from Ponselle's debut.

123. Author's interview of Carle A. Jackson, March 1978.

CHAPTER NINE: Some Enchanted Evening

1. Author's interview of Libbie Miller, September 1978.
2. Worcester *Evening Post*, 9 October 1937.
3. Atlanta *Constitution*, 15 October 1937.
4. Columbus *Dispatch*, 13 November 1937.
5. Columbus *Citizen*, 13 November 1937.
6. Charleston *Daily Mail*, 24 November 1937.
7. Letter of E. W. Evenett to Sir Thomas Beecham, 3 August 1937. (Copy of the letter courtesy of the Royal Opera Archives, Covent Garden, used with their permission. The author is grateful to William Ashbrook for obtaining the copy.)
8. Author's interview of Libbie Miller, November 1978.
9. Ibid.
10. Ibid.
11. Discographer Bill Park learned this the hard way. Having discovered Libbie's name during some of his research, Park innocently asked Ponselle who she was, which prompted the reaction quoted here. (Bill Park to the author, May 1995.)
12. Author's interview of Libbie Miller, November 1978.
13. Letter of Rosa Ponselle to Edith Prilik Sania, 6 June 1939. (Copy of the letter courtesy of the late Edith Prilik Sania.)
14. Ibid.
15. Letter of Rosa Ponselle to Edith Prilik Sania, 14 November 1939. (Copy of the letter courtesy of the late Edith Prilik Sania.)
16. Ibid.
17. Ibid.
18. Ibid.
19. Letter of Frederick R. Huber to Edward Ziegler, 31 October 1938. (The author is grateful to Robert Tuggle, Director of the Metropolitan Opera Archives, for providing access to this letter.)

20. Baltimore *Sun*, 31 October 1938.

21. Author's interview of Carle A. Jackson, March 1978.

22. Ibid. According to Carle, who reconstructed his father's words for the author, the senior Jackson put this ultimatum in a letter.

23. From the personal papers of Rosa Ponselle. The closing, conducted by the Piper & Hill Realty Company, took place a week earlier, on Monday, 15 January 1940.

24. Palmer and Lamden Architects, a Baltimore firm, designed the villa and grounds from Rosa's specifications. Consecutive sets of blueprints were housed in Ponselle's personal papers when the author reviewed them in 1978.

25. Author's interview of Carle A. Jackson, March 1978.

26. Alda, in *Men, Women, and Tenors* (Boston: Houghton Mifflin Company, 1937), described Ponselle's Carmen (p. 299) as "a lovely, slim, graceful gypsy," but criticized her for having "pushed [her] voice down" as a result of severe dieting.

27. Ibid.

28. Author's interview of Sonia Parr, February 1978.

29. Ibid.

30. The ceremony to which Ponselle refers took place at Arlington Cemetery on Armistice Day, 11 November 1919. Three other Metropolitan artists—Louise Homer, Morgan Kingston, and Adamo Didur—also had been invited by President Harding to sing sacred selections at the ceremony. (New York *World*, 12 November 1919.)

31. The concert took place aboard the *S.S. Aquitania* on 11 May 1931.

32. The event Ponselle recalled was a dinner commemorating the end of President Roosevelt's third year in office. It was held at the Mayflower Hotel in Washington, D.C., on 4 March 1935.

33. As historians of the Roosevelt presidency have written about extensively, James Farley eventually broke with FDR. Many of Ponselle's long-time friends, including Myron Ehrlich and James M. Alfonte, believed that her closeness to the Farleys led her to distance herself from Roosevelt and the Democratic party he all but defined.

34. After the master tapes of all selections were recorded, Ponselle delegated to Igor Chichagov and James M. Alfonte the responsibility for determining the sequence of the selections for *Rosa Ponselle Sings Today*. Before recording the masters, then, she could not have chosen which songs would follow one another on the published album. (James M. Alfonte to the author, 21 July 1995.)

35. Forty years afterward, Alfonte recalled this incident differently: "Rosa got curious about some recordings I brought to Villa Pace one afternoon. Afterward, she said, 'Bring some interesting lieder the next time.' I thought 'Von ewiger Liebe' would appeal to her because, like the 'Erlkönig,' it required a singer to create different voices. I don't recall that the RCA albums were in the offing then, although that's possible. I certainly don't remember saying 'Rosa, you *must* sing this.' I wouldn't have been so presumptuous. Furthermore, as anyone who knew her would attest, telling Rosa that she 'must' do something usually guaranteed that hell would freeze over first." (James M. Alfonte to the author, 21 July 1995.)

36. Ponselle did two "takes" of the "Erlkönig," James M. Alfonte recalled. "She did one with what I would call a traditional or 'quiet' ending, and another version which she ended with a pronounced gasp after the word *todt*. That gasp was so out of keeping with the way lieder singers do the 'Erlkönig' that I felt it would create problems for her if it was released on the LP. But Rosa kept saying, 'No, that's the way I *feel* it!' She had the last word, so the 'gasp' version was the one that RCA published." (James M. Alfonte to the author, August 1995.)

37. In her interview with Ruby Mercer (1955), from which this excerpt is taken, Ponselle said that she thought Tetrazzini had been the only other woman to have recorded "Bois epais." But she must have been thinking of Tosti's "Aprile" when she made the comment, and her response has been amended accordingly.

38. James M. Alfonte and discographer Bill Park recalled that Ponselle and Chichagov had actually recorded two versions of "The Night Wind" during the same session, each in a different key and with some other variations separating them. (James M. Alfonte and Bill Park to the author, July 1995.)

39. For a detailed history of the land on which Villa Pace was eventually built, see Dawn F. Thomas, *The Green Spring Valley: Its History and Heritage* (Baltimore, Maryland: Maryland Historical Society, 1978), pp. 343–46.

40. Ibid., p. 346. Thomas states that the Jacksons purchased a 155-acre tract, but the deed (a copy of which was located in Ponselle's personal papers at Villa Pace) specified 150 acres for a total price of $60,000, with Rosa and Carle paying $20,000 for their fifty-acre parcel and Raymond S. and Louise M. Clark paying the remaining $40,000 for their hundred-acre share.

41. Thomas, *The Green Spring Valley*, states (p. 346), "The $500,000 house they built was designed by Miss Ponselle and contains seventeen rooms."

42. Author's interview of Sonia Parr, February 1978.

43. Baltimore-Washington area USO performances were well covered by the Baltimore *Sun*, the Washington *Post*, and other newspapers in both cities between 1942 and 1946. Ponselle's recollections were drawn from the author's

interviews of March, August and December 1978. For typical vaudeville billings of the specific performers mentioned, see: *Variety*, 26 September 1915 (Davis Theater, Pittsburgh) for Sophie Tucker; *Variety*, 25 January 1918 (Avenue B Theater, New York City) for Burns; *Variety*, 17 January 1916 (Orpheum Theater, Grand Rapids, Michigan) for Frawley. Jack Pearl's recollections are taken from an interview recorded by Myron Ehrlich, a longtime friend, which Ehrlich played for Ponselle at her eightieth birthday celebration. (Copy of the interview courtesy of Myron Ehrlich.)

44. See p. 000. Goddard, like Ponselle, was dressed by Valentina.

45. Interview of Letitia Bernhardt by Hugh M. Johns (undated).

46. Author's interviews of Edith Prilik Sania (July 1977) and Myron Ehrlich (July 1977).

47. Ibid.

48. Author's interviews of Myron Ehrlich (July 1977) and James M. Alfonte (August 1995).

49. For detailed accounts of filmmaking during World War II, see Robert Sklar, *Movie-Made America: A Cultural History of the Movies* (New York: Vintage Books, 1976); Roy Pickard, *The Hollywood Studios* (London: Frederick Muller, Ltd., 1978); and Ethan Mordden, *The Hollywood Studios* (New York: Alfred Knopf, 1987).

50. Author's interview of Ruth Romani, July 1980.

51. Romani made this remark to James M. Alfonte at Villa Pace in the early 1950s. (James M. Alfonte to the author, June 1995.)

52. Author's interview of Ruth Romani, July 1980.

53. Author's interview of Carle A. Jackson, March 1978.

54. Author's interview of Sonia Parr, February 1978.

55. Author's interview of Carle A. Jackson, March 1978.

56. Ibid. Ida Cook, who visited Ponselle immediately after her stay at Seton Institute, noted in her diary that Rosa had been released on Wednesday, 5 February 1947. (Letter of Ida Cook to the author, 17 August 1978.) She had been hospitalized on Friday, 29 November 1946.

57. Author's interview of Walter E. Afield, M.D., January 1980.

58. Author's interview of Edith Prilik Sania, October 1978.

59. Ibid.

60. Ibid.

61. Author's interview of Sonia Parr, February 1978.

62. Author's interview of Hugh M. Johns, June 1993.

63. Author's interview of Lena Angle, July 1977.

64. Author's interview of Rosa Ponselle, March 1978.

65. Author's interviews of Rosa Ponselle (October 1978) and Antonio P. Ponzillo (July 1977).

66. Author's interviews of Carle A. Jackson (March 1978) and Walter E. Afield, M.D. (September 1979).

67. Author's interview of Sonia Parr, February 1978.

68. Ponselle told this to at least four persons who knew her, all of whom repeated it to the author: Sonia Parr, Myron Ehrlich, Anne O'Donnell, and Hugh M. Johns.

69. Author's interview of Sonia Parr, February 1978.

70. Author's interview of Carle A. Jackson, March 1978. The petition for divorce was filed in the Second Circuit Court of Baltimore on 17 August 1950. In the petition Rosa was named as complainant and Carle as defendant. The decree, which was granted on 27 February 1951, specified that (1) the property settlement agreement that they had signed on 22 April 1949 would become a part of the decree, (2) Carle was to pay Rosa no alimony in exchange for her retaining Villa Pace as her residence, and (3) Rosa was authorized to resume the use of her maiden name.

71. Author's interview of Sonia Parr, February 1978.

72. Author's interview of Anne J. O'Donnell, March 1992.

73. James M. Alfonte to the author, August 1995.

74. Baltimore businessman Gideon Stieff, at whose home the party was held, captured the selections on a home-type wire recorder. The recording was dubbed from wire to audiotape by Lloyd Garrison in the 1950s and was housed at Villa Pace at one point. But the tape reel had disappeared by the mid-1970s when discographer Bill Park began to chronicle Ponselle's known private recordings. (Bill Park to the author, May 1995.)

75. Author's interview of Myron Ehrlich, May 1978.

76. Author's interview of Robert Merrill, November 1985.

77. Author's interview of Leonard Bernstein, November 1985.

78. See chap. one, n. 28.

79. Author's interview of Ida Cook, October 1977.

80. Ida Cook later interpreted Ponselle's remark to refer to the condition of her voice, rather than to the poor reproduction of the recorder. After Rosa made

the remark, Louise Cook purportedly said to her, "There's nothing that a few weeks of practice wouldn't put aright," which led the Cooks to conclude that Louise's comment was the impetus for Ponselle's renewed interest in singing. Charitably, Ponselle went along with their well-meaning interpretation—as did this author, who incorporated it into *Ponselle: A Singer's Life* (pp. 186–87) out of deference to the Cook sisters. But realistically, Ponselle, who had performed at Fannie Hurst's and Constance Hope's parties, and had begun singing with Romani as her accompanist at Villa Pace by then, had no doubts about the condition of her voice in 1949.

81. Little is known about the exact dates or circumstances in which the six selections that Ponselle and Romani recorded in 1949 were made. The consensus among her friends and close associates was that they were made under studio conditions, rather than at Villa Pace. Some believe that they were recorded at the studios of radio station WFBR in Baltimore, which was partly owned by her long-time friend Joe Imbroguglio, who was then music director at WFBR. (Author's interview of Lloyd Garrison, February 1996.)

82. The Capitol offer was made in early August of 1952 when Richard C. Jones, of Capitol's Classical Division, extended the offer in a letter. On 20 August 1952 she replied that "although my schedule precludes the possibility of making records for you at the present, you may be sure that your interest is appreciated."

83. Author's interview of Igor Chichagov, January 1977.

84. Quoted in J. B. Steane, *Voices: Singers & Critics* (Portland, Oregon: Amadeus Press, 1992), p. 141. Chichagov's comment that Ponselle "never sang the same way twice" may have been an accurate description in 1954 when he recorded with her, but as is verified by alternate "takes" of her Victor recordings of the 1920s, this was not characteristic of her performances in the prime of her career.

85. Aida Favia-Artsay, "Flashes of Greatness Present and Past," in *Hobbies Magazine* (June 1955), p. 20.

86. *The Saturday Review*, 30 April 1955.

87. *The Saturday Review*, 30 March 1957.

88. Letter of Nina Morgana Zirato to Bidù Sayão, 15 November 1957. (Access to the letter courtesy of the late William Seward.)

89. Author's interview of Rose Bampton, January 1977.

90. RCA executive Alan Kayes, who had negotiated the LP contract for RCA with Ponselle, subsequently told James M. Alfonte that song-recital albums not only by Ponselle but other well-established singers had not sold well for RCA at that time. The buying public, Kayes reportedly said, seemed to want to buy arias and ensembles rather than collections of songs. (James M. Alfonte to the author, September 1995.)

91. According to documentation in Ponselle's files at Villa Pace, which the author examined in 1978, she and Schang corresponded about the quartet in the summer and autumn of 1955. She agreed to license the use of her name to Columbia Artists Management in October 1955.

92. *Baltimore Opera, 1950–75* (privately published by the Baltimore Opera Company, 1975), Part I (unpaginated).

93. Author's interview of Dr. Leigh Martinet, March 1978.

94. From the author's interviews of Gilda Cruz-Romo (November 1982) and Adriana Maliponte (November 1982). Information concerning Raina Kabaivanska courtesy of the late Ida Cooke; and concerning Carol Neblett, courtesy of Hugh M. Johns.

95. According to the opera company's official history, "Baltimore Opera Company" became its legal name after a change of charter in the 1968–69 season. (*Baltimore Opera, 1950–1975*, Part I [unpaginated]).

96. In the autumn of 1972, Ponselle was hospitalized and received electro-convulsive therapy at the Henry Phipps Psychiatric Clinic in Baltimore. Her illness was summarized by C. Timothy Golumbeck, M.D., in a letter to Ponselle dated 12 June 1979. (Copy of the letter courtesy of Dr. Golumbeck, through Walter E. Afield, M.D.) Both Afield and Golumbeck were critical of what they labeled the "unconventional" therapy and "mysterious" medications used by Dr. Nick Ballich when treating Ponselle for depression.

97. Bruce Burroughs, "Rosa Ponselle," in C. Steven LaRue and Leanda Shrimpton, eds., *International Dictionary of Opera* (London: St. James Press, 1993), Vol. II, p. 1035.

98. Author's interview of Rosa Ponselle, August 1978.

99. Jerome Hines, *Great Singers on Great Singing* (New York: Doubleday and Company, 1982), pp. 250–51.

100. Author's interviews of Hugh M. Johns (August 1982) and Jerome Hines (November 1989).

A Rosa Ponselle Bibliography

BY ANDREW FARKAS

I. Autobiographical Writings

A lifelong preference for the spoken rather than for the written word led Rosa Ponselle to leave behind, during her active career, no known diaries, no unpublished memoirs, not even much handwritten correspondence of a personal nature. In addition to her 1982 autobiography (in which the actual writing, as noted in the preface to this book, was entirely the work of her collaborator), a total of six articles identifying her as author have been located in various periodicals. But according to her secretary Edith Prilik Sania and to her manager Libbie Miller, none involved Ponselle's participation in any direct way and were instead written either by them or by staff members of the periodicals that had solicited and eventually published the articles.

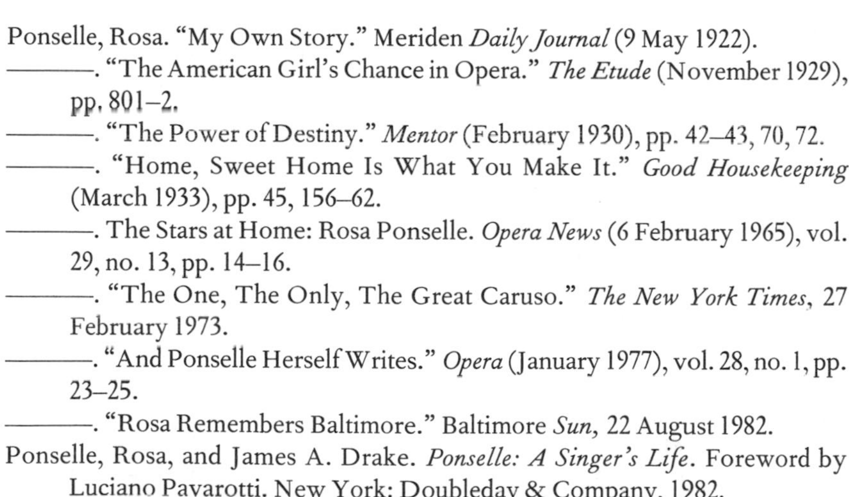

Ponselle, Rosa. "My Own Story." Meriden *Daily Journal* (9 May 1922).

———. "The American Girl's Chance in Opera." *The Etude* (November 1929), pp. 801–2.

———. "The Power of Destiny." *Mentor* (February 1930), pp. 42–43, 70, 72.

———. "Home, Sweet Home Is What You Make It." *Good Housekeeping* (March 1933), pp. 45, 156–62.

———. The Stars at Home: Rosa Ponselle. *Opera News* (6 February 1965), vol. 29, no. 13, pp. 14–16.

———. "The One, The Only, The Great Caruso." *The New York Times*, 27 February 1973.

———. "And Ponselle Herself Writes." *Opera* (January 1977), vol. 28, no. 1, pp. 23–25.

———. "Rosa Remembers Baltimore." Baltimore *Sun*, 22 August 1982.

Ponselle, Rosa, and James A. Drake. *Ponselle: A Singer's Life*. Foreword by Luciano Pavarotti. New York: Doubleday & Company, 1982.

II. Monographs Concerning Rosa Ponselle

Because of both the artistic stature she achieved and the public acclaim she was accorded during her career, Ponselle is often referred to in the biographies and autobiographies of her contemporaries and is also discussed (at varying lengths) in most surveys and histories of opera that deal topically with artists and performances heard during the first half of this century.

Alda, Frances. *Men, Women, and Tenors*. Boston: Houghton Mifflin Company, 1937.

Aldrich, Richard. *Concert Life in New York, 1902–1923*. New York: G. P. Putnam's Sons, 1941.

Aloi, Enrico. *My Remembrances of Rosa Ponselle*. New York: Vantage Press, 1994.

Armitage, Merle. *Accent on America*. New York: E. Weyhe, 1944.

Armstrong, William. *The Romantic World of Music*. New York: E. P. Dutton Company, 1922.

Baltimore Opera: 1950–1975. Baltimore: Baltimore Opera Company, 1976.

Block, Adrienne Fried, and Carol Neuls-Bates, eds. *Women in American Music*. Westport, Connecticut: Greenwood Press, 1979.

Blyth, Alan, ed. *Opera on Record*. London: Hutchinson of London, 1979.

Briggs, John. *Requiem for a Yellow Brick Brewery*. Boston: Little, Brown, and Company, 1969.

Celletti, Rodolfo. *Le grandi voci*. Rome: Istituto per La Collaborazione Culturale, 1964.

Christiansen, Rupert. *Prima Donna: A History*. New York: Viking Press, 1987.

Cook, Ida [Mary Burchell, pseud.). *We Followed Our Stars*. Toronto: Harlequin—Mills & Boon, 1976.

Davenport, Marcia. *Too Strong for Fantasy*. New York: Scribner, 1967.

Davidson, Gladys. *Opera Biographies*. London: W. Laurie, 1955.

Douglas, Nigel. *Legendary Voices*. London: André Deutsch Ltd., 1992.

Downes, Olin. *Olin Downes on Music: A Selection from His Writings During the Half-Century 1906 to 1955*. Edited by Irene Downes. Preface by Howard Taubman. New York: Simon and Schuster, 1957.

Eby, Gordon M. *From the Beauty of Embers: A Musical Aftermath*. New York: Speller, 1981.

Ewen, David. *Living Musicians*. New York: H. W. Wilson, 1940.

———. *Musicians Since 1900: Performers in Concert and Opera*. New York: H. W. Wilson Company, 1978.

Farrar, Geraldine. *Such Sweet Compulsion: The Autobiography of Geraldine Farrar*. New York: The Greystone Press, 1938.

Fitzgerald, Gerald. *Annals of the Metropolitan Opera: Chronology 1883–1985*. Boston: The Metropolitan Opera Guild/G. K. Hall, 1989. 2 vols.

Gatti-Casazza, Giulio. *Memories of the Opera*. New York: Charles Scribner's Sons, 1941.

Gigli, Beniamino. *Memoirs*. Translated by Darina Silone. London: Cassell, 1957.

Harvith, John, and Susan Edwards Harvith, eds. *Edison, Musicians, and the Phonograph: A Century in Retrospect*. New York: Greenwood Press, 1986.

Henderson, William James. *The Art of Singing*. Introduction by Oscar Thompson. New York: The Dial Press, 1938.

Heylbut, Rose, and Aimé Gerber. *Backstage at the Opera*. New York: Thomas Y. Crowell, 1937.

Hines, Jerome. *Great Singers on Great Singing*. New York: Doubleday & Company, 1982.

Homer, Anne. *Louise Homer and the Golden Age of Opera*. New York: W. Morrow, 1973.

Jackson, Paul. *Saturday Afternoons at the Old Met*. Portland: Amadeus Press, 1992.

Kesting, Jürgen. *Die grossen Sänger*. Düsseldorf: Claassen, 1986. 3 vols.

Klein, Herman. *Herman Klein and The Gramophone*. Portland, Amadeus Press, 1990.

Kolodin, Irving. *The Metropolitan Opera, 1883–1966: A Candid History*. New York: Alfred Knopf, 1968.

———. *The Story of the Metropolitan Opera, 1883–1950*. New York: Alfred A. Knopf, 1953.

Kostelanetz, André, and Gloria Hammond. *Echoes: Memoirs of André Kostelanetz*. New York: Harcourt Brace Jovanovich, 1981.

Lauri-Volpi, Giacomo. *Voci parallele*. Milan: Garzanti, 1955.

Lawrence, Robert. *The World of Opera*. New York: T. Nelson, 1956.

Leider, Frida. *Playing My Part*. London: Calder & Boyars, 1966.

Marafioti, Pasqual Mario. *Caruso's Method of Voice Production: The Scientific Culture of the Voice*. Preface by Victor Maurel. New York: D. Appleton, 1922.

Martens, Frederick H. *The Art of the Prima Donna and Concert Singer*. New York: D. Appleton and Company, 1923.

Mercer, Ruby. *The Tenor of His Time: Edward Johnson of the Met*. Vancouver: Clarke, Irwin, 1976.

Mesta, Perle. *My Story*. New York: McGraw-Hill Book Company, 1960.

Moore, Grace. *You're Only Human Once*. New York: Doubleday, Doran & Company, 1944.

Natan, Alex. *Primadonna: Lob der Stimmen*. Basel: Basilius Presse, 1962.

Noble, Helen. *Life with the Metropolitan*. New York: G. B. Putnam's Sons, 1954.

Null, Gary, and Carl Stone. *The Italian-Americans*. Harrisburg, Pennsylvania: Stackpole Books, 1976.

Pahlen, Kurt. *Great Singers From the Seventeenth Century to the Present Day*. Translated by Oliver Coburn. New York: Stein and Day, 1974.

Patrón Marchand, Miguel. *100 grandes cantantes del pasado*. Santiago: Andrès Bello, 1990.

Pelletier, Wilfrid. *Une symphonie inachevée* . . . Ottawa: Leméac, 1972.

Pleasants, Henry. *The Great Singers: From Jenny Lind and Caruso to Callas and Pavarotti*. New York: Simon and Schuster, 1981.

Rosenthal, Harold. *Two Centuries of Opera at Covent Garden*. Foreword by the Earl of Harewood. London: Putnam, 1958.

Schonberg, Harold C. *The Great Ones*. New York: Times Books, 1985.

Scott, Michael. *The Record of Singing: Volume Two, 1914–1925*. London: Duckworth & Company, 1977.

Shaman, William, William J. Collins, and Calvin M. Goodwin. *EJS: Discography of the Edward J. Smith Recordings: "The Golden Age of Opera," 1956–1971.* Westport: Greenwood Press, 1994.

Sheean, Vincent. *First and Last Love.* New York: Random House, 1956.

Spitzer, Marion. *The Palace.* New York: Atheneum, 1969.

Steane, John B. *The Grand Tradition: Seventy Years of Singing on Record.* London: Gerald Duckworth & Company, 1974. 2d ed., Portland, Oregon: Amadeus Press, 1993.

———. *Voices: Singers & Critics.* Portland, Oregon: Amadeus Press, 1992.

Taubman, H. Howard. *Opera Front and Back.* New York, Charles Scribner's Sons, 1938.

Thomas, Dawn F. *The Green Spring Valley: Its History and Heritage.* Baltimore: Maryland Historical Society, 1978.

Thompson, Oscar. *The American Singer.* New York: The Dial Press, 1937.

Tuggle, Robert. *The Golden Age of Opera.* Foreword by Anthony A. Bliss. New York: Holt, Rinehart, and Winston, 1983.

Valenti Ferro, Enzo. *Las voces: Teatro Colón, 1908–1982.* Buenos Aires: Arte Gaglianone, 1983.

III. Selected Periodicals and Newspaper Features

Especially during the 1920s, Ponselle's name was frequently seen in newspaper columns and in commercial as well as professional periodicals. The list below centers on feature articles that illumine various incidents and aspects of her professional career and, in some cases, her personal life as well.

Alfonte, James M. "Opera Sub Rosa." *Opera News* (28 March 1955), vol. 19, no. 21, pp. 12–13.

———. "Ponselle on LP." *Opera News* (1 December 1962), vol. 27, no. 4, p. 36.

———. "Three Heroines for Ponselle." *Opera News* (24 December 1956), pp. 26–27.

Ardoin, John. "Dramatic Soprano's Death Severs Link to Operatic Past." Dallas *Morning News,* 31 May 1981.

———. "A Footnote to Ponselle's *Norma. Opera* (March 1976), vol. 27, no. 3, pp. 225–28.

———. "A Happy Birthday to Rosa Ponselle." Dallas *Morning News,* 8 February 1972.

———. "Metropolitan Salutes Soprano Rosa Ponselle. Dallas *Morning News,* 11 February 1979.

"Baltimore Opera Tribute to Rosa Ponselle." *Pan Pipes,* vol. 69, no. 4, 1977, p. 15.

"Baltimore: Rosa Ponselle Honoured on Her 75th Birthday." *Opera* (March 1972), vol. 23, no. 3, p. 218.

"Baltimore's Blessing." *Opera News* (26 December 1964), vol. 29, no. 7, p. 31.

Bologna, Sando. "Triumphs and Heartaches of a Diva." Waterbury *Sunday Republican*, 17 October 1982.
"Carmela Ponselle—The Comeback of a Star of the Metropolitan." *Musician* (February 1943), pp. 27, 31.
"Carmela Ponselle To Tour the East." *Musical Courier*, 12 September 1931.
"A Chat with a Great Artist of Yesteryear." *Opera, Concert, and Symphony* (May 1946), pp. 22–23, 25.
Cook, Ida (Mary Burchell, pseud.). "Ponselle's London Debut." *Opera* (January 1977), vol. 28, no. 1, pp. 21–23.
———. "Rosa Ponselle." *Opera* (February 1952), vol. 3, no. 2, pp. 75–81.
———. "Rosa Ponselle: A Memoir." *Opera* (1981), vol. 32, no. 8, pp. 798–801.
Crutchfield, Will. "A Century of Operatic Glories Pours Forth." *The New York Times*, 13 October 1985.
de Schauensee, Max. "The Art of Rosa Ponselle." *High Fidelity* (December 1957), vol. 7, no. 12, p. 90.
———. "Caruso in Petticoats," *Opera* (January 1977), vol. 28, no. 1, pp. 19–20.
———. "Rosa Ponselle: January 22, 1897–May 25, 1981." *Opera News* (1981), vol. 46, no. 1, p. 22.
Drake, James A. "Carmela Ponselle Legacy." Meriden *Morning Record and Journal*, 16 July 1977.
———. "Ponselle Sisters Triumphed at the Met." Meriden *Morning Record and Journal*, 22 January 1977.
———. "The 'Real' Voice of Caruso?" *High Fidelity* (October 1976), pp. 86–90.
———. "Rosa." Baltimore *Sunday Sun*, 21 January 1979.
———. "Rosa Ponselle." *Italian Americana* (Spring/Summer 1979), pp. 178–95.
———. "Rosa Ponselle Recalls Roles and Colleagues." *Opera Quarterly*, vol. 10, no. 1, [Autumn] 1993, pp. 85–108.
———. "Rosa Ponselle Reminisces." *High Fidelity* (April 1977), pp. 75–78.
———. "The Seasons Abroad." *Opera Quarterly*, vol. 10, no. 4, [Summer] 1994, pp. 73–90.
Dreher, Carl. "Rosa Ponselle Before the Microphone." *Radio Broadcast* (April 1928), pp. 429–30.
Dyer, Richard. "A Lively Recording of an Opera Singer's Life." Boston *Globe*, 23 November 1982.
Emmons, Shirlee. "Rosa Ponselle." *Bulletin of the National Academy of Teachers of Singing* (November–December 1984), pp. 41–47.
Fassett, Stephen. "Ponselle Discoveries." *Hobbies* (19 June 1951).
Favia-Artsay, Aida. "The Art of Rosa Ponselle." *Hobbies* (March 1958), pp. 26.
———. "Flashes of Greatness Present and Past." *Hobbies* (June 1955), pp. 20–21.
———. "Grace Notes." *Hobbies* (November 1957), pp. 30–32.
———. "Open House with Rosa Ponselle." *Hobbies* (August 1954), pp. 23–24.
———. "Ponselle 'By Request.'" *Hobbies* (7 August 1959), pp. 26–27.
———. "Rosa Ponselle." *Hobbies* (October 1952), pp. 21–23.
Forbes, Marie. "A Diva's Legacy: Rosa Ponselle's Villa Pace Is Now a Bustling Museum." *Opera News* (1983), vol. 48, no. 1, pp. 32–33.

———. "Risen From the Ashes: The Spirit of Rosa Ponselle Lives On in the Restored Villa Pace." Baltimore *Sun,* 22 August 1982.

Gilman, Lawrence. "Farewell for Gatti-Casazza." New York *Herald Tribune,* 23 March 1935.

Hamilton, David. "Five Metropolitan Opera Stars, 1918–66 (Odyssey reissues)." *High Fidelity/Musical America* (July 1972), vol. 22, no. 7, pp. 68–70.

———. "The Ponselle Miracle." *High Fidelity* (September 1970), vol. 20, no. 9, pp. 81–82.

Henderson, William James. "Female Song Birds Duly Noted." *American Record Guide* (May 1959), p. 569 ff. (Reprinted from *Singing,* February 1926.)

———. "Miss Ponselle and Violetta." New York *Sun,* 24 January 1931.

Hendricks, Theodore W. "Court Order Stops Ponselle Sale." Baltimore *Sun,* 30 October 1980.

Hiller, C. "Zum Tode von Rosa Ponselle." *Opernwelt* (July 1981), vol. 22, no. 7, p. 10.

Höslinger, C., and R. Teuchtler. "Primadonna des Jahrhunderts; ein Hinweis auf Rosa Ponselle." *Opernwelt* (September 1967), no. 9, pp. 39–41.

Hume, Paul. "Remembering Rosa Ponselle." Washington *Post,* 27 May 1981.

———. "Rosa Ponselle of Villa Pace." *Saturday Review* (25 July 1953), vol. 36, no. 30, pp. 39–43.

Jacobson, Robert. "Viewpoint: Rosa Ponselle." *Opera News* (1981), vol. 46, no. 1, p. 6.

Jellinek, George. "The Ponselle Legacy: A Survey of Her Incomparable Recordings." *Opera News* (12 March 1977), p. 30.

Kanski, J. "Rosa Ponselle 1897–1981." *Ruch Muzyczny* (1981), vol. 25, no. 19, pp. 10–11.

Katz, Ivan. "Connecticut's Gift to the Opera World." New Haven *Register,* 3 October 1982.

Kearse, David. "Rosa Ponselle at 80 Feted by Opera Stars." Baltimore *Sunday Sun,* 23 January 1977.

Knerr, R. M. "Rosa Ponselle Makes a Record—and a Few Remarks." *Musical America* (15 July 1922), p. 15.

Lauri-Volpi, Giacomo. "Giacomo Lauri-Volpi Writes." *Opera* (January 1977), vol. 28, no. 1, pp. 23.

Legge, Walter. "La Prima Donna Assoluta." *Opera* (January 1977), vol. 28, no. 1, pp. 13–19.

———. "Rosa: An Eightieth Birthday Homage." *Opera News* (12 March 1977), pp. 10–15.

Low, Stuart. "Ponselle and Her Career of 'Truly Operatic Sweep.'" Baltimore *Sun,* 3 October 1982.

Maguire, Jan. "Callas, Serafin, and the Art of Bel Canto." *Stereo Review* (30 March 1968), pp. 47–49.

Mercer, Ruby. "Rosa Ponselle Reigns Supreme." *Opera Canada,* vol. 10, no. 4, 1969, pp. 18–19.

Miller, Philip L. "The Incomparable Ponselle." *American Record Guide* (June 1979), p. 45.

Mooney, Elizabeth C. "Visiting a Divine Diva's Delightful Digs." Washington *Post*, 31 August 1984.

Newman, Edwin. "In Her Glory." *Opera News* (22 December 1990), pp. 11–14.

Obituaries. *Gramophone* (July 1981), vol. 59, no. 698, p. 123.

Osborne, Conrad L. "A Plain Case for the Golden Age." *High Fidelity* (October 1967).

———. "Rosa Ponselle: A Singer's Life." *High Fidelity* (September 1983).

Pasatieri, Thomas. "From the Villa Pace: Rosa Ponselle Tells Her Story to Thomas Pasatieri." *Opera News* (12 March 1977), pp. 16–18.

Pavarotti, Luciano. "Pavarotti Remembers Ponselle." Baltimore *Sunday Sun*, 22 August 1982.

Peel, Tom. "Rosa Ponselle." *The Record Collector*, vol. 36, no. 3, (July, August, September 1991), pp. 218–19.

Robinson, Francis. "Rosa Ponselle: A Grand Tradition." *Musical America* (April 1963), p. 14.

"Rosa Ponselle." *Newsweek* (8 June 1981), p. 83.

"Rosa Ponselle." *Time* (8 June 1981), p. 75.

Rosa Ponselle Foundation. "Rosa Ponselle Foundation Changes Direction." *Opera* (February 1988), vol. 39, no. 2, pp. 161–62.

"Rosa Ponselle: They Stand Out From the Crowd." *The Literary Digest* (22 July 1933), p. 9.

Schonberg, Harold C. "Are These the All-Time Great Voices?" *The New York Times*, 16 October 1983.

———. "Memories of a Baritone Who Set Records at the Met." *The New York Times*, 6 November 1977.

———. "There Was Nothing Like the Ponselle Sound, Ever." *The New York Times*, 23 January 1972.

Secrist, J. B. "Rosa Ponselle." *The Record Collector* (December 1950), p. 288.

———. "Rosa Ponselle: Biography and Discography." In *The Record Collector* (May 1950), pp. 104–17.

Sills, Beverly. "Studying with Garden and Ponselle." *Opera* (March 1988), vol. 39, no. 3, pp. 270–75.

"Singers on Marriage and Mates: Lawrence Tibbett and Rosa Ponselle." Press Release: NEA Service, 8 February 1927.

Smith, Vernon L. (photographer). "The Stars at Home: Rosa Ponselle." *Opera News* (6 February 1965), pp. 14–16.

Sternberg, Gertrude. "Rosa on Rosa." Meriden *Morning Record and Journal*, 15 October 1982.

Stevens, Elisabeth. "Ponselle's Opera Memories Echo at Villa Pace." Baltimore *Sunday Sun*, 26 September 1982.

Suleyman, M. "Rosa Ponselle." *Opernwelt* (Yearbook 1978), pp. 6–14.

Tehan, Arline B. "Native Diva Sings a Song of Herself." Hartford *Courant*, 7 November 1982.

Valentina. "Designing for Opera." *Opera News* (10 March 1941), pp. 22–25.

Villella, Tom. "The Incomparable Ponselle." *Le Grand Baton* (September 1975), pp. 29–41.

———. "An Interview with Rosa Ponselle." *Le Grand Baton* (undated), pp. 25–32.

———. "The Story of Ponselle's Premature Retirement." *Le Grand Baton* (undated), p. 3.

Weidensaul, Jane Bennett. "Alberto Salvi: His Family, His Concert Career." *Journal of the American Harp* (Summer 1980), pp. 6–9.

Wright, A. "American Artists at Covent Garden." *Opera News* (6 April 1953), vol. 17, no. 23, p. 7.

IV. Microformat Materials

Rosa Ponselle: a collection of 17 scrapbooks, news clippings, photographs, 1911–December 1935. Microfilm. Bethlehem, Pennsylvania, Mid-Atlantic Preservation Service, 1990. 6 microfilm reels; 35 mm.

A Chronology of Ponselle's Appearances

BY THOMAS G. KAUFMAN

This chronology has afforded a special opportunity and special challenges. The special opportunity was a simple one: because most of Rosa Ponselle's operatic appearances were well-documented, a complete, day-by-day listing of them can be provided.

Concerts played a substantial part in Ponselle's career, which creates special problems for the researcher. Had it not been for the welcome assistance of any number of people, but especially of the author and also of Richard Miller of Brooklyn, this listing of concerts would have been a skeleton of what it now is. Unfortunately, however, it is still far from complete. Verifying known concert dates would have been only one facet of the challenge involved in creating an exhaustive listing. Attempting to locate any possible additional cities where Ponselle's manager may have scheduled concerts would have been an extended exercise in trial and error.

As I have done in other chronologies of singers' careers, I have arranged this one by season rather than by year. Full casts, which are available in the *Annals of the Metropolitan Opera*, are not listed here; to provide them would make this listing unwieldy and overlong. However, when major singers occasionally sang minor roles in one of these casts, their names are included because it was felt that the interest would be sufficient to justify it. In all cases, every singer is identified as to vocal register, using the following symbols:

s.	soprano
ms.	mezzo-soprano or contralto
t.	tenor
b.	baritone
bs.	bass
cond.	conductor

World premieres are indicated with two asterisks (**), while local premieres (where known) are designated by one asterisk (*). Matinee performances are signified by an M next to the date.

A few words are in order about the language in which Ponselle's performances were given. In some cases, earlier French operas such as *L'africaine* and *La Vestale* were customarily performed in Italian. Later French works, such as *Carmen*, were usually given in French. A notable exception among earlier operas is *La Juive*, for which the French version was used at the Metropolitan during Ponselle's tenure. In the case of *Don Carlo*, the four-act version, which was given to an Italian text, was heard in that language during Ponselle's Metropolitan career. The Meyerbeer and Verdi works, however, were performed in Italian; therefore, it would have been misleading to list them by their French titles in these pages. *William Tell* was also performed in Italian but is referred to by its English title in the chronology in order to be consistent with the text.

ACKNOWLEDGMENTS

As is always the case with such an undertaking, this chronology would not have been possible without the assistance of many persons. Most prominent among them are: the author, James A. Drake, for providing information about Ponselle's vaudeville career and a number of her concerts; Robert Tuggle of the Metropolitan Opera Archives for providing access to concert dates that had been gathered by the late Charles Jahant; Charles B. Mintzer for sharing his encyclopedic knowledge of concert life in the United States between the world wars; and Richard Miller for spending many days at the Lincoln Center Library searching their archives for these concert dates.

Thanks are also due to James M. Alfonte for providing the concert dates at the end of Ponselle's career; to Jack Belsom of New Orleans for some key dates in that city; to George Dansker of that same city; to Andrew Farkas, to Lloyd Garrison for checking the text; to Hugh M. Johns, also, for proofreading the text; to Lim Lai; to Francois Nouvion; and to Elisabeth Schaaf of the Peabody Institute. Equally important are the invaluable contributions of Janet Bone, Ruth Schultz, and Susan Rowe, of the Morris County Free Library, who helped me locate the numerous newspapers needed to reconcile the minor discrepancies between the various listings of the concert dates I had been given.

I also want to express my sincere thanks to the staffs of the following institutions and, at the same time, to apologize to anyone whom I may inadvertently omit: The Ball State University Library, The Music and Newspaper Divisions of the Library of Congress, The Music Division of the Library of the Performing Arts, The Princeton University Library, The Rutgers University Library, The University of Illinois Library, The University of Minnesota Library, The University of North Carolina Library, The University of Missouri Library.

Finally, I am indebted to my wife, Marion, without whose patience, support, and encouragement this listing would not have been possible.

Opera and Concert Appearances

AUTUMN, WINTER, AND SPRING 1915–16 VAUDEVILLE TOUR

The Ponzillo Sisters performed in: New York City (Royal Theater: Sept. 13–18); Paterson, N.J. (Majestic Theater: Sep. 27–Oct. 2); Allentown, Pa. (Orpheum Theater: Oct. 4–9); Altoona, Pa. (Orpheum Theater: Oct. 18–23); New Haven, Conn. (Poli's Theater: Nov. 22–27); Philadelphia (William Penn Theater: Dec. 6–11); Bridgeport, Conn. (Poli's Theater: Dec. 20–24 and Jan. 10–15); Baltimore (Maryland Theater: Mar. 20–25); Brooklyn (Flatbush Theater: Apr. 4–9); Philadelphia (Grand Theater: Apr. 24–29); Baltimore (Maryland Theater: May 1–6); New York City (Colonial Theater: May 8–13); Atlanta (Forsythe Theater: May 16–21) and New York City (Colonial Theater: June 5–10).

AUTUMN, WINTER, AND SPRING 1916–17 VAUDEVILLE TOUR

The Ponzillo Sisters performed in: Brooklyn (Bushwick Theater: Sep. 4–9 and Orpheum Theater: Oct. 2–7); Allentown (Orpheum Theater: Oct. 16–21); Atlantic City (Keith's Theater: Nov. 6–11); Cleveland (Keith's Theater: Nov. 20–25); Buffalo (Shea's Theater: Dec. 4–9); New Haven (Poli's Theater: Jan. 29–Feb. 3); Providence (Keith's Theater: Mar. 26–31); Montreal (Orpheum Theater: Apr. 2–7); Hamilton, Ont. (Temple Theater: Apr. 9–14); Chicago (Majestic Theater: Apr. 16–21); Milwaukee (Majestic Theater: May 7–12); Grand Rapids (Empress Theater: May 14–19); Detroit (Temple Theater: May 21–26); Youngstown (Hip Theater: May 25–30).

AUTUMN, WINTER, AND SPRING 1917–18 VAUDEVILLE TOUR

The Ponzillo Sisters performed in: New York City (Riverside Theater: Sep. 3–8); Brooklyn (Orpheum Theater: Oct. 15–20); New York City (Palace Theater: Oct. 29–Nov. 3, Century Theater: Nov. 26, Winter Garden Theater: Jan. 6, Royal Theater: Mar. 18–23, Alhambra Theater: Apr. 1–6, and Colonial Theater: Apr. 8–13).

AUTUMN 1918 NEW YORK CITY—METROPOLITAN OPERA

Nov. 15	*La forza del destino*	A. Gentle ms. E. Caruso t. G. de Luca b. T. Chalmers b. J. Mardones bs. G. Papi cond.
Nov. 28	*La forza del destino*	A. Gentle ms. E. Caruso t. G. de Luca b. T. Chalmers b. J. Mardones bs. G. Papi cond.

AUTUMN 1918 PHILADELPHIA—ACADEMY OF MUSIC

Dec. 10	*Cavalleria rusticana*	S. Braslau ms. P. Althouse t. M. Laurenti b. G. Papi cond.

WINTER 1918–19 NEW YORK CITY—METROPOLITAN OPERA

Dec. 21	*La forza del destino*	S. Braslau ms. E. Caruso t. G. de Luca b. T. Chalmers b. J. Mardones bs. G. Papi cond.
Dec. 28	*Oberon*	A. Gentle ms. G. Martinelli t. P. Althouse t. A. Reiss b. A. Bodanzky cond.

WINTER 1919 NEW YORK CITY—CARNEGIE HALL

Jan. 2	Concert	

WINTER 1919 NEW YORK CITY—METROPOLITAN OPERA

Jan. 4	*La forza del destino*	A. Gentle ms. E. Caruso t. G. de Luca b. T. Chalmers b. J. Mardones bs. G. Papi cond.
Jan. 9	*Oberon*	A. Gentle ms. G. Martinelli t. P. Althouse t. A. Reiss b. A. Bodanzky cond.
Jan. 17	*Oberon*	A. Gentle ms. G. Martinelli t. P. Althouse t. A. Reiss b. A. Bodanzky cond.
Jan. 27	*La forza del destino*	A. Gentle ms. E. Caruso t. G. de Luca b. T. Chalmers b. J. Mardones bs. G. Papi cond.
Jan. 29	*Oberon*	K. Howard ms. G. Martinelli t. P. Althouse t. A. Reiss b. A. Bodanzky cond.
Feb. 5	*La forza del destino*	S. Braslau ms. E. Caruso t. L. Montesanto b. T. Chalmers b. J. Mardones bs. G. Papi cond.

WINTER 1919 MERIDEN, CONN.—POLI'S THEATER

Feb. 7	Concert	

WINTER 1919 NEW YORK CITY—METROPOLITAN OPERA

Feb. 9	Concert	
Feb. 23	Concert	

WINTER 1919 BROOKLYN—ACADEMY OF MUSIC

Mar. 8	*La forza del destino*	A. Gentle ms. E. Caruso t. L. Montesanto b. T. Chalmers b. J. Mardones bs. G. Papi cond.

SPRING 1919 NEW YORK CITY—METROPOLITAN OPERA

Mar. 12	*The Legend***	K. Howard ms. P. Althouse t. L. d'Angelo bs. R. Moranzoni cond.
Mar. 20	*The Legend*	K. Howard ms. P. Althouse t. L. d'Angelo bs. R. Moranzoni cond.
Mar. 24	*Oberon*	K. Howard ms. G. Martinelli t. P. Althouse t. A. Reiss b. A. Bodanzky cond.

WINTER 1919 PHILADELPHIA—ACADEMY OF MUSIC

Mar. 25	*La forza del destino*	R. Delaunois ms. E. Caruso t. G. de Luca b. T. Chalmers b. J. Mardones bs. G. Papi cond.

SPRING 1919 NEW YORK CITY—METROPOLITAN OPERA

Apr. 3	Gala Concert	

Apr. 4	*The Legend*	K. Howard ms. P. Althouse t. L. d'Angelo bs. R. Moranzoni cond.
Apr. 6	*Messa di Requiem*	M. Matzenauer ms. C. Hackett t. J. Mardones bs. G. Setti cond.
Apr. 12	*Oberon*	K. Howard ms. G. Martinelli t. P. Althouse t. A. Reiss b. A. Bodanzky cond.

SPRING 1919 ATLANTA—AUDITORIUM

Apr. 21	*La forza del destino*	R. Delaunois ms. E. Caruso t. G. de Luca b. P. Malatesta bs. J. Mardones bs. G. Papi cond.
Apr. 26	*Cavalleria rusticana*	R. Delaunois ms. P. Althouse t. T. Chalmers b. R. Moranzoni cond.

SPRING 1919 CONCERT TOUR

Ponselle was accompanied for the first three concerts by Riccardo Stracciari and was later joined by Carmela Ponselle. Cities visited include: Richmond (Apr. 29); Norfolk (May 2); Charlotte (May 3); Macon (May 5); Ann Arbor (May 14); Springfield, Mass. (May 17); Meriden, Conn. (May 22); and Evanston, Ill. (June 6).

SUMMER 1919 NEW YORK CITY—LEWISOHN STADIUM

June 30	Concert
Aug. 28	Concert

SUMMER 1919 NEW YORK CITY—CENTRAL PARK MALL

Sep. 10	Concert

AUTUMN 1919 NEW YORK CITY—MADISON SQUARE GARDEN

Sep. 28	*Cavalleria rusticana*	F. De Gregorio t. M. Valle b.

AUTUMN 1919 CONCERT TOUR

Ponselle was accompanied for at least a part of the tour by Riccardo Stracciari. Cities visited include: Detroit (Oct. 7); Chicago (with Stracciari: Oct. 9); St. Louis (Oct. 11); Pittsburgh (Oct. 14); and Portsmouth, Va.

AUTUMN AND WINTER 1919–20 NEW YORK CITY—METROPOLITAN OPERA

Oct. 25	Gala Concert	
Nov. 22M	*La Juive*	E. Scotney s. E. Caruso t. O. Harrold t. L. Rothier bs. A. Bodanzky cond.
Nov. 28	*La forza del destino*	R. Delaunois ms. E. Caruso t. P. Amato b. T. Chalmers b. J. Mardones bs. G. Papi cond.
Dec. 1	*Oberon*	J. Gordon ms. G. Martinelli t. R. Diaz t. O. Dua b. A. Bodanzky cond.

Dec. 4	*La Juive*	E. Scotney s. E. Caruso t. O. Harrold t. L. Rothier bs. A. Bodanzky cond.
Dec. 15	*La Juive*	E. Scotney s. E. Caruso t. O. Harrold t. L. Rothier bs. A. Bodanzky cond.
Dec. 24	*Oberon*	J. Gordon ms. G. Martinelli t. R. Diaz t. O. Dua b. A. Bodanzky cond.
Dec. 31	*La forza del destino*	J. Gordon ms. E. Caruso t. P. Amato b. T. Chalmers b. J. Mardones bs. G. Papi cond.
Jan. 4	*Stabat Mater*	G. Besanzoni ms. C. Hackett t. J. Mardones bs. G. Setti cond.

WINTER 1920 PHILADELPHIA—ACADEMY OF MUSIC

Jan. 6	*La Juive*	E. Scotney s. E. Caruso t. O. Harrold t. J. Mardones bs. A. Bodanzky cond.

WINTER 1920 NEW YORK CITY—METROPOLITAN OPERA

Jan. 21	*La Juive*	E. Scotney s. E. Caruso t. O. Harrold t. L. Rothier bs. A. Bodanzky cond.
Jan. 26	*La forza del destino*	G. Besanzoni ms. E. Caruso t. R. Zanelli b. T. Chalmers b. J. Mardones bs. G. Papi cond.
Jan. 30	*Oberon*	K. Howard ms. G. Martinelli t. R. Diaz t. T. Chalmers b. A. Bodanzky cond.
Feb. 6	*La Juive*	E. Scotney s. E. Caruso t. O. Harrold t. J. Mardones bs. A. Bodanzky cond.
Feb. 22	Concert	

WINTER 1920 BROOKLYN—ACADEMY OF MUSIC

Feb. 24	*La Juive*	E. Scotney s. E. Caruso t. R. Diaz t. L. Rothier bs. A. Bodanzky cond.
Mar. 6	*Aida*	J. Gordon ms. G. Crimi t. P. Amato b. G. Martino bs. L. d'Angelo bs. R. Moranzoni cond.

WINTER 1920 NEW YORK CITY—METROPOLITAN OPERA

Mar. 11	*La forza del destino*	J. Gordon ms. E. Caruso t. P. Amato b. T. Chalmers b. J. Mardones bs. G. Papi cond.
Mar. 14	*Stabat Mater*	M. Matzenauer ms. M. Kingston t. J. Mardones bs. G. Setti cond.
Mar. 15M	Gala Concert	
Mar. 20	*La forza del destino*	J. Gordon ms. E. Caruso t. P. Amato b. T. Chalmers b. J. Mardones bs. G. Papi cond.

SPRING 1920 PHILADELPHIA—ACADEMY OF MUSIC

Mar. 30	*La forza del destino*	J. Gordon ms. E. Caruso t. P. Amato b. T. Chalmers b. J. Mardones bs. G. Papi cond.

SPRING 1920 NEW YORK CITY—METROPOLITAN OPERA

Apr. 4	*Messe Solennelle*	M. Matzenauer ms. C. Hackett t. J. Mardones bs. G. Setti cond.
Apr. 7	*La Juive*	E. Scotney s. E. Caruso t. O. Harrold t. L. Rothier bs. A. Bodanzky cond.
Apr. 12M	Gala Concert	
Apr. 18	Concert	
Apr. 23	*La Juive*	E. Scotney s. E. Caruso t. R. Diaz t. L. Rothier bs. A. Bodanzky cond.

SPRING 1920 ATLANTA—AUDITORIUM

Apr. 29	*La Juive*	E. Scotney s. E. Caruso t. R. Diaz t. L. Rothier bs. A. Bodanzky cond.

SPRING 1920 CONCERT TOUR

Cities visited include: Charlotte (May 3); Nashville (May 10); Birmingham (May 13); Jackson, Miss. (May 14); St. Louis (May 17); Houston (May 20); Norfolk (May 24); Roanoke (May 26); and Cleveland (May 28).

AUTUMN 1920 CONCERT TOUR

Cities visited include: Waterbury, Conn. (Oct. 5); Worcester (Oct. 8); Columbus (Oct. 11); Evansville; Chicago (Oct. 18); Detroit (Oct. 19); Nashville (Oct. 21); and St. Louis (Oct. 27).

AUTUMN 1920 NEW YORK CITY—METROPOLITAN OPERA

Nov. 15	*La Juive*	E. Scotney s. E. Caruso t. O. Harrold t. L. Rothier bs. A. Bodanzky cond.
Nov. 21	Concert	
Nov. 27M	*La forza del destino*	R. Delaunois ms. E. Caruso t. G. Danise b. T. Chalmers b. G. Martino bs. G. Papi cond.

AUTUMN 1920 PHILADELPHIA—ACADEMY OF MUSIC

Nov. 30	*La Juive*	E. Scotney s. E. Caruso t. R. Diaz t. L. Rothier bs. A. Bodanzky cond.

AUTUMN AND WINTER 1920–21 NEW YORK CITY—METROPOLITAN OPERA

Dec. 13	*La forza del destino*	J. Gordon ms. E. Caruso t. G. Danise b. T. Chalmers b. J. Mardones bs. G. Papi cond.
Dec. 23	*Don Carlo*	M. Matzenauer ms. G. Martinelli t. G. de Luca b. A. Didur bs. L. d'Angelo bs. G. Papi cond.
Jan. 2	Concert	
Jan. 3	*Don Carlo*	M. Matzenauer ms. G. Martinelli t. G. de Luca b. A. Didur bs. L. d'Angelo bs. G. Papi cond.

Jan. 6	*Oberon*	J. Gordon ms. M. Kingston t. R. Diaz t. O. Dua b. A. Bodanzky cond.
Jan. 9	Concert	
Jan. 12	*Don Carlo*	M. Matzenauer ms. G. Martinelli t. G. de Luca b. A. Didur bs. L. d'Angelo bs. G. Papi cond.
Jan. 14	*Cavalleria rusticana*	F. Perini ms. B. Gigli t. T. Chalmers b. R. Moranzoni cond.

WINTER 1921 PHILADELPHIA—ACADEMY OF MUSIC

Jan. 25	*Don Carlo*	J. Gordon ms. G. Crimi t. G. de Luca b. A. Didur bs. L. d'Angelo bs. G. Papi cond.

WINTER 1921 NEW YORK CITY—METROPOLITAN OPERA

Jan. 29	*Don Carlo*	J. Gordon ms. G. Martinelli t. G. de Luca b. A. Didur bs. V. Reschiglian bs. G. Papi cond.
Jan. 30	Concert	
Feb. 5	*La forza del destino*	R. Delaunois ms. G. Crimi t. G. Danise b. T. Chalmers b. J. Mardones bs. G. Papi cond.
Feb. 6	Concert	
Feb. 25	*Don Carlo*	J. Gordon ms. G. Martinelli t. G. de Luca b. A. Didur bs. V. Reschiglian bs. G. Papi cond.

WINTER AND SPRING 1921 CONCERT TOUR

Cities visited include: Jacksonville (Mar. 8); Savannah (Mar. 11); Atlanta (Mar. 14); Montgomery (Mar. 16); New York City (Mar. 19); Boston (Mar. 20 and 27); Schenectady (Mar. 29); Ithaca (Mar. 31); Providence (Apr. 4); Washington (Apr. 8); New Haven (Apr. 13); Springfield (Apr. 15); Bridgeport (Apr. 17); Washington (Apr. 19?); and Rock Hill (Apr. 21).

SPRING 1921 ATLANTA—AUDITORIUM

Apr. 25	*Andrea Chénier*	F. Perini ms. G. Crimi t. G. Danise b. A. Didur bs. G. Martino bs. R. Moranzoni cond.
Apr. 29	*Aida*	J. Claussen ms. G. Crimi t. G. Danise b. G. Martino bs. L. d'Angelo bs. R. Moranzoni cond.

SPRING 1921 CONCERT TOUR

Cities visited include: Houston (May 4); Hays, Kans. (May 8); Denver (May 10); and Yonkers (May 14).

SUMMER 1921 MERIDEN, CONN.—ST. JOSEPH'S CATHEDRAL

Aug. 7	A Requiem Mass in memory of Caruso	

AUTUMN 1921 CONCERT TOUR

Cities visited include: Bangor (Oct. 6); Worcester (Oct. 7); Portland, Maine (Oct. 10); Reading, Pa. (Oct. 14); Newark, N.J. (Oct. 16); Columbus (Oct. 18); Cleveland (Oct. 21); Charlotte (Oct. 25); and New Castle, Pa. (Oct. 28).

AUTUMN 1921 BROOKLYN—ACADEMY OF MUSIC

Nov. 22	*Aida*	M. Matzenauer ms. G. Crimi t. G. de Luca b. A. Didur bs. W. Gustafson bs. R. Moranzoni cond.

AUTUMN 1921 NEW YORK CITY—METROPOLITAN OPERA

Nov. 30	*Cavalleria rusticana*	F. Perini ms. B. Gigli t. T. Chalmers b. R. Moranzoni cond.
Dec. 8	*Ernani*	G. Martinelli t. G. Danise b. J. Mardones bs. G. Papi cond.
Dec. 11	Concert	

AUTUMN 1921 PHILADELPHIA—ACADEMY OF MUSIC

Dec. 13	*Ernani*	G. Martinelli t. G. Danise b. J. Mardones bs. G. Papi cond.

WINTER 1921–22 NEW YORK CITY—METROPOLITAN OPERA

Dec. 26	*Cavalleria rusticana*	F. Perini ms. B. Gigli t. M. Picco b. R. Moranzoni cond.
Dec. 31	*La forza del destino*	R. Delaunois ms. M. Salazar t. G. Danise b. T. Chalmers b. A. Didur bs. G. Papi cond.
Jan. 5	*Le Roi d'Ys*	F. Alda s. B. Gigli t. G. Danise b. A. Wolff cond.
Jan. 7	*Cavalleria rusticana*	F. Perini ms. B. Gigli t. M. Picco b. R. Moranzoni cond.
Jan. 13	*Ernani*	G. Martinelli t. G. Danise b. J. Mardones bs. G. Papi cond.
Jan. 15	Concert	
Jan. 18	*Don Carlo*	J. Gordon ms. G. Martinelli t. G. de Luca b. A. Didur bs. L. d'Angelo bs. G. Papi cond.
Jan. 21	*Le Roi d'Ys*	F. Alda s. B. Gigli t. G. Danise b. L. Hasselmans cond.
Jan. 27	*Le Roi d'Ys*	F. Alda s. B. Gigli t. G. Danise b. L. Hasselmans cond.
Jan. 28M	*Ernani*	G. Martinelli t. T. Ruffo b. J. Mardones bs. G. Papi cond.

WINTER 1922 PHILADELPHIA—ACADEMY OF MUSIC

Feb. 7	*Don Carlo*	M. Matzenauer ms. G. Crimi t. G. de Luca b. A. Didur bs. L. d'Angelo bs. G. Papi cond.

WINTER 1922 NEW YORK CITY—METROPOLITAN OPERA

Feb. 15	*Le Roi d'Ys*	F. Alda s. B. Gigli t. G. Danise b. L. Hasselmans cond.
Feb. 18	*Don Carlo*	J. Gordon ms. G. Martinelli t. G. Danise b. A. Didur bs. L. d'Angelo bs. G. Papi cond.
Feb. 19M	Concert	
Feb. 26	Concert	
Feb. 27	*Ernani*	G. Martinelli t. G. Danise b. J. Mardones bs. G. Papi cond.

WINTER AND SPRING 1922 CONCERT TOUR

Cities visited include: Evansville (Mar. 17); Kansas City (Mar. 20); St. Joseph, Mo. (Mar. 21); Durham (Mar. 25); and Norfolk (Mar. 27).

SPRING 1922 NEW YORK CITY—METROPOLITAN OPERA

Mar. 31	*La forza del destino*	J. Gordon ms. G. Martinelli t. G. Danise b. T. Chalmers b. J. Mardones bs. G. Papi cond.

SPRING 1922 CONCERT TOUR

Cities visited: Boston (Apr. 10); and New York City (Apr. 15).

SPRING 1922 ATLANTA—AUDITORIUM

Apr. 24	*Ernani*	G. Martinelli t. G. Danise b. J. Mardones bs. G. Papi cond.

SPRING 1922 MERIDEN, CONN.

May 8	Concert

SPRING 1922 SPRINGFIELD, MASS.—MUSIC FESTIVAL

May 13	Concert

AUTUMN 1922 CONCERT TOUR

Cities visited include: Denver (Oct. 2); Colorado Springs (Oct. 5); Nashville (Oct. 8); Memphis (Oct. 16); Oklahoma City (Oct. 20); San Antonio (Oct. 24); Austin (Oct. 26); Toledo (Oct. 29); Detroit (Nov. 1); Grand Rapids (Nov. 2); Cleveland (Nov. 5); Waterbury, Conn. (Nov. 9); Boston (Nov. 12); Hartford (Nov. 15); Lynchburg, Va. (Nov. 17); St. Joseph, Mo. (Nov. 24); Dallas (Nov. 27); Kansas City (Nov. 30); Jacksonville (Dec. 4); Orlando (Dec. 6); New Britain (Dec. 10); Nashville (Dec. 12); and New York City (Dec. 15).

AUTUMN AND WINTER 1922–23 NEW YORK CITY—METROPOLITAN OPERA

Dec. 16M	*Ernani*	G. Martinelli t. T. Ruffo b. J. Mardones bs. G. Papi cond.
Dec. 25	*Ernani*	G. Martinelli t. T. Ruffo b. J. Mardones bs. G. Papi cond.
Dec. 31	Concert	
Jan. 5	*William Tell*	M. Sundelius s. F. Perini ms. G. Martinelli t. G. Danise b. J. Mardones bs. A. Didur bs. G. Papi cond.
Jan. 11	*Ernani*	G. Martinelli t. T. Ruffo b. J. Mardones bs. G. Papi cond.
Jan. 15	*William Tell*	M. Sundelius s. F. Perini ms. G. Martinelli t. G. Danise b. J. Mardones bs. A. Didur bs. G. Papi cond.
Jan. 20	*Andrea Chénier*	F. Perini ms. B. Gigli t. G. Danise b. A. Didur bs. L. d'Angelo bs. R. Moranzoni cond.
Jan. 21	Concert	

WINTER 1923 BROOKLYN—ACADEMY OF MUSIC

Jan. 30	*William Tell*	E. Dalossy s. F. Perini ms. G. Martinelli t. G. Danise b. J. Mardones bs. P. Ananian bs. G. Papi cond.

WINTER AND SPRING 1923 NEW YORK CITY—METROPOLITAN OPERA

Feb. 2	*Ernani*	G. Martinelli t. T. Ruffo b. J. Mardones bs. G. Papi cond.
Feb. 10M	*William Tell*	M. Sundelius s. F. Perini ms. G. Martinelli t. G. Danise b. J. Mardones bs. I. Picchi bs. G. Papi cond.
Feb. 16	*Andrea Chénier*	F. Perini ms. B. Gigli t. G. Danise b. A. Didur bs. L. d'Angelo bs. R. Moranzoni cond.
Feb. 22	*Cavalleria rusticana*	F. Perini ms. G. Lauri-Volpi t. M. Picco b. R. Moranzoni cond.
Feb. 25	Concert	
Feb. 28	*Andrea Chénier*	F. Perini ms. B. Gigli t. G. Danise b. A. Didur bs. L. d'Angelo bs. R. Moranzoni cond.
Mar. 4	Concert	
Mar. 9	*Cavalleria rusticana*	F. Perini ms. G. Lauri-Volpi t. M. Picco b. R. Moranzoni cond.
Mar. 21	*L'africana*	Q. Mario s. B. Gigli t. G. Danise b. A. Didur bs. L. Rothier bs. A. Bodanzky cond.

Mar. 31M	*Andrea Chénier*	F. Perini ms. B. Gigli t. G. de Luca b. A. Didur bs. L. d'Angelo bs. R. Moranzoni cond.
Apr. 2	*L'africana*	M. Sundelius s. B. Gigli t. G. Danise b. A. Didur bs. L. Rothier bs. A. Bodanzky cond.
Apr. 3	Gala Concert	
Apr. 8	*Cavalleria rusticana*	F. Perini ms. M. Chamlee t. M. Picco b. G. Setti cond.

SPRING 1923 SHIMOKEN, PA.

Apr. 9	Concert	

SPRING 1923 NEW YORK CITY—METROPOLITAN OPERA

Apr. 11	*William Tell*	M. Sundelius s. F. Perini ms. G. Martinelli t. G. Danise b. J. Mardones bs. I. Picchi bs. G. Papi cond.
Apr. 13	*L'africana*	Q. Mario s. B. Gigli t. G. Danise b. A. Didur bs. L. Rothier bs. A. Bodanzky cond.

SPRING 1923 PHILADELPHIA—ACADEMY OF MUSIC

Apr. 17	*L'africana*	M. Sundelius s. B. Gigli t. G. Danise b. A. Didur bs. L. Rothier bs. A. Bodanzky cond.

SPRING 1923 NEW YORK CITY—METROPOLITAN OPERA

Apr. 19	*William Tell*	E. Dalossy s. F. Perini ms. G. Martinelli t. G. Danise b. J. Mardones bs. P. Ananian bs. G. Papi cond.
Apr. 21M	*L'africana*	Q. Mario s. B. Gigli t. G. Danise b. A. Didur bs. L. Rothier bs. G. Bamboschek cond.

SPRING 1923 ATLANTA—AUDITORIUM

Apr. 26M	*Don Carlo*	M. Telva ms. G. Martinelli t. G. de Luca b. F. Chaliapin bs. L. Rothier bs. G. Papi cond.
Apr. 27	*L'africana*	Q. Mario s. B. Gigli t. G. Danise b. A. Didur bs. L. Rothier bs. G. Bamboschek cond.
Apr. 28	*William Tell**	E. Dalossy s. H. Wakefield ms. G. Martinelli t. G. Danise b. J. Mardones bs. P. Ananian bs. G. Papi cond.

SPRING 1923 CONCERT TOUR

Cities visited include: Los Angeles (May 7); San Francisco (May 13); San Francisco (May 24); and Los Angeles (June 3).

AUTUMN 1923 CONCERT TOUR

Cities visited include: Syracuse (Oct. 2); Grand Rapids; Columbus; Toledo (Oct. 14); Louisville; Omaha; Lincoln (Nov. 8); Tulsa; Denver; Shreveport (Nov. 12); New Orleans; Havana (two concerts); Macon; Charlotte; and Sharon, Pa. (Dec. 3).

AUTUMN AND WINTER 1923–24 NEW YORK CITY—METROPOLITAN OPERA

Dec. 17	*Andrea Chénier*	F. Perini ms. B. Gigli t. T. Ruffo b. L. Tibbet b. A. Didur bs. R. Moranzoni cond.
Dec. 22	*Cavalleria rusticana*	F. Perini ms. M. Chamlee t. M. Picco b. R. Moranzoni cond.

WINTER 1923–24 BROOKLYN—ACADEMY OF MUSIC

Dec. 25	*Ernani*	G. Martinelli t. T. Ruffo b. J. Mardones bs. G. Papi cond.

WINTER 1923–24 NEW YORK CITY—METROPOLITAN OPERA

Dec. 28	*Ernani*	G. Martinelli t. T. Ruffo b. J. Mardones bs. G. Papi cond.
Jan. 3	*Cavalleria rusticana*	F. Perini ms. M. Chamlee t. M. Picco b. R. Moranzoni cond.
Jan. 6M	Concert	
Jan. 12M	*Ernani*	G. Martinelli t. G. de Luca b. J. Mardones bs. G. Papi cond.
Jan. 20	Concert	

WINTER 1924 PHILADELPHIA—ACADEMY OF MUSIC

Jan. 22	*L'africana*	Q. Mario s. B. Gigli t. G. Danise b. J. Wolfe bs. L. Rothier bs. A. Bodanzky cond.

WINTER 1924 NEW YORK CITY—METROPOLITAN OPERA

Jan. 27	Concert	
Jan. 31	*L'africana*	Q. Mario s. B. Gigli t. G. Danise b. A. Didur bs. L. Rothier bs. A. Bodanzky cond.
Feb. 2	*Ernani*	G. Martinelli t. G. Danise b. J. Mardones bs. G. Papi cond.
Feb. 3	Concert	
Feb. 4	*L'africana*	Q. Mario s. B. Gigli t. G. Danise b. A. Didur bs. L. Rothier bs. A. Bodanzky cond.
Feb. 10	Concert	
Feb. 12	*L'africana*	Q. Mario s. B. Gigli t. G. Danise b. A. Didur bs. L. Rothier bs. A. Bodanzky cond.
Feb. 15M	*Cavalleria rusticana*	M. Telva ms. G. Lauri-Volpi t. M. Picco b. R. Moranzoni cond.

WINTER AND SPRING 1924 CONCERT TOUR

Cities visited include: Hartford (Feb. 17); Waterbury (Feb. 19); New Castle, Pa.; Youngstown (Mar. 4); Akron; Mansfield; Raleigh (Mar. 11); Orlando; Tampa (Mar. 20); St. Petersburg; Miami; Jacksonville (Mar. 28); and Chattanooga.

SPRING 1924 NEW YORK CITY—METROPOLITAN OPERA

Apr. 9	*Cavalleria rusticana*	F. Perini ms. G. Lauri-Volpi t. M. Picco b. R. Moranzoni cond.
Apr. 16	*L'africana*	Q. Mario s. B. Gigli t. G. Danise b. J. Wolfe bs. L. Rothier bs. A. Bodanzky cond.
Apr. 17	*Cavalleria rusticana*	M. Telva ms. G. Lauri-Volpi t. M. Picco b. R. Moranzoni cond.
Apr. 19	*Il trovatore*	K. Branzell ms. G. Martinelli t. G. Danise b. L. d'Angelo bs. R. Moranzoni cond.

SPRING 1924 ATLANTA—AUDITORIUM

Apr. 22M	*Il trovatore*	M. Telva ms. G. Martinelli t. G. Danise b. L. Rothier bs. R. Moranzoni cond.
Apr. 26	*Cavalleria rusticana*	M. Telva ms. B. Gigli t. M. Picco b. R. Moranzoni cond.

SPRING 1924 CLEVELAND—PUBLIC AUDITORIUM

Apr. 28	*Aida*	J. Claussen ms. G. Martinelli t. G. Danise b. J. Mardones bs. L. d'Angelo bs. R. Moranzoni cond.

SPRING 1924 PHILADELPHIA—ARENA

May 1	Concert	G. Martinelli t.

SPRING 1924 CLEVELAND—PUBLIC AUDITORIUM

May 3	*Il trovatore*	M. Telva ms. G. Martinelli t. G. Danise b. I. Picchi bs. R. Moranzoni cond.

SPRING 1924 CONCERT TOUR

Cities visited include: Newark (May 5 with Martinelli); Spartanburg, S.C. (May 9); Los Angeles (May 15); and Philadelphia (May 23).

AUTUMN 1924 CONCERT TOUR

Cities visited include: Montreal (Sep. 21); Pine Bluff, Ark. (Sep. 29); Shreveport (Sep. 30); Denton, Tex. (Oct. 4); Kansas City (Oct. 6); and Cleveland (Oct. 19).

AUTUMN 1924 NEW YORK CITY—METROPOLITAN OPERA

Nov. 29M	*Andrea Chénier*	M. Telva ms. B. Gigli t. G. Danise b. L. Tibbett b. A. Didur bs. T. Serafin cond.

Dec. 7	Concert	

AUTUMN 1924 PHILADELPHIA—ACADEMY OF MUSIC

Dec. 9	*La gioconda*	J. Gordon ms. M. Alcock ms. B. Gigli t. G. Danise b. J. Mardones bs. T. Serafin cond.

AUTUMN AND WINTER 1924–25 NEW YORK CITY—METROPOLITAN OPERA

Dec. 13M	*Cavalleria rusticana*	M. Telva ms. A. Tokatyan t. M. Picco b. G. Papi cond.
Dec. 15	*Andrea Chénier*	H. Wakefield ms. B. Gigli t. T. Ruffo b. L. Tibbett b. A. Didur bs. T. Serafin cond.
Dec. 19M	*La gioconda*	J. Gordon ms. M. Alcock ms. B. Gigli t. G. Danise b. J. Mardones bs. T. Serafin cond.
Dec. 21	Concert	
Dec. 25	*Aida*	I. Bourskaya ms. M. Fleta t. G. de Luca b. L. Rothier bs. L. d'Angelo bs. T. Serafin cond.
Dec. 27	*L'africana*	Q. Mario s. B. Gigli t. G. Danise b. A. Didur bs. L. Rothier bs. T. Serafin cond.
Dec. 29	*Cavalleria rusticana*	I. Bourskaya ms. B. Gigli t. V. Ballester b. G. Papi cond.
Jan. 2	*Aida*	J. Gordon ms. M. Fleta t. T. Ruffo b. J. Mardones bs. L. d'Angelo bs. G. Bamboschek cond.
Jan. 7	*L'africana*	Q. Mario s. B. Gigli t. G. Danise b. A. Didur bs. L. Rothier bs. T. Serafin cond.
Jan. 9	*La gioconda*	J. Gordon ms. M. Alcock ms. B. Gigli t. T. Ruffo b. J. Mardones bs. T. Serafin cond.
Jan. 11	Concert	

WINTER 1925 NEW YORK CITY—HOTEL WALDORF

Jan. 12	Concert	

WINTER 1925 NEW YORK CITY—METROPOLITAN OPERA

Jan. 17	*Andrea Chénier*	H. Wakefield ms. M. Fleta t. G. Danise b. T. Serafin cond.

WINTER AND SPRING 1925 CONCERT TOUR

Cities visited include: Hartford (Jan. 18); Worcester (Jan. 20); Boston (Jan. 25); Springfield, Mass. (Jan. 27); Detroit (Jan. 30); Bridgeport (Feb. 1); Syracuse (Feb. 3); Columbus (Feb. 6); Akron (Feb. 9); Youngstown (Feb. 10); New London (Feb. 13); Trenton (Feb. 15); Westfield, N.J. (Feb. 20); Lynchburg, Va. (Feb. 25); Columbia, Mo. (Feb. 28); Lincoln (Mar. 6); Independence (Mar. 9); Galveston (Mar. 16); Tucson (Mar. 20); Pomona (Mar. 23); San Diego (Mar. 25); Los Angeles (Mar. 26 and 28); Oakland (Mar. 30);

Sacramento (Apr. 2); Seattle (Apr. 6); Vancouver (Apr. 7); Portland (Apr. 9); and San Francisco (Apr. 18).

SPRING 1925 ATLANTA—AUDITORIUM

Apr. 25	*Cavalleria rusticana*	M. Telva ms. A. Tokatyan t. M. Picco b. G. Papi cond.

SPRING 1925 CLEVELAND—PUBLIC AUDITORIUM

Apr. 27	*L'africana*	Q. Mario s. G. Lauri-Volpi t. G. Danise b. A. Didur bs. L. Rothier bs. T. Serafin cond.
Apr. 29	*Il trovatore*	M. Telva ms. G. Martinelli t. G. Danise b. L. d'Angelo bs. G. Papi cond.

SPRING 1925 CONCERT TOUR

Cities visited include: Newark (May 6); Spartanburg, S.C. (May 8); Wilson, N.C. (May); and Chicago (May 26).

AUTUMN 1925 CONCERT TOUR

Cities visited include: Dayton; Grand Rapids (Oct. 5); Detroit (Oct. 9); Bristol Conn.; Boston (Oct. 11); Stamford; Springfield; and Bridgeport.

AUTUMN 1925 NEW YORK CITY—METROPOLITAN OPERA

Nov. 2	*La gioconda*	M. Matzenauer ms. M. Telva ms. B. Gigli t. G. Danise b. J. Mardones bs. T. Serafin cond.
Nov. 7	*L'africana*	Q. Mario s. B. Gigli t. G. de Luca b. G. Martino bs. L. Rothier bs. T. Serafin cond.
Nov. 12	*La vestale*	M. Matzenauer ms. E. Johnson t. G. de Luca b. J. Mardones bs. T. Serafin cond.
Nov. 15	Concert	
Nov. 21M	*L'africana*	Q. Mario s. M. Chamlee t. G. de Luca b. A. Didur bs. L. Rothier bs. T. Serafin cond.
Nov. 22	*Il trovatore*	M. Telva ms. V. Fullin t. M. Basiola b. G. Martino bs. G. Bamboschek cond.
Nov. 25	*La gioconda*	M. Telva ms. M. Alcock ms. B. Gigli t. G. Danise b. L. Rothier bs. T. Serafin cond.
Nov. 27	*La vestale*	M. Matzenauer ms. E. Johnson t. G. de Luca b. J. Mardones bs. T. Serafin cond.
Nov. 29	Concert	

AUTUMN 1925 PHILADELPHIA—ACADEMY OF MUSIC

Dec. 1	*L'africana*	Q. Mario s. B. Gigli t. G. Danise b. A. Didur bs. L. Rothier bs. T. Serafin cond.

AUTUMN 1925 NEW YORK CITY—METROPOLITAN OPERA

Dec. 7	*La vestale*	M. Matzenauer ms. E. Johnson t. G. de Luca b. J. Mardones bs. T. Serafin cond.
Dec. 11M	*La gioconda*	J. Gordon ms. M. Telva ms. B. Gigli t. T. Ruffo b. L. Rothier bs. G. Setti cond.
Dec. 16	*Andrea Chénier*	M. Telva ms. B. Gigli t. T. Ruffo b. A. Didur bs. G. Bamboschek cond.
Dec. 18	*La Juive*	C. Ryan s. G. Martinelli t. R. Errolle t. L. Rothier bs. L. Hasselmans cond.

AUTUMN 1925 BROOKLYN—ACADEMY OF MUSIC

Dec. 22	*Cavalleria rusticana*	I. Bourskaya ms. A. Tokatyan t. M. Basiola b. G. Papi cond.

WINTER 1925–26 NEW YORK CITY—METROPOLITAN OPERA

Dec. 24	*La gioconda*	J. Gordon ms. M. Alcock ms. B. Gigli t. M. Basiola b. J. Mardones bs. T. Serafin cond.
Dec. 26M	*La vestale*	M. Matzenauer ms. A. Tokatyan t. G. de Luca b. J. Mardones bs. T. Serafin cond.
Dec. 27	Concert	
Jan. 1	*La gioconda*	J. Gordon ms. M. Alcock ms. M. Chamlee t. G. de Luca b. J. Mardones bs. T. Serafin cond.
Jan. 4	*La Juive*	N. Morgana s. G. Martinelli t. R. Errolle t. L. Rothier bs. L. Hasselmans cond.
Jan. 6	*La vestale*	M. Matzenauer ms. E. Johnson t. G. de Luca b. J. Mardones bs. T. Serafin cond.
Jan. 8M	*Cavalleria rusticana*	M. Telva ms. B. Gigli t. M. Basiola b. G. Papi cond.

WINTER 1926 CONCERT TOUR

Cities visited include: Washington; and New Bedford, Mass. (Jan. 17).

WINTER 1926 NEW YORK CITY—METROPOLITAN OPERA

Jan. 21	*Requiem*	M. Alcock ms. B. Gigli t. J. Mardones bs. T. Serafin cond.

WINTER 1926 CONCERT TOUR

Cities visited include: Montclair, N.J. (Jan. 22); New Haven (Jan. 24); Worcester, Mass.; Hartford, Conn. (Jan. 31); Waterbury, Conn. (Feb. 4); Providence (Feb. 7); Lynn, Mass. (Feb. 14); Lowell, Mass.; Canton, Ohio (Feb. 19); Dayton, Ohio; Springfield, Ohio (Feb. 23); Bloomington, Ind. (Feb. 25); and Minneapolis.

WINTER 1926 NEW YORK CITY—METROPOLITAN OPERA

Mar. 1	*L'africana*	Q. Mario s. G. Lauri-Volpi t. G. Danise b. A. Didur bs. L. Rothier bs. T. Serafin cond.

SPRING 1926 CONCERT TOUR

Cities visited include: Denver; Colorado Springs; Bristol, Va.; Asheville, N.C.; and Ithaca (Apr. 13).

SPRING 1926 ATLANTA—AUDITORIUM

Apr. 19	*Aida*	J. Claussen ms. G. Martinelli t. M. Bohnen b. J. Mardones bs. L. d'Angelo bs. T. Serafin cond.
Apr. 24	*Il trovatore*	M. Telva ms. G. Martinelli t. M. Basiola b. L. Rothier bs. T. Serafin cond.

SPRING 1926 CLEVELAND—PUBLIC AUDITORIUM

Apr. 28	*La gioconda*	M. Telva ms. M. Alcock ms. G. Lauri-Volpi t. G. Danise b. J. Mardones bs. T. Serafin cond.
May 1	*Cavalleria rusticana*	D. Flexer ms. A. Tokatyan t. M. Basiola b. G. Bamboschek cond.
May 5	*Aida*	J. Claussen ms. G. Martinelli t. M. Basiola b. J. Mardones bs. L. d'Angelo bs. T. Serafin cond.

AUTUMN 1926 CONCERT TOUR

Cities visited include: Toronto (Oct. 1); Birmingham (Oct. 6); Little Rock (Oct. 8); Tulsa (Oct. 11); Atlanta (Oct. 14); Cleveland (Oct. 17); and Boston (Oct. 24).

AUTUMN 1926 NEW YORK CITY—METROPOLITAN OPERA

Nov. 1	*La vestale*	M. Matzenauer ms. G. Lauri-Volpi t. G. de Luca b. E. Pinza bs. T. Serafin cond.
Nov. 7	Concert	

AUTUMN 1926 PHILADELPHIA—ACADEMY OF MUSIC

Nov. 9	*L'africana*	N. Guilford s. B. Gigli t. G. Danise b. A. Didur bs. L. Rothier bs. T. Serafin cond.

AUTUMN AND WINTER 1926–27 NEW YORK CITY—METROPOLITAN OPERA

Nov. 12	*La Juive*	C. Ryan s. G. Martinelli t. A. Tedesco t. L. Rothier bs. L. Hasselmans cond.
Nov. 20	*La gioconda*	J. Gordon ms. M. Alcock ms. B. Gigli t. M. Basiola b. E. Pinza bs. T. Serafin cond.
Nov. 22	*L'africana*	N. Guilford s. B. Gigli t. G. Danise b. A. Didur bs. L. Rothier bs. T. Serafin cond.

Nov. 25	*La vestale*	M. Matzenauer ms. A. Tokatyan t. G. de Luca b. E. Pinza bs. T. Serafin cond.
Dec. 3	*La vestale*	M. Matzenauer ms. G. Lauri-Volpi t. M. Basiola b. E. Pinza bs. T. Serafin cond.
Dec. 11M	*La forza del destino*	M. Telva ms. G. Martinelli t. G. Danise b. L. Tibbett b. E. Pinza bs. V. Bellezza cond.
Dec. 15	*La Juive*	Q. Mario s. G. Martinelli t. A. Tedesco t. L. Rothier bs. L. Hasselmans cond.
Dec. 20M	*Cavalleria rusticana*	M. Alcock ms. A. Tokatyan t. M. Picco b. V. Bellezza cond.
Dec. 23	*La gioconda*	M. Telva ms. M. Alcock ms. B. Gigli t. T. Ruffo b. E. Pinza bs. T. Serafin cond.
Dec. 29	*L'amore dei tre re*	B. Gigli t. G. Danise b. A. Didur bs. T. Serafin cond.
Jan. 2	Concert	

WINTER 1927 PHILADELPHIA—ACADEMY OF MUSIC

Jan. 4	*La vestale*	M. Telva ms. G. Lauri-Volpi t. M. Basiola b. E. Pinza bs. T. Serafin cond.

WINTER 1927 NEW YORK CITY—METROPOLTAN OPERA

Jan. 8	*La gioconda*	J. Gordon ms. H. Wakefield ms. B. Gigli t. G. Danise b. E. Pinza bs. T. Serafin cond.
Jan. 9	Concert	
Jan. 13	*La forza del destino*	I. Bourskaya ms. G. Martinelli t. G. Danise b. L. Tibbett b. E. Pinza bs. V. Bellezza cond.
Jan. 15	*L'africana*	N. Morgana s. G. Lauri-Volpi t. G. de Luca b. P. Ludikar bs. T. Serafin cond.

WINTER AND SPRING 1927 CONCERT TOUR

Cities visited include: Philadelphia (Jan. 16); Baltimore (Jan. 17); Washington (Jan. 21); Pittsburgh (Jan. 23); Worcester (Jan. 25); Troy (Jan. 27); Hartford (Jan. 29); Waterbury (Jan. 30); Havana (Feb. 3 and 5); Tampa (Feb. 9); St. Petersburg (Feb. 11); Miami (Feb. 14); San Antonio (Feb. 18); Phoenix (Feb 23); Pomona (Feb. 28); Palo Alto (Mar. 3); Los Angeles (Mar. 8); Pasadena (Mar. 10); San Diego (Mar. 12); Santa Barbara (Mar. 14); San Francisco (Mar. 16); Oakland (Mar. 18); San Francisco (Mar. 19); Portland (Mar. 21); Tacoma (Mar. 24); Bellingham (Mar. 28); Salt Lake City (Apr. 1); Minneapolis (Apr. 5); Youngstown (Apr. 8); and Dayton (Apr. 11).

SPRING 1927 NEW YORK CITY—METROPOLITAN OPERA

Apr. 14M	*Cavalleria rusticana*	I. Bourskaya ms. A. Tokatyan t. M. Picco b. V. Bellezza cond.
Apr. 16	*La gioconda*	K. Branzell ms. M. Alcock ms. B. Gigli t. M. Basiola b. E. Pinza bs. T. Serafin cond.

SPRING 1927 BALTIMORE—LYRIC THEATER

Apr. 19	*Il trovatore*	J. Claussen ms. G. Martinelli t. M. Basiola b. L. Rothier bs. T. Serafin cond.
Apr. 21	*Cavalleria rusticana*	I. Bourskaya ms. A. Tokatyan t. L. Tibbett b. G. Bamboschek cond.

SPRING 1927 WASHINGTON—AUDITORIUM

Apr. 23	*Il trovatore*	J. Claussen ms. G. Martinelli t. M. Basiola b. L. Rothier bs. T. Serafin cond.

SPRING 1927 ATLANTA—AUDITORIUM

Apr. 26	*L'amore dei tre re*	G. Martinelli t. L. Tibbett b. E. Pinza bs. T. Serafin cond.
Apr. 29	*La forza del destino*	I. Bourskaya ms. G. Martinelli t. M. Basiola b. M. Picco b. E. Pinza bs. V. Bellezza cond.

SPRING 1927 CLEVELAND—PUBLIC HALL

May 2	*Aida*	J. Claussen ms. G. Martinelli t. G. de Luca b. E. Pinza bs. W. Gustafson bs. T. Serafin cond.
May 5	*La forza del destino*	I. Bourskaya ms. G. Martinelli t. M. Basiola b. M. Picco b. E. Pinza bs. V. Bellezza cond.
May 7	*Il trovatore*	J. Claussen ms. G. Martinelli t. M. Basiola b. L. d'Angelo bs. T. Serafin cond.

SPRING 1927 ROCHESTER—EASTMAN THEATER

May 9	*La forza del destino*	I. Bourskaya ms. G. Martinelli t. G. de Luca b. M. Picco b. L. Rothier bs. V. Bellezza cond.

SPRING 1927 CONCERT TOUR

Cities visited include: Allentown (May 11); New Haven (May 13); and Grand Rapids (May 17).

AUTUMN 1927 CONCERT TOUR

Cities visited include: Detroit (Oct. 1); Saginaw; Toronto; Buffalo (Oct. 7); Erie; Columbus; and Cincinnati (Oct. 14).

AUTUMN 1927 PHILADELPHIA—ACADEMY OF MUSIC

Nov. 1	*La gioconda*	M. Telva ms. M. Alcock ms. B. Gigli t. G. Danise b. L. Rothier bs. T. Serafin cond.

AUTUMN 1927 NEW YORK CITY—METROPOLITAN OPERA

Nov. 4	*La forza del destino*	I. Bourskaya ms. G. Martinelli t. M. Basiola b. P. Malatesta b. E. Pinza bs. V. Bellezza cond.

AUTUMN 1927 PHILADELPHIA

Nov. 13	Concert	

AUTUMN 1927 NEW YORK CITY—METROPOLITAN OPERA

Nov. 16	*Norma*	M. Telva ms. G. Lauri-Volpi t. E. Pinza bs. T. Serafin cond.
Nov. 19	*Cavalleria rusticana*	M. Alcock ms. A. Tokatyan t. M. Basiola b. V. Bellezza cond.
Nov. 23	*L'africana*	Q. Mario s. B. Gigli t. G. de Luca b. A. Didur bs. L. Rothier bs. T. Serafin cond.

AUTUMN 1927 BROOKLYN—ACADEMY OF MUSIC

Nov. 26	*Norma*	E. Vettori ms. G. Lauri-Volpi t. L. Rothier bs. T. Serafin cond.

AUTUMN 1927 NEW YORK CITY—METROPOLITAN OPERA

Nov. 28	*La forza del destino*	I. Bourskaya ms. G. Martinelli t. G. Danise b. P. Malatesta b. E. Pinza bs. V. Bellezza cond.

AUTUMN 1927 BROOKLYN—ACADEMY OF MUSIC

Dec. 1	*Norma*	M. Telva ms. G. Lauri-Volpi t. E. Pinza bs. T. Serafin cond.

AUTUMN 1927 NEW YORK CITY—HOTEL WALDORF

Dec. 5	Concert	

AUTUMN 1927 NEW YORK CITY—METROPOLITAN OPERA

Dec. 7	*Il trovatore*	M. Telva ms. G. Lauri-Volpi t. M. Basiola b. E. Pinza bs. V. Bellezza cond.
Dec. 12	*Norma*	M. Telva ms. G. Lauri-Volpi t. E. Pinza bs. T. Serafin cond.

AUTUMN 1927 NEW YORK CITY—PLAZA HOTEL

Dec. 15	Concert	

AUTUMN 1927 NEW YORK CITY—METROPOLITAN OPERA

Dec. 17	*Il trovatore*	I. Bourskaya ms. G. Lauri-Volpi t. G. Danise b. L. Rothier bs. V. Bellezza cond.
Dec. 18	Concert	
Dec. 21M	*Norma*	M. Telva ms. G. Lauri-Volpi t. E. Pinza bs. T. Serafin cond.
Dec. 24M	*L'africana*	L. Lerch s. B. Gigli t. G. Danise b. P. Ludikar bs. E. Pinza bs. T. Serafin cond.

WINTER 1927–28 PHILADELPHIA—ACADEMY OF MUSIC

Dec. 27	*Norma*	M. Telva ms. F. Jagel t. L. Rothier bs. T. Serafin cond.

WINTER 1927–28 NEW YORK CITY—METROPOLITAN OPERA

Dec. 29	*La gioconda*	L. Homer ms. M. Alcock ms. B. Gigli t. T. Ruffo b. E. Pinza bs. T. Serafin cond.
Jan. 7	*Andrea Chénier*	D. Flexer ms. B. Gigli t. T. Ruffo b. A. Didur bs. T. Serafin cond.

WINTER 1928 PHILADELPHIA

Jan. 10 Concert

WINTER 1928 NEW YORK CITY—METROPOLITAN OPERA

Jan. 11	*La gioconda*	M. Telva ms. H. Wakefield ms. M. Chamlee t. G. Danise b. L. Rothier bs. T. Serafin cond.
Jan. 14M	*Norma*	M. Telva ms. F. Jagel t. E. Pinza bs. T. Serafin cond.
Jan. 21	*La forza del destino*	I. Bourskaya ms. F. Jagel t. G. Danise b. P. Malatesta b. E. Pinza bs. V. Bellezza cond.
Jan. 27	*Norma*	M. Telva ms. G. Lauri-Volpi t. E. Pinza bs. T. Serafin cond.

WINTER AND SPRING 1928 CONCERT TOUR

Cities visited include: Washington (Feb. 1); Brockton, Mass. (Feb. 10); Worcester (Feb. 14); Schenectady (Feb. 16); New York City (Feb. 18); Williamsport (Feb. 21); Baltimore (Feb. 24); Waterbury (Feb. 25 or 26); Akron (Feb. 28); Toledo (Mar. 2); Duluth (Mar. 8); Des Moines (Mar. 10); Warrensburg, Mo. (Mar. 14); St. Louis (Mar. 16); Marietta, Ohio (Mar. 19); Louisville (Mar. 21); Dayton (Mar. 23); Bristol, Va. (Mar. 26); Norfolk (Mar. 28); Richmond (Apr. 2); and Troy (Apr. 12).

SPRING 1928 BALTIMORE—LYRIC THEATER

Apr. 16	*La forza del destino*	M. Telva ms. G. Martinelli t. G. de Luca b. P. Malatesta b. E. Pinza bs. V. Bellezza cond.

SPRING 1928 WASHINGTON—POLI'S THEATER

Apr. 18	*Norma*	M. Telva ms. F. Jagel t. L. Rothier bs. V. Bellezza cond.

SPRING 1928 ATLANTA—AUDITORIUM

Apr. 23	*L'africana*	Q. Mario s. B. Gigli t. M. Basiola b. P. Ludikar bs. L. Rothier bs. G. Bamboschek cond.

Apr. 27	*Norma*	M. Telva ms. F. Jagel t. E. Pinza bs. V. Bellezza cond.

SPRING 1928 CLEVELAND—PUBLIC AUDITORIUM

Apr. 30	*Aida*	J. Claussen ms. G. Martinelli t. L. Tibbett b. E. Pinza bs. L. d'Angelo bs. V. Bellezza cond.
May 2	*Norma*	M. Telva ms. F. Jagel t. E. Pinza bs. V. Bellezza cond.
May 5	*Il trovatore*	J. Claussen ms. G. Martinelli t. M. Basiola b. P. Ludikar bs. V. Bellezza cond.

SPRING 1928 ROCHESTER—EASTMAN THEATER

May 8	*Norma*	M. Telva ms. F. Jagel t. L. Rothier bs. V. Bellezza cond.

SPRING 1928 CONCERT TOUR

Cities visited include: Passaic, N.J. (May 14); Harrisburg (May 16); Springfield, Mass. (May 18); Keene; N.H. (May 25); Norwich, Conn.; Staten Island; Lynchburg, Va.; and Greensboro, N.C.

AUTUMN 1928 CONCERT TOUR

Cities visited include: New Haven (Oct. 2); Buffalo (Oct. 4); Toronto (Oct. 6); Detroit (Oct. 8); Ann Arbor (Oct. 10); Dayton (Oct. 12); Philadelphia (Oct. 14); Rochester (Oct. 19); and Bangor (Oct. 24).

AUTUMN 1928 NEW YORK CITY—METROPOLITAN OPERA

Oct. 29	*L'amore dei tre re*	G. Martinelli t. G. Danise b. E. Pinza bs. T. Serafin cond.
Nov. 7	*Norma*	M. Telva ms. G. Lauri-Volpi t. E. Pinza bs. T. Serafin cond.
Nov. 10	*L'africana*	Q. Mario s. B. Gigli t. M. Basiola b. A. Didur bs. E. Pinza bs. T. Serafin cond.
Nov. 17M	*La gioconda*	M. Matzenauer ms. M. Alcock ms. B. Gigli t. G. Danise b. E. Pinza bs. T. Serafin cond.

AUTUMN 1928 PHILADELPHIA—ACADEMY OF MUSIC

Nov. 20	*L'africana*	L. Lerch s. B. Gigli t. M. Basiola b. A. Didur bs. L. Rothier bs. T. Serafin cond.

AUTUMN 1928 BROOKLYN—ACADEMY OF MUSIC

Nov. 24	*Norma*	E. Vettori ms. F. Jagel t. L. Rothier bs. T. Serafin cond.

AUTUMN 1928 NEW YORK CITY—METROPOLITAN OPERA

Nov. 26	*Norma*	M. Telva ms. G. Lauri-Volpi t. E. Pinza bs. T. Serafin cond.
Dec. 6M	*Il trovatore*	L. Homer ms. G. Lauri-Volpi t. G. Danise b. E. Pinza bs. V. Bellezza cond.
Dec. 8M	*Andrea Chénier*	H. Wakefield ms. G. Martinelli t. T. Ruffo b. A. Didur bs. T. Serafin cond.

AUTUMN 1928 PHILADELPHIA—ACADEMY OF MUSIC

Dec. 11	*Ernani*	G. Martinelli t. G. Danise b. E. Pinza bs. V. Bellezza cond.

AUTUMN AND WINTER 1928–29 NEW YORK CITY—METROPOLITAN OPERA

Dec. 14M	*Norma*	M. Telva ms. G. Lauri-Volpi t. L. Rothier bs. T. Serafin cond.
Dec. 17	*Ernani*	G. Martinelli t. T. Ruffo b. E. Pinza bs. V. Bellezza cond.
Dec. 20	*La gioconda*	J. Claussen ms. M. Alcock ms. F. Jagel t. G. Danise b. E. Pinza bs. T. Serafin cond.
Dec. 28	*Ernani*	G. Martinelli t. G. Danise b. E. Pinza bs. V. Bellezza cond.
Dec. 30	Concert	
Jan. 5	*L'africana*	N. Morgana s. B. Gigli t. G. Danise b. A. Didur bs. L. Rothier bs. T. Serafin cond.

WINTER 1929 NEW YORK CITY—PLAZA HOTEL

Jan. 10	Concert	

WINTER 1929 NEW YORK CITY—METROPOLITAN OPERA

Jan. 12	*La gioconda*	J. Claussen ms. M. Alcock ms. B. Gigli t. M. Basiola b. P. Ludikar bs. T. Serafin cond.

WINTER 1929 PHILADELPHIA—ACADEMY OF MUSIC

Jan. 15	*L'amore dei tre re*	E. Johnson t. L. Tibbett b. A. Didur bs. T. Serafin cond.

WINTER 1929 NEW YORK CITY—METROPOLITAN OPERA

Jan. 17	*Ernani*	F. Jagel t. G. Danise b. E. Pinza bs. G. Bamboschek cond.
Jan. 24M	*Ernani*	F. Jagel t. M. Basiola b. E. Pinza bs. G. Bamboschek cond.
Jan. 26M	*Norma*	M. Telva ms. F. Jagel t. E. Pinza bs. T. Serafin cond.

WINTER AND SPRING 1929 CONCERT TOUR

Cities visited include: Washington (Feb. 6); Brockton, Mass.; Boston (Feb. 11); Hartford; Baltimore (Feb. 15); Washington (Feb. 19); Richmond (Feb. 21); Knoxville; Cleveland; Lansing; Kalamazoo (Mar. 1); Chicago; Appleton, Wis.; Cincinnati; Denver; San Francisco (Mar. 12 and 15); Los Angeles; Fresno; Portland (Mar. 25); Seattle (Mar. 27); Milwaukee (Apr. 2); Urbana; and Pittsburgh.

SPRING 1929 NEW YORK CITY—METROPOLITAN OPERA

Apr. 12M	*Norma*	M. Telva ms. F. Jagel t. E. Pinza bs. T. Serafin cond.

SPRING 1929 BALTIMORE—LYRIC THEATER

Apr. 16	*Norma*	M. Telva ms. F. Jagel t. E. Pinza bs. T. Serafin cond.

SPRING 1929 WASHINGTON—POLI'S THEATER

Apr. 18	*Cavalleria rusticana*	M. Telva ms. A. Tokatyan t. L. Tibbett b. V. Bellezza cond.
Apr. 20M	*Aida*	M. Telva ms. G. Lauri-Volpi t. G. Danise b. E. Pinza bs. L. d'Angelo bs. T. Serafin cond.

SPRING 1929 ATLANTA—AUDITORIUM

Apr. 23	*Aida*	J. Claussen ms. G. Lauri-Volpi t. M. Basiola b. E. Pinza bs. J. Macpherson bs. T. Serafin cond.
Apr. 25	*La gioconda*	M. Telva ms. H. Wakefield ms. G. Lauri-Volpi t. G. Danise b. E. Pinza bs. T. Serafin cond.

SPRING 1929 CLEVELAND—PUBLIC AUDITORIUM

Apr. 29	*Norma*	M. Telva ms. F. Jagel t. L. Rothier bs. T. Serafin cond.
May 1	*La gioconda*	J. Claussen ms. M. Telva ms. G. Lauri-Volpi t. G. Danise b. E. Pinza bs. T. Serafin cond.

SPRING 1929 LONDON—COVENT GARDEN

May 28	*Norma*	I. Minghini-Cattaneo ms. N. Fusati t. L. Manfrini bs. V. Bellezza cond.
June 3	*La gioconda*	I. Minghini-Cattaneo ms. B. Castagna ms. A. Pertile t. G. Inghilleri b. F. Autori bs. V. Bellezza cond.
June 7	*Norma*	I. Minghini-Cattaneo ms. N. Fusati t. L. Manfrini bs. V. Bellezza cond.

June 11	*La gioconda*	I. Minghini-Cattaneo ms. B. Castagna ms. F. Merli t. G. Inghilleri b. F. Autori bs. V. Bellezza cond.
June 19	*Norma*	I. Minghini-Cattaneo ms. N. Fusati t. L. Manfrini bs. V. Bellezza cond.

WINTER 1929–30 NEW YORK CITY—METROPOLITAN OPERA

Dec. 21M	*Luisa Miller*	M. Telva ms. G. Lauri-Volpi t. G. de Luca b. T. Pasero bs. P. Ludikar bs. T. Serafin cond.
Dec. 27	*Andrea Chénier*	D. Flexer s. G. Lauri-Volpi t. G. Danise b. V. Bellezza cond.
Dec. 30	*Luisa Miller*	G. Swarthout ms. G. Lauri-Volpi t. G. de Luca b. T. Pasero bs. P. Ludikar bs. T. Serafin cond.
Jan. 2	*Don Giovanni*	E. Fleischer s. E. Rethberg s. B. Gigli t. E. Pinza bs. L. d'Angelo bs. L. Rothier bs. P. Ludikar bs. T. Serafin cond.
Jan. 6	*Don Giovanni*	E. Fleischer s. E. Rethberg s. B. Gigli t. E. Pinza bs. L. d'Angelo bs. L. Rothier bs. P. Ludikar bs. T. Serafin cond.
Jan. 10M	*Norma*	M. Telva ms. G. Lauri-Volpi t. E. Pinza bs. T. Serafin cond.

WINTER 1930 PHILADELPHIA—ACADEMY OF MUSIC

Jan. 14	*Luisa Miller*	G. Swarthout ms. G. Lauri-Volpi t. G. de Luca b. T. Pasero bs. P. Ludikar bs. T. Serafin cond.

WINTER 1930 NEW YORK CITY—METROPOLITAN OPERA

Jan. 16	*Luisa Miller*	M. Telva ms. G. Lauri-Volpi t. G. de Luca b. T. Pasero bs. P. Ludikar bs. T. Serafin cond.
Jan. 22	*Luisa Miller*	M. Telva ms. G. Lauri-Volpi t. G. de Luca b. T. Pasero bs. P. Ludikar bs. T. Serafin cond.
Jan. 25	*Il trovatore*	J. Claussen ms. G. Lauri-Volpi t. G. Danise b. T. Pasero bs. V. Bellezza cond.
Jan. 27	*La gioconda*	K. Branzell ms. M. Telva ms. G. Lauri-Volpi t. G. Danise b. T. Pasero bs. T. Serafin cond.
Jan. 31	*Norma*	M. Telva ms. F. Jagel t. T. Pasero bs. T. Serafin cond.
Feb. 2	Concert	

WINTER AND SPRING 1930 CONCERT TOUR

Cities visited include: Boston; Brockton (Feb. 13); Hartford (Feb. 16); Washington (Feb. 19); Baltimore (Feb. 21); Philadelphia (Feb. 23); Utica; Northampton, Mass.; York, Pa.; Rochester (Mar. 7); Toronto (Mar. 10); Flint; Saginaw; Cleveland (Mar. 17); Memphis; Charlottesville (Mar. 24); Roanoke; Staten Island; Syracuse; Columbus (Apr. 4); and Pittsburgh (Apr. 7).

SPRING 1930 BALTIMORE—LYRIC THEATER

Apr. 21	*Aida*	J. Claussen ms. G. Martinelli t. L. Tibbett b. E. Pinza bs. L. d'Angelo bs. V. Bellezza cond.

SPRING 1930 WASHINGTON—FOX THEATER

Apr. 24	*Andrea Chénier*	H. Wakefield ms. G. Swarthout ms. G. Martinelli t. G. de Luca b. V. Bellezza cond.

SPRING 1930 BALTIMORE—LYRIC THEATER

Apr. 26	*La Juive*	Q. Mario s. G. Martinelli t. A. Tedesco t. L. Rothier bs. L. Hasselmans cond.

SPRING 1930 RICHMOND—MOSQUE AUDITORIUM

Apr. 29	*Aida*	J. Claussen ms. G. Martinelli t. G. Danise b. E. Pinza bs. J. Macpherson bs. V. Bellezza cond.

SPRING 1930 ATLANTA—AUDITORIUM

May 2	*Il trovatore*	J. Claussen ms. G. Martinelli t. G. Danise b. P. Ludikar bs. T. Serafin cond.

SPRING 1930 CLEVELAND—PUBLIC AUDITORIUM

May 5	*La gioconda*	J. Claussen ms. G. Swarthout ms. B. Gigli t. G. Danise b. E. Pinza bs. T. Serafin cond.
May 7	*Cavalleria rusticana*	G. Swarthout ms. B. Gigli t. M. Basiola b. V. Bellezza cond.

SPRING 1930 LONDON—COVENT GARDEN

May 26	*Norma*	I. Minghini-Cattaneo ms. T. Verona t. E. Pinza bs. V. Bellezza cond.
May 29	*Norma*	I. Minghini-Cattaneo ms. T. Verona t. E. Pinza bs. V. Bellezza cond.
June 13	*La traviata*	B. Gigli t. G. Inghilleri b. V. Bellezza cond.
June 18	*La traviata*	A. Minghetti t. G. Inghilleri b. V. Bellezza cond.
June 24	*La traviata*	B. Gigli t. G. Inghilleri b. V. Bellezza cond.

June 30	*L'amore dei tre re*	F. Merli t. G. Inghilleri b. F. Autori bs. V. Bellezza cond.
July 4	*L'amore dei tre re*	F. Merli t. G. Inghilleri b. E. Pinza bs. V. Bellezza cond.

AUTUMN 1930 PHILADELPHIA—ACADEMY OF MUSIC

Oct. 28	*La gioconda*	J. Claussen ms. G. Swarthout ms. B. Gigli t. G. Danise b. E. Pinza bs. T. Serafin cond.

AUTUMN 1930 NEW YORK CITY—METROPOLITAN OPERA

Oct. 31	*L'africana*	N. Guilford s. B. Gigli t. M. Basiola b. P. Ludikar bs. L. Rothier bs. T. Serafin cond.
Nov. 5	*Il trovatore*	J. Claussen ms. G. Martinelli t. M. Basiola b. P. Ludikar bs. V. Bellezza cond.
Nov. 7M	*Don Giovanni*	M. Müller s. E. Fleischer s. B. Gigli t. E. Pinza bs. L. d'Angelo bs. L. Rothier bs. P. Ludikar bs. T. Serafin cond.
Nov. 14	*Norma*	M. Telva ms. F. Jagel t. T. Pasero bs. T. Serafin cond.
Nov. 17	*Don Giovanni*	M. Müller s. E. Fleischer s. B. Gigli t. E. Pinza bs. L. d'Angelo bs. L. Rothier bs. P. Ludikar bs. T. Serafin cond.
Nov. 21M	*La forza del destino*	O. Didur ms. G. Martinelli t. M. Basiola b. A. Gandolfi bs. T. Pasero bs. T. Serafin cond.

AUTUMN 1930 PHILADELPHIA—ACADEMY OF MUSIC

Nov. 25	*Andrea Chénier*	I. Bourskaya ms. G. Swarthout ms. B. Gigli t. M. Basiola b. G. Sturani cond.

AUTUMN 1930 NEW YORK CITY—METROPOLITAN OPERA

Nov. 27	*L'africana*	Q. Mario s. B. Gigli t. M. Basiola b. P. Ludikar bs. T. Pasero bs. T. Serafin cond.
Dec. 1	*La forza del destino*	O. Didur ms. G. Martinelli t. M. Basiola b. A. Gandolfi bs. T. Pasero bs. T. Serafin cond.
Dec. 5M	*La gioconda*	M. Telva ms. F. Petrova ms. B. Gigli t. G. Danise b. E. Pinza bs. T. Serafin cond.

AUTUMN 1930 PHILADELPHIA—ACADEMY OF MUSIC

Dec. 9	*Don Giovanni*	M. Müller s. E. Fleischer s. B. Gigli t. E. Pinza bs. L. d'Angelo bs. L. Rothier bs. P. Ludikar bs. T. Serafin cond.

AUTUMN AND WINTER 1930–31 NEW YORK CITY—METROPOLITAN OPERA

Dec. 13M	*Norma*	M. Telva ms. G. Lauri-Volpi t. T. Pasero bs. T. Serafin cond.
Dec. 17	*L'africana*	Q. Mario s. B. Gigli t. G. Danise b. P. Ludikar bs. L. Rothier bs. T. Serafin cond.
Dec. 20	*La gioconda*	J. Claussen ms. F. Petrova ms. G. Lauri-Volpi t. G. de Luca b. T. Pasero bs. T. Serafin cond.
Dec. 22	*Luisa Miller*	M. Telva ms. G. Lauri-Volpi t. G. de Luca b. T. Pasero bs. P. Ludikar bs. T. Serafin cond.
Dec. 27	*Don Giovanni*	M. Müller s. E. Fleischer s. B. Gigli t. E. Pinza bs. L. d'Angelo bs. L. Rothier bs. P. Ludikar bs. T. Serafin cond.
Dec. 31	*Norma*	M. Telva ms. A. Tokatyan t. T. Pasero bs. T. Serafin cond.
Jan. 3	*La forza del destino*	O. Didur ms. G. Martinelli t. M. Basiola b. A. Gandolfi bs. T. Pasero bs. T. Serafin cond.
Jan. 16M	*La traviata*	G. Lauri-Volpi t. G. de Luca b. T. Serafin cond.
Jan. 18	Concert	
Jan. 23M	*Norma*	M. Telva ms. A. Tokatyan t. E. Pinza bs. T. Serafin cond.
Jan. 26	*La traviata*	G. Lauri-Volpi t. L. Tibbett b. T. Serafin cond.

SPRING 1931 BALTIMORE—LYRIC THEATER

Apr. 18	*La traviata*	G. Lauri-Volpi t. L. Tibbett b. T. Serafin cond.

SPRING 1931 WHITE PLAINS

Apr. 20	*La traviata*	G. Lauri-Volpi t. L. Tibbett b. T. Serafin cond.

SPRING 1931 CLEVELAND—PUBLIC AUDITORIUM

Apr. 27	*La traviata*	G. Lauri-Volpi t. L. Tibbett b. T. Serafin cond.
May 1	*Norma*	G. Swarthout ms. A. Tokatyan t. L. Rothier bs. T. Serafin cond.

SPRING 1931 S.S. AQUITANIA

May 11	Concert	

SPRING 1931 LONDON—COVENT GARDEN

June 1	*La forza del destino*	G. Pederzini ms. A. Pertile t. B. Franci b. T. Pasero bs. T. Serafin cond.
June 4	*La forza del destino*	G. Pederzini ms. A. Pertile t. B. Franci b. T. Serafin cond.
June 9	*La traviata*	D. Borgioli t. D. Noble b. T. Serafin cond.
June 12	*La forza del destino*	G. Pederzini ms. A. Pertile t. B. Franci b. T. Serafin cond.
June 15	*La traviata*	D. Borgioli t. D. Noble b. T. Serafin cond.
June 18	*Fedra**	E. Casazza ms. A. Cortis t. C. Formichi b. T. Serafin cond.
June 23	*Fedra*	E. Casazza ms. A. Cortis t. C. Formichi b. T. Serafin cond.
June 26	*La traviata*	D. Borgioli t. D. Noble b. T. Serafin cond.
June 29	*Fedra*	E. Casazza ms. A. Cortis t. C. Formichi b. T. Serafin cond.

AUTUMN 1931 CONCERT TOUR

Cities visited include: Washington (Oct. 19?); and Hartford (Nov. 12?).

AUTUMN 1931 NEW YORK CITY—METROPOLITAN OPERA

Nov. 2	*La traviata*	G. Lauri-Volpi t. G. de Luca b. T. Serafin cond.
Nov. 14M	*La forza del destino*	G. Swarthout ms. G. Martinelli t. M. Basiola b. A. Gandolfi b. T. Pasero bs. T. Serafin cond.

AUTUMN 1931 BROOKLYN—ACADEMY OF MUSIC

Nov. 17	*La gioconda*	J. Claussen ms. F. Petrova ms. B. Gigli t. M. Basiola b. E. Pinza bs. T. Serafin cond.

AUTUMN 1931 NEW YORK CITY—METROPOLITAN OPERA

Nov. 19	*Don Giovanni*	M. Müller s. E. Fleischer s. B. Gigli t. E. Pinza bs. L. d'Angelo bs. L. Rothier bs. P. Ludikar bs. T. Serafin cond.

AUTUMN 1931 HARTFORD—BUSHNELL THEATER

Nov. 24	*La traviata*	B. Gigli t. G. de Luca b. T. Serafin cond.

AUTUMN AND WINTER 1931–32 NEW YORK CITY—METROPOLITAN OPERA

Dec. 2	*La notte di Zoraima***	F. Jagel t. M. Basiola b. L. d'Angelo bs. T. Serafin cond.
Dec. 5	*La traviata*	A. Tokatyan t. G. de Luca b. T. Serafin cond.
Dec. 9	*La notte di Zoraima*	F. Jagel t. M. Basiola b. L. d'Angelo bs. T. Serafin cond.

Dec. 12	*L'africana*	Q. Mario s. B. Gigli t. G. Danise b. T. Pasero bs. L. Rothier bs. T. Serafin cond.
Dec. 14	*La notte di Zoraima*	F. Jagel t. M. Basiola b. L. d'Angelo bs. T. Serafin cond.
Dec. 18	*Don Giovanni*	M. Müller s. E. Fleischer s. B. Gigli t. E. Pinza bs. L. d'Angelo bs. L. Rothier bs. P. Ludikar bs. T. Serafin cond.
Dec. 26M	*Norma*	G. Swarthout ms. G. Lauri-Volpi t. E. Pinza bs. T. Serafin cond.
Dec. 28	*L'africana*	N. Guilford s. B. Gigli t. M. Basiola b. A. Didur bs. E. Pinza bs. T. Serafin cond.
Dec. 31	*La notte di Zoraima*	F. Jagel t. M. Basiola b. L. d'Angelo bs. T. Serafin cond.
Jan. 6	*La forza del destino*	G. Swarthout ms. G. Martinelli t. M. Basiola b. A. Gandolfi b. T. Pasero bs. T. Serafin cond.
Jan. 8	*La gioconda*	J. Claussen ms. F. Petrova ms. G. Lauri-Volpi t. G. Danise b. E. Pinza bs. T. Serafin cond.

WINTER 1932 PHILADELPHIA—ACADEMY OF MUSIC

Jan. 12	*La notte di Zoraima*	F. Jagel t. M. Basiola b. L. d'Angelo bs. T. Serafin cond.

WINTER 1932 NEW YORK CITY—METROPOLITAN OPERA

Jan. 16	*Il trovatore*	F. Petrova ms. G. Lauri-Volpi t. G. Danise b. T. Pasero bs. V. Bellezza cond.
Jan. 22	*La forza del destino*	I. Bourskaya ms. G. Martinelli t. A. Borgioli b. A. Gandolfi b. T. Pasero bs. T. Serafin cond.
Jan. 25	*Norma*	G. Swarthout ms. F. Jagel t. T. Pasero bs. T. Serafin cond.

WINTER 1932 WASHINGTON

Feb. 1 Concert

WINTER 1932 NEW YORK CITY—METROPOLITAN OPERA

Feb. 7 Concert

WINTER AND SPRING 1932 CONCERT TOUR

Cities visited include: Hartford (Feb. 14); Washington (Feb. 17); Buffalo (Feb. 24); Rochester (Feb. 26); London, Ont. (Feb. 29); Detroit (Mar. 2); Columbus (Mar. 7); Indianapolis (Mar. 14); Ann Arbor (Mar. 16); Pittsburgh (Mar. 28); New Haven (Mar. 30); Orange, N.J. (Apr. 1); and Boston (Apr. 3).

SPRING 1932 BALTIMORE—LYRIC THEATER

Apr. 20	*L'africana*	A. Doninelli s. B. Gigli t. M. Basiola b. P. Ludikar bs. L. Rothier bs. T. Serafin cond.

SPRING 1932 CLEVELAND—PUBLIC AUDITORIUM

Apr. 23	*La gioconda*	C. Ponselle ms. H. Wakefield ms. G. Martinelli t. M. Basiola b. E. Pinza bs. T. Serafin cond.

SPRING 1932 CONCERT TOUR

Cities visited include: Detroit (May 1); Ann Arbor (May 8); Oberlin (May 11); Cleveland; Grand Rapids; Indianapolis (May 16); Baltimore (May 18); New York City (May 21); Brooklyn; and New Haven.

AUTUMN 1932 CONCERT TOUR

Cities visited include: Buffalo (Oct. 10); Cleveland (Oct. 14); Hartford(Oct. 16); Cincinnati (Oct. 18, cancelled because of her mother's death); Hartford; Reading; Toronto (Oct. 21); Toledo; Akron (Oct. 25); and Montreal.

AUTUMN 1932 PHILADELPHIA—ACADEMY OF MUSIC

Nov. 22	*La gioconda*	R. Bampton ms. F. Petrova ms. G. Lauri-Volpi t. A. Borgioli b. T. Pasero bs. G. Sturani cond.

AUTUMN 1932 NEW YORK CITY—METROPOLITAN OPERA

Nov. 25	*Andrea Chénier*	F. Petrova ms. G. Lauri-Volpi t. A. Borgioli b. V. Bellezza cond.
Nov. 28	*La gioconda*	R. Bampton ms. F. Petrova ms. G. Lauri-Volpi t. A. Borgioli b. T. Pasero bs. T. Serafin cond.
Dec. 1	*La traviata*	T. Schipa t. R. Bonelli b. T. Serafin cond.

AUTUMN 1932 BROOKLYN—ACADEMY OF MUSIC

Dec. 6	*La traviata*	T. Schipa t. L. Tibbett b. T. Serafin cond.

AUTUMN AND WINTER 1932–33 NEW YORK CITY—METROPOLITAN OPERA

Dec. 15M	*La traviata*	G. Lauri-Volpi t. L. Tibbett b. T. Serafin cond.
Dec. 17M	*Don Giovanni*	M. Müller s. E. Fleischer s. T. Schipa t. E. Pinza bs. P. Malatesta bs. T. Pasero bs. L. Rothier bs. T. Serafin cond.
Dec. 21	*La gioconda*	C. Ponselle ms. F. Petrova ms. G. Lauri-Volpi t. A. Borgioli b. T. Pasero bs. T. Serafin cond.

Jan. 2	*Don Giovanni*	M. Müller s. E. Fleischer s. T. Schipa t. E. Pinza bs. L. d'Angelo bs. T. Pasero bs. A. Anderson bs. T. Serafin cond.
Jan. 8	*Cavalleria rusticana*	G. Swarthout ms. A. Tokatyan t. A. Borgioli b. W. Pelletier cond.

WINTER 1933 BALTIMORE

Feb. 8 Concert

WINTER 1933 NEW YORK CITY—METROPOLITAN OPERA

Feb. 26 Gala Concert

WINTER 1933 CONCERT TOUR

Cities known to have been visited include: Washington (Mar. 3); and Kansas City (Mar.).

SPRING 1933 FLORENCE—MAGGIO MUSICALE FIORENTINO

May 4	*La vestale*	E. Stignani ms. A. Dolci t. P. Biasini b. T. Pasero bs. V. Gui cond.
May 7	*La vestale*	E. Stignani ms. A. Dolci t. P. Biasini b. T. Pasero bs. V. Gui cond.

SUMMER 1933 NAPLES

July 4 Concert

AUTUMN 1933 CONCERT TOUR

Cities visited include: Worcester (Oct. 6); Philadelphia; Harrisburg; Toronto (Oct. 11); Detroit; Indianapolis (Oct. 22); Rochester (Oct. 27); Peoria; Lawrence, Kans. (Nov. 8); Hartford (Nov. 17); Schenectady (Nov. 27); Hanover, N.H. (Dec. 5); Brooklyn (Dec. 8); and Cleveland (Dec. 26).

WINTER 1933–34 NEW YORK CITY—METROPOLITAN OPERA

Dec. 28	*L'africana*	N. Morgana s. G. Martinelli t. A. Borgioli b. V. Lazzari bs. L. Rothier bs. T. Serafin cond.
Jan. 3	*Don Giovanni*	M. Müller s. E. Fleischer s. T. Schipa t. E. Pinza bs. L. d'Angelo bs. V. Lazzari bs. L. Rothier bs. T. Serafin cond.

WINTER 1934 TOLEDO

Jan. 12 Concert

WINTER 1934 NEW YORK CITY—METROPOLITAN OPERA

Jan. 13M	*L'africana*	N. Morgana s. F. Jagel t. A. Borgioli b. V. Lazzari bs. L. Rothier bs. T. Serafin cond.

Jan. 20M	*Don Giovanni*	M. Müller s. E. Fleischer s. T. Schipa t. E. Pinza bs. L. d'Angelo bs. V. Lazzari bs. E. List bs. T. Serafin cond.

WINTER 1934 HARTFORD—BUSHNELL THEATER

Jan. 30	*Cavalleria rusticana*	G. Swarthout ms. F. Jagel t. A. Borgioli b. V. Bellezza cond.

WINTER 1934 NEW YORK CITY—METROPOLITAN OPERA

Feb. 2M	*La traviata*	T. Schipa t. J. C. Thomas b. T. Serafin cond.
Feb. 5	*Don Giovanni*	M. Müller s. E. Fleischer s. T. Schipa t. E. Pinza bs. L. d'Angelo bs. V. Lazzari bs. L. Rothier bs. T. Serafin cond.
Feb. 11	*Cavalleria rusticana*	G. Swarthout ms. F. Jagel t. A. Borgioli b. W. Pelletier cond.
Mar. 2	*La gioconda*	C. Ponselle ms. G. Swarthout ms. G. Martinelli t. A. Borgioli b. V. Lazzari bs. T. Serafin cond.
Mar. 11	Gala Concert	

SPRING 1934 CONCERT TOUR

Cities visited include: New Orleans (Mar. 17); St. Louis; Lawrence, Kans.; Dallas (Mar. 20); Birmingham (Mar. 23); San Francisco (Apr. 5); Los Angeles (Apr. 6); and Des Moines.

SPRING 1934 NEW YORK CITY—METROPOLITAN OPERA

Apr. 14	*Cavalleria rusticana*	G. Swarthout ms. F. Jagel t. A. Gandolfi b. W. Pelletier cond.

SPRING 1934 CONCERT TOUR

Cities visited include: Ann Arbor (May 10); Pittsburgh (May 16 and May 24); Providence (May 25); and Meriden (May 31).

SUMMER 1934 ST. MORITZ—PALACE HOTEL

Aug. 10	Concert

AUTUMN 1934 CONCERT TOUR

Cities visited include: Pittsburgh (Oct. 10); and Ann Arbor (Oct. 24).

WINTER 1934–35 NEW YORK CITY—METROPOLITAN OPERA

Dec. 27	*La gioconda*	C. Ponselle ms. G. Swarthout ms. G. Martinelli t. A. Borgioli b. V. Lazzari bs. E. Panizza cond.
Jan. 5M	*La traviata*	F. Jagel t. L. Tibbett b. E. Panizza cond.

WINTER 1934–35 BROOKLYN—ACADEMY OF MUSIC

Jan. 8	*La gioconda*	C. Ponselle ms. M. Leonard ms. G. Martinelli t. A. Borgioli b. E. Pinza bs. E. Panizza cond.

WINTER 1935 NEW YORK CITY—METROPOLITAN OPERA

Jan. 18	*Don Giovanni*	M. Müller s. E. Fleischer s. D. Borgioli t. E. Pinza bs. L. d'Angelo bs. V. Lazzari bs. L. Rothier bs. E. Panizza cond.
Jan. 21	*La gioconda*	R. Bampton ms. G. Swarthout ms. G. Martinelli t. A. Borgioli b. V. Lazzari bs. E. Panizza cond.
Jan. 31	*La traviata*	R. Crooks t. G. de Luca b. E. Panizza cond.
Feb. 3	Concert	
Feb. 9M	*Don Giovanni*	M. Müller s. E. Fleischer s. T. Schipa t. E. Pinza bs. L. d'Angelo bs. V. Lazzari bs. E. List bs. E. Panizza cond.
Feb. 13	*Cavalleria rusticana*	I. Petina ms. F. Jagel t. A. Borgioli b. V. Bellezza cond.
Feb. 15	*La traviata*	T. Schipa t. R. Bonelli b. E. Panizza cond.
Mar. 19	Gala Concert	

WINTER 1935 WASHINGTON—MAYFLOWER HOTEL

Mar. 4	Concert	

WINTER 1935–36 NEW YORK CITY—METROPOLITAN OPERA

Dec. 27	*Carmen*	H. Burke s. G. Martinelli t. E. Pinza bs. L. Hasselmans cond.
Jan. 6	*Carmen*	H. Burke s. C. Kullmann t. E. Pinza bs. L. Hasselmans cond.

WINTER 1936 HARTFORD—BUSHNELL THEATER

Jan. 14	*Carmen*	H. Burke s. C. Kullmann t. E. Pinza bs. L. Hasselmans cond.

WINTER 1936 NEW YORK CITY—METROPOLITAN OPERA

Jan. 25	*Carmen*	H. Burke s. G. Martinelli t. E. Pinza bs. L. Hasselmans cond.

WINTER 1936 PHILADELPHIA—ACADEMY OF MUSIC

Jan. 28	*Carmen*	L. Bori s. G. Martinelli t. E. Pinza bs. L. Hasselmans cond.

WINTER 1936 NEW YORK CITY—METROPOLITAN OPERA

Feb. 1	*Carmen*	S. Fisher s. C. Kullmann t. E. Pinza bs. L. Hasselmans cond.

Feb. 12	*Carmen*	Q. Mario s. R. Maison t. E. Pinza bs. L. Hasselmans cond.
Feb. 16	Concert	

WINTER 1936 BROOKLYN—ACADEMY OF MUSIC

Feb. 25	*Carmen*	S. Fisher s. R. Maison t. E. Pinza bs. L. Hasselmans cond.

WINTER 1936 NEW YORK CITY—METROPOLITAN OPERA

Mar. 14	*Carmen*	S. Fisher s. R. Maison t. J. Huehn b. L. Hasselmans cond.

SPRING 1936 BOSTON

Mar. 28M	*Carmen*	H. Burke s. R. Maison t. E. Pinza bs. L. Hasselmans cond.

SPRING 1936 NEW YORK CITY—METROPOLITAN OPERA

Mar. 29	Gala Concert	

SPRING 1936 BALTIMORE—LYRIC THEATER

Apr. 4	*Carmen*	H. Burke s. R. Maison t. J. Huehn b. L. Hasselmans cond.

AUTUMN 1936 NEW YORK CITY—CARNEGIE HALL

Sep. 27	Concert	

AUTUMN 1936 CONCERT TOUR

Cities visited include: Worcester (Oct. 19); and Columbus, Ohio (Nov. 12).

WINTER 1937 NEW YORK CITY—METROPOLITAN OPERA

Jan. 9M	*Carmen*	N. Bodanya s. S. Rayner t. J. Huehn b. G. Papi cond.
Jan. 21	*Carmen*	N. Bodanya s. R. Maison t. E. Pinza bs. G. Papi cond.
Feb. 4M	*Cavalleria rusticana*	I. Petina ms. S. Rayner t. C. Morelli b. G. Papi cond.
Feb. 15	*Carmen*	H. Burke s. R. Maison t. E. Pinza bs. G. Papi cond.

WINTER 1937 BROOKLYN—ACADEMY OF MUSIC

Feb. 23	*Cavalleria rusticana*	H. Olheim s. F. Jagel t. J. Royer b. G. Papi cond.

WINTER 1937 NEW YORK CITY—METROPOLITAN OPERA

Mar. 14	Concert	

SPRING 1937 BALTIMORE—LYRIC THEATER

Mar. 31	*Cavalleria rusticana*	I. Petina ms. S. Rayner t. C. Morelli b. G. Papi cond.

SPRING 1937 CLEVELAND—PUBLIC AUDITORIUM

Apr. 12	*Cavalleria rusticana*	I. Petina ms. S. Rayner t. C. Morelli b. G. Papi cond.
Apr. 17	*Carmen*	H. Burke s. R. Maison t. J. Huehn b. G. Papi cond.

AUTUMN 1937 CONCERT TOUR

Cities visited include: Worcester (Oct. 8); Atlanta (Oct. 14); Washington (Oct. 17); Pittsburgh (Oct. 23); Boston (Nov. 4); Columbus, Ohio (Nov. 12); Baltimore (Nov. 19); and Charleston (Nov. 23 or 24).

AUTUMN 1938 CONCERT TOUR

Cities visited include: Long Beach (Oct. 7); Seattle (Oct. 21); Vancouver (Oct. 22); and Portland (Oct. 25).

WINTER 1939 FINAL CONCERTS

Ponselle's final two concerts were given in Baltimore (Feb. 7) and Washington (Feb. 9), both with the National Symphony.

AUTUMN 1952 BALTIMORE ARMORY (RALLY FOR DWIGHT D. EISENHOWER)

Sep. 25	Special Appearance

Rosa Ponselle's Repertoire

OPERAS IN CHRONOLOGICAL ORDER BY ASSUMPTION OF ROLE

World premieres sung by Rosa Ponselle are underlined.

OPERA AND COMPOSER	ROLE	CITY	THEATER	DATE	TOTAL TIMES SUNG
La Forza del destino, Verdi	Leonora	New York	Metropolitan	15 Nov. 1918	38
Cavalleria rusticana, Mascagni	Santuzza	Philadelphia	Academy of Music	10 Dec. 1918	38
Oberon, Weber	Rezia	New York	Metropolitan	28 Dec. 1918	10
The Legend, Breil	Carmelita	New York	Metropolitan	12 Mar. 1919	3
La Juive, Halevy	Rachel	New York	Metropolitan	22 Nov. 1919	17
Aida, Verdi	Aida	Brooklyn	Academy of Music	6 Mar. 1920	14
Don Carlo, Verdi	Elisabetta	New York	Metropolitan	23 Dec. 1920	10
Andrea Chénier, Giordano	Maddalena	Atlanta	Auditorium	25 Apr. 1921	16
Ernani, Verdi	Elvira	New York	Metropolitan	8 Dec. 1921	19
Le Roi d'Ys, Lalo	Margared	New York	Metropolitan	5 Jan. 1922	4
William Tell, Rossini	Mathilde	New York	Metropolitan	5 Jan. 1923	7
L'africana, Meyerbeer	Selika	New York	Metropolitan	21 Mar. 1923	35
Il trovatore, Verdi	Leonora	New York	Metropolitan	19 Apr. 1924	15
La gioconda, Ponchielli	La gioconda	Philadelphia	Academy of Music	9 Dec. 1924	38
La vestale, Spontini	Julia	New York	Metropolitan	12 Nov. 1925	11
L'amore dei tre re, Montemezzi	Fiora	New York	Metropolitan	29 Dec. 1926	6
Norma, Bellini	Norma	New York	Metropolitan	16 Nov. 1927	34
Luisa Miller, Verdi	Luisa Miller	New York	Metropolitan	21 Dec. 1929	6
Don Giovanni, Mozart	Donna Anna	New York	Metropolitan	2 Jan. 1930	15

La traviata, Verdi	Violetta	London	Covent Garden	13 June 1930	21
Fedra, Romani	Fedra	London	Covent Garden	18 June 1931	3
La notte di Zoraima, Montemezzi	Zoraima	New York	Metropolitan	2 Dec. 1932	5
Carmen, Bizet	Carmen	New York	Metropolitan	27 Dec. 1935	15

OPERAS IN ALPHABETICAL ORDER BY COMPOSER

Bellini: *Norma*
Bizet: *Carmen*
Breil: *The Legend*
Giordano: *Andrea Chénier*
Halevy: *La Juive*
Lalo: *Le Roi d'Ys*
Mascagni: *Cavalleria rusticana*
Meyerbeer: *L'africana*
Montemezzi: *L'amore dei tre re* and *La notte di Zoraima*
Mozart: *Don Giovanni*
Ponchielli: *La gioconda*
Romani: *Fedra*
Rossini: *William Tell*
Spontini: *La vestale*
Verdi: *Aida*, *Don Carlo*, *Ernani*, *La forza del destino*, *Luisa Miller*, *La traviata*, and *Il trovatore*
Weber: *Oberon*

RELIGIOUS WORKS

Rossini: *Messe Solennelle*, *Stabat Mater*
Verdi: *Messa di Requiem*

Discography

BY BILL PARK

The recording career of Rosa Ponselle neatly divides itself into three periods. The initial one began with a test recording she made for the Columbia Graphophone Company a few months before her Metropolitan debut in 1918 and concluded with a final series of selections she recorded for the Victor Talking Machine Company's prestigious Red Seal label early in 1929. The second period took place in the autumn of 1939, when Ponselle briefly resumed her recording career for RCA Victor while staying in Hollywood. Her pianist during that week-long session was her mentor, Romano Romani, who had accompanied her and had conducted the studio orchestra at all her Columbia recording sessions two decades earlier.

The third period was long in coming but, in the estimation of record reviewers of the time, was well worth the wait. In 1954, when she was approaching sixty, Ponselle signed a new contract with RCA Victor and recorded enough selections for two long-playing albums. Harking back to the earliest days of the recording industry when pioneer technicians traveled to Tamagno's villa and Patti's castle to capture their voices during their twilight years, RCA sent its sound engineers to Villa Pace to record the voice of Ponselle nearly two decades after she had last appeared at the Metropolitan Opera House.

This discography is an updated, summary version of the one appearing in *Ponselle: A Singer's Life* (Doubleday, 1982). Part I of this version chronicles the Ponselle Columbia recordings. Part II lists all known information pertaining to her Victor recordings, from the first of her Red Seal sessions in December 1923 through the LP sessions at Villa Pace in October 1954. Because Ponselle recorded both acoustically and electrically for the Victor Company, the discography entries carry this identifying information to enable the reader to distinguish between them.

As with those of other legendary singers, most of Ponselle's commercial recordings were transferred from their original 78 r.p.m. format onto long-playing albums. In recent years, however, the compact disc recording has relegated the long-playing record to the same fate as the shellac discs of Ponselle's day. Accordingly, all Ponselle CD releases that have been published as of April 1996 are listed in this discography. Many new Ponselle CDs, however, are anticipated during the Ponselle centennial in 1997. In Part III, these CDs are listed by label, catalog number, and title. In Parts I and II, the contents of each CD are listed with the original recordings they contain.

In Part IV, all known performances that Rosa Ponselle sang on radio are listed in chronological order. A number of these were preserved through "air checks," or discs that were recorded by networks and sponsors in order to monitor the quality of the broadcast signal. Where known from newspapers or other sources, all selections Ponselle performed on each broadcast are also listed. (Newspaper accounts of selections Ponselle was to sing on a broadcast often differed from those she actually performed.) If part or all of the broadcast was preserved and has been issued in compact-disc form, the CD catalog number is listed accordingly.

Because this discography is the first and only one that Rosa Ponselle herself not only commissioned but also authorized, I was fortunate to have been able to express to her my special appreciation for her encouragement and assistance. In updating my earlier work, I am indebted to John Pfeiffer and Bernadette Moore of BMG Records, Louise Rice and Virginia Barder of Romophone, Paul Gruber of the Metropolitan Opera, William R. Moran, Thomas G. Kaufman, James A. Drake, James M. Alfonte, H. Ward Marston, Jeffrey Miller, Dan Hladik, Lawrence F. Holdridge, Raymond Horneman, and Susan Halfhill. I am similarly indebted to the staffs of Nimbus, Legato Classics, and Fono Enterprise SRL. I am also grateful to Aida Favia-Artsay, whose tribute to Rosa Ponselle and her recordings captures the sentiments of all who have been enchanted by her uniqueness:

> To listen to these recordings is to be enchanted by a voice never equalled for its bewitching beauty, first giving shape to the musical composition with the care of a master sculptor and then, like him, passing on to the details, vivid or subdued, as the object being created may require. . . . We have samples of her art in its progressive developments, and as hers was a perfectly phonogenic voice, we can enjoy it to our heart's content in all its resplendent glory.

I. Columbia Records

1. Abide With Me (Monk) [Eng.]
   With B. Maurel (Orch. R. Romani)
   78557-1, -*2*; 36000D; X245 (U.K.)
   9 July 1919
2. *Africana* (Meyerbeer): Figlio del sol [It.]
   (Orch. R. Romani)
   98059-*1*, -2; 68000D CDS 9964
   1 Feb. 1923
3. *Aida* (Verdi): Ritorna vincitor [It.]
   (Orch. R. Romani)
   98092-*1*, -2 68084D; 7066M CDS 9964, NI 7878
   19 Sept. 1923

4. *Aida* (Verdi): O patria mia [It.]
(Orch. R. Romani)
49557-1, -2, -3, -4, -*5*; 68036D; 8910M CDS 9964
29 Nov. 1918
5. *Aida* (Verdi): O terra, addio! [It.]
With C. Hackett (Orch. R. Romani)
49734-*1*; 71000D; 9010M CDS 9964
14 Jan. 1920
6. Blue Danube Waltz (Strauss) [Eng.]
(Orch. R. Romani)
49988-1, -2, -3, -*4*; 68078D; 7062M CDS 9964, VA 1120, MIN 7
17 Sept. 1921
7. *Bohème* (Puccini): Sì, mi chiamano Mimi [It.]
(Orch. R. Romani)
98062-1, -*2*; 68000D; 7035M CDS 9964, NI 7878
13 Feb. 1923
8. Carolina Sunshine (Hirsch-Schmidt) [Eng.]
With C. Ponselle (Orch. R. Romani)
78927-1, -2; (Unpublished)
15 Jan. 1920
9. *Cavalleria rusticana* (Mascagni): Ave Maria (Intermezzo) [It.]
(Orch. R. Romani)
49556-1 (unpublished)
29 Nov. 1918
10. *Cavalleria rusticana* (Mascagni): Voi lo sapete [It.]
(Orch. R. Romani)
49570-1, -*2*; 68039D 8089M CDS 9964, NI 7878, MET 218CD
9 Jan. 1919
11. Comin' Thro' the Rye (Traditional) [Eng.]
With C. Ponselle (Orch. R. Romani)
78847-1, -2, -*3*; 36002D CDS 9964, MET 218CD
9 Dec. 1919
12. *Ernani* (Verdi): Ernani! Ernani, involami [It.]
(Orch. R. Romani)
98028-*1*, -2; 68037D; 7034M NI 7878
9 June 1922
13. Flower of the Snow (E. Brown) [Eng.]
(Orch. R. Romani)
49756-1 (unpublished)
20–27 Feb. 1920
14. *Forza del destino* (Verdi): La Vergine degli angeli [It.]
With Chorus (Orch. R. Romani)
49558-1, -2, -4, -5, -*6*, -7, -*8*; 68038D; 8910M; 7227, 7340 (U.K.) CDS 9964 (-*6*), NI 7846 (-*6*)
2 Dec. 1918

15. *Forza del destino* (Verdi): Pace, pace, mio Dio [It.]
(Pf. R. Romani)
Test record, matrix number unknown
3 Apr. 1918
16. *Forza del destino* (Verdi): Pace, pace, mio Dio [It.]
(Orch. R. Romani)
49859-1, -*2*; 68038D; 7033M CDS 9964
5 July 1920
17. *Gioconda* (Ponchielli): Suicidio!
(Orch. R. Romani)
49735-1, -2, -*3*; 68039D; 7034M CDS 9964, MET 218CD
14 Jan. 1920
18. Good-Bye (Tosti) [Eng.]
(Orch. R. Romani)
49560-1, -2, -*3*; 68064D 7035M CDS 9964, NI 7846, VA 1120, MIN 7
2 Dec. 1918
19. Home, Sweet Home (Bishop) [Eng.]
(Orch. R. Romani)
49935-*1*; 68065D; 7064M CDS 9964
16 Feb. 1921
20. *Juive* (Halévy): Il va venir [Fr.]
(Orch. R. Romani)
98096-1, -2
28 Sept. 1923
-*3*; AF 1 CDS 9964, NI 7846
11 Jan. 1924
-4
14 Jan. 1924
21. Keep the Home Fires Burning (Novello) [Eng.]
With Quartet: Harrison, Miller, Croxton, Sarto (Orch. R. Romani)
49585-1, -2, -*3*; 7038M CDS 9964, VA 1120, MIN 7
15 Feb. 1919
22. Little Alabama Coon (Starr) [Eng.]
With Quartet: Harrison, Miller, Croxton, Sarto (Orch. R. Romani)
79980-1, -2, -3
10 Sept. 1921
4, -*5*; 33003D; 2024M CDS 9964
13 Apr. 1922
23. *Lohengrin* (Wagner): Einsam in trüben Tagen [Ger.]
(Orch. R. Romani)
98093-*1*, -2; AF 1 CDS 9964, NI 7846, BIM 701-2
21 Sept. 1923
24. *Madama Butterfly* (Puccini): Un bel dì vedremo [It.]
(Orch. R. Romani)
49571-1, -*2*; 68059D; 7065M; 7234; 7340 (U.K.) CDS 9964, NI 7846, NI

7802
9 Jan. 1919

25. *Mademoiselle Modiste* (Herbert): Kiss Me Again [Eng.]
(Orch. R. Romani)
49869-1, *-2*; 68077D; 7061M CDS 9964, NI 7846, NI 7851, MET 218CD
26 July 1920

26. *Manon Lescaut* (Puccini): In quelle trine morbide [It.]
(Orch. R. Romani)
79971-1, *-2* MET 218CD
7 Sept. 1921
-3; 36001D; 2014M (with recitative) CDS 9964, NI 7846
19 Sept. 1923
-4
11 Oct. 1923

27. Maria, Marì (Di Capua) [It.]
(Orch. R. Romani)
49870-1, *-2*; 68064D; 7035M CDS 9964, VA 1120, NI 7878, MIN 7
26 July 1920

28. *Maritana* (Wallace): Scenes That Are Brightest [Eng.]
(Orch. R. Romani)
49982-1, *-2*; 68078D, 7062M CDS 9964, MET 218CD
9 Sept. 1921

29. *Norma* (Bellini): Casta diva [It.]
(Orch. R. Romani)
49720-1, -2, -3, *-4*; 68060D; 7063M CDS 9964
11 Dec. 1919

30. Oh! That We Two Were Maying (Nevin) [Eng.]
With C. Ponselle (Orch. R. Romani)
80391-1, -2, -3 (Unpublished)
9 June 1922

31. Old Folks at Home (Foster) [Eng.]
(Orch. R. Romani)
49934-*1*; 68065D, 7064M CDS 9964
15 Feb. 1921

32. 'O Sole Mio (Capurro-Di Capua) [It.]
With C. Ponselle (Orch. R. Romani)
49983-*1*; 9007M CDS 9964, VA 1120, MIN 7
9 Sept. 1921

33. *Otello* (Verdi): Ave Maria [It.]
(Orch. R. Romani)
98029-1, *-2*, -3; 68060D; 7063M CDS 9964
9 June 1922

34. *Pagliacci* (Leoncavallo): Stridono lassù [It.]
(Orch. R. Romani)
98063-1, -2

13 Feb. 1923
-3, -4, -5
22 Sept. 1923
-*6*, -7; 68084D; 7066M CDS 9964, NI 7878, MET 218CD
11 Jan. 1924

35. Rachem (Mana-Zucca) [Yid.]
(Orch. R. Romani)
49925-1, -2, -*3*; 7025M CDS 9964
8 Jan. 1921

36. Rose of My Heart (Löhr) [Eng.]
(Orch. R. Romani)
49987-1 (unpublished)
17 Sept. 1921

37. Rose of My Heart (Löhr) [Eng.]
(Orch. R. Romani)
80307-*1*; 33003D; 2024M CDS 9964
13 Apr. 1922

38. *Sadko* (Rimsky-Korsakov): Song of India [Eng.]
(Orch. R. Romani)
49920-1, -*2*; 68077D; 7061M CDS 9964, NI 7846
30 Dec. 1920

39. *Tales of Hoffmann* (Offenbach): Barcarolle [Eng.]
With C. Ponselle (Orch. R. Romani)
78846-1, -*2*, -3; 36001D CDS 9964
9 Dec. 1919

40. *Tosca* (Puccini): Vissi d'arte [It.]
(Orch. R. Romani)
49569-1, -2, -3, -4, -*5*; 68059D; 7065M CDS 9964, NI 7846, NI 7851
7 Jan. 1919

41. *Trovatore* (Verdi): Tacea la notte [It.]
(Orch. R. Romani)
98051-*1*, -2; 68036D; 7033M CDS 9964, NI 7878
16 Nov. 1922

42. *Trovatore* (Verdi): D'amor sull'ali rosee [It.]
(Orch. R. Romani)
49559-1, -2, -3, -*4*; 68058D 8089M CDS 9964, NI 7846, MET 409CD, CD MOIR 428
10 Dec. 1918

43. *Trovatore* (Verdi): Mira d'acerbe lagrime [It.]
With R. Stracciari (Orch. R. Romani)
49922- 1, -*2*, -3; 71000D CDS 9964, MET 218CD, CD MOIR 428
30 Dec. 1920

44. Values (Vanderpool) [Eng.]
(Orch. R. Romani)
78920- 1, -2, -*3* CDS 9964

10 Jan. 1920
45. *Vespri Siciliani* (Verdi): Mercè, dilette amiche [It.]
(Orch. R. Romani)
49686-1, -2, -*3*; 68037D CDS 9964, MET 218CD
4 Nov. 1919
46. Where My Caravan Has Rested (Löhr) [Eng.]
With C. Ponselle (Orch. R. Romani)
80392-1
2 June 1922
-2, -*3*; 36002D; 2019M CDS 9964
13 June 1922
47. Whispering Hope (Hawthorne) [Eng.]
With B. Maurel (Orch. R. Romani)
78325-1, -2, -3
1 March 1919
-*4*, -5, -*6*; 36000D; 2019M; X242 (U.K.)
9 July 1919
48. *William Tell* (Rossini): Selva opaca [It.]
(Orch. R. Romani)
98058-*1*, -2; 68058D; 7026M CDS 9964, NI 7878, MET 218CD
1 Feb. 1923

II. Victor Records

49. *Africana* (Meyerbeer): Figlio del sol [It.]
(Orch. R. Bourdon)
C 31710-*1*; 6496B MET 218CD, ROM 81006-2 (B)
-*2* BMG 7810-2-RG, ROM 81006-2 (B), NI 7878
14 Jan. 1925
50. Agnus Dei (Bizet) [Lat.]
(Org. I. Chichagov)
(No Matrix Number Assigned) ROM 81023-2
20 Oct. 1954
51. *Aida* (Verdi): Ritorna vincitor [It.]
(Orch. R. Bourdon)
C 29063-1, -*2*; 74860; 6437A ROM 81006-2 (A)
5 Dec. 1923
-3, -*4* ROM 81006-2 (A)
11 Dec. 1923
CVE 29063-5, -*6*; VIC 1507 ROM 81007-2 (A)
20 May 1926
-7, -8
8 Dec. 1927

-*9*; 7438A; 8993; DB 1606 NI 7846, BMG 7810-2-RG, ROM 81007-2 (B), CD MOIR 428
18 Jan. 1928

52. *Aida* (Verdi): Qui Radamès verà . . . O patria mia [It.]
(Orch. R. Bourdon)
C 29061-1, -*2*; 74861; 6437B DB 854 NI 7805, MET 218CD, BMG 7810-2-RG, ROM 81006-2 (A), CD MOIR 428
5 Dec. 1923
-3, -4
11 Dec. 1923
CVE 29061-5, -*6* VIC 1507 ROM 81007-2 (B)
20 May 1926

53. *Aida* (Verdi): Pur ti riveggo, mia dolce Aida [It.]
With G. Martinelli (Orch. R. Bourdon)
C 29446-1, -*2*, -3; IRCC 126; VB 73 NI 7805, ROM 81006-2 (A), MET 706CD, CD MOIR 428
7 Feb. 1924

54. *Aida* (Verdi): Là tra foreste vergine [It.]
With G. Martinelli (Orch. R. Bourdon)
C 29447-1, -*2*; VB 73 NI 7805, ROM 81006-2 (A), MET 706CD, CD MOIR 428
7 Feb. 1924

55. *Aida* (Verdi): La fatal pietra [It.]
With G. Martinelli (Orch. R. Bourdon)
C 29451-*1* ROM 81006-2 (A)
-*2*; ABHB 3 ROM 81006-2 (A), NI 7878
8 Feb. 1924

56. *Aida* (Verdi): O terra, addio! [It.]
With G. Martinelli (Orch. R. Bourdon)
C 29450-*1*, -2; ABHB 3 ROM 81006-2 (A), NI 7878
8 Feb. 1924

57. *Aida* (Verdi): La fatal pietra [It.]
With G. Martinelli (Orch. R. Bourdon)
BVE 35459-1, -2, -*3*; 3040A; 1744A; DA 810 NI 7846, ROM 81007-2 (A), MET 503CD, CD MOIR 428
17 May 1926

58. *Aida* (Verdi): Morir! Si pura e bella! [It.]
With G. Martinelli (Orch. R. Bourdon)
BVE 35460-1, -2, -*3*; 3040B; 1744B; DA 810 NI 7846, ROM 81007-2 (A), MET 503CD, CD MOIR 428
17 May 1926

59. *Aida* (Verdi): O terra, addio! (Part 1) [It.]
With G. Martinelli & Chorus (Orch. R. Bourdon)
BVE 35461-*1*, -2; 3041A; 1745A; DA 809 NI 7846, ROM 81007-2 (A), MET 503CD, CD MOIR 428

17 May 1926

60. *Aida* (Verdi): O terra, addio! (Part 2) [It.]
With G. Martinelli, E. Baker & Chorus (Orch. R. Bourdon)
BVE 35462-1, -*2*, -3; 3041B; 1745B; DA 809 NI 7846, ROM 81007-2 (A), MET 503CD, CD MOIR 428
17 May 1926

61. A l'aime (de Fontenailles) [Fr.]
(Pf. R. Romani)
PBS 042207-2, -3, -*5*; 2053A NI 7839, BMG 7810-2-RG, ROM 81022-2 (A)
31 Oct. 1939

62. *Amadis* (Lully): Bois epais [Fr.]
(Pf. I. Chichagov)
E 4-RC-0701-1, -*2*; LM 1889 ROM 81022-2 (B)
16 Oct. 1954

63. Amuri, amuri (Sadero) [It.]
(Pf. R. Ponselle)
E 4-RC-0707-*1*, -2; LM 1889 BMG 7810-2-RG, ROM 81022-2 (B)
17 Oct. 54

64. An die Musik, Op. 88, No. 4 (Schubert) [Ger.]
(Pf. I. Chichagov)
E 4-RC 0723-*1*; EJS243 ROM 81023-2
20 Oct. 1954

65. Aprile (Tosti) [It.]
(Pf. I. Chichagov)
E 4-RC-0710-*1*; LM 1889 ROM 81022-2 (B)
18 Oct. 1954

66. Asturiana (*Seven Popular Spanish Songs*, No. 3) (de Falla) [Sp.]
(Pf. I. Chichagov)
E 4-RC-0727-1, -*2* ASCO A-125 ROM 81023-2
18 Oct. 1954

67. Ave Maria (Bach-Gounod) [Lat.]
(Orch. R. Bourdon)
CVE 35470-1, -*2*; 6599A; DB 1052 NI 7846, BMG 7810-2-RG, ROM 81007-2 (A)
19 May 1926

68. Ave Maria (Kahn) [Lat.]
(Orch. R. Bourdon)
BVE 38856-1
2 June 1927
-2, -3, -4
13 June 1927
-5, -*6*; 1456A ROM 81007-2 (A)
16 June 1927

69. Ave Maria (Luzzi) [Lat.]

(Org., I. Chichagov)
(No Matrix Number Assigned) ASCO A-125 ROM 81023-2
20 Oct. 1954

70. Ave Maria (Millard) [Lat.]
(Org., I. Chichagov)
(No Matrix Number Assigned) 81023-2
20 Oct. 1954

71. Ave Maria (Sandoval) [Lat.]
(Org., I. Chichagov)
(No Matrix Number Assigned) ASCO A-125 ROM 81023-2
20 Oct. 1954

72. Ave Maria, Op. 52, No. 6 (Schubert) [Lat.]
(Pf. R. Romani; violin, M. Schmidt)
PCS 42212-2, -3, -*5*; VB 74 NI 7861, ROM 81022-2 (A), MET 206CD
1 Nov. 1939
-9, -*10* ROM 81022-2 (A)
7 Nov. 1939

73. Ave Maria (Tosti) [It.]
(Pf. I. Chichagov)
E 4-RC-0722-*1* EJS 243 ROM 81023-2
20 Oct. 1954

74. 'A vucchella (Tosti) [It.]
(Orch. R. Bourdon)
BVE 35466-1, -*2*, -3; 1164A; DA 1035 (U.K.) ROM 81007-2 (A),
MET 210CD
18 May 1926

75. 'A vucchella (Tosti) [It.]
(Pf. I. Chichagov)
(No Matrix Number Assigned) LM 2047 ROM 81022-2 (A)
18 Oct. 54

76. Battitori di grano, I (Sadero) [It.]
(Pf. I. Chichagov)
E 4-RC-0706-*1*; LM 1889 ROM 81022-2 (A)
-*2* ROM 81023-2
17 Oct. 1954

77. Beau soir (Debussy) [Fr.]
(Pf. I. Chichagov)
(No Matrix Number Assigned) LM 2047 ROM 81022-2 (A)
17 Oct. 1954

78. Beloved (Silberta) [Eng.]
(Orch. J. Pasternack)
BVE 32852-1
1 June 1925
-2, -3, -4
4 June 1925

-*5*, -6; VA 67 LCD 179-1, ROM 81006-2 (B)
5 June 1925

79. Bonjour, Suzon (Delibes) [Fr.]
(Pf. I. Chichagov)
(No Matrix Number Assigned) LM 2047 ROM 81022-2 (A)
17 Oct. 1954

80. Carmè (arr. De Curtis) [It.]
(Orch. R. Bourdon)
B 29878-1, -*2*, -3; 66256; 1013B NI 7805, ROM 81006-2 (B)
11 Apr. 1924

81. Carmen-Carmela (arr. Ross) [Sp.]
(Pf. I. Chichagov)
(No Matrix Number Assigned) LM 2047 BMG 7810-2-RG, ROM 81022-2 (A)
21 Oct. 1954

82. Carry Me Back to Old Virginny (Bland) [Eng.]
(Orch. J. Pasternack)
CVE 32856-1, -2, -*3*; 6509-A; DB 872 ROM 81006-2 (B), NI 7878
2 June 1925

83. Chevelure, La (Debussy) [Fr.]
(Pf. I. Chichagov)
(No Matrix Number Assigned) LM 2047 ROM 81022-2 (A)
17 Oct. 1954

84. Colombetta (Buzzi Peccia) [It.]
(Pf. I. Chichagov)
E 4-RC-0725-1 ROM 81023-2
20 Oct. 1954

85. Could I (Tosti) [Eng.]
(Pf. R. Ponselle)
(No Matrix Number Assigned) LM 2047 ROM 81022-2 (A)
21 Oct. 1954

86. Cradle Song, Op. 49, No. 4 (Brahms) [Eng.]
(Orch. R. Bourdon)
B 29453-*1*; 66240; 1002A ROM 81006-2 (A)
8 Feb. 1924

87. Cradle Song, Op. 49, No. 4 (Brahms)
(Pf. R. Bourdon)
B 29454-1 (Unpublished)
8 Feb. 1924

88. Dicitencello vuie (Falvo) [It.]
(Pf. R. Ponselle)
(No Matrix Number Assigned) LM 2047 ROM 81022-2 (A)
21 Oct. 1954

89. Drink to Me Only With Thine Eyes (Jonson) [Eng.]
(Pf. I. Chichagov)

E 4-RC-0719-*1*; LM 1889 ROM 81022-2 (B)
19 Oct. 1954

90. Elégie (Massenet) [Fr.]
(Orch. R. Bourdon)
CVE 35469-*1*, -2; 6599B ROM 81007-2 (A), NI 7846
-*3*; DB 1052 (U.K.) ROM 81007-2 (A)
19 May 1926

91. Erlkönig, Der, Op. 1 (Schubert) [Ger.]
(Pf. I. Chichagov)
E 4-RC-0715-*1*, -2; LM 1889 ROM 81022-2 (B)
19 Oct. 1954

92. *Ernani*: Sorta è la notte . . . Ernani! Ernani, involami! [It.]
(Orch. R. Bourdon)
C 29062-*1* ROM 81006-2 (A)
5 Dec. 1923
-2, -3
11 Dec. 1923
-*4*; 74867; 6440B NI 7805, MET 218CD, ROM 81006-2 (A)
23 Jan. 1924
CVE 29062-*5* ROM 81007-2 (A)
16 June 1927
-*6*; 6875B; DB 1275 BMG 7810-2-RG, ROM 81007-2 (B), CD MOIR 428
17 Jan. 1928

93. Extase (Duparc) [Fr.]
(Pf. I. Chichagov)
(No Matrix Number Assigned) (Unpublished)
17 Oct. 1954

94. Fa la nana bambin (Sadero) [It.]
(Pf. R. Ponselle)
E 4-RC-0708-1, -*2*; LM 2047 ROM 81022-2 (A)
17 Oct. 1954

95. *Forza del destino* (Verdi): La vergine degli angeli [It.]
With E. Pinza & Chorus (Orch. G. Setti)
CVE 41636-*1*; 8097B; DB 1199 NI 7805, MET 105CD, CD 9351, ROM 81007-2 (B), CD MOIR 428
23 Jan. 1928

96. *Forza del destino* (Verdi): Pace, pace, mio Dio [It.]
(Orch. R. Bourdon)
C 29060-1, -2
5 Dec. 1923
-*3* ROM 81006-2 (A)
-*4* ROM 81006-2 (A), NI 7878
11 Dec. 1923
-*5*; 74866; 6440A MET 218CD, ROM 81006-2 (A), BMG 0926-61580-2
23 Jan. 1924

CVE 29060-6
13 June 1927
-7
16 June 1927
-*8*; 6875A; DB 1275 NI 7818, BMG 7810-2-RG, CD 9351, ROM 81007-2 (B), CD MOIR 428
-*9* ROM 81007-2 (B)
17 Jan. 1928

97. *Forza del destino* (Verdi): Io muoio! [It.]
With G. Martinelli & E. Pinza
(Orch. R. Bourdon)
CVE 41625-*1* ROM 81007-2 (B)
-*2*; 8104A; DB 1202 BMG 7810-2-RG, CD 9351, ROM 81007-2 (B), CD MOIR 428
18 Jan. 1928

98. *Forza del destino* (Verdi): Non imprecare [It.]
With G. Martinelli & E. Pinza
(Orch. R. Bourdon)
CVE 41626-*1* ROM 81007-2 (B)
-*2*; 8104B; DB 1202 BMG 7810-2-RG, CD 9351, ROM 81007-2 (B), CD MOIR 428
18 Jan. 1928

99. *Gioconda* (Ponchielli): Suicidio! [It.]
(Orch. R. Bourdon)
C 31709-*1*; 6496A; DB 854 NI 7805, BMG 7810-2-RG, ROM 81006-2 (B)
-*2* ROM 81006-2 (B)
14 Jan. 1925

100. Good-Bye (Tosti) [Eng.]
(Orch. R. Bourdon)
C29876-*1* ROM 81006-2 (B)
-*2*; 74886; 6453A ROM 81006-2 (B)
11 Apr. 1924
CVE 29876-3, -4
2 June 1927
-5, -*6*; 6711B ROM 81007-2 (A)
13 June 1927

101. Guitares et mandolines (Saint-Saëns) [Fr.]
(Pf. I. Chichagov)
E 4-RC-0702-*1*; LM 1889 ROM 81022-2 (B)
20 Oct. 1954

102. Happy Days (Strelezki) [Eng.]
(Orch. J. Pasternack)
BVE 32839-1, -2, -3
1 June 1925
-4, -5, -6

4 June 1925
-7, -8
5 June 1925

103. Home Sweet Home (Bishop) [Eng.]
(Orch. J. Pasternack)
CVE 32866-1, -*2*; VB 74 LCD 179-1, ROM 81006-2 (B)
3 June 1925

104. Homing (Del Riego) [Eng.]
(Pf. I. Chichagov)
E 4-RC-0718-1, -*2*; LM 1889 ROM 81022-2 (B)
18 Oct. 1954

105. Ideale (Tosti) [It.]
(Pf. I. Chichagov)
E 4-RC-0709-*1*; LM 2047 ROM 81022-2 (A)
18 Oct. 1954

106. In questa tomba oscura (Beethoven) [It.]
(Pf. I. Chichagov)
E 4-RC-0726-*1*, -2; LM 1889 ROM 81022-2 (B)
17 Oct. 1954

107. In the Luxembourg Gardens (Lockhart-Manning) [Eng.]
(Pf. I. Chichagov)
(No Natrix Number Assigned) ROM 81023-2
19 Oct. 1954

108. Invitation au voyage, L' (Duparc) [Fr.]
(Pf. I. Chichagov)
(No Matrix Number Assigned) ROM 81023-2
17 Oct. 1954

109. Jeune fillette (18th Cent. Bergerette; harm. Weckerlin) [Fr.]
(Pf. I. Chichagov)
E 4-RC-0703-*1*; LM 2047 ROM 81022-2 (A)
17 Oct. 1954

110. Little Old Garden, The (Hewitt) [Eng.]
(Orch. J. Pasternack)
BVE 32850-1, -*2*, -3; VA 67 LCD 179-1, ROM 81006-2 (B), VA 1120, MIN 7
1 June 1925

111. Love's Sorrow (Shelley) [Eng.]
(Orch. R. Bourdon)
B 29875- 1, -*2*; 1057A ROM 81006-2 (A)
11 Apr. 1924

112. Lullaby (Scott) [Eng.]
(Pf. R. Bourdon)
B 29412-1
23 Jan. 1924

113. Lullaby (Scott) [Eng.]

(Orch. R. Bourdon)
B 29452-*1*, -2; 66241; 1002B MET 218CD, ROM 81006-2 (A)
8 Feb. 1924

114. Luna d'estate (Tosti) [It.]
(Orch. R. Bourdon)
BVE 35467-1, -*2*, -3; 1164B; DA 1035; VA 68 MET 218CD,
ROM 81007-2 (A), NI 7878
18 May 1926

115. Marechiare (Tosti) [It.]
(Pf. I. Chichagov)
(No Matrix Number Assigned) LM 2047 ROM 81022-2 (A)
18 Oct. 1954

116. Maria, Mari! (Di Capua) [It.]
(Orch. R. Bourdon)
B 29411-1, -2
23 Jan. 1924
-3, -*4*; 66255; 1013A NI 7805, ROM 81006-2 (B)
11 Apr. 1924

117. Mirar de la Maja, El (Granados) [Sp.]
(Pf. I. Chichagov)
(No Matrix Number Assigned) LM 2047 ROM 81022-2 (A)
18 Oct. 1954

118. Mir träumte von einem Königskind, Op. 4, No. 5 (Trunk) [Ger.]
(Pf. I. Chichagov)
E 4-RC-0712-*1*; LM 1889 ROM 81022-2 (B)
18 Oct. 1954

119. *Molinara* (Paisiello): Nel cor più non me sento [It.]
(Pf. I. Chichagov)
E 4-RC-0721-*1*; LM 2047 ROM 81022-2 (A)
18 Oct. 1954

120. Morgen, Op. 27, No. 4 (Strauss) [Ger.]
(Pf. I. Chichagov)
E 4-RC-0717-*1* ASCO A-125 ROM 81023-2
19 Oct. 1954

121. My Dearest Heart (Sullivan) [Eng.]
(Orch. J. Pasternack)
BVE 32853-1, -2
1 June 1925
-3, -4
2 June 1925
-5, -6, -7
4 June 1925
-8, -9, -10
5 June 1925

122. My Lovely Celia (Higgins) [Eng.]

(Orch. R. Bourdon)
B 29877- 1, *-2*; 1057B ROM 81006-2 (B)
11 Apr. 1924

123. My Lovely Celia (Munro) [Eng.]
(Pf. I. Chichagov)
(No Matrix Number Assigned) ASCO A-125 ROM 81023-2
18 Oct. 1954

124. My Old Kentucky Home (Foster) [Eng.]
(Orch. J. Pasternack)
CVE 32857-*1*, -2, -3; 6509B ROM 81006-2 (B), NI 7878
2 June 1925

125. Nana (*Seven Popular Spanish Songs*, No. 5) (de Falla) [Sp.]
(Pf. I. Chichagov)
E 4-RC-0728-*1* ASCO A-125 ROM 81023-2
18 Oct. 1954

126. Nightingale and the Rose, The (Rimsky-Korsakov) [Eng.]
(Orch. R. Bourdon; flute, C. Barone)
BVE 38857-1, *-2*; 1456B ROM 81007-2 (A)
2 June 1927

127. Nightingale and the Rose, The (Rimsky-Korsakov) [Eng.]
(Pf. R. Romani)
PBS 042208-2, *-3*; 16451A NI 7805, BMG 7810-2-RG, ROM 81022-2,
VA 1120, MIN 7
31 Oct. 1939

128. Night Wind, The (Farley) [Eng.]
(Pf. I. Chichagov)
E 4-RC-0720- 1; ROM 81023-2
-2, LM 1889 ROM 81022-2 (B)
19 Oct. 1954

129. *Norma* (Bellini): Sediziose voci . . . Casta diva (Part 1) [It.]
(Orch. G. Setti, with Metropolitan Opera Chorus)
CVE 49031-1
31 Dec. 1928
-2, *-3*, -4; 8125A; DB 1280 NI 7805, NI 7801, BMG 7810-2-RG, CD 9317,
ROM 81007-2 (B)
30 Jan. 1929

130. *Norma* (Bellini): Ah! bello a me ritorna (Part 2) [It.]
(Orch. G. Setti, with Metropolitan Opera Chorus)
CVE 49032-1, *-2*; 8125B; DB 1280 NI 7805, NI 7801, BMG 7810-2-RG,
CD 9317, ROM 81007-2 (B)
31 Dec. 1928

131. *Norma*: Mira, o Norma (Part 1) [It.]
With M. Telva (Orch. G. Setti)
CVE 49703-1, *-2*; 8110A; DB 1276 NI 7805, MET 218CD, CD 9317,
ROM 81007-2 (B)

30 Jan. 1929

132. *Norma*: Cedi . . . deh cedi! (Part 2)
With M. Telva (Orch. G. Setti)
CVE 49704-*1*, -2; 8110A; DB 1276 NI 7805, MET 218CD, CD 9317, ROM 81007-2 (B)
30 Jan. 1929

133. *Nozze di Figaro* (Mozart): Voi che sapete [It.]
(Pf. I. Chichagov)
(No Matrix Number Assigned) ASCO A-125 ROM 81023-2
21 Oct. 54

134. Nur wer die Sehnsucht kennt, Op. 6, No. 6 (Tchaikovsky) [Ger.]
(Pf. I. Chichagov)
(No Matrix Number Assigned) ASCO A-125 ROM 81023-2
16 Oct. 1954

135. O del mio amato ben (Donaudy) [It.]
(Pf. I. Chichagov)
E 4-RC-0714-1, -*2*; LM 1889 ROM 81022-2 (B)
19 Oct. 1954

136. Old Folks at Home (Foster) [Eng.]
(Orch. J. Pasternack)
CVE 32865-1
3 June 1925
-2, -*3*; IRCC 126 ROM 81006-2 (B), NI 7878
-*4*; DB 872 ROM 81006-2 (B)
4 June 1925

137. On Wings of Dream (Arensky) [Eng.]
(Pf. R. Romani; violin, M. Violin)
PCS 042213-1, -3, -*5*; 16451B NI 7805, ROM 81022-2 (A), BIM 701-2, VA 1120, MIN 7
1 Nov. 1939

138. *Otello* (Verdi): Salce! Salce! [It.]
(Orch. R. Bourdon)
C 29410-*1*, -2; 6474A; DB 807 NI 7805, BMG 7810-2-RG, ROM 81006-2 (A)
23 Jan. 1924

139. *Otello* (Verdi): Ave Maria [It.]
(Double string quartet, R. Bourdon)
C 29409-*1*, -2, -3; 6474B; DB 807 NI 7805, MET 207CD, ROM 81006-2 (A)
23 Jan. 1924

140. Panis angelicus (Franck) [Lat.]
(Org., I. Chichagov)
(No Matrix Number Assigned) (Unpublished)
20 Oct. 1954

141. Partida, La (Alvarez) [Sp.]

(Pf. I. Chichagov)
E 4-RC-0713-*1*; LM 2047 ROM 81022-2 (A)
18 Oct. 1954

142. Perfect Day, A (Bond) [Eng.]
(Orch. J. Pasternack)
BVE 32867-*1*, -2, -3; 1098B NI 7805, ROM 81006-2 (B)
3 June 1925

143. Plaisir d'amour (Martini) [Fr.]
(Pf. I. Chichagov)
(No Matrix Number Assigned) LM 2047 ROM 81022-2 (A)
17 Oct. 1954

144. Psyché (Paladilhe) [Fr.]
(Pf. I. Chichagov)
(No Matrix Number Assigned) ASCO A-125 ROM 81023-2
21 Oct. 54

145. Rispetto (Wolf-Ferrari) [It.]
(Pf. I. Chichagov)
E 4-RC-0724-*1*; ROM 81023-2
-*2*; LM 1889 ROM 81022-2 (B)
20 Oct. 1954

146. Rosary, The (Nevin) [Eng.]
(Orch. J. Pasternack)
BVE 32864-1, -2, -3
3 June 1925
-4, -5, -6
4 June 1925
-*7*, -8; 1098A ROM 81006-2 (B)
5 June 1925

147. Rosemonde (Persico) [Fr.]
(Pf. I. Chichagov)
E 4-RC-0704-*1*; LM 1889 ROM 81022-2 (B)
17 Oct. 1954

148. Rosita, La (Dupont, pseud. G. Haenschen) [Eng.]
(Orch. J. Pasternack)
BVE 32851-1, -2, -3
1 June 1925
-4, -*5*; VA 69 LCD 179-1, ROM 81006-2 (B), VA 1120, MIN 7
4 June 1925

149. Se (Denza) [It.]
(Pf. I. Chichagov)
(No Matrix Number Assigned) ASCO A-125 ROM 81023-2
18 Oct. 1954

150. Serenade (Tosti) [Eng.]
(Harp, F. Lapitino)
C 29879-*1*, -2; 74887; 6453B ROM 81006-2 (B)

-*3* ROM 81006-2 (B), NI 7878
12 Apr. 1924
CVE 29879-4, -*5*; 6711B ROM 81007-2 (A)
2 June 1927

151. Since First I Met Thee (Rubinstein) [Eng.]
(Orch. R. Bourdon; 'cello, Lennartz)
BVE 41624-1, -2, -*3*; 1319B; DA 1023 ROM 81007-2 (B)
17 Jan. 1928

152. Si tu le voulais (Tosti) [Fr.]
(Pf. R. Romani)
PBS 042206-2, -3, -*5*; 2053B ROM 81022-2 (A), NI 7878
31 Oct. 1939

153. Songs My Mother Taught Me, Op. 55, No. 4 (Dvorák) [Eng.]
(Orch. R. Bourdon)
BVE 41623-*1*; 1319A; DA 1023 ROM 81007-2 (B)
17 Jan. 1928

154. Spagnola, La (Di Chiara) [Eng.]
(Orch. J. Pasternack)
BVE 32873-1, -*2*, -3; VA 69 BIM 701-2, LCD 179-1, ROM 81006-2 (B), VA 1120, MIN 7
5 June 1925

155. Ständchen (Schubert) [Ger.]
With C. Ponselle (Orch. R. Bourdon)
CVE 35471-1, -2; VIC 1507 ROM 81007-2 (A) (composite of both takes)
19 May 1926

156. Star vicino (Attr. Rosa) [It.]
(Pf. I. Chichagov)
E 4-RC-0715-*1*; LM 2047 ROM 81022-2 (A)
19 Oct. 1954

157. Temps des lilas, Le (Chausson) [Fr.]
(Pf. I. Chichagov)
E 4-RC-0705-*1*; LM 1889 ROM 81022-2 (B)
17 Oct. 1954

158. Tod und das Mädchen, Der, Op. 7, No. 3 (Schubert) [Ger.]
(Pf. I. Chichagov)
(No Matrix Number Assigned) ASCO A-125 ROM 81023-2
18 Oct. 1954

159. Träume (*Wesendonck Lieder*, No. 5) (Wagner) [Ger.]
(Pf. I. Chichagov)
(No Matrix Number Assigned) ASCO A-125 ROM 81023-2
19 Oct. 1954

160. Tre giorni son che Nina (Ciampi) [It.]
(Pf. I. Chichagov)
(No Matrix Number Assigned (2 takes) ASCO A-125 ROM 81023-2
19 Oct. 1954

161. Tristesse éternelle (Vocal Air of *Études*, Op. 10, No. 3) (Chopin-Litvinne) [Fr.]
(Pf. I. Chichagov)
(No Matrix Number Assigned) ASCO A-125 ROM 81023-2
21 Oct. 1954
162. *Trovatore* (Verdi): Miserere [It.]
With G. Martinelli and Metropolitan Opera Chorus (Orch. G. Setti)
CVE 41637-*1*; 8097A; ROM 81007-2 (B), CD MOIR 428
-*2*; DB 1199 ROM 81007-2 (B)
23 Jan. 1928
163. *Vestale* (Spontini): Tu che invoco [It.]
(Orch. R. Bourdon)
CVE 35464-*1*, -2; 6605A; DB 1274; VB 3 NI 7805, MET 218CD, ROM 81007-2 (A)
18 May 1926
164. *Vestale* (Spontini): O nume tutelar [It.]
(Orch. R. Bourdon)
CVE 35465-*1*; 6605B; DB 1274; VB 3 NI 7805, BMG 7810-2-RG, ROM 81007-2 (A)
-*2* ROM 81007-2 (A)
18 May 1926
165. Von ewiger Liebe, Op. 43, No. 1 (Brahms) [Ger.]
(Pf. I. Chichagov)
E 4-RC-0711-*1*; LM 1889 ROM 81022-2 (B)
18 Oct. 1954
166. When I Have Sung My Songs (Charles) [Eng.]
(Pf. R. Romani)
PBS 042209-*1*; VA 68 NI 7846, BMG 7810-2-RG, ROM 81022-2 (A)
-2, -*3*; VA 68 ROM 81022-2
31 Oct. 1939

III. Compact Disc Releases

Label: RCA/BMG
Catalog Number: 7910-1-RG
Title: *Rosa Ponselle–Verdi, Bellini, Meyerbeer, Ponchielli*

Label: RCA/MET
Catalog Number: 0926-61580-2
Title: *100 Singers–100 Years*

Label: ROMOPHONE
Catalog Number: 81006-2
Title: *Rosa Ponselle: The Victor Recordings (1923-25)*

Label: ROMOPHONE
Catalog Number: 81007-2
Title: *Rosa Ponselle: The Victor Recordings (1926-29)*

Label: ROMOPHONE
Catalog Number: 81022-2
Title: *Rosa Ponselle: The Victor Recordings (1939-54)*

Label: ROMOPHONE
Catalog Number: 81023-2
Title: *Rosa Ponselle: The Victor Recordings (1954 Unpublished Titles)*

Label: PEARL GEMM
Catalog Number: CDS 9964
Title: Rosa Ponselle: The Columbia Acoustical Recordings

Label: PEARL GEMM
Catalog Number: CD 9317
Title: *Rosa Ponselle in La traviata*

Label: PEARL GEMM
Catalog Number: CD 9351
Title: *La forza del destino–Giovanni Martinelli*

Label: NIMBUS PRIMA VOCE
Catalog Number: NI 7805
Title: *Rosa Ponselle–Volume 1*

Label: NIMBUS PRIMA VOCE
Catalog Number: NI 7846
Title: *Rosa Ponselle–Volume 2*

Label: NIMBUS PRIMA VOCE
Catalog Number: NI 7878
Title: *Rosa Ponselle–Volume 3*

Label: NIMBUS PRIMA VOCE
Catalog Number: NI 7801
Title: *The Great Singers (1909-1938)*

Label: NIMBUS PRIMA VOCE
Catalog Number: NI 7802
Title: *Divas*

Label: NIMBUS PRIMA VOCE
Catalog Number: NI 7839
Title: *Prima Voce Party*

Label: NIMBUS PRIMA VOCE
Catalog Number: NI 7851
Title: *Legendary Voices*

Label: NIMBUS PRIMA VOCE
Catalog Number: NI 7861
Title: *The Spirit of Christmas Past*

Label: METROPOLITAN OPERA
Catalog Number: MET 218CD
Title: *Rosa Ponselle–Portraits in Memory*

Label: METROPOLITAN OPERA
Catalog Number: MET 706CD
Title: *Met Centurians–Giovanni Martinelli*

Label: METROPOLITAN OPERA
Catalog Number: MET 105CD
Title: *Ezio Pinza–Great Artists at the Met*

Label: METROPOLITAN OPERA
Catalog Number: MET 207CD
Title: *A Sunday Night Concert at the Met*

Label: METROPOLITAN OPERA
Catalog Number: MET 503CD
Title: *Great Operas–Aida*

Label: METROPOLITAN OPERA
Catalog Number: MET 409CD
Title: *Great Operas–Il trovatore*

Label: METROPOLITAN OPERA
Catalog Number: MET 210CD
Title: *Songs Our Mothers Taught Us*

Label: BIOGRAPHIES IN MUSIC
Catalog Number: BIM 701-2
Title: *Rosa Ponselle: When I Have Sung My Songs*

Label: BIOGRAPHIES IN MUSIC
Catalog Number: BIM 179-1
Title: *Rosa Ponselle: The Cross-Over Album*

Label: LEGATO CLASSICS
Catalog Number: LCV 017 (VIDEO)
Title: *Legends of Opera*
(Includes Ponselle's M-G-M Screen Test, 1936)

Label: EKLIPSE
Catalog Number: EKR 51
Title: *Rosa Ponselle in Concert (1936–1952)*

Label: EKLIPSE
Catalog Number: EKR CD 6
Title: *Carmen (Boston, 1936)*

Label: WALHALL
Catalog Number: WHL15
Title: *Carmen (17 Apr. 1937)*

Label: FORTIES RADIO
Catalog Number: FT 1513.14
Title: *La traviata (1935)*

Label: RADIO YEARS
Catalog Number: RY 17
Title: *Rosa Ponselle on Radio (1934-36)*

Label: RADIO YEARS
Catalog Number: RY 10.02
Title: *La traviata (1935)*

Label: VOCAL ARCHIVES
Catalog Number: VA 1120
Title: *Rosa Ponselle: Rare Songs Recorded (1918-1939)*

Label: MINERVA
Catalog Number: MINERVA 7
Title: *Rosa Ponselle–Songs and Operettas (1918-1939)*

Label: MEMOIR CLASSICS
Catalog Number: CD MOIR 428
Title: *Rosa Ponselle and Giovanni Martinelli Sing Verdi*

IV. Radio Broadcasts

I January 1927
VICTOR TALKING MACHINE HOUR
New York, WEAF, 9-11:00 P.M.
Other artists: J. McCormack, A. Cortot, and M. Elman
(Orch. N. Shilkret)
Ave Maria (Bach-Gounod?)
La forza del destino: Pace, pace mio Dio
Elégie (Massenet)
Lullaby (?)
The Rosary (Nevin)
This broadcast was billed as "The radio debut of Rosa Ponselle."

1 January 1928
VICTOR TALKING MACHINE HOUR
New York, WEAF, 9-11:00 P.M.
Other artists: G. Martinelli, E. Pinza, Metropolitan Opera Orchestra & Chorus
(Orch. G. Setti)
Aida: Ritorna vincitor
Il trovatore: Miserere (with G. Martinelli)
La forza del destino: Trio finale (with G. Martinelli and E. Pinza)

3 December 1928
GENERAL MOTORS HOUR
New York
(Orch. E. Goossens)
La forza del destino: Pace, pace mio Dio
Norma: Casta Diva
Carmen: Habanera
Mighty lak' a Rose (Nevin)
Fa la nana bambin (Sadero)
Swiss Echo Song (Eckert)
(Pf. R. Romani)

13 October 1929
ATWATER KENT RADIO HOUR
New York, WEAF, 8:15-9:15 P.M.
(Orch. J. Pasternack)
La forza del destino: Madre pietosa Vergine
La vestale: O nume tutelar
I vespri siciliani: Bolero (with orch.)
Rosalinda: Meco sulla verrai (Veracini)
Tristesse eternelle (Chopin)
Heine (Blech)

La Chanson de la Cigale (Lecocq)
Swiss Echo Song (Eckert)
The Night Wind (Farley)
My Old Kentucky Home (Foster)
(Pf. R. Romani)

10 April 1930
RCA VICTOR HOUR
New York, WEAF, 10-11:00 P.M.
(Orch. ?)
Ave Maria (Composer?)
By the Waters of Minnetonka (Cavanass-Lieurance)
Mademoiselle Modiste: Kiss Me Again
The Night Wind (Farley)
Il trovatore: Tacea la notte
The Fairy Pipers (Brewer)
Lullaby (Composer?)
Swiss Echo Song (Eckert)
The Rosary (Nevin)

23 October 1930
RCA VICTOR HOUR
New York, WEAF
(Orch. ?)
La forza del destino: Pace, pace mio Dio
Angel's Serenade (Braga)
In the Luxembourg Gardens
Come Unto These Yellow Sands (La Forge)
Carmen: Chanson bohème

7 December 1930
ATWATER KENT RADIO HOUR
New York, WEAF
(Orch. J. Pasternack)
Fedra: O divina Afrodite
Mariä Wiegenlied (Reger)
Elégie (Massenet)
La traviata: Addio del passato
I vespri siciliani: Bolero
Annie Laurie (Scott)
The Cuckoo (Lehmann)
Ständchen (Schubert)
Swiss Echo Song (Eckert)
Carmen: Habanera
Billing: "Mr. Romano Romani will conduct the Romanza from his opera Fedra *and accompany Miss Ponselle at the piano."*

1 June 1931
ROYAL OPERA HOUSE, COVENT GARDEN
London, WABC, 3:00 P.M.
Transatlantic broadcast
La forza del destino (Orch. T. Serafin)
With A. Pertile, B. Franci, T. Pasero

9 June 1931
ROYAL OPERA HOUSE, COVENT GARDEN
London, WABC, 3:00 P.M.
Transatlantic broadcast
La traviata (Orch. T. Serafin)
With D. Borgioli, Noble

18 October 1931
ATWATER KENT RADIO HOUR
New York, WEAF, 9:15-10:15 P.M.
(Orch. J. Pasternack)
Ständchen (Schubert)
I vespri siciliani: Bolero
But Lately in Dance (Arensky)
The Fairy Pipers (Brewer)
Angel's Serenade (Braga)
The Night Wind (Farley)
Fedra: O divina Afrodite
Marechiare (Tosti)
'O Sole Mio (Di Capua)
(Pf. R. Romani)

26 December 1931
METROPOLITAN OPERA
New York, WEAF, 3:45-5:15 P.M.
Norma (Acts II and III) (Orch. T. Serafin)
With Lauri-Volpi, Swarthout, Pinza

16 January 1932
METROPOLITAN OPERA
New York, WEAF, 3.00-4:00 P.M.
Il trovatore (Orch. V. Bellezza)
With Lauri-Volpi, Danise, Petrova

27 March 1932
GENERAL ELECTRIC TWILIGHT HOUR
New York, WEAF
(Orch.?)

The Rosary (Nevin)
I Passed by Your Window (Brahe)
Elégie (Massenet)
The Cuckoo Clock (Griselle-Young)
Ave Maria (Schubert)
Comin' Thro' the Rye (Trad.)
Mariä Wiegenlied (Reger)
Marechiare (Tosti)
The Last Rose of Summer (Moore)

17 December 1932
METROPOLITAN OPERA
New York, WJZ, 1:45-5:15 P.M.
Don Giovanni (Orch. T. Serafin)
With Pinza, Müller, Fleischer, Schipa, Pasero, Malatesta, Rothier

19 January 1933
Waldorf-Astona
New York, 2:00 P.M.
Harlem Philharmonic (Cond.?)
(With D. Borgioli)
Chi vuol comprar (Jomelli)
Die Tote Stadt: Mariettas Lied
Rispetto (Wolf-Ferrari)
Alceste: Divinités du Styx
La traviata: Parigi, o cara
Freschi luoghi prati aulenti (Donaudy)
On Wings of Dream (Arensky)
Dedication (Schumann)
The Doll's Cradle Song (Moussorgsky)
Come Unto These Yellow Sands (La Forge)

22 January 1933
GENERAL ELECTRIC SUNDAY CIRCLE
New York, 9:00-9:30 P.M.
WEAF Orchestra (Cond.?)
Swiss Echo Song (Eckert)
Home, Sweet Home (Bishop)
Naughty Manetta: Ah, sweet mystery (Herbert)
The Nightingale and the Rose (Rimsky-Korsakov)
Carmen: Habanera
Rose Marie: Indian Love Call

19 February 1933
GENERAL ELECTRIC SUNDAY CIRCLE

New York, WEAF
WEAF Symphony (Cond.?)
Carmen: Chanson bohème
Cavalleria rusticana: Ave Maria
The Chocolate Soldier: My hero
Drink to Me Only with Thine Eyes (Jonson)
Ich liebe dich (Grieg)
Lullaby (Brahms)
Good-Bye (Tosti)
Aida: Ritorna vincitor!

3 March 1933
PRE-INAUGURAL CONCERT
Washington, D.C., WEAF, 8.30-9:30 P.M.
National Symphony Orchestra (Cond. H. Kindler)
Aida: Ciel! mio padre! (with L. Tibbett)
Die Tote Stadt: Mariettas Lied
Swiss Echo Song (Eckert)
Der Erlkönig (Schubert)
The Night Wind (Farley)

19 March 1933
GENERAL ELECTRIC SUNDAY CIRCLE
New York, WEAF, 9:00-10:00 P.M.
WEAF Symphony (Cond.?)
Liebesträume (Liszt)
La vestale: Tu che invoco
Comin' Thro' the Rye (Trad.)
I vespri siciliani: Bolero
Serenade (Moszkowski)
In the Luxembourg Gardens (Lockhart-Manning)

7 May 1933
FLORENCE MAY FESTIVAL
Florence, Italy, 9:00 P.M.
La vestale (Cond. V. Gui)
With Dolci, Pasero, Stignani, Pierobiasini

15 November 1933
NBC SEVENTH ANNIVERSARY GALA
New York, WEAF, 10:30-11:00 P.M.
Drink to Me Only with Thine Eyes (Trad.)
The Cuckoo Clock (Griselle-Young)

11 December 1933
New York, WEAF?

With J. Heifetz
La vestale: O nume tutelar
La trauiata: Addio del passato
Carmen: Chanson bohème
Freschi luoghi prati aulenti (Donaudy)
Die Tote Stadt: Mariettas Lied
Rispetto (Wolf-Ferrari)
Slumber Song of the Madonna (Head)
My Lover He Comes on a Ski (Clough-Leighton)

24 December 1933
CADILLAC HOUR
New York, WJZ, 6:00-7:00 P.M.
With Metropolitan Opera Chorus (Cond. A. Bodanzky)
Norma: Casta diva
Good-Bye (Tosti)
Der Erlkönig (Schubert)
Mariä Wiegenlied (Reger)
The Cuckoo Clock (Griselle-Young)
Adeste Fideles (Trad.)

13 January 1934
METROPOLITAN OPERA
New York, WEAF
L'africana (Cond. T. Serafin)
With Jagel, Borgioli, Morgana, Rothier

20 January 1934
METROPOLITAN OPERA
New York, WEAF
Don Giovanni (Cond. T. Serafin)
With Pinza, Müller, Fleischer, Lazzari, Schipa

28 January 1934
HEINZ HALL OF FAME PROGRAM
New York, WEAF, 10:30-11:00 P.M.
(Cond. N. Shilkret)
Naughty Marietta: Ah, Sweet Mystery of Life (Herbert)
Cavalleria rusticana: Voi lo sapete
Mademoiselle Modiste: Kiss Me Again (Herbert)
Angel's Serenade (Braga)
Carmen: Habanera

2 April 1934
CHESTERFIELD HOUR

New York, WABC
(Cond. A. Kostelanetz)
Swiss Echo Song (Eckert)
Fedra: O divina Afrodite
A Perfect Day (Bond)

9 April 1934
CHESTERFIELD HOUR
New York, WABC
(Cond. A. Kostelanetz)
Carmen: Chanson bohème
Comin' Thro' the Rye (Trad.)
La traviata: Addio del passato
Home, Sweet Home (Bishop)

16 April 1934
CHESTERFIELD HOUR
New York, WABC
(Cond. A. Kostelanetz)
Songs My Mother Taught Me (Dvorák)
I vespri siciliani: Bolero
La Paloma (Yradier)
The Nightingale and the Rose (Rimsky-Korsakov)

23 April 1934
CHESTERFIELD HOUR
New York, WABC
(Cond. A. Kostelanetz)
Come Unto These Yellow Sands (La Forge)
The Old Refrain (Kreisler)
La vestale: Tu che invoco

30 April 1934
CHESTERFIELD HOUR
New York, WABC
(Cond. A. Kostelanetz)
Naughty Marietta: Ah, sweet mystery (Herbert)
Die Tote Stadt: Mariettas Lied
Carry Me Back to Old Virginny (Bond)
Fa la nana bambin (Sadero)

7 May 1934
CHESTERFIELD HOUR
New York, WABC
(Cond. A. Kostelanetz)

Here's to Romance: I Carry You in My Pocket
Alceste: Divintés du Styx
Ständchen (Schubert)
Love's Old Sweet Song (Molloy)

14 May 1934
CHESTERFIELD HOUR
New York, WABC
(Cond. A. Kostelanetz)
Carmen: Habanera
The Chocolate Soldier: My hero (Straus)
Fa la nana bambin (Sadero)
Blue Danube Waltz (Strauss)

21 May 1934
CHESTERFIELD HOUR
New York, WABC
(Cond. A. Kostelanetz)
Mademoiselle Modiste: Kiss Me Again (Herbert)
La bohème: Mi chiamano Mimi
My Old Kentucky Home (Foster)

28 May 1934
CHESTERFIELD HOUR
New York, WABC
(Cond. A. Kostelanetz)
Sadko: Song of India (Rimsky-Korsakov)
Ave Maria (Kahn)
The Night Wind (Farley)

4 June 1934
CHESTERFIELD HOUR
New York, WABC
(Cond. A. Kostelanetz)
Cavalleria rusticana: Voi lo sapete
The Cuckoo Clock (Griselle-Young)
The Rosary (Nevin)

11 June 1934
CHESTERFIELD HOUR
New York, WABC
(Cond. A. Kostelanetz)
Der Erlkönig (Schubert)
I Passed by Your Window (Brahe)
Danny Boy (Trad.)

18 June 1934
CHESTERFIELD HOUR
New York, WABC
(Cond. A. Kostelanetz)
'O Sole Mio (Di Capua)
La forza del destino: Pace, pace, mio Dio
Good-Bye (Tosti)

25 June 1934
CHESTERFIELD HOUR
New York, WABC
(Cond. A. Kostelanetz)
La forza del destino: Pace, pace
Here's to Romance: I Carry You in My Pocket
The Fairy Pipers (Brewer)
Annie Laurie (Trad.)

2 July 1934
CHESTERFIELD HOUR
New York, WABC
(Cond. A. Kostelanetz)
Marechiare (Tosti)
The Red Mill: I'm Falling in Love with Someone (Herbert)
True (Samuels)

9 July 1934
CHESTERFIELD HOUR
New York, WABC
(Cond. A. Kostelanetz)
Dicitencello vuje (Falvo)
In the Luxembourg Gardens (Lockhart-Manning)
The Fortune Teller: Gypsy Love Song
Home, Sweet Home (Bishop)

1 October 1934
CHESTERFIELD HOUR
New York, WABC, 9:00-9:30 P.M.
(Cond. A. Kostelanetz)
Don Giovanni: Batti, batti BIM 701-2
I Love You Truly (Bond) BIM 701-2, LCD 179-1, VA 1120, MIN 7
The Cuckoo Clock (Griselle-Young) LCD 179-1, VA 1120, MIN 7
Homing (Del Riego)

8 October 1934
CHESTERFIELD HOUR

New York, WABC, 9:00-9:30 P.M.
(Cond. A. Kostelanetz)
The Chocolate Soldier: My hero (Straus) BIM 701-2
Cavalleria rusticana: Ave Maria BIM 701-2
In the Luxembourg Gardens (Lockhart-Manning)
Carmen: Chanson bohème

15 October 1934
CHESTERFIELD HOUR
New York, WABC, 9:00-9:30 P.M.
(Cond. A. Kostelanetz)
Blue Danube Waltz (Strauss) LCD 179-1
La Golondrina (Serradell)
Wiegenlied (Brahms)
Will-o'-the-Wisp (Spross)

22 October 1934
CHESTERFIELD HOUR
New York, WABC, 9:00-9:30 P.M.
(Cond. A. Kostelanetz)
Otello: Ave Maria
Swiss Echo Song (Eckert)
Ouvre ton coeur (Bizet)
CD:

29 October 1934
CHESTERFIELD HOUR
New York, WABC, 9:00-9:30 P.M.
(Cond. A. Kostelanetz)
La violetera (Padilla)
Samson et Dalila: Printemps qui commence
The Last Rose of Summer (Moore) BIM 701-2

5 November 1934
CHESTERFIELD HOUR
New York, WABC, 9:00-9:30 P.M.
(Cond. A. Kostelanetz)
Humoresque (Dvorák)
The Cuckoo Clock (Griselle-Young)
Der Erlkönig (Schubert)

12 November 1934
CHESTERFIELD HOUR
New York, WABC, 9:00-9:30 P.M.
(Cond. A. Kostelanetz)

Jeanne d'Arc: Adieu forêts
Clavelitos (Valverde)
In the Gloaming (Harris)
Santa Maria (Lara)

19 November 1934
CHESTERFIELD HOUR
New York, WABC, 9:00-9:30 P.M.
(Cond. A. Kostelanetz)
Ave Maria (Sandoval)
The Merry Widow: Waltz Song
Estrellita (Ponce)
The Sleigh (Tchervanow-Kountz)

26 November 1934
CHESTERFIELD HOUR
New York, WABC, 9:00-9:30 P.M.
(Cond. A. Kostelanetz)
Carmen: Habanera
A Dream (Bartlett) LCD 179-1
What Is in the Air Today (Eden)
The Rosary (Nevin)

3 December 1934
CHESTERFIELD HOUR
New York, WABC, 9:00-9:30 P.M.
(Cond. A. Kostelanetz)
Alceste: Divinités du Styx
Mariä Wiegenlied (Reger)
Big Brown Bear (Mana-Zucca)
Good-Bye (Tosti)

10 December 1934
CHESTERFIELD HOUR
New York, WABC, 9:00-9:30 P.M.
(Cond. A. Kostelanetz)
Angel's Serenade (Braga)
Comin' Thro' the Rye (Trad.)
Fedra: O divina Afrodite

17 December 1934
CHESTERFIELD HOUR
New York, WABC, 9:00-9:30 P.M.
(Cond. A. Kostelanetz)
The Fairy Pipers (Brewer)

The Old Refrain (Kreisler)
Elégie (Massenet)
Don Giovanni: Mi tradi

24 December 1934
CHESTERFIELD HOUR
New York, WABC, 9:00-9:30 P.M.
(Cond. A. Kostelanetz)
Adeste Fideles (Trad.)
La forza del destino: La Vergine degli angeli
Der Erlkönig (Schubert)

5 January 1935
METROPOLITAN OPERA
New York, NBC
La traviata (Cond. E. Panizza)
With Jagel, Tibbett PEARL CD 9317, FT 1513.14, RY 10.02

9 February 1935
METROPOLITAN OPERA
New York, NBC
Don Giovanni (Cond. E. Panizza)
With Pinza, Müller, Fleischer, Lazzari, Schipa

17 March 1935
FORD SUNDAY EVENING HOUR
Detroit, CBS, 9:00-10:00 P.M.
Ford Symphony (Cond. Kolar)
Jeanne d'Arc: Adieu forêts
Il trovatore: Miserere (with de Filippi)
Carmen: Habanera
Sagesse (Panizza)
Ouvre ton coeur (Bizet)
Believe Me, If All Those Endearing Young Charms (Moore)

27 October 1935
GENERAL MOTORS SYMPHONY
Detroit, WEAF, 10-11 P.M.
(Cond. E. Rapée)
Carmen: Habanera
Carmen: Chanson bohème
Dicitencello vuje (Falvo)
Blue Danube Waltz (Strauss)

21 November 1935
"TO ARMS FOR PEACE"

New York, WABC
(Cond. ?)
Carmen: Seguidilla
Jeanne d'Arc: Adieu forêts (Honegger)

1 February 1936
METROPOLITAN OPERA
New York, WABC
Carmen (Cond. L. Hasselmans)
With Kullman, Pinza, Fisher

26 February 1936
CHESTERFIELD HOUR
New York, WABC
(Cond. A. Kostelanetz)
Carmen: Seguidilla BIM 701-2
Carmen: Air des cartes BIM 701-2
Here's to Romance: I Carry You in My Pocket LCD 179-1, VA 1120, MIN 7
None but the Lonely Heart (Tchaikowsky) BIM 701-2

4 March 1936
CHESTERFIELD HOUR
New York, WABC
(Cond. A. Kostelanetz)
Carmen: Chanson bohème bim 701-2
Clavelitos (Valverde)
Danny Boy (Trad.) LCD 179-1, BIM 701-2
Der Erlkönig (Schubert)

11 March 1936
CHESTERFIELD HOUR
New York, WABC
(Cond. A. Kostelanetz)
The Old Refrain (Kreisler) BIM 701-2, LCD 179-1, VA 1120, MIN 7
L'ultima canzone (Tosti)
Comin' Thro' the Rye (Trad.) BIM 701-2, LCD 179-1
Cavalleria rusticana: Voi lo sapete BIM 701-2

18 March 1936
CHESTERFIELD HOUR
New York, WABC
(Cond. A. Kostelanetz)
Humoresque (Dvorák) BIM 701-2, LCD 179-1, VA 1120, MIN 7
Ouvre ton coeur (Bizet)
Fedra: O divina Afrodite
When I Have Sung My Songs (Charles) LCD 179-1, BIM 701-2

25 March 1936
CHESTERFIELD HOUR
New York, WABC
(Cond. A. Kostelanetz)
Ave Maria (Sandoval)
The Night Wind (Farley) LCD 179-1
Carmen: Habanera BIM 701-2
Ich liebe dich (Grieg)

28 March 1936
METROPOLITAN OPERA
Boston, NBC
Carmen (Cond. L. Hasselmans)
With Maison, Pinza, Burke EKR CD 6

1 April 1936
CHESTERFIELD HOUR
New York, WABC
(Cond. A. Kostelanetz)
Good-Bye (Tosti) BIM 701-2, LCD 179-1
The Cuckoo (Lehmann) LCD 179-1, VA 1120, MIN 7
Morenita (Buzzi-Peccia)
La vestale: Tu che invoco BIM 701-2

24 May 1936
LOS ANGELES PHILHARMONIC
Hollywood Bowl, WEAF, 10-11:00 P.M.
(Cond. E. Rapée)
Semiramide: Bel raggio
La traviata: Addio del passato
Cavalleria rusticana: Voi lo sapete
Morenita (Buzzi-Peccia)
Carry Me Back to Old Virginny (Bland)
Marechiare (Tosti)

31 May 1936
GENERAL MOTORS HOUR
San Francisco, WEAF, 10-11:00 P.M.
San Francisco Symphony (Cond. E. Rapée)
Alceste: Divinités du Styx
Ave Maria (Schubert)
Carmen: Seguidilla
Marechiare (Tosti)
Annie Laurie (Trad.) LCD 179-1, VA 1120, MIN 7
Morenita (Buzzi-Peccia)

15 June 1936
ERNESTINE SCHUMANN-HEINK; 75th BIRTHDAY PARTY
Los Angeles, WEAF
Wiegenlied (Brahms)
Home Sweet Home (Bishop)

27 September 1936
GENERAL MOTORS HOUR
Carnegie Hall, New York, WEAF, 10-11:00 P.M.
(Cond. E. Rapée)
Aida: Ritorna vincitor
Dicitencello vuje (Falvo) BIM 701-2
Otello: Ave Maria BIM 701-2
Homing (Del Riego) BIM 701-2, LCD 179-1
Ouvre ton coeur (Bizet)

10 December 1936
"THEN AND NOW"
New York, WABC, 10:00-10:30 P.M.
Sears Orchestra & Chorus (Cond. C. Kelsey)
Moonlight Bay (Madden-Wenrich) EKR 51
La forza del destino: La Vergine degli angeli EKR 51
Carmè (Arr. de Curtis)
Mademoiselle Modiste: Kiss Me Again (Herbert) ERK 51

9 January 1937
METROPOLITAN OPERA
New York, NBC
Carmen (Cond. G. Papi)
With Rayner, Huehn, Bodanya

17 April 1937
METROPOLITAN OPERA
Cleveland, NBC
Carmen (Cond. G. Papi)
With Maison, Huehn, Burke WHL 15

25 April 1937
CINCINNATI SYMPHONY PROMS CONCERT
Cincinnati, WLW
(Cond. E. Goossens)
Ave Maria (Kahn) EKR 51
The Chocolate Soldier: My hero (with F. Forest) LCD 179-1, EKR 51, VA 1120, MIN 7
The Old Refrain (Kreisler) EKR 51

The Night Wind (Farley) EKR 51
None but the Lonely Heart (Tchaikovsky) EKR 51

2 May 1937
RCA MAGIC KEY
New York, WJZ 2:00-3:00 P.M.
(Cond. F. Black)
Drink to Me Only with Thine Eyes (Trad.)
Fedra: O divina Afrodite BIM 701-2
Carry Me Back to Old Virginny (Bland) LCD 179-1, BIM 701-2
Mademoiselle Modiste: Kiss Me Again (Herbert) LCD 179-1, VA 1120, MIN 7
My Old Kentucky Home (Foster)
Home, Sweet Home (Bishop) LCD 179-1, VA 1120, MIN 7

17 March 1954
Rosa Ponselle and Boris Goldovsky discuss Bellini's *Norma* EKR 51

11 March 1960
Rosa Ponselle and Boris Goldovsky discuss Verdi's *La forza del destino* EKR 51

Index

Italicized references denote plate numbers for illustrations. The entry "Rosa Ponselle" does not appear in this index.